Wage Rage for Equal Pay

Jocelynne A. Scutt

Wage Rage for Equal Pay

Australia's Long, Long Struggle

palgrave
macmillan

Jocelynne A. Scutt
University of Buckingham
Buckingham, UK

ISBN 978-3-031-42177-8 ISBN 978-3-031-42178-5 (eBook)
https://doi.org/10.1007/978-3-031-42178-5

This Palgrave Macmillan imprint is published by the registered company Springer Nature Switzerland AG.
The registered company address is: Gewerbestrasse 11, 6330 Cham, Switzerland

Paper in this product is recyclable.

Remembering Val Buswell (1922–2005) and Di Graham (1912–2001), staunch fighters for women's rights—recognising that women's economic independence and financial status inside and outside the home are vital to women's equality and freedom.

Thanking Penn State Dickinson Law (Visiting Professor 2013–2014), University of Buckingham (Senior Teaching Fellow (2014–present) and UNSW (PhD 2004–2007, Adjunct Professor 2022–2025).

Case List

Adoption Leave Test Case 1985 (1985) 298 CAR 321 (Print F9852)

Alexander [sic] Gregg v. Tasmanian Trustees Ltd [1997] 128 FCA (28 February 1997)

Application by United Voice and the Australian Education Union [2018] FWCFB 177, 274 IR 1

Atkinson and Atkinson v State of Victoria (Department of Community Services (Aboriginal Affairs)) [1994] VCAT

Australian Municipal, Administrative, Clerical and Services Union and Ors v Australian Business Industrial [2012] FWAFB 1000

Automotive, Food, Metals, Engineering, Printing and Kindred Industries Union v HPM Industries Pty Ltd **(1998) 94 IR 129**

Australian Iron and Steel Pty Ltd v. Banovic (1989) 168 CLR 165 (FC 89/052)

Australian Theatrical and Amusement Employees' Association v. J.C. Williamson Ltd and Ors (1916) 11 CAR 133; (1917) 11 CAR 665

Automotive, Food, Metals, Engineering, Printing and Kindred Industries Union v HPM Industries case 1997 (*HPM case 1997*), C.No. 23933 of 1995, The first HPM case 137—A legislative entitlement to equal remuneration 135 (1library.net) (accessed 1 June 2009)

Automotive, Food, Metals, Engineering, Printing and Kindred Industries Union v HPM Industries case (HPM case 1998 (No 2)), Equal Remuneration—The Reality (actu.org.au) (accessed 1 June 2009)

Awards of the Court Binding Upon the Australian Railways Union and Others (Basic Wage and Wage Reduction Inquiry 1930–1931) (1931) 30 CAR 2

R. v. Barger; Commonwealth v. McKay (1908) 6 CLR 41
Basic Wage and Wage Reduction Inquiry 1930–1931 (1931) 30 CAR 2
Basic Wage Inquiry 1934 (1934) 33 CAR 144
Basic Wage Inquiry 1937 (1937) 37 CAR 583
Basic Wage Case 1940 (1941) 44 CAR 41
Basic Wage Case 1949–1950 (1949–50) 68 CAR 698
Basic Wage and Standard Hours Inquiry 1952–1953 (1953) 77 CAR 477
Basic Wage Case 1957 (1957) 87 CAR 437
Basic Wage Case 1973 (1973) 149 CAR 75 (*National Wage Case 1973*)
Bebb v. The Law Society (1914) 1 Ch. 286
In re the Boilermakers' Board (1917) 18 ALR 399.
In re Brewery Employees Union [1910] AR 258
Broken Hill Proprietary Limited case (1909) 6 CAR 71 (*Broken Hill PL case*)
Re Childcare Industry (ACT) Award 1985; Childcare Industry (NT) Award 1986 case 1990 (1990) 39 IR 194 (Print J4316) (December 1990)
Childcare and Kindergarten Employees' Award—State (1991) 137 QGIG 399
Clothing Trades case (1918) 2 SAIR 23 (*Clothing Trades case*)
R. v. Coldham; Ex parte Australian Social Welfare Union (1983) 153 CLR 297 (*Social Workers case*)
In re Commercial Clerks' Board (1918) 19 ALR 142
Commonwealth v Introvigne (1982) 150 CLR 258; 56 ALJR 749
Commonwealth v. Tasmania (Tasmanian Dams Case) (1983) 158 CLR 1, Commonwealth v Tasmania ("Tasmanian Dam case") [1983] HCA 21; (1983) 158 CLR 1 (1 July 1983) (austlii.edu.au) (accessed 29 May 2023)
Crown Employees (Librarians, Library Assistants, Library Technicians and Archivists) Award 2002 [2002] NSW IR Comm. 55, 111 IR 48
Crown Librarians, Library Officers and Archivists Award—Re Applications under the Equal Remuneration Principle [2002] NSW IRComm 55 (28 March 2002)
Danfoss Case, http://www.coc-law.org.uk/Defaultaspx?page=3150&theme=print (accessed 15 April 2006); *Handels~ og Kontorfunktionaeremes Forbund I Danmark v. Dansk Arbejdsgiverforening* (*Danfoss case*), ECJ 109/88 (17 October 1989).
Dunn-Dyer v. ANZ (1997) EOC §92–897
In re Edith Haynes (1904) 6 WAR 209
Equal Pay Case 1969 (1969) 127 CAR 1142
Equal Pay Case 1972 (1972)) 147 CAR 172

Equal Remuneration Case 2010–2012 (AMACSU case) [2012] FWAFB 514 (22 June 2012).
Re Equal Remuneration Decision 2015 [2015] FWCFB 8200, 256 IR 362
Re Equal Remuneration Principle 2000 (2000) 97 IR 177
Family Court of Australia v. Public Sector, Professional, Scientific Research, Technical, Communications, Aviating and Broadcasting Union, Professional Officers Association, Australian Government Employment, Professional and Executive Salaries Award 990, P 127 Dec 700/93 S (Print K8020)(11 June 1993)
Family Leave Test Case 1994 (1994) 57 IR 121 (Print L6900)
Federated Clothing Trades of the Commonwealth of Australia v. J.A. Archer and Ors (1919) 13 CAR 647 (*Federated Clothing Trades case*)
Gas Employees case (1921) 16 CAR 4
Gas Employees case (1922) 16 CAR 82
Geyer v. Downs (1977) 138 CLR 91
In re Government Railways and Tramways (Coachmakers &c) Award [1928] IR 475.
GrainCorp Operations Limited and Anor; S. Markham v. GrainCorp Operations Ltd AIRC (C2002/3380)(U2001/4990) 2002 (29 October 2002), http://www.airc.gov.au/decisionssigned/PR924103.doc, pp. 1–17 (accessed 3 August 2006)(Print 924103)
HPM Industries case 1998 (1998), Dec 553/98 N Print Q1002 (C No. 21025 of 1998)
Ex parte H.V. McKay (*Harvester case, Harvester, Harvester judgment, Harvester decision*) (1907) 2 CAR 1
In re Hairdressers &c. Females (State) Award [1929] IR 39 (*Hairdressers case*)
Handels-oq Kontorfukionaererness Forbund i Danmark v. Dansk Arbejdsgner Forening [1989] IRLR 532 (the *Danfoss case*)
Harvester, *Harvester case*, *Harvester* judgment or *Harvester* decision (1907) 2 CAR 1
Hickie v. Hunt & Hunt (1998) EOC §92–910 (HREOC No. 96/185, 7 March 1998)
Hopper v. Mt Isa Mines (1997) EOC §92–879
Horne & McIntosh v. Press Clough Joint Venture (1994) EOC §92–556
Independent Education Union of Australia (C2013/6333 and AM2018/9) [2021] FWCFB 205.
Re Kitson [1920] SASR 230

McKenna v. State of Victoria (1998) EOC §93–927

Maternity Leave case 1979 (1979) 218 CAR 120 (Print D9576)

In the Matter of Seven Applications by the Broken Hill Pty. Co. Ltd. (Nos 81, 122, 152, 165, 172, 173 and 255 of 1942) and other applications under Regulations 6, 7 and 11 of the Schedule to the *Women's Employment Act* 1942 (Cth) (No. 55 of 1942) (1943) 49 CAR 62 (*Metal Trades (Broken Hill) case*')

In the Matter of an Application by the British Australasian Tobacco Company Pty. Ltd. and W.D. & H.O. Wills (Australia) Ltd (under Regulation 6 of the Schedule of the *Women's Employment Act* (No. 55 of 1942)(No. 267 of 1942))(1943) 49 CAR 45, p. 48 (*British Australasian Tobacco Company case*)

In the Matter of an Application by Noyes Bros., Sydney under Regulation 6 (1943) 49 CAR 14 (*Crockery and Glassware case)*

In the Matter of an Application by the Amalgamated Postal Workers' Union under Regulation 7 of the Schedule to the *Women's Employment Act; In the Matter of an Application by the Commonwealth Public Service Board* under regulation 6 of the Schedule to the W*omen's Employment Act* (Nos 91 and 96 of 1942) (1943) 49 CAR 36, pp. 36–37 (*Postal Assistants case*)

In the Matter of an Application by the Commonwealth Public Service Board under Regulation 6 (No. 6 of 1942) (1943) 49 CAR 34 (*Broadcasting Control Booth Operators case*)

In the Matter of an Application by Apex Bedding & Wire Mattress Co. Pty Ltd, Melbourne under Regulation 6 (1943) 49 CAR 10 (*Bedding and Mattress case*)

In the matter of an Application by the Victorian Railways Commissioners under Regulation 6 (No. 5 of 1942) (1943) 49 CAR 78 (*Car Cleaners and Porters case*)

In the Matter of an Application by the Commonwealth Public Service Board under Regulation 6 (No. 143 of 1942) (1943) 49 CAR 26 (*Postal Clerks case*)

In the Matter of an Application by the Commonwealth Public Service Board under Regulation 6 (1943) CAR 29 (*Counter Officers case*)

In the Matter of an Application by the Commonwealth Public Service Board under Regulation 6 (1943) 49 CAR 31 (*Mechanics Grade 1 case*)

In the Matter of an Application by the Commonwealth Public Service Board (1942) 48 CAR 242 (*Mail Officers case*)

In the Matter of an Application by The Alba Petroleum Co. of Aust. Pty. Ltd. under Regulation 6 of the Women's' Employment Regulations (1943) 49 CAR 146, p. 162 (*Commercial Travellers' case*)

In the Matter of an Application by Ivy Moray under Regulation 7 (1943) 49 CAR 119 (*Ivy Moray's case*)

In the Matter of an Application by Sims Cooper (Freezing Works) Pty. Ltd. (1943) 49 CAR 153 *(Meat Trade case)*

In the Matter of Applications by the Federated Municipal and Shire Council Employees' Union, N.S.W. Branch under Regulation 6 (1943) 49 CAR 244 (*Sydney County Council case*)

In the Matter of an Application by the Public Service Board of New South Wales under Regulation 6 (1943) 49 CAR 124 (*Miss Goldsmith's case'*)

Metal Trades Award, 1941; Motor Body and Coachbuilding Award, 1939; Federated Furnishing Trade Society of Australasia v. Australian Glass Manufacturers Co. Ltd. and Ors; Federated Rubber and Allied Workers Union of Australia v. Australian Rubber Mills Pty Ltd and Ors; Advanx Tyre and Rubber Co. Pty. Ltd. and Ors v. Federated Rubber and Allied Workers Union of Australia (1948) 60 CAR 1405, p. 1417 (*Female Minimum Rates Case 1948*).

In re Metalliferous Miners &c General (State) Award [1928] IR 466

Minimum Wage Case 1974 (1974) 157 CAR 293

Re Miscellaneous Workers Kindergartens and Childcare Centres &c (State) Award [2006] NSW IRComm 64 (*Childcare Centres case*)

Nadjovska v. AI&S [1985] EOC §92–140

Nadjovska and Ors v. AI&S Pty Ltd (1988) EOC §92–223

National Wage Case 1973 (1973) 149 CAR 75 (*Basic Wage Case 1973*)

National Wage Case (April) 1975 (1975) 167 CAR 18

National Wage Case 1976 (1976) 182 CAR 225

National Wage Case (Wage Fixing Principles Case) 1978 (1978) 211 CAR 399 (*Wage Fixing Principles Case 1978*)

National Wage Case (Inquiry into Wage Fixing Principles) 1981 (1981) 250 CAR 79.

National Wage Case 1983 (1983) 291 CAR 3

National Wage Case 1986 (1986) 301 CAR 611; (1986) 14 IR 187.

National Wage Case 1987 (1987) 17 IR 65

National Wage Case 1988 (1988) 25 IR 170

National Wage Case 1989 (1989) 30 IR 81

National Wage Case February 1989 Review (1989) 27 IR 201

National Wage Case 1990–1991 (1991) 36 IR 120

National Wage Case 1991 (1991) 39 IR 127 (30 October 1991) (Print KO300)
New South Wales v. Commonwealth of Australia; Western Australia v. Commonwealth of Australia [2006] HCA 52 (14 November 2006)
Nurses Comparable Worth case 1985–1986 [1986] 13 IR 108
Nurses Comparable Worth case No. 2 [1987] 20 IR 420
Osland v The Queen Osland v R [1998] HCA 75; 197 CLR 316; 159 ALR 170; 73 ALJR 173 (10 December 1998) (austlii.edu.au) (accessed 29 May 2023)
Parental Leave case 1989–1991 (1989–1991) 36 IR 1 (Print J3596)
Parental Leave—Casual Employees—Test Case (2001) 107 IR 71 (Print PR904631)
Paternity Leave Test Case 1990 (1990) Parting J3596 (26 July 12990)
Pay Equity Inquiry: Reference by the Minister for Industrial Relations pursuant to Section 146(1)(d) of the Industrial Relations Act 1996 (1998), Matter No. IRC6320 of 1997, NSW Industrial Commission, http://202.02.124.6/workandfamily/payequity/report/index.html (accessed 12 June 2006)
Personal/Carer's Leave Test case—Stage 2 (1995) 62 IR 48 (Print M6700);
Printing Trades case (1918) 2 SAIR 31
Re Private Hospitals and Doctors' Nurses (ACT) Award 1972 [1986] 13 IR 108 (*Nurses Comparable Worth case*)
Re Private Hospitals' and Doctors' Nurses (ACT) Award 1972 and Other Awards [1987] 20 IR 420 (*Nurses Comparable Worth case No. 2*)
Re Private Hospital Nurses (State) Award [1972] AR 156
Registered Nurses (Salaries and Career Structure) Reference 1986 (1986) 2 VIR 205 (*Registered Nurses (Vic.) case 1986*).
Rural Workers' Union and United Labourers' Union v. Mildura Branch of the Australian Dried Fruits Association and Others (1912) CAR 61 (*Fruitpickers case*)
Shaw v. Commonwealth of Australia (1992) 110 FLR 379
In re Shop Assistants Union [1910] AR 279
In re Shop Assistants, &c. (Metropolitan) Award [1927] AR 23, 25 (*Shop Assistants case*).
Shop Assistants case (1960) 59 AR 112
In re Standard of Living and Living Wages for Adult Males and Adult Females (Standard of Living and Living Wages Case 1932) (1932) IR 91
Re State Equal Pay Case [1973] AR 425

State of New South Wales v. Amery [2006] HCA 14 (13 April 2006)
State of Victoria v. McKenna (2000) EOC §93–080
State Wage Case 1974 [1974] AR 195
State Wage Case 1976 [1976] AR 329
State Wage Case 2005 (2005) 142 IR 337 (*State Wage Case 2005*)
State Wage Case 2000 Tasmanian Industrial Commission, Matters No. T8413, T8483, T8624, http://www.tic.tas.gov.au/decisions_issued/state_wage-case-Decisions/t8413,_t8483_and_t8624 (accessed 12 October 2023)
Supplementary Award Simplification case 1998 (1998) (Print Q5596) (15 September 1998)
United Voice and AEU, Application by [2018] FWCFB 177, 274 IR 1.
Wage Case 2005 (2005) 142 IR 337 (*State Wage Case 2005*).
Wardley (Lawrie) v. Ansett Transport Industries (Operations) Pty Ltd (1979) EOC
Watchel v. Watchel [1973] FD 72, [1973] 2 WLR 366, [1973] 1 All ER 829
Waters v. Public Transport Corporation (1992) 173 CLR 349, FC 91/038
Work and Family Test Case [2003] CAR 18.
Work and Family case 2005, Print PR082005, http://www.airc.gov.au/fullbench/PR082005.htm, pp. 1–132 (accessed 10 August 2006)
Working Hours case 2002 (2002) 114 IR 390 (Print PR072002)
Women's Employment Board (WEB) cases (1942) 48 CAR, (1943) 49 CAR.)
Yaruga v State of Victoria (Department of Community Services (Aboriginal Affairs)) [1994] VCAT

Contents

List of Abbreviations[1]

AAA	Affirmative Action Agency
AAB	Aboriginal Arts Board
AAC	Affirmative Action Committee
AAESDA	Association of Architects, Engineers, Surveyors and Draughtsmen of Australia
AAF	Australian Aboriginal Fellowship
AAL	Australian Aborigines League
AAMWS	Australian Army Medical Women's Service
AASW	Australian Association of Scientific Workers
ABC	Australian Broadcasting Commission/Corporation
ABS	Australian Bureau of Statistics
ACAC	Australian Conciliation and Arbitration Commission
ACE	Australian College of Education
ACEF	Australian Council of Employers Federation
ACF	Australian Conservation Foundation
ACMA	Associated Chamber of Manufacturers Australia
ACOA	Australian Clerical Officers Association
ACOP	Australian Council of Professionals
ACP	Australian Consolidated Press

[1] Biographical Sources—Interviews, Personal Communications, Personal Knowledge; Women's Voices, Women's Lives series (Scutt, ed.); Australian Women's Register; NLA, *Trove*; ***Australian Dictionary of Biography;*** Andrea Lofthouse, ***Who's Who of Australian Women***, Methuen, Sydney, 1982; NFAW, ***Australian Women—Biographical Entry; Who's Who in Australia 2006***, D&B Marketing/BWW, Melbourne, Victoria.

ACR	Australian Council of Retailers
ACSPA	Australian Council of Salaried and Professional Associations
ACT	Australian Capital Territory (Canberra)
ACTU	Australian Council of Trade Unions
ACW	Aircraft Woman
AEMWF	Arms Explosives and Munition Workers Federation
AESDA (now ACSPA)	Association of Engineers, Surveyors and Draftsmen of Australia
AEU	Amalgamated Engineering Union
AEU	Australian Education Union
AFBPW	Australian Federation of Business and Professional Women
AFEI	Australian Federation of Employers and Industries
AFPC	Australian Fair Pay Commission
AFUW	Australian Federation of University Women
AFWV	Australian Federation of Women Voters
AI	Amnesty International
AIDA	Australian Industry Development Association
AIF	Australian Infantry Forces
AIFS	Australian Institute of Family Studies
AIRC	Australian Industrial Relations Commission
AIS	Australian Iron & Steel
AJA	Australian Journalists Association
ALGWA	Australian Local Government Women's Association
ALLY	Australian Labor League of Youth
ALP	Australian Labor Party
ALRA	Abortion Law Reform Association
ALRM	Aboriginal Legal Rights Movement
AMACSU	Australian Municipal, Administrative, Clerical and Services Union
AMC	Australian Maritime College
AMFSU	Amalgamated Metals, Foundry and Shipwrights Union
AMG	Angliss Meat Group
AMIA	Australian Meat Industries Association
AMIEU	Australasian Meat Industry Employees Union
AMWSU	Amalgamated Metal Workers and Shipwrights Union
AMWU	Australian Manufacturing Workers Union
ANESBWA	Association of Non-English Speaking Background Women of Australia
ANHLC	Australian Neighbourhood Houses and Learning Centres
ANU	Australian National University
ANTaR SA	Australians for Native Title and Reconciliation South Australia
APA	Aborigines' Progressive Association
APEA	Association of Professional Engineers Australia

APS	Australian Public Service
APSA	Australian Public Service Association
APTU	Australian Postal and Telecommunications Union
ARM	Australian Republican Movement
ARU	Australian Railways Union
ASU	Australian Services Union
ASWU	Australian Social Workers Union
ATNA	Australian Trained Nurses Association
ATO	Australian Taxation Office
ATSIC	Aboriginal and Torres Strait Islander Commission
ATUC	All-Australian Trades' Union Congress
AWAs	Australian Workplace Agreements
AWAS	Australian Women's Army Service
AWGE	Australian Women's Guild of Empire
AWLA	Australian Women's Land Army
AWM	Australian Women's Movement
AWP	Australian Women's Party
AWU	Australian Workers Union
AWUEQ	Australian Workers Union of Employees Queensland
AWW	Asian Women at Work
BallaratU	Ballarat University
BEU	Brewery Employees Union
BHP	Broken Hill Proprietary Ltd
BLF	Builders Labourers Federation
BPW	Business and Professional Women
BSS	Bachelor of Social Sciences
BSW	Bachelor of Social Work
BTUC	British Trade Union Council
BWIU	Builders Workers Industrial Union
CA	Certified Agreement
CAE	College of Advanced Education
CAEP	Council of Action for Equal Pay
CAI	Confederation of Australian Industries
CAIS	Centre for Aboriginal Indigenous Studies (now Monash Indigenous Centre [MIC])
CAPOW!	Coalition of Australian Participating Organisations of Women!
CAR	Council for Aboriginal Rights
CATUA	Clothing and Allied Trades Union of Australia
CAWSA	Council of Aboriginal Women of South Australia
CBW	Council of Business Women
CCFU	Commonwealth Council of Federated Unions
CEDA	Committee for Economic Development of Australia

CEDAW	UN Convention on the Elimination of All Forms of Discrimination Against Women
CEPC	Combined Equal Pay Committee (Western Australia (WA))
CEPO	Council for Equal Pay and Opportunity (Western Australia (WA))
CFMEU	Construction Forestry Maritime Mining and Energy Union
CIDA	Council of Intellectual Disability Agencies
CLS	Community Legal Service
CMA	Chambers of Manufacturers of Australia/Associated Chambers of Manufacturers of Australia
CPA	Communist Party of Australia
CPI	Consumer Price Index
CPS	Commonwealth Public Service
CPSA	Commonwealth Public Service Arbitrator
CPSB	Commonwealth Public Service Board
CPSO	Commonwealth Public Service Officers
CPSU (SPSF/SPSFT)	Community and Public Sector Union (State Public Services Federation/Tasmania)
CSA	Civil Service Association
CTU	Clothing Trades Union
CWA	Country Women's Association
CWTA	Combined Women Teachers' Association
CYSS	Commonwealth Youth Support Scheme
DEET	Department of Employment, Education and Training
DLitt	Doctor of Literature
ECCV	Ethnic Communities Council of Victoria
EcoSoC	UN Economic and Social Council
EEC	European Economic Community
EEO	Equal Employment Opportunity
EOB	Equal Opportunity Board
EOWA	Equal Opportunity for Women Agency
ERO	Equal Remuneration Order
ET	Embryo Transfer
ETUA	Electrical Trades Union of Australia
EYL	Eureka Youth League
FAAH	Federation of Australian Associations of Housewives
FAUSA	Federated Australian University Staff Association
FCAATSI	Federal Council for the Advancement of Aborigines and Torres Strait Islanders
FCTU	Federated Clothing Trades Union
FCU	Federated Clerks Union
FMWU	Federated Miscellaneous Workers Union

FPA	Family Planning Association
FPC	Fair Pay Commission
FPEPLPEAA	Federated Photo Engravers, Photo Lithographers and Photogravure Employees Association of Australia
FPU	Food Preservers Union
FRWU	Federated Rubber Workers Union
FSOG	Female Scientific Officers' Group
FTCWU	Federated Tobacco and Cigarette Workers Union
FU	Flinders University
FUA	Federated Unions of Australia
FWA	Fair Work Australia
FWC	Fair Work Commission
GDR	German Democratic Republic
GNP	Gross National Product
GPO	General Post Office
GRI	Global Reporting Initiative
GST	Goods and Services Tax
HCCPSO	High Council of Commonwealth Public Service Organisations
HCREU	Hotel, Club and Restaurant Employees' Union
HEF	Hospital Employees Federation
HEIU	Hospital Employees Industrial Union
HEU	Hospital Employees Union
HRC	Human Rights Commission
HREOC	Human Rights and Equal Opportunity Commission
HSU	Health Services Union
IAG	Industrial Action Group
IAW	International Alliance of Women
ICFTU	International Confederation of Free Trade Unions
ICW	International Council of Women
IEU	Independent Education Union
IFBPW	International Federation of Business and Professional Women
ILO	International Labour Organisation
IPA	Institute of Public Affairs
ITUC	International Trade Union Confederation
IVF	In Vitro Fertilisation
IWD	International Women's Day
IWSA	International Woman Suffrage Alliance
JCEP	Joint Committee for Equal Pay
JIR	Journal of Industrial Relations
JSNL	Jessie Street National Library
LGA	Local Government Association

LHMWU/LHMEU	Liquor Hospitality and Miscellaneous Workers Union/ Liquor Hospitality and Miscellaneous Employees Union
LSMA	London School Masters' Association
LTA	Lady Teachers' Association
LTU	Liquor Trades Union
LWV	League of Women Voters
MACOVI	Ministerial Advisory Council on Veterans' Issues
MacquarieU	Macquarie University
MEAA	Media, Entertainment and Arts Alliance
MEU	Mining and Energy Union
MIEU	Meat Industry Employees Union
MLHA	Master Ladies' Hairdressers Association
MonashU	Monash University
MTEA	Manufacturing Transport and Engineering Australia
MU	Murdoch University
MUA	Maritime Union of Australia
MWG/MWM	Militant Women's Group/Militant Women's Movement
MWU	Miscellaneous Workers Union
NAC	National Advisory Committee for IWY
NACSR	National Advisory Council on Strategy and Resources
NAP	National Australia Party
NAWC	National Association of Women in Construction
NCW	National Council of Women
NCWV	National Council of Women Victoria
NDA	Non-Disclosure Agreement
NEPC	National Employers Policy Committee
NFAW	National Foundation for Australian Women
NPEC	National Pay Equity Coalition
NRTs	New Reproductive Technologies
NSW	New South Wales
NSW COSS	Council of Social Service
NSW DEOPE	Director of Equal Opportunity in Public Employment
NSW WAC	Women's Advisory Council
NT	Northern Territory
NTEU	National Tertiary Education Union
NWAC	National Women's Advisory Council
NWFE	National Network of Women in Further Education
NWWC	National Working Women's Conference
OEA	Office of Employment Advocate
OECD	Organisation for Economic Cooperation and Development
OSW	Office of the Status of Women

OWA	Office of Women's Affairs
OWN	Older Women's Network
PMG	Post Master General
POA	Professional Officers Association
PSA	Public Service Arbitrator
PSA	Public Service Association
PSB	Public Service Board
PSC	Public Service Commission
PSF	Public Services Federation
PTWU	Public Transport Workers Union (now TWU)
QNA	Queensland Nurses Association
QU	Queensland University
QWA	Queensland Workplace Agreement
RAF	Royal Air Force
RAAF	Royal Australian Air Force
RANF	Royal Australian Nursing Federation
RMO	Resident Medical Officer
RSL	Returned Services League (now Returned and Services League of Australia)
RTA	Retail Traders Association
RWU	Rural Workers' Union
SA	South Australia
SACS	Social, Community and Disability Services (originally Social and Community Services)
SCC	Sydney City Council
SCEGGS	Sydney Church of England Girls' Grammar School
SDA	Shop Distributive Association
SDAEA	Shop Distributive and Allied Employees Association
SPS	Social Purity Society
SPSF	State Public Services Federation
SRN	State Registered Nurse
SSTU	Southern State Teachers Union
SU	Students Union
SUC	State Unemployed Council
SWU	Socialist Workers Union
TAFE	Technical and Further Education
TCCI	Tasmanian Chamber of Commerce and Industry
TCFU	Textiles Clothing and Footwear Union
TGWU	Tailors and Garment Workers' Union
THC	Trades Hall Council
TLC	Trades and Labour Council

TPCU	Telegraphist and Postal Clerks Union
TSIT	Tasmanian State Institute of Technology
TTLC	Tasmanian Trades and Labour Council
TUERC	Trade Union Employee Relations Commission
TUTA	Trade Union Training Authority
TWU	Transport Workers Union
UA	United Associations
UAW	Union of Australian Women
UAdel	University of Adelaide
UCWS	United Council for Women's Suffrage
ULU	United Labourers' Union
UMacq	Macquarie University
UM	University of Melbourne
UN	United Nations
UNA	United Nations Association
UNAA	United Nations Association of Australia
UNewcastle	University of Newcastle
UNHCR	United Nations High Commissioner for Refugees
USyd	University of Sydney
UTas	University of Tasmania
UTLC	United Trades and Labour Council
UTS	University of Technology Sydney
UV	United Voice
UWA	University of Western Australia
UWM	Unemployed Workers Movement
UWU	Unemployed Workers Union
UWU	United Workers Union
VBU/VBEF	Vehicle Builders Union/Vehicle Builders Employees Federation
VCA	Victorian College of the Arts
VCAT	Victorian Civil and Administrative Tribunal
VCOSS	Victorian Council of Social Service
VEF	Victorian Employers Federation
VLTA	Victorian Lady Teachers' Association
VTHC	Victoria Trades Hall Council
VTU	Victorian Tailoresses Union
VTU	Victorian Teachers Union
VWC	Victorian Women's Coalition
VWT	Victorian Women's Trust
WA	Western Australia
WAAAF	Women's Auxiliary Australian Air Force
WAC	Women's Action Committee
WAC	Women's Advisory Council

WATA	Women Assistant Teachers' Association
WCM	Women's Charter Movement
WCTU	Women's Christian Temperance Union
WCU	Women's Coordination Unit
WEAC	Women's Employment Action Committee
WEB	Women's Employment Board
WEFA	Woman's Equal Franchise Association
WEL	Women's Electoral Lobby
WETTANK	Women's Economic Think Tank
WFE	Women in Further Education
WFL	Women's Franchise League
WFTU	World Federation of Trade Unions
WHC	Women's Health Centre
WICH	Women in Community Housing
WICH	Women in Industry and Community Health
WIDF	Women's International Democratic Federation
WILPF	Women's International League for Peace and Freedom
WIRE	Women's Information Referral Exchange
WIS	Women's Information Switchboard
WLA	Women Lawyers Association
WL/WLM	Women's Liberation/Women's Liberation Movement
WM	Women's Movement
WPA	Women's Progressive Association
WPEL	Women's Political Education League
WRAAF	Women's Royal Australian Air Force
WRANS	Women's Royal Australian Navel Service
WSG	Women's Service Guilds
WSEL	Women's Suffrage and Education League
WSL	Women's Suffrage League
WSPU	Women's Social and Political Union
WSVE	Work Skills Value Enquiry
WTUC	Women's Trade Union Conference
WTUL	Women's Trade Union League
WUS	Women's Union of Service
WWC	Working Women's Centre
WWCC	Working Women's Charter Campaign
WWPO	Women Workers Political Organisation
WWTU	Working Women's Trades Union
YWCA	Young Women's Christian Association

CHAPTER 1

Introduction: Work, Theory, Scholarship—Equal Pay, Pay Equity, and the Sex of Gendered Work

> [O]ne of the first demands of enfranchised women in New Zealand and South Australia was equal pay … in all State departments. In Victoria women teachers are paid less than men of the same grade, although very often teaching more subjects; and, moreover, a woman, no matter how skilled, is not allowed to reach the highest position in the State schools. Our Women Factory Inspectors are paid less than men, and one might multiply these cases indefinitely. I saw [recently] it was a 'matter of principle in the boot-making trade to pay women less than men'. How is it that men do not see how this principle, or rather want of principle, affects them?
>
> 'Suffragist', Letter to ***Tocsin***, a Victorian Socialist Journal
> 28 October 1897

Introduction

From the nineteenth century, Australian women demanded equal pay. As claimants, witnesses, interveners, and advocates, women contested wage injustice as discrimination, exploitation, and undermining work value in federal, state, and territory arenas. Through trade unions, women's organisations, conferences, and workshops, women advocated locally, nationally, and internationally. Women used press releases, press articles, and interviews. Through non-fiction and fiction, documentary, docu-drama and features, radio, film, and television, women demanded industrial

J. A. Scutt, *Wage Rage for Equal Pay*,
https://doi.org/10.1007/978-3-031-42178-5_1

justice. Despite the struggle's longevity, in 1975—finding Australia's major school text, FK Crowley's ***A New History of Australia***, published 1974, referred to women simply 'as wives, mothers and novelists', with men's wages referenced 'at least seven times'—Peter Spearritt discovered one article alone on women's employment published in ***Labour History***, founded in 1961.

Such historical distortion is not isolated. The twentieth-century's last quarter had women's employment more frequently recorded in mainstream research and writing. Yet even today, women are too often ignored and, educated and socialised in a world where men still hold most positions of power and predominate in publishing, women are not immune from the dominant discourse. Historian Heather Radi says 1920s working women 'seemed to accept their situation "without obvious discontent"', although records repudiate such passivity. Kate White endorses Women's Movement waves theory, saying Australia's first-wave feminism ended with the 1936 breakdown of the working relationship between two well-heeled, assertive feminists, Bessie Rischbieth and Jessie Street. Yet many activists and organisations existed beside those of Rischbieth and Street, who worked with other Women's Movement activists through the 1940s and 1950s.

Nevertheless, some scholarship does challenge traditional history. Affirming women's citizenship and agency, Jennie Bremner observes that despite portrayal of the 1930s Depression as determinedly anti-feminist, the 'first consistent' women's Australia-wide equal pay campaign occurred then, Muriel Heagney a pivotal figure. Even then, equal pay demands emerged well before the 1930s, and Bremner rightly questions '... the historical caricature [confining] female activism to the "Two Great Waves of Feminism" leaving in limbo everything between the suffragette campaign and the [1960s] women's liberation movement ...'. This applies equally to assertions of 1950's women eschewing activism and public life. Far from retreating into domesticity, abandoning the world, women's 1950s equal pay activism eclipsed the 1960s. Media reports appeared throughout the 1950s and into the early 1960s, 1950s women activists sustaining 1960s reportage.

Constance Lamour's Women's Employment Board (WEB) wage-fixing work refers to women's 'failure ... to capitalise on the advantages of their wartime organisation and advancement'. For Lamour, women did not seize on 'wartime conditions and ... post-war ... labour shortages [with] unsatisfied demands for goods and services' to press equal pay. Yet far from ignoring the possibilities, Heagney worked with the Australian Council of

Trade Unions (ACTU)'s Harold Souter in the ***Basic Wage Case 1949–1950***. Their equal pay claim gained women rates at 75 per cent of the male basic wage. The League of Women Voters, Australian Federation of Business and Professional Women (AFBPW), and National Council of Women (NCW) intervened, explicitly claiming equal pay. The Arbitration Court's three-fourths of a man's wage, rejecting equal pay, cannot negate women's presence, render their initiative meaningless, or undercut the wage gain, directly contradicting 'failing to capitalise on equal pay'.

Even when placed centre-stage, women and women's working lives are distorted or misrepresented when one group of women or women's activity is authenticated at the expense of another. Winifred Mitchell records women's 1890s activism during the NSW and Queensland miners' strikes, centering women in the historical frame, yet denies women as independent activists demanding workers' rights. Her analysis has women demonstrating, picketing, and lobbying against blacklegs and strike-breakers, so husbands, brothers, and fathers can retain their jobs. Accepting as 'justifiable' the description of women's trade union participation as 'trivial', she depicts women's organisations as 'less strong' than women's auxiliaries to mine worker (men's) organisations. Yet this elevates some women and women's organisations at the expense of others. Validating one group of women does not require others to be nullified, or asserting one exists only in the other's absence. Whilst professing to deny traditionalist history, this simultaneously reads women's history through traditionalist eyes. As activists, women standing firm against mining companies and governments determined to break the (male) miners' will existed alongside women activists advocating working women's rights. Often, they were both. Women trade unionists were active in 'men's unions' and in women's unions and organisations, Heagney one of many.

Although the bulk of visible research and writing on Australian women's history dates from the 1970s, earlier records exist alongside journals and diaries, letters, and scribbled notes hidden in escritoires or destroyed by unthinking or unknowing relatives or bailiffs. Today, a solid and ever-expanding core recounts women's history from myriad perspectives, in many mediums. Despite history's overwhelming male focus, equal pay history and analysis appears in texts and articles recounting women's engagement as workers and industrial activists. Some research advances theories and insights into women's equal pay claims and the struggle to achieve it. Theories of bias in comparable worth and work value assessment, including interaction between paid and unpaidwork, exist alongside critique of decision-makers' approaches to women's industrial conditions and wage setting. So, too, conjecture in research and literature surrounding equal pay progress and retreat. Women's fiction as a mirror and means of exposing industrial injustice and advancing pay equity provides a rich body of work, too.

Pursuing Equal Pay Through Jurisprudence

Australia's industrial relations system is crucial. Centralised wage fixing set pay rates from the end of the nineteenth century and federally from 1904 until abandoned at century's end. The conciliation and arbitration system came from a belief, confirmed by the 1890s miners' strikes, that industrial disputation required a workable mechanism for lasting, or at least consistent, resolution. Mostly, the impact on women's wages has been a by-product of male-dominated unions seeking higher wages and better conditions for male workers. However, sometimes the system has resolved industrial conflicts surrounding women workers' wages. There, impact has been direct, women's wages adjusted or settled through arbitration explicitly as women's rates of pay. Today, because women's wages are generally low and women predominate in low-paid industries, setting a minimum, 'living' or 'fair' (sic) wage (alongside enterprise bargaining) applies mainly to women's jobs.

Three principal areas of dispute have surrounded women's wage rates. First, during wartime, discontent amongst women earning women's wages, seeing women in essential industries taking men's jobs and gaining a higher percentage of the male wage. Secondly, disputes around women's rates versus men's rates, unions seeking to shore-up men's wages by keeping women out in fear of women's wages depressing men's or women taking men's jobs. Thirdly, disputes about women's right to equal rates as men: claims for the rate for the job, equal pay for equal work or equal pay for work of equal value or pay equity.

Reviewing changing feminist perspectives on equal pay and the impact of legal institutions, Raelene Frances considered feminist historians' contributions to Australian arbitration history. Until recently these scholars' verdict was, she wrote, '… uniformly critical' of arbitration in 'reinforcing the subordinate position of women within Australian society'. Frances cites Edna Ryan and Anne Conlon's ***Gentle Invaders—Australian Women at Work 1778–1975***, mapping differentials in male and female wages and 'setting the tone for subsequent work'. However, in 2001, the move to enterprise bargaining brought a shift, with feminists reassessing arbitration as generating progressive results for women. This, wrote Frances, balanced Ryan and Conlon's 'overwhelmingly negative view', Ryan ironically a leader in this shift.

Frances quotes Ryan's saying that in the Arbitration Court workers 'had access to law, if not equality before the law' so 'did not have to feel so threatened'. The shift occurred simultaneously with 1980s calls for labour market deregulation: facing a prospect of no awards or protection for unionists, feminists 'began to realise … the arbitration system was the lesser of several evils', at least ensuring a 'floor of protection', 'preventing differentials from widening further'.

In 1975, the ***Gentle Invaders*** was a landmark. Tracing Australian wage fixing from the 1907 ***Harvester*** decision, Ryan and Conlon argued that for 60 years ***Harvester*** thwarted equal pay. Commonwealth Conciliation and Arbitration Court president Higgins promoted the living or family wage—determined by a family man's needs as father of two dependent children, husband to a dependent wife, spending his income on family upkeep. Then, in the ***Clothing Trades case 1919***, Higgins fixed women's wages at 54 per cent of the male or family wage, referencing women workers as single, living at home, lacking financial responsibilities for family or dependants. Between these decisions, in the ***Fruitpickers case 1912***, Higgins established the 'equal pay for equal work' principle: women doing men's work, alongside men, should receive the male rate.

For Ryan and Conlon, ***Harvester***, endorsing the fallacious notion that all male workers had (or would have) a wife and two children to support—using their income to support them, came from misogyny or male chauvinist dogma. Support for this proposition—an arbitration system tainted by ideology inimical to women's rights and equal pay—they located in state and federal decisions.

Depicting Higgins as a colonial 'acolyte', in 2006 Mark Hearn analysed his decisions as founded in a bourgeois paternalistic vision of nation-building women and men, '… intended as a prescription of what sort of citizens they should become and how they should behave'. His ideals evolved from 'a middle-class liberalism' centred in British 'ideological and cultural roots'.

Some 20 years earlier, Laura Bennett's short rejoinder to ***Gentle Invaders*** argued that neither culture nor patriarchy explained Arbitration Court women's wage determinations. Principles set by colonial and state industrial bodies before 1907 did. For Bennett, truth lay in Higgins following these precedents, elevating men's industry above women's. Frances agrees an explanation for male-female wage differentials lies in the characterisation of male workers' jobs as skilled, male job components being skills, but said judicial reluctance 'to award women more for their skills owed more to ideology than Bennett allows'.

Frances' view is the more persuasive. It is unlikely that Higgins would follow colonial or state decisions. Architect of the Arbitration Court, appointed simultaneously to it and the High Court, with his experience and standing Higgins would not consider himself bound by other bodies' decisions, particularly state wages boards or commissions. They created no precedents and, in any event, the NSW Industrial Commission set the family wage at three children plus parents, not Higgins' two. Higgins applied his own mind (its socialisation, cultural context, moral and ethical ideals), generally showing a disposition toward considering, or at least bearing in mind, what today would be community values, influenced by social justice focussed on his envisioned working class. Inevitably, this carried patriarchal implications, but ***Harvester*** requires analysis and critique beyond this.

Ryan and Conlon framed Higgins' male chauvinism on excerpts from his male/female wage decision. However, a more complex interpretation lies in concerns that employers should pay sufficient wages for families to live, coupled with an ethical perspective that workers should not be exploited by receiving less than a fair share of profits in wages. Higgins' judgments confirm male chauvinism was not his only motivator, nor the sole foundation for the family or living wage. They affirm a desire for industrial fairness and an acute consciousness of employers' exploitative power, albeit accompanied by a paternalistic concern for women (rather than recognition of women's rights as equal). Commonly, women live double lives: workers in their own right, but married women attached to a male worker upon whom they may be dependent at least some time in their lives, through social mores and physiological or biological realities, viz childbearing and suckling of infants. For Higgins, this meant women required protection from exploitation not by (generally) granting them a living wage or family wage alongside male counterparts, but by promoting a paidwork world where men's wages could relieve women from the need to compete in industry as wage earners, often under poor industrial conditions.

In the ***Broken Hill Proprietary Limited (BHP) case 1909***, evidence showed labourers' wives expending 'more than [the] receipts' (wages) of their husbands. Significantly, 'the mother of the household is so often found leaving her home, even her young children, for a day's work ...', supplementing a husband's wages. Ryan and Conlon cite this as confirming an anti-women's-right-to-work dogma. Yet Higgins' words constitute a clear indictment of a powerful employer—BHP Industries—exploiting (male) labourers meaning they cannot afford to support themselves or their families.

The original ***Harvester*** judgment relates to a manufacturing industry (Harvester Industries made agricultural machinery) earning substantial profits while workers were paid 6s (shillings) a day. How they might survive on 6s, when Higgins' rate of 7s was based on a minimal cost of living estimate: rent, grocers' bill, bread, meat, milk, fuel, vegetables and fruit, omitting light, clothing, boots, furniture, utensils, rates, life insurance, savings, accident or benefit societies, loss of employment, union dues, books and newspapers, tram and train fares, sewing machine, mangle, school requisites, amusements and holidays, intoxicating liquors, tobaccos, sickness and death, religion or charity, or expenditures for contingencies is unfathomable. HV McKay, Harvester's owner and employer, was notorious for anti-union opinions and behaviour. Responding to a union protest when he paid overtime at ordinary rates, McKay asserted that as the firm paid a bonus at previous year's end, it was 'not fair to expect extra payment for overtime'. Yet the bonus was paid, in the main, to foremen—not labourers, apparently designed to promote their extracting 'the greatest amount of work from the men' in the future. Writing to William Morris Hughes, Australia's prime minister, McKay declared he did 'not believe in the basic wage' and 'God did not make men equal—... no use trying to pretend He did, or to make laws as though He did ...'

For Higgins, running an undertaking 'as a marvel of enterprise, energy and pluck ...'meant McKay was 'allowed ... to make any profits ... he can'. But an employer is not, Higgins added, entitled 'in the course of his economies, to economise at the expense of human life ...' This discloses a Higgins' balancing act. Of necessity, considering industrialists' power and Higgins' sympathetic leanings towards labour, capitalists' rights were acknowledged but curtailed in the affirmation of workers' rights.

In upholding working-class rights, Higgins was bound by traditional socialism—the fight for the working-class man alone being necessary to free the working-class woman. Higgins was trapped, too, by his middle-class values—seeking to extend them to working-class women so that, like (some) middle-class women, they would not need paid employment. He overlooked the realities of working-class women's lives, by necessity needing paidwork, and of middle-class women abjuring the middle-class ideal, whatever their husbands or fathers' views. He supported university education for women, championing niece Nettie Palmer and as a University of Melbourne Council member supporting women's full admission. His wage determinations reveal him as paternalistic, rather than patriarchal. Wanting working-class women to be freed, he promoted a remote possibility, thereby locking them into dependency or poverty. Yet for the times, Higgins' decision was monumentally radical—so proven when the High Court struck it down the following year. His professed bow to capitalism and language he used to lift the wage by what seems a bare minimum were clearly designed to preserve the higher rate. This failed, and it is unsurprising that in the High Court appeal, which McKay won 3:2, the dissenting judges were Higgins and Isaacs.

For Ryan and Conlon, the ***BHP case*** again evidences Higgins' male chauvinism. Atop other remarks, he deemed it 'fortunate' that the 'greater number of breadwinners still are men', so women were 'not all dragged from the home to work', leaving the men 'loafing at home'. Yet was this really a splenetic response to middle-class women's goal of entering the professions and public life, Higgins believing they conflated working-class women's interests with their own, or imposing their goals upon working-class sisters? Or was it a concern about men shirking their breadwinner responsibilities? Or a caustic remark directed not to keeping women at home and out of the paid workforce, but pointedly aimed at a large capitalist employer, BHP, setting wages so low that women-as-wives had no choice except working to supplement the husband's wage?

Taking Higgins' comment on excess of essential expenditure over Broken Hill workers' income, this last explanation seems the more plausible, bearing in mind his championing of women's independence professionally and intellectually. His position arguably rested on desiring economic stability and protection for (married and prospectively married) working-class women rather than denying them the right to work. Paternalistic and sex/gender discriminatory, yes. Yet a paternalism associated with upholding (what he saw as) the rights of the working-class–women and men.

Employee power was subordinated to employers. Higgins sought to adjust this status quo. (As he said so explicitly in ***Harvester***.) Thus, if power differentials place all bargaining chips in one party's hands (here, BHP), whether being 'dragged out' to work expresses the reality for women in the workplace or is what women wish or not; whether women seek careers in trades or professions to secure an independent income and economic freedom or not—this is subordinated to employer diktat. Where a powerful company can dictate, workers having little or no protection or capacity to bargain for fair and reasonable wages, both adult members must enter paidwork, whatever their preferences. This reality underlies Higgins' critique, informing his decision.

Rightly, Ryan and Conlon emphasise through Commonwealth Bureau of Census and Statistics, Royal Commissions, and living and industrial conditions inquiries that not all men had wives and children. Those who did often did not support them—frequently deserting. Many women relied on their own income or resources for supporting not only themselves but children and, not infrequently, parents or elderly, disabled, or indigent relatives. As ***Gentle Invaders*** attests, setting a family wage as if men alone have dependants is unfair on women whose own expenses equal a man's and sometimes man-and-family, although in all fairness Higgins referred throughout to worker and workers never *male* workers.

House rent or accommodation costs, rates, electricity, board, clothing, travel expenses, and other life necessities are no lesser expense for women than men. Industrial bodies also ignored women's *right* and *need* to work (for money), and women's right to a fair day's pay for a fair day's work. Wage fixing leaving women out in the cold to starve or make do as they can, or relying on welfare or church charity, is inexcusable. However, Higgins' decision-making seems not to be informed by, or to be, *active* misogyny. It was misguided and, hence, sexist—paternalistic or 'benign' discrimination being equally negative for women as active sexism. Simultaneously, however, it was a radical challenge to laissez faire notions of employers' entitlement to fix wages regardless of workers' capacity to survive on them.

More than one reading applies to the ***Fruitpickers case 1912***, too. Higgins' equal pay for equal work decision (mirrored in the ***Equal Pay Case 1969***) is touted as designed to keep women out of men's jobs. Yet the alternative ***Harvester*** analysis can apply. The union claimed rises for all workers. Seeking to extract maximum wages from reluctant and even recalcitrant employers, whilst facing a High Court that can overturn him on appeal (as with ***Harvester***), Higgins sets the wage level for jobs mainly done by men at as high a level he estimates the High Court will tolerate. He offsets this by fixing wage levels lower for jobs mainly done by women. The rationale is sustainable in the context of the times. Traditionally, women were paid less than men. Therefore, he calculates, the decision survives an appeal: the employer (though grumbling and reluctant) pays wages at a family or living level for some jobs, at least.

In a system where trade-off is inherent—the very words conciliation and arbitration import negotiated outcomes—unions aim for the highest levels of pay possible for their members. Employers aim to keep wage levels down. For a judge sympathetic to workers' rights, the aim is finding a solution satisfying the goal of increasing workers' incomes to a liveable level. In the ***Fruitpickers case***, this meant some women, at least, gained equal pay. Quite properly, Ryan and Conlon focus on the women missing out. Yet this should not negate, ignore, or sideline the 1912 advance. After all, the argument that some women were entitled to a family wage opened an argument that *all* women in paidwork were entitled. Ultimately, it is for unions, workers, and advocates to advance wage-fixing arguments. Industrial bodies cannot manufacture arguments or support for decisions in the absence of parties' submissions. Higgins and the Arbitration Court do not alone bear responsibility for decisions underpaying women workers.

As women generally have constituted one-third of the Australian workforce 'at any time and never less than 20 per cent', Ryan and Conlon found women confronted an invidious decision: '... the necessity of demanding either the right to work or the right to be paid the rate for the job'. Getting a foot in the door, much less on the promotions ladder, tempted women to take jobs at lower wages simply to gain economic independence. Yet taking a job at lower wages meant mere survival, not financial freedom. Ryan and Conlon concluded that women should have focussed from the outset on the rate for the job, not equal pay. This echoed Heagney's cry from the 1920s into the 1950s, Kath William's call from the 1950s and 1960s, and AFBPW's in 1965.

Thirty years before ***Gentle Invaders*** explored wage fixing denying women a fair reward for their work simply because women did the work, in 1942 Council of Action for Equal Pay/Australian Education Union (CAEP/AEU) published Heagney's ***Are Women Paid Men's Rates?*** Earlier, in 1935, Heagney's ***Are Women Taking Men's Jobs?*** declared the 'only means of equalising the position of the sexes as wages earners' is fixing 'occupational rates based upon the nature of the work' (not whether women or men did it). An employer could not pay women's wages and men's wages, or a basic wage (for men) and a woman's wage, or pay less for a job done by a woman, or more because a man did it. For Heagney, economic independence was a human right, women 'consciously demanding recognition', not categorised as 'protected in the home' as a 'man's appendage'. Women's right to work should rest 'not on the number of dependants, nor [whether] she does or does not compete with men, but in the absolute right of a free human being, taxpayer and voter, to economic independence'.

Adamant that economics was fundamental to women's rights struggle, she persuaded unions to support equal pay and the rate for the job. 'There can be no emancipation for women,' the May 1937 Equal Pay Conference resolved, until 'economic equality [is secured] for women through equal pay for the sexes. *This is our primary and most important interest.*'

Contrary to contentions that women and unions failed to pursue equal pay as women's right—either not at all, or by bolstering men's claims to jobs and keeping women out of them—Heagney noted that despite 'few pressures' on the union movement 'as a whole' to fight for equal pay in pre-war years, unions with substantial female memberships, including the Clerks and the Clothing Trades, regularly initiated equal pay cases. In 1926, the Clothing Trades Union argued '... every woman should enjoy the highest possible standard of living in her own right and not merely share in the pleasure and comforts of life through her men folk'.

Until the 1940s, women's groups argued consistently for the rate for the job. As job segregation by sex/gender could lead to women receiving less than men, activists demanded the claim's extension to 'the same or similar work'. Then Jessie Street and the UA opposed rate for the job, creating a split in the Women's Movement and between Street and Heagney. Ultimately, rate for the job did not bring equal pay, notwithstanding ACTU Congress resolutions, unions adopting the principle, equal pay conferences, pressure from women's organisations and women.

Even during wartime, the male rate for the job for men, not women, persisted. As ***Gentle Invaders*** noted, during the First World War it was suggested that women's work performance would influence peacetime pay rates. Thus, 'influenced by the fervour of the time, ... and in a generous mood acknowledging women's ability in a crisis ..., in 1916 Mr Justice Powers suffered a slight aberration ...' Noting women's contribution, he said it would 'be hard, after the war ... to refuse to acknowledge [equal pay] claims for equally good work, solely on the ground [of being] done by a woman'. Yet, with the war over, Powers found it 'not hard at all'. Having 'chucked them under the chin' for their war work, he didn't hesitate 'in wanting to boot women out of the industry by 1921 ...'. Saying the community would be better served if men responsible for wives and children worked at employment suitable for them, rather than girls and women 'tempted to take up men's work in factories and workshops', Powers determined the Court would not '... encourage employers to employ women at work ... men can reasonably claim to be men's work'.

During the Second World War, the Women's Employment Board (WEB), established by the Curtin Labour government to set women's wages in men's industries, generally paid up to 90 per cent of the male rate only, and often much less. A woman's rate persisted, even when women did (enlisted) men's work.

Reviewing WEB's approach, Constance Lamour suggests outcomes would have been different, had the Arbitration Court retained jurisdiction over men's work performed by women for the war effort. The Arbitration Court '... was greatly influenced by its concept of the traditionally different nature of work performed by females'. Hence, if it controlled the setting of women's wages and conditions in essential war work (traditionally men's work), '... the whole structure and rationale of wage fixation would have been irretrievably altered'.

Yet convention has it that WEB's wartime wage-fixing role was best for women's wages in male industry, because rates increased for women all around. As women in men's work received higher wages than those in women's work, industrial disputation generated higher rates in women's industries. Critiquing this, Ryan and Conlon identify an irony, as women with longer work histories could be paid less than newcomers taking on male jobs. Furthermore, rarely awarding full male rates, the WEB failed women. Would the Arbitration Court have differed?

First, employers. Twice launching High Court challenges against the federal Parliament's power to create the WEB, employers resisted WEB's decisions informally, too. Referencing Heagney's logbooks, Lynn Beaton describes them as 'full of discontent, stoppages and disputes created by employers' refusal ... to pay WEB rates'.

Would employers have resisted Arbitration Court decisions similarly? The Court's standing, its existence for almost 40 years, may have given its decisions greater weight. Employers may have acceded more readily to paying women rates closer to the male rate than previously. However, Beaton records the Chamber of Manufactures reporting some members facing prosecution for refusal to pay WEB rates—albeit compliance meant additional profits. That employers in essential industries filled government contracts 'on a cost-plus basis, ... the government [paying] employers a percentage of their costs as a profit' meant paying women higher wages would increase costs and, therefore, create higher profits. Deep-seated prejudice evidently operated amongst at least some employers. Would prejudice disappear with the Arbitration Court ordering higher wages?

What of Lamour's suggestion that in fixing women's wages in essential industries (men's jobs) the Arbitration Court would likely have awarded 100 per cent? History defies any belief of much difference between the two forums. WEB decisions are infused with notions of women as less skilled, more prone to injury, more susceptible to fatigue, and, although euphemisms abound, at menstruation's mercy. The Arbitration Court used identical factors to reduce women's working hours. Such assumptions would govern its assessment of women's work in essential (male) industries, surely, rather than precedents covering men's industries and men's jobs prior to war being applied to women workers in essential industries during war.

Arbitration Court division of work into male and female, with male and female wage rates was fatal to women's universal equal pay claims. So long as the Arbitration Court classified (some) work as men's work—whether women or men did it—this hindered any real increased valuation of women's work during the war or when, at war's end, women returned to it. Women remaining in or at men's work would retain men's wages (WEB decisions no longer applying), but the system would remain bifurcated into women's and men's rates for women's and men's work.

Lamour's confidence in better Arbitration Court outcomes matches Ryan's contemporary support for the arbitration system and centralised wage fixing, despite her critique 25 years earlier. This revision corresponds, too, with that of others familiar with the wage-fixing system and wary of negative consequences for women without it. Yet confidence in the arbitration system does not require showing the Arbitration Court and WEB would have responded differently in wartime. As Carol O'Donnell and Philippa Hall emphasise in ***Getting Equal***, changes in wage-fixing principles can lift or lower women's and men's wage relativities. Reintroduction of the minimum wage in 1966 is one example. The minimum wage applied to men only, in 'unskilled' jobs, with no male employee paid less than the minimum wage. Women in jobs classed unskilled had no such protection. The key is centralised wage fixing versus alternatives.

From 1967 to 1974 and 1980 to 1983, when the Commonwealth Conciliation and Arbitration Commission adopted a more decentralised approach to wage fixing, lower paid workers—the majority women—fell behind. The ***Equal Pay Cases 1969*** and ***1972*** and ***Minimum Wage Case 1974*** delivered some catch up, women's wages rising appreciably in some sectors. But the 1969 decision's limitations and union failure to pursue claims under the 1972 decision meant that despite 'equal pay', women did not generally get it.

From the ***National Wage Case 1983***, women's organisations focussed beyond the basic or national wage, considering over-award payments (replacing margins and loadings, abolished with introduction of the total wage), bonuses, and fringe payments. Then, from the ***Nurses Comparable Worth case 1985–1986*** and onwards through appearances in the ***National Wage Cases 1988, 1990–1991*** and ***1991***, and ***Family Court Counsellors case 1993***, attention turned to valuation of women's work, valuing skills, and value set on women's skills contrasted with skills value attributed to men's work or deemed inherent in work done by men.

Calculating Women's Work as Worthy of Equal Pay

The pervasive belief that women's work is not as valuable as men's, and 'women's industries' are not worthy of remuneration, status, or prestige accorded industries predominantly male, is replicated in all institutions, at all levels of society. In 'every known human society, the male's need for achievement can be recognised' (she might have said male's need for recognition of achievement), anthropologist Margaret Mead noted, observing that if men 'cook or weave or dress or hunt humming-birds', if these are accepted male occupations, then 'the whole society, men and women alike, votes them as important'. Yet if performed by women, these occupations 'are regarded as less important':

> In a great number of human societies men's sureness of their sex role is tied up with their right, or ability, to practise some activity women are not allowed to practice.

Defining women as non-persons, Australia followed British precedents denying women the right to practice law and medicine. Working-class men relied on regulations or custom banning women from occupations: jobs redefined as male. Professional men had judicial support: where laws and regulations conferred rights and privileges, making no distinction between the sexes (referring to 'persons'), judicial interpretation barred women. This denied women prestige, status, and access to arcane knowledge conferring power and lucrative prospects. No surprise, then, that judges led in classifying work and wages—whether labouring or trade—along sex/gender lines.

The rate for the job gained credence amongst equal pay proponents who believed setting a wage rate irrespective of the worker's sex/gender would remove wage-fixing bias, restoring or affirming sex/gender neutrality. Yet a jurisprudence capable of defining person as 'man' and woman as 'non-person' had little difficulty in applying the rate for the job along sex/gender lines. The simple expedient was to nominate one rate for jobs done by men (the family or living wage), one for jobs done by women (the family or living wage minus x per cent). Then, so long as male fields excluded women, the rate for the job operated to deny women male rates.

Similarly, equal pay for equal work can deny women equal pay. Working alongside men, doing the work men do, women will receive the (male) rate for the job: the rate for that job, equal pay for that work—the rate set at the family or living wage. Working at some other job, alongside women, doing the work women do, women will receive the rate for the job—set by what the work is worth, with a built-in indicator that it must be worth the family or living wage minus x per cent. Next, reclassify jobs as male and female, moving women from 'male' jobs. Thus, the rate for the job, like equal pay for equal work, could promote workplace segregation. This followed the ***Equal Pay Case 1969***. However, equal pay for work of equal value as in the ***Equal Pay Case 1972*** provided greater possibilities: women doing men's jobs gain the male rate, and women doing women's jobs gain it if those jobs are assessed as equal in value to men's jobs.

Work value is a long-accepted method of determining value of job components to fix upon a composite wage for the job. The 1972 decision enabled cross-award and cross-job assessments, meaning components of jobs traditionally done by women could be compared with components of jobs traditionally done by men. If components matched, the man's job rate would accrue to the woman's job. Yet as with any job evaluation scheme, problems hover. How are different jobs compared? How can assumptions that women's work is inherently worth less than men's, and hence components are not comparable, be overcome?

In the 1980s, dissension flared: did comparable worth fit the Australian system? Would it hold women back, adding complexities and biases more difficult to shift than those already existing? Women's Movement critics worried about in-built bias measuring comparable worth; proponents saw it as a focussed way to apply a principle already in the Australian system, namely, equal pay for work of equal value. In the ***Nurses Comparable***

Worth case 1985–1986, the ACAC dismissed comparable worth saying that, coming from the US, it had no relevance to Australia.

The ***Equal Pay Case 1972*** definitively affirmed cross-award and cross-job assessments to determine work value. As sex/gender bias is pervasive, whatever system of assessment is used, whatever terminology employed, comparable worth supporters wanted focus on addressing sex/gender bias. In the ***Pay Equity Inquiry 1997***, the NSW Industrial Relations Commission heard expert evidence on bias affecting job evaluation and assessment. The NSW Commission sought counteracting methods to eliminate or at least ameliorate its operation and effects.

In ***The Promise and the Price***, Clare Burton identifies bias associated with organisational politics, resulting from embedding a gendered workplace culture, continuously replicating itself. Organisations are 'saturated with masculine values' because men have played 'internal organisational politics through both formal and informal structures' since their foundation. Values 'derived from men's experience, massively contribute to women's inequality at the workplace' because 'certain positions, or qualifications for advancement, demand time and activity [assuming] domestic support' or job definitions are grounded in constructions of masculinity. Burton attributes arrangements in work organisations to the cumulative outcome of bargains and compromises between parties, excluding women from playing a significant or influential role in this bargaining.

The workplace automatically promotes employees embodying or representing existing (masculine) values. Managers and supervisors notice and approve of their work, supporting their promotion and pay rises. Jobs they do and how they do them are more valued, attracting higher pay. Promoted into decision-making positions, these workers operate as did their managers and supervisors, promoting and rewarding employees performing identically or as much like the masculine norm as possible. Position descriptions attract workers of similar ilk, job interview panels are constructed to accommodate that norm, and selections are made consistent with inherited masculine workplace values.

Within this context, industrial bodies assess the value of work, what are 'skills', what skills are worth. Burton, Raven Hag, and Gay Thompson see objectivity as a key problem: subjective judgements 'inevitably form a part of the evaluation process'. Yet decision-makers see their decision-making and assessments as objective. Alerting them to their biases and reliance upon assumptions is crucial. Decision-makers accepting this is equally crucial.

Bennett describes how unions ensured members' work was labelled 'skills' or skilled, thereby securing wage rises, margins for skill, and over-award payments. Unions worked to ensure their members and jobs they did would avoid 'unskilled' classification depriving them of 'skilled work' wage benefits. Burton says the politics of skill explains and is the problem. Power relationships 'govern determination of appropriate qualifications for positions, ... whether some qualities, essential for performance in a job, [will] be acknowledged at all and, if they are, whether they [will] be paid for and at what rate'. Women's skills employers consider as natural female attributes, not skills accruing 'through training and experience'—say, 'manual dexterity, social skills and caring qualities—so do not warrant compensation'. Perceptions of ability and performance are crucial. Merit takes centre stage, purportedly introducing fairness and objectivity. However, 'common understanding' that merit is measured by reference to the candidate's ability or capacity to perform is, Burton avers, misplaced. Research shows men assessed as more able than women, with more (desirable) 'natural' ability 'in many areas' or possessing 'more of the important *kinds* of ability'. This stereotyping Burton identifies as mainly resulting from 'attitudes and practices' categorising women as 'better at emotional work (say) required in looking after children, men at hard physical work or hard mental work' for paid jobs. Thirty-five years on, Mary Ann Sieghart's ***The Authority Gap*** recognises similarly the undervaluing, by undermining, of women's authority.

The *unpaid* factor impacts on women's paidwork participation in juggling family responsibilities, broken work patterns through maternity, childbearing and childrearing, and responsibility for ageing parents and other relatives. It also affects assessments of work women do in paid employment, modifying valuation of women's work and fields where women predominate. Voluntary work plays a part, a resume referencing voluntary work in Zonta, Soroptomists, Probus or Quota, Women and Management, AFBPW, or Women Leaders conveying a different message from one listing Lions, Rotary, Apex, Chamber of Commerce, Young Business Leaders, or Youth Chamber of Commerce. Women's organisations may be unfamiliar to appointment and promotions committees, or assessors of skills and abilities. Organisation titles may lack resonance or meaning; if recognised, existing attitudes towards women's workplace capacities—and women's organisations—influence valuing.

Besides subjectivity/objectivity, Burton, Hag, and Thompson identify three keys to assessing cross-job or cross-award job value or comparable worth:

- Influence of the chairperson of, or senior people in, an evaluation committee on final job ranking
- Effect of 'rater familiarity' with the job
- Consistency in format and length of written position descriptions

Paraphrasing this troika, transposing them into work value assessment in Australian industrial bodies:

- Influence of judge or presiding commissioner in final job ranking
- Effect of 'rater familiarity' of a commissioner assessing work value regularly in particular industries or fields, becoming (overly) familiar with particular jobs, weighting judgements towards them
- Consistency in format and composition of jobs compared for work value assessments.

Influence, effect, and consistency are definitive in the industrial system. Judges or presiding commissioners exercise *determinative* power, not just 'influence'. Ultimately, they *decide definitively* job worth, skills' worth, valuation of skills as against other skills, of jobs relative to other jobs. This within a system imbued with Burton's masculine workplace culture, just more so.

Traditionally, the arbitration system assigned judges or commissioners to particular trades and industries to resolve disputes. This ensured judges or commissioners were familiar with those industries and trades in components and type of work done, workplace history, past disputes, wage fixing, and dispute settlement. However, it harbours the risk Burton, Hag, and Thompson identify for workplace 'raters'. Judges or commissioners doing work value assessments regularly in industries or trades assigned to them could 'become (overly) familiar with particular jobs, [weighting] judgements towards the better known or well-known jobs'.

The arbitration system necessarily developed greater familiarity in men's jobs and fields traditionally male-dominated. The strongest—male industry—unions brought work value assessment claims. As Frances, Burton, and Bennett observed, 'skills' applies to components of jobs done by workers unions represent. This contrasts with lesser knowledge of women's fields of work, stereotypical views of women and work, what women can and cannot do physically, physiologically and/or intellectually according to ascription. Plus a moral or prejudiced undertow—'we cannot allow women to do that', 'can't allow women to get dirty', 'women shouldn't work late nights' or even 'women can't work alongside men'.

Such thinking infuses legal system decision-making, from parliaments to courts. Parliamentary debates on married women's property, women's suffrage, guardianship of infants replicated '… prevailing attitudes to women's status and role within the family', as Susan Edwards notes, exposing gender's function in excluding women from public participation. Inconsistencies 'between social and legal reality' prevail. On the one hand, the 'wife and mother role is extolled … glorifying maternity'. Yet traditionally husbands and brothers held legal authority, with no legal authority in a wife's domestic status. ***Watchel v. Watchel*** (1973) showcases this stereotypical thinking. Denning MR saw the divorced husband, going 'out to work all day', as needing 'some woman to look after the house—either [new] wife … or housekeeper', child maintenance adding to his financial burden. The 'wife will not usually have so much expense'. Even if in paidwork, doing 'most of the housework herself, perhaps with some help, she will not usually employ a housekeeper'. Hence, her material needs are the less.

Last century, yes, but abandoned? Denning's exposition of income needs and financial sustainability relies on what women should do, versus what men should not (have to) do; men's (greater) rights and entitlements as against women's. Identical ideas persist in wage fixing. Nonetheless, transparency of legal system decision-making contrasts starkly with confidential job assessment and evaluation, skills estimates, and valuing work done by interview and selection panels, employers, and job search consultants. Commission, court, and wage-fixing tribunal decisions are open to parties and subject to media scrutiny. Work value and (un)equal pay decisions are published. Just as Denning's decision is open to read or be read about in press or law journals, so with industrial bodies' decisions.

Openness allows not only for critique but possibility of change by dislocating inherent sex/gender bias. It affords the chance that work value, women's work, and equal pay decisions can incorporate a less biased perspective. This has been women's goal in intervening in industrial bodies.

The educative effect of women's engagement, though slow, is evidenced by changes over time.

Urging Equal Pay Through Unions and Women's Organisations

Transparency is a compelling reason for supporting the arbitration system. Yet ambivalence accompanies women's interaction with legal and political institutions. Often Women's Movement antagonism or hostility challenges the legal system. Some aspects are deplored, some tolerated or even supported, despite the system's limitations. As Edwards says, 'feminist realists' traditionally 'engaged with the law and campaigned politically through trade unions, and political parties', feminist *campaigners* having '... always seen some laws as capable of improving [women's] position ...'. She cites nineteenth-century feminist reformers regarding the law 'as a major lever in campaigns and struggles for great participation of women in public life and social reform ...' This reflects the contest: use law to change society, or abjure it—'perpetuating inequality'. The 'feminist idealists' versus 'feminist realists'.

Trade unionists Heagney and Kath Williams remained committed to the conciliation and arbitration route for achieving equal pay. Women's Movement activist Street expressed scepticism, yet fought within the system. Women's organisations time and again sought leave to appear, wanting to be heard. With applications for leave granted almost consistently, every time equal pay was refused or partially granted, women fashioned new arguments, challenged inconsistent rationales. Every intervention meant the bench faced women's demands.

Decisions are not immutable—though influencing future decision-making, their rationale and effects can be rejected in future cases, too. Decision-makers' predisposition to outcomes can be changed or at least impacted by stating and restating arguments, as women did in ***Basic Wage, Equal Pay, Minimum Wage,*** and ***National Wage Cases***. Though men predominated as decision-makers, lawyers, interveners, and parties' representatives, openness and transparency gave women's claims a chance.

Unions are central to arbitration. Women's unions, and women in unions, have had a problematic relationship with men's unions, and men in unions. An initial, substantial impediment was union registration under the Conciliation and Arbitration Act 1904 (Cth): registered unions alone could appear in the Arbitration Court or its successors. Women workers organised first, often taking industrial action more persistently. In the nineteenth century, match girls in England and tailoresses in Australia went on strike, tailoresses establishing their own union. Yet the arbitration system which could have supported women's trade unions failed them. Men's unions registered first. Once one union was registered, another could register only if representing workers not covered by the registered union. Women's unions were absorbed by men's unions or fell into desuetude. Women workers had to find representation in men's unions.

Women's industrial rights, pay, and conditions would have been on the agenda immediately had women's unions been registered. Even if male-dominated unions pushed ahead, Arbitration Court dispute processes would have assured women's application hearings. Even if women's wages were, despite female union representation, set below men's, women workers would still be better inside than outside the system. Even with male union representation, women were better off in it. Take outworkers: without unionisation and lacking arbitrated awards, pieceworkers were notoriously underpaid. Sweated work prompted establishment of Victoria's wages boards to regulate conditions, and sweating was a major women's organisation concern.

With women's unions registered, a dichotomy could nonetheless have infused work value calculations under arbitration, due to male dominance. However, three elements might have militated against this. First, women's pursuit of the issue politically and in the industrial arena: equal pay indivisible from equal opportunity. Secondly, women in male-dominated unions had impact despite fewer numbers, gaining positions from which they operated cooperatively with women's organisations. Thirdly, where opportunities exist, women's perspectives impact the mainstream.

Women's unions continued operating in some states; however, federally women were limited to male unions, with greater male membership and all-male or male-dominated executives. Yet as women had honed organising and negotiating skills in their own unions, they found ways of using the Arbitration Court's key wage-fixing role. Outcomes between state bodies and the Arbitration Court meant workers receiving less under either system led to industrial disputes. The higher rate was a lever for advocates to raise the lower rate. In the equal pay struggle, this signified. For Heagney and Williams, Sara Lewis, Helen Robertson, Maude O'Connell, Minnie Felstead, and their confreres, union meetings, executive decision-making, and ACTU Congresses with few women delegates meant lesser likelihood of getting the call to speak. In the Arbitration Court, with leave granted, or as witnesses, they could speak. Heagney and, later, Williams, Zelda D'Aprano and others devised equal pay arguments from union ranks and within the Women's Movement, advancing them in conferences, state industrial bodies and the Arbitration Court. Maintaining strong union loyalties and taking an active role in union affairs as union members did not inhibit their voicing doubts about unions' approach to the struggle. Though less stark today, women taking prominent union positions, issues remain.

A loyal union and ALP member from 1918, Heagney staunchly adhered to a publicly expressed belief that equal pay, or 'rate for the job', would come through unions and Women's Movement activism. Nonetheless, by 1942 she 'frankly [had] given up hope of achieving anything worthwhile immediately', writing to a woman activist friend that in Australia 'the Labour Movement and ACTU executive officers are so terribly reactionary in their views on women workers'. This meant commencing 'about half a mile behind the starting post in a mile race when women are involved in any issue ... trade union officials and Labor ministers as a rule [being] more difficult to deal with than many bad employers of labour'.

Yet as D'Aprano observes and the record shows, neither Heagney nor Williams gave up on the unions. This seems attributable to their commitment to organised labour and the chance for women's wage justice, and that not all unions, not all male members, denied women's industrial rights and union rights as important. Women unionists did not work without male unionists or union officials and organisers. NSW Teachers Federation equal pay debates evidence this.

With the teachers and other unions, the split for and against equal pay was not all one way: sometimes, women opposed, male members in favour; sometimes, men argued adamantly for 'real issues' leading the agenda (their wages), not the 'distraction' of equal pay. In the 1990s, this was replicated during women's efforts to retain centralised wage fixing, when the ACTU wanted enterprise bargaining. Women advocates and activists arguing that enterprise bargaining would damage lower-paid workers' prospects (mainly women) earned ACTU ire. The ACTU disappointed and frustrated them when, as predicted, enterprise bargaining blocked progress toward equal pay, a decline beginning with the mid-1980s two-tier wage system.

Despite the Women's Movement and unions' problematic relationship, trends are apparent. From 1937, membership lists confirm the CAEP successfully drew together unions and women's organisations, many women holding dual membership. Some periods saw women's organisations invited to ACTU conferences, making equal pay resolutions and policy. Equal Pay Week, initiated by union Equal Pay Committees, hailed speakers from unions and women's organisations. During the 1950s, relationships between women's organisations and the ACTU were particularly strong, equal pay a motivator.

Simultaneously, unions harboured antagonisms to the Women's Movement, dismissing it as middle-class (despite union and working-class women in both) or antagonistic to unions and working-class industrial rights. This became particularly evident during the 1970s and 1980s, with women's agitation for anti-discrimination, equal opportunity, and affirmative action laws. In NSW, the Trades and Labour Council (TLC) campaigned to remove employment discrimination from Anti-Discrimination Board jurisdiction to the NSW Industrial Commission. Unsuccessful, the campaign simmered for years.

Conversely, women's organisations have sometimes viewed unions as a barrier to women's equal pay, equal union involvement, and improving women's industrial conditions. In the 1970s, male domination and women's absence from executives in women's industry unions—retail (Shop Distributive and Allied Employees Association (SDA)) and clerical work (Federated Clerks Union (FCU))—were focal points. In the 1980s, CAEP members experienced ACTU betrayal in the ***Nurses Comparable Worth case 1985–1986***. Behind the scenes, prior to the hearing, the ACTU sought CAEP support. The CAEP believed this meant comparable worth would be pivotal to the ACTU's claim. The CAEP's submissions advocated comparable worth. When the Commission rejected it, disparaging its US origins, the CAEP bore the brunt, inferring that the ACTU blamed it for 'antagonising' the Commission and undercutting the ACTU's claim.

Introduction of enterprise bargaining through the ***National Wage Case 1991*** and the Industrial Relations Amendment Act 1992 (Cth) by the Hawke Labor government did generate a rise in women's union membership. Having intervened against enterprise bargaining, once adopted, AFBPW (generally professionals or small business entrepreneurs), promoted union membership, advocating union representation as crucial in bargaining negotiations. But the 1990s–2000s Howard Liberal National Coalition government stymied equal pay. Still, states gave some hope. Then Labor's return federally in 2007, 2010, and 2022 heralded change. But was it enough?

Advocating Equal Pay Through Fictional Foresight

Atop all this, equal pay activism proves multifaceted. Women's organisations, unions, paid jobs or voluntary work, women working together or independently through the centuries, agitating at grassroots, working on the ground, in small groups, in unions or against them, in fiction and fantasy, and in the international arena. Women's organisation and trade union records, and women's papers, all providing insights, alongside diaries and letters, just as women's history is preserved in literature—novels, short stories, poetry, plays. In ***Writing a New World*** (1988) and ***Heroines*** (1991), Dale Spender shows women gaining voice through myriad styles and avenues, recording their own and other women's lives, informing, politicking, proselytising.

Writing signifies in all political and economic change movements. Texts create or lead shifts in thinking or relate underlying tensions influencing action. Just as women's literature is weighty in Women's Movement activism generally, it registers the equal pay struggle. As H. Aram Veeser relates, the New Historicism accepts literary works as 'a product of [their] time, … place of writing and circumstances of composition'. Yet literature influences more than time and place, often heralding changes to the external circumstances of its composition. The influence of mass-market popular fiction is a common field of research, feminist writers analysing reality shows, film and magazines including the ***Women's Weekly*** and ***New Idea***. Simone de Beauvoir and Kate Millett reviewed fiction's projection of women as objects of male desire. The influence of literature on equal pay warrants scrutiny.

For centuries, women as poets, playwrights and fiction writers have been significant Women's Movement players. Writer Dymphna Cusack spoke at a UA meeting when visiting Sydney, requiring organiser Vivienne Newson's swift action to quell rumblings about Cusack's 'Commie' ideas. In Perth, newspaper articles and correspondence with Irene Greenwood affirm Katharine Susannah Prichard's active membership of the Combined Equal Pay and Equal Opportunity Committee. Their novels provide a rich source for literary critics, writers, activists, and historians.

With universities favouring male academics, how could women write history from academic posts? Denied access to academic and non-fiction publishers, women wrote women's struggle for citizenship, economic independence, equal pay, and political worth into fiction. In the nineteenth and early twentieth century, Catherine Helen Spence, Louisa

Lawson, Henry Handel Richardson, Stella Miles Franklin, Barbara Baynton, Jessie Couvreur ('Tasma'), Marie Bjelke-Petersen, Rosa Praed, and Ada Cambridge wrote women's political, social, economic, and romantic reality. Later, Cusack, Prichard, Dorothy Hewett, Eve Langley, Florence James, M (Marjorie) Barnard Eldershaw, Jean Devanny, Kylie Tennant, and Eleanor Dark explored women's realities—more acceptable to publishers and critics in fiction. When women figured in history as a grey background, muted tones against which men's exploits were writ large, or as audience to male warriors, gamblers, workers, explorers, exploiters, leaders, and lunatics, it was near to impossible to publish women's history qua history. This meant writing, publishing, preserving in other ways.

Cusack, Tennant, James, Hewett, Langley provide insights into lives and struggles of their times. Real stories—based on real women's lives, circumstances confronting real women. They struggled, too—to live as full-time writers, sustained through an income from writing, faced the impossibility of doing so. As artists, writers, filmmakers, poets, women mostly rely on modest incomes. In the 1930s, 1940s, 1950s, and into the 1960s this was even more so. Being female preordained relative penury. This, they knew. Equal pay and decent industrial conditions were crucial for them, too.

As litterateurs, Australian women recount women's struggle for industrial rights and pay equity, fiction firmly grasping reality. Working in a Sydney factory for a year created Hewett's record in ***Bobbin Up*** of life and lives of those around her, of dustups and putdowns, strikes and strike breakers, back-breaking work for meagre reward. She recorded the camaraderie between workers, support for one another and disdain for the bosses. Her book galvanised women into joining the struggle. Langley picked peas, packed apples, harvested sweetcorn, and wrote ***The Pea Pickers***. With sister June, she followed the women of Higgins' ***Fruitpickers case 1912*** 30 years earlier. For novelist Ruth Park, ***The Pea Pickers*** came from a writer of 'dazzling' ideas who, in 'careless drifting manner, filled my mind with treasure that still delights me', the 'first woman I ever saw who constantly wore slacks', with 'thick leather sandals of a Franciscan type' encasing her 'bare, scratched, brown feet ...'

'Every character and every incident was taken from life ...' Cusack on her ***Come in Spinner*** collaboration with James, resonating alongside other accounts of women campaigning for wage justice, women's lives as workers, as characters in fiction, as individuals surviving as secretaries, clerks, and support staff, deprived by patriarchal rules of the right to work their chosen professions. Australian women's literary writing has influenced the politics and history of women's rights for a fair day's pay for a fair day's work. It lies crucial in recounting the long, long struggle for equal pay.

Women as theorists, historians, writers, philosophers, lawyers, and activists have construed and conveyed the campaign multifariously, through trade unions, in women's organisations, and in novels and song. All provide a footing for understanding the equal pay struggle and how, over time, the rate for the job, equal pay for equal work, equal pay for work of equal value, comparable worth, and pay equity have shaped and continue to shape women's wage justice demands.

Taken up by women of the nineteenth century, building on women's activism of earlier decades in laying the foundation, the equal pay fight catapulted women into union and political activism. Building on this, the twentieth century saw women committed to wage justice campaigning through each decade and into the new millennium.

Women spoke out, spoke up, and worked with others, collectively, to advance equal pay. An understanding of the battles fought through the industrial system rests in seeing these women actors as individuals and members of organisations they established or joined to claim women's rights. Without individual women acting collectively, the women's wage justice campaign would not have begun, nor continued. Recognition of women dedicating themselves is an essential part of equal pay's history of struggle. Just who were these women, how did they work, and what skills, experience, and understandings did they bring to the struggle? Chapter 2, 'Intermission—Pay and Personalities I' relates some of the many, known and unknown, in the equal pay story.

References

Cases—See Case List

AFBPW, ***The Rate for the Job***, BPW Australia, Melbourne, Victoria, 1965.

Lynn Beaton, 'The importance of women's paid labour', in Bevege, James and Shute (eds), ***Worth Her Salt***, 1982, pp. 84–98.

Simone de Beauvoir, ***The Second Sex***, 1949, Jonathan Cape, London, UK, 1953.

Laura Bennett, 'The Construction of Skill', ***Law in Context***, vol. 2, 1984a, pp. 118–32.
Laura Bennett, 'Job Classification and Women Workers', ***Labor History***, vol. 51, 1986, pp. 11–23.
Laura Bennett, 'Legal Intervention and the Female Workforce', ***International Journal of the Sociology of Law***, vol. 12, no. 1, 1984b, pp. 23–35.
Margaret Bevege, Margaret James and Carmel Shute (eds), ***Worth Her Salt***, Hale & Iremonger, Sydney, NSW, 1982.
Jennie Bremner, 'In the cause of equality—Muriel Heagney' in Bevege, James and Shute (eds), ***Worth Her Salt ...***, 1982, pp. 286–98.
Clare Burton, ***The Promise and the Price***, Allen & Unwin, Sydney, NSW, 1991.
Clare Burton, Raven Hag and Gay Thompson, ***Women's Worth***, AGPS Press, Canberra, ACT, 1987.
Val Buswell, ***Personal Communication***, Sydney, NSW, 1991; ***Interview***, Sydney, NSW (24 June 1996).
CAEP Members, ***Interview***, Melbourne, Victoria, 1996 (June 1996).
CAEP/AEU, ***Are Women Paid Men's Rates?*** CAEP, Sydney, NSW, 1942.
HK Crowley (ed), ***A New History of Australia***, William Heinemann, Melbourne, Victoria, 1973, 1986.
Ann Curthoys, Susan Eade and Peter Spearritt (eds), ***Women at Work***, Australian Society for the Study of Labour History, Canberra, ACT, 1975.
Zelda D'Aprano, ***Kath Williams***, Spinifex Press, Nth Melbourne, Victoria, 2001.
Susan SM Edwards, ***Sex and Gender in the Legal Process***, Blackstone, London, UK, 1996.
Susan SM Edwards, ***Women on Trial***, Manchester University Press, Manchester, UK, 1984.
Bradon Ellem, ***In Women's Hands?*** UNSW Press, Kensington, NSW, 1989.
Raelene Frances, 'Gender, Working Life and Federation' in Hearne and Patmore (eds), ***Working ...***, 2001, pp. 32–47.
Raelene Frances, 'One Hundred Years of Women's Wage Fixing', ***Journal of Interdisciplinary Gender Studies***, vol. 5, no. 2, 2000 (December), pp. 84–93.
Muriel Heagney, ***Are Women Taking Men's Jobs?*** Hilton & Veitch, Melbourne, Victoria, 1935.
Muriel Heagney Papers, Latrobe Library, Melbourne, Victoria.
Mark Hearn, 'Securing the Man—Henry Bournes Higgins', ***Australian History Studies***, vol. 37, no. 127, 2006, pp. 1–24.
Mark Hearne and Greg Patmore (eds), ***Working the Nation***, Pluto Press, Annandale, NSW, 2001.
Constance Lamour, 'Women's Wages and the WEB', in Curthoys, Eade and Spearritt (eds), ***Women ...***, 1975, pp. 47–58.
Margaret Mead, ***Male and Female***, Penguin, New York, NY, USA, 1962.
Kate Millett, ***Sexual Politics***, Doubleday & Co., New York, NY, USA, 1970.

Winifred Mitchell, 'Wives of the Radical Labour Movement' in Curthoys, Eade and Spearritt (eds), ***Women …***, 1975, pp. 1–14.

NPEC Members, ***Interview***, Sydney, NSW, 2006 (26 June 2006).

Carol O'Donnell and Nerolie Golder, 'A Comparative Analysis of Equal Pay', ***Australian Feminist Studies***, no. 3, 1996 (Summer 1986), pp. 76–87.

Carol O'Donnell and Philippa Hall, ***Getting Equal***, Allen & Unwin, Sydney, NSW, 1988.

Ruth Park, quoted Joy Thwaite, ***The Importance of Being Eve Langley***, Angus & Robertson, Sydney, NSW, 1987.

Heather Radi, 'Women in Sydney', in Crowley (ed), ***A New History …***, 1973, pp. 357–14.

Edna Ryan, 'Equal Pay, Comparable Worth and the Central Wage-Fixing System', ***Australian Feminist Studies*** no. 6, p. 9, 1988.

Edna Ryan and Anne Conlon, ***Gentle Invaders—1778–1975***, Nelson, Nth Melbourne, Victoria, 1975.

Penny Ryan and Tim Rouse, 'Women, Arbitration and the Family' in Curthoys, Eade and Spearritt (eds), ***Women …***, 1975, pp. 15–30.

Mary Ann Sieghart, ***The Authority Gap***, Transworld/Doubleday, London, UK, 2021.

Peter Spearritt, 'Women in Sydney Factories c. 1920–50' in Curthoys, Eade and Spearritt (eds), ***Women …***, 1975, pp. 31–46.

Dale Spender, ***Writing a New World***, Pandora Press, London, 1988.

Dale Spender (ed.), ***Heroines***, Penguin, Ringwood, Victoria, 1991.

H. Aram Veeser (ed.), ***The New Historicism***, Routledge, New York, NY, USA, 1989.

WEL, *Submission to the National Wage Case 1983*, WEL Sydney, NSW, 1983.

Kate White, 'Bessie Rischbieth, Jessie Street …' in Bevege, James and Shute (eds), ***Worth Her Salt …***, 1982, pp. 319–29.

CHAPTER 2

Intermission: Pay and Personalities I

TO WHOM IT MAY CONCERN

These notes of evidence in the Commonwealth Arbitration Court ***Basic Wage Inquiry*** of 1937 are made available so that, ... with the transcript notes of the Clerks' Union Equal Pay Case before the NSW Industrial Commission in 1940, all concerned with future wage negotiations have clear and definite knowledge of these important cases relating to women's wages.

Muriel Heagney
Council of Action for Equal Pay
3 January 1941

Introduction

Muriel Heagney left a paper trail behind her. The trail began in 1906 with her Victorian Political Labor Council membership card when, at twenty-one, she joined. It led from the Richmond branch of the Victorian Council, to NSW, to Queensland, to WA and SA. It tracked her to Honolulu for the first Pacific International Conference, from Russia to Geneva, then London and the first British Commonwealth Labour Conference. It followed her into the NSW Industrial Commission and Commonwealth Arbitration Court, through her years with AB Piddington's 1920 Inquiry into Poverty, the NSW Clerks' Union ***Equal Pay Case 1937***, federal ***Basic Wage Case 1937***, and ***Basic Wage Case 1949–1950***, with equal pay run but not won. From a Richmond convent to primary school teaching, to

J. A. Scutt, *Wage Rage for Equal Pay*,
https://doi.org/10.1007/978-3-031-42178-5_2

clerking in the Department of Defence, standing unsuccessfully in the Boroondara federal seat by-election, initiating Council of Action for Equal Pay (CAEP) meetings, then from women's organisation meetings to speaking on the factory floor, dynamic in trade union meetings and congresses, onward to rallies and conferences, next Equal Pay Week celebrations, so back to the CAEP …

A dull bronze wall plaque mounted outside Melbourne's Trades Hall Council Chamber celebrates Heagney's name and work. In 1974, Elizabeth Reid lamented that Heagney and her exploits remained so little known, now. As Australia's 'most effective advocate for the … rate for the job', wanting a rate 'without regard for the sex of the person', Heagney's slogan was 'equal status, equal pay, and equality of opportunity'. Yet a week after women won an adult minimum wage in the ***National Wage Case 1974***, she 'died neglected and forgotten …'. Heagney was not 'baggage too heavy for us to carry … for we had never heard of her. If we had she may well have been able to help us see our way ahead'. Ignorance not only deprived Heagney of her rightful affirmation but denied women a direct knowledge of past strategies for advancing women's rights.

Ten years later, in 1984, Trades Hall and the Working Women's Centre (WWC) hosted an exhibition on working women and trade unionists' lives. Heagney featured then, and at Women and Labour Conferences in the late 1970s–early 1980s her name appeared in occasional scholarly papers published in conference collections. Texts now acknowledge her existence and theses pay tribute to her importance. Despite this, Heagney was largely abandoned by the Women's Movement to which she devoted her life, argued with, decried, denied, nurtured, and led over decades of equal pay struggle. Her work was even dismissed as 'leading to showy but unfortunately short-lived resolutions in favour of equal pay and opportunity'.

Yet Heagney was a giant of her times, initiator of women's actions and activism, a women's organiser who recognised labour movement backing of equal pay for women was essential. Who believed women's industrial rights and wage justice would be gained not by gradualism, but by demands made head on. Feisty, and wilful too, whatever the opposition she was never averse to standing her ground.

A major 1930s–1940s Women's Movement rift arose because Heagney openly disdained Jessie Street's softly, softly approach. Street was prepared to endorse incremental women's wage increases rather than matching men's wages overnight. Unaccustomed to being disagreed with—by women fighting women's cause—Street never forgave Heagney. Nor did Heagney forgive her.

Difficult Women? Personalities, Principles, and Internecine Struggles

Traditionally, differences between women are attributed to an inability to work together, competitiveness or, colloquially, spats between cats. Rarely are differences seen for what they are: ideological arguments over principle, or disputes about practicalities of advancing a case or promoting a cause through a designated strategy. Often, arguments combine both. As in all political disputes, personality features. Women in the equal pay struggle are strong-minded—of necessity. Often, individualistic even whilst working in groups and endorsing group action. Little wonder differences, even schisms, arose between and amongst women and women's groups in wage campaigns.

Heagney and Street's dispute was not isolated. Adela Pankhurst Walsh and Rose Scott gained notoriety over mutual disdain for their respective positions on a range of subjects and argued fervently with others—simultaneously devoted to economic justice and women's rights. Bessie Rischbieth, working closely with Street particularly through the AFWV, took exception to Street's support of Russian workers. Labelling radical Jessie a Red and a Communist, conservative Bessie declined further collaboration.

Albeit agreeing on women's wage justice, approaches differed. Sometimes, women worked harmoniously for long periods, then fell out. Sometimes, differences in ideology and outlook persisted perennially. Yet conservative organisations included women's industrial conditions and equal pay in their objects, however else differing from progressive women's groups. The principle of women's economic independence through rate for the job, equal pay for equal work, then equal pay for work of equal value, was a founding tenet from the nineteenth century onward. Despite disparate positioning on the political divide, through into the twenty-first century, women from varying backgrounds and beliefs united around equal pay.

Nor was the struggle geographically isolated. In Queensland, heralded as Brisbane's first women's trade union organiser, Emma Miller was a key figure, in 1890 playing a founding role in the Tailoresses Union. Later, Kath Thomas worked with her Queensland confreres within and outside the union movement. In WA, Rischbieth was prominent alongside Molly Driver and Ethel Rose Paterson Joyner. Whilst following Driver, her mother, and preserving records of her work and times, agreements, disagreements and lobbying efforts and outcomes WA women engineered, Irene Greenwood in her own right upheld rights to equal pay, independence, and autonomy.

Brave Ways, Grand Days—Picture Portraits in a Thousands-Strong Gallery

Naming every equal pay campaigner is impossible. Some names leap from history's pages, arbitration cases, union records, government documents, women's organisation minutes, and membership lists. Some stand immortalised in state or university libraries, local libraries, or women's own collections, at home. Some remain overlooked or omitted. Yet the breadth of women's equal pay struggle demands illustration, honouring the named for their contribution alongside unnamed sisters, mothers, aunts, grandmothers, great-grandmothers, colleagues, friends and, sometimes, enemies.

Choosing names means exercising discretion, every list created with additions or subtractions. In this ongoing uncovering/discovering of women's campaigns, naming the well-known alongside lesser known affirms women's activism, its scope, the links between, individuals being part of a huge diverse movement demanding women's wage justice. Without the named and unnamed, known and unknown, the struggle would not have been waged. It is this foundation upon which women have built and continue to build.

From Brisbane, Queensland, ***Muriel Heagney*** **(1885–1974)** moved with her family to Melbourne, Victoria, at century's end. Annie Agnes Currie, her mother, with her father, Pat, an early Australian Workers' Union (AWU) member, was a Queenslander. Publican and later carpenter, in 1902 Pat Heagney was a Richmond branch, Victorian Political Labor Council founding member then Victorian Central Executive secretary (1904–1910). In 1906, Heagney joined the Richmond branch, becoming a Political Labour Council Women's Organising Committee delegate (1909), attending the first Victorian Labor Women's Conference at Victorian Trades Hall (July 1909). Working at her primary school teacher post until 1915, when (she disliked the job) she resigned, as a Department of Defence clerk she earned the same wage as male clerks—there was no female rate of pay. In 1930s' Sydney, founding member, research convenor, and major moving force in the Council of Action for Equal Pay (CAEP), as joint president then secretary-treasurer from 1939, she maintained her CAEP work with a full-time position in the Queensland Tourist Bureau. As an Australian Education Union (AEU) organiser, working in Queensland, NSW, and Victoria, maintaining links with women in all states and overseas, Heagney frequently travelled to speak and support women's organisation work and trade union activism. In 1950, returning to Victoria after the

CAEP disbanded, she published ***Arbitration at the Crossroads*** (1954), adding to a publications record established at least thirty years earlier. Her intellectual and strategic contributions were often prescient, analysis and arguments in ***Are Women Taking Men's Jobs*** (1935) remaining relevant today, as with ***Equal Pay for the Sexes***, published in 1948. Of foresight and courage, Heagney was a dynamo, her contribution as thinker, writer, activist to women's equal pay struggle unmatched. In tribute to her and her CAEP colleagues' work, Melbourne women Kate MacNeill, Sue Jackson, Barbara (Barb) Jennings, Fiona Smith, and Anne Delaney revived the CAEP, intervening in the ***Nurses Comparable Worth case 1985–1986***.

Formed in 1929, the United Associations (UA), which ***Jessie Street* (1889–1970)** made her own, amalgamated the NSW Women Voters' Association, Women's Service Club, and NSW Women's League. From a wealthy pioneering family, Jessie Mary Grey Lillingston married Kenneth Street, barrister son of NSW's chief justice; her husband, then her son Laurence, succeeded to the post. Independent woman, intellectual and activist, with the courage to take a stand when courage was necessary, Street fought for women's and Indigenous Australian rights. Joining the Australian Aboriginal Fellowship (AAF), she campaigned for the 1967 referendum amending the Australian Constitution to remove Australian Aborigines from subjection to racist state laws. But family dualities remained. Street gained economic independence through her family of origin and the financial and social backing of her marriage, with the luxury few women had to take up causes. Yet she faced conflicts in balancing family demands and social dictates against personal and political rights, resisting establishment influences and traditionalist wife-and-mother demands, and role as wife-and-daughter-in-law of the NSW legal profession's leading lights. Her domestic affairs managed by servants, her class origins inevitably shaping and shading her ideas and ideals, she nevertheless supported Russia's working-class after the 1917 Revolution, derided and decried by anti-Communists as Red Jessie, and twice in the 1940s stood as Australian Labor Party (ALP) candidate for Wentworth (NSW federal seat). The annual ***Jessie Street Luncheon*** affirms her life and work, the centenary of her birth celebrated by establishing the ***Jessie Street National Library*** 'to heighten awareness of women's issues; preserve documents on women's lives and activities; support women's history; and highlight women's contribution to Australia's development'. The ***JSNL*** provides a launching platform for women to continue the struggle.

A founding member of the NSW Teachers Federation (amalgamating several teachers unions) in 1919, ***Lucy Woodcock* (1889–1968)**, BA, BEc (USyd), elected to the union executive (1924), senior vice-president, then president (1932), first woman in these posts. She represented the Teachers' Federation on the NSW Trades and Labour Council (TLC) and Australian Council of Trade Unions (ACTU), as a founding member of CAEP and its precursor, the Trade Union Equal Pay Committee. Over its lifetime, she held CAEP positions (1937–1943) and, as NSW Teachers' Federation representative, with Mr RL Day was Federated Rubber Workers' Union (FRWU) joint president (1942–1943). She, like Heagney, joined the UA, working with Street and other middle-class women, determined that working-class women's demands remained part of collective Women's Movement action. Woodcock supported International Women's Day (IWD), held on 8 March, recognising women's struggle for personhood, citizenship, equal rights, employment rights, industrial conditions, and fair rates of pay. In the early 1950s, meetings and concerts at the Conservatorium of Music or Teachers Federation hall being the main Sydney-based IWD activities, she was an invited speaker, alongside Della Elliot (then Della Nicholas), Vivienne Newson, Ada Bromham, and others. For IWD 1954, Woodcock launched an international jewellery and handcrafts exhibition televised at Sydney department store Anthony Hordern's. In 1960, an IWD speech she wrote as a brief history of NSW women up to contemporary times, including Indigenous Australian women and convict women, was read by Nellie Lamport. Woodcock's equal pay struggle encompassed pay equity and work and permanency, whatever a woman's status, campaigning for married women teachers' right to professional standing and income rather than being forced to resign upon marriage, then (re-)employed as temporaries.

Aboriginal leader and activist ***Pearl (Gambanyi) Gibbs* (1901–1983)**, Gambanyi in her Ngiyamba language, grew up in country NSW (Yass and Brewarrina), attending segregated schools at Yass and Cowra. An Aboriginal rights movement leader from the 1920s, she organised protests with Aboriginal and non-Aboriginal people for Indigenous Australian rights, establishing and joining organisations including the Aborigines Progressive Association (APA), Australian Aborigines League (AAL), Council for Aboriginal Rights (CAR), and AAF. Her work as a maid, cook, and single parent of three children underpinned her acute awareness of women's (lack of) industrial and socio-political rights. The first Aboriginal woman to broadcast Aboriginal issues on radio, Gibbs sought women's advancement, workers' rights, and civil rights for all. Campaigning to end racist state laws founding the Aboriginal Protection Board, she highlighted Aboriginal girls' employment as domestic servants and the spurious apprenticeship system depriving Aboriginal girls of income: long unregulated hours, no pay at all or confiscated on the Board's contentions that young women couldn't handle their own finances. Gibbs lobbied against school and hospital segregation—pregnant women were restricted to local hospital verandahs, away from 'white' women's wards—and for adequate health provision for girls and women. In an April 1938 speech, she demanded justice for all women—Indigenous and non-Indigenous, saying: 'A country must needs be Great that is Just. A country must needs be Noble that believes in women and trusts them gladly with every Liberty it has already given to its men. I would have my country all this. I would have my country be the Noblest country upon Earth. The Purest, the Most Free, Just, loving, generous and unselfish. And do you think it can attain to all this without the direct aid of its women?' Role model Gibbs precipitated many into an activism for a just world, including women's wage justice.

Margaret Windeyer* (1866–1939)** always started big. Calling a public meeting in Sydney Town Hall in 1896 typified her approach. No more prominent nor more public structure existing, it was fitting, she believed, for NSW's first National Council of Women (NCW) to begin there. Inaugurated on 26 June, with Windeyer (supported by Rose Scott, also taking a leading role in NCW's formation) elected first honorary secretary, the organisation initially comprised eleven affiliated groups (sixty-eight by 1936), including the Women's Club, the Women's Christian Temperance Union (WCTU), and the Women's Suffrage League (WSL). In 1895, president of the WSL Maybanke Anderson invited her friend Windeyer to assume publishing the ***Women's Voice: Anderson's son Arthur having drowned, in her distress Anderson could not sustain it. Windeyer declined. Spurred by her 1893 visit to the Chicago World Fair and Chicago Exhibition, her activism took her in another direction. In Chicago, she presented a paper to the Congress of Women held in the Woman's Building, World's Columbian Exposition, meeting women from the 1848 Seneca Falls Women's Convention. Neither writer nor publisher, her practical organiser's bent meant she determined to cultivate similar energies in NSW to eliminate all women's disabilities—legal, economic, social. NCW was her vehicle, equal pay an original constitutional plank. Her mother, Mary Elizabeth Windeyer, also firmly centred in getting-things-done practicalities, was first WSL president. Independent thinkers, Windeyer and her mother formed a formidable team, often travelling together overseas, pursuing women's rights interests and activism individually and together.

Growing up on the WA goldfields, working as kitchen maid in a Kalgoorlie miners' boarding house, brought ***Cecilia Shelley* (1893–1986)** into trade unionism. A strong women's rights and equal pay proponent, moving to Perth with her family she worked as a domestic servant, then in hotel and catering work. In 1917, she joined the Hotel, Club, Caterers, Tearooms, and Restaurant Employees' Industrial Union, by 1919 as a union organiser leading her first strike, and again in 1921. That year, the workers had twenty-two weeks out, campaigning on union preference, strikers dubbed Shelley's Army. In 1925, it was a demand for the forty-four hour week and a wages increase. Holding the post until 1968, Shelley was one of the first women in Australia elected as a paid union secretary. Under her tutelage and organising power, in the 1920s, the Hotel, Club, Caterers, Tearooms and Restaurant Employees Industrial Union became one of the largest WA female unions. Her Arbitration Court telling-it-as-it-is policy, shocking opponents with scathingly realistic accounts of workers' conditions, earned her the title 'Tigress of Trades Hall'. She campaigned tirelessly for women's membership of trade unions and equal pay, directing concern not only to women in paid employment, but encompassing unemployed women and girls. With Katharine Susannah Prichard, in 1932 she organised the Unemployed Girls' and Women's Defence Committee. In the 1950s, she supported revival of IWD celebrations, speaking alongside Greenwood at an 8 March 1957 Trinity Church Hall meeting before a thronging audience of 400—women and men.

***Irene Longman* (1877–1963)** was the first woman to win a Queensland Parliament seat. In 1929, nominated by Queensland Women's Electoral League, endorsed by the Country Progressive National Party, she defeated the sitting Labor member in the seat of Bulimba with a swing exceeding 10 per cent: a majority of 401 for Longman replaced the absolute majority of 1027 votes in the previous election. Holding the seat for one term, she lost when Labor returned to power after a short hiatus in the lengthy period of Queensland Labor governments. Believing that women, like men, had a right to paid employment informed her parliamentary career and lifelong women's organisation work, with an equally powerful commitment to the principle that marriage should not hamper but affirm women's particular and specific knowledge and experience, enhancing women's status, with motherhood a recognised profession, and work of married women remaining at home remunerated by the state. She lobbied for, and achieved, appointment of Queensland policewomen, yet was unable to persuade the authorities that equal recognition as male police and equal rates of pay should be theirs.

Australian Federation of Business and Professional Women (AFBPW) branch president in 1944, obstetrician and gynaecologist ***Constance Elizabeth D'Arcy* (1879–1950)** practiced as honorary surgeon at Paddington's Royal Hospital for Women, with a private practice in Sydney's Macquarie Street. Believing nursing had a key healthcare role, wanting continuing high standards of nursing care and nurses accepted as professionals, she jointly founded the Royal Australian Nursing Federation (RANF) and played a founding role in NCW's project to establish school sex education programs. As a University of Sydney clinical obstetrics lecturer (1925–1939), D'Arcy understood the importance of education and equal pay for educators. Yet because 'women lecturers got the same pay as men', she said they suffered no sex discrimination. Supporting Street's Australian Women's Charter, D'Arcy suffered for her stand. St Joan's Alliance was established 'to offset the damage done to the Catholic image by the association of one of Sydney's most prominent Catholic women, Dame Constance D'Arcy, with Street': Street's sheepskins-for-Russia campaign and her political position informed this attack. Scheduled to open the 1946 Women's Charter conference, D'Arcy withdrew under pressure. As a pioneer in women's struggle to enter medicine, a building named for her at Paddington Royal Hospital for Women stood as a memorial to her work, she being appointed to Paddington Women's Hospital as resident medical officer (RMO) and honorary surgeon, first woman ever to hold these posts. When relocated to Randwick in the 1980s, despite the Women's Hospital complex covering several blocks, the Constance D'Arcy memorial building was demolished, disappearing entirely. No acknowledgement of D'Arcy appeared at the new complex.

Eileen Powell* (1913–1997)** worked with the Australian Railways Union (ARU) NSW branch, as clerk then organiser with the Refreshment Services Branch covering Railway Refreshment Rooms (RRR) staff (1937–1944). On 11 September 1925, Victorian Railways waitresses went out on strike when a retired naval officer in a senior railways post declared refreshment staff 'girls from Melbourne' were 'unlikely to give satisfaction', being 'lazy, dirty and unmanageable'. He was contacting Immigration Authorities 'to ascertain the possibilities of getting suitable servants'. An apology took two days of negotiating with the ARU's male leadership. In 1938, before the NSW Industrial Commission Full Bench, Powell argued that RRR staff, mostly women living in railway towns lacking award coverage, should have their own award. Travelling all over NSW gathering evidence, meeting women workers on country railway stations, she won an award, increased wages, overtime, abolition of compulsory board and lodging payments, and a cut in spread of hours. A compelling advocate and dedicated grassroots worker, from eight years Powell was active in the ALP and at Trades Hall with her mother, Margaret Powell, who—separating from her husband, Powell's father, in 1918—joined the ALP. At fifteen, Powell joined, by sixteen elected Stanmore branch assistant secretary. Beginning in retail at Grace Brothers, then Trades Hall secretarial and clerical work and on ***Labor Daily, in 1944 upon retiring from the ARU she returned to Trades Hall. Broadcasting on Radio 2KY, covering living standards, cost of living, women and work, women in parliament, community centres, and women's international work and rights, she focused on the United Nations (UN). Her column 'Labor Women' appeared in ***ALP News*** (1964) and 'Women and Work' in ***ETU News*** (1971–1972). Member of the ALP Women's Central Organising Committee, UA, and CAEP founding member, Powell stood as ALP candidate for North Sydney (NSW state seat—1951). Male opponents contested her preselection, claiming an irregularity—she nominated in her own name (used throughout her life), not her husband's (a late forties marriage). The challenge failed, she polled well, though not winning the seat. In 1954, she addressed the Australian Federation of Women Voters (AFWV) Conference in Adelaide on 'Economic Equality—Goal of the Second Half Century', and her appearance in the NSW ***Female Wage Case 1935*** and the ***Equal Pay Case 1969*** confirm the longevity, breadth, and scope of her work.

First woman winning a Victorian parliamentary seat in a contested general election, ***Ivy Lavinia Weber* (1892–1976)** represented Nunawading as an Independent through 1937, 1940, and 1943 elections. With the League of Women Voters (LWV) 'Women for Canberra Movement', she resigned her state seat after the 1943 election, standing as an Independent for Henty, a federal seat. The sitting member retained Henty, Weber next unsuccessfully contesting the Victorian state seat Box Hill (1947). Mother of eleven children—three from marriage to Clarence Weber, widower and father of seven, one from an earlier marriage, she was widowed seven years before her parliamentary election. An executive NCW member, active in the Australasian Women's Association and WCTU, the WCTU encouraged her to stand as an Independent, endorsed by the League of Women Electors of Victoria under their manifesto 'Mother, Child, Family, Home and Health'. Her electoral agenda called for a true democracy providing economic security to alleviate distress and unemployment; free education—kindergarten to university; a National Health Scheme raising general health standards; abolition of slum dwellings, with construction of homes 'suitable for families'; and a comprehensive National Insurance scheme, including hospital treatment. Despite professing herself 'not a feminist', she campaigned for women-on-juries, local councils and government boards, and teachers' equal pay. Just as differences in principle and policy may arise between women, women can carry internal contradictions. Weber's 'women teachers' rights' platform included married women working only if in desperate circumstances.

Born in the Victorian country town of Lara, ***Cathleen (Kath) Williams* (1895–1975)** joined the Communist Party of Australia (CPA) (1936). In 1948, invited by acting secretary Jim Coull and following her trade union family tradition—her father, Arthur Chambers, was Victorian Clerks' Union foundation secretary—she became a Liquor Trades Union (LTU) organiser. In 1954, when Trades Hall Council (THC) delegates numbered 150 males to some 8 females, Williams made it 9. Later, as an ACTU Congress Lady Teachers' Union (LTU) delegate, she breached another male bastion. In November 1954, she took a request to Trades Hall from a special meeting of women union members, asking that the THC establish an Equal Pay Committee to comply with the 1953 ACTU Congress motion. In March 1955, a meeting of unions with women members, held by the THC executive, resolved to establish the Committee, with Williams elected unanimously as honorary secretary/organiser. With fellow members G. Hayes of the Boot Trades, D. MacSween, Clothing Trades, A. Williams, Electrical Trades, G. Collaretti, Hospital Employees Federation (HEF), W. Steel, Federated Clerks Union (FCU)—all men—she launched the Committee with press releases, radio and television campaigns, leaflets, and meetings. Another equal pay stalwart, her union and Women's Movement activism spanned decades.

Jean Arnot* (1903–1995)** served in positions of authority at NSW Public Library from 1921 until retiring in 1968. As for other women librarians, she was denied equal pay. From 1937, campaigning for equal pay, lobbying through her union, the Public Service Association (PSA), speaking publicly at conferences, seminars, rallies, and workshops; debating on the Australian Broadcasting Commission (ABC), winning hands down in a performance broadcast nationally; working through AFBPW and NCW as a member and office holder. Arnot was paid less than a male junior staff member. Then, notwithstanding being acting chief librarian, exhibiting the ability indicative of her capacity for the job, the position went to a man. Following retirement, skills in demand, she assisted Berkelouw booksellers and advised on private library cataloguing. Dying at ninety-two, still campaigning, knowing that despite equal pay decisions, regardless of apparently gaining pay-rate parities, reality differed. The ***Jean Arnot Luncheon recognised Arnot's key contribution to the equal pay struggle. Jointly hosted at Parliament House, originally under then Legislative Council president, the Hon. Meredith Burgmann, by AFBPW's Val Buswell and NCW's Joan Ellison, with Marlene Arditto stepping into AFBPW's role upon Buswell's death in 2004, the first celebrated Arnot's ninetieth birthday, annually honouring by invitation NSW women contributing to women's rights and attaining ninety years. Women of all ages working for equal opportunity and equal pay, including young and younger women, affirmed Arnot's devotion to ensuring young women have opportunities for learning and being supported in political activism to advance women's rights, particularly equal pay, on the principle that the cause is theirs, too.

Standing on a women's rights platform, ***Vida Goldstein* (1869–1949)** was one of four women candidates in the 1903 Australian federal election. First in the southern hemisphere to nominate, first in the (then) British Empire to run for national election, she was first to cast her vote, choosing the St Kilda polling booth closest to her Alma Road home. At thirty-three years on that December day, she stood in pouring rain at the head of the voting queue. She did not win a seat, but won 51,497 votes: 51,497 female and male voters wanted to be represented in the Senate by a woman. She stood again in 1910, 1913, 1914, and 1917, but not until 1943 did a woman, WA's Dorothy Tangney, become a senator. Goldstein nonetheless had national and international recognition. In 1902, delegate to the first International Woman Suffrage Conference in Washington, DC, she addressed both US Houses of Congress, meeting with president Theodore Roosevelt who sought her out as the only woman in the country with a national vote. In 1911, invited by the radical suffrage movement, in London she addressed an Albert Hall audience of 10,000. She door-knocked with hundreds of women, garnering 30,000 signatures on the women's-right-to-vote Monster Petition, tabled in Victoria's Parliament in 1891 as the largest petition ever lodged, edited ***Women's Sphere*** (1898–1905) and ***The Woman Voter*** (1908–1911). In the 1890s, with her sister, Goldstein opened a preparatory school in Inkerman Street,

St Kilda, campaigned for equal pay for female teachers, and was appointed United Council for Women's Suffrage (UCWS) general secretary. Member of the Women's Franchise League (WFL) and Women's Peace Army, a founding member of NCW Victoria, at a meeting at her St Kilda home Goldstein made one of the first Women's Shilling Fund donations for building Melbourne's Queen Victoria Hospital for Women, William and Little Lonsdale Streets, later moved to Lonsdale and Swanston Streets. In 2003, the Women's Electoral Lobby (WEL) Victoria established the ***Vida Goldstein Awards*** to acknowledge feminists advancing Goldstein's aims, including equal pay, equal property rights, equal parental rights; improved child laws and protection for neglected children; women police; and correcting injustices. Awardees include Eve Mahlab, Gwen Goedecke, and Diane Alley. A plaque in Parliament House Gardens, Melbourne, commemorates Goldstein's women's rights and political democracy commitment with (in December 2022) a statue foreshadowed.

After devoting herself to education and community work, in 1948, ***Margaret Edgeworth McIntyre*** **(1886–1948)** began a second career as first woman in Tasmania's Parliament, a career cut short when, returning from a NCW conference in Brisbane, Queensland, she died in an aircraft crash. Before her death, she worked to open trades and professions to women, for employment opportunities with commensurate rates of pay, and concentrated upon schemes to improve esteem and wellbeing of young women and opportunities. This followed from encouragement in her own education and development, her mother being first woman principal of Hurlstone Teachers Training College, campaigning for social reform and women's further education. Graduating BA (USyd, 1907), McIntyre returned to Tasmania, was president and producer of Launceston Players, involved with Launceston's Progressive Education Group and establishing Brooks Community School, established a youth drama group, and worked with Girl Guides and the Young Women's Christian Association (YWCA). As NCW president, in a 1948 speech to Anzac Hostel Women's League of Remembrance Launceston, she emphasised teachers' and mothers' important influence on policy and the nation. 'As the world has been run by men for so long, and they do not appear to have made a very good job of it,' she said, 'isn't it time we women tried to use more influence in national affairs?' Girl Guides named Launceston's ***Margaret McIntyre House*** as their northern headquarters in her memory.

Mary Lee **(1821–1909)**, born on 14 February in County Monaghan, Ireland, landing in 1879 at the Port of Adelaide as a widow with her nineteen-year-old daughter Evelyn, quickly engaged with local SA issues, particularly as affecting women and girls. Consistent with contemporary religious backing for women's actions, in a 14 April 1890 letter she observed 'home is women's sweetest sphere' but 'wherever woman can be of best and wisest usefulness to her fellow men and women there, by God's providence, is her allotted sphere; and whatever her best gifts of wealth or influence—of head or hand—these are ... the instruments, of the work which God expects of her'. Her Social Purity Society (SPS) work focused on girls and women's rights to bodily integrity and freedom from mistreatment and abuse. Advocating equality of education for girls, almost one hundred years before the term 'sexual harassment' emerged, she agitated against industrial and sexual exploitation of young women servants, factory workers, or newspaper street-sellers. Her December 1889 women's trades union proposal initiated the Working Women's Trades Union (WWTU) in 1890, with Lee as secretary (1890–1893) then vice-president, attending TLC meetings, serving on the Distressed Women and Children's Committee, distributing clothes and food to families through the 1890s economic depression, and working on the sub-committee examining clothing industry conditions. For Lee, ending exploitation of women workers and improving industrial conditions and wages for women, particularly in piecework, was essential. When in 1886 the first Woman Suffrage Bill went before the SA Parliament, Lee joined inaugurating the SA Women's Suffrage League (WSL), believing the vote meant women would 'redress women's wrongs—moral, social, industrial and educational'.

At twenty-two, ***Irene Adelaide Driver Greenwood*** **(1899–1992)** mounted the activist stage, joining Perth's first civil servants strike. Attuned to injustices women and Indigenous Australians confronted through disadvantage and oppression, social justice was high on her campaign demands. She recognised the importance of women's economic independence, publicising and proselytising, particularly through broadcasting, beginning in 1931 in Sydney, continuing upon returning to Perth in 1935, first the ABC's Women's Session, then her 'Woman-to-Woman' commercial radio program, until retiring from radio in 1953. A founder of WA's Council for Equal Pay and Opportunity, Greenwood edited ***Equal Pay News*** from the Council's inception until its demise, maintaining a wealth of papers, including minutes, newsletters, radio program transcripts, and correspondence with Dymphna Cusack, Newson, Prichard, Mary (Molly) Driver (her mother), and others. Committed peace activist, longtime Women's International League for Peace and Freedom (WILPF) member, she lobbied successfully for a chair of Peace Studies at Murdoch University (MU). During the 1950s Greenwood chaired Perth International Women's Day (IWD) committees, speaking with Prichard at the first major Perth gathering in 1938. Active in Women's Liberation/ Women's Liberation Movement (WL/WLM) and WEL, Family Planning Association (FPA), and Abortion Law Reform Association (ALRA), she saw the ***MV Irene Greenwood***, flagship of WA's fleet, launched in her honour, and was first woman to receive an honorary doctorate from MU. Affirming her commitment to women's right to political participation, Greenwood publicly changed her date of birth from 1898 to 1899, the year non-Indigenous women won the vote in WA.

***Emma Miller* (1839–1917)** took a principal role in the 2 February 1912 general strike, leading a women's contingent marching upon Parliament House, Brisbane. Avoiding police on the forward journey, on return women met police flourishing bayonets and rifles, on horseback and on foot, standing as a wall against them. Police charged. Crossing the police line, brandishing their only protection: umbrellas and hatpins, Miller (at seventy-three) led again. Earlier, in 1903, she formed the Queensland Women Workers' Political Organisation (WWPO). Then, as Women's Peace Army president, in 1916 she headed the Queensland delegation to the Australian Peace Alliance conference in Melbourne. Shirtmaker by trade, foundation ALP member, she was president of the Women's Equal Franchise Association (WEFA) from start to finish: 1894 to 1905 when Queensland women won the state vote. Active in 1914–1918 anti-conscription struggles, she died committed to women's rights, labour's right to organise, workers' industrial rights, and equal pay. The state funeral proposed by the state government upon her death was declined by her only surviving son, George Calderwood. The journey taking her coffin from her home to Toowong Cemetery led a procession of several hundred mourners walking by her side. Miller was renowned as Mother Miller and the grand old Labour woman of Queensland.

Past, Present, Future

Links between activist women persist over time, in agreement, in struggle, argument, anger, encouragement, in both heated and comforting words, through and beyond differences. The equal pay campaign, like all women's rights struggles, deserves more than a romanticised history, a false vision of women working always together, always in agreement, ever surging forward toward the chartered goal or, contrarily, ever at loggerheads. It demands recognition that women identifying primarily as unionists worked solidly with women identifying with women's organisations, fighting for women's goals. Divisions came along union and women's group lines, yet crossovers in membership, unity in aims, and joining together in a unified equal pay demand was real, too.

Through more than two centuries of Australian history, women from multiple backgrounds came together, fought together, fell out, reconciled. Boosting one another, bolstering arguments. Letting one another down, too. Yet - reviving, surviving, acting.

Without them, women of today's equal pay—or pay equity fight would have no past. The present would not comprise trade union women working alongside—sometimes together, sometimes less so, even divided — women of women's organisations and Women's Movement in all its diversity, advocating in the same forums for equal pay. Without the women of the past urging sympathetic men and male-dominated unions on, listening to men who were, sometimes, prepared to go further, labour movement support would be less developed, less advanced.

Without them, future gains in equal pay—however remote appearing to be in confronting a withered job market, or insecure jobs, changes through the Covid 19 pandemic, sometime government 'slash and burn' policies or cuts in the name of economic prudence—would be less assured. The history of equal pay in industrial courts, commissions, and tribunals rests against the backdrop of Women's Movement activism and women, named and unnamed, leading and supporting the struggle.

Early Autumn, 1973

In Melbourne at an equal pay conference, Jean Arnot sets out to post letters over which she laboured the evening before. Buys stamps from the concierge, moistens them on the sponge standing in glass on a rosewood desk beside the foyer's umbrella stand. Fixing each to the top right-hand corner of its envelope, she presses down with the flat of her hand then, coat tugged firmly to throat, short strap of her handbag looped over her arm, she takes up the slim, stamped envelopes.

Walking down Little Collins Street from the Victoria Hotel, she turns up Swanston Street, proceeds briskly past Buckley & Nunn and Myer Emporium. A short five minutes more, and she's at the corner of Bourke and Elizabeth Streets. Towards the posting boxes, along the General Post Office (GPO) colonnade, a figure stoops by the steps, sheltering against the wind.

From a distance, Arnot has thought it no more than a bundle of rags. Surrounded by hessian sacks topped with rubbish, it's an eyesore awaiting council rubbish truck attention. But the bundle moves … she discerns it as human.

In deference to the personal sensitivities of yet one more woman consigned to bag-lady status and, in truth, to her own reluctance to acknowledge the destiny falling easily on too many women, she averts her gaze. But in the very instant of her turning away, the features of the figure on the steps register. Arnot looks back.

A flash of recognition, repeated.

'It's Muriel Heagney, isn't it?' she says. The inauspicious nature of the setting makes her no less sure of her ground. Perhaps, in a fleeting instant of the certain knowledge possessed by all women, deep down, of their prospects in a world where economic independence is assured for no woman, with unequal pay, inferior industrial conditions, unequal job opportunities entrenched, and facing the pensions gap, she is even more certain.

The woman looks at her, looks away. 'No, it's not', says Muriel Heagney.

Arnot's letters arrive at Sydney NCW offices and NSW Teachers' Federation in Bathurst Street later that week. Post to Perth travels less swiftly. Irene Greenwood receives hers, addressed to the CAEP, WA Branch, at her Shenton Park home the following Monday.

The envelopes lie in their respective letterboxes until collected, still firmly sealed, no tampering, no re-opening by their writer. No second thoughts, she has had no more to write, added no postscript. But more than twenty years on, she remembers.

And, so it is that today Heagney, the socialist, is overlooked in favour of Street, the woman of (her father's and husband's) means. Heagney, woman of the Women's Movement and labour movement, pushed aside for UA's founder and president, Street. Even then, both are passed over in favour of a reworked history of the equal pay struggle, locating its centre in the 1970s. Both lose out against a pean of praise to more recent campaign activists, as if the past and their work don't exist, even in memory, or do not count. As if to remember the women of the past and their times detracts from contemporary campaigns, more contemporary women.

No commemorative dinner, no memorial lecture, no women's library or trust, no prizes, no bequest or bounty remembers Heagney's death, a pauper. Ironically, family money—as for Street—and late twentieth-century feminist clout for her and more recent women's wage justice claimants—speak louder than pain, persistence, and fortitude crowned by material poverty. Too often they speak to smother the struggles of nineteenth and early twentieth century, women who led, followed, fought, and won—or failed—along the way. Too often a language omitting to name past failures and regroupings, campaigns and successes. Drowning out Heagney's impoverished circumstances, her striving to improve women's lot, recognising that without economic independence won through her own labour, no woman would ever be free to speak, act, think independently, live independently of men.

Federally, women won the vote in 1902, SA and WA earlier (1894 and 1899), NSW (1902), Tasmania (1903), Queensland (1905), Victoria (1908), Indigenous women's voting rights variously gained into the 1960s. Predating and stimulated by these wins, women galvanised unionists like Edward Chambers, FCU Australia secretary, writing on 17 April 1912 to prime minister Andrew Fisher that 'commercial experience' and the FCU's 'considerable acquaintance' with the work, confirmed '[no] inequality or dissimilarity' in 'typing or stenography and typing' other than the worker's sex, with 'equally competent women … available'. Evidence ready, Chambers emphasised its being 'of high importance to our calling … no distinction in pay should be considered'. So, forward to Chap. 3, 'A Nineteenth Century Legacy—Early Days, Equal Pay and Radical Women' illuminating women's continuing struggle, undaunted.

References

Cases—See Case List

Biographical information additionally Australian Dictionary of Biography, Australian National Library 'Trove'.

Jean F. Arnot Papers 1916–1969 ML MSS 3147, ADD On 2070/4, Mitchell Library, Sydney, NSW.

Pearl Gibbs, 'Woman Today', 1938 (April 1938), quoted Bain Attwood and Andrew Markus, ***The Struggle for Aboriginal Rights***, Allen & Unwin, Sydney, 1999.

Irene Greenwood, 'Chronicle of Change' in JA Scutt, As a Woman – Writing Women's Lives, Artemis Publishing, Melbourne, 1992, pp. 107–20.

Helen Jones, 'Mary Lee', in ***Australian Dictionary of Biography***, vol. 10, 1891–1939, MUP, Melbourne, Victoria, Australia.

Elizabeth Mansutti, ***Mary Lee 1821–1909***, State Library SA, Adelaide, SA, 1994.

Papers of the Scott Family, Printed Material, State Library of NSW, Sydney, NSW, 1863–1924 (CY2231, CY 3673).

Elizabeth Reid, 'Muriel Heagney', ***Refractory Girl***, no. 6, Sydney, NSW, 1974 (June 1974), 1937–1940.

Women Tasmania, ***Significant Women Project—Margaret Edgeworth McIntyre, OBE (1886–1948)***, Hobart, Tasmania.

CHAPTER 3

A Nineteenth-Century Legacy—Early Days, Equal Pay, and Radical Women

> 1070 … Similar work is adapted for males and females, and they ought to be employed and kept together as much as possible … The wife is just as good at herding cattle or sheep, and other work as the man, as a rule …
>
> 1082 … I initiated the following state of wages, which many of the neighbours adopted, viz—Boys and men, 10s., 15s., or 20s. per week, with rations and cook, according to their capacity, and their wives 5s. per week …
>
> Queensland pastoralist Donald McLean
> Evidence, Select Committee on the Aborigines Bill
> ***South Australian Parliamentary Papers***, 1899, 77a 871

The year is 1906. Four years earlier, Ada E. Evans graduates from Sydney University (USyd), the first Australian woman qualifying in law. Barring Indigenous Australian women, on 27 August 1902 and following federal election rights gained earlier that year, alongside other NSW women she wins state voting rights, but is refused professional practice rights. The Legal Practitioners Act 1898 (NSW) entitles qualified *persons* to practice—yet the all male board approving candidates determines, upon legal authority, women are not persons. ***In re Edith Haynes***, the WA Supreme Court does likewise. Edyth Haynes applies for admission, claiming to be a person under the Legal Practitioners Act 1893 (WA). The Supreme Court says she isn't.

J. A. Scutt, *Wage Rage for Equal Pay*,
https://doi.org/10.1007/978-3-031-42178-5_3

The year is 1906. The NSW state election is announced, the third with NSW women voting, although Indigenous Australian women must wait until 1926. No women run for election, disqualified until 1918. Yet defying traditional woman's place—as women's organisations have for over a century—the Women's Progressive Association (WPA) lobbies MPs and public. Letters, leaflets, and petitions instruct MPs and prospective MPs that the requirements of office include candidates' commitment to women's rights as non-negotiable, voters bearing women's social, political, and industrial rights in mind.

Industrial Rights for Women

In 1906, education, training and access to trades and professions, and equal pay headed women's organisation agendas. Candidates were asked to declare support for Bills before Parliament at prorogation. The Truancy Bill (later the Free Education Act 1906) required school enrollment and regular attendance for girls and boys, promoting girls' education rights over being kept at home doing housework and household chores, including grandparents' or ill parents' care. The WPA demanded that, once educated, girls and boys, women and men should benefit equally, with qualifications dictating equal pay.

On 16 June, attracting candidate, government, and press attention, the WPA's petition, headed like a parliamentary Bill, contained its 1906 platform incorporating women's industrial rights:

> Sir,
>
> You are earnestly requested to endeavour to have the following Measures of Social and Domestic Reform passed into law during the ensuing Session:
>
> 1. … legislation against sweating by enacting that no child on beginning work in a workroom, shops or factory shall receive less than 5/- per week; and no worker over 20 years of age less than 25/- per week.
> 2. … the Factories' and Shops' Act be amended to include all country districts; Early Closing to include all who engaged in or about, … shops, storerooms, distributing depots, refreshment rooms, hotels and restaurants.
> 3. Equal pay for women with men for work of equal merit.
> 4. The right of women to enter the legal profession …

WPA president Annie Golding, secretary Miss Beck, treasurer Mrs T. Chapman, honorary general secretary Mrs K. Dwyer featured in their campaign.

Four years later, across the Nullabor, 1910 federal election candidates received a list of questions from the Women's Service Guilds (WSG), one asking:

> Are you, if elected, prepared to support equal pay with equal [promotion] chances ... for women with men in the Federal Civil Service?

Like the WPA and National Council of Women (NCW), WSG identified equal pay as crucial to women's economic equality. When Labour won both houses with clear-cut majorities, women speculated whether Andrew Fisher's incoming government would legislate fair industrial conditions and a fair day's pay for a fair day's work for women, or they'd have gained more under Alfred Deakin's Liberal Protectionists and Joseph Cook's Free Traders. They plotted, planned and acted.

In 1912, WSG chairing, the Clerks' Union held a mass public meeting for equal pay. Flyers distributed widely, the Literary Institute overflowed. Representatives of both major political parties and prominent women and men spoke, the meeting carrying a unanimous resolution for clerks' equal pay. In ***March of Australian Women*** (1964), Bessie Rischbieth recalled '... a crowded platform, a crowded hall, and an enthusiastic meeting ... fifty years ago, we ... believed equal pay was just around the corner ...'

Demanding Women

Almost 10 years before the WPA interrogated NSW politicians, 15 before WSG pursued federal candidates, Victoria's socialist journal ***Tocsin*** published Suffragist's 28 October 1897 reply to a correspondent opposing equal pay. Suffragist denounced support for unequal pay as not only embracing social and industrial injustice, but spawning grave consequences for tradesmen and labourers, getting men sacked and excluding them from most trades, lower-waged women preferred. Such inevitability was 'not difficult to foretell', for 'women are every day becoming more skilled and competent', women simply requiring the opportunity to match any man. Men in the higher professions sufficiently alert to this principle, Suffragist continued, 'an immediate outcry' would erupt should women doctors charge lower fees.

The minimum wage 'for equal work, irrespective of sex' should replace the present system, a 'most shortsighted policy' and 'simply suicidal' for workers. Advocating 'injustice to half the human race' shows 'how far we can get from the true ideal of Democracy ...'

Suffragist's demand for women's economic and industrial rights through equal pay for equal work crossed class lines. In 1882, Sydney established the first Australian Women's Christian Temperance Union (WCTU) branch, later the National WCTU of Australia, while in 1891, Melbourne women formed the WCTU of Australasia. Mary Leavitt's 1885 visit from US headquarters prompted Queensland, SA, Tasmania, and NSW branches, and in 1892 journalist Jessie Ackerman of the US WCTU on her second Australian visit led WA to follow. Albeit the WCTU's principal aim was abstinence, or prohibition of alcohol, by 1893 equal pay—'a matter of justice for both sexes'—was a firm tenet. The 1890s Depression and sweated labour in ill-lit sheds and rooms thrusting women into prostitution, men's pay rates for women aimed at undermining the sex trade. Then some 10 years after WCTU began campaigning, the NCW gained its first Australian branch, characterised by party political neutrality, though it favoured the establishment and conservative politics. Often the state's governor's wife was patron, with conference receptions at Government House. From 1904 to 1918, NCW Victoria's president was wife of the presiding governor. Equal pay was, however, a founding principle.

In 1893, Miss Margaret Windeyer attended the first International Council of Women (ICW) Quinquennial Council Meeting at its Chicago world congress. In the US attending a Librarianship Council conference coincidently in Chicago, meeting members of US NCW, Windeyer was impressed with the forthright approach demanding 'equality between man and woman'. Ambitious to establish NCW in Australia, Windeyer set sail for home.

Following the inaugural meeting of NCW NSW in 1896, in George Street at Sydney's Town Hall, members attended the 1899 ICW London Quinquennial Congress. The agenda included equal pay, access by men and women to all professions, maternity allowances, appointment of women factory inspectors, and relieving women from 'household drudgery' through developing 'modern household machinery'.

NCW branches formed throughout Australia, not replacing women's state organisations, rather aiming to join them to create a strong collective voice for all women. The Princess Ida Club, formed in 1888 by University of Melbourne (UM) women graduates, was a foundation NCW Victoria member, together with the WCTU, Association of Domestic Economy,

Austral Salon (women writers and artists), Collingwood Crèche and Collingwood Girls' Club, Daughters of Court, Gentlewomen's Aid Society, Victorian Lady Teachers' Association (VLTA), and 26 more voluntary societies.

The first NCWV congress, 28–29 October 1903, was attended by country and interstate representatives, delegates, and associates. Amongst papers on 'Epileptic Colonies' by Dr Mary Page Stone, Miss Alice Henry's 'The Rejected Contribution', Mrs FA Long's 'The Work of the District Nursing Association', and 'The Rights of the Child' by Miss Clara Weeks, were 'Factory Legislation' by Miss MG Cuthbertson (later a factory inspector and expert witness in the ***Federated Clothing Trades case 1919***) and Mrs EF Allan (Aotearoa/New Zealand NCW) on 'Equal Pay for Equal Work'.

Theory and practice drove the campaign, propelled by women working in factories and shops, as telegraphists, and postal clerks. In the 1880s, Melbourne seamstresses went on strike for improved industrial conditions and rates of pay. In 1886, factory inspectors approved factories in Flinders Street, Melbourne, and workrooms in the Horderns Building, Elizabeth and Goulburn Streets, Sydney as 'well ventilated and well kept'. Yet (if true) this was not the norm. Well into the 1880s and beyond, machinists, cutters, and pressers worked in damp, dank conditions in cellars and basements, ramshackle shops, airless rooms dusty with the steady drumming of sewing machine treadles. In 1882, an ***Age*** series recounted low pay and long hours worked by women in the industry, 500 to 600 women workers marching to Trades Hall on 10 December, demanding better conditions and equal pay. On 15 December, around 300 formed the Victorian Tailoresses' Union (VTU), claiming uniform rates of pay. Negotiations faltered. On 15 February 1883, roughly 1200 women went on strike, out until April, when some had their claims met, others forced to accede to other employers' lower rates.

In Victoria, like the Clothing Trades Union (CTU) and Telegraphists and Postal Clerks Union (TPCU) launching official demands for equal pay in 1900 and 1902, teacher unions pursued the claim. In August 1912, demanding male-female parity in teachers' salaries, the VLTA sought NCWV's cooperation. Replicated in schools around Australia, the doctrine 'God created men and women differently' restricted women's teaching opportunities, women's legitimacy in the profession being closely associated with rights to equal pay. Holding identical qualifications and doing the same or similar work rendered distinctions spurious, yet female teachers' equal pay claims were ignored.

Nevertheless, in 1913, VLTA, with NCW, succeeded in having a public service commissioner, GC Morrison, appointed to report to Victoria's Parliament on female teachers' conditions and differentials in male-female rates of pay. Ultimately declaring women were not equally qualified, nor did the same work, Morrison rejected VLTA and NCW arguments.

His proposition that most female teachers lacked university degrees so should be denied equal pay was curious, because neither did most male teachers. Skating over this, Morrison focused on equal work. No woman headed a school teaching level six or over, meaning female teachers did not do 'the same' work as male teachers, indicating lack of capacity, he said. Yet this overlooked policy and practice reserving higher status and higher paid jobs for men, preventing women from developing the skills or showing off those they had. Morrison also ignored that women worked as teachers alongside men, and specialised in infants' teaching, equally dependent upon intellect and communication skills, and equally taxing, as teaching older age groups or managing schools—or more so. Furthermore, women teachers did the most difficult work: classes at the hierarchy's base. Male teachers taught classes with the 'top' students, women had the 'difficult' ones.

Employing stereotypical assumptions and mere assertion, Morrison held unacceptable as 'unimpeachable doctrine' notions of women's equality with men 'from a physical or an intellectual viewpoint'. Whilst 'freely admitting' that 'woman has done a great deal in her own sphere of womanhood', she is, 'by reason of her natural frailty of body, unfitted to bear … the physical strain inseparable from the vocation of a teacher …'. Men, 'with rare exceptions', have achieved 'the world's great things' and in a crisis 'endure strain better than women'. Hence, no equal pay for women in teaching.

The Federal Industrial Response

In the Commonwealth Arbitration Court, at first glance a different approach emerged. Justice Higgins, addressing women working Mildura and Renmark orchards as fruitpickers alongside men, acknowledged that a fruitpicker is a fruitpicker. In other words, albeit men more often worked as fruitpickers, women more often consigned to fruitpacking, fruitpicking is not a sex-linked skill, hence not justifying different levels of remuneration for women and men.

The ***Fruitpickers case*** addressed equal pay for equal work for women in the dried fruits industry. The Rural Workers' Union (RWU) and SA

United Labourers' Union (ULU) argued for workers, on strike for fair rates of pay for an 8-hour day with additional overtime rates. The RWU wanted piecework or the 'task system' outlawed, and no overtime for women, girls, and boys. The ULU wanted growers to provide accommodation, wood, and water as workers' industrial entitlements. Mildura and Renmark growers rejected the unions' rates of 7s for men and women over 17 or 18 years, 6s for boys and girls of 16 to 18 years. Growers wanted a many-tiered system depending upon age and sex, seeking an adult male rate of 7s per day, 5s 6d for women, boys (17–19) 6s a day, girls 4s 6d. Below 17, the differential was boys – 5s, girls – 4s. Hut accommodation, wood or other allowances should come out of workers' wages.

A compulsory conference failed. This meant that, the dispute came before the Arbitration Court.

Fruitpicking industry work was classed unskilled, casual, and light, with an hourly rate. Payment for unskilled work rested on cost of living, higher in Renmark and Mildura than Melbourne or Adelaide, due to distance and goods and labour transport costs. This, said Higgins, was relevant to wage setting, as well as 'discrimination based on sex' in fruitpicking wages and a minimum wage for women doing fruitpacking.

Higgins travelled to Mildura and Renmark to see the picking fields and packing sheds. For the first time, the Arbitration Court dealt explicitly with what Higgins called 'the problem of female labour'. Most industry workers were men, 'even in the simple process of picking'. Nonetheless, women and girls outnumbered men and boys in packing—wrapping citrus in paper, or trimming and placing paper in boxes, packing fruit in cartons, fashioning neat facings to boxes for shop windows.

The phrase 'equal pay for equal work' had 'an attractive sound', said Higgins, 'seeming to carry justice on its face; for, obviously, where a woman produces as good results as a man in the same kind of work, she ought not [receive] less remuneration'. Yet the phrase implied that unequal work should receive unequal pay. Higgins therefore adopted an interpretation of equal pay restricting it to men and women doing work 'of the same character', a minimum wage accruing to all doing the work, whatever their sex. Employers could not lawfully undercut this but could pay *above* the minimum rate to 'exceptionally good workers whose services he desires to secure'. Employers were also 'free to dispense with the services of any worker ... not com[ing] up to his standard'. For Higgins, if blacksmiths 'are a class of workers', the minimum rate should recognise they are usually men. The minimum rate for fruitpickers, a 'class of workers' must recognise that, 'to the present at least, most … pickers are men (although women have been usually paid less)', and 'men and women are fairly in competition' in that 'class of work'.

By setting the minimum wage for fruitpicking at the male rate, Higgins said, employers would be precluded from driving men out of the industry or forcing fruitpickers' wages down. The 'tendency to substitute women for men in industries, even in occupations … more suited for men' resulted in lower wages for women workers. He concluded that men and women pickers' earnings should be set on a 'substantial level', with identical wage rates. Employers would be 'at liberty freely to select whichever sex and whichever person he prefers for the work', resulting in 'greater efficiency' with 'true and healthy competition—not competition as in a Dutch auction by taking lower remuneration, but competition by making oneself more useful to the employer'.

Victory for women in the fruitpicking industry? For some, yes, women fruitpickers' wages rose to the male level. The decision could even be read as anticipating equal pay for women doing work of equal value. Yet it can be interpreted as securing fruitpicking jobs for men alone—obliged to pay women men's wages, they could take men, dispensing with women. This is a traditional feminist reading assigned to Higgins.

What of an alternative analysis? Higgins' decision emphasises that employers should be deterred from driving wages down, leaving workers no real choice: take jobs at lower wages, risking wages being undercut again and again, or refuse the work. This would advantage neither women nor men, for reduced wages would affect both: if women entered the industry at lower wages, driving men out, nothing would prevent employers from reducing women's wages even more drastically. A snowball effect would have implications for industries employing women in preference to men, and for men working in male dominated industries. Alternatively, setting rates based in women's work and men's work could damage men's job prospects and wage rates overall. Employers could transmute men's work into women's work, reducing wages. Lowered women's wages could be a base mark for arguing that if women could survive on less, so could men. Here, however, Higgins' rationale becomes evident: as the social norm was that women needed less, that justified increasing men's wages and not setting them at the level acceptable (traditionally) for women. The decision to increase men's wages where they were doing 'men's jobs' (because more men than women were fruitpickers) could be justified on this argument: women needed less, men needed more. This made it more difficult for the employer (here, the growers) to hold to their maximum of 7s for all-male adult workers, 6s for males 17 to 19, and 5s under 17, with greater negative differentials for adult women, women between 17 and 19, and women under 17 years. Ultimately, Higgins' decision finessed the employer growers.

Both unions claimed equal rates for women and men, whatever jobs they were doing, and equal rates for boys and girls, whatever their jobs: were unions wanting parity for women and men workers, or seeking to price women out of fruitpicking? The growers' claim was for unequal male-female rates, whatever the jobs. Higgins rejected the proposition that whatever work women and girls did, it must be worth (much) less than that of men and boys. He didn't give women and men (or girls and boys) equal rates in all their jobs, whether done mainly by men (or boys) or mainly women (or girls). Yet he secured higher rates all around—not the lower rates and wide differentials employers sought. He secured in part what the unions wanted, simultaneously giving growers in part what they wanted. He formulated a trade-off. So, is it fair to say his decision aimed at driving women out of men's jobs, or driving down women's wages? The decision did encourage a likelihood that people (women or men) seeking higher pay rates would move into fruitpicking, meaning men content to work at fruitpacking may no longer be so, with more furious competition in the industry's fruitpicking side. By fixing a minimum wage at the union-proposed higher level (not the employer-advocated lower level) Higgins' decision prevented such competition precipitating lower wages.

The decision was framed in the employers' right to choose workers by skill and capacity: those with greater skill and capacity, women or men, were open to fruitpickers' jobs, earning higher wages. Yet higher pay was allocated not by the nature of the work nor upon greater or lesser skills for the job (whether exercised by women or men) but on whether women or men were more concentrated in the work. This made the decision problematic, particularly for women, as well as disclosing an aspect not previously pursued in ***Fruitpickers case*** analyses—skills.

First, problematics vis-à-vis women. If in the short-term women risked being driven out of fruitpicking, with men gaining and retaining jobs at the higher wage rate whilst women lost those jobs along with the superior pay rates, the long-term effect was even more telling. Simultaneously with establishing women's right to equal pay for work of the same character as that performed by men, Higgins cemented into the federal arbitration system a substantial inequality in rates of pay for women and men, along with the notion that unequal wages based on sex/gender of the worker—not on actual job components, nor on skill or capacity required for the job—was appropriate and fair. Not only did the ***Fruitpickers case*** refuse to countenance, so eliminate, unequal pay rates for women in fruitpicking. It confirmed unequal pay rates for fruitpacking (predominantly done by women): the minimum rate for men and women pickers 'in competition' with one another was fixed at 1s per hour, but the minimum for workers in fruitpacking, 'in which men are hardly ever employed', was fixed at 9 pence. This was on the basis that women had lesser costs of living than men, albeit no evidence was admitted.

Next to skills. Higgins' analysis harboured contradictions. Observing that picking was a simple process, he concluded that women were particularly suited to packing work. Having 'had the advantage of seeing the women performing the lighter operations of packing at a factory', he had 'no doubt' that the work was 'adapted for women with their superior deftness and suppleness of fingers'. The 'best test', he said, was that if wage rates for women were identical to those of men, employers 'would always, or nearly always, employ the women' as packers. This meant that he 'must, therefore, endeavour to find a fair minimum wage for these women, assuming they must find their own food, shelter, and clothing'.

Why not pay the women at a rate recognising their ability? If women predominate in packing (rather than the 'simple process' of picking), through 'superior deftness and suppleness of fingers', why not a rate commensurate with the work's superior nature? Higgins classes packing as 'lighter' work, as compared to (presumably) the heavier work of fruitpicking. With unskilled work, 'lighter' is traditionally regarded as 'easier' than 'heavier' work and hence paid at a lower rate. Yet Higgins says 'lighter', simultaneously with assessing the (women's) work as requiring superior skill. Ultimately, however, this does not inform his wage setting. Sex/gender is crucial to the rate of pay, not the nature of the work or the skill required.

Herein lies an irony. Ultimately skill is irrelevant not because Higgins rules out wage rates based on women's capacities, but because work in the dried fruits industry excluded skill as an issue. Despite his comments, these jobs—all of them—were already classed unskilled. The union did not contest it. The question was what pay rates were due to unskilled labourers and unskilled labouring. 'Better' or not, 'superior' abilities or not, women in packing, along with men (and women) in picking, were not classed as 'having skills' or 'being skilled'. Because the case was about *unskilled* workers (both women and men), according to wage-fixing principles, Higgins could set a minimum rate of pay only in accordance with 'cost of living'. This, he said, had to be seen as different for a woman than that set for a man. Why?

Higgins is implicated by his own reasoning back in 1907. In ***Harvester***, H.V. McKay sought relief from excise duties in selling harvesting and other farm machinery overseas. To be exempt, H.V. McKay had to show that remuneration it paid workers was 'fair and reasonable' under the 1906 Excise Tariff Act.

Higgins said the question was not whether H.V. McKay or any other export company was making profits, or how much they made in profits. Rather, the Arbitration Court must focus on wages and conditions. The Excise Tariff Act did not define 'fair and reasonable'. In the first instance, interpretation was for the Arbitration Court. Higgins was critical that such a 'controversial problem, with ... grave social and economic bearings' was 'committed to a Judge' lacking responsibility 'at least directly' and who 'ought not to be responsible to public opinion'. Aware of the potential for appeal, he added prophetically that even if his interpretation was initially accepted, that would not necessarily follow in the future.

Women fighting for equal pay continually confronted the Higgins' ***Harvester*** stumbling block. The principle of 'a living wage' as fair and reasonable payment to workers ought not in itself to have promoted any male-female divide. Higgins' own words created no obstacle to *women* workers seeking (or obtaining) a living wage (equal to men's). But the ***Harvester*** living wage and workers' rights or needs were applied differentially to women and men, despite ***Harvester*** not precluding unions from arguing that women, like men, have dependents, nor tribunals from recognising this.

Higgins focused first on relative bargaining strengths of employee vis-à-vis employer, saying provision for fair and reasonable remuneration was set to benefit industry employees, to gain what they could not get through individual bargaining with employers. The provision of 'fair and reasonable' would be unnecessary if it meant only what could be gained in terms of contracts of service and what 'employees will accept and employers will give'. In that case, remuneration 'could safely have been left to the usual, but unequal, contest, the "higgling of the market" for labour', and 'pressure for bread on one side, ... pressure for profits on the other'. Therefore, '"fair and reasonable" must be something else ...'

The 'something else', Higgins framed initially in sex/gender neutral terms: the everyday needs of the average employee 'a human being living in a civilised community'. He then cited 'workman' and 'fair and reasonable'. Denoting 'fair' as the method of gaining agreement between employee and employer, he said 'reasonable' meant payment should be commensurate with work done. An employer and workman don't contract on an equal footing or make a 'fair' wages agreement, he said, when 'the workman submits to work for a low wage to avoid starvation or pauperism (or something like it) for himself and his family'. Nor is an agreement 'reasonable' if it 'does not carry a wage sufficient to insure the workman food, shelter, clothing, frugal comfort, provision for evil days, &c., as well as reward for the special skill of an artisan if he is one'.

Higgins heard evidence of terms and conditions of work and living costs for average workers. Seasonal signing-off of significant numbers 'of men' led to inconstancy of employment, to be considered with cost of living, calculating payment for food, shelter, clothing, for an average labourer with normal wants, under normal conditions. The wife of a former vatman in candleworks said his then wages of 36s weekly meant she could not provide him (*sic*) with meat some 3 of 7 days. Higgins labelled this 'certainly not conducive to the maintenance of the worker in industrial efficiency ...' Further undisputed evidence 'by working men's wives and others' confirmed the usual labourer's rent, as distinguished from an artisan, as 7s. Evidence varied in amounts and computation methods of cost of living but, averaging lists of nine 'housekeeping women' for groceries, bread, meat, milk, fuel, vegetables, and fruit, and taking rent at 7s, Higgins set the essential average weekly expenditure for a labourer's home of some five persons as £1 12s 5d. This excluded light (some lists omitted it), clothes, boots, furniture, utensils ('casual', not weekly expenditure), rates, life insurance, savings, accident or benefit societies, loss of unemployment, union pay, books and newspapers, tram and train fares, sewing machine, mangle, school requisites, amusements and holidays, intoxicating liquors, tobacco, sickness and death, domestic help, 'unusual contingencies', religion, or charity. Setting weekly wages at 36s left 3s 7d to pay for all of these, said Higgins, declaring this a rather large call for 3s 7d to cover—even for non-drinkers and non-smokers—as were most of the men.

Despite the words 'workman' and 'vatman', and recourse to evidence from workers' wives, nothing in Higgins' decision indicates that 'fair and reasonable' and 'a living wage' meant 'men only', nor that it had no application to women in paidwork. All workers in question were men making machinery. However, 'workman' arguably applied generically. The Excise Tariff Act did not distinguish between male and female workers or pay rates, referring only to fair and reasonable wages. The Interpretation Act 1901 (Cth) said legislation included female in the male form.

However, the 1912 ***Fruitpickers case*** hinged the ***Harvester*** living wage upon a legal obligation to male workers. According to Higgins, a 'living wage' meant the wage upon which a man (rather than 'worker'), his wife and children could adequately live, not a woman with dependent children and spouse (or dependent parents or siblings). Referencing ***Harvester***, Higgins noted the obligation—'even a legal obligation' resting upon the man—although Australia was notorious for desertion by men of their families. Women he saw as under no obligation, 'unless perhaps in very exceptional circumstances', on which the minimum could not be based. He considered employers free from being 'told to pay a particular employee more because she happens to have parents and brothers and sisters dependent on her'. Nor, however, could employers pay less because a woman had a legacy from grandparents, or free board and lodging from parents, and 'merely wants some money for dress'. Employers could not be asked by the state to familiarise themselves (atop all other anxieties) with employees' 'domestic necessities'. Neither could the state allow 'girls with comfortable homes' undercut wage standards required by 'less fortunate girls [having] to maintain themselves'.

Yet with no evidence in the ***Fruitpickers case*** that women's cost of living was any less than men's, Higgins assumptions (supposition and traditional expectations, not facts) led to assertions that men still comprised most bread winners. Higgins assumed board and lodging costs (17s or 18s) were 'primarily applicable to males'. Evidence of 'considerable differ ence between males and females—say, from [fifteen years] onwards—on the expense of dress' was not applied by Higgins to increase the women's minimum rate, or at least equalise it to men's. The argument for holding women's wages down in work dominated by women (packing sheds) was that raising women's wages to male rates would be too costly to the employer. Generally put by employers, this was reiterated whenever equal pay for women arose.

However, lack of evidence of women's cost of living ultimately lies with the unions. Parties must submit evidence upon which they rely. If, in claiming equal pay for female and male workers, the union evidence was intended to stand for both, that costs for women were identical should have been argued. Prudence dictates bringing women not only as wives, but as workers. Unions left Higgins to his assumptions. The union hierarchy being male, male interests being visible and, hence, privileged, explains the breach.

Awaiting the hearing, unions obtained temporary agreements through the Arbitration Court. Employers consented to the unions' full 8s per day claim as the minimum wage for all workers in the industry, women and men. Consent ensued upon Higgins' 'distinct assurance that [he] would leave [his] mind open and unaffected by the rate … employers conceded for peace at a crucial time'—the strike coincided with the picking season. When the agreements expired, the old rates resumed, women persuaded by union leaders to continue working a full day at rates of 3s 6d to 4s 6d, pending arbitration. Contemplating the effect of reinstating rates won under the temporary agreements, Higgins said that increases from 3s 6d, 'or even 4s. 6d. or 5s. for a full day', to 8s, 'certainly seems violent'. If 26 women were employed at 4s 6d, this meant a massive increase in output cost. He concluded that with a minimum of 1s per hour for men and women pickers in competition, the minimum for women workers in packing sheds, where men rarely worked, should be 9d per hour.

Women's serious underpayment made it more difficult to award them fair and adequate wages: raising their rates to parity meant comparatively huge increases. Higgins should not have bowed to a system that left women with inadequate wages. Yet awarding women wage rates equal to their true entitlement would likely bring the whole outcome—increases across the board, against employers' wishes—crashing down. Higgins worked the balancing act the arbitration system required, running a continuing battle against employers generally (to benefit downtrodden employees whom he recognised as lacking in power), and High Court conservative forces, which saw the Arbitration Court as a challenge to its own authority. Whilst Higgins' overriding aim was to have Arbitration Court authority recognised, enabling it to stand as a bulwark against rapacious employers and for workers' rights, Arbitration Court decisions not infrequently suffered reversals in High Court appeals (as in ***R v Barger*** overturning ***Harvester***).

Yet this cannot absolve Higgins from the industrial consequences for women. His bias in favour of man-as-breadwinner and overlooking women with breadwinner responsibilities was exemplified when he noted, in ***Fruitpickers***, that 'fortunately for society' male breadwinners outnumber women heads-of-household. If he was concerned about women's lack of economic and socially sanctioned resources to head households and be breadwinners, his decision served only to lock women into their already existing position of need. His argument was circular: the 'fortunate' became a self-fulfilling prophecy.

Women responsible for dependants were left coping on a female wage Higgins acknowledged did not match support-a-family level. His decision maintained and affirmed the very conditions making it (in his eyes) 'fortunate' that most families were headed by a male breadwinner. Whether women were 'breadwinners' or not, 'heads-of-household' or not, Higgins consigned all women workers to living on a wage leaving them dependent upon others for survival, or at least living frugally. Nonetheless, he did leave open the possibility of setting the minimum wage for women doing women's work at a level more akin to men's. Alluding to the paucity of evidence of women's needs and requirements, he classed his finding 'tentative', open to correction on better materials. This signalled unions in all industries to acquit their responsibility in future (too often honoured in the breach), calling comprehensive evidence of women's living needs, costs, and family responsibilities.

But the male-female living wage disparity held. Women's entry into male industries during the 1914–1918 war years brought no lasting shift. Despite Higgins' continuing to express apparent doubts, or leaving the door open to another approach, in 1917 and 1918 the Arbitration Court confirmed different male and female 'living' wages.

Justice Powers in ***Australian Theatrical and Amusement Employees' Association v. J.C. Williamson Ltd and Ors*** set women's living wage at 35s per week against 65s for men, but said equal rates of 65s applied to women 'employed to do men's work' *and* if the work done by a woman was 'of as great a value' as a man's. This ran alongside setting the male living wage on the assumption that the average man has or will have a wife and family of three children whatever the value of his work. Contrarily, the living wage of the woman doing woman's work was calculated as if she were single. But this case left open at least two possibilities for women and unions supporting equal pay. They could argue that women's work in a women's industry had 'as great a value' as men's work in a male industry. They could also introduce evidence disputing assumptions about women's and men's family responsibilities, showing that far from all women—or even most—in paidwork being single without dependants, many (unmarried, deserted, or wives or mothers of the profligate, ill, alcoholic or unemployed) had family responsibilities equalling men's. First World War demands and ravages added to women's responsibility for supporting husbands, children, and parents.

Equally, evidence would show many men, albeit receiving a wage based on wife-and-three-children, single and without family responsibilities or, having a family, not conforming to the wife-plus-three model. This gained passing recognition in Arbitration Court cases, but like Powers in ***J.C. Williamson***, concerns were that paying single men less than married men meant employers would favour cheaper labour, who could not then provide for marriage. But refusal to extend equal pay to women with dependants left women heads-of-household struggling to provide for their families. Fixing wages on male family responsibilities (real, presumed or projected) ensured that workers classed 'unskilled' had a minimum or living wage. Including women would not, or not necessarily, mean reducing pay rates. Nonetheless, the Arbitration Court was captive of its time, Higgins, particularly, seeking outcomes favouring workers by a rationale socially and culturally acceptable, lessening the possibility of appeals overturning decisions.

In 1919, Higgins reviewed his ***Fruitpickers*** decision. In ***Federated Clothing Trades of the Commonwealth of Australia v. J.A. Archer and Ors***, his ability to review male-female wage disparity was limited when the Federated Clothing Trades Union (FCTU) claim was for a lower rate for female workers. Yet the case projected some hope for future claims. Higgins held that the burden lay upon employers to show that sex should found differential rates for the same occupation, and differential female rates should apply to the basic rate only, not the secondary rate (or margins) for skill or danger and poor conditions.

The FCTU claimed 65s weekly as the basic male wage (set at 50s by Victorian Wages Board determinations), and 40s for women. Echoing his ***Fruitpickers case*** concerns, Higgins queried lack of cogent or comprehensive cost of living evidence for women. This time, the union was not at fault. Women workers gave income and expenses evidence, revealing their ingenuity in scraping a living. Higgins appeared to approve of W. Jethro Brown's 1918 claim in the SA ***Clothing Trades case***, of being 'unable to arrive at any other conclusion than that the bedrock living wage for women should be 27s. 6d. per week', without 'giving precise details' of his calculation.

The ***Advertiser*** of 22 October 1931 reported Brown's failure being 'reticence on the part of a "mere man" dealing with a problem so intricate and so delicate': public testing of witnesses on the 'more intimate articles of women's underwear'. This undermines confidence in the process and the judge's competence. Women's wages require determination by qualified tribunal. Judicial determinations having precluded women from legal practice, the first woman appointed to a Supreme Court (SA) in 1965, for years male judges demonstrated their inadequacies vis-à-vis 'women's matters'. Higgins called for research and 'scientific evidence' from the Commonwealth Statistician in women's wage claims, he and Powers repeatedly suggested this to government. In its absence: 'I must do my best on the materials available'.

Witnesses before Higgins included Miss Brenda Sutherland, Melbourne's Domestic Arts Hostel superintendent, factory inspector Miss Cuthbertson, and seven women operatives the union called to testify on their 1918 expenditure. The women made do—one paying for her own laundry and fuel, sewing for her landlady's family to supplement board and lodging payment; another did evening sewing for extra money; a third boarded with her mother; a fourth had 'considerable money gifts [from] her sister in Sydney'; a fifth lowered accommodation costs, 'sleeping on a balcony'. All made their own clothes.

Higgins determined 35s a week would cover board and lodging and clothes, without monies for sickness or old age, union fees, amusements or church, stamps or journals or books, no tram or train fares, nor for 'giving assistance to others'. The FCTU advocate Mr Carter asked for a modest £2 only, necessary expenditure being calculated at £2 6s 6d per week.

Consistent over jurisdictions is the recurring theme of women's clothing as a wage component and item of expenditure, visions of women spending their own or husbands' money on 'fripperies' exercising many a judicial brain. Higgins thought employers shouldn't be 'compelled ... to pay 15s. per week for clothes alone ...'. It was the 'girls' business' if wanting 'finery at the sacrifice of [necessities] ...'.

Unfortunately, Higgins missed his own non sequitur. If women were going without necessities to clothe themselves, then if awarded less money for clothing, surely they ought to be awarded more for necessities foregone. Yet besides missing out on what they sacrificed for finery (and gaining nothing for those necessities), women were to clothe themselves to 'be respectable'. Betraying bourgeois notions of conformity and expectations of women's comportment, Higgins declared the 'important social function of girls' dress as a bulwark for self-respect' should be remembered, 'women [showing] simplicity and good taste' in dress to their economic inferiors.

Having criticised the women's evidence, Higgins bluntly set the living wage for women at 35s a week, not even providing women workers the same percentage increase as the men. Had he raised the women's basic wage in the same ratio—50s:60s, women's wages would have risen from 28s to 36s 5p.

The States Industrial Response

Around Australia, the unequal pay rationale ranged from protecting women's jobs outside the home by not pricing women out of work; contending women would rather be married and out of the paid workforce than unmarried and in it; claiming women lacked dependants; saying they might but it lacked relevance to wage setting; emphasising the male breadwinner role; asserting men had no right to use equal pay to manoeuvre women's dismissal from jobs male workers (and unions) wanted to keep for themselves. Whatever the argument, mostly men's higher pay won, women's unequal rates remained.

On 11 March 1913, 'Women Must Take Less—"Equal Pay for Equal Work" Principle Set Aside in Victoria' headed the Sydney ***Sun*** report on the Victorian Court of Industrial Appeal's latest decision. Justice Cussen in ***In re Commercial Clerks' Board*** set aside the Commercial Clerks' Wages Board determination that a minimum of 48s weekly go to clerks 'irrespective of sex'. Dismayed, women's organisations reacted. The VTU and NCW were running a claim for equal pay in the teaching profession, and this was the first time the Industrial Court had addressed occupational—as distinct from trade or industry—pay rates.

The Commercial Clerks' Board was appointed by the Victorian Parliament to decide minimum rates for cashiers, typewriters, stenographers, bookkeepers, and a range of clerks—collecting, time-keeping, dispatch, store, and weighing clerks. Cussen applied principles set by the Industrial Court in ***In re the Boilermakers' Board***, requiring correcting 'what is wrong or anomalous', with 'justice … administered, not benevolence at other people's expense'. Change 'for the mere love' of it, or to 'give effect to the economic or sociological views of the individual or individuals constituting the tribunal, or of some writer on economic or sociological subjects' was deprecated. Wages for trade or occupation before a board or tribunal could be compared with the wages paid in 'cognate trades or occupations', principally in Victoria or (with great caution) trades or occupations in other states.

That *male* adult clerks' base rate should be 48s per week of 48 hours did not worry Cussen. The problem lay in extending a male rate to women doing the self-same clerical work. Stenographers, typewriters, and operators of calculating or billing machines—classed 'clerks', were mostly female. What rate should apply when men did that work? For the few men in these occupations, the Board fixed the base rate as 45s, saying it should apply across the board, giving women 45s, too. Previously, women received under 30s weekly whilst 'almost all' male clerks, whatever their work, got over 40s.

The Board's argument was that male adult wages shouldn't go below 42s per week, that being the amount 'found [to] support in frugal comfort a man, his wife and ... a reasonable or average family of three children'. By this standard, the Board considered male adult clerks in male dominated areas, then men in female dominated areas, deciding for the former a weekly rate of at least 48s and the latter, 45s, fixing women's wages accordingly. This meant 45s weekly in female dominated areas, and with males and females in male dominated areas 'doing clerical work, and there should be equal pay for equal work, female adults also should receive the same 48s for forty-eight hours'.

Cussen concluded on this reasoning it would be 'equally logical, or ... equally illogical and absurd' for employers to argue—'Females are under no obligation to support a husband and family, and thirty shillings for forty-eight hours would be enough to support a single female or a female considered singly, and as both males and females do clerical work, on the principle of equal pay for equal work, male adults should also receive as the lowest wages not more than thirty shillings'. Here, he articulated a fear driving some unions to argue for equal rates for women in male dominated areas in the first place, and with greater logic. At the time, fixing the rate, as Higgins had, in family obligation was more easily sustained. 'Wife and family to support' was an historical catch cry, supporting male worker awards not through the nature of the work, but by assumed obligations. The argument against Cussen is that not all men are yet married with children, but this did not affect the established rate of pay or its rationale. Industrial tribunals did not argue it should. Hence, that some women doing the same work may, like some men, not have the same family obligations (albeit some do) should not undercut the established rate of pay. In framing the argument as he did, Cussen put the focus on women workers as potentially undermining men's right to a liveable wage, a focus unlikely to foster positive working relations between male and female clerks or women and men in other occupations concerned to preserve wages at fair and liveable rates.

Cussen failed to address alternative ways of fixing rates. He relied upon the ambiguity Higgins identified in the ***Fruitpickers case***, in 'the proposition, "equal pay for equal work"', when Higgins set women packers' weekly wages at 36s. In refusing to uphold equal pay, Cussen concluded that if rank and file female clerks (not higher-grade female clerks) performed equally as male clerks, at least by results, women would be employed 'to a much greater extent'. As they were not, this meant applying the male rate, 'many females would lose their employment'. Further, 'a large class of female employees was opposed to the increase .... [O]ne young lady was independent enough to say that the minimum should not be fixed higher than 35s a week, [as] if a girl was worth more, she would get more'.

When he challenged the Clerks' advocate, saying equal pay 'was in many cases disastrous', the advocate responded 'these girls must be sacrificed for the good of the cause as a whole'. Cussen replied that those 'sacrificed' could be 'numbered probably by hundreds', a 'dear price for the State to pay to uphold the majority'. Nothing he could find in the legislation led him 'to think … any such wholesale slaughter of innocents' was intended.

Was Cussen's aim women's job preservation? His decision raises doubts, whatever he said. He applauded women's restriction to narrow paidwork fields—24,000 of 30,000 women recorded as in paid employment worked in ten fields: boots, clothing, confectionery, drapers, dresses, millinery, bookbinding, shirts, underclothing, and woollens, most paid one-half to two-thirds of men's wages. He saw no cause to change this, being the general rule. Nor could he envisage considering women's responsibility for 'helping' (*sic*) support a parent or other relative. Where women were in 'complete or nearly complete control' of an occupation or trade, wages were rightly fixed at a lower rate, 'equal pay for equal work' being a 'fallacious expression'.

Cussen considered 'certain exceptional women … do work of the kind ordinarily allotted to females above the ordinary value, or … do work, such as bookkeeping, ordinarily allotted to males'. Such women generally received above the lowest wages and 'might be specially provided for'. But, following 'general lines' meant he 'should not specially provide for them now …' That a female clerk might be employed with male clerks would not show her work as necessarily of equal value, rendering unnecessary pursuing the subject further. Nonetheless rates for men in jobs mainly done by women required attention. Rejecting the idea that work women generally did merited lower wages, he concluded it was less difficult here to make a distinction purely on sex lines. The practical outcome was to set women's rates lower than men's in any event. A man doing typing or stenography would warrant the male clerk's rate, but a woman whatever type of clerking she did qualified for the female base rate only. The whole tenor of Cussen's judgment was that women's wages should be set by reference to wages of other women, whatever the work, not be compared with men's, in male or female occupations. For men, working in male occupations they merited the male rate. In female occupations, they qualified for a male rate, not the lower rate set for women beside whom they worked but, it being women's not men's work, men would not be paid the rate for men in male occupations. Hence, three rates: men's rates, men-in-women's-occupations, and women's—in descending order.

Ostensibly the equal pay problem lay, for Cussen, in terminology. Did 'equal pay for equal work' mean 'equal results'—in terms of piecework, or 'equal results' assessed by employers, or 'equal effort' calculated by the worker's assessment? Yet the difficulty truly lay in his failure to accept women's right to paidwork, to economic self-sufficiency, and freedom to choose employment. He excoriated the union for attempting (as he saw it) to exclude women by pricing them out of the market—employers rejecting them at men's rates. However, he set women's wages low for the same end—getting women out of paidwork. They were, for him, temporarily in the labour market, their aim an escape into marriage. Evidently believing this was women's rightful goal, Cussen set wages to enforce economic reality through a slimmer pay packet for them, a fatter one for men as husbands and prospective mates. Economics should prompt women to opt for marriage. Unreasonable women wanted equal pay. Cussen maintained the status quo—women gaining a higher standard of living through a husband's wage. 'Most reasonable people,' he opined, 'would agree'.

In ***In re Brewery Employees Union***, the NSW Industrial Court saw preventing male workers from using industrial tribunals to drive women out of an industry as central. The Brewery Employees Union (BEU) appealed against a Brewers Board determination that the award rightly differentiated between female and male pay rates for women employed alongside men. Disallowing the appeal, the president observed that the union's 'expressed fear' that employing women in work 'seeming to be well within their capabilities' may result in fewer men employed might be well-founded. Nonetheless the Court had no remit for 'protecting men against women any more than protecting women against men'. Wage boards 'represented the whole community', all workers' rights being 'entitled to equal consideration ...'

Here, 'equal consideration' meant maintaining women's wages at lower rates where women did the same work as men because this would (purportedly) preserve women's right to do that work. Perhaps more tellingly, it preserved the employers' right to hire (women) workers at lower rates. Seven days later, this was repeated in ***In re Shop Assistants' Union***, the Board being required to reconsider award terms granting female shop assistants identical rates with males, whilst male office assistants were paid higher rates than female office assistants. The president speculated there were 'very few female grocery shop assistants', so 'men were anxious to protect themselves from ... possible [future] intrusion ...'. With office work, female office assistants being relatively high in number, he thought the Board did not want to burden employers with a large wages increase, nor put women at 'considerable risk of dismissal'. If his theory were right, he must inform all Boards they 'must [exercise wage-fixing power] by legitimate principles'. Wage scales 'must not be drawn up [to] exclude either sex'.

Setting wage scales to encourage women's dismissal—by requiring employers to pay a male wage (as with the grocery assistants' rate) was unfair. That few women worked as grocer's shop assistants, though employers could employ them at 'decidedly lower wages than men' under the existing award seemed to indicate the role as 'unsuited to females'. Thus men 'already have a handicap in their favour without supporting themselves by a wage scale ... probably absolutely prohibitory to females'. Further, the argument 'where economic value of the work done by the female is equal to that done by the male, the wages should be the same' could embroil arbitration in contested economic and political principles, such to be avoided, as awards would vary according to boards' 'varying political views'. It was 'evident' the Board was not 'influenced in the instant case by [the equal pay for work of equal economic value] argument, because they have given different wages to the male and female office assistants'.

This echoes women's continuing struggle then and in the future, caught between industrial tribunals professing a lack of power over equal pay, directing proponents to the political arena, governments declaring power lay with industrial tribunals. Upholding male-female differentials and women's lower wages was just as political as deciding 'for' equal pay. It is at least equally political to maintain the status quo as it is to upset it. Equally, economic consequences flow from both. Deciding women's rates should be less than men's gave employers a lower wage bill if they increased their female labour force. Granting higher rates for men in women's occupations, whilst retaining lower wages for women again advantaged employers: paying a few men more impacted little, yet paying many women the higher rate presaged significant economic impact.

Brown's rationale in the 1918 SA ***Printing Trades case*** was blunt. Like Cussen in the ***Clerks case*** that year, women should not have equal wages as men, because men's 'life's vocation' lies in their occupation, women's occupation—'beyond the domestic sphere'—being 'in most cases transitory':

> It is not that women are not conscientious; they are often pathetically so. If … a dreary, monotonous task [is] to be performed, [needing] constant and minute attention, … a woman's service is unsurpassed. It is not that women are not intelligent; individual women again and again … proved their worth. It is not that women are physically weak; individually they may be stronger than individual men, and, [anyway], physical strength is no longer the greatest factor in industry. Women are inferiors in the industrial world because they have not decided (except individually) they desire to be otherwise, or at least that they desire to pay in training the price of efficiency.

Women lost out every time. If retaining their jobs, as tribunals assured them these decisions would allow, they worked alongside men earning more for identical work requiring equal attention, attendance, persistence, and skill. All of them, reliant upon the minimum or basic wage for women, earned less than it took to keep themselves, and far less than to meet any family obligations.

On Being 'Fair'

Nineteenth-century activists campaigned for more than the vote. Equal pay featured for women, unions, industrial courts, and tribunals. Women acted as paidworkers, supporters, lobbyists, and in women's organisations, participated as trade union members, officials, experts, and witnesses in equal pay and living wage claims. Yet the greatest stumbling block was a case aiming to grant workers fair and reasonable wages. Arguably made in the spirit of fairness for all workers, ***Harvester*** redounded against women's rights to fair pay and industrial conditions. It was used by tribunals unsympathetic to workers' rights and disposed to promote business or employer rights. Man-as-worker and worker-as-man held primary position in the Arbitration Court and other industrial tribunals. The world outside these forums was crucial. Having no wife, a woman was not entitled to the 'family wage'. Whatever her responsibilities, lacking legal rights to her children, she could be classed not responsible for them—therefore disentitled from claiming a wage based in financial responsibility for dependants.

Many women were primarily responsible for children's upkeep (and frequently aged parents, aunts, uncles, grandparents, unemployed adult children, those with disabilities, ne'er do well husbands or, simply, a man-out-of-work). Not being the traditional (male) head of household, Higgins' family wage eluded them.

In the ***Fruitpickers case***, Higgins' failure to extend his appreciation of workers' needs to incorporate *all* women workers as equally entitled, meant he treated women-doing-men's-work as just that. Men's work—men, or primarily men, did. Sometimes women did it and must be paid men's wages—but not on an identical basis as men. Men got men's wages through family responsibilities or (theoretically) having them in the future. Whether they did, in fact, was irrelevant. Women doing men's work got men's wages—because they did men's work, if they got it. A woman in a man's job qualified for a man's pay because of the work she did, not because she had, or might have, dependants. Like all women in paidwork, she was classed a single entity, oddity (in men's work) or necessity (in women's work) but without family relationships, at least not responsible for them. Single (or not), she was responsible only for herself.

Higgins was not alone in denying women workers equal entitlements to a living wage based on economic survival. Whilst couching decisions in language purporting to defend women's rights as wage earners and, more particularly, as candidates for marriage, state judges were frequently more retrograde. The male minimum or basic wage was paid to men because of their (presumed and assumed) family circumstances, family circumstances defined being a man. *What* work a man did didn't matter: being a man meant automatic qualification for the (male) basic wage—or the male basic wage for men in women's work. Men needed a living wage. Contrarily, when paid to women, the male basic or minimum wage was paid because of the work they did, not because they needed a living wage.

Meanwhile, women doing women's work were paid women's wages. Supporting a family was irrelevant. The focus was on the work they did, indicated by women's workforce composition. Even if work women did alongside women was seen as requiring special skill—'nimble fingers', or 'pathetic' conscientiousness—it warranted less pay. Neither Higgins, praising women packers' work, nor Brown, in one breath acknowledging women's skill—capable of 'constant and minute attention'—whilst damning it for use in 'dreary' and 'monotonous' tasks, saw this as warranting women higher pay. It meant only that women were suited to the work they did. This had immediate and long-term effects on women's wages and workforce composition. Whatever they did, women's work was deemed worth less because women were deemed not to bear male family responsibilities. That women were classed as especially suited to particular work created and compounded the practice of confining women to particular work. Workforce stratification, men in a wide range, women a narrow band of jobs persisted. The stage was set, too, for women missing out again, when family responsibilities was replaced by skills and the nature of work to determine wage setting.

Where women *were* single, despite overwhelming evidence of living away from home, boarding in the city or following jobs into country, ***Harvester*** and its state equivalents held otherwise. The woman worker, being single, was deemed to have parents with whom she could live, presumed living at home with them. The man of that household (her father), employed (in theory), had the family wage. Under this theorising, for the single woman to receive *any* independent income put her in an advantaged position. Why an independent income when she lived at home? If an income, why more than pin money—a token amount for female fripperies, the head of household shouldering household bills and responsibilities.

The promise held out by Powers in the ***J.C. Williamson case***, for equal pay for work of equal value, created no precedent. It took another 55 years for unions to pursue this opening. Setting men's wages and assumptions about men's family circumstance as the reference point spoke against the ***J. C. Williamson case*** challenge.

In the 1919 ***Federated Clothing Trades case*** Higgins relied upon B. Seebohm Rowntree's ***The Human Needs of Labour***, published in England (1918), for his assumptions. An investigation of 516 women workers in York, of whom 430 (according to Rowntree) supported no dependants 'partially or entirely', whilst the remaining 87 (*sic*) 'partially or entirely maintained others than themselves', concluded that men, whatever their family circumstances, should receive higher pay rates. Rowntree asserted it was normal for men to marry and support families, men deemed to provide. Not being 'normal' for women to have dependants, women needed no minimum wage, or it should be less than men's.

Australian women rejected Rowntree's figures and analysis, just as they rejected Higgins and his colleagues' presumptions about men's family responsibilities and dedication to them, and women's corresponding lack. Time and again, women argued against differential pay rates for women and men. Yet time and again, orientated toward workers' rights or employer privilege, governments, courts, and industrial tribunals relied upon assumptions, presumptions, and stereotypes to gain from women a fair day's work, whilst denying women in return a fair day's pay.

Before the 1920s—Women in 1919

By 1920, women had fought and won rights to vote, enter university, be admitted to professional practice, and hold public office. Formal rights achieved through legislative change did not mean, however, that women completed university degrees, entered professions, and practiced alongside men with identical benefits, incomes and support. Nor did it mean women entering public office or appointed to posts ordinarily held by men, unless just occasionally.

Four years of these two decades absorbed the war effort or, for the Women's International League for Peace and Freedom (WILPF) and Women's Peace Army, the cause of peace. For women, as for men, the war ended at the Palace of Versailles, victors dividing the conquered world. The Paris Treaty concluded with a win for women: the principle that women and men be paid equally for equal work. The motion was put by Australia's prime minister, Billy Hughes. Surely women played a part in this and founding the International Labour Organization (ILO)? Women lacked equal pay, but were intent on achieving it. Chapter 4, 'Alarums and Excursions—Infiltrating at the Palace of Versailles', considers what might women have done about it in Paris in 1919.

References

Cases—See Case List

Jean F. Arnot Papers 1916–1969 ML MSS 3147, ADD On 2070/4, Mitchell Library, Sydney, NSW.

Raymond Brooks, 'The Melbourne Tailoresses' Strike 1882–1883: An Assessment', ***Labour History***, no. 44, 1983, pp. 27–38.

Kay Daniels and Mary Murnane (eds), ***Up Hill All the Way***, UQP, Brisbane, Qld, 1980.

Bradon Ellem, ***In Women's Hands?*** UNSW Press, Sydney, NSW, 1989.

Raelene Frances, *The Politics of Work—Case Studies in Three Victorian Industries 1880–1939*, PhD Thesis, MonashU, Melbourne, Victoria, 1988.

Bessie M. Rischbieth, ***March of Australian Women***, Paterson Brokensha Pty Ltd, Perth, WA, 1964.

Edna Ryan and Anne Conlon, ***Gentle Invaders***, Thomas Nelson, Sydney, NSW, 1975.

Suffragist, 'Letter to the Editor', ***Tocsin***, 28 October 1897, p. 4; reprinted Marian Aveling and Joy Damousi (eds), ***Stepping Out of History***, Allen & Unwin, Nth Sydney, NSW, 1991.

Victorian Parliamentary Papers, Victorian Parliament, Melbourne, Victoria, vol. 3, 1887.

CHAPTER 4

Alarums and Excursions: Infiltrating at the Palace of Versailles

> The Principle that men and women should receive equal remuneration for work of equal value is of social and urgent importance.
>
> 'General Principles'
> *Treaty of Versailles*, Paris, 1919

> The delegates will meet again
> Perhaps very soon
> To see if it is possible
> To stop the sun and moon.
>
> William M. Hughes
> Australian Prime Minister, 1918

In Alan Bennett's play ***The History Boys***, an exchange between the boys and sole female character, history teacher Mrs Lintott, sees her rhetorically asking can they, 'for a moment' imagine the dispiriting experience of 'teaching five centuries of masculine ineptitude …' History is 'not such a frolic for women as it is for men', she says, asking—again rhetorically: 'Why should it be?' Illustrating women's reality through describing women's lot as 'never getting round the conference table' she refers to 1919, observing women 'just arranging the flowers', then 'gracefully retiring'. History, she remarks, 'is a commentary on the various and continuing

J. A. Scutt, *Wage Rage for Equal Pay*,
https://doi.org/10.1007/978-3-031-42178-5_4

incapabilities of men'. Finally, 'What is history? History is women following behind with the bucket …'

Yet is this truly history? The only history? Glenda Strachan and John Burgess observe that in 'industrial relations and management history, and many other disciplines, men's experience has been privileged …':

> Men's experience was seen as the only experience. Women's experience when recorded was seen of lesser importance or seen through the prism of men's experience and compared with it …

So it is with fiction and Bennett.

True, in 1919 the Treaty of Versailles was negotiated around a table seating men only. But did women simply arrange the roses, and go?

From 1880, Australian women entered universities. By 1919, women held university qualifications and professional status. Discrimination remained, preventing them from practicing professions despite their qualifications. Restrictions imposed by custom, prejudice and legal decisions calling them 'non-persons' did not stop them using their knowledge, abilities, and skills. They took work where they could get it: they had to; they had to live. Earning money as secretaries and clerks and administrators, they did more than toss out dead flowers to replace them with new ones, or change the water.

That the Treaty of Versailles contains a provision not only affirming equal pay but explicitly an urgency about implementing it is surely significant. Is it likely that the men around the table at Versailles thought this up all by themselves? Or women had no role in getting it on the agenda? The great changes in political, social, and cultural rights of women have, it's true, come about because men affirmed the justice of those rights. There was no alternative. It occurred in Parliaments around the world, where men alone exercised rights to be and men alone had a vote—until they passed legislation confirming women's voting rights and right to run for political office. In women's absence, no women there to speak, no women's voices heard, no right to register votes … passage of women's rights Acts depended upon men. Men alone could table the Bill, make second reading speeches, engage in debate and, in the end, vote aye or nay.

Yet these Bills, debates, votes, and laws would not have evolved without women initiating them. Surely this follows for equal pay and the Treaty of Versailles?

At Versailles

'What are you laughing at?'

Shoulders shaking, Enid Russell hunches over a file. Momentarily speechless, she points a finger at the letter atop an orderly pile, wipes her eyes with a handkerchief, gulps down the last of her laughter.

'It's a copy of correspondence between the Minister for Defence and the Council of Churches. You know—all that bother about the Prophylactic Tent and ***Facultative Motherhood***. The P.M. wrote to Watt, saying that as Acting P.M. he should take responsibility for it all. The gist is, he asked Watt to follow up the Tent *and* the pamphlet. Now Watt's offsider has sent us all the letters. Wanting the P.M. to wear all the flack, I expect.'

Ada Evans bends to look over her shoulder. 'Not that old Reverend Worrall again!' She reads aloud: '... when we pointed out to you that in our opinion a thrill of horror would run through the community when parents knew that their soldier sons, many of them in their teens, were instructed in the use of Prophylactic Tents by the direct orders of the Defence Department, you gave us to understand that the thing would stop ...' Laughter suppressed, her shoulders begin to heave.

Leaping to her feet, Enid grabs the letter from under Ada's nose. Taking up the file, she strides across the office, head flung back, papers held in one hand, stretched out in front of her. At the desk beside the door leading onto the patio, the pen Edyth Haynes has been scratching across a pad ceases its scrawl. She looks up, lips twitching. Enid's bulk fills the space between desk and doorway. Her hair blazes red in the light.

'I personally presented you with the analysis of Govt Medico-Legal Analyst ... who expressed his opinion of "505": "If "505" is used in a cold blooded manner before and after each sexual act, it will mitigate but not eliminate the risk"', declaims Enid, taking up where Ada had left off. Ada covers her face in her hands, doing her best to smother the loud hoots threatening to bring the office staff next-door to see what is going on.

'"The use of such prophylactics may increase rather than diminish the prevalence of venereal disease as a false feeling of security is engendered and prudence vanished".' Portentously, Enid's tones ring out. She glances at Ada, then upon Edyth.

'What do you think the P.M.'ll make of all this? A bit strong, isn't it?'

Edyth nods. Ada shakes her head, uncertain any words she might attempt will emerge beyond a splutter. Enid turns the page. Reads on.

'"It is evident that your Government has really done nothing nor has it intimated any intention of doing anything to remove this blot from our civilisation—the blot of providing youths in their teens with what is really an incentive to moral degradation."' Striding back to the desk, waving the file: 'And he's talking about the whole of the Methodist Church of Australasia and the Council of Churches withdrawing support from the war effort—or at least demonstrating against Defence Department policy.'

For the moment, at least, Ada has recovered. She takes the letter from Enid's hands. 'What's he saying?'

She flaps the pages, then reads sonorously, imitating the P.M.'s correspondent: '"I hoped that our representations to you personally would have taken away the necessity of a public agitation against this filthy condition of public morals, but I have been disappointed. A Government that contaminates the minds and morals of brave lads who have enlisted to defend the nation has no right to expect support from such a Council as the Council of Churches." Whew! Then he asks Watt's forgiveness, no less, for letting fly with his "personal abhorrence at this unwarranted uncleanness of military administration". Well, Enid, what *do* you think the P.M.'s response will be?'

Law graduates from the University of WA and University of Sydney, Enid Russell, Edyth Haynes, and Ada Evans chanced upon secretarial work in the Prime Minister's office in London. The Hon. William Hughes had arrived at the Australia House offices on the Strand, ready for the 1918 British Empire Conference, this year styled 'Imperial War Conference', and for meetings of the British War Cabinet and the Supreme War Council of the Allies in Paris, not to mention the Peace Talks, only to find himself down two staff. Ada had been taken a week or so earlier, located beside Edyth in the typing pool. Enid had just walked in, enquiring about the possibilities of temporary work, when the Prime Minister's Principal Private Secretary was prowling about on the other side of the counter, demanding *someone* do *something*. After all, they all *knew* what the P.M. was like. If his entourage was smaller than that of the Canadian Prime Minister, someone would pay. The Principal Private Secretary was determined it wouldn't be him.

So it comes to pass that the trio is ensconced at the Paris Villa Majestic as part of the staff of the Office of the British Empire Delegation Secretariat at the Conference of Versailles. If only the boys and men who had studied law with them at their respective universities, sailing into practice and partnerships with the best law firms in Sydney and Perth, could see them now.

Sure, secretaries, not delegates. Paid to do shorthand-typing and keep the P.M.'s appointment book, not play the role of Principal Minder. Overlooked in matters the Australian delegation deemed 'Paris Peace Talks' important. Like being included in group photographs, chatting around the bar at the Astoria. And there was no room for them at any of the conference room desks, or around conference tables where policies and positions are argued out before going to the conference chamber for putting to a final vote.

But not all the work is done by the important names. So much behind the scenes, Assistant Secretaries playing a key role. On Tuesdays, Australia supplies the Assistant Secretary. On Thursday, it's Aotearoa/New Zealand's turn. Mondays, Wednesdays, and Fridays are allotted to Canada, South Africa, and India, guaranteeing the British Empire Delegation is fully serviced.

Where do Edyth, Enid, and Ada fit? Afternoon each Monday, one or other of them accompanies Sir Robert Garran or Lieutenant-Commander J.G. Latham, whichever is scheduled to be Assistant Secretary next day, to the Villa Majestic where, their assistance vital, he prepares the agenda and arranges circulation of memoranda. Sometimes, depending on workload, two go, leaving one *in situ*, dealing with whatever might arise, or visitors appear, in the others' absence.

On the Tuesday, in Room 802 adjoining the Conference Room, Enid and Ada sit at their typewriters, shorthand notebooks ready. Edyth is already sorting a pile of documents, making notes on the pad beside her. Garran or Latham attends the British Empire Delegation meeting next-door, calling upon the women's shorthand skills when necessary. Meeting over, Garran and one or other of them work as a team, composing draft minutes for the Secretary's approval, prior to their being circulated.

On the Wednesday, Enid, Ada, or Edyth collects returned draft minutes, proofs them, takes them to Garran or Latham for final approval before printing.

Mondays and Wednesdays, all three meet with women attached to Canadian and South African delegations, at first nodding, growing more chummy as days and weeks pass. One of the Canadians, Clara Brett Martin, introduces them to her colleague Maud Penery French and New Zealanders Harriet Newcomb, Anna Paterson Stout, and Kate Sheppard. Olive Schreiner, from South Africa, asks them to supper, where they meet Jesmini Fonseca, clerical support to India's delegation. Mithai Lam, together with her mother giving evidence at a British Status of Women inquiry run by the Women's Labour League (later the Labour Party Women's Organisation as part of the British Labour Party) some months earlier and stayed on in England to study law, is tied up in taking dictation from one of the Indian delegates. They meet her later, tea drinking at the Astoria. Swift typist she is, Mithai has completed the job and corralled the most comfortable chairs in the lounge. Not only that, somehow she's extracted Lapsang Souchang from a waiter and is sipping delicately from fine bone china. Beside her stands a plate covered with bright red and green jelly-like lozenges, sweet as concentrated sugar. Jesmini and Kate Sheppard pounce upon them eagerly, as Mithai shares them around.

A tendency to lord it over the colonials initially dogs the British delegation, right down to support staff. But arrival of Miss Bebb, LLB, and Edmee Plunkett, arts graduate amongst these women lawyers (BA, London 1914) and, for a time, secretary to Lord Edward Cecil in Egypt, puts an end to that. Miss Bebb strides about mustering the troops, as she calls it—ensuring secretarial and clerical staff are happy, well-housed, and well-fed. Her no nonsense style and bag of Ballard's Strong Mints carried in a capacious handbag permit of no anorexia or other eating disorders, whoever comprises the delegation. Banting is out, so woe betide any woman whom she catches with leftovers on her plate. 'The starving millions in China,' she intones. 'Think!' 'Yes, and if we don't eat our crusts, our hair won't curl,' Enid mutters to Ada, sotto voce, tugging at her straight brown locks in fun. They have a great time writing to Ethel Benjamin in Dunedin, filling her in on front and back of house activities. Ethel hadn't been able to come, being tied up in a case as junior to a KC. Something of a miracle, this: no woman has ever appeared in court beside a KC before. Turning that down meant not only would Ethel be cut by the KC, bench, and Bar. She'd never get a brief again.

As for Edmee Plunkett, she has a special affinity for the women from the antipodes, as Miss Bebb described them. It was in Egypt, when on Lord Cecil's staff, she met husband-to-be (although she didn't know it then, daring only to hope), Melbourne-born Lieutenant-Colonel George Langley DSO, Gallipoli veteran and commander of the 1st Australian Camel Battalion. When he eventually popped the question by telegram delivered by a charming young man on a motor bicycle, the news went around like wildfire. A grand farewell, secretaries and clerks seeing off, returning to Cairo and into the arms of the delicious George as they named him, sight unseen—ready to accept Edmee's assessment of his charms. What better recommendation? Tall, tanned, Australian—and a war hero to boot!

But all that was months ahead. Meanwhile, work was to be done in Paris, and Edmee, all the while harbouring romantic dreams starring herself and George Langley DSO, which she thought, but did not quite know, were reciprocated, put her fingers to the typewriter, her pen to the shorthand pad, alongside the rest of them.

The Politics of Power

In Paris, the women quickly learn that not all the power lies in the arms of those raising their hands to signify 'aye' or 'nay' at a conference vote, or a recommendation argued out. Nor does it lie only with Prime Ministers and Foreign Secretaries of the Four Great Powers (as they're known) participating in the series of Conversations arranged by Lord Hardinge, Organising Ambassador having charge of administration of the whole of Departmental Missions. As women, Enid Russell, Edyth Haynes, and Ada Evans along with the others, know, of course knew long before.

More than 70 years later, a woman sitting at a desk in the Dickson Archives Office in Canberra, Australia, reading the Treaty of Versailles provisions, realises it too. She had known it when, some years before, in 1992, she interviewed Jean Arnot, reading papers Jean accumulated over years of her work in the equal pay struggle. There, amongst journals and photocopied articles, minutes of meetings, correspondence back and forth (within Australia and without), was a speech Arnot delivered in support of a motion proposed in 1937 by the Public Service Association (PSA) professional section. Subsequently published in public sector journal ***Red Tape***, the speech called upon justice, trade unionism, economic principles, and practicalities of women's and men's paidwork to argue equal pay as not only a necessity but a principled notion, its time surely come. In her speech and ***Red Tape*** article, Arnot declared that the idea of women receiving lower wages than men is not new, nor particularly of the industrial age. Nor was the idea new, she said, that women and men should receive equal pay for equal work, irrespective of sex. After all, 20 years before, in Paris, the Great Powers had agreed.

Nearly 60 years after her speech, in that 1992 interview, Arnot demonstrated the support the Great Powers had conferred. Plucking a paper out of the filing cabinet beside her, waving it triumphantly, she flourished her copy of the 1919 Peace Treaty of Versailles. 'There it is,' she said, interviewed in her Double Bay flat in Sydney, Australia, eighty years on, 'they included that very proposition in its General Principles.'

Meanwhile, In Paris

'Enid!'

Concentrating on the papers before her, at first the voice doesn't register. Her Olivetti typewriter, used in London and now with her in Paris, is playing up. The ribbon needs changing, and she is loath to add to the ink already spilt generously onto her fingers from a fountain pen that leaks.

'Drat! Why do I always manage to get mess everywhere?'

'Enid! Psst!'

Miss Bebb's voice. Miss Bebb has, Enid is sure, never before allowed such a familiar expression pass her lips—particularly not with the now elongated 'sssssss' sounding loud. Her head shoots up.

'Have you finished?'

Enid shakes her head. 'It's this jolly Olivetti. Usually, it's a dream, but today …!'

'Captain Jones is finalising agenda papers. We've just *got* to get it into this lot. We'll not get another chance.'

Opening the top left-hand drawer of the desk, Enid takes out a packet, removes the typewriter ribbon. Waving it in Miss Bebb's direction, motions at the machine.

'Okay, Miss Bebb. *You* do it.'

When the item on equal pay arises on the agenda at Tuesday's meeting of the British Empire Delegation, under a listing indicating its origins in the papers of the Australian Prime Minister, comes a pause. All eyes turn to William ('Billy') Hughes. His irascible tones have already flayed most of those sitting around the table that day. Who dares risking the whip of his tongue again?

Hughes looks at the item, looks around the table, wonders where it has come from, and why it should be listed under matters *he* and *his* delegation are raising. Glances at Garran, sitting beside him. Garran's face is inscrutable. Latham sits one row back, and across the table. Hughes raises an eyebrow. Latham's face is blank. If he hasn't known it's there, he's not about to admit to error now.

All eyes go to it, as the agenda item comes into focus on the pages in the sheaves before each of them.

> The Principle that men and women should receive equal remuneration for work of equal value is of social and urgent importance.

Next, they see in unison the neatly typed executive summary, supporting documentation lying beneath, impeccably presented.

'Why is this …' The Rt. Hon. Sir R.L. Borden, G.C.M.G., K.C., Prime Minister of Canada gets no further. The Rt. Hon. W.M. Hughes, Prime Minister of Australia is not ready to lie down or let the Canadians do him over. He glares around at Prime Ministers assembled. General The Rt. Hon. Louis Botha, Prime Minister of the Union of South Africa sits beside Lieut.-General The Rt. Hon. J.C. Smuts, K.C., Minister for Defence, Major-General His Highness The Maharaja Sir Ganga Singh, Bahadur, G.C.V.O, K.C.B., G.C.S.I., G.C.I.E., A.D.C., Maharaja of Bikaner and The Rt. Hon. Sir S.P. Sinha, K.C., Member of the Executive Council of the Governor of Bengal are ranged alongside the Rt. Hon. A. Bonar Law, M.P., The Rt. Hon. A.J. Balfour, O.M., M.P., The Rt. Hon. E.S. Montagu, M.P., Secretary of State for India, and General Sir H.H. Wilson, G.C.B., D.S.O., Chief of the Imperial General Staff. The Prime Minister of the United Kingdom, Lloyd George, is in the Chair.

William Hughes looks down at his papers, flicks through them, lifts the one sporting the equal pay proposal.

'Clear as day,' he says. 'Here it is.' The paper flaps up and down several times, as if daring anyone to challenge the content. 'All here. Every argument clear. Any opposing proposition discounted. No earthly reason why it shouldn't be in our endorsed list of principles. On the contrary, every reason why it must.'

Casts his sharp glare around once again. 'Anyone against?'

It's not really a question.

Silence.

'Very well, passed unanimously. Let's get on.'

He looks toward the Chair. Bonar Law leans toward the Prime Minister, as if to speak, hesitates, falls back. Smuts spits out a few words. Cook, G.C.M.G., Australian Minister of the Navy, glances first at Hughes, then at Smuts.

Hughes slaps his left hand down on the table. The British Prime Minister, poised to acknowledge Smuts, changes direction. Looks at him, changes his mind.

'Harrumph. Next item?'

The meeting moves on, down the agenda.

They do not know, the others around that table, that the resolution is not entirely unexpected. When he saw it, after the first shock his brain began pumping away, remembering all the signs. He'd sensed there'd been something brewing amongst the women. They'd been direct enough with him, let's face it. Telling him women shouldn't be overlooked, require explicit mention in the Treaty. Said it often, and pointedly. Well, as often and as pointedly as they could, he thought.

And why not equal pay? The women deserve it, they've struggled long enough …

He couldn't have sat all that time on the British War Cabinet after Asquith was P.M. without thinking of inhumanity to women, after all. It was Asquith who'd led the anti-Suffragette movement, all those women arrested, thrown into prison, force fed. And why? Because they wanted a vote that women in Australia had without the world's collapse. What was wrong with Asquith? What wrong with the rest of 'em, that they'd let Asquith get away with it? Supporting him with speed, those Cabinet members. Imprisoning women. Torturing them—force feeding is that, surely? All the while pretending they're gentlemen. Hughes laughs inwardly … Gentlemen, my foot!

Then, mid-way through the Great War, as some already called it, Asquith had got his, resigning in 1916, Lloyd George grabbing the office.

Well, the women have done over Asquith over in Paris, make no mistake. Given Lloyd George his, too, Hughes reflects.

And he, Prime Minister Billy Hughes, is the one the women chose as the vehicle by which to do it. He almost slaps his thigh in delight.

For after all, he muses, as Australian Prime Minister how could he not support it? Women he knows at home—like Bessie Rischbieth and Muriel Heagney, then Annie Kennie over in London—worth more than some men he knows. Some round this table. And Mary, his very own worldly-wise wife—well, she'd brought Christabel Pankhurst home to Russell Square, where they lived in London. What tales *she* had to tell of the Cat and Mouse Act. Asquith's doing—the entire Cabinet for that matter, with Lloyd George going along with it, whatever his support for the workers. All of them, implicated.

Then as P.M. Lloyd George has done nothing about it, either. Christabel and her W.S.P.U. women burnt down his house early on, with no cause to thank him upon his taking over the reins.

Thus, when the item appears so suddenly atop his file with those words:

> The Principle that men and women should receive equal remuneration for work of equal value is of social and urgent importance ...

he'd thought of those women, and the package stored amongst his papers, back in Melbourne.

Safe in his cabin trunk, returning with him back in 1916, three large rolls of vellum carrying signatures in their thousands of British women, placed beneath an illuminated address. The petition was headed:

> Women's Memorial to the Rt Hon. W.M. Hughes Prime Minister of Australia urging his immediate return to London, that he may share in the management of the War, as a member of the inner and supreme War Council of the Empire.

Dated October 1916.

How could he ignore the women now? Their arguments are persuasive enough, by God!

How could he let Lloyd George and the other buggers think it was fighting fair to cut women out?

Later, Enid Russell and Ada E. Evans, with solemn and sober air, type up the minutes. Edyth Haynes files background documents whilst Mr Deane, Hughes private secretary, standing in for Sir Robert, stands by, ready to deliver the finished papers to the Astoria. There, he and Cecil Hurst, legal advisor to the Foreign Office and of the Conference Drafting Committee, share an office with staff members Maurice Hankey and Gustav Bauer. Absently drumming his fingers, he waits. Does he wonder why the Villa Majestic atmosphere suddenly seems lighter, the heady air of achievement swirling?

The PM stuck his head in, just for a moment, after the meeting. Said something jolly. Was that it? Got the women stirred up with his rough-cut charm, the blighter ...

After all, they aren't bad lookers, either, Enid with that red hair of hers, Ada's ankles ... Edyth's eyes ...

Or was it something more? An air of excitement mingles with satisfaction ... a job done well.

Resolution Passed

In his second thoughts, Deane would not have been wrong. There was no chance of anything going amiss now, and hair, ankles, and eyes had nothing to do with it.

As first woman law graduate from Oxford University, where would Miss Bebb be better placed than the office of Mr C.J.B. Hurst, Legal Adviser of the Foreign Office and Drafting Committee member? Sure, just as for Miss Russell, Miss Haynes, Miss Evans—and the others. She'd have filled the role of Legal Adviser equally capably as Secretary to the Legal Adviser, even more so. As Legal Advisor, she (like the rest) would have ensured that the Treaty of Versailles contained a lasting statement of principle proclaiming women's right to equal remuneration with men. But she, like Ada Evans, Edyth Haynes, Enid Russell and all well knew that, with thoughtful planning, the power of the shorthand secretary could finesse those with more impressive titles. Impressive argument requires no title.

So it was that while the women of the future stood poised to stand on the shoulders of their sisters of the past and thus to burst through the glass ceiling to take the roles of the men around the table, secretarial Miss Bebb, like her secretarial colleagues, law graduates all beside their accomplished sisters, pressed and pushed and by slight of typewriter-tapping hand saw that 21 word statement take its place in the Treaty of Versailles.

> The Principle that men and women should receive equal remuneration for work of equal value is of social and urgent importance.

Seventy years on, Jean Arnot and her interviewer look at the paper drawn from her files, look at one another, smile. Through the triumphal words on the page, Ada E. Evans, Miss Bebb, Enid Russell, Edyth Haynes and their confreres smile back.

Explanation—Over and Out

The Treaty of Versailles contains this statement—women and men should be paid equally for equal work. The motion was put by Australia's prime minister, Billy Hughes. This is recorded in papers from the Versailles Conference held by Australian Archives and at the International Labour Organization (ILO).

Some 20 years later, at the 1941 ILO conference in New York Albert E. Monk, Australian Workers' Union (AWU) delegate, put forward a motion requiring all governments to adopt equal pay within their administrations and public services. Muriel Heagney was with the Australian delegation, appointed by the federal government. No one could doubt, upon reading the 1941 resolution, that her words are incorporated into it.

Gaining their law degrees early in the twentieth century, Edyth Haynes and Ada E. Evans were prevented, by judicial interpretations determining that women, not being 'persons', from practicing in their chosen profession. Enid Russell graduated several decades after them. By that time, the law enabled her to take out a practicing certificate. How could women with law degrees and no practicing certificate, or with such a certificate and no entre to a law firm, earn a living wage? The inability of law firms' heads, principals, and partners to overcome sex prejudice forced many professionally qualified women to look elsewhere—yes, taking up secretarial or clerical work alongside men with whom they graduated: not as their equals but as secretaries or personal assistants to their bosses.

The equal pay resolution got into the Prime Minister's papers.

We know, from experience of women at other times, in other places, other fields, that women's ingenuity results in achievements for women by overturning long-existing prejudices, rules and regulations. Hence, this foray into 'The Treaty of Versailles' has its foundation in women's real lives, women's ways of working, determination and achievements gained through ingenuity and courage in attempting that from which others might shy.

Women as secretaries and occupying support roles or roles not at the top of an organisation had—and where they work in these roles today have—huge repositories of knowledge fundamental to male institutional workings. Often, women in these roles are assigned to training up young men to take over top-level positions—which the women themselves could do, if given the chance. Often, the women do the work without the title, prestige or salary.

Just as at Versailles?

So it is, from a position of strength, equal pay acknowledged at the highest international level, that Australian women end the first two decades of the twentieth century. The following 20 years see women engage with the industrial system and continue their lobbying. More freedom for women expressed through the 1920s, a reaction to the war years. Then the years of Depression. Chapter 5 considers 'The Fortunes of the Flappers—The 1920s Generation Confronts the '30s'. How did women continue the equal pay struggle between the wars?

References[1]

Jean Arnot, ***Interview***, Double Bay, NSW, 1992 (6 April 1992).

Jean F. Arnot, 'Embedded in the Soul' in JA Scutt (ed.), ***Taking a Stand—Women in Politics and Society***, Artemis Publishing, Melbourne, Victoria, 1994, pp. 116–28.

Jean F. Arnot Papers 1916–1969 ML MSS 3147, ADD On 2070/4, Mitchell Library, Sydney, NSW.

Alan Bennett, ***The History Boys***, Faber & Faber Limited, London, UK, 2004.

MS 1538 Papers of William Morris Hughes, Series 16 Prime Minister, 1916–1923, item V. Petition, NLA.

Glenda Strachan and John Burgess, 'Gender and Workplace Reactions: Introduction', ***Journal of Interdisciplinary Gender Studies***, vol. 5, no. 2, 2000 (December 2000), pp. 3–9.

The Paris Peace Conference and the Treaty of Versailles: The Remaking of Europe in 1919, Australian Archives, Dickson Repository, Canberra, ACT.

Preamble, Part XIII, Versailles Treaty 1919, Paris, France, 1919, Australian Archives, Dickson Repository, Canberra, ACT.

Letter Reverend Worrall, Australian Council of Churches, to acting PM William Alexander Watt, Australian Archives, Dickson Repository, Canberra, ACT.

[1] Fictional extrapolation from information contained in Paris Peace Talks 1919 documents. Language, expressions and style early twentieth century, capitals and contemporary punctuation, say P.M., for consistency. Earlier version published *The Rationalist*, 75–76, Spring 2006/Summer 2006–2007, 50–57.

CHAPTER 5

The Fortunes of the Flappers—The 1920s Generation Confronts the '30s

> One wonders if the persons presiding in the Arbitration Courts and on Boards of Trade consider women have two commodities for sale when making an award, and ... whether the organised Trade Union Movement thinks along those lines; that no organised protest is made against 39/6 as a living wage for women would lead to such belief.
>
> If 39/6 is all craft unions can win for a woman doing a job [when] a man gets 85 shillings, it is high time women take direct action ... instead of telling themselves they're only filling in time before their weddings. Economics force them back into the workplace after marriage, and they must learn to fight for themselves. An all-Australian Trade Union League of Women would be a [start] ...
>
> Nellie Rickie, shop assistants' representative, NSW Labor Council
> ***Workers Weekly***, 28 August 1925

The year? 1920. Two years after NSW women win the right to practice law and stand for state Parliament, the Holman government is defeated. Despite her fifteen-year campaign for the Women's Legal Status Act 1918 (NSW), Ada E. Evans declines to enter legal practice, protesting she is now too old. In May, after a 12-year hiatus, the National Council of Women (NCW) SA is re-established, focusing on equal pay and women's political representation. Adelaide's lady mayoress Deborah Hackett-Moulden, arrived two years earlier from WA to marry the lord mayor, presides. On the east coast, NSW's state election sees no women standing.

J. A. Scutt, *Wage Rage for Equal Pay*,
https://doi.org/10.1007/978-3-031-42178-5_5

On 13 April, John Storey forms a Labor ministry. With no women members of Parliament, none can lobby from within for equal pay.

On 10 July, striking over wages, WA civil servants and teachers stay out until month's end. On 30 October 1920 the Communist Party of Australia (CPA) is founded in Sydney. Back across the Nullabor, twenty-one years after winning voting rights, the Parliament (Qualification of Women) Act 1920 (WA) wins women's right of election to state Parliament. On 12 March 1921 Edith Dirksey Cowan, National Australia Party member, becomes the first woman member of an Australian Parliament. Elected to the WA Legislative Assembly, she defeats both male candidates, sitting member TP Draper, attorney-general in the Mitchell National Party government, and an independent Nationalist.

The Australian Federation of Women Voters (AFWV), initially the Australian Federation of Women's Societies for Equal Citizenship, asserts women's civil, political, and economic rights, including equal pay. In Sydney on 21 April 1922, promising to be a formidable force for women's country causes, the Country Women's Association (CWA) is promoted by the ***Stock and Station Journal***: notices and articles advise curious and potential members of its officers and activism. By 1936, the NSW branch endorses equal pay for women.

In 1923 Cowan ferries the Women Legal Practitioners Act 1923 (WA) through Parliament. With legal practice rights, WA women can agitate for equal pay from inside the profession. In Victoria, the Parliamentary Elections (Women Candidates) Act 1923 follows. In NSW, Millicent Preston-Stanley wins for the Nationalists, while in 1925, May Holman becomes first Labor woman in an Australian Parliament, claiming Forrest, a state seat. On 17 June, JT Lang becomes NSW Labor premier. In 1924, WA's Beryl Mills is crowned first Miss Australia.

Are women MPs, teacher and civil service militants, and respectable women prowling the catwalk precursors to a disruptive and demanding decade? Rebellion bubbles. The establishment shudders. On 16 March 1926, a Crimes Act 1914 (Cth) amendment proclaims federal power over Communists and political agitators.

By decade's end, the 1929 election sees John Curtin and Ben Chifley enter federal Parliament. Irene Longman is Queensland Parliament's first woman elected. Britain's Ramsay MacDonald becomes Labour prime minister. The League of Nations is ten-years-old. In Sydney, Adela Pankhurst Walsh founds the Australian Women's Guild of Empire (AWGE) to abolish class warfare and create industrial peace. Miles Franklin's ***Up the Country*** appears under pen-name Brent of Bin Bin, ***Ultima Thule***, third volume of

Henry Handel Richardson's ***The Fortunes of Richard Mahoney***, is published, M. Barnard Eldershaw publishes ***A House Is Built***, Katharine Susannah Prichard's ***Coonardoo*** wins acclaim, and together they win the ***Bulletin*** £500 literature prize. Meanwhile, in Germany, unemployment reaches three million. In Australia, four-and-a-half million working days—second highest figure in the country's industrial history and highest since the 1917 general strike—lost through strikes. On 13 January 1929, Henry Bournes Higgins dies at seventy-seven, while on 9 December, RJL (Bob) Hawke is born.

1920s Activism Meets 1930s Depression

From early 1922 until 1933, the NSW CPA cell rented Communist Hall at 393 Sussex Street, Sydney. Almost next door to Trades Hall, the Labor Council building near Goulburn Street, it accommodated the entire CPA national membership of 700–800. In 1919, women teachers' associations and associations of men teachers—primary, secondary, teaching, and principal classes amalgamated as the Teachers Federation, owning its own building on Sussex and Bathurst Streets. Equal pay claims ran through the 1920s and 1930s, mingled with the Depression and buffeting of human lives and hopes.

In 1925, Hepworth Press, at 218 Castlereagh Street not far from the Teachers' Federation, published a sell-out book's second edition. Prepared by the Women's Propaganda Committee for the NSW Combined Women Teachers' Association (CWTA), ***Justice versus Tradition*** was a spirited response to ***Equal Pay and the Teaching Profession***, produced by the London School Masters' Association (LSMA) shortly before. Billed 'A reply to the attack on the principle of equal pay for equal work', ***Justice versus Tradition*** was 'Dedicated to all men and women interested in true human progress'. NSW women teachers were not intimidated nor deterred, despite 'some men teachers ... seem[ing] to think ... London School Masters have said the last word ...'. A plank in the Federation platform, equal pay, supplemented by child endowment, was 'not merely to women, but to men, ... ethically and economically ... a huge step forward in human evolution'.

Leading the struggle, on 18 November 1919 Miss Carr and Miss Mackintosh convened the NSW Women Assistant Teachers' Association (WATA):

1. To inculcate high ideals of character and citizenship;
2. [M]utual welfare of the Teaching profession;
3. [E]quality of remuneration for equal work.

By 1920, women teachers won three-fourths of male teachers' pay. Increases on 15 February brought women to £33 annually, against £44 for men. In April, ***Education*** reported the 'three-fourths principle' negotiated with the Department of Education meant 80 per cent for mistress salaries. For assistant teachers, that the 'lowest grade man ... received more than the highest woman assistant' was condemned, for women and men assistants in charge of classes did the same work, tested by the same standards, sitting identical classification examinations. In Victoria, for almost forty years the Lady Teachers' Association (LTA), affiliated with NCW, campaigned. In 1893 Victorian women teachers lost entitlement to four-fifths of male teachers' salaries. On 15 February 1921, ***Education*** reported Miss McDonald confirming 'only after working for twenty-seven years is this ratio ... restored'.

For nursing, the Australian Trained Nurses Association (ATNA) and Queensland Nurses Association (QNA) sought shorter hours and higher pay, QNA's first industrial award application meeting criticism that it ignored patients. '[A]lready overcrowded ..., deficient equipment ... no increase of one bed or any accommodation for the sick poor ...', 'frequent changes and loss of continuity of work', nurses 'gain nothing' apart from 'reduction of work from fifty-six to forty-eight hours of work per week and increase of salaries ...', came QNA's response. The exchange anticipated Victoria's 1980s nurses strike, and nurses, like teachers, persisted.

By 15 February 1921, ***Education*** was reporting the first Public School Teachers of Australia interstate conference at the Education Building, Bridge Street, Sydney Assembly Room. Commencing 4 January 1921, NSW delegates included eight men alongside three women—Mrs Taylor, Misses Simpson and Aston. From Tasmania—one delegate, male; Queensland, two men; SA, one; WA, one man, one woman (Miss Ashton); and Victoria's five male delegates with three women—Misses McDonald, Reid, and Gray. Taylor and McDonald reported on Acts passed in 1918 (NSW) and 1920 (Victoria), delivering 2400 classified primary women teachers four-fifths of male rates in similar classifications. Increments for women in each class were increased, making their salaries equivalent to men's. For infants school teachers, Simpson said women 'are doing the work, but you are not giving them the honour', but more freedom means 'you will get better citizens'. Noting 'her girls' attended school, even if 'scarcely able to get out of bed ...': their leave for ill-health didn't average five days a year.

Equal pay for equal work for teachers Australia-wide was agreed, McDonald saying the Paris Convention included it, the British War

Cabinet Reconstruction Committee recommended it for the Civil Service, it was advocated for the Commonwealth Public Service (CPS), and 'women teachers of Victoria believe [its] adoption in the teaching service [upholds] men and women teachers' [and the community's] best interests'. Under the heading 'Passion of Women Teachers', McDonald and Taylor said promotion and rising through the ranks were fundamental to equal pay. A women's 'Class I' enabled women teachers to advance, 'if qualified', to the highest posts available to men, yet outnumbering men above two to one (including classified, union teachers, and sewing mistresses—over 4000) 90 per cent were in the fifth or lowest class. Teaching was evidently 'more attractive to women than men', so equal opportunity claims were 'only reasonable'. Furthermore, boards should reserve a seat for at least one woman 'where her or the interests of children' lie.

TH followed up under 'Men and Women' in ***Education*** of 15 August 1921, deeming 'economic difference' between men and women's pay 'unjustifiable'. If increased responsibilities justified the difference, increasing pay would increase responsibilities 'until the sexes are as they should be—equal'. Only 'usage and perhaps expediency' saw women and mothers as 'less responsible' for their own career and children's welfare than men and fathers for theirs. Getting women 'cheaper' was a 'slur of civilisation'.

'Comparable worth' (a term not used) was an imperative for 1920s equal pay activists: paper qualifications and educational elitism should not eclipse skills learnt and practiced in the field. TH questioned Morrison's 1913 Victorian women teachers' pay inquiry assertion that men—falsely designated graduates—should be paid more. In teaching 'it matters not what high degrees a man possess, no matter how long or what it cost ..., unless he can do the work and shoulder the responsibility ...' Comparing teachers with university lecturer, demonstrators, and tutors was inappropriate, for though their work 'might be of a high class in knowledge, it carries less responsibility, ... than the headmaster of a big Primary School [with] 1000 children ... and staff of 30 teachers ...'. Even an Oxford or Cambridge degree counted little without 'the prime qualities [making] a teacher ...'. Payment should be made on what people 'do do, rather than what they can do', with 'equal pay accompany[ing] equal responsibility'.

Activism was Australia-wide. On 15 January 1925 in Glen Innes, teachers voted: 'That women teachers of similar classification and efficiency be paid equal salaries to ... men teachers—carried'. On 15 April, NSW Teachers Federation established the 'Equal Pay for Equal Work' committee, electing Misses Woodcock, Stuart, E. Symons, Fordyce, R. Symonds,

Taylor, Cunningham, and Mrs Ogilvy with five men—one (Mr Bendeich) speaking against equal pay at a later meeting. Despite his dissent, the majority held firm, a month later releasing its first 'Equal Pay for Equal Work Report': the committee disavowed setting a woman teacher rates schedule as contradictory to 'our holding of the principle of equal pay for equal work …'.

By 1927, equal pay was before the NSW Industrial Commission, Misses R. Symonds and F. Cohen initially in charge, then Miss Stuart, Women Assistant's Association president. In April 1928 Miss Lucy Woodcock took over, in June 1929 the case being referred for hearing. By close of 1929, the case had run almost two years, ***Education*** reporting on 15 January 1930 that Dr Evatt, KC, for the Federation, had applied for an interim award pending a Full Court hearing. Yet the claim was modest: for women's salaries on a four-fifths ratio of men's. Women were back to the ratio ten years before. Would they even get that? Evatt outlined the 1920 Federation and director of education, Mr P. Board, agreement to extend the four-fifths ratio for a ten-year period, 'to stabilise the position and counter the [1919] equal pay application'. For the government, Mr JA Ferguson opposed an interim award as 'payment in advance of … a large sum amounting to £750 per week, amounting … to £21,000 of public money [by the time of the hearing], which would be irrecoverable'. Justice Piddington's sole dissent stood against Cantor and Street's majority ruling. It was not said women would force men from jobs, higher pay would rob women of jobs, women were incapable of doing the job or unable to reach their male counterparts' standards, that men teachers were university qualified (whatever the reality), women (whatever the reality) were not. The spectre of women laying claim to public moneys ruled (partial) wage justice for women an intolerable burden on the economy.

Despairing but undaunted, the Federation anticipated the full claim hearing. But economic arguments holding sway in 1929 against a four-fifths ruling—much less equal pay—the stock market spiralling downwards, recession setting in—and depression threatening, they loomed ineluctably. Yet Street, at least, did not escape lightly. On 27 November 1934, heralding a new round of equal pay agitation, Jessie MG Street, United Associations (UA) vice president and Street's daughter-in-law, wrote that, the UA's object being 'equality of status and opportunity for men and women', equal pay for equal work was fundamental.

Depression, Despair, and Dissent

'Women Cheaper than Cattle' 'Sydney's Auction Block; Girls Work for 10/-' In December 1934 ***Truth*** ran an expose of women's industrial exploitation. Subjection to 'slave labour' and wages denying more than subsistence were target by a dedicated newspaper campaign. Street and UA were in the thick of it.

From 1929 to 1934, the World Slump dictated rise and fall of governments and government policy. By 1932, Australia's mass unemployment mirrored job losses throughout the industrialised world: US 13.7m, Germany 5.6m, Britain 2.8m. The agricultural market vanished, hitting Australian farmers badly. Timberworkers protested, striking over increased working hours (to forty-eight), wages reduction (manipulated by introducing piecework), and employment on youth wages of young, inexperienced workers, risking workers' safety. The Militant Women's Group (MWG) flooded Sydney streets, mass Belmore Park meetings preceding marching into the city distributing leaflets emblazoned: 'Not a minute on the day, not a penny off the pay'.

Labor's 1930 state conference precipitated an Unemployed Workers' Movement (UWM) statement 'denounc[ing] all labour organisations … clinging to bourgeois illusions [about] women's place in the home … denying working women their rightful place'. Published in August's ***Working Woman***, it charged the labour movement with ignoring working women's conditions, proclaiming as UWM's policy 'the energetic struggle to unite unemployed women workers in [its] movement'.

Earlier, on 13 February 1930, the ***Sydney Morning Herald*** reported a 'three-line advertisement' offering employment to 'two girls experienced in bottling and labelling'. '… 200 girls stormed the offices of Mr Knight, toilet preparations agent …', many 'well educated [with] references from leading city firms …', telling 'pitiful tales' of family job-loss privations, 'almost begging for the position'. But when British aviator Amy Johnson arrived to an awed yet tumultuous Darwin welcome on her solo flight, none anticipated the depths of poverty and despair set to sear the world, marking the decade, joy replaced by ***Truth*** headlines hollered by newsboys on street corners: 'Vast Tragedy of Cheap Female Labor', 'Strong Support Given Timely Articles in "Truth"', 'What Hope … of Any Work for Jobless Youths Adrift in the City?'

On 2 December 1934 ***Truth*** called women 'undoubtedly [equally] capable as men in many occupations' yet instead of 'equal rates of pay …

are used to cheapen production costs'. Mr James Graves, SA Labor Party general secretary exposed 'the danger of continued employment of cheap female labor'. ***Truth*** agreed:

> IN MANY FAMILIES TO-DAY WE FIND THE DAUGHTER GOING TO WORK, WHILE THE FATHER AND BROTHER REMAIN AT HOME WITHOUT WORK ... A GROTESQUE SITUATION.
>
> Lots of girls are working to secure a base existence. They can't get married because their out-of-work boyfriend cannot keep them.

By 30 June 1934, NSW male unemployment numbered 189,666, paid employment 647,380 males, 193,126 females. ***Truth*** proposed 'a mighty stroke of the pen' abolishing female labour. Men would have jobs, women a 'happy home of their own', as women's employment destroyed 'the whole economic fabric of society', their low wages 'cheapen[ing] production costs'. The 'practicable solution!': 'EQUAL PAY FOR EQUAL WORK FOR WOMEN'. This topsy turvy argument spurred Street to write 'Equal Pay for Males and Females: How It Can Readily Be Secured'. Appearing on 9 September, ***Truth*** headlined: 'The United Associations of Women Put Their Views Of the Case' 'FACTS FOR INDUSTRIAL COMMISSION—by Jessie M.G. Street, President, …'

Street argued 'any … differential treatment on account of sex reacts … UNJUSTLY ON BOTH MEN AND WOMEN WORKERS'. The economic downturn favoured equal pay claims, she said. With men dismissed, rather than a male wage, the family must live on a female wage, resulting in a 'much reduced' living standard. 'Even more serious' is 'purchasing power reduction of the family', when 'everything possible' should be done to 'increase community purchasing power'. With equal pay, whether male or female were employed, families' '… standard of living and purchasing power … would be the same'. Besides, women, if 'more efficient', could 'get employment when the men cannot'. Incapacity, illness, or 'detention in some institution' had women supporting families on less pay. Equal pay would end 'unfair competition of cheap female labor' inhibiting men's job search, whilst women 'would not be condemned to a lower return for their labor …'.

Footnoting Street's article 'not necessarily… ***Truth***'s views', though ***Truth*** 'whole-heartedly favours equal pay …', this illustrated differing rationales for equal pay and its implementation. Dissension amongst women activists festered between Street and Heagney camps. UA membership was diverse. Campaigning against the Married Women Teachers' and Lecturers' Dismissal Bill (passed in 1932), NSW Teachers Federation member Woodcock joined in 1931. Transferring from Melbourne to Sydney, Federated Clerks' Union (FCU) official Heagney joined in 1935. From very different class backgrounds, Street's family monied professionals, Heagney's father a publican and carpenter, each wrote conference papers, resolutions, journal, magazine, and newspaper articles. Heagney's influential ***Are Women Taking Men's Jobs?*** appeared alongside Street's pamphlets, including ***The Justice of Equal Pay and Equal Opportunity***. Both visited the Soviet Union, Heagney in 1923, Street fifteen years later.

In 1937, supported by trade union women and women's organisations, Heagney and confreres established the Council of Action for Equal Pay (CAEP). In NSW, Woodcock and Street were delegates, Heagney honorary secretary. However, simmering differences spilled into a public denunciation of Street and UA, culminating in an Equal Pay Council resolution proposed by Heagney at its September 1939 conference. Should Street and UA's gradualist approach, or Heagney and the CAEP demand for the basic wage for all be urged upon governments, tribunals, commissions, and wages boards. The trade unionists considered UA's approach attacked the basic wage. UA members and president Street, it was argued, were 'bowing to their bourgeois husbands' dictates'. Street resigned, UA departing with her.

For UA and Street, the family wage (Higgins' living, minimum or basic wage—paid to a man and his family in a civilised society) required revision. Again in ***Truth***, on 2 July 1936 under 'Equal Pay for Men and Women and Child Endowment' Street advocated the dependants' component being a state family allowance or child endowment paid directly to workers. The rationale was that with men alone classed as having dependants (wife and children) or responsible for them, or (as single men) anticipating that responsibility, women would never gain equal pay. Whilst women were presumed totally dependent upon husbands, lacking financial responsibility for domestic upkeep; or single at home or boarding (modestly), wages for finery, fripperies, and pin money only, the (male) basic wage would be denied them.

Street's ***Truth*** article explained why, in 1936, feminists hoped a living wage inquiry would advance equal pay. For her, the feminist position was distorted, particularly by female trade unionists (Heagney most prominent). Unfortunately, the 1936 inquiry resulted in a wages reduction for single women from 54 to 51 per cent of the male basic wage. Street said it was 'grossly unfair' to suggest feminists advocated reducing the man's wage to the single woman's wage. Feminists wanted an adult minimum wage based on two adults' needs, child endowment meaning the 'amount of money paid in wages would be the same, but … distributed differently', parents 'getting more, their gain [being] the loss of those without children—but would not such preferment be right and proper?' Every child qualifying for endowment, family standards would remain with each child's arrival. Some 59,000 women supporting children through a husband's refusal or unemployment would receive an income increase.

Street demanded the Australian Labor Party (ALP) and trade union movement engage with her proposal realistically, not 'mouth shibboleths', wanting cooperation, not a feminist-labour (trade unionist) breakdown. Equal pay being 'admitted policy of both feminists and labour', 'damaging and wrong criticism' towards feminists' suggestions would 'not achieve constructive criticism'. Calling for 'mutual understandings', her analysis and complaint were directed at Heagney more than anyone. Heagney saw it as undermining basic wage rates fixed according to male wage earners' wellbeing, potentially an excuse for reducing minimum wages. She wanted equal pay to raise all women's wages to male levels, a rate of pay for the job, whoever did it.

On 9 September 1937, CAEP planned state and federal government approaches. Woodcock wrote asking Street to join prime minister and NSW premier deputations to present the endorsed proposal:

> The respective Arbitration Acts be immediately amended to provide for occupational rates in all awards and industrial agreements. Such wage or salary rates not conditioned in any way by employee sex.

Nominated speakers were Woodcock, NSW Labour Council's Mr RL King, Heagney, and Street. A sting came at the end of Woodcock's invitation. Speakers would 'meet and discuss the points they will mention', these 'conform[ing] with the [Council] policy …'. Precipitating the final split, this emphasised the unequivocal approach resolved at the 22 May 1937 CAEP conference, opposing UA and Street's gradualist approach.

Men's Clothes, Women's Hair—Fashion and 1920s Wage-Fixing

The 1920s and 1930s afforded openings for equal pay. Opportunity arose through 1920s buoyancy, then the 1930s economic collapse underlining women's equal need for subsistence. Both decades provided for recognition of women's equal household contributions and responsibilities. Yet neither possibility of these decades was fulfilled. At best problematic, slow, and mostly muted, the equal pay contest, hobbled by assumptions of women's (purportedly) lesser needs and (purportedly) lesser value of women's work, lost out. Economy strong, under pressure, or overwhelmed by deficits and downturns, it made no difference.

From 1914 to 1918, women's work in industry and commerce was increasingly visible. Having always worked, Australian women did no more work than in the years preceding mobilisation or in earlier centuries. Aboriginal women worked in the cattle industry and on pastoral leases, for minimal wages or payment in kind. Many were bartered or boarded out as white-household servants. Aboriginal and non-Aboriginal women worked in factories, shops, schools, and offices, work paid for yet concealed through lacking acceptance that without it, productivity would decline, enterprises fail through lack of women's work and absence of secretarial, clerical, and other support for men's jobs. Women worked in households and boardinghouses where, paid or unpaid, housework, laundry, cooking of meals, and psychological support is invisible, seen only when not done. But with men on the battlefield, women, particularly in paidwork, could no longer be discounted as insignificant or rudely ignored.

From 6 December 1919 to 23 November 1920, AB Piddington KC headed the Royal Commission into the Basic Wage (***Basic Wage Inquiry 1919–1920***), Heagney working as an investigator and on the Federated Unions of Australia (FUA)'s submission. The Commission recommended basic wage adjustments to contemporary price levels measured by index numbers (CPI), with wages calculated on an 'accurate estimate of the cost of living of a unit of man, wife, and three dependent children according to reasonable standards of comfort'. Saying the Commission's basic wage level exceeded what employers could pay, the government rejected it.

In the 1920s, NSW Industrial Commission deputy commissioner then president, AB Piddington sat on appeals against equal pay rulings complying with the Industrial Arbitration (Amendment) Act 1926. Reflecting concerns previously expressed, he said equal pay should not be manipulated to 'drive women out of jobs', reflecting continuing tensions arising from:

- unions demanding equal pay to exclude women from men's jobs or displace women workers encroaching upon male domains;
- women demanding equal pay for equal work or 'rate for the job';

- assertions women would lose jobs through equal pay, employers preferring male workers if obliged to pay the higher rate;
- assertions that paying women lower wages deprived men of jobs, employers preferring women as cheaper workers;
- woman-headed households, fathers/husbands absent by desertion, death, unemployment, illness, or disability (including alcoholism);
- women's need to support themselves and dependants, just as men should;
- injustice of sex setting women's wages below men's.

The Industrial Arbitration Act 1901 (NSW) 1926 amendment aligned it with Queensland's Industrial Arbitration Act 1916, the NSW Industrial Commission gaining power to:

- determine, no more than six monthly, a standard of living and living wage for male and female employees; and
- conduct equal pay adjudication for the same work or work producing the same return of profit or value to the employer.

In ***In re Shop Assistants &c (Metropolitan) Award 1927***, the Retail Traders' Association (RTA) appealed against an award provision granting male shop assistants' rates, less 20 per cent, to female shop assistants selling 'Special Goods' for over half their hours a week in men's mercery, men's and youths' hats, men's clothing (excluding juveniles), dress goods, manchester (except fancy linens), furnishing drapery, furniture, carpets, linoleums, bedding, ironmongery (household and general). Employers with fewer than twenty-five shop assistants in any one shop were excluded.

Upholding the appeal, deputy commissioner Piddington said power to award equal pay under the 1926 amendment should be exercised only if 'satisfied beyond all doubt as to the value of work performed', the aim being justice for women workers, not 'injury' of removing her employment. Here, he said, 'whatever the intention', the effect would be to cut women out of employment in the departments named.

So—according to Piddington, equal pay legislation should not apply *against* women's interests. Yet his purported protection of women workers disadvantaged them. In stamping on spurious equal pay claims made to reserve jobs for men, Piddington overlooked women's equal pay rights or rate for the job. The award provision didn't grant equal pay—just 80 per cent (men's rates *minus* 20 per cent), not in all instances, and small firms or large ones with small shops escaped altogether.

Piddington had no evidence that equalising wages would exclude women from an industry or the jobs in the instant claim, nor of causing unemployment or dismissal of women already there. Assuming employers would not employ women if they received fair rates (or, here, partially 'fair')—the men's rate, and that employers would dismiss women rather than pay them fairly, Piddington applied speculative paternalism. Further, in raising work value, he effectively questioned women's work capacity, standard, and output.

Not addressing the appeal by reference to *evidence* of women's interests, overlooking what women themselves experienced, simultaneously Piddington said that the impact on women worker's rights was so serious that a 'thorough and exhaustive inquiry by a committee or tribunal of male and female members' was essential. Yet he didn't return the claim to the relevant committee for it to hear evidence from industry women, give women's organisations leave to intervene, or call for them or equal pay unionists to come forward. He *assumed* women's interests, and failed to question whether—as 'equal pay'—wages could be set at 20 per cent *below* men's rates.

Further, requiring 'satisfaction beyond all doubt' (not even 'reasonable' doubt) of value of work performed before ruling women's entitlement to men's rates set a potentially enormous obstacle to success in any claim. Although Piddington saw the satisfaction beyond all doubt standard as protecting women's interests, invariably it would operate to hold women's wages down. A favourable outcome—men's wages—required a strong case for women's work as equally valuable as the men's. Difficult in any circumstance (tradition, custom, stereotyping), surely impossible without women as witnesses. Conversely, if unions used the provision to keep women out of men's jobs or getting women out who already were in the jobs, operating ostensibly in women's favour (saving their jobs) it would hold women's wages down. Each time, women lost the chance of men's wages. The civil standard of proof—balance of probabilities—applies to disputes other than crime. Why not assess value of work done by women on the balance of probabilities? Why introduce a test even more stringent than the criminal standard into wage fixing?

The spectre of women losing jobs through equal pay persisted alongside the notion that women would steal men's jobs if entering men's industries without equal pay. Was this cover for a deep-seated reluctance to recognise women's equal skills as equal and equally due for reward? A concern that women paid equally, so economically free, might disrupt the natural order? Paternalism—or patriarchy?

On 5 April, ***In re Hairdressers &c. Females (State) Award 1929*** (***Marcel Wave case***) claims of female employee hairdressers doing marcel waving, water waving, permanent waving, dyeing, or tinting came before the NSW Industrial Commission. Fashion—'20s women adopting the bob, shorter skirts, snappy box-pleated dresses, peplums, bangles, and seemingly-endless strings of beads—influenced a hairdressing industry expansion. Permanent waving became 'a separate and well-defined division of the industry ... generally'. For the Commission, consequences of fashion counted. More tellingly, minimal research into the changing industry showed that raising women's wages to men's level did *not* mean men replaced women. Still, women's wages were reduced by that argument: women's wages should be pegged low to save women's jobs. But *men's* wages in hairdressing were not set on that basis.

Until April 1927, no award covered women's hairdressing or prescribed rates of pay. On 1 April, the hairdressers conciliation committee prescribed wages and employment conditions by dividing female hairdressers into two classes—those doing haircutting, shaving, or men's work generally, and those in ladies' haircutting, manicuring, waving, dyeing, tinting, chiropody, facial work, scalp treatment, electrolysis, wig-making, or hair work generally. The committee said workers in the first category warranted male hairdressers' rates, payable under the employee male hairdressers' award. For the second category, without employers' consent, the committee awarded the rate payable under the male award for male hairdressers doing ladies' hairdressing. The NSW Master Ladies Hairdressers' Association (MLHA) appealed. The deputy commissioner held that because the employers had conceded the male rate to women doing haircutting and shaving, it necessarily followed that 'a lower rate should not be awarded to females doing ladies' hairdressing, which ... was ... at least as skillful as ... haircutting'. The rationale applied was that once equal pay for equal work 'was conceded' for one female employee classification, it was 'locally impossible to confine [it] to that one class'. That 'the same principle must be applied in fixing the rate for females doing ladies' hairdressing only' necessarily followed.

Two years later, employers applied to the Full Commission to have wages awarded to journeywomen doing marcel and other forms of waving, dying, or tinting reduced from £5 10s 0d to £3 3s 0d, with consequential alterations in casual journeywomen, apprentices, and improvers' rates.

In ***In re Hairdressers &c Females (State) Award*** Piddington (now president), Cantor, and Street held that the state's equal pay legislation should be applied according to all the circumstances of each case. Over some seven years, expansion in ladies' hairdressing was 'very extensive', led by changes 'in the prevailing fashions [following] modern adoption by women of short hair'. Demand driven, employee numbers had 'increased at an enormous rate ...'. Permanent waving was deemed a 'woman's industry'—employing women 'almost exclusively'. A 'ladies' hairdressing expert' called by the union said '... the industry is and ought to be carried on by women'. This did not mean women were 'expert' or 'highly skilled'. The (male) expert spoke of 'different waving processes' only, not the industry generally, nor most particularly 'actual cutting of the hair ... still almost wholly' in men's hands. The Commission's baffling conclusion was that permanent waving, 'although calling for a certain degree of care and intelligent use of the appliances', being 'work eminently suited to women and not difficult ... to learn', could be 'carried out by girls without very lengthy training'. The only concession: 'some time' might be required 'to enable them to attain complete proficiency ... to ... work without supervision'. Would a woman expert have helped?

Expansion generated no increased employment of women in senior positions. Fifty-five establishments in August 1926, pre-dating the first award, expanded to eighty-two by August 1928. The number of journeywomen went from 108 to 101. Clearly, the Commission said, hairdresser numbers increased by 'employment of apprentices and improvers' whilst 'seniors or journeywomen numbers reduced ...'. Thus, whatever the Commission surmised about equal pay driving women from jobs didn't follow in hairdressing, as reduction predated the award. Concurrently, from 1926 to 1928, numbers of men employed at haircutting or cutting and waving fell from 61 to 47—far more than the journeywoman reduction.

Nonetheless, saying it was protecting senior women's hairdressing jobs, the Commission *reduced their wages*—leading to reduced *junior women* wages, preserving adult, junior and apprentice wage-relativities. No evidence showed this reduction would—or even might—lead to a journeywoman increase. Anyway, why should women retaining their jobs suffer a wage reduction, whilst *men* kept their higher wages, despite their numbers reducing far more?

The decision augured ill for equal pay, effectively undermining the 1926 legislation, which now had no universal, consistent application, albeit some consistency lay in Commission rulings denying women workers equal pay. According to the Commission, the 1926 law should apply case-by-case, decided according to individual or peculiar features. Any application of the equal pay principle was, effectively, restricted to margins—payments over and above the living wage. The lower living wage rate for women was to be retained—whatever women's real costs of living—simply because women were women.

The 1926 definition of industrial matter as including equal pay claims drew no distinction between the living wage for women and men. However, the Commission interpreted it as if it did. The Act required the Commission to determine a standard of living and declare living wages based on that standard for adult male and female employees. It did not require the Commission to set those standards differently by sex. After all, the Commission, not the legislature, had originally determined upon a sex-differential in living wages for women and men. In setting the living wage under the Act the Commission had the power to undo this. The law directed the Commission's attention to wage setting by reference to women and men performing the same work, or producing the same return or profit or value to the employer, an opening and a legislative directive. This repudiated the Commission's sex-based living wage approach. The Commission reinstated it.

In the ***Hairdressers case***, journeywomen's hairdressing wages were set by the female living wage plus an additional 21s, bringing journeywomen's wages down to £3 7s 0d weekly. Despite the Act's not limiting equal pay to margins, the Commission did just that. The 21s payment was equivalent to the 21s margin added to the male living wage making up a hairdresser journeyman's wages. The Commission concluded with an unsubstantiated contention that the high rate (men's rate—male living wage plus male margin) previously awarded to journeywomen was effectively illusory, 'largely a paper award, [for] ...as soon as employees become entitled to the journeywomen's rate they are dismissed'. The Commission rendered invisible, too, the 101 journeywomen to whom the Committee's award of equal pay was not 'illusory'—they had retained their jobs at the higher rate. Not being asked, what they thought about their wage reduction on appeal, on the false basis that equal pay had lost them their jobs, is not recorded. Nor did the Commission ask, much less research, how these journeywomen would continue to bear their family responsibilities and pay their own living expenses, with their wages peremptorily cut. Nor any enquiry as to how female juniors and apprentices would survive on wages cut even further through adult women workers' 'equal pay' recast as equal pay for margins, unequal pay for the living wage.

This decision also provided no joy for 'comparative wage justice' between women and men, although the Commission had no difficulty addressing this between men under section 26—as in ***In re Metalliferous Miners &c General (State) Award*** and ***In re Government Railways and Tramways (Coachmakers &c) Award***. In the women's case, no evidence was presented on whether perms and waves, now so fashionable and almost exclusively done by women, produced the same return or profit or value as cutting of bobs, proclaimed as dominated by men. Nor was consideration given to whether women cutting bobs produced the same return or profit or value—why should a bob cut by a man be any more valuable or profitable than by a journeywoman? Equally, the notion permanent waving is more eminently suited to women than cutting hair, or is easier to learn, is inexplicable—but was accepted without demur. Whatever the standard of proof—beyond (reasonable) doubt or on the balance of probabilities—lacking evidence of components, skill or value of the work, or its profitability, how could any informed decision be made?

Just as for Higgins in the 1912 ***Fruitpickers case*** fruitpicking (male work) should be more highly paid than fruitpacking (women's work—though 'more skilled'), and millinery (women's work) was purportedly less skilled and less valuable—because women did it, for Piddington, Cantor, and Street, if women did it, the work automatically qualified as less valuable, less skilled, less profitable: women could do it, therefore 'not difficult ... to learn', they said. Automatic assumptions, grounded in sex bias, not only undermined, but rendered inoperative, what was written explicitly into the 1926 legislation—comparable worth.

If industrial bodies were unable to appreciate, investigate fairly and without prejudice or investigate at all comparable worth of women's work, the onus was on women to establish women's work value by ensuring the evidence was there. Heagney prepared cost-of-living schedules for the Clothing Trades Union (CTU) in 1923 and 1927 Arbitration Court equal pay claims. Yet the 1929 fall of Wall Street was looming, the Depression adding another dimension to equal pay.

Subsistence and Survival: Arbitrating Wages in the 1930s

On 15 August 1930, summonses were issued by Victorian and NSW Railways Commissioners for variation of industry awards (Daily Paid Grades and Salaried Officers'), claiming:

- variation of the basic wage;
- employment rationing; and
- percentage reduction of wages and/or salaries.

The ***Basic Wage and Wage Reduction Inquiry 1930–1931*** (***Basic Wage Inquiry 1930–1931***) was one of the first major volleys by Great Depression employers to downgrade worker provisions, most particularly wages. Already at less advantaged wage levels, women's industrial conditions, wellbeing and economic independence were even more at risk. Yet equal pay arguments did not change fundamentally, whatever the market changes. Women's needs were less, women's work lesser.

The ***Basic Wage Inquiry 1930–1931*** employers asked the Arbitration Court to 'correct' the standard for adjusting wages under the 1907 ***Harvester case***. Arguing 'a sudden and violent change in the economic condition of the Commonwealth' made 'maintaining existing wage standards impossible', employers bluntly sought a wage reduction. In mid-1930, Australia's raw products fell almost to pre-war levels, wool by 40 per cent, butter 35 per cent, mutton and copper 20 and 25 per cent, spelter 35 per cent, and hides by 27 per cent. Overseas prices fell or bottomed out earlier, borrowing maintaining higher levels in Australia, but suddenly prices of wool, wheat, metals, and other primary products 'came tumbling down', bringing 'the day of reckoning'. Disputing this, unions asserted Australia had 'allowed the surplus and world parity to dominate the internal situation'. Australia should work, they said, 'to a large extent independently of … international or foreign parity in prices', learning 'to do without exports', becoming 'a self-contained nation'. This, replied the Court, might be an attractive solution—but ignored reality.

The unions argued that rather than reducing wages, 'those in control of industry … should [maintain] their operations at reduced profits …' Having netted 'such large profits in the past, and hav[ing] such stores of accumulated reserves', this solution would be fairer. Providing substantial detail of various companies' operations, they said workers' rewards had lacked proportionality to productivity, and '… undistributed profits [required] distribut[ion] in wages'. The Court responded that it was 'not Parliament', and what the unions wanted, only the legislature could do: unions must 'not live in the past', but face the 'present situation and future prospects'. Raising wages, giving workers greater spending power, would not engineer an economic upturn.

With both employee organisations and employers no longer accepting Higgins' ***Harvester*** family wage to calculate wages, the Court focused on production costs and productivity. Considering debate amongst women since 1907, the Court might have added women's organisations as challenging 'fixation of a basic wage on family units' creating 'serious anomalies'. Variations included federally—'man, wife and three children', NSW—'man, wife, and one child, plus certain provision for child endowment', other states—'an average family of man, wife and two children', whilst for Queensland, productivity was determinative.

The Court's function was not, it said, 'merely to ascertain … the predominant family unit cost of living' but to 'fix a basic wage for adults, single, married without children, or married with children whatever the number …'. 'Productive capacity … must … be considered, whatever the ascertained cost of living at a certain standard of comfort …'. Parties 'admitted' it was 'beyond industry's capacity' to extend to all single men and men without children a basic wage factored on 'the average needs of a man, wife, and three children …' Legislating an endowment scheme for extra children alongside wage determinations based on a minimum for a man, wife and one child (as in NSW), was supported as 'the only method' for 'equitably fixing' the wage.

However, concluding that no variations in basic wage or existing method of calculation should be made 'without further inquiry', the Court, 'after much anxious thought' was 'forced to [conclude] that for … twelve months and … until further order' a general wages reduction was required. From 1 February 1931, all wage rates were reduced 10 per cent. This overlooked women, already receiving lower pay, and the family wage, disadvantaging women, continued to persist, both federally and (Queensland and NSW variation apart) in the states. Nonetheless, in urging a national endowment scheme, the Court endorsed Street's UA proposal.

In 1932, the NSW Industrial Commission invited employers and unions to address whether wages set to the 1929 standard of living were inadequate or excessive. Canvassing principles established by the ***Basic***

Wage Inquiry 1920–1921 (endorsed by the NSW Commission in 1926, 1927 and 1929, but not the Arbitration Court), in ***In re Standard of Living and Living Wages for Adult Males and Adult Females*** (***Standard of Living and Living Wages Case 1932***) the Commission studied food and grocery costs, rent, clothing and 'miscellaneous', plus 'unemployment relief tax' (1s in every £1 of personal earnings), 'rationing' (companies furloughing unpaid employees for one in every four weeks, sometimes five or six, through ten), and unemployment (the period stood-down employees earned nothing).

Wages could not be set to compensate for unemployment relief tax, said the Commission, which 'could not adjust wages to cover periods of unemployment through rationing'. However, it carefully reviewed living wage components, endorsing the ***Basic Wage Inquiry 1920–1921*** 'calorific standard' that the food component shall:

1. … be sufficient in food values, expressed in calories, to provide warmth and energy, renew tissue to maintain [body] weight …, and satisfy [growing and developing children's] requirements …
2. … contain a proper proportion of three main constituents …, viz., proteins, … fats and carbohydrates … necessary to obtain a proper physiological balance … to maintain [body] functions …
3. … permit of a sufficient variety of food for … palatable and digestible meals.
4. … conform generally to [community] habits …

The 'number of calories necessary for a man' (engaged in 'moderate muscular work': 3500—eliminating 'unavoidable waste such as the bones, parings, husk etc., of food') was determinative, other family members' needs calculated by 'man unit calories'. 'A wife' measured 0.80 'man units', boy ten years, six months 0.60 'man units', seven-year-old girl 0.50 units, and boy of three years, six months 0.40 units. On rent, unions wanted the living wage to include an equivalence of rent for a four-roomed house-with-kitchen. Employers said the 1929 rent on a 'house containing three rooms and a kitchen' was 'excessive'. At the unions' request, the Commission's statist gave evidence of 'distribution of over 2,000 houses comprising three rooms and kitchen according to rental payments during the 1932 first quarter, from metropolitan area collections'. The Commission then ruled out the excessive rent claim, simply maintaining the 1929 standard. The employers challenged the clothing rate. Satisfied the 1929 standard 'must be regarded as ... liberal', the Commission nonetheless adopted it. With 'miscellaneous', denoting a sum in the 1929 standard (excluding 'domestic assistance'), the 1932 Commission endorsed it, despite acceding to employer 'excessive wages' protestations. The (male) living wage—'expenditure necessary to produce for an adult male employee in [NSW] requirements [for] a husband, wife and one child under the age of 14 years'—shrank from £4 2s 6d to £3 10s 0d per week.

Employee organisations argued that adult female employees' standard of living should be based on a female employee outside the parental home. The Commission rejected their proposal for detailing actual cost, saying the legislation required setting 'a standard of living of universal applicability, suitable to females as well as males, and to men without families as well as men with families'. This was bolstered by the 1929 finding that in NSW male and female living wage 'are now to be measured from the same standard'.

Yet this did *not* mean that women received £3 10s 0d per week. Women's living wage was a 'percentage of the cost of obtaining the same standard of living by an adult male employee'. An 'adequate amount' set according to the 1926 Act was calculated 'by taking 54 per cent of the living wage rate ... for adult male employees', namely £1 18s per week. Thus, the Commission decided men required more money because they were men, declined to study women's economic needs, and arbitrarily decided on 54 per cent. It could just as well have stuck a pin in one of the calorific charts spread before it in its search for the quotient of calories due to the man-of-moderate-muscular-work.

The NSW Parliament didn't trouble itself with women's dietary or clothing needs, housing or miscellaneous expenses either. In 1936, the Industrial Arbitration (Amendment) Act section 5 set the Commission's '54 per cent' rule in concrete. The provision enjoined the Commission to 'declare the living wage for adult female employees in the State at fifty-four percentum (to the nearest sixpence)' of the adult male employee living wage set on requirements of man, wife, and child under fourteen years. Nor did the Parliament ask itself about women's responsibilities for adult or minor dependants—or whether all men bore a wife-and-child burden, indeed whether a wife *was* an economic burden. Neither it nor the Industrial Commission asked whether calculating wages by family responsibilities should concede to some other measure. This failure lasted well over twenty years—until, by 1950s end, the Industrial Arbitration Act 1958 made yet another equal pay provision law in NSW.

Federally, the principle was about to change. In the ***Basic Wage Inquiry 1934*** the Arbitration Court considered cost of living, national productivity, family endowment, and the basic wage. On 23 November 1920, the Piddington Royal Commission (***Basic Wage Inquiry 1920–1921***) had recommended a 25 per cent basic wage increase. The Arbitration Court in the ***Gas Employees case*** awarded 3s only (the Powers 3s), saying industry could afford no more. In 1925, the Queensland Industrial Court received a report recommending wages should be adjusted on productivity variations but took no action. Ten years later, in the ***Basic Wage Inquiry 1934***, the Arbitration Court decided to endorse productivity for federal award wage fixing.

Setting and adjusting the 'new' basic wage was to accord with standard of living based on the Commonwealth Statistician's 'All Items' Price Index Numbers—compiled from retail figures. Dethridge and Drake-Brockman (chief justice and justice) held existing award rates should provide the starting point then, by a percentage and points mechanism, be adjusted upward via 'All Items' retail prices, moving wage fixing from the ***Harvester*** 'family wage' to a productivity base.

Justice Beeby wanted a new approach, but not Dethridge and Drake-Brockman's rate-fixing. Nor did he agree they had introduced a new principle. Beeby wanted a basic wage set by reference to production, not cost of living. Noting it 'may be so'—to the contention that the Court 'is not competent to find a true economic wage', the task 'better left to a board of independent statistical experts'—he said the Court itself could consult experts and state tribunals to reach 'a far more satisfactory method of fixation'.

The economic recovery justified 'more substantial restorations' than his colleagues proposed, but didn't reference women wage earners. Dethridge and Drake-Brockman did—one word over seven lines, determining it was 'not necessary or desirable, at any rate at the present time', to set a female basic wage for 'generally speaking they carry no family responsibilities'. Acknowledging the minimum wage should 'never be too low' for the employee's 'reasonable needs', they observed 'those needs may vary in different industries', preserving proportionate variations in each award between the female and male minimum wage.

So, restoring the male basic wage, however poor, and adoption of a 'new' approach or not, failed again to address the question women in trade unions and women's organisations asked: when would industrial courts and tribunals competently determine equal pay vis-à-vis women's economic rights?

Intervening Women

The ***Basic Wage Inquiry 1934*** was hailed as lifting the ***Harvester*** family wage burden from the equal pay argument. Fixation on men alone with dependants or obliged to plan for them meant women missing out in any wage fixing system reliant on ***Harvester***. Yet whatever was said in 1934, Beeby's view that the family wage was not really abandoned proved correct. Subsequent cases showed the 1907 principle as not so easily dislodged, no doubt because the (male) family wage fitted not only industrial mindsets, but dominant community assumptions.

Yet the 1934 decision, like the NSW ***Standard of Living and Living Wages case 1932***, held out one hope. The Court emphasised the NSW family endowment effectively increasing the basic wage for workers with children—the (male) basic wage covering one child, family endowment put money in parents' pockets for the second and third. The Court appeared to be asking when would the federal government follow the NSW legislative lead. Women pre-empted and echoed the Court, wanting federal government payments for dependants, meaning women with children, like men financially responsible for children's upkeep, would no longer be obliged to stretch the female basic wage to accommodate responsibilities their wage-rates ignored?

Far from being deterred by two decades of boom and bust, in 1937 women anticipated action. In the NSW ***Living Wage Case 1934***, wanting women's voices heard, Street's UA had gained leave to intervene with a threefold plan to have the Industrial Commission:

- base the female minimum wage on actual costs and expenditure by investigating a single women's cost of living, rather than aggregating male worker costs and expenditure, then allocating an arbitrary percentage of his base-wage for her;
- retain setting the living or basic wage in conjunction with endowment—a government payment—covering 'wives and children', rather than wages incorporating a component for 'dependant responsibilities' (for male workers only);
- reinstate within the living or basic wage—and incorporate into the female wage—the amount included under 'miscellaneous', until

1929—an amount predicated on paying someone to do domestic work done by a 'wife'.

UA's 1934 submission said female workers should not have to do two jobs, 'after a day's work, her own marketing, cooking, washing, mending, or making her own clothes'. A man's wife did it, or single men paid boardinghouse keepers to do it. This component should be included in the female living or minimum wage.

When the FCU took the case for higher wages to the NSW Industrial Commission in the ***Living Wage Case 1937***, women again took the stage, Street and UA briefing barrister Nerida Cohen, whilst Heagney prepared as expert witness. UA's proposal—phasing-in equal pay, awarding women a 5 per cent increase annually until reaching male basic wage level—failed. Three years later, Street and UA once more briefed Cohen, seeking leave in the Arbitration Court's ***Basic Wage Inquiry 1940***. Garnering support from twenty women's organisations (including each state NCW), Street failed to consult with Heagney or the CAEP (possibly cocking a snook at contentions of bending beneath bourgeois husbands' demands).

Responding to UA's letter, the Industrial Registrar telegrammed that on 21 November 1940 at 2.30pm, UA would have its application for leave to intervene heard. On 19 November, Cohen left for Melbourne, Street the following day.

When called on, Cohen submitted that before reaching a final decision on the male wage, the Arbitration Court should consider women's claims for equal pay in all new industries or occupations women were entering for the first time. The Court should hear UA on the automatic fixing of the woman's wage at a male rate percentage. More, it should consider a periodic progressive female basic wage increase until attaining equal pay. Her eloquence did not sway Dethridge. None of the seventy unions behind the Australian Council of Trade Unions (ACTU) application made 'any reference whatever' to 'the women's wage', so the Court 'could not hear her'. 'After argument on this point', runs Street's report, 'Miss Cohen asked that the matter be held over to allow us to consult the Unions'. Permitted, consult they did.

Officials called a Trades Hall meeting of all unions having women members, for Wednesday morning, 27 November. Union officials and 'other interested persons' held interviews Monday and Tuesday. On Wednesday, Street and Cohen addressed representatives of thirty-one unions. Street argued that if new industries and occupations women newly entered were 'geared down' to the female rate of pay, 'it would be impossible at any time for men to be employed in them'. The Depression experience would be repeated, 'men unemployed and women working at female rates of pay supporting unemployed husbands and families'. If industries 'started on cheap female wage rates', she said, 'we run the future risk of standards of living and community health being undermined'. Additionally, assessing women's work as of less value than men's required reconsideration. Following trade unions officials on the need to press equal pay claims and a better rate of pay for women, a unanimous resolution suggested the ACTU make a 'simultaneous application in common form' by all unions representing industries with women employed—then or prospectively. The claim for:

- equal pay in all new industries;
- equal pay in all industries women were entering for the first time,
- an increase in the female minimum wage, to cover all other women workers.

Despite this, no equal pay application followed, so no intervention. But, Street's report attested, women emerged from the 1930s with women's organisations combining publicly to support an equal pay claim in the Arbitration Court, with power to grant it, and trade unions could lead a combined equal pay application. Still, Street declared:

> … *unless women themselves*, whether Trades Unionists or members of social organisations, *are prepared to take an active part in pressing the claim for equal pay* and the improvement of the rates of pay for women workers in proper quarters, … *such claims will not be pressed.*

This was echoed when in the mid-1970s Ryan and Conlon ended ***Gentle Invaders*** with a call to action. From 1930s end, women embraced Heagney and Street's resolve for action as trade unionists and members of women's organisations, within their groups and intervening in industrial commissions. Thirty-five years on, this had made a difference. In 1975 the exhortation was for women not only to be active in trade unions and organisations, or as advocates in industrial commissions, but to be *on* commissions as decision-makers.

Notwithstanding refusal to allow UA's intervention in the ***Basic Wage Inquiry 1940***, for the CAEP, UA, NCW, Women's Christian Temperance

Union (WCTU), and fellow organisations, members and all women burdened by the iniquity of unequal pay, the 1920s and 1930s had triumphs. NSW equal pay legislation held out hope, as earlier in Queensland, that women's wage earner role and productive contributor to the nation may be recognised. Legislative endorsement mattered, despite, in purporting to support women, the law was undermined. Women and women's organisations built upon their knowledge of the system and constructed new arguments. Well-armed with counterarguments and determination, they faced the 1940s.

The 1920s began on the tail-end of war. The 1930s ended with war. Men mobilised for the front. Women mobilised into war industries. The Great Depression behind them, new conditions of work and industry confronting them, entering male industries electrified the equal pay struggle. Collective action imperative yet, as in any campaign, not everyone on the same side. As Chap. 6 'Alarums and Excursions: Women Versus Men Versus Women' asks: Who stood where? Would women fight it out alone?

References

Cases—See Case List

Jean F. Arnot, 'Embedded in the Soul' in JA Scutt (ed.), ***Taking a Stand –***, Artemis Publishing, Melbourne, Victoria, 1994, pp. 116–28.

Jean F. Arnot Papers 1916–1969 ML MSS 3147, ADD On 2070/4, Mitchell Library, Sydney, NSW.

CAEP, ***Are Women Paid Men's Rates***, CAEP/AEU, Sydney, NSW, 1942.

Rosemary Francis, *Muriel Heagney and the Council of Action for Equal Pay 1937–1948*, MA Thesis, UM, 1989.

Audrey Johnson, ***Bread & Roses***, Left Book Club, Sydney, NSW, 1990.

Glenda Law, '"I have never liked Trade Unionism" ...' in E. Windschuttle (ed.), ***Women, Class and History***, Fontana, Sydney, NSW, 1980, pp. 192–211.

Brian McKinlay, ***Australian Labor***, Drummond, Carlton, Victoria, 1979.

Winifred Mitchell, ***Fifty Years of Feminist Achievement***, UAW, Sydney, NSW, 1979.

NFAW, ***Australian Women—Archival/Heritage Resources—CAEP (1937–1948)***, http://www.womenautralia.info/archives/AWE0499a.htm (accessed 14 June 2021).

NSW Teachers Federation, ***Education***, NSW Teachers Federation, Sydney, NSW, 1920 (March 1920).

NSW Teachers Federation, ***Education***, NSW Teachers Federation, Sydney, NSW, 1921 (15 August 1921).

NSW Teachers Federation, ***Education***, NSW Teachers Federation, Sydney, NSW, 1930 (15 January 1930).
Edna Ryan and Anne Conlon, ***Gentle Invaders***, Thomas Nelson, Sydney, NSW, 1975.
Peter Sekuless, ***Jessie Street***, UQP, Brisbane, Qld, 1978.
Jessie Street, 'Equal Pay', 1936; copy ***Jean F. Arnot Papers 1916–1969 ML MSS 3147, ADD On 2070/4***, Mitchell Library, Sydney, NSW.
Jessie Street, 'Equal Pay for Males and Females: How It Can Readily Be Secured', ***Truth***, Melbourne, Victoria, 1934 (9 December 1934).
Jessie Street, 'Federal Basic Wage Hearing'—report on the application by women's organisations for leave to intervene in the basic wage inquiry on 21 November 1940, reprinted in ***Jessie Street***, 1990, pp. 87–89.
Jessie Street, ***Truth or Repose***, Australasian Book Society, Sydney, NSW, 1966.
Beverley Symons, ***The Hummer—Muriel Heagney …***, http://www.asslh.org.au/sydney/hummer/vol3no1/heagney.htm, pp. 1–7 (accessed 14 June 2021).
Lucy Woodcock, Letter to Jessie Street, Sydney, NSW, 1937 (9 September 1937); copy ***Jean F. Arnot Papers***, Mitchell Library, Sydney, NSW.
Women's Propaganda Committee, ***Justice***, 1925, in A. Johnson, ***Bread …***, 1990.

CHAPTER 6

Alarums and Excursions: Women Versus Men Versus Women

> Equal pay for equal service is affirmed at every conference, but no progress is made. In W.A. the Minister of Education refuses to recognise women give equal service. In N.S.W. Mr James says the position would be better understood if the women went out to work and 'the old man' stopped at home to do the woman's work.
>
> ... Mr McKinnon was hailed as a very brave man when he got up to oppose ... 'equal pay for equal work for men and women'. A headmaster stated that when a young man, his pupil teacher was removed, and he asked that a girl be sent instead of a boy. (Loud applause.)
>
> When Mr Board remarked that the Department could absorb more women teachers, there were general comments of 'It costs less'.
>
> Mr Jacobs ... suggested another alternative—that Mr Board might think them better than men.
>
> ***Education—The Journal of the New South Wales Teachers Federation***
> Sydney, NSW, 25 January 1920

As telegraphists, 'females very rarely acquire the highest degree of proficiency', says Victorian deputy postmaster general in his 1880 ***Report to the Inter-Colonial Conference of the Heads of Postal and Telegraph Departments***. 'Extremely few' women become 'sound' or 'thoroughly expert' operators, for even the very best cannot endure 'continuous exertion to anything like the extent young men are capable of ...' Nor, 'as

J. A. Scutt, *Wage Rage for Equal Pay*,
https://doi.org/10.1007/978-3-031-42178-5_6

assistants, engaged in simple clerical or routine duty', can women produce 'the same amount of work, or perform it with equal accuracy and despatch'. Female rates 'do not average more than half those paid to males', and service rendered by five men equates to that of ten women.

Thus, male equals automatic ability, female the opposite. What sympathy, then, for late twentieth-century slogans claiming women must work twice as hard as men, or that a woman wishing to be a man's equal lacks ambition? What about worker solidarity: could women expect support from the men alongside whom they worked?

Professions Are for Women?

On 18 May 1961, Miss Jean Randell of WA's Equal Pay Committee contests employers' claim that equal pay would be 'an intolerable burden on Australia's economy'. Perth's afternoon newspaper, ***Daily News***, reports Randell's words under 'Woman hits back': 'Equal pay is the law in NSW. Why not here?' The International Labour Organization (ILO) 'equal remuneration … for work of equal value' Convention supports the Combined Equal Pay Committee (CEPC) campaign, she adds, with France, Holland, Sweden, Norway, twenty US states, seven Canadian provinces, Aotearoa/New Zealand, and NSW introducing equal pay and 'show[ing] no sign of any intolerable burden'. Ultimately, says Randell, employers, not male workers, profit from paying women lower rates.

Male workers don't necessarily agree. Male-dominated organisations often stand firm against women's equality claims, while some suffer internal dissent over equal pay and equal opportunity. Alice Henry, writing in 1915 in ***The Trade Union Woman***, reports male workers, unionist or non-unionist, single or married, are 'just the same', yet 'how different it is with a girl …'. Proposals 'to organise the girls with whom they work' reveals 'mingled apathy and impatience'. Henry quotes men taking the attitude: 'These girls have come into our shop. We can't help it. We didn't ask them. They should be at home. Let them take care of themselves'.

In 1960, the Association of Professional Engineers Australia (APEA) splits over a move to encourage women into the profession. On 21 March, the Sydney ***Sun*** reports 'A Win for Women'. Lengthy discussion, some 'strongly' against, has the organisation's Federal Council recommending women's membership. Melbourne's Mr RH Richmond says 'the trained and practical mind', not 'the trousers' make an engineer, noting some forty women are graduate engineers already and universities will 'weed out' 'unsuitable women' as with unsuitable men. Mr NG Young, also of Melbourne, objects, 'quite sure' women have 'untidy minds', there's 'no room for that kind of person in engineering'. From Tasmania, Mr RF Ford declares women's place is 'at home—looking after children'; women are 'too emotional and unstable for engineering', and 'juvenile delinquency started when women left their homes and families and went to work'. A Sydney delegate, Mr RJ Brickhill, sums up: 'The only branch of engineering … suited to women [is] gold-digging'.

Forswearing women's skills, intellect, and right to equal pay and opportunity brands the decades. Yet when women enter male-dominated fields, holding their own, arguments are turned on their head, rhetoric condemning women 'taking men's jobs' and demanding women be legislated out of the field. Talk of women's purported inefficiency is silenced, without complementary affirmations of women's expertise. If women are acknowledged as having expertise, it is generally not in men's jobs, but 'simple' jobs requiring ability to engage in monotonous tasks. During wartime, the rhetoric changes. Men's absence requires workers. Women's ability is recognised, even lauded. Nonetheless, women are rarely granted men's wages for doing men's work.

Across the sex divide, women and men confront each other. Yet dissenters do not stand unchallenged. Justice and fairness draw some men to women's struggle, it is this simple: women must not be denied rightful reward for their work. For others, the fear that women's lower wages undermine male industrial conditions and access to jobs. The men's rights camp argues alongside equal pay proponents—but with a different rationale—setting women's wages at male rates saves men's jobs and pay rates. Some fear paying women equally to men means employers will choose male over female workers, underpinned by claiming men need (paid) jobs, women don't. Wanting women out of men's jobs, this propels support for, even initiating, equal pay claims.

Agreement, Disagreement, Opposition, Confluence, and Confrontation

Women's activism and industrial campaigns propel differences and divisions. Men's role in unions, government, business, and political parties counts. Difference in male and female positions on equal pay? Yes. Sometimes. Often. Why then some men with women 'for' equal pay, both seemingly united in facing men (alongside some women) against?

Differences between men and men? Some adamantly opposed and proud of it, relishing scorn or ridicule. Others with economic and intellectual arguments—meeting rigorous critique, for opposition means women hone their arguments and air them, an opportunity otherwise denied.

In 1950, the NSW Public Service Board (PSB) increases male public service salaries by £1 0s 0d, women (on 54 per cent of men's wages) gain 16s only. In December, the NSW Teachers' Federation applies to the Industrial Commission to have women's pay rates set equally to men's. By November 1951, the PSB uses the claim to sidestep discussion with the Federation on salary levels generally.

To keep wages down and undercut equal pay claims, employers promote conflict between equal pay and general wage rises, as if general pay rises should take precedence over women's wage justice, and are fair if women's pay differentials are ignored. Promoting potential differences amongst union members and between unions and women's organisations advantages employers wanting to hold down wages and deny equal pay. In 1951, the NSW PSB pursues this strategy, forcing unions to decide between pursuing women's claims for wage justice and general pay claims.

'You are apparently not aware of the proceedings before the Industrial Commission on October 23, 1951', writes a sarcastic Board secretary, 'when it was agreed that the [Federation's] claim ... involves an examination of male teachers' [work], and ... determination of [female teachers'] proper minimum rates involves a review of ... male and female teachers' [salaries]'. He says the PSB could 'properly' have raised an objection to the application under the existing Public Service Act agreement, but chose not to.

State government and PSB acknowledged inflation, raising PSB members' salaries retrospectively to 1 July 1951 and proposing increases in MPs' salaries. This reinforces the message: the Teachers' Federation pursues equal pay to its peril; if teachers act on equal pay, all teachers suffer the consequence—no general wage increase. The Teachers' Federation drops its equal pay claim.

A Case Study in Teachers and the Teaching Profession

NSW Teachers Federation history encapsulates the crossing of sex lines in the equal pay struggle. Thirty years before the 1951 claim, the Federation Constitution was amended. A motion by Miss Cunningham (Assistant Teacher), incorporated 'To obtain equal pay for equal service for men and women' in the objects. Upon amalgamation in 1919, the understanding was that the Federation would 'always stand for equal pay'. Contrarily, some members were now saying women should receive a percentage of men's pay only. Absence of any equal pay reference in the objects could be used against women, for however much male members might be supportive, in the future some might 'make themselves a menace to the principle of equal pay for equal work'. Seconder Mrs Taylor said women teachers in high schools and primary schools 'were as good at the profession as any man'. Mr Cook and Mr McDonald proclaimed support, McDonald affirming that on 'no account could the Association [adopt] the attitude that women [should] be paid less than men for equal service'. Miss Symonds said if work done by women 'were classed as skilled labour', women should 'receive the same as men'.

However, Mr McKinnon spoke against the motion. For women (not being breadwinners) to be paid equally was 'profiteering'. The additional amount paid to single men should attract a 'bachelor tax'. He justified this in economics and male responsibilities, seen as exclusively borne by men who 'might have a wife and six children—I have three, and have to clothe and keep a wife and children ...'. In turn, he met opposition. Miss Miller protested: 'How can it be "profiteering" for a woman to be paid for her work?' It was 'a matter of simple honesty: is the work worth so much or not?'

The motion was won, yet equal pay did not follow. Nor did debate end. McKinnon had a history of supporters.

In 1920, NSW female teachers' pay was £33 0s 0d annually, men's £44 0s 0d. Reviewing salaries that year, the PSB determined the rate should be four-fifths, not three-fourths. Anti-equal pay rumblings bred the proposition that 'making a woman self-supporting' is 'an economic mistake' because unwillingness to give up their salaries left 'splendid wives and mothers lost to the State'. On 15 December, C.A.B. responded in ***Education***: 'Fancy saying women ought to be starved into marriage!' Contending a man 'should get twice a woman's wage at least, to make a home and keep a wife and family' had 'nothing to do with the pay a woman gets, unless it follows the first puerile argument!' As for notions that women 'do not work as hard as men', with headmasters and inspectors 'not expecting so much of them', C.A.B. said women teachers were 'on the whole much more concerned' for pupils' welfare. And why isn't 'the old bachelor' paid the same wage as a spinster? The four-fifths quota would entitle a woman 'to do only four-fifths of [the man's] work' but there would be 'no wisdom' in this, for the Education Department 'cannot do without women [and] would be a laughing stock to the world if it tried ...'

The debate continued into 1921. On 21 August, ***Education*** published 'Tally-Ho's letter contending 'a good deal of parrot cry' about equal pay for equal work creates '—a lot of ... noise, but only a little truth'. Taken up 'years ago by Women Teachers or their Champion, then Miss Annie Golding ... the fight ... in season and out of season, has rightly raised women teachers' salaries and status, but wrongly imbued the minds of many with a false idea'. Challenging declarations that women's responsibilities as teachers were akin to a man's, Tally-Ho declared the 'weakness is that it should be equal pay for equal work, and equal responsibility, or equal pay for equal responsibility'. The headmaster 'bears all the responsibility and women cannot make the claim until the headmistress is solely in charge and not reliant on the guidance of the headmaster ...'.

Three months later, a 15 November letter to ***Education*** contradicts Tally-Ho. Schools 'conducted on common sense lines' find the headmaster confers with department mistresses 'glad of their help and advice ...' Claims that a headmaster carries full responsibility apart from 'ordinary class routine' emanate from a man 'imagining himself (for we presume it could only be a man who would hold this ... view) back in our Educational system's Dark Ages ..., when Mistresses of Departments really held the status of upper grade assistants, dutifully carrying out the Headmaster's behest ...'. As for contentions that 'any derelict ... can find safe harbour in the peaceful waters of an infant school', meaning infant teachers be paid less than anyone else in teaching, this was simply untrue, 'from modern educators' point of view' and 'knowledge of the facts [from] experience'. Infants required '...discipline, subjects, preparation and correction of work ... equal to ... older children'.

Debate shaped the 1920s, 1930s, and 1940s, through letters, at conferences and meetings. Men and women (preponderantly women) wrote and spoke in favour. Women and men (men far outweighing women) spoke and wrote against. Reported in ***Education*** on 22 May 1937, at Sydney's Equal Pay Conference, Federation member Mr McGuinness moved that respective remuneration Acts 'immediately be amended to provide occupational rates in all awards and industrial agreements', wages or salary rates 'not to be conditioned in any way by sex of employees'. Carried by majority, this was the first policy plank of the Council of Action for Equal Pay (CAEP), established by the Equal Pay Conference.

Resolutions going nowhere hardly satisfied women. Ten years later, with no equal pay, were the Teachers Federation and its members genuine? On 25 July 1945, Edith Wilson put the case in ***Education***, saying opponents of equal pay justify the remuneration gap by arguing 'a man normally has greater responsibilities than a woman'. Superficially this 'may have some appeal' in teaching, 'as with other forms of employment', yet bears no investigation. A 'tremendous struggle' over 'little more than a hundred years' has 'extended women's range of work into almost every kind of occupation'. The fight continues, she said, with victory 'only when "Equal Pay for Equal Work" advances' from slogan to practice. In the same issue, 'Croesus' responded to another Federation member's 'enlightening statements', exposing the salary of a fully certificated, non-graduate, secondary department woman assistant as insufficient for a 'self-respecting person' to live. No working woman could board or 'dress even presentably' on less than 15s weekly. Cutting out reading newspapers, belonging to a library or 'buying decent books' left her 'in a mental vacuum [un]fitted to give precisely the kind of education her present salary warrants'.

Resolutions, motions, and letters to ***Education*** showed the anti-equal pay contingent was a minority, at least publicly. Paucity of opposition numbers showed in June 1945, when the Federation circulated the year's salaries claim, including equal pay. ***Education*** reported seventy-six Federation associations fully supporting, eight advancing suggestions for implementing equal pay. One association wanted an extra principle, 'differential rates in accordance with work done' included, whilst two opposed equal pay. Four years on, ***Education*** of June 1949 saw the salaries campaign and negotiations again incorporating equal pay, a 'last resort' position seeking at least some rise in women teachers' pay, bringing it nearer to male teachers.

In 1953, debate on an equal pay motion saw the usual differences. For some thirty years the Constitution included equal pay, yet the implication was that it must be affirmed anew. Miss Farr supported the motion. Mr Barnes said he 'would not cry' if it were passed. No one 'recognised the value of ladies in their work more' than he, and although (citing a 50 per cent figure) 'many of the ladies' entered teaching without the intention of permanency, he (to the accompaniment of 'laughter') did not blame them. Women teachers risked nervous breakdown more than men and 'filled a much higher sphere when they [left] the profession'. Subsidising the family man was, he agreed, a national question requiring answer by the state through pensions or benefits, not wages and salaries.

Mr Jacobs favoured the principle, but not the motion. Mr Davies called the principle 'incontrovertible'. But cautioned equal pay meant men would be preferred to women. Mr Brigden said the principle would 'wipe out' some wage claim resolutions already passed by conference that morning. What's more, the scheme was 'impracticable'. Miss Johnson argued that with women constituting over 50 per cent of the Federation, the principle should unquestionably be a Constitution plank. Otherwise, '... things would drift back to their old state'. Mr Board wanted women in school. Dropping equal pay for equal work, he said, meant men jeopardised their own position.

Miss Cunningham spoke in reply. Thirty-two years after moving the original 1921 motion putting equal pay into the Federation's Constitution, she said 'camouflaging of the issue' requires opposition. She hadn't 'noticed women "breaking down" more than men, but if so it would be due to financial constraints under which they work'. On family responsibilities, these 'belong to the person himself' and 'No private employer would want a man with private responsibilities if he had to pay for them. The state should pay'.

By majority, equal pay went forward, reinstating the claim dropped in favour of the general pay claim, when in 1951 the PSB said it would not address both. Back then, continual delays in negotiations required an explanation to Federation members. On 17 May 1951, members learned through ***Education*** that the PSB was opposed to any increase in salaries, by equal pay or otherwise, 'in brief': 'Nothing doing; we don't want to break an agreement'. This referenced the 1949 Salaries Agreement, used by the Board to deny any general pay claim salary increases, so long as equal pay remained in the negotiations.

On 1 March 1952, ***Education*** reported 'by an overwhelming majority' a Federation Council resolution was carried to withdraw the equal pay application and call on the PSB to grant the general salaries claim immediately. The resolution ended with a clause 'emphasising' the 'right and duty of the NSW Teachers' Federation to campaign and work for implementation of equal pay for the sexes in the teaching service'. Subtext: just not now.

Women occupied an invidious position. Why relinquish a claim to equal pay, in the name of support for 'all' teachers? A general pay rise covered them as well as men, yet women would never benefit as would their male colleagues. Without equal pay, women's base salary supporting the percentage rise was smaller. Yet pressing their claim might lose support for the principle itself. Women could be depicted as selfish, greedy, and grasping, ignoring male teachers' families' needs—deserving a general pay rise, particularly with inflation. Yet when *would* the time be right for the women's claim? If equal pay were always subjugated to claims for a general rise, male-female salaries would never be equalised. In the 1970s, 1980s, and 1990s, this problem arose across the board in ***National Wage*** and ***Basic Wage Cases***, confronting women just as it faced 1950s and earlier women.

To maintain the equal pay claim, in March 1952, ***Education*** published Teachers' Federation secretary, SP Lewis' open letter to premier the Hon. J. McGirr (Labor), condemning the PSB's using equal pay to excuse its failure to act on the general claim. Teachers could be left without a new Salaries Agreement for months or years, awaiting Industrial Commission hearing of the equal pay case. Why should a Labor government be dictated to by the PSB's approach to equal pay, he asked.

Yet 'dumping' the equal pay case (as ***Education*** described it on 19 February 1952) didn't work. The PSB refused to negotiate *despite* the withdrawal. Contrary to its earlier protestation against negotiating for one part of the teaching profession alone—women—it now said negotiation on wages for the whole profession was possible only after determining women teachers' minimum rates of pay.

The immediate prompt to the Federation's claim was a PSB decision raising women's pay by a significantly smaller amount than men's. As ***Education*** explained on 19 March 1952, the claim was filed to put the equal pay claim before the Court, so exposing 'the differentiation between the increased rates' the PSB set for its employees and those set by the Industrial Commission.

From December 1950 to 1 March 1952, the Federation case had three mentions in the Industrial Commission. At the third, the chief judge declared the Commission's lists 'jammed' with no hearing date available. Scepticism abounded. Was the Federation treading softly, or at least dragging its feet? A week before the ***Education*** item of 19 March, on 11 March 'Action' wrote to the editor demanding a 'full explanation' for lack of a Commission hearing of the equal pay case. Action asked '… why, in truthful detail, … "it is more than 12 months since the application for equal pay was filed"?' Furthermore, what 'approximate date for hearing' did the Federation request?

Mindful of legal system delays, Action nonetheless posited that it 'would not be for more than a very few weeks', any union gaining a hearing 'in either Court within three months—usually about three weeks—…'. Teachers were 'most vociferous in their dislike of the PSB's apparent reluctance to "come good"' with salary increases, so 'Why bother with such a crowd?' asked Action. '… far more sensible to go to the Court [as] 'the final authority …'. Then the premier ('Reluctant Dragon McGirr') 'must pay up …'.

On 23 April in ***Education***, twenty-six St George Girls' High School teachers declared lack of satisfaction with any sex-discriminatory salaries agreement. Demanding tenacious representation, they questioned how the Constitution could include equal pay for over thirty years, yet remain unfulfilled? The present system making no allowance 'for the man with six children to receive any higher rate … than the bachelor … the present male salaries scheme [set] the rate according to "the job", not … financial commitments'. Consistency required applying the principle 'to the whole teaching service—male and female'. Confused economic arguments didn't bear close examination, and the 'it's not the right time' argument was 'bankrupt'. If a 'period of economic adjustment—inflation or deflation' deemed it 'not a suitable time to press such claims, a pamphlet entitled: 'NOW is NEVER the Time', published some twenty years earlier by women teachers in England came to mind. 'Are we waiting for the millennium?'

Two months later, on 11 June 1952, ***Education*** published letters with a response from senior vice-president Woodcock (to some an apologist for the Federation executive) reciting the Federation's equal pay history, including the Equal Pay Committee inauguration in 1949. Newcastle Girls' High School teachers' letter emphasised 'No Salaries Agreement can be acceptable to women [teachers] which places them in the ignominious position of having their work remunerated at less than its assessed worth'. Paying women less than men rests on a dated concept that 'dependants and domestic responsibilities generally' lie with 'the male sections of society'. Burwood Home Science High School teachers concluded whatever the action, 'so far little has been achieved', despite the Federation's pressing equal pay in all salary negotiations and actively supporting the Equal Pay Committee. They agreed a rise to 85 per cent of the male rate, 'though inadequate', would be an improvement, but anomalies meant some women going to 82 to 83 per cent of male rates for several years, receiving 85 per cent only when on their maximum assistant teachers' salary. If precedent prevented adjusting rates of pay granting all women teachers 85 per cent from 1 April 1952, it was a 'bad precedent'. Women 'would not submit quietly'. Lacking justice or logic, it 'should be scrapped'.

In June, an 'overflow meeting' unanimously challenged women's rates. With less than two days' notice, the meeting filled the hall, women sitting on the platform and standing in the aisles. A long list of apologies was read, with overcrowding forcing some to leave. Another major meeting was held on 3 August, at the height of the controversy. In July 1952, Harry Bembrick of Randwick Boys' High School followed with a letter to ***Education*** saying his branch rejected equal pay, wanted a vote to drop it from the Constitution, and urged the Federation to concentrate on 'pay rates'. On 23 July, ***Education*** published Mary A. Reid's reply noting that despite his stated lack of 'desire to engage in polemics', Bembrick gave 'no reasons' for rejecting the claim. Was it, she asked, that 'staff of the aforesaid school consists of a group of misogynists? Possibly they consider the quality of women's work' in teaching 'is of a lower standard than that of the males ...' so 'their monetary reward should be less'. She surmised it 'would indeed be interesting to hear some sound arguments from this superior group of beings at Randwick Boys' High School to support the courses of action asked for in their resolutions'.

The same issue published Clare Kinsella's letter saying taking a vote and removing it would not prejudice the claim's justice but prove 'social consciences of the men and women teachers are not sufficiently sensitive to injustice and those teachers have yet to learn there can be no justification for discrimination against women'. Elizabeth Lawson added that the Women Assistant Teachers' Association (WATA), numbering 1600, 'wholeheartedly supports the claim', calling for support on the recently drafted UN Declaration of Human Rights. Noting equal pay in a range of government and private sector occupations, she said professional women and men in private practice 'demand identical fees'.

Next, Mr Elliott, in ***Education*** August 1952. The average woman teacher 'lives better than the average man'. On 10 September, S. Gallaway replied: 'Of course! ... she spends her spare time and money on cultural pursuits, ... improv[ing] her as a teacher and citizen; often she dresses better [by making] her own clothes. This should be contrasted with how some men teachers 'dedicate their spare time and money'. However, 'what a person does with his or her own money is his or her own business; unlike Mr Elliott, I do not presume to criticise ...'.

Elliot had mentioned male teacher's chagrin on seeing 'his schoolroom colleague ... set on a far higher level outside the schoolroom'. Yet that was 'nothing', responded Gallaway, 'compared with that felt by the female teacher, teaching the same work, in the same school, performing the same share of other tasks as her male colleague', knowing his cheque is about £6.0.0 higher, 'solely because he is a MALE'. As to Elliot's contention that 'Part of a man's wages belongs to his wife and children', the point 'has me baffled', for 'what happens to that part (a) when he has no children, (b) when he has no wife? Will you please tell me, Mr Elliot? But don't say he is putting away every spare penny for matrimony or children, because I know many are not'. Furthermore, women teachers contributed through taxes covering child endowment, 'to help support men teachers' wives and children', so 'surely their work' deserved payment 'regardless of Mr Elliott's considerations, which seem untenable, judged by any standards of logic and fairness'.

Simultaneously, debate raged in the Queensland Teachers' Federation. An early 1950s meeting at Ann Street Church Hall saw Viv Flannery, Olive McKeown and Ruth Don present equal pay arguments to female and male teachers. At the next annual conference, Don was asked to deliver a paper and, despite some murmuring, equal pay was reiterated in the union's aims and objects.

Don found most people 'not terribly antagonistic'. Some opposed equal pay, though with 'not terribly sound' arguments. One departmental official had asked, 'What do women want all that money for? They're single'. Yet they 'did not think it should be taken off the single men—… It was simply … women did not need the money and why should they be given it'. At the Arbitration Court she 'had a darned good fight with somebody arguing women did not take enough interest in the union, and they were not going to … fight for them to get more pay … it didn't occur to them that women perhaps didn't take an interest because they were regarded as somewhat inferior, treated as if they [lacked] capacity to contribute'.

As union president, working with general secretary Mr Daughtry, Don argued about equal pay. 'He called me up one day, saying he'd read the whole of my presentation and didn't agree with it. [H]e had to prepare a case for the Arbitration Court, and I … argued and argued and argued with him about it, and he was still against it. I said, "Well, you've got to prepare a case." And by the time he had finished preparing the case he said, "I've convinced myself".'

Meanwhile, in Sydney, Elliott's August 1952 contribution provoked a new correspondence round. Writing in ***Education*** of 22 October 1952, V. Shannon rejected Elliot's criticism of the phrase equal pay for equal work. Comparison of teaching profession work done by women with women's 'much more difficult, more skilled, more exacting work' in the home confused the issue. Some wives were not mothers; some found their home job 'so little exacting that they went out to work every day as well', whilst most 'cope with their home duties quite adequately with little more training than that given to the 15-year-old girl'. Just as with male teachers, female teachers are '... intensively trained for the occupation to ... 19 or 21 years'.

Alert to dangers of side-arguments, Shannon noted replacement of 'equal pay for equal work' by 'the much more apt "rate for the job—irrespective of sex", the job here being the teaching job'. Mr Elliott 'is paid a salary for being a teacher, not ... a father'. If he considered all women teachers should 'forgo some of their just salaries to help keep his children and those of his fellow-men teachers', did he also think this should apply to all childless men teachers? If so, Elliott should let the 'Stork Derby' rule, male teachers paid, not on classification, but for the number of children. Yet 'the unmarried or less prolific headmaster would not relish ... receiving less pay for his teaching job than his more procreative assistant; or [does] he visualise the ambitious male teacher concentrating more on the Stork Derby than on having his teaching classification raised?' Both women and men might support parents and invalid dependants, but 'men teachers receive extra money to keep the home and housekeeper, whereas women ... must do the housekeeping themselves, before and after their day's teaching ...'.

That equal pay would mean a decrease in men's pay met with the response that money 'secured from the public purse' for salaries of MPs and PSB members (some without wife-and-children to support) must also affect male teachers' pay rates. Why single out women teachers for disapproval? Should a woman doctor 'charge a smaller fee than her male counterpart?' The woman running a grocery shop or café 'make less profit than her male counterpart?' All are 'taking money from the community for service to the community'. So, Elliot's being 'sufficiently intelligent' to be a teacher, 'he must be capable of sufficient logic, free of all sentiment, to make up his mind: Are teachers to be paid according to—(a) the work they are responsible for doing or paying someone else to do outside the school: that is, their commitment; or (b) the work they do in the school?' If (a), this would be 'a most complicated matter'. Arguments for both—but *sex* alone should not rule. If doctors, dentists, MPs, grocery and hardware shop assistants, transport workers, police, musicians have *one rate* for the job, why not teachers?

For Elliot, equal pay advocates raised a 'sectional' issue and should concentrate on 'general rates of pay'. This echoed H. Bambrick and Randwick Boys High School—with 'general rates of pay' meaning, for them, men's rates. Indeed, Shannon noted 'men like Mr Elliott' always 'restrict[ing] the sacrifice to *women*, irrespective of [their] commitments—who is being sectional now?' The 'saving up to be married' mantra was unrealistic, because women 'save up' equally as men—perhaps more; and what guarantee men will marry—even less have children. Many men teachers, said Shannon, are unmarried, many without children and 'a great many' married to women teachers—in paidwork, not dependent on their husbands. Women teachers doing their own housework ought not 'be expected to contribute to providing housekeepers for these men'.

VO McKeown and 'AB' of Robertson, one for, one against, joined in. McKeown disputed women teachers earning 85 per cent of men teachers' pay, as most received 80 per cent only. Equal pay legislation required supplementary measures, including tax concessions and social security measures. AB said equal pay must be addressed according to the female basic wage. Female workers 'so vociferous in their demands for "equal pay"' should fight for housewives' payments, too. AB would 'fight shoulder to shoulder with fellow unionists for the equal pay principle ... when the housewife is on the payroll ...' Until then, 'while mere men, generally speaking, bear the brunt of financial responsibility in rearing of families, I [don't] favour ... equal pay' ...

The 1952 Teachers Federation annual conference saw equal pay and opportunity as first of three topics. On 12 November 1952, ***Education*** carried the Federation Equal Pay Committee's article, 'Why Equal Pay for Teachers', canvassing old and new arguments around lesser numbers of women entering teaching through more attractive employment as doctors, dentists, nurses, masseuses, radiologists, physiotherapists, pathologists, dietitians, social welfare officers, librarians, radio announcers, private secretaries. Lack of equal pay infused this exodus.

By 1953, 803 delegates to the thirty-fourth annual conference debated equal pay. Whilst paying lip service, Randwick High School opposed equal pay for women. Writing in ***Education*** of 1 April 1953, Federation representative Nicholas McDonough said staff 'recently carried a resolution deploring the amount of money and energy' the Federation expended in 'continuing to press for equal pay for the sexes'. Those carrying the motion 'questioned whether printing and distribution of stacks of literature on this topic, forwarded periodically to schools, can be justified', no one suggesting 'the equal pay clause be deleted from the Federation Constitution ...' but 'staffing and accommodation shortages should be regarded ... as of more importance ...'. McDonough concluded by calling it 'axiomatic' that the more the Federation 'pushes' for equal pay, the less attention given to 'working conditions'. Equal pay should go to 'the background for the time being', enabling the Federation 'to improve our [sic] conditions and achieve reforms'.

Did McDonough believe that avoiding mention of equal pay and conditions confronting women members would somehow bring about reforms and women's wage justice? Or was women's pay really irrelevant? With other opponents, McDonough appeared not to appreciate women members' conditions were a key issue, equal pay central. McDonough's reference to 'our' conditions and reforms ignored women teachers, nullifying or negating the Federation's responsibility to represent women members alongside male colleagues.

Taking on the Dual Revolution

Arguments exposed means prejudice and myth countered. That general wages should take pre-eminence over equal pay elevates men's desire for (their own) pay packet increases, demoting women's wage rights. The fallacy of favouring general pay rates as if women's and men's pay inequality has no relationship to general pay rate setting is revealed.

Yet throughout these NSW Teachers Federation debates or the teaching profession generally, amongst clerical workers, in banking and insurance, transport or shop assistants, pharmacists, public service and university sector, in libraries, factories, and hospitals, women seeking pay equity bounce between optimism and despair. Women are torn between hopes of male dominated unions supporting equal pay justice, despair when they don't. Between male trade unionists' comradeship in acknowledging unbegrudgingly skills of women working alongside them—and rendered invisible, with their claims for wage justice, at meetings, rallies, and wage hearings. Between commitment to equal pay in resolutions and motions at union conferences and congresses—and failure to action and implement them. Between prospect of equal pay cases advanced to public service boards, industrial commissions, wages boards, Arbitration Court and Commission—and delayed outcomes.

Women are angered at commissions and boards, employers, and professional associations' ignorance in depreciating women's qualifications. Enraged at payments less than men with lesser or no more than equal talents and abilities. Bitterly disappointed when employer organisations raise the 'it will cost too much' and 'the economy can't afford it' shibboleth. Saddened when industrial boards and tribunals, the Conciliation and Arbitration Commission, its predecessors and successors fail to grasp the economic justice of women's claims.

Women work through the system, outside the system, against the system, and with the system. They resolve to do it without men. Resolve to do it alongside men. Resolve to do it despite men. They determine to change the law, lobbying parliamentarians. Demand industrial rulings, intervening in the public interest—explain women workers' interest in a fair wage for a fair day's work.

Amid this, men hold the ultimate key to women's wage justice, dominating unions and union decision-making bodies, parliaments, ministry and cabinet, holding positions of power in bureaucracies, courts, and commissions.

In 1950s Queensland, for Don, Queensland Teachers' Federation president, it was 'not any thought of men against women, it was a case of women getting paid what was paid for the job elsewhere'. Yet every decision denying women equal pay—or declaring equal pay means something less than the remuneration paid to men—all-male or male-dominated benches makes it. When women say the problem is men—this highlights the pattern and practice fostered and cultivated by men, a cultural reality underpinning the charge.

'Maybe you're one of those guys who don't like women in your shop', says a union leader in a September 1943 ***Metal Trades Journal*** article. 'That's too bad, brother'. Why?

> With 'em this country will win the war. Without 'em we stand a darn good chance of losing it. So pocket that grouch for the duration … women have a lot of pride … Tell 'em they're doing fine. You'll be surprised at the results …

Women cannot be blamed for feeling patronised. Why pocket that grouch for war's duration only? Where does the grouch originate? Where its legitimacy? Why not women as equals? After all, women are there before the war, will be there after—in paid employment whether men want them there or not.

The women versus men versus women struggle continues. Women respond with intellect, humour, confrontation, assertiveness, and satire. This time, the struggle must be won. Like women before them, they claim equality as their entitlement—and that of their brothers.

In her opening address at the Australian Women's Trade Union Conference (WTUC) in Sydney on Friday 6 August 1976, Patricia (Pat) Giles of the Hospital Employees' Industrial Union (HEIU) (WA) is emphatic. Women want a dual revolution, the battle 'on two main fronts: we must speed the occupational revolution *and* the domestic revolution'. Giles expresses belief that men need support, too, to embrace equality in unpaidwork, along with equality in paidwork. Characteristic of the 1970s, she asks 'how can we be certain of securing … domestic bliss for males, making [housework] enjoyable, so they don't have to rush through their chores?' No man 'need fear disadvantage':

> He too has every right to deliciously soft 'Palmolive hands'; … can experience the hilarious delight of spraying that stuff on the frying pan before cooking his breakfast; … can claim the 'most concerned parent of the year' award by using Fabulon on the clothes before doing the ironing.

But this lies in the future.

Moving from the 1920s and 1930s into the 1940s, 'the rate for the job' sounds in women's ears, chorusing from their lips. No time to urge home duties on husbands. Nor for men to lather Palmolive, even did they wish. War looms. Men's hands called upon for service of King and country. No time for women to lament lack of help around the home, Palmolive becomes a utility, scrubbing factory floor oil stains and grit and grime from fingernails. As men join the war effort on the front, women join it in occupations men leave behind.

So, if women do men's work in the cause of fighting off Hitler, then striving against Japan's southward movement, shouldn't women be equally rewarded, too? As Chap. 7, 'Intruders on the Rights of Men? 1940s Women at War and Work' shows, debates favouring and opposing equal pay continue. Wartime does not make wage injustice disappear.

References

Cases—See Case List

Jean F. Arnot Papers 1916–1969 ML MSS 3147, ADD On 2070/4, Mitchell Library, Sydney, NSW.

Patricia Giles, 'Opening Address' in ***Unions are for Women Too!—a report of the first Australian Women's Trade Union Conference***, 1976, WTUC, Sydney, NSW.

Muriel Heagney, 'The Council of Action for Equal Pay', in CAEP/AEU, ***Are Women Paid Men's Rates?*** CAEP, Sydney, NSW, 1942.

NSW Teachers Federation, Conference Minutes, 1953 (June 1953).

Metal Trades Journal, 1943 (September 1943), p. 243.

NSW Teachers Federation, ***Education***, vol. 32, no. 15, 1951 (14 November 1951).

Secretary, NSW State Public Service Board, Letter, Sydney, NSW, 1951 (October/ November 1951); reproduced NSW Teachers Federation, ***Education***, 1951.

'Woman hits back', ***Daily News***, Perth, WA, 1961 (18 May 1961); copy ***Irene Greenwood Collection***, MU Library, Perth, WA.

CHAPTER 7

Intruders on the Rights of Men? 1940s Women at War and Work

7th August 1939

The Hon. Minister for Defence,
Canberra

Dear Sir,

The following resolution carried at the annual conference of the Women's Service Guilds of W.A. Inc. held … on July 25th and 26th is forwarded to you for your information and consideration.

> "The Women's Service Guilds of W.A. in conference assembled believe the lives and work of those serving their nation in time of need should be of equal value, irrespective of sex, and ask the Federal Government for assurance that rates of payment shall be equal for men and women doing civil defence work or engaged on industrial or military service in time of actual war, and this shall apply to pensions in the event of disablement or death."

Resolution
WSG WA Inc 1939

Yours faithfully,
D. Cass
Secretary

J. A. Scutt, *Wage Rage for Equal Pay*,
https://doi.org/10.1007/978-3-031-42178-5_7

> The federal Labor Women's Conference required for any section of work in the Army, Navy or Air Force units, that equivalent male rates automatically apply, with all privileges and status of men enlisted for service in the same group, and no sex differential of any kind permitted to be introduced into pay, conditions and privileges of defence force ranks.
>
> ***Resolution***
> ACTU Annual Congress, Melbourne 1941

At 2.15 pm, Miss Nicholas rises to put a resolution to trade union delegates at the 1947 Australian Council of Trade Unions (ACTU) Congress. Held from 1 to 5 September, the ninth session addresses women's rates and conditions. Nicholas calls for Congress to reaffirm its policy and objective of the rate for the job, irrespective of sex .... Executive and affiliated unions must take immediate steps to campaign for:

1. Arbitration Act Amendment ... for elimination of the limitation on Conciliation Commissioners prohibiting ... dealing with the minimum rate of remuneration for adult females.
2. Complete abolition of Wage Pegging Regulations.
3. Pending abolition ... Government be requested to continue rates awarded by the Women's Employment Board [WEB] and under Female (Minimum Rates) Regulations.

   Further, existing Female (Minimum Rates) Regulations be amended to allow 75% of the corresponding male rate or 75% of the minimum adult rate plus full male margins.
4. [I]n all applications for increased wages in [female labour] industries, Trade Unions seek the rate for the job, irrespective of sex.
5. ... State and Commonwealth Governments be approached to introduce ... equal pay for their employees.
6. Repeal of legislation and regulations and alteration of Government policy limiting employment rights of women.
7. [Seeking] from Commonwealth Government [introduction] of an adequate uniform industrial code covering conditions and amenities.

Del O'Driscoll seconds. Carried unanimously, the resolution requires union deputations to government: ACTU to the prime minister, ACTU branches to state governments. Legal opportunities under still existing wartime regulations are urged to be taken, with the resolution roneod and forwarded to all unions employing women and all Trade Union Equal Pay Committee delegates. Yet the following year, the Equal Pay Committee Annual Report acknowledges little real action. Delivering her report on Tuesday, 6 April 1948, M. Anderson, secretary, says the resolution stands without implementation. Affiliated trade unions have failed to implement it, not sought equal pay for inclusion in any new awards, nor addressed equal pay in any other measures.

Yet every reason exists for unions to pursue wage justice, particularly women workers' industrial rights. The war years make a difference. Fighting from the ranks for equal pay in the services came naturally for some. Demobilised, knowing their strengths and skills are equal to servicemen, they demand entitlements as of right in a restructured workforce. Working in men's jobs when men enlisted, taking jobs in factories converted from peacetime manufacturing to munitions or domestic goods for the services. Finding 'canteen' jobs—keeping Australian troops happy during breaks from training or war-service; entertaining US officers and men on R&R between Pacific war theatre skirmishes. Remaining in pre-war jobs or moving from unpaidwork at home into jobs vacated when women workers enlisted or swapped for jobs created in response to war.

From 1942, reconstruction is highlighted. In 1948, the Trade Union Equal Pay Committee does not intend defeat, nor to let ACTU resolutions languish. With bank nationalisation proposed on 16 August that year, the Committee lobbies women bank officers and entreats prime minister, Ben Chifley, to include equal pay for bank workers. Meanwhile, federal government programs target retraining and return to 'civvy street'. A Gazette advertisement for a reconstruction course targeting returned teachers attracts Kath Dickson, demobbed from the Army (granted leave for active service). She applies to join. Told that, being a woman, 'it's not open' to her, she responds it 'specifies "returned teachers" and [she] is a returned teacher'. Going 'around the corner' to the union office, the first time she 'has ever been in the Union office or appealed to the Union for anything', she asks for help. Not having addressed it previously, they 'did some checking'. The next session three returned women join. 'Probably if I had not gone to the Union we would not have been "reconstructed" at all'.

So, at decade's end. What of the beginning?

Equal Pay for Women in Service?

Like other industrial struggles and life itself, the 1940s battle for equal pay fell under the shadow of international conflict. On 3 September 1939, immediately on Britain's entry into war, Australia declared war on Germany. The Commonwealth basic wage was £3 18s 0d. Women took up men's work in factories and offices, went into the services and the Australian Women's Land Army (AWLA), worked as volunteers knitting socks and balaclavas, packing and posting care packages, weaving camouflage nets. Attracted by relaxed job-market rules, Anglo-Australian women began leaving domestic service. Requests from middle and upper-class women for Aboriginal domestic servants deluged the native affairs commissioner. But Indigenous Australian workers had no industrial incentives, no guaranteed conditions, their pay was minimal. Racism dictated denial of regulation wages, on grounds of 'native mentality', a euphemism for 'the walkabout'. Authoritarianism increased. Few Anglo-Australian women's civilian life benefits extended to them.

When women demanded the right to join the military, prejudice precipitated a dual struggle. Claiming the right to be paid equally with men serving their country, women faced entrenched beliefs in women's inferiority in war and peace.

On 27 October 1941, the ***Sydney Morning Herald*** editorialised 'Women's War Service', saying the claim that any extension of women's service auxiliaries was 'unlikely', had 'surprised and disappointed a large section of the pubic'. Quoting AS Drakeford, minister for air, as 'speaking particularly of the W.A.A.A.F., the Air Force auxiliary', the editorial observed the remarks appeared to 'represent an important section of Ministerial opinion':

> How could Cabinet reconcile this … with its pledge to wage war with the maximum of Australia's capacity?

In 1941, Clare Stevenson worked in Sydney at Berlei, the underwear manufacturer. Summonsed to Government House by the governor (Wakehurst)'s wife, she was told she would head a Royal Australian Air Force (RAAF) women's auxiliary. Despite the Advisory War Council's reluctance, the War Cabinet approved the Women's Auxiliary Australian Air Force (WAAAF). Recruitment began, lack of ground staff, essential for the RAAF, providing the immediate impetus: women could do the jobs.

Opposition lay in two arguments: first, women's motherhood role was challenged by women performing in any war-capacity at all; secondly, so long as women were recruited for work otherwise done by men, men's jobs were at risk. Necessity won out. Then, with women employed as an Air Force auxiliary, it was not long before women were recruited to Australian Women's Army Service (AWAS) and Women's Royal Australian Naval Service (WRANS).

What of pay? Servicewomen did men's work. WAAAFs worked as mechanics and armourers, in air-force hangars, signals sections, operations rooms, stores depots, administrative offices, and messes. Reflecting on her wartime experience, after initial training in Sydney, with time at Ultimo, Val Buswell was transferred to Newcastle as an Aircraftwoman (ACW), the lowest rank. In stores, a corporal (male) was in charge. Buswell became a corporal, then sergeant running her own department—electrical goods, stationery, and aircraft parts—without equal pay. In Newcastle, she did 'exactly the same work' as the 'nice old bloke': 'no difference in stores, … women and men did identical work, but women received two thirds of the men's wages'—*of what they actually received*. Men's allotments were sent home, women's pay was only two thirds of the pay in their pockets. Clare Stevenson 'tried to have it changed, but couldn't'.

Returning from Germany and London, in late 1938 Joyce Opie (later Thomson) joined the Australian Women's Flying Club in Sydney. When WAAAF began recruiting, she enrolled as a teleprinter operator, becoming acting squadron officer until discharged late 1944. In ***The WAAAF in Wartime Australia***, she outlines women and women's organisations' solid support for women's auxiliary services, wanting identical conditions of service and salary as men. Government, military, and sometimes unions demurred.

In Britain, emergency conditions precipitated women into the services early. In Australia, resistance loomed from some unions and within the services. In Canada and London to negotiate joining the Empire Air Training Scheme and finalising RAF air marshal Charles Burnett's appointment as chief of staff, JV Fairbairn, minister for air, observed the readiness, through necessity, of these governments to recruit servicewomen. In Australia, he alerted the RAAF Air Board, which obtained information about the women's auxiliary. On 13 January 1940, the ***Argus*** reported Fairbairn's listing jobs women 'could successfully execute'—transport, driving and 'many others'. He endorsed the UK Women's Auxiliary Air Force, saying any Australian scheme 'would be similar'.

On 12 March 1941, ***Hansard*** recorded Maurice Blackburn, Labor MP, pursuing equal pay for servicewomen employed on the same class of work as airmen. The concern was for men's jobs if women received lower wages. Yet women were not displacing men: vacancies—particularly for wireless and teleprinter operators and cypher clerks—exceeded male and female enlistments. On 3 April, minister for air and civil aviation, John McEwan, 'without promising', agreed to reconsideration of equal pay. Rates were equivalent to women's rates doing similar work in the public service, where men earned approximately £50 0s 0d more annually than women. No allowance applied for higher skills, like wireless telegraphy, and no penalty rates for shiftwork or overtime. Most servicewomen took home less pay than their civilian sisters and far less than servicemen in equivalent jobs.

Once women entered the auxiliary forces, the labour movement was vital. On 23 April 1941, twenty-four unions with women members met at Trades Hall, seeking ACTU and Australian Labor Party (ALP) support for equal pay, targeting federal parliamentarians. Women's organisations lobbied within the services, too. The Joint Committee for Equal Pay, United Associations (UA) and National Council of Women (NCW) led. Servicewomen, conscious of conditions confronting servicemen overseas, fighting in poor conditions with far from princely wages, were less adamant. Nonetheless Stevenson headed WAAAF's push for pay and conditions, going direct to her superior officers and director, and encouraging women's organisations, ensuring pressure from outside and inside the service.

In 1940, pending women's auxiliary services formation, the Finance Committee opposed setting servicewomen's wages by RAAF rates of pay. Arguing that Royal Air Force (RAF) rates were lower than RAAF rates, ruling out comparison between Britain and Australia, (women's) civilian rates were touted as the comparable measure. Instead of comparing women's wages with men's, women's wages should be compared with women's wages—albeit women did men's jobs—like men, serving their country. The Committee also rejected servicewomen's right to Repatriation Act 1920 (Cth) pensions (more generous than civilian entitlements) and recommended women's take-home pay should be cut-down even more, factoring in benefits—free medical treatment and uniform issue—all available to men at the higher rate of pay. Different pay rates for minors (a civilian distinction not existing in (male) military services) should apply too. Joyce Thomson concludes that all this was designed to ensure 'traditionally lower pay of women in civilian employment was [not] jeopardised by granting servicemen's pay and conditions to servicewomen'. So, servicewomen should be denied equal pay, despite equal work, for fear of discord amongst non-servicewomen driving equal pay claims outside.

In July 1941, McEwan proposed WAAAF members receive identical rates of pay with airmen doing the same class of work. Curtin, Labor opposition leader, said consultation with unions and a non-government War Council member should precede the War Cabinet's decision. In September, full male rations plus uniform and clothing issue were established for women, alongside scales for officers confirmed at 5s to 5s 6d a day less than male rates. Officers' travel allowances were set on the nurses', not RAAF, scale. Replicating industrial tribunals, making pay rates and conditions between WAAAF, WRANS and AWAS uniform took precedence over uniform pay and conditions for servicewomen doing work equivalent to servicemen.

Women maintained the pressure. On 27 January 1942, NCW Victoria supported a general protest against servicewomen's rates of pay. Victorian president, Ivy Brookes, with members Louise Burton and ME Williamson, became a delegation to the minister for air, AS Drakeford, through the Air Board. Mrs LB Marfield asked that equal pay and compensation be added. The minister peremptorily refused the delegation. Vowing to go above him to the prime minister, NCW recorded a strong protest. On 11 April 1942, an ***Age*** report shamed Drakeford into seeing the women, but not into acknowledging servicewomen's right to equal pay.

Meanwhile, Joint Committee for Equal Pay (JCEP)'s Julia Rapke, with UA president and vice-president Erna Keighley and Jessie Street, went to Canberra to see the prime minister or minister for air. Meeting with head bureaucrat, MC Langslow, the delegation uncovered his opposition to equal pay, arguing 'women could live on smaller allowances than single men, travel more cheaply, stay in cheap boarding houses while men stayed at hotels'. Women were precluded from repatriation benefits and access to industrial tribunals for pay adjustments, and 'minors should be paid less than adults', while 'the WAAAF were only an auxiliary and not really a part of the defence forces'.

Angry, checking her letter with Stevenson, Keighley protested to Drakeford that she was 'appalled' at Langslow's 'viewpoint' on women's 'status and their pay etc.'. It was 'quite unfitting, most unfortunate, and absolutely unjust' he should exercise power over women workers. Langslow had 'views and opinions of the Crimean War …', with 'decisions made by your Ministry show[ing] evidence of the influence of his antiquated ideas', and he 'is doing your Party infinite harm …' Saying he 'advocates everything to lower the standard of living for Australian women', she concluded this was 'a serious state of affairs' which the Labour government 'should [act] to remedy'.

So long as civilian women suffered unequal pay, it seemed, servicewomen would miss out, with the additional hurdle that postings overseas or to the field of war were severely restricted. Nurses might go to the front. Women in men's jobs in non-combat roles did not. Women joined up, wanting to contribute to the war effort. Restriction to non-combat roles was not their choice but denied them equal pay, cementing the link to women's pay in jobs outside the services, not men's jobs within them.

Equal Pay for Women in Women's Jobs in the War Effort?

January 10, 1940. From Sydney the first contingent of the Australian Infantry Forces (AIF), 6th Division, sails for the Middle East. From 11 March to 16 May, coalminers strike for higher wages and shorter hours. As severe drought conditions settle over the country, the prison ship ***Dunera*** arrives at Sydney carrying 2000 German and Austrian internees, exiles from Britain and home. A year earlier, Kylie Tennant's ***Foveaux*** is published. Christina Stead publishes ***The Man Who Loved Children*** and ***Forty Thousand Horsemen***, Charles Chauvel's film starring Chips Rafferty and Grant Taylor, plays in Australian cinemas. Meanwhile, women doing men's work ask for men's pay for men's jobs. They get the jobs—but the pay?

On 24 March 1943, ***In the Matter of the National Security (Industrial Peace) Regulations and of The Arms Explosives and Munition Workers Federation of Australia and the Director-General of Munitions*** (***Arms Explosives and Munition Workers case***), the federal minister for labour and national service referred women's wages to the Arbitration Court. Industrial unrest loomed through 'differences and inconsistencies … in … wages [of] female members of the [Arms, Explosives and Munition Workers' Federation] AEMWF … at the Government Small Arms Ammunition Factories'. Women employed in the factories *before* the war—doing women's jobs—'women's work', and paid women's wages, received lower wages than women entering the factories to do men's jobs *because* *of* the war. Doing men's jobs, pay was set by the Women's Employment Board (WEB) at rates akin to men's. Women in men's jobs earned more than the women in women's jobs—despite the latters' greater experience and expertise.

The 17 June 1943 decision is understood only against wage-fixing for war-time production. Three wage-setters existed for munition factory workers:

- Arbitration Court—wage fixing generally (including men doing men's work in munitions factories);
- WEB—from 1942, wage fixing for women workers in new jobs—existing since the war, and men's jobs where women worked in men's absence at war;
- Commonwealth Public Service Arbitrator (CPSA)—wage fixing for women workers doing women's jobs—jobs in munitions factories done by women prior to war.

When war began, some munitions factories manufactured weapons. One manufactured small arms exclusively. One made ammunition, including for small arms, with women workers. Another manufactured explosives. A fourth was an ordnance factory. The fifth comprised laboratories concerned with supply. Departmental policy required 'providing work and income for the family man and potential family man', hence—male workers. The exception was small arms ammunition. Women represented some 12¼ per cent of the total munitions industry workforce.

Being women's work, CPSA determinations regulated wages and conditions in small arms manufacture. Industrial rights of other employees, including any making small arms ammunition, fell under Minister-employee organisation agreements, the most recent dated 4 December 1939, for three years. Outbreak of hostilities meant munitions factories and their output increased. The 4 December agreement covered incoming workers. In September 1939, for the first time, women worked at more than manufacturing small arms ammunition. Specific classifications were included under the December 1939 agreement. In October 1941 and subsequently, women's employment extended into other areas. By 1943, women constituted 75 per cent of small arms ammunition manufacturing and 40 per cent of other categories, covering numerous classes of work, some previously exclusively male, some not done previously by women or men. None was deemed unsuitable for women.

Unions resisted women's employment, but after March 1942, with the Department's announcement it would employ women at small arms making, unions withdrew opposition. Women would be paid male rates—following two weeks' probation on 60 per cent male pay. But except for small arms, women were employed at pay rates like those prescribed for female employees by the 4 December agreement.

The Department notified the WEB of the women's employment, as 1942 Statutory Rules required WEB permission for women's employment on work where male employee rates were set by an industrial award, order, determination, or agreement and was (at that time) 'customarily performed by males'. The WEB determined women's pay rates in manufacturing of fuzes, primers, tubes, vents and allied components, brass cartridge cases, shell and allied components, guns, percussion caps, explosives, paper components, pyrotechnics, and detonators; shell and bomb filling, fuze filling, cartridge bundling and assembling; operations in rolling mills, and several miscellaneous occupations. Adults secured 65 per cent of male rates for similar work—basic wage and margin, plus male war loading—for the probation period, then 90 per cent of the male rate for similar work—basic wage and margin, plus loading. Juniors had 90 per cent of the junior male rate, plus war loading for junior males. WEB covered all female employees 'replacing males at various dates' after war commenced, which excluded women in small arms ammunition manufacturing whose rates of pay remained under CPSA decisions.

With three wage-setters, disputes inevitably arose when women in women's jobs earned less than women in men's jobs, particularly pre-war industry workers versus women coming into war munitions. This background to the ***Arms Explosives and Munition Workers case*** meant the Arbitration Court must consider what women in various categories earned. It considered ***Harvester*** principles, 1930s Depression years, and early 1940s ***Basic Wage Cases***, plus WEB decision-making, saying historically two methods applied in basic and minimum wage setting:

- ***Harvester***: living wage for 'normal needs of an average employee', one needs a domestic life (wife and children);
- Depression: foundational wage on industry capacity to pay.

Never had the basic or minimum wage related to value of work done by employees. Margins or other payments over and above basic or minimum rate accommodated this. As the ***Fruitpickers case*** and ***Harvester*** principle applied, women working men's jobs got the average employee wage (man with a domestic life) or something set by that measure, those in women's jobs a basic rate calculated for a single woman paying for board and lodgings, maintaining herself from earnings, minus dependants.

The only exception, said the Court, was in WEB calculation of wages under its charter. Women working men's jobs in industries not worked by women prior to war or in jobs created by war, under Statutory Rule 132 of 1942, WEB assessed rates referencing women's 'efficiency and productivity' when 'engaged upon the specified classes of work, as compared with efficiency and productivity of males doing similar work'.

WEB's calculation set a basic or minimum wage for women's work in the particular job or industry. The Arbitration Court said it was not within their province to question WEB's approach or decisions, authorised by the Women's Employment Act 1942 and Regulations, where Parliament 'clearly decided that, to encourage [women's] employment … [to aid] prosecution of the present war', women workers in particular classes of work could have 'exceptional treatment' in pay rates. Discretion in fixing those rates was 'limited only [on] minimum and maximum [rates WEB] … may fix …'. This set different pay rates for women in munitions factories but did not create any anomaly under the Regulations.

The ***Arms Explosives and Munition Workers case*** rationale was that war did not change women's work on small arms ammunition manufacture. Prior to war that work was suitable for women—women worked at it, so it remained suitable for them. No evidence or suggestion arose of men competing with women for small arms ammunition work. Pay rates under the 4 December agreement applied according to the general rule setting *women's* wages. Hence, rates were not anomalous. Even if it followed, as the AEMWF suggested, that government policy decreed a general comparability of wages according to relative efficiency and productivity, the Court said that unless the legislation required, it was not the Court's role to expedite expressions or intentions of government policy.

The Court left open whether, consistent with 'comparative justice', a case could support all munitions jobs filled by women to be set at WEB rates. If so, all circumstances of the employment must be considered. Additionally, an assessment would be required of the effect on all women throughout Australia, in whatever jobs, of paying WEB rates for all munitions work. But WEB's job was to address pay rates of specified classes of work only. If all women's rates were raised, concluded the Court, 'the very purpose of the Women's Employment Act would ... be frustrated'.

Thus, a body ostensibly created to support valuing of work done by women, undercut the valuation of work women already did in industry, and particularly in industries dominated by men (at least prior to war)—with women consigned to particular jobs or particular parts of the munitions industry or factory. Ultimately, women in women's jobs—jobs held by women before and during the war—remained at the lower women's rate, determined solely on the 'percentage of the male Basic Wage' basis. Women in men's jobs and jobs specifically for the war effort continued to be paid the special WEB rate. That women in women's jobs might be equally skilled as women and men working in the same factory or industry, or more skilled than new workers, was irrelevant. That little distinction existed between some of the jobs mattered not at all. Nor did it matter that all women had been working at the lower (women's) rate from their entry into munitions work: those doing women's, those doing men's, and those doing new jobs.

That these differentials might promote industrial unrest was ignored—astonishing when the federal industrial relations power under Constitution section 51 (xxxv) is centred in resolution of disputes, recognising wage setting is a vital component. Differences in women's pay obviously engendered industrial disputation—the reason the case came before the Arbitration Court in the first place!

Yet not only potential but actual industrial unrest—potent causes of increases in men's wages and improvement in conditions—was bluntly ignored. The stereotype of women's conformity to expectations of womanly behaviour and war-effort devotion—choosing loyalty to the nation over industrial fairness for themselves and fellow (women) workers—appears to have prevailed.

So women in all industries, whatever their jobs, were denied equal pay, classed alongside servicewomen refused servicemen's rates. Women's skill, efficiency, and productivity were irrelevant to women's wage setting, just as no attention was paid to *real* costs for women—including responsibilities for children and other dependants. Contradictions adhere in government-established childcare centres and a wartime childcare program. That women had worked in women's munitions jobs preceding declaration of war told against them: working without government support for their non-war childcare needs, their responsibility for dependants remained invisible to wage-fixing.

What of women doing men's work (not women's work) in munitions and outside the armed services?

Equal Pay for Women in 'Men's Jobs'?

8 December 1941. Japan attacks Kota Bharu, Thailand, Singapore, and Guam and bombs Pearl Harbour. Australia is at war with Japan, Finland, Hungary, and Romania. Some three months before, on 27 August 1941, as a war measure, Melbourne trams run with women conductors for the first time. But everyday events go on. On 5 February that year, Banjo (AB) Patterson dies at seventy-six years. On 19 April in Adelaide, Ola Cohn's memorial statute *Pioneer Women*, is unveiled; Eleanor Dark's ***The Timeless Land*** appears alongside Tennant's ***The Battlers*** and Ernestine Hill's ***My Love Must Wait***. Commencing 1 July, the Commonwealth introduces child endowment, 10s a fortnight for each child under fourteen, except the first. This emolument, lobbied for by women's organisations for years and linked to the equal pay quest, could presage success or a future wedge, encouraging women to bear more children, jeopardising stability in recognised paidwork roles. War suspends this as a possible outcome.

Women working men's jobs in wartime Australia wanted their work to be recognised equally as the men whose jobs they filled. Employers, driven by profits—even (sometimes even more) in war—wanted women for less, whilst maintaining productivity. Sometimes, unions faced a dilemma. Not wanting women to undercut men's pay and conditions provided an incentive to demand women receive the wages of men who left. Yet what of the men's inevitable return to 'civvy street' when war ended? Could wage rates be maintained at the men's rate—if women proved equal to men's jobs and employers chanced on retaining women as worthy substitutes? Could men reclaim their jobs? Wage justice for women might even be a worthy goal: some men and some unions saw equal pay thus. Nonetheless, with women in the services and in men's jobs, the masculine mystique imbuing 'men's work' was jeopardised. During wartime, this may have been even more telling. Distinctions between men entering the services and men left behind drew even more firmly upon notions of masculinity.

What constitutes a man's job? Can women do it just as well? When doing it, what rate for women? WEB cases came from a wide variety of union, employer, and government sources. All showed the difficulty—even impossibility—of assessing women's labour objectively. In 1943 ***In the Matter of Seven Applications by the Broken Hill Pty Co. Ltd***, BHP applied for a common rule for NSW, Victoria, SA, and the ACT to employ women, then set women's hours, pay, and conditions. Work included clerical, storeroom and checking jobs, machinery jobs—setting up machinery and apparatus, repetitive and mechanical work—and driving machinery. Additionally, WEB included jobs classed 'general engineering' (window-frame and agricultural implement making); boiler-making and steel construction; and welding.

Inspecting or investigating each shop or factory's conditions was impossible. The WEB referred to its earlier metal trades decisions, operative since 23 September 1942, covering large numbers of women. It 'noted a variation in relative productivity and efficiency of females as compared with males' and 'marked variations' in productivity and efficiency between individual women doing similar work in different factories. However, employers and employees agreed on a uniform flat rate, covering 'all factors of differentiation between productive capacity of the sexes as well as averaging out as nearly as possible "highs and lows" of the different groups of females' in the industry.

Productivity differences were not entirely attributed by WEB to women workers' deficiency. Sometimes fault lay with employers '... poor supervision, bad surroundings, unsatisfactory or obsolete plant, poor organisation, bad set-up, failure to intelligently utilise females in their most efficient capacity, failure to provide adequate and proper conveniences, amenities and rest periods, [or] psychological factors [making] so pronounced a difference not only in well being of the females but in their productivity'. WEB said it would not 'penalise females whose productivity and efficiency are lessened by no fault of their own' but expected employers 'in their own interests' and those of the 'war effort' to bring labour power up to full capacity. Still, women did not gain 100 per cent of men's rates.

Themes of output, productivity, and efficiency recurred. Statutory Rules, then the Women's Employment Act required it. Almost consistently, women were classed less productive, less efficient, and generating lesser output, despite lack of any clear basis. Invariably, wages settled at below the male rate. In ***In the Matter of an Application by the British Australasian Tobacco Company Pty. Ltd. and W.D. & H.O. Wills (Australia) Ltd*** (***British Australasian Tobacco Company case***), seeking rates of pay, hours and conditions of work, and permission for female workers in various classifications is illustrative.

The work in question was 'well within the capacity of females and of the kind [to] be performed by them without any detriment', WEB said.

Employer and employee organisations conceded they lacked 'actual experience of [females'] capacity in classifications covered by the application' because 'no females had heretofore performed these operations'. Nevertheless, 'upon [their] experience' (unspecified), an estimate was calculated. 'Relative efficiency and productivity of females' was agreed at 80 per cent. Women's purportedly lower productivity, efficiency, and output lay in comfortable agreement between employers and unions based in assumption or prejudice, 80 per cent plucked out of the air.

In this case, absent evidence of women's work, productivity, or efficiency in the field, the WEB at least acknowledged the possibility that the parties' estimate was 'inaccurate'. Yet the agreement was accepted 'as a tentative determination', operative for six months. The WEB would then reconsider and, 'in light of the parties' experience', fix 'with greater accuracy and precision' the relative efficiency and, so, the percentage rate. Any change would be retrospective to the date of the WEB's original decision.

This provided employers and unions an opportunity to assess performance and productivity. Yet so much of the work being unremarkable, standard production line, why six months' probation, why a negative assumption against women's capacity for the work and entitlement to men's rates. Men brought in to replace men leaving for military service entered on the male rate, with no six-month, 80 per cent trial. Evidently, the operative factor was that these incoming workers were female.

In the ***Metal Trades (Broken Hill) case***, for Broken Hill, Australian Iron and Steel (AIS), and Rylands Bros. workers, WEB favoured the uniform flat rate approach of earlier metal trades cases. This sparked some resistance. With crane drivers, WEB was pressed strongly to recognise equal or greater capacity shown by some females in the job. In other cases, say cleaners in mixed male-female teams, emphasis lay on asserting women workers displayed less than 90 per cent efficiency, warranting a less than 90 per cent rate.

The flat rate prevailed, so again women missed out. Those adjudged equal or better than male workers did not receive the male rate—albeit their work should have credited them (at least) the full 100 per cent. Those deemed less efficient were, ironically, women doing work which in the household devolves (generally) to women—seen as women's work. The WEB did not ask why women doing women's work in a male domain might purportedly produce substandard results. Lacking logic, all things being equal, for women to be poor or lesser cleaners than men, warranted scrutiny. Working in mixed teams, women may endure sexual harassment, generating absenteeism, poor performance, negative reports about their work by disgruntled co-workers, requiring changes to workplace standards, and eliminating unhealthy work practices, including occupational health and safety risks, not lesser pay for women cleaners. Alternatively, afraid that work classed as female when done at home may be so (re) defined when women do it on the shopfloor, male cleaners may have sought to downgrade women's capacity for the work, preserving its masculinity. This phenomenon should not deny women equal pay and opportunity.

In the ***Metal Trades (Broken Hill) case***, WEB reflected upon employers, women, men, and work. The decision canvassed a range of arguments for and against women workers. First, 'a reluctance and failure to appreciate woman's new place in industry', despite women's entering and working in fields 'surprisingly well', 'amazing' employers and community. Next, stereotypes took centre-stage in suggestions that women should be denied 'dirty work' potentially 'soiling her face and hands … by … grease and grime', or 'jeopardising her comfort by … work in constrained or uncomfortable places and positions'. WEB challenged this, observing that knight-in-shining-armour chivalry was 'as out of date as the shining armour', 'humiliating to women [resenting] patronizing condescension'. Further, the sexes might not be equal '—heaven forbid—', but 'their respective contributions … though different are not so very unequal'. Who, WEB declaimed, 'shall say which sex weighs down the scale?' Furthermore, 'everywhere' women were claiming 'they can do most jobs as well as males'. Apart from 'obvious limitations associated with their sex and physical limitations' women were, said WEB, 'content to be judged and paid by results they achieve—a fair field and favour to none …'. Post-war, the 'greatly increased reservoir of labour' mobilised and achieving 'production of materials and services of war in abundance', would remain at the community's disposal and would require attention, with returned servicemen considered, but claims of women and the community would merit attention, too. Some cases suggested that labour power 'called into existence by the war then suddenly released' would 'work disastrous results', particularly to men 'fearing loss of their place in industry'. Productive capacity in a 'well-ordered State' was not 'evil', WEB concluded, but should generate a higher standard of living, 'greater culture', and 'more leisure'.

Yet 'equal pay for equal work' bypassed BHP's women workers. This was a consistent WEB feature: treading with enormous caution, rarely accepting women could work as well as men, or women working men's jobs should be, even generally, equally rewarded. Nor, having oversight of a wide range of employments and observation of women's participation, did it use its position to encourage experience or development of expertise in jobs previously held by men. Justice Foster, chairing the WEB, compiled a list of men's occupations with women's productivity calculated on a percentage basis, the implicit assumption being that women's productivity in men's jobs did not equals men's. Whatever limitations imposed by WEB's legal foundation, it had an opportunity (arguably responsibility) to provide soundly-based information, insights, and guidance for post-war transition yet, acting ad hoc, it failed.

At Broken Hill Pty Ltd (BHP), the WEB permitted women's employment, setting hours and conditions consistent with men doing substantially similar work. It applied standard provisions for juvenile females: in almost all WEB cases, rates for juvenile females of similar age doing work of a substantially similar nature were set at 100 per cent of the juvenile male rate, with no probationary period, applying the standard rule that no juvenile female could be employed at a rate below that fixed for seventeen-year-old males. For adult workers, however, a one month probationary period (calculated as twenty days paidwork if worked in aggregate with an employer covered by the decision, a week's employment being five or five-and-a-half days), with wages at 66.6 per cent of the adult male rate for substantially similar work. Thereafter, the rate was 90 per cent of the adult male rate for work substantially similar.

With rare exceptions, below-male-rate plus probation were standard WEB decisions, though none went below the 60 per cent limit set by the Act and Statutory Rules. Post-probation, the rate generally rose to 80 (as in the ***British Australasian Tobacco Company case***) or 90 (as in the ***Metal Trades (Broken Hill) case***) per cent of the male rate. In 1943, 'reception, sorting and assembling of crockery, glassware, cutlery and fancy goods and work ancillary thereto' provided a rare instance of 100 per cent. In ***In the Matter of an Application by Noyes Bros., Sydney***, workers gained 65 per cent for the first six weeks' probation, 80 per cent for the second six weeks, and thereafter 100 per cent of the male rate under the Industrial Arbitration Act 1940 (NSW) and the Warehouse Employees, other than Soft goods and Drug Warehouses (Cumberland and Northumberland) Award, for a five-day week. Yet why this lengthy sixty days aggregate delay pending the full amount? A sop to employers, WEB not wishing to impose immediate payment of men's wages to women, making 100 per cent more palatable? A nod to male workers' pre-eminence in the world of men's work? A statement to women workers, emphasising a fitting deference to male superiority as opposed to envisioning themselves unquestionably equal? Foster's persuasion in negotiating a union-employer result, union representatives seeking 100 per cent, the employer consistently against?

Postal workers gained a 100 per cent award, the employer admitting there was 'no reason to suppose females employed upon this class of work would not be equally as efficient and productive as males'. ***In the Matter of an Application by the Amalgamated Postal Workers' Union*** (***Postal Assistants case***), the Commonwealth Public Service Board (CPSB) employed women as 'Postal Assistants Grades 1 and 2', equally responsible with male officers for carrying 'stock advances of substantial values'. WEB said females needed time to 'acquire the efficiency and productivity of the average male', estimated as four weeks 'in a special training school', then a fortnight's practical experience in a post office. The Postmaster-General's Department (PMG) provided special recruit training for these positions, with no special rate. The measure of efficiency and productivity of the average male was made after a training period with practical experience in a post office. In omitting a probation requirement (not a WEB initiative), the Department made no special concession, simply restoring women to positions where fifty years before they had held employment, even (as postmistress) in the exalted position of postmaster.

Sometimes, health and safety featured. ***In the Matter of an Application by Apex Bedding & Wire Mattress Co. Pty. Ltd, Melbourne*** (***Bedding and Mattress case***), work was approved for women, but 'amenities' were substandard: '… no dining room nor rest room provided, seating accommodation inadequate, no lockers nor warm water for washing, change room primitive', with 'sanitary conveniences' location and access 'unsatisfactory'. The Department of Labour and National Service Industrial Welfare Division was called to enable employer compliance.

For some jobs, health and safety requirements played no part, whilst for others they did. Thus, the ***Postal Assistants case*** determinations on hours, conditions, and rates of pay for women in various positions (broadcasting mechanics, postal clerks, counter officers, and mechanics grade 1) in the PMG passed without any 'special conditions regarding safety, health and well-being'. However postal assistants were employed subject to provision that 'no female shall be required to make a greater lift than 35lb except that females under … eighteen years shall not be required to … lift

[more] than 25lb'. This applied in ***In the matter of an Application by the Victorian Railways Commissioners*** (***Car Cleaners and Porters case***), too.

In some cases, as in the ***Metal Trades (Broken Hill) case***, WEB said State Shops and Factories Acts provisions would apply 'unless inconsistent'. To safeguard women against employment where factory conditions and amenities were 'below standard', a 'liberty to apply' order in wide and general terms meant a dissatisfied party could return to the WEB at any time 'for adjustment, rectification or variation'. However, this provides no guidance for why women's wages were set below the male rate in so many jobs, little or no evidence of inability to perform equally well as the men. Despite assertions that women's 'physical limitations' underpinned the failure to grant women equal pay rates, health and safety requirements, including weight-lifting limitations, do not explain the WEB regime. Too many exceptions prevailed. Not only were juvenile wages almost invariably set equally for males and females although health requirements applied equally to juvenile and adult women workers, some (few) adult women were awarded wages at 100 per cent of the male rate, without consistency in which jobs.

In the Matter of an Application by the Commonwealth Public Service Board (***Mail Officers case***) this occurred, and ***In the Matter of an Application by The Alba Petroleum Co. of Aust. Pty. Ltd.*** (***Commercial Travellers case***) where WEB approved women filling jobs in Melbourne:

- arranging return of empty drums to ocean terminals;
- inspecting and arranging maintenance of the company's equipment—petrol pumps, tanks, oil equipment;
- checking consignment stocks;
- collecting moneys owing;
- selling lubricating oil …

The probationary period comprised two three-month terms, wages rising from £5 0s 9d per week to £5 12s 0d, then to 100 per cent of the rate prescribed under the Victorian Determination for Commercial Travellers for adult males doing work of a substantially similar nature. Yet women's employment was subject to 'safeguarding the safety, health and well-being of the said females'—by a weight limit requirement of 35lb.

Employed by Kenneth Wright Pty Ltd as motor car driver and collector and subject to the 35lb weight restriction, ***In the Matter of an Application by Ivy Moray*** Miss Moray's salary was set at 100 per cent of the prescribed adult male rate under the Carters and Drivers' Board of Victoria Determination. Similarly, when in ***In the Matter of an Application by Sims Cooper (Freezing Works) Pty. Ltd.***, Sims Cooper applied for permission to employ juvenile females in the meat trade:

- affixing pins and strings of tails of carcasses of lambs and mutton;
- affixing tickets and grade strings to carcasses of lambs and mutton;
- branding carcasses with the small stamp 'AUSTRALIA';
- packing smallgoods—that is, sweetbreads, brains, and c.

WEB granted the industry male basic wage. The 35lb limitation applied, and employment of an adult female supervisor was required.

'Lesser efficiency' or 'lesser productivity' provided no legitimate reason for setting women's rates lower than men's, either. Most cases involved no analysis at all. Regulations and Act provided WEB should undertake inspection or oversight of women at work. Rarely do cases disclose this was done. The few cases commenting substantively on 'efficiency' and 'productivity':

- asserted without supporting evidence, apparently based in prejudice or comfortable agreement between parties; or
- acknowledged women workers' efficiency and productivity exceeded men's in some categories of work, while in other categories in the same workplace didn't match it; or
- acknowledged that some women workers doing specified jobs exhibited more efficiency and productivity than men, whilst other women workers in the same workplace, doing the same jobs, exhibited less efficiency and productivity than the men; or
- gave a generalised acknowledgement of differences in efficiency and productivity existing between women doing the same male jobs.

The ***Metal Trades (Broken Hill) case*** is a fine example of the first two—assertions followed by confession of no inspection or no women observed in the work, then contentions that some women are better than the men, some worse. There was no gain in the employee organisation asserting the women were just as good as the male crane drivers—WEB set a flat rate, anyway—at 90 per cent of the male rate for all women workers (after probation). Contrarily, nothing was gained by assertions that women cleaners were not as productive as men cleaners in mixed cleaning teams—for the flat rate was applied without regard to that (purported) specifically-targeted lesser efficiency.

In ***In the Matter of Applications by the Federated Municipal and Shire Council Employees' Union, N.S.W. Branch (Sydney City Council case)***, when the Sydney City Council (SCC) employed women as:

- clerical assistants;
- office assistants, typists, and machine operators on work ordinarily performed by males;
- telephonists other than those employed on the main telephone switchboard;
- cashiers;
- one on work ordinarily performed by an assistant engineer,

documentary and oral evidence was given of their performance, tasks, and modifications claimed as made to the jobs because women now filled them. 'Exhibit "C"' was said to show workers performing part only of work done by the replaced male, many 'requiring a great deal more supervision than necessary for the male'. In some instances, 'an appreciable lessening of responsibility' was asserted; in others 'some slight changes in … work performed'.

This is a variation on the fourth approach, for it meant that in at least *some* cases the female worker was performing the *whole* of the work formerly done by the male she replaced; in *some* cases at least she did *not* require more supervision; there had been *no changes at all* in the nature of some work and in many cases no change in responsibility. The ruling was not that *no one* was entitled to 100 per cent—as it was clear that those performing to the same standard, in the same way, identical jobs of males ought to have been so entitled. Rather, WEB said: 'It is obvious they were *not all* entitled to 100 per cent …'. Then, from 'not all' entitled to 100 per cent, moves to *none* so entitled.

Yet when in 1943 Miss LJ Goldsmith's salary in her NSW Public Service Board (PSB) post arose ***In the Matter of an Application by the Public Service Board of New South Wales***, WEB said there was 'no reason' why she, a legal clerk determined as *more* efficient and productive than her predecessor, 'should not receive *as the Women's Employment Regulations intended* the 100 per cent of the rate of payment' the enlisted Mr White had received. Why then were crane drivers at Broken Hill and more efficient and productive women workers at the SCC not granted 100 per cent? Why was Miss Goldsmith not paid more? Why were supervisors granted 100 per cent in the ***Meat Trade case 1943***? Why was probation set in some instances and not others: ***Optical Munition … Technicians***; ***Crockery and Glassware case*** (1943) (probation included); ***Postal Assistants case*** (1943) (no probation); ***Broadcasting Control Booth Operators case*** (1943) (no probation).

As in the ***Sydney County Council case***, the WEB presumption was that women workers *not* be paid 100 per cent of the male rate. Neither Act nor Regulations required WEB to make assumptions against award of the full male rate. No legislative or jurisdictional requirement prevented women gaining 100 per cent as a few women did. The legislation could—even should—lead to that conclusion. The Women's Employment Act enjoined WEB to decide a rate it 'considers to be just and proper in all the circumstances' and 'as far as practicable' to assess it 'by reference to such factors as it thinks fit' including 'efficiency of females in performance of the work' and 'any other special factors which may be likely to affect the productivity of their work in relation to that of males'. That balancing these factors might result in findings that women in men's jobs did them better (as did Miss Goldsmith) was clearly envisaged, for the Schedule said no adult female employee should be paid less than 60 per cent *nor more than 100 per cent* of the payment to adult males doing work of a substantially similar nature. This confirms (if necessary) that no presumption against women being paid men's rates was authorised—just that whatever their performance they not be paid more.

Something other than efficiency, productivity, and so-called special requirements—including health measures, appears to underlie wartime determinations. For wage fixing, women's worth and women's work value were influenced by generalised views of women in paidwork and unpaidwork, and notions about men's rates being men's rates. Being a woman is central to wage-fixing, whether the Arbitration Court, CPSB, or WEB. Unsurprising, then, that industrial and wage-fixing experience of women in men's jobs, women's jobs, and new jobs parallels that of women who embraced voluntary work in the war effort, and those going on the land.

Knitting for Centipedes?

November 9, 1942. Three months after the Australian Women's Land Army (AWLA) is established, Edward Leonski, a US serviceman, is hanged for rape and murder of three women, the press dubbing the crimes as 'the brownout murders'. On 3 December, women aged eighteen to thirty are called up for war work. The ban on the Communist Party of Australia (CPA) is lifted. Chifley becomes minister for Post-War Reconstruction. Langley's ***The Pea Pickers*** is published. In 1943, Tennant's ***Ride on Stranger*** and 1944 Stead's ***For Love Alone*** appear. Gwen Meredith's long running ABC serial 'The Lawsons' begins, ending as 'Blue Hills' thirty-two years later, on 30 September 1976, upon its 5795th episode. Where did women as volunteers fit?

On 6 September 1941, the ***Australian Women's Weekly*** published a letter written by one of many women doing women's work outside the home—for no pay:

> Like all the other wives, sweethearts and mothers, I wanted to do something. There didn't seem to be much else to do but knit and knit and knit. Jim had to protest, 'after all dear, I'm not a centipede,' …

Women worked with Red Cross or established branches, fundraising through dances, balls, bridge-nights, paddy's markets, penny-sticker campaigns, talent contests, cake stalls, concerts and auctions, and direct requests through door-knocking and rattling tins on street corners. Women wrapped bandages, sewed pyjamas, threaded camouflage nets, visited the wounded recuperating in Australian hospitals, taking chocolates and cigarettes. Thousands of women volunteered for emergency duties, without thought—on either side—of payment. The federal government's Women's National Voluntary Register listed volunteers doing factory work, staffing canteens, or providing entertainment. Men *did* join the war effort in fund raising and other unpaidwork—such as coast watch—particularly through the Returned Services League (RSL), but with a significant difference. Men in voluntary unpaidwork were beyond active service age, disabled, or classed unfit for the services or paidwork. Women doing voluntary unpaidwork were—quite simply—women.

Women joining the AWLA stood at a crossover between paid and unpaidwork. Doing farm work—not domestic work in farmhouses—their work was classed as specifically 'war effort', replacing enlisted farmworkers. Receiving 'minimal pay' and initially none of the benefits of other services, they were given no uniforms, providing their own kit. Regulations ruled out domestic work as part of their (regular) work. Workers cleaned and tidied their own rooms, washed their own laundry, and made their own beds. Rules emphasised: '*If she volunteers to assist in any other household duties, this is her own concern*'. Yet AWLA workers were vulnerable to exploitation in ways women in auxiliary services were not. Whatever the regulations said, realistically, rules fixed by a distant authority could not (and did not) stand between Land Girls and their employers. If the woman of the house expected housework, the Land Girl complied—running the risk of losing her position or suffering poor treatment to hasten her going.

Wartime tensions existed between how women saw themselves as members of the regular forces—albeit auxiliary services rather than regular army, navy, or airforce. War conditions and service hierarchies precipitated women into seeing themselves as superior because they *were* associated with the regular services, distancing themselves from Land Girls, seen as lesser in status through lacking the cachet of such an association, and their position contrasting with unpaid volunteers. This compounded equal pay problems. So did tensions between women taking men's jobs or newly created jobs in factories, working alongside women remaining in women's jobs.

Muriel Heagney, like Kath Williams, advocated women's collegiality in the equal pay struggle as crucial. For women in the professions or heading occupational hierarchies to gain equal pay or wages akin to it whilst leaving other women behind, she saw as fatal. In April 1941, the CAEP approach, identical with ACTU policy, of 'rate for the job' resolved to gain equal pay for the sexes across the board. However, wartime developments tended to militate against joint or concerted action. Artificial divisions between the various groups—force auxiliaries, AWLA, unpaid volunteers, women doing women's jobs in munitions, women doing men's jobs in essential services, women doing men's or women's work in support services—emphasised difference rather than prompting unified action.

Some women saw the inequity of assessing wages differently, when working in jobs they had never done before, in factories where women on different pay rates did similar jobs—which women had always done. The tendency was for women on lower rates to compare and contrast their wages with wage rates of other *women*, rather than recognising men's wage and salary rates as the true measure of value of their paidwork. That women were willing voluntary workers exacerbated the problem: the federal government early saw advantage in recruiting women's voluntary services, however false the assertion that women were kept by their husbands, and (through wages policy) that wages of women in paidwork were irrelevant to the household's financial upkeep.

Populist campaigns condoned the contradiction. Posters cautioned against relaxing strict care of wartime secrets: 'Talking Causes Loss of Life—Do As Dad Does, Keep Mum', WEB's approach concurring. To qualify for the (male) basic wage, no man had to prove his efficiency or productivity. Being a (male) worker was enough. The (male) basic wage accrued to men in paidwork simply because they were men in paidwork.

After the War

On 3 July 1945, prime minister John Curtin dies. Elected ALP leader, on 13 July JB Chifley replaces caretaker FM Forde as prime minister. Late August, the Liberal Party of Australia is formally inaugurated, its first federal council meeting held in Sydney. That day, the Labor government increases taxes to cover increased social services. On 1 October, two months after the US drops atom bombs on Hiroshima and Nagasaki—6 and 9 August—general demobilisation begins.

At 1940s end, trade union women and women's groups re-grouped around equal pay. Women's role in reconstruction, demobilised women's claims, and women's industrial rights rode high on their agenda. This enthusiasm was not matched by federal or state governments, Arbitration Court, state tribunals, or ACTU.

On 4 August 1946, the Second Women's Charter Conference opened in Sydney. Street and UA led in lobbying governments and women's groups, nationally and internationally, to endorse the women's rights platform. With new impetus, following consultation between trade union representatives, Street was asked to call a meeting of unions having women members to initiate active campaigning for rate for the job and equal pay for the sexes immediately. On 20 November 1946, with Street chairing, the first meeting of what became the Trade Union Equal Pay Committee occurred at Federation Hall, Phillip Street, Sydney.

NSW Teachers' Federation, Federated Clerks' Union (FCU), Australian Association of Scientific Workers (AASW), Public Service Association (PSA), Ironworkers, Miscellaneous Workers, Hospital Employees, NSW Nurses Association, Hotel Club and Restaurant Workers, Sheet Metal Workers representatives, Actors Equity, and Australian Journalists' Association (AJA) observers attended. Ill health absented Lucy Woodcock; an apology came from the Council for Scientific and Industrial Research's Mr Cranwell. Unanimous resolutions called for all representatives to promote equal pay through their unions, union journals, and 'other suitable channels', the ACTU to include in its campaign 'the demand that [the] Basic wage apply to all workers, irrespective of sex' and that awards be varied by eliminating sex differences and establishing the 'rate for the job'; the Trade Union Equal Pay Committee to support the ACTU 'in all matters concerning employment of women'; that other unions with women members be invited to appoint committee representatives; and that 'possibilities of interstate organisation' be investigated.

Street and Woodcock were elected joint chairmen, Miss Nicholas (Clerks), Miss Davis (Hotel Club), Miss Newham (Hospital Employees), Mr Ockenden (Sheet Metal Workers), Miss Crane (PSA), and Mrs Hibberd (Association of Scientific Workers) committee members. The principal resolution, moved by Miss Mills (Clerks Union), seconded Miss Newham (Hospital Employees), supported a 40-hour week and improved basic wage, exhorting all workers to join 'rate for the job' and 'equal pay for the sexes' campaigns for immediate implementation, meanwhile retaining WEB and wartime regulation rates.

Federal minister for labour, Mr Holloway, confirmed the prime minister would 'interview [a] deputation'. Street, Woodcock, Nicholas, and Miss Eileen Powell (Actors Equity) were nominated, Powell withdrawing and Miss Barclay of the Teachers' Federation nominated by Miss H. Ross to stand in for Woodcock if necessary.

By 10 December, the delegation described prime minister Chifley's 'very courteous and cordial hearing' of their main points, namely that 'all forces within Australia' favoured equal pay, participation in the UN Charter and International Labour Organization (ILO) Conference indicated ALP approval, and the Liberal Party also approved. That trade unions with women members 'be permitted to approach [the Arbitration] Court for 100% of the male rate' met with advice that the ACTU requested 75 per cent. That a basic wage rise 'apply equally to men and women' met with Chifley's saying he could 'recognise A.C.T.U. requests' only. He conceded 'some merit in equal pay for the Public Service', though lifting the ban on married women's employment had not been raised previously. The deputation wanted a House of Representatives resolution but accepted the prime minister was 'to some extent correct' in saying this 'would not mean anything ...' The ACTU was his (and the government's) female minimum rates and basic wage guide, so resolutions must come through unions, to the ACTU and prime minister.

Street reported her follow-up with the ACTU's Mr Clary, asking that wage-pegging regulations be amended enabling unions to seek the 100 per cent rate for women. To the argument that it would 'give women and deny men the right of applying for further increases', transgressing the ACTU's 'equal rights for women and men' principle, Street responded that a woman from the equal pay campaign should sit on any committee investigating the basic wage. Clary's response was not recorded.

However, joining union women with women active in women's organisation equal pay campaigns, the Equal Pay Trade Union Equal Pay Committee had extraordinary success, exemplified by its original claims, the ACTU's original position, and the outcome. At the September 1947 ACTU Congress, Miss Nicholas put and had carried a resolution affirming the ACTU's commitment to campaigning for women's industrial claims and wage rates, including equal pay. Perth and Melbourne committees, and the NSW Trades and Labour Council (TLC), had convened a conference of all interested unions to discuss women's rates of pay and conditions, preceding the ACTU Congress.

The ACTU resolution differed from the Equal Pay Committee's July 1947 Program of Action, which included 'overhaul of protective legislation' to improve or eliminate 'obsolete provisions affecting women's employment'; repeal of all legislation and regulations limiting women's employment rights; full equality of the sexes for training and promotion rights 'in all spheres of employment', with equal pay retained for public service jobs: the Committee fixed on Chifley's acquiescence that equal pay for the Public Service had merit. However, the ACTU resolution changed 'equal pay for men and women' generally to 'the rate for the job'. This portended no retreat: rather, 'rate for the job' was used consistent with equal pay, fitting with industrial claims for rates and considered more precise so less subject to repudiation or misunderstanding. From late 1946, when Street reported upon her meeting with the ACTU's Clary, the Committee had not changed its demands. The ACTU (or at least Clary) had.

Nonetheless in 1948, claimants for equal pay and identical calculation of women and men's wages once again confronted legalism. On 22 July, the Arbitration Court determined women's minimum rates of pay. What did 'minimum rate of remuneration for adult females in an industry' mean? How could minimum rates—for women—be set? The Commonwealth Conciliation and Arbitration Act 1904–1947 section 13 said a commissioner lacked power to *make an order or award* altering *the minimum rate* of adult female remuneration in an industry. Sections 25 and 40 said the Arbitration Court could, 'to prevent or settle an industrial dispute', make such an order or award.

In the ***Female Minimum Rates Case 1948***, Foster held the Arbitration Court, not commissioners, could *alter* the minimum rate—but couldn't *create* any minimum rate, hence no point in ACTU or unions making claims for a universal minimum rate. If minimum rates for women existed federally, they were peculiar to each group of women under a federal award, the minimum being the lowest amount paid under that award. Foster said no universal minimum rate ever set meant no standard—women's position varying employment differing—meaning nothing the Arbitration Court could find to adjust as a standard minimum rate. Lacking power to create a minimum rate, it could not fix any minimum rate as a universal concept for women. Further, it was not for the Arbitration Court to decide whether it had power to compute a minimum rate as distinct from altering the amount of such rate.

Unions could have tried going to individual commissioners for creation of minimum rates for women in relevant industries or workplaces, then joining a collective application to alter minimum rates, hoping the Court would set a universal standard as a minimum wage. The ACTU could have done this, once minimum rates had been set by commissioners for women, trusting to the Court's seeing itself as able, in the circumstances, to set a universal minimum wage. Considering statements in the ***Female Minimum Rates Case 1948***, however, this was not assured.

Foster appeared to question whether principles could be set for a female minimum rate, in the name of altering the rate set in one industry, or for one group of women workers. This left women employees in limbo: no basic wage—only amounts set as a percentage of the male basic wage—nor any minimum wage. For that, they waited another twenty-five years. For a basic wage, they had to change the law, to at least qualify for a basic wage set in the Arbitration Court. In 1949, women secured a Conciliation and Arbitration Act amendment. Yet this did not get women equal pay.

The 1950s struggle was about to begin, to maintain the right to paidwork and gain equal payment for that work. Five years before the new decade began, Street and UA began campaigning for an Australian Women's Charter. This ambit claim aimed to secure women's rights in industry, the professions, and public life. Women took the struggle overseas. The Australian Women's Charter was adopted as a universal Women's Charter for women rights everywhere. Australian governments were pressured, too, by international perspectives entering the Australian debate.

Chapter 8, 'Alarums and Excursions—Out of Bounds in the International Arena', explores the peripatetic investigations, conferencing, and travelling of Australian women in the equal pay and women's rights struggle.

References

Cases—See Case List

All-Australian Trade Union Congress, ***ACTU Congress Papers—Minutes 7th Session***, NBAC/ANU, S784 Box 1, Melbourne, Victoria, 1947 (4 September 1947).

Zelda D'Aprano, ***Kath Williams***, Spinifex Press, Nth Melbourne, Victoria, 2001.

Val Buswell, 'Eighty-Eight's Fair Enough' in JA Scutt (ed.), ***Glorious Age—***, Artemis Publishing, Melbourne, Victoria, 1993, pp. 11–22.

Sara Buttsworth, 'Women Colouring the Wartime Landscape' in J. Gregory (ed.), ***On the Homefront***, UWA Press, Nedlands, WA, 1996, pp. 56–70.

Kath Dickson in Roberta Bonnin (ed), ***'Dazzling Prospects'—***, QUT, Brisbane, 1988.

Patricia T. Fallon, *So Hard the Conquering: A Life of Irene Longman*, MPhil. Thesis, Griffith University, Brisbane, QLD, 2002.

Muriel Heagney, *Equal Pay for the Sexes—*, June 1948, copy UM Archives.

Heagney, Muriel Agnes (1885–1974) Papers, Melbourne Trades Hall Council—Equal Pay Committee 1940–1967, Ref. 84/145, UM Archives, Melbourne, Victoria.

Claire McCuskey, 'Women in the Victorian Post Office' in M. Bevege, M. James and C. Shute (eds), ***Worth Her Salt***, Hale & Iremonger, Sydney, NSW, 1982, pp. 49–61.

Ada Norris, ***Champions of the Impossible***, Hawthorne Press, Melbourne, Victoria, 1978.

Edna Ryan and Anne Conlon, ***Gentle Invaders***, Nelson, Melbourne, 1975.

Jessie Street, ***Truth or Repose***, Australasian Book Society, Sydney, NSW, 1966.

MS 2683—Papers of Jessie Street (1889–1970)—1929–49, Folder 7, NLA, Canberra, ACT.

MS 2683—Papers of Jessie Street (1889–1970), 1927–68, Folder 25, NLA, Canberra, ACT.

Kylie Tennant, ***Ride on Stranger***, 1941, A&R Classics, 1991, Sydney, Australia.

Joyce Thomson, ***The WAAAF in Wartime Australia***, UM Press, Carlton, Victoria, 1991.

A. Wright, 'The *Australian Women's Weekly*: Depression and the War Years. Romance and Reality', ***Refractory Girl***, 1973 (Winter, 1973), p. 11.

CHAPTER 8

Alarums and Excursions: Out of Bounds in the International Arena

TRADE UNION EQUAL PAY COMMITTEE

166 Phillip Street,
SYDNEY, N.S.W.
28 June, 1948.

CIRCULAR
TO ALL TRADE UNIONS AND DELEGATES:

The next meeting of the Committee will be held on Tuesday, 6th July, 1948 at 8 p.m., Room 505, Fifth Floor, Federation House, 166 Phillip Street, Sydney …

The last meeting … discuss[ed] a comprehensive report, forwarded through the good offices of Mrs. Street, submitted by the World Federation of Trade Unions, dealing in detail with the conditions of women workers throughout the world … [C]orrespondence from the W.F.T.U. to the United Nations, is attached. The full report is available for perusal should any union or delegate so desire, and application should be made to the Secretary …

Yours faithfully,

D. Nicholas
ACTING SECRETARY.

J. A. Scutt, *Wage Rage for Equal Pay*,
https://doi.org/10.1007/978-3-031-42178-5_8

> Alice Henry is a woman whose vigorous writings and stirring lectures on the manifold phases of industrial economics have made her conspicuous as an international character.
>
> ***St Louis Star***
> St Louis, Missouri, USA
> September 1912

From 120 Paine Avenue, New Rochelle, her home in New York, Carrie Chapman Catt writes to Mrs Ashby, International Woman Suffrage Alliance (IWSA) member and colleague in the women's rights struggle. The date? 1 August 1945. The subject? The Australian Women's Charter.

Street is the Charter's major proponent. In August, she is to be in London, following her attendance as Australia's delegate at the San Francisco Conference of the United Nations (UN).

'I am anxious that you should give her a good chance to see and talk with you privately and at length', writes Chapman Catt. 'Australian women have a dream that they should be able to get women all over the world to endorse their Charter and try to get it adopted in their respective lands … Please read the Australian Charter carefully'.

Women and Australian Women— The Internationalists

Thirty years earlier, Rose Schneiderman of New York, NY, calls for international cooperation, too. In the April 1915 issue of ***Life and Labour***, journal of the US Women's Trade Union League (WTUL) edited by Alice Henry with Stella Miles Franklin, she promotes women's economic rights, noting suffragists 'have blazed the way for recognition of women's economic value', unenforceable without 'political freedom backed by economic organization'. Advocating equal pay and women's industrial rights, Schneiderman affirms the broader dimensions of women's struggle across international boundaries.

Across centuries and across decades, Schneiderman, Chapman Catt, and Street find support. In London in 1840, the International Convention on Slavery sees Elizabeth Cady Stanton and Lucretia Mott meet British and Empire women. Banned from being delegates, speaking rights denied them, from behind a curtain in the gallery, affronted and outraged, they listen to the debate.

The snub causes international rumblings. US women plan their first women's conference for Seneca Falls, 1848. Women's wage justice is high on the agenda, as almost one hundred years later in Street's Australian Women's Charter. Chapman Catt proposes incorporating the Seneca Falls Declaration into the World Women's Charter as Chapter one. The Australian Women's Charter would follow immediately as Chapter two.

Fifty years after women meet at Seneca Falls, and almost fifty before debates about the Women's Charter, ***Life and Labor*** publishes articles promoting internationalist labour movement demands and women's industrial struggle. Moving from Melbourne to Chicago in January 1906, as first editor Alice Henry introduces journalistic expertise and respect. She brings support of confederates and mentors, Catherine Helen Spence amongst them, carrying letters of introduction from Spence to Susan B. Anthony, Jane Addams, and Anna Garlin Spencer, knowing from direct experience, working internationally from the nineteenth into the twentieth century, that the women's rights movement necessarily crosses national boundaries. So does Franklin, joining Henry in October that year, via England, as ***Life and Labor***'s joint editor.

Over decades of absence from Australia, Henry maintains her links with women at home. Corresponding with Muriel Heagney, in 1935 Henry's words are the forward to ***Are Men Taking Women's Jobs?*** Now, she writes, 'the national conscience has ... been touched regarding women ...' The 'whole field of industry' may be affected, with men, too, 'sharing in the benefits'.

Travellers Transcending Class

Nor is travel restricted to women sporting middle-class backgrounds. In 1956, Kath Williams responds with alacrity to suggestions she sail to Europe, boarding a train for Budapest, Hungary, for the World Conference of Women Workers, under World Federation of Trade Unions (WFTU) and Women's International Democratic Federation (WIDF) auspices. Williams' pamphlet, ***Equality will be Won***, describes her observer experience. Getting there, tacking on two weeks in the Soviet Union, a month in China, is eased by Union of Australian Women (UAW) fundraising. Joint action between UAW and trade union women raises sufficient for Williams' fare and modest living allowance: she cannot be left stranded, or starving.

Williams and her fellow delegates ensure equal pay conference resolutions are emphatic. International Labour Organization (ILO) Convention No. 100 must be ratified and 'accompanied by its practical implementation'. 'Energetic and persevering action' is demanded, all workers and women's organisations 'in the broadest possible unity necessary to win the most important demands, application of … "Equal Pay for Equal Work" for all [women worker] categories, including young girls, … a guaranteed minimum wage equal for both men and women', and associated industrial claims. Individual women are not let off the hook. They must join their trade unions in 'drawing up programs of demands … applicable to each country's conditions', being more active in 'struggles of the working-class for increased wages, trade union rights and democratic liberties'.

In Budapest, Williams joins hands with Cecilia Shelley, arrived from Perth, Esther Taylor and Flo Davis, from Sydney. State chauvinism creeps in as, joining a welcoming gesture for the working women meeting in Budapest, the photograph sent home displays a message writ large on a pillowcase: 'Melbourne women greet the World Congress of Working Women'. Some thirty years earlier, Heagney preceded them, setting off by sea for Hawaii, presenting a paper, 'The Trade Union Woman', to the First Pan-Pacific Women's Conference held in Honolulu from 9 to 19 August 1928.

This international perspective, traversing generations, class, status, and nation-state lines, boosts morale across boundaries. Women exchange information and tactics. Australian initiatives spread through international forums, building support and accelerating demands. Working across the globe, women press them on local and national governments, and international agencies. Initiatives and strategies devised by women oceans away are adopted at union and women's conferences, and pursued by government deputations. Australian women present international statistics in industrial commission, wages board and Arbitration Court submissions. From at least the nineteenth century, women propound international arguments to state and federal governments.

Equal opportunity, like equal pay, is promoted locally, nationally, and internationally. Men have no monopoly on jobs. Women have rights to enter men's occupations and do their jobs just as well. These themes are universal.

International Leverage—Public Service, Equal Pay

In 1897, a year after Sydney's National Council of Women (NCW) is formed on Margaret Windeyer's initiative, just back from Chicago and Toronto, Melbourne newspaper the ***Leader*** devotes two columns to a London ***Daily Telegraph*** report on women's 'invasion' of city offices. Republished as 'Chivalry Died 65 Years Ago' in Perth's ***Weekend News*** of

22 April 1961, the article asserts women have an economic advantage 'in nine cases out of ten', living with parents, 'drinking very little, never smoking' and, 'accepting a relatively small wage', are pushing male clerks aside.

Claiming women 'meet favour from employers' through punctuality, making no 'excuses to go out or take unfair advantage of the lunch interval', being 'quiet and obedient' in the office, neither ***Leader*** nor ***Daily Telegraph*** acknowledges that exploitation, not advantage, lies in the economic bargain between women office workers and their employers. What's more, the 'lady clerk' wears neat and sensible dress, 'not only because her employers would deprecate anything tawdry or showy', but because office attendance is necessary 'in all weathers' and, having 'superior strength and activity', men 'always secure the inside place on the omnibus when it rains'. Women might complain, but men 'might reply that chivalry towards ... their rivals is hardly to be expected!'

Protesting women's entitlement to both equal pay and good manners, NCW contacts British Civil Service women, exchanging notes. Over decades, correspondence and in-person discussions accompany Australian women's travels to London, New York, Eastern Europe, the Continent, and Pacific. In the 1930s, women's organisations correspond with US and European counterparts, exchanging arguments to counter media attacks. When newspaper articles demand women take wage cuts or exit jobs for men, the United Associations (UA) contacts the Government Workers' Council of Washington, DC and National Women's Party of America. On 17 October 1934 ***Nation***, published in New York, bureaux in Budapest, London, and Southern Africa, contributors including Albert Einstein, Martin Luther King Jnr, Gore Vidal, and Jean Paul Sartre, runs an article by Alma Lutz. Challenging an earlier story, in 'Women and Wages' she argues against moves toward a minimum wage for women and children. Women, she says, are demeaned by classification with children, and minimum rates restrict women's opportunities for higher wages.

In November 1934 ***Current History*** publishes Helena Hill Reed's 'The New Deal that Women Want'. Castigating minimum wages and laws dismissing married women, Reed declares Roosevelt's New Deal as 'not the one women want'. Under Roosevelt's plan, women must 'fight against determined assaults on their right to earn a living, not only [for rights to fair] industrial conditions'. The Economy Act 1932 (USA) marital status clause, albeit written in sex-equality terms, targets married women 'for the unemployment heap', simply because they've taken marriage vows. Not for married men: they're deemed worthy of higher pay, promotion, and even high office, simply by marriage. Reed adapted the adage 'Marriage vows maketh the man'—but destroy a woman's career chances, even her right (if it could even be called a right) to work—for an income. Under the New Deal, for a couple in government service, the wife is first to be dismissed. Despite protests, the marital status clause becomes permanent. Australia, the UK, Aotearoa/New Zealand, and Canada follow suit.

As for the US women's minimum wage, it creates a barrier to women's employment, just as protective legislation denied women jobs. Yet men and boys take jobs from women. In dining-rooms, hotel and café kitchens, men and boys replace women 'at an alarming rate', despite preference for women in that work. Reed argues in favour of minimum wages for all adult workers.

Through correspondence with US organisations, Street incorporates Lutz's arguments into Australian debates. When Reed's article is republished in pamphlet form, Street obtains a copy. Alongside Heagney, whose 1935 monograph ***Are Women Taking Men's Jobs*** figures highly, Street, Mavis Woodford, and fellow activists organise joint UA and NSW Teachers Federation public meetings and government delegations, bolstering overseas work with their own arguments. David Jones' reception hall, fifth floor, on Sydney's Market and Elizabeth Streets corner, hosts meetings decrying laws banning married women from paidwork or scheduling them as first to go.

Equal Pay and International Advocacy

During the war years, the Council of Action for Equal Pay (CAEP) relied heavily upon international action in advocating 'rate for the job'. Women entering men's industries, doing men's work, should gain men's rates, and women's work in women's industries should be recognised as equally productive as men's, rates set by job, not sex. In deploring the Women's Employment Board (WEB)'s performance in rarely setting women's rates at 100 per cent of the male rate, in ***Are Women Paid Men's Rates?*** CAEP quoted statistics, constitutions, and equal pay laws or regulations from Soviet Russia, Mexico, Brazil, Colombia, Peru, China, the US, and Great Britain, and cited women's appointment to Women's Consultative Committees in the US and Britain. The Australian government was chastised for failing to extend the rate for the job to women in essential and wartime industries. In castigating WEB, the British option was declared superior.

Under WEB guidelines, organisations 'are confronted with … almost insuperable obstacles' said the CAEP, the onus lying principally on respondent unions, not employer applicants, to demonstrate the rate should be higher. Further, unions faced WEB assumptions that women in industry are less efficient than men. During parliamentary debate on WEB, Labour's Arthur Calwell read CAEP's telegram to ministers and members, advocating substitution of 'the prevailing male rate for the job instead of 60 to 100 per cent' as specified in the Bill plus a clause making employers bear the burden of proof where claiming women workers' ineptitude for the work, based on recommendations of Lloyd George's British War Cabinet Committee on Women in Industry appointed in 1919.

When Jean Arnot marshalled her arguments for 'Employment of Women in the Civil Service', an August 1945 address to the NSW regional Institute of Public Affairs (IPA) group, she incorporated Australian, British, and US claims back to nineteenth century international support for equal pay. It was mistaken, she said, to believe women played a 'very unimportant part in the community's economic life' until the Second World War. Women worked 'from earliest times in every known economic system', essential for the economy and women's maintenance, happiness, and well-being. Child-bearing, 'tying women to the home', meant women's 'contribution to the wealth of the community often was made from [there]', prompting contentions that women's work is 'of lesser value and so worthless, ... very often unpaid altogether'. She referred to British Civil Service supervisory posts, created in 1880 'at rather better rates of pay' than clerical positions previously denoted for women, with promotions 'remarkedly improving' women's health. When advised, Postmaster-General Henry Fawcett responded: 'Because they are able to dine more frequently'.

From 1853, US Congress set a uniform federal clerks pay scale yet, Arnot advised her audience, simultaneously established a separate class for women, restricted to subordinate clerical work or temporary clerking posts. In 1870, equal pay for equal work was legislated, but department heads applied it—according to whim. Jobs women traditionally held were deemed not designated for equal pay, nor reclassified to secure women a living wage. The Classification Act 1923 (USA) stipulated equal compensation for equal work irrespective of sex was mandatory but did not achieve equal pay: women remained confined to women's work, classed as unequal to men's.

As for the UK, the ***British Royal Commission into the Civil Service 1929–1931*** recommended no differentiation by sex in civil service remuneration rates; all appointments open to men and women 'by the same methods and on the same terms'; and training and experience opportunities equally available. Albeit British and US women lacked equal pay, at least laws existed to 'stamp out the injustice', Arnot observed. In Australia, 'despite repeated election promises', no federal, state, Labor, or Liberal government has 'despite repeated election promises' grasped courage sufficient to 'face up to the issue' through a scheme to ensure payment of work for its worth, no matter who performs it, addressing responsibility for dependants separately. If governments led, she concluded, private industry would follow quickly.

Arnot's incorporation of overseas policies and laws reflects Australian women's internationalism. Twenty years after Arnot's speech, on 12 July 1962 the ***Sydney Morning Herald*** publishes Doris Osborne's letter 'Women Migrants And Equal Pay'. Active in the NSW Teachers' Federation and Australian Federation of Business and Professional Women (AFBPW), Osborne uses media reports of a speech by Alexander Downer, immigration minister, to rebuke government's equal pay failures. Recently returned from Paris, he 'expects an influx of French women into Australia', yet did he explain 'most would be paid 75 per cent of the male rate only?' The 1946 and 1958 French Constitutions proclaim equal rights for men and women, in 1953 France ratified ILO Equal Remuneration Convention No. 100, and the 1960 UN publication ***Equal Pay for Equal Work*** says the French Public Service applies it. The Treaty of Rome Article 119 pledges European Economic Community (EEC) nations to implementing equal pay by 1964. What are French women to think of Australia? Unless the government acts, they'll leave for Europe the instant Australian women's wages are advised them.

Earlier, Heagney applied foreign government statistics and policies to equal pay. Working with the 1919 Piddington Royal Commission into the Basic Wage reinforced her industrial credentials. Her labour movement and women's organisation authority ultimately spanned more than five decades. Representing the Federated Clerks' Union (FCU), she was a CAEP founding member with Australian Women's Movement (AWM)'s Mrs M. Beirnes, the Feminist Club's Grace L. Scobie and Ruby Rich, UA's Street, Miss HF Bennett of the Women's Union of Service (WUS), Public Service Association (PSA)'s Arnot and Charles Drummond, Mr S. Ford of the Food Preservers' Union (FPU), Mr J. McDowell for the State Unemployed Council (SUC), Mr WE Rhodes, Mr BH McClure, Mr AE Evers and John Hughes for the FCU, and the Australian Railways Union (ARU)'s Eileen Powell. Representing the Australian labour movement overseas, as Secretary of the Australian Relief Fund for Stricken Europe, in 1921–1923 Heagney travelled to Russia. In Geneva, she worked for the ILO; some twenty years later she was first woman appointed by the Australian government as unofficial adviser to the Australian Delegation to the 1941 ILO conference in the USA. As a federal ALP and Victorian trades union delegate, in 1925 she attended the first British Commonwealth Labor Conference in London. In 1928 she and Powell represented the Victorian ALP, Victorian and NSW trade unions at the first Pan-Pacific Women's Conference in Honolulu, Rischbieth leading the delegation.

CAEP pamphlets and papers—drafting and production falling to Heagney—quote Russian and US legislation and regulations on pay rates, exhorting readers to demand emulation of those countries' standards and conditions as more advanced. In her ***Clothing Trades case 1927*** submission, she quoted Fredric Engels, calling for Arbitration Court affirmation of a woman's contribution to production as equally valuable as a man's, and to recognise equal pay as women's right to complete economic independence. In the ***Basic Wage Inquiry 1949–1950***, she relied on US equal pay investigations, alongside the Piddington Royal Commission findings.

Following Heagney's lead, in the ***Wages and Hours Case 1953***, AFBPW and the Australian Federation of Women Voters (AFWV) submission put international obligations and world trends to the fore. After addressing the economic consequences of women as cheap labour, under 'International Obligations', AFWV argued that Australia's commitment as a UN and ILO member was jeopardised by a 'widening of the gap between male and female wage rates' with 'consequent lowering of the status of women'.

Foregrounding world trends, AFBPW ended by asserting the 'social and political implications of a reduced female basic wage—at national and international levels—as well as its immediate economic effects' must be decisive in the Court's deliberations. US and Canadian advances, including states and provinces. By April 1952, AFBPW's Sydney Club had a copy of Ontario's Female Employees Fair Remuneration Act 1951 and Saskatchewan's adoption of equal remuneration for work of equal value, with New Jersey following twelve other US states enacting equal pay laws in 1952. AFBPW cited its membership of the International Federation of Business and Professional Women (IFBPW), a non-government organisation with UN EcoSoC consultative status, noted ILO Convention No. 100, then quoted the UN Charter's Preamble and Universal Declaration of Human Rights, Article 23(a): 'Everyone, without any discrimination, has the right to equal pay for equal work'. The Arbitration Court should, said AFBPW, comply with these international instruments, effecting equal pay through the ***Wages and Hours Case 1953***.

Equal Pay and Equal Opportunity

Overseas advances spurred campaigning beyond ***Wage Case*** interventions. Believing the story behind the Ontario Female Employees Fair Remuneration Act 1951 'should inspire and strengthen campaigns in all countries', Business and Professional Women (BPW) Sydney Club disseminated it widely. Australian women found parallels, for when a BPW Canada Equal Pay Committee deputation waited upon the Ontario premier 'they met with the familiar excuse': the principle approved of, 'but … impracticable at the present time'. Fighting back, Miss Margaret Hyndman, KC, 'refuted all arguments with great skill …' Finally, 'formal opposition crumpled, Miss Hyndman being asked to prepare a suggested Bill'. Copies of the Hyndman draft went with alacrity from Ontario's Club president to all House of Commons members. At the Female Employees Fair Remuneration Bill's first reading, members received a copy of the Declaration of Human Rights, relevant sections marked in red ink.

Women used these tactics when lobbying successive Australian governments for an office equivalent to the Canadian Women's Bureau and US Department of Labour Women's Bureau. On 5 June 1920, congressional legislation established the US Bureau, headed by a woman appointed by the president, setting standards and policies 'promoting wage-earning women's welfare' focused on working conditions, efficiency, and women's opportunities 'for profitable employment'. From 1920 onwards, Heagney, Greenwood, Street, Arnot, Leonora Polkinghorne—Women's Charter Movement (WCM) vice-president—received a wide range of Women's Bureau publications, including investigations into women's wages.

Persistence won out when in 1963 the Department of Labour and National Service established a Women's Section. On 10 February 1964, Alison Stephen of Melbourne head office wrote to Miss EM Ross, WA Council for Equal Pay and Opportunity honorary secretary, saying she had, in 1963, met in Canada with Miss Royce, Women's Bureau director, the 'purpose and operation' of the Women's Section being akin to the Canadian Bureau. The Women's Section would 'expand', 'consolidate and coordinate' work already underway on economic and social problems facing women in employment, she said. This was a direct result of women's organisations' connections.

In 1952 Dorothy Hewett Flood attended a Vienna conference, fellow UAW members including Vena Barton (later UAW's first national president) and Mary Lewis, Hotel, Club and Restaurant Employees' Union (HCREU) delegate and Young Women's Christian Association (YWCA) member. Flood (Hewett) 'was struck by the many attractive magazines and publications produced by leftwing magazines and newspapers throughout the world (particularly the French) …' Writing articles and reports to Australia with 'nowhere to publish them', once home she persuaded UAW to produce a national magazine—'no small undertaking, financially and otherwise'. ***Our Women*** was launched with Flood as editor and Noreen Hewitt from ***Common Cause*** her offsider.

Our Women's first issue publicised employers' push through the Arbitration Court for a wages reduction. Cooperation between women's organisations, despite disparate class origins, meant a full page was allotted to Caroline Scrimgeour, UA president, attacking the employers' case for reduction of the male:female differential from 75 to 60 per cent. Equal pay, she wrote, 'is undoubtedly the major bone of contention and most glaring example of inequality of status in present day Australia'.

Women shared morale boosting, tactics, and information from abroad to defeat opponents. Debate raged in newspapers, news and feature articles, and 'Letters to the Editor'. On 25 April 1960, Leila S. Roberts led an equal pay deputation to WA premier David Brand, pressing for equal pay in the state public service. N. Sampson, Teachers' Union president, presented the teachers' case. Mr AJ Fraser, past Civil Service Association (CSA) president, addressed economic aspects. Roberts reviewed WA's existing situation, comparing it with conditions interstate and overseas. The following day the ***West Australian*** and ***Daily News*** reported on the deputation's 'comprehensive written submission, including information … from other countries'. Lodging the submission with State Archives, Roberts stressed 'it [was] a key document … in the social history of WA'.

In the 1960s, both local WA papers—***Daily News*** and ***West Australian***—played a key role. On Wednesday 1 June 1960, the ***Daily News*** ran the headline 'Bessie Rischbieth calls for international perspective'. Rischbeith was in Persia, representing AFWV at an International Alliance of Women (IAW) conference. 'Holding on to our small local views' was retrograde, 'learning to have world-wide ideas' essential. Otherwise 'Eastern women … will outstrip European women'. Internationalism would 'gradually … equalise women's position in the world'.

Equal Pay and International Standards

Earlier, on 6 April 1960, the ***West Australian*** published Greenwood's article 'Economics of Equal Pay', urging attention to international standards and outcomes. From an equal pay rally at Perth Town Hall, she quoted US Manpower Council chairman, Mr Erwin Cabham, saying women were an essential part of 'an economic revolution erupting at the turn of the century and … altering the economic scene ever since'. To Mr N Dufty's contention that equal pay would 'put women out of jobs' Greenwood lobbed Mr Cabham's words: 'If all the women of America walked off their jobs tomorrow it would be a catastrophe of incredible magnitude'. Industrialisation and specialisation made women indispensable 'because of their skill and dexterity in machine processes' and in the professions. Sex differences were subordinate to efficiency, employers everywhere giving preference to those providing 'best value for his money'. Women would not be replaced by men; rather, the opposite.

Rejoinder was rapid. On 9 April 1960 the ***West Australian*** published 'Campaign for Equal Pay for Women'. Avoiding international data, Dufty cited 'four main arguments against equal pay'—women are 'lower in output, higher in labour turnover and absenteeism, and not potential executives'. Re-emphasising that raising female wages would promote male employment to women's detriment and, generating increased men's wages, would cause inflation, technical changes making women able to do men's work meant women's pay would rise, anyway, he said.

Roberts' reply, 'Women's Claim for Equal Pay', appeared on 14 April. Countries with equal pay suffer 'neither inflation nor detriment', she wrote, nor did women 'have a lower output than men'. In some jobs, 'women's output is even greater'. High labour turnover, rather than an argument against equal pay, is one for employing women in suitable jobs. Employed 'on vital work' during wartime, 'women's absenteeism [was] no higher than men's'. The real equal pay barrier is 'custom and prejudice' which, if 'allowed to impede progress … would [see us] still living in the Stone Age'.

Perhaps distance meant WA women led in using overseas connections. Singapore, Malaya, and Djakarta were closer than Sydney and Melbourne. Canberra could seem as remote as New York. Geography meant Australian women, particularly in the West, were acutely aware of developments elsewhere and the importance of being leaders and representatives for Australia in international forums. In 1922, when prime minister William Morris

Hughes visited Perth following League of Nations negotiations, a Women's Service Guilds (WSG) and AFWV deputation met him, led by Miss Ada Bromham and Mrs Mary (Molly) Ann Driver, appealing for at least one woman in any federal government delegation attending the third League of Nations General Assembly. Despite prime ministerial assurances of support and a promise the request would go to cabinet, time passed without confirmation or appointment.

Visiting Melbourne, where federal Parliament was sitting, Rischbieth sent in her card to the five WA MPs. When they asked 'what they could do' for her, 'I wish to see the Prime Minister', she replied. Eventually 'received by the Prime Minister ... Mr Hughes greeted me with "Madam, do you realize you have called a Prime Minister out of Parliament at a quarter of an hour's notice?"' 'Yes, Mr Hughes, but I have come nearly two thousand miles, and we hardly ever see a Prime Minister'. Hughes relayed cabinet's refusal, 'writing on an official envelope ... the names of those ministers not in favour of including a woman in the ... delegation', saying: 'You must see these men'. WA's MPs would arrange it. Next day, at a roundtable conference of five or six cabinet ministers at Parliament House, Littleton Groom presiding, Rischbieth outlined 'why a woman representing Australia', to be 'assured, after speaking for some time, that a decision would be made ...' Next day, the prime minister advised: 'You can go on your way to Sydney rejoicing. The Government has agreed to include a woman in the Delegation'.

Margaret Dale, of NSW AFWV, went to the League of Nations Assembly in 1922, the first Australian woman with federal government accreditation. In 1923, Melbourne University's Jessie Webb followed. In 1935, Rischbeith was appointed an alternate delegate to the League of Nations then, seven years later, Heagney—then FCU (NSW Branch) councillor and CAEP honorary secretary—went to the 1941 US ILO conference, a federal government appointment as unofficial Australian delegation advisor, the first woman in the role. Her presence had a profound effect. Albert E. Monk, AWU delegate, put women's work and equal pay firmly into play by resolution showing clear signs of Heagney's fine hand. Acknowledging economic injustice and detrimental impact of unequal wages, it concluded conference should 'consider ... male occupational standard rates for the job, irrespective of sex [as] the basic principle ...' with immediate steps to eliminate sex differentials in wage standards. Further, the ILO should 'resume ... investigation of women's work, [formulating] plans to combat ... exploitation of this pool of efficient and underpaid labor', circulating information to every government, requesting 'legislative and administrative action' to eliminate sex differentials.

When Street attended at UN conferences from the late 1940s into the 1950s, when women are said to have been so invisible, uninformed, inactive in women's and world affairs, she followed in these women's footsteps. When 1970s women learned of Street's presence, women setting the precedent decades before went unnoticed. As Rischbieth said thirty years earlier, sending Australian women as official delegates to League of Nations conferences was 'the first act in the drama of the new world pattern as affecting' Australian women. She was right.

In 1975, an Australian government delegation was off to the International Women's Year (IWY) UN Conference in Mexico City. Elizabeth Reid, prime minister Whitlam's women's advisor, headed the delegation with Margaret Whitlam. In 1980, the International Decade for Women, prime minister Malcolm Fraser sent a delegation to Copenhagen headed by RJ Ellicott, home affairs and women's affairs minister, with Beryl Beaurepaire, National Women's Advisory Council (NWAC) convenor. They signed the UN Convention on the Elimination of All Forms of Discrimination (CEDAW), 'condemn[ing] discrimination against women in all its forms', including economics, equal pay and opportunity. UN conferences in Nairobi, Kenya, and Beijing, China, saw women appointed government delegates.

Informal links between and amongst women and women's organisations internationally continued, connections developing over decades between women and in their women's organisation roles. These formal and informal relationships had not needed UN or government fostering, nor government imprimatur. Yet developments through UN initiatives influenced women outside government and government delegations, too. Simultaneously with official UN conferences, grassroots women and women's organisations maintained international links or freshly developed them. In the 1970s, new women's rights organisations sprang up. Together or competing for funds, sponsorship, and support, they launched into non-government internationalism, attending parallel conferences held simultaneously with UN official conferences.

Women went to Mexico, Copenhagen, Nairobi, and Beijing, scrabbling together what money they could, saving for months, borrowing—and getting there. Kate MacNeill, working on submissions the reconstituted CAEP made to the Australian Industrial Relations Commission (AIRC) in the ***Nurses Comparable Worth case 1985–1986***, gained Victorian Women's Trust (VWT) funding for the 1985 Nairobi conference.

Just as women's international activism was significant in women's suffrage struggle, it was key in the equal pay campaign. Although her connection with Russia and the Cold War ended major support for Jessie Street's Australian Women's Charter, her work in widely circulating it and gaining trade union endorsement profited decades later. In the 1970s the Women's Charter advanced by union women gained Australian Council of Trade Unions (ACTU) support. The 1970s Australian Women's Charter shared a history in its namesake, and Street's internationalism ensured the idea did not die, progressing under later women's guidance, of a new time.

Across the world, UK women used the 1941 ILO New York Heagney-Monk resolution to promote equal pay in wartime industries. Ann Loughlin, national Tailors' and Garment Workers' Union (TGWU) organiser, chairing the British Trade Union Council (BTUC) Women's Advisory Committee, acknowledged its impact on the 'rate for the job' in a number of industries and services, 'regardless of the workers' sex, and sometimes regardless of the workers' age ...' Loughlin paid tribute to Australia, noting Monk's support for universal application of equal pay.

Jennie Duncan, in 'The Rate for the Job', London ***Post*** article of 11 January 1941, referenced minister for labor and national services, Mr Ernest Bevin, in his support for 'the rate for the job', declaring to a gathering of businesswomen that people should 'be wise enough not to allow Parliament to escape that principle in future'. Duncan said the need for struggle 'should not deter us, but inspire us', as 'the ruling class' must be pressed into 'worthwhile reform' through 'courage, initiative and imagination', eschewing 'cautiousness and timidity'.

Courage, initiative, and imagination shone in international perspectives infusing Australia's equal pay struggle. Highlighting internationalism, in 1941 Heagney wrote of CAEP's 'historic' formation in 1937—fifty-three organisations and many eminent citizens represented—officers formally elected on 14 July. This, she laconically yet triumphantly noted was the anniversary 'of the Fall of the Bastille, surely a most appropriate date to commence an onslaught on one of the very deeply entrenched injustices of our day and generation'. A decade later, into the 1950s, women wanting wage justice were backed by international statistics, laws, and policies, well-primed for another round of struggle. A clear vision of wage (in)justice and industrial legitimacy, women faced the 1950s—a decade ripe with potential. No dead Women's

Movement, nor women moribund, Chap. 9, 'A Decade of Darkness—or into the Light? The Struggles and Success of the 1950s Woman' traces 1950s women's campaigning throughout the decade following the Second World War, that led into the 1960s.

References

Cases—See Case List

Jean Arnot, *Employment of Women* ..., Presentation to IPA, Sydney, NSW, ***Public Administration***, vol. v, no. 8 (new series), 1945 (December 1945), p. 365 and 'Official Organ of the Public Service Association of NSW', ***Red Tape***, Sydney, NSW, 1945 (25 September 1945).

Jean F. Arnot Papers 1916–1969 ML MSS 3147, ADD On 2070/4, Mitchell Library, Sydney, NSW.

Margaret Bevege, Margaret James and Carmel Shute (eds), ***Worth Her Salt ...***, Hale & Iremonger, Sydney, NSW, 1982.

Val Buswell and Chris Rapp, ***Milestones—Equal Pay—Probate***, AFBPW, Sydney, NSW, 1988.

CAEP/AEU, ***Are Women Paid Men's Rates***, CAEP/AEU, Sydney, NSW, 1942.

Barbara Curthoys and Audrey McDonald, ***More Than a Hat and Glove Brigade***, UAW, Sydney, NSW, 1996.

Muriel Heagney, ***Are Women Taking Men's Jobs?*** Hilton & Veitch, Melbourne, Victoria, 1935.

Alice Henry, 'Foreword' in Heagney, ***Are Woman Taking Men's Jobs?*** 1935.

Beverley Kingston, 'Yours Very Truly, Marion Phillips', *Labour History—Women at Work*, vol 29, 1975, pp. 123–131.

Marie Muir, ***Interview***, Sydney, NSW, 1993 (12 November 1993).

Marion Phillips, 'Appeal to the Women of England', ***Labour Woman***, London, UK, 1919 (September 1919).

Elizabeth Reid, 'The Child of Our Movement: A Movement of Women' in JA Scutt (ed.), ***Different Lives*** -, Penguin, Ringwood, Victoria, 1987, pp. 8–20.

Bessie Rischbieth, ***March of Australian Women***, Paterson Brokensha, Perth, WA, 1964.

Caroline Scrimgeour, ***Our Women***, UAW, Sydney, NSW; copy ***Jean F. Arnot Papers 1916–1969 ML MSS 3147, ADD On 2070/4***, Mitchell Library, Sydney, NSW.

Kate White, 'Bessie Rischbieth, Jessie Street ...' in M. Bevege, M. James and C. Shute (eds), ***Worth Her Salt ...***, 1982, pp. 319–29.

CHAPTER 9

A Decade of Darkness—Or Into the Light? The Struggles and Successes of 1950s Women

C100—Equal Remuneration Convention, 1951 (No. 100)
The General Conference of the International Labour Organisation … having met in its Thirty-fourth Session on 6 June 1951, …

Adopts … the Equal Remuneration Convention, 1951.

Article 1

For … this Convention—

(a) The term ***remuneration*** includes the ordinary, basic or minimum wage or salary and any additional emoluments whatsoever payable directly or indirectly, … by the employer to the worker and arising out of the worker's employment.
(b) The term ***equal remuneration for men and women workers for work of equal value*** refers to rates of remuneration established without discrimination based on sex.

'Equal pay for men and women … It's the talk of the town in London and Sydney, Canberra, Melbourne, and Brisbane'. The 23 January 1958 ***Sydney Morning Herald*** highlights a British equal pay puzzle. A civil servant 'changed her sex'—becoming entitled to a man's salary. So how could unequal pay be rationalised by 'ineptitude' or women's 'lack of

J. A. Scutt, *Wage Rage for Equal Pay*,
https://doi.org/10.1007/978-3-031-42178-5_9

ability' to work with a man's 'skill and fortitude'? 'Never' has unequal pay 'appeared so ludicrous or indefensible'.

Australian Federation of University Women (AFUW) president Dr Lorna Lloyd-Green tells the ***Herald*** that women should 'tough it out', boycotting jobs if denied the wage when doing equal work. Mrs EW Potter and Gladys Hain of Melbourne and Brisbane Federation of Australian Associations of Housewives (FAAH) branches weigh in. Many women would be jobless 'if they boycotted lower-paid jobs', says Mrs Potter. Mrs Hain says equal pay 'is only fair', but gaining it 'is another matter altogether'. Jean F. Arnot and Elsa Brooks of Sydney and Brisbane Business and Professional Women (BPW) clubs focus on women's need for a regular pay packet. 'A girl has to eat', says Brooks. 'She must have a job before she can start fighting for the same pay as men'. Arnot observes that boycotting 'may sound all right' but need precludes it. A woman 'can't just refuse a job' paying her an Arbitration Court wage. NSW Labour Council Equal Pay Committee's Mavis Woodford seconds Arnot but sees both sides. Women's 'economic position makes accepting prevailing conditions imperative', but a financially independent woman who can 'refuse a job [through] pay inequality … strikes a definite blow in the right direction'. For FAAH, Hain concludes there 'must be a revolution'—a peaceful one—before equal pay arrives.

Talk of revolution contradicts conventional views. Traditional and mainstream feminist history depicts the 1950s as a decade of retreat, returning soldiers pushing women back into domesticity, women absorbing a barrage of government propaganda, docilely submitting to their destined role at hearth and home, wartime work an aberration. By this account, women were not only removed from wage-earning, but removed themselves from political activism, public protest, and agitation. Yet just as history has overlooked women at other times, the 1950s as a decade of women's silence, voicing no demands, failing to speak out or in speaking out not being heard, is false. The equal pay struggle says otherwise.

The Female Basic Wage

The ***Basic Wage Inquiry 1949–1950*** began the decade. The lead up is crucial. The ***Basic Wage Inquiry 1940*** saw no female basic wage claim advanced by any of the seventy unions. The Arbitration Court ruled women's wages irrelevant. United Associations (UA)'s barrister Nerida Cohen was denied leave. UA's submissions went unheard. This time, the Australian Council of Trade Unions (ACTU) lodged an equal pay claim. Heagney was an expert union witness. The Australian Federaton of Business and

Professional Women (AFBPW) and National Council of Women (NCW) intervened.

Historically, the Arbitration Court had denied itself power to set a woman's basic wage, determining women's pay as a percentage of the male basic wage. At AFBPW's 2 October 1948 annual conference in Sydney, a resolution supported a Conciliation and Arbitration Act 1901–1947 (Cth) section 25 amendment, whereby the Arbitration Court could fix a minimum basic wage for all adult employees, male and female, under federal awards. Like other equal pay proponents, AFBPW also wanted the Court, in fixing the minimum basic wage, to disregard dependants. An Employees' Family Allowances Act should replace the Child Endowment Act 1941–1945 (Cth), covering dependent wives, children, and other prescribed dependants. Then, wage fixing would drop assumptions of men as husbands, fathers, and breadwinners, women lacking dependants and family financial obligations. The living or family wage abolished, equal pay would succeed.

On 29 October 1949, the Conciliation and Arbitration Act amendment passed, incorporating a basic wage definition: it should be 'just and reasonable' for an adult male or female 'without regard to any circumstance pertaining to the work upon which, or industry in which, [s/he] is employed ...' This was a landmark achievement. When women's groups had lobbied federal government for equal pay, the response was 'go to the Conciliation and Arbitration Court'. Yet amending section 25 was as far as government would go. No Employees' Family Allowances Act eventuated. This left the Court stuck with the obsolete notion that men alone have dependants and rejecting a universal minimum or basic wage. Still, the Court was empowered unequivocally to determine a male *and* a female basic wage on identical principles, assessed as just and reasonable. When prime minister Robert Menzies told AFBPW by letter of 26 November 1949: 'A decision ... rests with the Court', the ***Basic Wage Case 1949–1950*** provided the opportunity.

The ACTU began with claims for a basic wage set by actual living costs and equal pay, wanting the claims heard together, with the Court investigating actual living costs of a family of five—man, wife, and three dependent children. The male and female basic wages should be based on a standard of living 'related to socially necessary requirements' and 'the nation's productive capacity', adjusted by productive capacity increases. The adult basic wage should be £10 0s 0d weekly for capital cities, with higher or lower amounts according to actual cost of living differences in those cities. Country-city differentials should be discontinued, one basic wage for city and country. Annual wage adjustments would be calculated by Australian industry's productive capacity increase, quarterly adjustments, and additional earnings covering costs over and above the standard.

Increased industry capacity was a key equal pay argument, meaning a 'greatly increased and progressively increasing standard of living as a national minimum' was possible, with no material difference between the states. Workers, 'irrespective of sex', should 'be paid at the same rate', essential to preventing 'unfair discrimination by employers as between male and female workers'.

In proposing workers be paid regardless of sex, logic rested with the ACTU. If wages calculated for all male workers treated all men as if exercising financial responsibility for dependants they had or would have, whatever the facts, why shouldn't the female basic wage apply similarly? Some men had dependants and supported them; some men did not and would not; some women were financially responsible for dependants; some were not. Why should women miss out, particularly those with needs based in real family circumstances?

However, in framing the claim for a basic wage in terms of children and *wives*, the ACTU undercut its own argument, conjuring the notion that *male* responsibilities were real and really the issue in basic wage setting. Feeding into existing assumptions and prejudices about men's role as breadwinner and head of household, employers used this to influence the decision, pressing competing arguments. First, justification for computing the basic wage on a family unit of five was lacking, because average male wage and salary earners (earning the basic wage, or above) supported no family of that size. Secondly, basic wage fixation should take account not only of productive capacity, but also:

- actual production and return from production;
- proportion of production going to wage and salary earners otherwise than as basic wage;
- proportion of production owed to other sections of the community;
- calls of public finance; and
- national welfare.

On equal pay, employers contested identical basic rates for males and females, saying that if basic wages were fixed by socially necessary requirements, child endowment payments should be factored in. They warned that claims for a general increase were ill-timed, the basic wage being 'as high as, or higher than, the economy can sustain'. The age-old argument—the nation cannot afford equal pay and neither can we—was back.

Victoria, SA, and WA intervened, opposing equal pay. The Railways Commissioner and SA government contended the basic wage for adult female employees and juvenile employees (male and female) should 'continue [at] much the same proportion' to the adult male basic wage. Victoria argued, bluntly, 'the same basic wage should not be fixed for men and women'. WA's attorney-general said computing the basic wage on family units and their living costs should factor in 'all additions and concessions available … social service benefits or otherwise', and the claim for basic wage additions proportionate to productive capacity should be rejected. Further, equal pay 'would be inequitable', and the Court should hear all ACTU claims before deciding on any basic wage alteration. WA's aim seems to have been delaying flow-on effect to the states if the Court decided 'for' equal pay, women's public sector employment being significant.

Evidence and 'Equal Pay'—*Basic Wage Inquiry 1949–1950*

Kelly, Foster, and Dunphy (chief justice and justices) resisted the ACTU's desire to retain, as the basic wage:

- calculation by 'needs' of a 'family man' (plus prosperity loading);
- including dependants' support, whether a man had dependants or not.

saying this set the basic wage too high. It interpreted the ACTU's claim not for all workers to receive the same basic wage but as importing differential pay levels based on male and female workers' actual financial responsibilities.

Kelly considered no distinction should apply to a male worker as married or unmarried, childless though married, or with fewer or more than three dependent children. This did not mean, however, that wage fixing should ignore family responsibilities. An employer 'should not [be concerning] himself with the man's domestic affairs or … choose men [without] children or few children in preference to men [with] many'. Therefore, 'some reasonable allowance for family life and children' (meaning 'men's family life and children') should apply.

Dunphy's rationale referenced its traditional base more starkly. Impossible to reconcile any claim for equal male and female basic wages with the ACTU's 'emphatic demand' that the male basic wage should remain based on worker and family requirements, he said. Laws and 'social demands' might explain an unmarried man's family wage, but women could 'hardly expect wage recognition' for responsibilities they 'can never incur'.

Ultimately Foster and Dunphy supported a basic wage increase. Kelly disagreed. All opposed equal pay. Dunphy and Foster saying parties and interveners provided no evidence for setting a female basic wage rate. As a female basic wage must be set, they decided on a male-female basic wage relativity of 75 per cent. Kelly stuck with 54 per cent of the adult male basic wage, as without 'specific evidence' on the 'just and reasonable' standard and costs of adult female employees, nothing warranted a change from the already existing 'proper' basis for adult female employees' basic wage element.

Yet substantial evidence was brought by unions and interveners AFBPW and NCW.

Bidding for equal pay with a scheme for dependants' financial support, AFBPW's Miss Audrey Turner presented basic male and female workers' living cost, including cost-of-living tables. Expert witness Heagney, giving evidence of British and US equal pay investigations, was acknowledged by the Court through her work with the 1919 Piddington Royal Commission into wages and equal pay (***Basic Wage Inquiry 1919–1920***). Harold Souter was 'female basic wage' unions advocate until the Court dismissed the Amalgamated Engineering Union (AEU) from proceedings: AEU industrial action during the case led to employers demanding its expulsion. Souter's disappearance left the ACTU's equal pay claim incomplete. Nonetheless, before going, Souter called twenty-one witnesses, all women, eliciting evidence of their incomes and actual costs of living. He also relied on evidence from departmental managers of two large department stores, and the recent English Royal Commission into equal pay, drawing substantially on the minority reports.

The Court unanimously rejected the evidence. Dunphy said the female witnesses' oral testimony dictated the 'immediately obvious' conclusion that 'without exception' their standards failed to conform 'to those accepted as applicable to the fictional male basic wage earner'. With witnesses all expressing 'conflicting views on matters of quality and quantity' of essential needs, it wouldn't have helped 'in the slightest' in a simple inquiry of female basic wage workers' needs, 'let alone [on] wage equality with the male', so 'without further comment' he 'rejected' equal pay.

Kelly said the ACTU submission that identical rates were 'necessary to prevent unfair discrimination by employers' between male and female workers lacked substance: 'no evidence' of unfair discrimination. His comment on women's lower wages was limited to the possible impact on men: '... when employment is ... endangered or reduced ... retention or employment of females (on lower wages ...) disadvantages the male employees'. Expressing nothing about impact on women denied pay rates equivalent to male colleagues, perhaps he chose to ignore it.

Foster's opinion was scathing. In an excoriating attack upon AFBPW's Turner, asserting she lacked understanding of the Court's task and even of her own statistics, he declared 'flaws' in her evidence and understanding meant he 'rejected her testimony entirely'. More mildly, but equally averse, he discounted Heagney, whilst dismissing as 'irrelevant' all Souter's witnesses. International claims, trends, or enquiries were snubbed. Heagney's US citations and Souter's English Royal Commission references Foster 'found ... entirely unsatisfactory': providing 'very little guidance upon any basis', the Court could base no 'needs' judgement on it.

As none of the women witnesses—from Melbourne, Sydney, and Adelaide—earned the female minimum rate, averaging annually—Melbourne £337 0s 0d, Adelaide £332 0s 0d, and Sydney £378 0s 0d, Foster objected to *all* the material. For him, the basic rate appropriate for women in 1949 was £190 0s 0d—54 per cent of the male basic wage. Yet asserting the evidence lacked assistance because none earned the basic wage was odd, for (apart from the purpose being to illustrate the inadequacy of women's unequal wage) simultaneously the Court acknowledged the extreme difficulty of locating a worker on the male basic wage, because of add-ons—loadings and margins. Foster's own shortcomings included no appreciation of women's expenditure for a reasonable living standard—food, clothing, rent, board, or other housing expenses; fares to and from work; health costs—dental, medical, chemist; holidays, sport, and recreation; reading material; union dues; sundry items and wages tax. As well, he failed to grasp the concept—women are entitled to the rate for the job—the same rate as men for the work they do. Nor did he grasp that if (a matter of contention) needs was the basis of wage calculation, no good reason lay in saying men *need* more money than women to live.

Further, the male basic wage then being £380 0s 90d, Souter's evidence showed that women's needs, as witnesses outlined, at least equated approximately the male basic wage. It showed women in 'superior' jobs earning below the male basic wage (paid to male labourers) and stretching earnings to accommodate their basic needs or going without. How did women survive? At minimum the evidence showed that women on £190 0s 0d, or 54 per cent of the male basic wage, would struggle to live, and payment of less than approximately £380 0s 0d annually left a woman unable to cover her needs.

Foster's criticism lay not only with the women workers' evidence. Repudiating the Myer Emporium managers, he discounted the former Foy and Gibson Ltd manager whose association with the textile industry continued. Advanced as experts on female basic wage workers' needs, the character, durability, and cost of clothing required, notwithstanding (as Foster acknowledged) their experience being 'greater than [his] in these matters', this didn't 'justify Mr Souter's claim that they should be regarded as experts'.

So, evidence deemed irrelevant, suspect, or misconstrued meant the Court must find another female basic wage principle. The ACTU proposed three alternatives: equality with the adult male basic wage; if rejected, then the highest industry can sustain; or the needs of an arbitrarily chosen female worker. The Court unanimously rejected them. A claim 'based on the present male basic wage' was unsustainable, said Foster, because:

- the male basic wage was a social wage for a man, his wife and family;
- it was socially preferable to pay men a higher wage due to 'social obligations to fiancée, wife and family';
- single women might want a higher wage, but on marriage at about 25 years their interest changed, wanting husbands bringing home the largest possible pay envelope';
- 'productivity, efficiency, needs, and responsibilities, etc., of females were substantially less than … males in this community';
- no claim was made for a unit wage upon which to base equality of wages, a 'failure easily understood as [possibly resulting] in a lower male basic wage', though this 'might furnish an acceptable and perhaps desirable basis for equality of reward but [requiring legislative action] is beyond the Court's power'; and
- redistributing 'the wage fund' meant young unmarried women's 'very substantial increased spending power', disturbing the economy

to disadvantage the married basic wage worker and his wife and family, and probably the whole community.

Furthermore, the wage fund being the notional percentage of national dividend absorbed or represented by wages and salaries, increasing female rates would (if the wage fund existed) be at the expense of other wages and salaries (men's wages and salaries), lowering wages for men, basic wage, and margins. This meant, said Foster a 'socially undesirable', 'complete wage structure recasting' would be required to effect equal pay, and equal pay based on the male basic wage would 'put intolerable strain on the economy'.

With every equal pay claim, this refrain—by employers or bench—was reiterated. But the essential evasion in Foster's judgment came in refusing to accept any of the evidence. 'If', he said, 'as I do, we reject the claim for equality and find no means of basing an award upon the reasonable needs of the humblest female worker, then upon what?'

What, indeed?

Judicial 'Wisdom', Women's Words

Between 8 and 11 June 1949, the International Federation of Business and Professional Women (IFBPW) (representing seventeen nations, including Australia) met in Helsinki. Reaffirming the 'rate for the job' in the Universal Declaration of Human Rights, article 2, IFBPW recommended action to advance (a) adoption of that principle, rather than rate based on sex; (b) women's technical training and guidance, access to jobs and promotion procedures, equal to men; and (c) eliminate legal or customary restrictions on women workers' pay. Turner incorporated this resolution into her ***Basic Wage Case 1949–1950*** submission, adding: 'Everyone, without any discrimination, has the right to equal pay for equal work'. The submission's 'first Request to the Court' for equal pay on that principle and 'in the public interest' was to:

(a) compute the male basic wage on an adult's needs without dependants;
(b) fix it at £6 12s 0d per week, being a basic wage rate for adult males as at 1 December 1949, and considered sufficient to meet an adult male or female's needs without dependants;
(c) fix it for adult females and adult males at the same figure, that is, £6 12s 0d per week.

Two tables covered existing cost of living, for the average unskilled male adult worker without dependants and the female adult worker without dependants. This relatively modest claim set the unskilled adult male workers level at £343 4s 0d, the same for women. Itemised needs (over two years) included, for men, overcoat and raincoat, two suits, six shirts, three sports shirts and two sports coats, plus trousers, khaki shorts, pullovers and ties, fifteen pairs of socks, handkerchiefs, hats, shoes and slippers, underwear—cotton singlets and underpants, woollen singlets and underpants, dressing gown, braces and belt, three pairs of cotton and woollen pyjamas. This list included laundry and £71 16s 0d for recreational purposes, totalling £15 0s 0d for annual holiday and transport and £56 16s 0d for weekend sport and midweek recreation including fares. For women, recreation totalled £54 0s 0d only, £15 0s 0d for annual holiday and transport, plus £39 0s 0d for weekend sport and midweek recreation, including fares.

Women's necessary clothing included overcoat and raincoat, umbrella and suit, good winter frock, woollen skirt, blouses, party frock, good summer frock, cotton frocks, summer skirt and blouses, light coat, and eight pairs of stockings annually. Women were expected to make clothing for themselves: £2 0s 0d covered 'wool for (knitting) jumper'. Gloves, handkerchiefs, handbags, swimsuit, hats, shoes, and slippers completed outer garments. Six vests (summer and winter), eight panties and four brassieres, two corsets, two slips, and six nighties or pyjamas (three winter, three summer), plus 'dressing gowns or housecoats' completed 'underwear'. Essential sanitary wear came to £4 10s 0d. Hairdressing, medical expenses, newspapers, cosmetics, toothpaste and brushes, toilet soap and powder, plus union dues and wages tax were listed. Allotted £5 0s 0d for dry cleaning, for their own laundry women required washing soap, Lux, and Blue—. For men, clothes upkeep, drycleaning, pressing, and laundry amounted to £15 8s 0d.

Neither diligence, nor modest calculations of living expenses, nor clarity in addressing dependants' cost paid off. The ***Basic Wage Inquiry 1949–1950*** canvassed the social security debate—child endowment, family allowance, and the basic wage, but despite Turner's submissions gave no indication that the Court read or heard them or even processed their essence. Community responsibility as part of good government for children's upkeep and wellbeing was Women's Movement policy for decades, Street and UA in the forefront, challenging wages policy and Arbitration Court decisions since ***Harvester***. Turner calculated cost of a higher level of benefits through government social services as against increased cost to industry of raising women's wages to the basic male rate, then deducted the amount by which wage levels would be reduced if the dependants' calculation went from wages to government.

In 1949, families with more than one dependent child received child endowment. Under the AFBPW scheme, removal of a basic wage component for support of dependent children was compensated by increased child endowment. Payment would apply to first and each child thereafter, rather than birth of a second dependent child. Extrapolating from census figures, Turner calculated total child endowment as £43,148,802, comprising £19,425,518 (amount for 1947–1948), plus £23,723,284 (for all first children). If the male basic wage formula continued providing for 'mythical children of single men', cost of children (real and mythical) would be £88,876,632. Turner's submissions provided a national saving. The Court lost sight of this.

On dependent wives, Turner's submission calculated 'probably one dependent wife in each of the ... 586,415 families with two or more children and approximately 326,019 in one-child families' (census figures), totalling 912,434 wives. Removing wives as dependants from male basic wage calculations, a government allowances scheme at £1 0s 0d weekly amounted to £47,446,568 per annum. Estimating 147,245 wives without children under 16 years, if included in the dependant wives category, added £7,656,740. AFBPW's proposal of £1 0s 0d plus 10/- per child was 'far from adequate' but accommodated the economy's 'current state', contemplating an increase upon 'the national economy stabilising' so 'able to carry the higher cost'. AFBPW's proposal was premised on the principle that continuing to calculate into the male wage 'real and mythical wives' militated against equal pay (women lacking real or mythical wives).

Foster's denunciation of Turner's evidence meant excluding her social services submissions—at least by acknowledgement. Yet employers saw them, and the debate, as germane. Even with his scathing comments, Foster incorporated government responsibility for dependants into his considerations, but his focus on *male* workers and a man's real or theoretical (mythical) responsibilities and his inability to appreciate women's paid-work and rights to a living wage, trapped him.

For social services payments, Foster noted their origin in payroll tax: theoretically, employers made social service payments, but price increases covered payroll tax, so consumers (including a large working-class sector) effectively paid for child endowment and social security generally.

Employers argued social services should be considered in setting wages, reducing the employers' burden. Unsurprisingly—unlike AFBPW, their aim was reducing wages, not promoting equal pay. The states as employers endorsed their approach.

Employers (including the states) weren't asking for wage reduction factored by the benefits, Foster observed, but for benefits to be 'considered and estimated before awarding any increase'. This he rejected: government policy shouldn't be allowed to disturb the Court's judgment in settling wage disputes, 'any more than … defence, conscription, tariffs, international relationships policy', all affecting wages in some way. Social benefits were for governments and legislation, not the Court.

Foster acknowledged social services 're-distribute Australian income after it is earned', but not that setting a male basic wage incorporating real and mythical dependants re-distributed income—inequitably —after it was earned. Women workers, contributing equally to the national economy through their labour, had their rightful payment for that labour taken before it reached their pay packets. If a set portion of Gross National Product (GNP) was allocated to wages, men gained their portion plus a portion properly due to women in paidwork. Alternatively, if the male basic wage was a fair measure of labour, employers benefitted by keeping the portion of wages properly due to their female workers: the difference between female and male basic wage.

In understanding that all taxpayers contributed to child endowment, 'the working-class [thus] providing their own endowment', and concluding it 'all comes out of industry … [from] which all wealth is poured …', Foster also saw 'industry' as not meaning 'corporations, factories or businesses in the sense of employers alone', including employees' industry, too. Yet ironically, in recognising employees' input to industry, Foster—and the Court as a whole—was unable to see (or admit) that employees included women, too. Alternatively, the Court collectively, Foster individually, disregarded that employees included women working equally hard, expending energy, talents, abilities, and capabilities in jobs they did or were allowed to enter.

For the Women's Movement, key to national economic policy lay recognition through adequate benefits of community responsibility for children's upkeep and wellbeing. For women's organisations, the family wage wrongly absolved government from social security provision and wealth redistribution. By supporting wages calculated according to private (and public) obligations of an individual for upkeep of his (sic) children (mythical or real), but not extending this to women, the Court ignored women's personal and human rights to a living wage and private (and public) obligations toward their children. It simultaneously ignored the public obligation for wellbeing and upkeep of children (and dependants—ill, infirm, aged, or with disabilities) lying with national government.

The Rate for the Job

In the immediate sense, the ***Basic Wage Inquiry 1949–1950*** was a setback. Equal pay remained elusive. The 54 to 75 per cent increase was awarded by Foster and Dunphy explicitly saying women were generally being paid that, anyway. State tribunals used the decision to confirm their own prejudices. Worse, it was used to minimise women's claims not only to men's basic wage, but to margins. The Court did not restrict margins over and above the basic wage to the 75 per cent differential. Nor did the ruling require employers to *limit* women's wages to 75 per cent. Nothing prevented employers from paying women *more* than 75 per cent of the basic wage. But state tribunals interpreted the decision restrictively. On 19 September 1951, in the ***Clerks and Telephonists case*** the SA Industrial Court held, citing the ***Basic Wage Inquiry 1949–1950***, that the margin for 'females performing substantially similar work' to males should not exceed 75 per cent of the male margin'. A differential between women's and men's basic wages was applied as a mandatory requirement that the *total* wage earned by women should be 25 per cent less than men's.

But court decisions have disparate impacts and multiple meanings. The ***Basic Wage Inquiry 1949–1950*** gave impetus to campaigns. Government ministers' claim they lacked power to act on equal pay was exposed as subterfuge. Now, with the Arbitration Court revealed as a limited and inadequate forum, women used the case to bolster demands for executive and legislative action. The 'rate for the job' became the universal equal pay slogan, the means to achieve it. If the Court refused one rate (for male and female), denying equal pay, governments must act. Public servants could gain equal pay through executive action—no legislation required. For non-government workers, laws requiring a general, not sex specific, rate for the job would force employers and tribunals to concede women's equal remuneration entitlement. Both avenues were pursued.

In 1938, the SA Women's Non-party Political Association, in a pamphlet ***The Case for Family Endowment***, attacked the standard 'needs' approach excluding women from equal pay, paying men as if their needs were greater, despite cost of living affecting both equally. A wage 'determined by NEED would surely see it costs a woman just as much to live as a man—she eats a little less certainly, but … probably evens up on clothes'. Further, '"Equal Pay for Equal Work" is an impossibility [for the working woman], while a man is paid enough for four or five people and she for one only …'.

Ten years later, on 13 February 1948, Street writes to Lean Spiegel, World Federation of Trade Unions (WFTU) consultant, that replacing 'equal pay for equal work' with 'rate for the job' is vital, for the former encouraged dividing women and men between jobs. So long as women workers 'are segregated from men into separate occupations or separate Trade Unions, by special conditions of work, or because they are married or have families, or for any other reasons', equal pay is impossible. Advocating women workers be treated 'first … as workers', she pressed for 'no discriminations of any kind …' Equal pay and equal opportunity being inextricably linked, if women and men accessed all trades, professions, and work equally, rate for the job would bring equal pay. If rate for the job was the men's rate, then that being the measure of job-value and work required for it, women should, and on this argument would, be paid that rate.

In 1949, equal pay topped the NSW Teachers Federation annual conference agenda. A resolution affirmed existing equal pay policy, expressing it as rate for the job and calling on state and federal governments to introduce legislation providing women teachers with identical pay rates as men in comparable positions. ***Education*** on 13 April 1951 reported deputations and representations to the premier, minister for education and Lower House members, plus joint action with public service organisations, including the federal and state Public and Essential Services Council. When the ACTU rallied in the Sydney Domain, Mr SP Lewis, NSW Teachers Federation president, called on all working people to unite for equal pay. At the state election, Teachers Federation members forwarded letters to candidates and sitting members, asking them to pledge support for equal pay. Favourable replies came from several candidates. Cabinet members' reply: for the minister for education, not for them.

In December 1950, the Teachers Federation's thirty-second annual conference included equal pay in its next year's action plan—alongside peace, civil liberties, students' allowances, salaries, school conditions, and recruitment and training. A 1950 ***Annual Report*** addendum called on government and Public Service Board to 'increase salaries paid to women teachers by an amount at least equal to' the difference between the former fifty-four and new seventy-five per cent women's to men's basic wage' ratio. During the 1951 federal election, ***Education*** reported leaders of all political parties receiving a questionnaire raising 'matters of vital concern to the people of the Commonwealth', including:

> [Will] your party lead … in granting equal pay … in all [Commonwealth Government] departments …, including educational agencies, and recommend this be followed by all State Governments?

Detecting negative rumblings, the executive warned members not to 'undermine the Federation equal pay campaign'. The phrase 'equal pay for equal work' causing confusion, the ***Annual Report*** confirmed its 'long ago abandonment', replaced by 'equal pay and employment rights for the sexes' and 'rate for the job'.

In WA, Rischbieth said the Australian Federation of Women Voters (AFWV) had by 1952 framed equal pay, plus family allowances, as 'a standard rate for the job, irrespective of sex of the worker'. In 1955, ***The Case for Equal Pay and Equal Opportunity for Men and Women Teachers***, a NSW Teachers Federation pamphlet, explained 'Rate for the Job' as occupation, training, and importance of a job, not family responsibilities, 'determin[ing] salary differentiation between different occupations'. Referencing a medical practitioner without dependants, his salary was set 'because of his training and quality of work he performs', his income exceeding that of a carpenter with five dependants. The doctor's salary 'would be no greater if he had five dependants, that of the carpenter no less if he had none', and employers don't ask 'the number of children … when determining pay envelope contents …'.

Economic factors had embedded women's lack of equal pay in the system, ran the argument. Because in the past (particularly in older occupations) women's labour 'was relatively less scarce' than men's, women received lower pay, said ***The Case for Equal Pay …*** Similarly because it was 'wasteful' for women to learn a skilled trade. Women trained to be teachers, however as one of the older occupations, convention influenced salaries, entrenching different male/female rates of pay. In occupations more recently opened to women—instancing pharmacy and the department of transport—'no difference [lay] in rates of pay for men and women doing the same job'. The teaching service should follow that example.

Education of 12 November 1952 foreshadowed the argument. E. Thorpe taught in the early 1920s, a widow with sole support of four children, working in a city school's boys' department. For eighteen years, with identical responsibilities, she worked equally efficiently as the men alongside, yet received four-fifths of the men's pay, 'regardless of work done or responsibilities shouldered'. Expressing amazement 'at the narrow-minded attitude of some men in the Service towards equal pay', she vowed no woman should relinquish the struggle 'till justice is done and women receive the rate for the job'.

Thorpe may have had the Public Service Board (PSB) in mind. In the same ***Education*** issue, the Board argued it could not be 'first' to recognise equal pay. In the following issue, AJS found the Board's argument fallacious. It would follow, not lead, if adopting the rate for the job:

> One rate is paid to women and men journalists, musicians, chemists, hospital technicians, university lecturers, some shop assistants, government employees such as transport workers, policewomen, radio announcers, orchestra members, members of parliament. Teachers in Denmark have received the same rate for over 50 years …

AJS said 'drudgery of household chores' was often the woman teacher's lot. She (as her male counterparts) 'would appreciate someone to do her housework … and the money to pay her'.

The Federation did not meekly accept the Board's rejection. ***Education*** of 15 November 1952 reported Federal Council resolving that the general secretary communicate with NSW premier, opposition leader, and Country Party leader, requesting they appear before the Federation's annual conference stating their preparedness—or not—to 'bring down [equal pay] legislation' endorsing 'rate for the job'. Motion moved Mrs J. Johnston, seconded Miss J. Dransfield: no politician accepted the challenge. The Board did not relent.

By mid-1950s, the entire union movement adopted 'rate for the job'. On 31 October 1954, Mr R. King, MLC, ACTU senior vice-president and NSW Labor Council secretary, observed one principle only 'on which it is possible to work, i.e., the rate for the job', workers married or single. Echoing women's organisations, he condemned the argument for family responsibilities and needs in wage fixing as illogical: 'many men have [no] family responsibilities', men responsible for children 'do not remain so permanently'. Assuming three children born within six years as the average, the entire length of family dependency 'is … about 21 years'.

Therefore, 'for about half the 45 years a man expects to earn a full adult wage, he has no dependent children to support'.

King quoted 1947 census figures showing 69.4 per cent of the male population over nineteen years as married, 36.5 per cent over nineteen with dependent children, and 85.6 per cent of men with dependent children between twenty-five and forty-nine. Of the total female population, 2.6 per cent over nineteen years had dependent children. No figures listed dependants other than children, but the Teachers Federation noted women teachers, more than any other section of the community, took responsibility for aged parents, invalid relatives and younger family members' education. This 'made a mockery' of basic wage fixation, for besides ignoring women's responsibilities, the childless widower 'gets a full male rate while the widow with dependent children receives only the female rate'.

The ***Basic Wage and Standard Hours Case 1952–1953***, employers wanting a reduction in male and female basic wages, unions seeking a rise, gave further impetus to the rate for the job. In what appeared to be a new departure, the Arbitration Court asserted that the federal basic wage had never been determined on needs. Since ***Awards of the Court Binding Upon the Australian Railways Union and Others (Basic Wage and Wage Reduction Inquiry 1930–1931)***, said the Court, capacity of industry to pay was the determinative basic wage fixing factor.

True, in response to the Great Depression, the ***Basic Wage and Wage Reduction Inquiry 1930–1931*** adopted capacity of industry to pay. Yet the Court's assertion flew in the face of ***Harvester*** since 1907, confirmed in the ***Basic Wage Inquiry 1949–1950***. History was rewritten. Passing over Higgins' rationale that needs—mythical or real—of a man-keeping-wife-and-family was what determined a 'proper' or 'fair and reasonable' wage in a 'civilised' community, the Court said ***Harvester*** did not establish 'a living wage designed to provide a particular standard of living to a typical family group …' The 7/- a day as 'fair and reasonable' was restricted to 'reputable employers in sheltered industries'.

'Sheltered industries' were, the Court said, those classed by Higgins as 'public bodies … not aim[ing] at profit, but which are responsible to electors or others for economy'. Yet McKay Harvesters was not a sheltered industry. It was very much concerned with making profit, as Higgins' decision noted.

In 1954, the Court acknowledged the 1930–1931 case as the first denoting capacity to pay as the predominant basic wage principle: Level of wages and the basic wage must be 'what the economy can sustain'. It then said the argument for a man's higher salary because of family responsibilities 'is not accepted by industrial tribunals in Australia when fixing the basic wage, nor … male rates for different occupations'. The presence or absence of family responsibilities was not, and ought not to be, taken into consideration when assessing a man's salary in any occupation.

Women could be rightly bewildered. If so, why, then, should it for so long have denied women equal pay?

Attacking Women's Gains

Throughout the 1950s, women concentrated not only on forward-looking claims, necessarily arguing against regression. In 1951, the International Labour Organization (ILO) adopted equal pay Convention 100. By the mid-1950s, some NSW government employees—tram and bus conductresses, police women, some railway employees, including ticket sellers and collectors, porteresses, parcels section workers, carriage cleaners, and anywhere work proved identical—scored male rates. Federally, Australian Broadcasting Commission (ABC) 'Sydney Singers' and announcers received equal basic rates, although salaries differed because women received two-thirds of cost-of-living adjustments only. Non-governmental employees on male rates included journalists, registered pharmacists (not in government hospitals), musicians, hospital technicians in metropolitan and some other hospitals—radiologists, laboratory technicians and the like, resident medical officers in most hospitals, actors, some university staff categories, shop assistants selling groceries, cooked provisions, hardware and certain other goods categories, and whitegoods manufacturer Malley's employees. As Arnot recounts, these lists were trotted out to illustrate inconsistency in claims women could not do men's work, the fallacy of decrying women's talents and capabilities as less valuable, and the nonsense that equal pay presaged a failed economy.

Yet employers saw a threat, as the Arbitration Court's 75 per cent rate did not cover workers under state awards or women denied the award rate—potentially generating industrial unrest. The ***Basic Wage Case 1949–1950*** decision came under attack.

In the ***Standard Hours and Basic Wage Case 1952–1953*** employers applied to the Court for a ruling for longer working hours, lower men's wages, and the female basic wage cut:

- forty-four hour working week restored;
- male basic wage reduced by £2 9s 6d;

- cost-of-living adjustments suspended;
- 75 per cent female rate reduced to 60 per cent of the male rate.

Not only did employers want women's wages reduced by the reduction in men's wages; they wanted an additional 15 per cent reduction specifically targeted at women.

In ***March of Australian Women***, Rischbieth nominated the case 'an historical milestone in the Australian Women's Movement for economic equality'. Intervening, NCW and AFBPW briefed barrister Mollie Kingston. Amy Wheaton, University of Adelaide (UAdel) social science director and AFWV federal president, applied, with FAAH joining AFWV. President Gladys Hain, senior ***Argus*** journalist, attending the hearing, briefing Joan Rosanove.

Fighting to retain the 75 per cent ratio, Miss Kingston told the Court that the ***Basic Wage Case 1949–1950*** recognised 'the important bargaining power of women in industry'. Women in industry increased during the war, with 'no appreciable decrease' after, women appearing 'able to stay ... in the industrial body of the country ...', paid 75 per cent of the male wage 'even before the Court gave it to them, ... the Court confirm[ing] the status quo'. Why, she asked, should women's wages be fixed on a needs basis only, strictly defined for single women, while male wages were fixed on industry capacity to pay. Women as a 'pool of cheap labour' created a 'vicious circle', low wages leading to poor training, poor training leading to low wages.

Rosanove emphasised that any lowering of women's economic status constituted 'direct denial of the principle of equality at International level'. She and Kingston referred the Court to women's improved status domestically and by UN, particularly ILO, principles. Pointedly highlighting the employers' witness failure: no evidence for wage reduction or hour increase, nothing supporting the alleged parlous state of Australian industry, nor that, if existing, women's 75 per cent wage was responsible, Kingston called two University of Melbourne (UM) witnesses: Miss Ruth Hoban, social studies director, and Mr JF Cairns, senior lecturer in economic history.

Rischbieth reported the 'protracted struggle' lasting 'well over a year'. The decision came down in 1953 'in favour of retaining the female wage at 75% ...'. Despite 'no increase in the women's wage, neither was there any decrease ... women had the satisfaction of knowing that by INTERVENING they prevented a wider gap'—sapping women even more. But the contest continued. One year after the Arbitration Court eliminated quarterly adjustments yet retained women's 75 per cent, Newcastle Union of Australian Women (UAW) supported women on strike at an Islington factory. ***New Woman*** wrote '... on your right neat office buildings, well-constructed, airy and light with many windows ... the offices of P.J. Bearings'. Down the side street to the rear, 'in the corrugated iron shed, badly ventilated, over crowded with machinery, is the factory [where] about 100 women workers, 60% of them women and girls ... make the ball bearings'. Work identical with the men's, they 'get as much as £5 0s 0d less'. Endorsing women's claims and explaining the strike, a leaflet was published and distributed widely by UAW. The women workers won a £1 0s 0d increase.

Agitation, Activism, and Equal Pay Acts

Writing as Brent of Bin Bin, Franklin's ***Prelude to Waking*** launched the 1950s. A year later, six years after winning the ***Daily Telegraph*** novel competition, Cusack and James' ***Come in Spinner*** appeared, Jean Lee was hanged in Melbourne alongside two male companions, for torture and murder of a seventy-three-year-old bookmaker met in a bar. The High Court declared the Communist Party Dissolution Act 1950 (Cth) invalid. Daisy Bates and JB Chifley died. Evonne Goolagong was born.

In 1955, the Australian Labor Party (ALP) weathered 'The Split', the Victorian branch expelling 104 Industrial Group members (the Groupers). Liberals Mabel Miller and Amelia Best became first women elected to Tasmania's House of Assembly. A year later UAW launched its 'Mother and Child' campaign, 2000 petitions demanding increased child endowment, higher wages, and equal pay. Following ***R v Kirby and Ors; ex parte the Boilermaker' Society of Australia***, the Commonwealth Industrial Court and Commonwealth Conciliation and Arbitration Commission replaced the Arbitration Court. The 1958 NSW equal pay legislation, and the ACTU's National Working Women's Conferences in Melbourne and Sydney, closed the decade.

At Sydney Trades Hall, from forty-five unions and fifty-one organisations, more than 200 delegates or observers—over two-thirds women—attended the Conference alongside Labor Councils from all states except WA. Albert E. Monk, ACTU president, declared equal pay for the sexes, consistent with ILO principles, the objective. In September 1957, he said, a 62,000 signature equal pay petition elicited an assurance from Mr Holt, labour and national service minister, that the federal government would announce—for the Conference—steps to implement the ILO Convention. Nothing eventuated.

On 21 March 1958, the ***Sydney Morning Herald*** heralded the ACTU's support for equal pay for equal work as a first step toward 'genuine equal pay'. Australian Railways Union (ARU) federal secretary, Mr O'Brien, told delegates that equal pay, a social and political matter, was not for industrial courts. It must be fought.

Women's organisations endorsed working with the union movement, with women trade unionists through union hierarchies, supporting ACTU equal pay moves. At the 1957 and 1958 Conferences, as trade union affiliated delegates or observers, all major women's organisations—NCW, Australian Federation of Women Graduates (now Australian Federation of University Women (AFUW)), UAW, United Nations Association (UNA), AFWV, AFBPW, Liberal Party women's groups, ALP Women's Organising Committee, and other political, non-party political, and non-political organisations sent representatives, heralding revival of 1930s and 1940s Equal Pay Weeks. Through the 1960s first half, trade unions and women's organisations participated equally, the ACTU providing information and speakers, sharing platforms with women's group speakers. Women's functions circulated union leaflets and flyers, women sent and distributed material to trade union functions.

Alongside Monk, NSW premier JJ Cahill opened the 1958 Conference. In the lead up, midway through March, ***Public Service Board Notices*** highlighted women's wage inequity, urging readers to 'get active', attend the conference. The day preceding, Wednesday 19 March, 'Vacancies' stirred debate:

> Theatre Sister, Randwick Auxiliary Hospital (General Division). Salary, £14.1s 11d. range £16.9s 6d. Experience in thoracic surgical work desirable.
>
> Gardener, Mental Hospital, Callan Park. (General Division). Pay, £16.15s 3d. range £18. 5s 2d. Appointee ... required to maintain bowling green. Greenkeeping experience essential. Preference to applicants with Certificate in Gardening and Horticulture ... Sydney Technical College or other appropriate qualifications. (P.S.B. 58/873)

Earlier, on 13 March, NSW Women Lawyers' Association (WLA) weighed in, Miss Joyce Shewcroft, Research Committee convenor, through the ***Daily Mirror*** 'having her say'. 'Women's pioneering days are not yet over', each woman, 'using her talents fully and extending herself to her utmost capacity', forever 'doing more than ensuring her own niche in life', working altruistically in charitable organisations. But more, she said, was necessary. Concerted lobbying must ensure ILO 100 'Equal Pay for ... Labour of Equal Worth' ratification. Even ratification was insufficient: voicing women's frustration since federation, the Commonwealth 'leaves it to the States, the States to the Commonwealth', she said, 'passing the buck'. However, with the 'entire equal pay question' on the Conference agenda, she anticipated wins.

Conference morning. In the ***Daily Mirror***, Mrs J. Metcalfe, Australian NCW president, confirmed equal pay as long-lived NCW policy, applauding growth of women 'employed in professional and business fields ..., [their] success [earning] them the right to equal pay'. Leila Roberts said WA women were 'probably worse off' than in any other Australian state, wage percentages 'as low as 70 per cent', women teachers' recent 100 per cent claim unlikely to succeed. Roberts lamented women's limited career range. Male university graduates could choose from many jobs, 'women from only about two-thirds ...'.

Second day. Cahill announced Mr JJ Maloney, minister for labour and industry, was 'examining ... an Equal Pay Act for men and women under state awards', projected introduction 'before the next election'. Did scepticism meet this replay of his almost-a-year-earlier announcement? At the June 1957 ALP state conference, Cahill had confirmed 'a belief in' equal pay, 'a major industrial reform still to be achieved', assuring delegates of 'the possibility of granting it' before forthcoming state elections.

With 300,000 NSW women in paidwork, some 200,000 under state awards, the initial proposal covered state government employees, a fair proportion of the total. By the 1958 Conference, the plan had developed into an Equal Pay Act, costing the government around £4m annually. Employer response was immediate. Friday 21 March, the ***Daily Mirror*** reported Mr PJ Self, Employers' Federation secretary, claiming this would 'tear up the whole wage structure around which industry was established'. The NSW wages bill would increase 'by £27m a year'. Extended to women under federal awards, wages upsurge would be 'about £47m a year'. No 'responsible Government would contemplate such a costly scheme at this stage in the [economy's] development ...'. Atop 'unemployment, rising costs and lower living standards' dangers, 'an exodus of employers from N.S.W. to other States [with] lower production costs' and 'reluctance by overseas investors to sink their money in N.S.W.' would ensue.

Mr A. Upjohn, Chambers of Manufacturers Association (CMA) secretary, claimed 'an automatic rise in [industry] costs and overheads'. An 'army' of women working under state awards, making unemployment inevitable, manufacturers could not afford paying women men's wages, and small manufacturers would be hit badly. RTA secretary Mr JB Griffin, reviving the family wage concept (despite women being told it no longer applied to male wages), called the plan 'outrageous'. Contradictorily, cases of women workers having equal responsibility with men were 'so limited they are negligible', he expostulated. Simultaneously, headlined 'Sack for Women', another ***Daily Mirror*** article had employers warning of women 'losing their jobs' in droves, plus 'a sharp fall in living standards and [rise in] prices, particularly food and clothing. Maloney persevered, insisting equal pay was 'much-needed'. Echoing women's organisations, he said unemployment 'is always predicted for social reforms', with 'gloomy forecasts never borne out …'.

Intense lobbying, nine months gestation, and 1 January 1959 the Industrial Arbitration (Female Rates) Act 1958 (NSW) commenced. Hotel Club and Restaurant Employees' Union (HCREU) secretary Flo Davis, UAW member, called it 'a step in the right direction', 'a tiny step towards equality'—useful for badgering governments. On 30 April 1959, Victoria Trades Hall Council (VTHC) Equal Pay Committee endorsed a raft of proposals, noting that although fewer than the ACTU wanted, 100,000 NSW workers had just received £1 0s 0d a week pay rise under the Act. Secretary Kath Williams and committee president G. Hayes circulated all organisations and unions with women members. Calling it 'an important first step in winning Equal Pay', with NSW trade unions 'demanding a better Act' and 'Melbourne THC supporting them …', Williams and Hayes said federal and state governments must implement ACTU policy, act on ILO Conventions, and provide federal aid for states granting equal pay.

In the 1950s spirit, WA Combined Equal Pay Committee (CEPC) planned a deputation to the premier. On Thursday 31 March 1960, over 500 people at the Perth Town Hall Equal Pay Rally called unanimously for equal pay. Civil Service Association (CSA) president Mr AJ Fraser presiding, Roberts, committee chair, Gordon Freeth, federal interior minister, Mr Dufty, heading Perth Technical College Management Department, Mr NE Sampson, Teachers' Union president, and Mr FE Chamberlain, ALP federal president and state secretary, shared the platform. Interior minister and ALP president engaging typically for the times, Freeth reiterated the federal government mantra that while 'not opposing' equal pay, it was 'for the Arbitration Court'. Chamberlain emphasised Australia's equal pay obligation as an ILO member. If Labor returned to government at the state election, it would introduce legislation similar to NSW.

On 28 April 1960, led by Roberts with Fraser and Sampson, the CEPC deputation met with David Brand, WA premier, who refused committing to State Public Service equal pay, but if 'satisfied economic difficulties and unemployment would not follow', the government would not be 'unsympathetic'. Told NSW's 10,000 women teachers were due for equal pay by 1963, through annual rises over a four-year period, Brand said this 'experiment' would be borne in mind. When he pledged to commit the deputation's case to 'expert' examination, the CEPC rightly could have asked who more expert than they?

The federal government stood firm in its noughts and crosses approach: refer equal pay advocates to the Arbitration Court (now Arbitration Commission), the Commission leaving equal pay in abeyance, asserting it was not their province. In May 1959, ten minutes after midnight, Mr Johnson, MP for Hughes, NSW, rose in the federal Parliament adjournment debate, deploring federal government equal pay inaction. Referencing 800,000 women throughout Australia denied equal pay, Johnson castigated the government legislative program's 'absence of imagination', evidencing 'no genuine desire for social reform' or any 'general concern for the welfare of human beings'.

Ending the 1950s

Highs and lows began and ended the decade. The ACTU's ***Basic Wage Inquiry 1949–1950*** equal pay claim and women's intervention crowned to-ing and for-ing between governments and the industrial relations system. Although the formal outcome confirmed what already existed: 75 per cent of men's wages, women were heard again in Australia's industrial hierarchy.

Throughout the 1950s, women questioned whether campaigning for legislation, or urging unions to claim equal pay through the industrial system with women's organisations intervening would win. But it was never a case of either/or. The media exchange when the British press described the woman who, changing her sex, gained the male rate albeit her work remained the same, illustrates the conundrum of women's right to equal wages.

The ***Sydney Morning Herald*** of 23 January 1958 reported Hain saying women would 'be surprised' if gaining equal pay, 'because it would mean a harsh, competitive world for them and many would not survive it'. While apathetic toward politics, women would 'get what they deserved'. Yet she not apathetic. Nor were Lloyd-Green, Arnot, Brooks, Woodford, or Potter, quoted alongside her. And women on meagre wages or considerably less than male colleagues were already struggling to survive in a harsh and competitive world—with less money and as many financial and other responsibilities.

Far from women marrying and deserting paidwork, leaving political agitation behind, giving up trade union membership, or forgetting their 1940s role as paid and unpaidworkers, throughout the 1950s numerous women retained their involvement and employment. In the mid-1950s, married women comprised 30 per cent of all women in officially recorded paid employment. The figure dropped from 33.8 per cent in 1947, but 1933's formal statistics recorded only 12.5 per cent of all women in paidwork as married. Between 1954 and 1961, married women increased to 38.3 per cent of all women officially recorded as in paid employment. The increase continued.

Being central to AFWV's intervention in the ***Hours and Wages Case 1952–1953***, why Hain's pessimism at decade's end? She, like so many other women, laboured for equal pay throughout the 1950s, joining women in women's organisations and trade unions, many 1940s activists and before. Yet the decade ended with no industrial tribunal embracing equal pay, and legislation in NSW alone—that a small step. Was this the reason for her gloom and the decade's misrepresentation as 'nothing happening', as Audrey Johnson describes, yet simultaneously refutes in ***Bread & Roses—***, published in 1990. Recounting the 'personal history of three militant women and their friends', 1902–1988, Johnson references 'the depressing 1950s', Australia's popular culture and identity 'almost submerged in the flood of American films, pop music and, after 1956, American television'. In observing UAW's ***Our Women*** 'must have been one of the very few places where Australian women could meet a serious treatment of ... their own life not considered more newsworthy by more popular magazines', she does allow of the possibility of other such places.

Our Women tackled 'equal pay, childcare, unions and the lives of Aboriginal women', running sheet metal workers' organiser Frank Bollins' series affirming unions' significance for women. Johnson notes these issues 'were to claim attention of the new women's movement from the late 1960s, some of its members UAW members' daughters'. So the activism of thousands of women in the 1950s struggles made 1960s and 1970s activism possible. Itself constructed on the work of earlier decades, the strong foundation built during the 1950s generated the following decades' achievements. Late 1960s and 1970s Women's Movement activists won advances through their own dedication and because women went before, so often working in women's organisations and the trade union movement.

Yet the cry 'what do women want' reverberates at the 1950s end and into the 1960s. Equal pay on the agenda, confluence and dissonance between and amongst women run alongside concord and dispute from men. Conflict and concession, obduracy and compromise are intrinsic to socio-political movements. On women's economic independence and capacity to live free, not all women agree. Where difference and convergence underlie the struggle, Chap. 10, 'Alarums and Excursions: Women versus Women versus Men' provides a snapshot.

References

Cases—See Case List

Jean F. Arnot, 'Embedded in the Soul', in JA Scutt (ed.), ***Taking a Stand*** -, Artemis Publishing, Melbourne, Victoria, 1994, pp. 116–28.

Jean F. Arnot ***Papers 1916–1969 ML MSS 3147, ADD On 2070/4***, Mitchell Library, Sydney, NSW.

Barbara Curthoys and Audrey McDonald, ***More Than a Hat and Glove Brigade—***, UAW, Sydney, NSW, 1966.

Zelda D'Aprano, ***Kath Williams***, Spinifex Press, Melbourne, Victoria, 2001.

Irene Greenwood Collection, MU, Perth, WA.

ALP State Conference, June 1957 Minutes in Mitchell and Dixon Libraries Manuscripts Collection, State Library of NSW, ***ML MS 9377***, Sydney, NSW.

NSW Teachers Federation, ***Education***, vol. 32, no. 4, 1951 (13 April 1951).

NSW Teachers Federation, ***Education***, 1952, copy ***Jean F. Arnot Papers 1916–1969 ML MSS 3147, ADD On 2070/4***, Mitchel Library, Sydney, NSW, month/page number obscured.

NSW Teachers Federation, Federal Council, Sydney, NSW, 1952 (15 November 1952), copy resolution and written statement (31 October 1954) provided by Marie Muir, Teachers Federation member and Labor Council delegate.

NSW Teachers Federation, 12 November 1954, copy provided by Marie Muir, Sydney, NSW.

Bessie Rischbieth, ***March of Australian Women***, Petersen Brokensha, Perth, WA, 1964.

CHAPTER 10

Alarums and Excursions: Women Versus Women Versus Men

Thank you for your letter of 28th June enclosing the Equal Pay Committee Report ... You will be interested to know that the City of Greater Wollongong Council has now granted equal pay to at least its four most senior girls. It is a wedge.

I am sorry to admit that quite a percentage of our Wollongong B.&P.W. members don't believe in Equal Pay—even our Secretary thinks it quite wrong, advising the Executive she is so much against it she would not sign any correspondence dealing with it. Oh dearie me!

Letter from Bessie Foskett of Wollongong BPW Club to
Jean Arnot, 15 July 1960

The problem will never be solved by a militant feminist majority. If the women of Australia want equality of pay and opportunity they must develop a separate political conscience instead of meekly duplicating the vote of their menfolk who, theoretically, prefer them to remain unpaid and at home.

Letter to the Editor
Sydney Morning Herald, Sydney, NSW, 1 November 1956

Would availability of housekeeper services help you return to professional employment?
Have you held a position of professional responsibility?
Did you give up work following your marriage?

J. A. Scutt, *Wage Rage for Equal Pay*,
https://doi.org/10.1007/978-3-031-42178-5_10

In 1961, the University of Sydney (USyd) surveys its married women graduates.

> Would you return to your profession with more encouragement from your husband?
> Did you find discrimination against you as a married woman?
> Do you send your children to pre-school kindergarten?
> Have you decided to abandon your profession permanently because you consider home and family a full-time responsibility?

Response to 84 detailed questions is huge. (Un)equal pay and lack of professional opportunities are high priority, along with a concern about attitudes limiting women's sphere.

On 13 February 1961, by letter headed 'Trials of Married Women Graduates', Marien Lidden, BA, LLB, of Lane Cover writes to the ***Sydney Morning Herald***, following up the study. With 3 years' training in psychology atop her university studies, having discussed 'problems of married woman graduates' from most faculties, obstacles are, she says, evident:

> … a woman pharmacist: 'Male colleagues have actually said to me we should be paid less because we are not expected to lift heavy boxes of shop supplies.'
> … a woman economist: 'My husband says a university education makes women try to ape men. According to his view, a woman should be content to act like a woman—i.e. drudge round the house all day.'
> … a woman lawyer: 'Men's professional organisations invariably state they are ready to accept you with open arms. Those declarations are often for display purposes only. When you get down to everyday work in your profession, you find the welcome far less eager.'
> … a woman Arts graduate: 'I know my husband would rather see me bake a cake than write a thesis. He is not interested in my opinions on anything outside the home …'

Contradiction Versus Conjunction

Yet the sex war, so called, is never isolated to warring camps of women and men. The equal pay campaign bore this out. Differences boiled between women holding politically opposing ideas and ideals, one group committed to women's civil, political, economic, and legal rights and necessity for action, and the other believing women should remain in the home and silent, without public voice or identity. Sometimes, women disagreed on tactics or took philosophical or practical exception to how women's rights were framed or ways of achieving them pursued. Women who had fought alongside one another sometimes fell out over unresolved differences. Women disagreed with women over the principle and over what method would win equal pay. Fallings out between former colleagues, male and female, years or decades later ended in rapprochement—or never did. Women's organisations opposed one another, as with the Council of Action for Equal Pay (CAEP) and United Associations (UA) at the ***Basic Wage Inquiry 1937***. Women inside and outside the unions and labour movement sometimes clashed. There were conflicts between women within individual unions and disagreements between unions, as D'Aprano recounts in ***Zelda—The Becoming of a Woman***, and ***Kath Williams—The Unions and the Fight for Equal Pay***. Differences were sharp, and sharply expressed. Anti-equal pay lobbyists argued that women were less productive workers than men, that women didn't need the money, men were breadwinners and had greater need—whatever their individual circumstances or those of their colleagues, male and female. Sometimes it was simply that a man is a man and needs more, just as sometimes women reserved meat for the man of the house, because that was his role and right. These arguments and rationales paralleled those in industrial commissions, wages boards, the Arbitration Court, and its successors.

Federal Parliament showcased one of the most public splits in women's solidarity. On 10 December 1960, Senate ***Hansard*** reported that of the five women senators, one alone supported equal pay for women in the federal Public Service. Voting 'yes' was Western Australia (WA) Labour senator, Dorothy Tangney, first woman elected to the Australian Senate, in the 1943 election. The others, all conservatives, voted 'no'. Response was instantaneous. Press releases, letters to the editor, and robust missives showered upon the senators' parliamentary and electorate offices. Women's organisations condemned the 'no' vote and, over 30 years later, Arnot recalled the episode vividly, speaking scathingly of the female senators 'wasting' their positions and 'going along with' the men and the party line. A long-time Liberal, she was incensed, maintaining her rage for more than three decades.

The media weighed in, too.

'Now They'll be Popular', reported the Brisbane ***Courier Mail*** on 11 December 1960, setting out naysayers' names and party affiliations:

> The move for equal pay was made by Senator Willisee (Labour, WA), on the third reading of the Public Service Bill.

> He said it was time the Government set a lead … [In] many places in Australia women were doing work equal to a man's.
> The four women who opposed the amendment were Senators Nancy Buttfield (Lib., SA), Dame Annabelle Rankin (Lib., Qld.), Ivy Wedgwood (Lib., Vic.), and Agnes Robertson (C.P., WA).

Division amongst women was not generational. The women who voted, and public responses, confirm it was not young progressives or new radicals up against old reactionaries or ossified conservatives. From nineteenth-century campaigns to the rambunctious 1960s, both young women and middle-aged women opposed and supported equal pay, old women, and very old women, amongst its greatest supporters.

Fair Pay for Service?

The armed forces entered the debate. On 19 June 1961, headlined 'WRAAF's ideas about equal pay', Sydney's ***Sun*** reported that most women in paidwork 'feel that the sexes should receive equal pay'. As Val Buswell, Australian Federation of Business and Professional Women (AFBPW) member and former Women's Auxiliary Australian Air Force (WAAAF) recounted, Claire Stevenson, WAAAF leader in the Second World War years, was solid in support of servicewomen's right to pay commensurate with male colleagues'. But as the ***Sun*** reported, discussion amongst 38 members of a Women's Royal Australian Air Force (WRAAF) recruit course revealed that some did not agree. Young women, all worried about 'loss of respect from men'.

'Loss of respect' related to 'encouragement' provided to married women by 'equality of the paycheck', meaning they'd leave the home for wages instead of sustaining full-time housewifery. Some claimed, too, that equal pay would boost the cost of living.

Marshalled into four groups (explained the ***Sun***), they discussed the subject independently, then wrote a short essay. Flight Officer L. Buckman and Aircraftwoman (ACW) Joy Calder, 18 years, Marion Oliver, 24 years, Valerie Dare, 20 years, and Christine Barrett, 18 years, were amongst organisers and discussants. The ***Sun***'s 'summary of the girls' thoughts on the subject' decreed:

> **Group 1**: It is the male's duty to provide a home for his wife and family and many men secretly resent their wives working. Higher wages for women would only encourage more wives to get a job.

Group 2: Only men and women with equal qualifications and experience should receive equal pay. However, equal pay generally 'kills' chivalry.
Group 3: Too many wives today are going out to work and equal pay would mean even more wives working. In any case, men take their careers more seriously than women because of family responsibilities and should be paid more.
Group 4: Men should get more pay as they have more responsibilities when starting on a career. A woman earning equal to her male escort should be expected to pay her own way, and why not?

This resonated with many older women who believed younger women often harboured conservative ideas about women's rights, including wage justice claims, and said so. On 29 September 1963, 2 years after the armed services survey, the Sydney ***Sun-Herald*** reported:

> Few women are bosses—but who is to blame?
> If women seldom are promoted to bosses in industry and business, just where does the fault lie—with the men passing them over, or the women who aspire to, but fail to attain these positions? The perennial problem [received] some new slants in the United States recently by the president of the National Federation of Business and Professional Women's Clubs, Miss Virginia Allan. She believes the blame probably lies with the women themselves.

According to the ***Sun-Herald***, Miss Allan, already impressive as educator and businesswoman, yet to come civic leader and stateswoman—chairing Richard Nixon's presidential Task Force on Women's Rights and Responsibilities 1969–1972, then deputy assistant secretary of state for public affairs and, in between, US delegation member for International Women's Year (IWY) Mexico Conference (1972) and Copenhagen Mid-Decade Conference for women (1980), believed men were 'more advanced in their thinking than women':

> If women are prepared for executive positions, men are prepared to accept them. Unfortunately women—especially of the younger generation—are not fully aware of this change in the male attitude. They are also not aware that men will welcome any equal-pay-for-equal-work legislation. Women will then be hired on their ability and not just because they provide cheap labour. This will mean a break for men as well as for women.

Reactions ranging from emphatic disagreement to its opposite. Dr Nell MacMahon said some truth may lie in these remarks as 'many women are not aware of the need of fitting themselves for executive positions and to take responsibility'. Still, she didn't think it 'entirely their fault that few occupy top positions'. Little opportunity, particularly in government departments and, presently:

> Australian men are still not prepared to accept women as bosses. The age-old prejudice against working under women lingers on. The only way to change this is by women slowly proving their efficiency and tact.

Miss Alice Brown, 'senior Public Service clerk, retired', thought prejudice against women was disappearing—'even if in some places old ideas die hard', for 'if women have the ability and necessary tact' in 'many cases … they would be quite acceptable as bosses'. Furthermore, women in Australia 'do fill equal pay positions', and 'few here have not been recognised simply because they're women':

> [Many] women manage their own business just as efficiently as men. We have women aldermen—and from what they've told me, there's been no prejudice against them. A woman … was recently chairman of a Sydney City Council committee … But it's probably true that if women want to occupy high technical positions they [must] be slightly more efficient than a man …

Contrarily, Miss Nancie Wicks, international hockey player and administrator, assistant publications secretary of the ***Australian Journal of Science***, claimed Allan's words had no Australian application: women 'are not given opportunities to hold top jobs … in the Public Service, libraries and banking world'. Universities were 'the only place where women are accepted without question': having qualifications, women professors and lecturers 'find no discrimination in the academic world'. Nor did Wicks agree with Allan about men's position on legislation for equal pay for equal work. 'I'd like to see the man here who is for it. We can't even get all members of the Labor Party to support it.'

But the last word went to Miss Marjorie Chalmers, Rural Bank examiner (the highest Rural Bank position a woman could occupy at that time), testifying to 'a definite change of attitude in her profession' over 12 months, men being 'more amenably prepared to accept women are capable of more responsible positions':

> Recently at a women's committee meeting, United Bank Officers' Association of N.S.W. president, Mr R.A. McKell, admitted … women are quite capable of holding senior and executive positions. This was the first time such a concession had been made.

Chalmers considered women's thinking executive positions were not for them led to their disentitlement from the two Rural Bank positions senior to examiner—loans officer and accountant. Women discounted their work as a career, yet 'proved to be quite as capable ... as soon as looking on it' in that light. With women 'now coming to accept opportunities', 'generally speaking ... lots exist'. With more qualifications, 'they become less diffident and more confident in assuming such positions as company secretary and accountant'. As for equal pay, Chalmers agreed with Allan:

> A lot of men are in favour of it. Any adjustment for a family person, compared with a single man or woman receiving equal pay for equal work, will automatically [come] with child endowment and greater tax benefits.

Class War, Wage War

Thirty years earlier, Great Depression rumblings found the ***Sydney Morning Herald*** reporting parrying between Street and Adela Pankhurst Walsh, pacifist, anti-conscription activist, Women's Progressive Association (WPA) Victoria member, 1920s foundation Communist Party of Australia (CPA) member then, in 1925 parting from the CPA, founder of the Australian Women's Guild of Empire (AWGE) branch of the British Guild of Empire.

In April-May 1933, a United Associations (UA) letter advocating equal pay plays a part. W. Feeney responds, arguing equal pay will give a single woman above her needs for necessities, the basic wage being based on needs of a man, wife, and child. Street's letter in reply, going unpublished, asks rhetorically whether Feeney also objects to a single man getting more than sufficient for his needs. This side of the question, she writes, is 'carefully avoid[ed]'. Nor does Feeney 'take cognisance of the fact that a married woman or widow [with dependent] children ... does not get the wage deemed necessary to keep a home and a family'. She protests at Feeney's 'amazing statement' that the woman's basic wage of £1 17s 0d should be further reduced by taxation 'as she spends a large amount of this wage on luxury':

> If your correspondent would budget £1.17.0 and show what amounts would be over for luxuries I feel sure that the women would be grateful.
>
> Would he also tax the single man on any amount he might be tempted to spend on luxury? If, as he states, a million could be saved by this tax on the

> meagre wages of the woman, how much could be saved by taxing the excessive wage of the single man?

Street concluded 'the time [having] arrived' for decisions about basing wages 'on the value of the work, or on the domestic responsibility of the worker'. If value of work, 'there is no argument against equal pay'. If domestic responsibilities, 'more adequate provision must be made for the family man'.

Published in the ***Sydney Morning Herald*** of 18 April 1933, adding to this chapter of the controversy, Street noted women's basic wage having 'just been declared at £1 17s 0d and men's at £3 8s 6d', one of 'the greatest anomalies' in NSW lay in 'the discrepancy between wages paid to men and women ...'. Observing 'injustice all around' from 'this inequitable system', declaring it 'most reprehensible that women should have to work the same hours as men and get paid a little more than half the amount men are paid', the letter continued:

> Firstly it is unjust to the woman worker as she does not get the same value for her work as a man gets; secondly it places the woman worker in the invidious position of being regarded as 'cheap labour' with resultant loss of dignity and status; thirdly it is ... responsible for much unemployment amongst men since women can be employed to do just as effective work as men for a little more than half the cost; a fourth injustice is ... great hardship to families where the woman is breadwinner, ... Should the husband be incompetent, intemperate, a gambler, or unreliable in any way it is often impossible for the wife to depend on him to support the family. Then responsibility falls upon her, and work as hard as she may, under the present system she can earn only half as much as she would were she a man.

Concluding with a demand that 'the politicians of this country' recognise it is 'quite time [to give] their attention to legislation governing the fixing of the Basic Wage', affirming equal opportunity and equal pay as inextricably linked, Street declared that justice lay in wages based on the value of work done, not on worker's sex: 'Let wages be fixed for the different occupations, and let everyone have an equal opportunity to engage in these occupations.'

Pankhurst Walsh expressed her views in the ***Sydney Morning Herald***, too. Suffragette alongside her mother Emmeline Pankhurst and sisters Christabel and Sylvia in England, having emigrated to Australia in 1914, by the 1930s her politics had transmogrified. She took to writing letters and articles bemoaning the 'Drift from Old Realities' to 'new values' destructive of 'family life'. On 7 August 1930, the ***Sydney Morning Herald*** published her AWGE protest that women should sacrifice their jobs and opportunities for employment to boys and men. The following year, the ***Sydney Morning Herald*** of 8 and 9 April published her saying 'child culture and home management give full scope to women if they are carried out with energy and ability' and 'are as necessary, and more difficult, than most of the work done by men'. She urged women to stay at home to pursue this 'worthy' role. Two years later, in a ***Sydney Morning Herald*** letter of 1932, Pankhurst Walsh challenged anything being 'wrong' in pay differentials between women and men. Equal pay would advance the already too prevalent breakdown of family life and deprive men of their breadwinner place. Married women didn't 'need' equal pay, particularly in teaching, for (ignoring laws forcing married women out) '...marriage intervenes and removes the women from the profession'. Furthermore, the vast majority of women in paidwork 'are single girls without responsibilities'. Joining issue with Street, she challenged UA and other women's groups—they were wrong, she said. Equal pay would be socially and politically detrimental to all.

On 11 May 1933, relying on the ***1933 Statistical Bulletin of New South Wales*** (December quarter), UA's president 'craved space for reply'. The ***Sydney Morning Herald*** declined to publish. UA declared that 'letters from working men and women' published in the ***Herald***'s columns supported equal pay, but 'Mrs. Pankhurst Walsh's letter is so full of unsubstantiated and misleading statements that it calls for an answer'. Pankhurst's position was 'totally opposed' to the Guild of Empire, the 'English body her organisation ... represents', one of their objects being 'To work for equality between men and women'.

The (unpublished) letter replied to 'a few of Mrs. Walsh's statements':

> We trust the single girls will raise in their wrath and assure Mrs. Walsh that if she took a census she would find the majority of single girls to-day on the princely wage of 37s. are trying to keep fathers and brothers who cannot get work because an employer prefers to engage the cheaper labour—the woman. Mrs. Walsh assumes industry cannot afford to pay a living wage to a woman as ... to a man, and ... will collapse ... Is this not reminiscent of the days when the abolition of child labor in factories and mines was discussed, and many well known Englishmen said England's greatness would decline were she prohibited from employing children (see British Hansard 1842). Did England decline?

As to women teachers:

> If the women freely resign their jobs on marriage why was it necessary to pass a law to force them to do so? The women do not forsake it; a man made law obliges them to do so.

Believing equal pay would solve many unemployment problems, UA's position was that it would further 'help to fund many more of those homes Mrs. Walsh so desires', 'help men regain their self-respect', and, 'above all', establish 'the great principle' that a worker's sex was not the issue in setting of pay rates; rather, 'all work should be paid for according to the nature of the work'.

UA vice-president Street wrote again. Relenting, the ***Sydney Morning Herald*** of 22 May 1933 published. Street noted the nub of the criticism was that a man's wage 'is calculated to cover the cost of maintaining himself and his family, whereas a woman has only herself to keep'. Saying the argument 'may sound all right in theory', she went on to look at census statistics. Women were far from having 'only themselves to keep', whilst men were far from universally being responsible for 'families' or 'wives and children'. From the most recent census, of men between 21 and 65 years of age, 35 per cent were single, with 'no more responsibility than single women, for in both cases to the extent of their ability they contribute towards their family's incomes'. As for men of the same age, married without children, they comprised 22 per cent:

> If people were paid according to their responsibilities, these men as well as the single men are overpaid. And what is the position of the men with families? According to the statistics only 45% are fathers of families and responsible for the maintenance of children. If wages are to be paid according to domestic responsibilities, many of these [may be] underpaid.

The time had come for governments and industrial commissions to concretely recognise women's just claims by entrenching equal pay in legislation and basic wage determinations.

When the ***Sydney Morning Herald*** refused to publish further UA correspondence, Street went to the ***Labour Daily***, her letter, signed by UA's president, was published on 7 June 1933. The gist was that 'discussion of methods adopted to arrive at the Basic Wage should be of interest to every wage earner'. Incorporating statistics from an unpublished ***Sydney Morning Herald*** letter, she concluded 'the time had come' for a fundamental minimum wage calculation review of 'worker responsibilities' versus 'value of work done'. 'Value of work done' meant 'equal pay for equal work, and an equal opportunity in performance of that work', and that should be the measure.

By 14 February 1934, the argument continued, equal pay a 'hot topic' amongst correspondents. That day, the ***Sydney Morning Herald*** published another UA letter:

> The disparaging attacks on women workers by your correspondents are most unfair. That they are cheap labor is not [women workers'] fault … who have repeatedly stressed their claim for equal pay. The lower wage these women are paid is imposed on them by the laws of the State. The declared basic wage for men being £3 6s. 6d. and for women £1 16s. 0d.
>
> As for the accusation that the girls are 'scarlet lipped' and 'overdressed', I would draw the attention of our correspondents to the fact that girls must compete in the open market for jobs, and that if they are as described it must be that the employers prefer them so.

Unemployment, the letter went on, 'is a tragedy', more so 'for a man with dependants and woman with dependants' than for those without. The money women earns is 'as necessary to her and her family as [that of] a man is necessary for him and his family'. Expelling women workers simply shifts the burden to 'shoulders of a class already handicapped by sex prejudice, custom and lack of status and opportunity'.

(Un)Equal Pay and (No) Emancipation

The Pankhurst Walsh-Street differences were reminiscent of those aired in the ***Australian Economist*** almost half a century earlier. A similar split emanated from a discussion chaired by the Reverend Dr Bevan, hosted by the Women's Suffrage and Education League (WSEL) (known also as the Women's Political Education League (WPEL)). In the ***Economist*** of 23 April 1895, under the heading 'Women and Womanhood Suffrage', Miss EA Badham in her own phrase 'attacked' the WSEL for its argument that should women gain their rightful place as voters, the new millennium would be the 'Century of the Woman'.

A retort was not long in coming. The ***Economist*** of 21 June saw the argument laid out in full. Miss Badham, linked with girls' school Sydney Church of England Girls' Grammar School (SCEGGS) and Sydney

University (SydU), received a sharp rebuke. Rose Scott, WPEL NSW leader and foundation member, replied in blunt fashion, the exchange comprehensively reported:

Miss Badham: In rejecting women's emancipation, including equal pay, she did not stand alone, she said, with 'some of [her] friends' requesting she 'explain to those who care to hear' why 'a very large number of women feel themselves utterly averse to this movement'. Rejecting 'certain stock arguments' relied upon by 'rank and file' womanhood suffrage proponents, who 'repeat them somewhat in parrot fashion to all and sundry'.

Surely, women's work 'is subject to other ordinary conditions of supply and demand'. Any commodity less well paid is so, 'because it is not worth so much'. To their own detriment, and that of 'women's skills', contemporary women renounced their grandmothers' approach. Whereas their grandmothers 'followed few arts', in those they 'strove to attain to a high degree of excellence', evident in their 'detailed elaborate cookery books', needlework—'treasured as relics of a lost art', and well-written letters, praiseworthy both for calligraphy and language. 'Not one woman in fifty can boil rice,' she added, 'or be trusted to grill a chop when it is easier to fry it':

> We can scarcely ... complain when men reproach us with a want of finish and exactness in our work, [refusing] to allow it the same market value as their own. That [this] presses heavily on many individuals, whose work, judged by itself, is worthy of the highest market price, is unfortunate ..., but can be remedied only by a marked improvement in women's work in general.

A man banning women from his trade 'fights not only for his own livelihood', but for women dependent upon him. For Badham and friends, it was not the time to discuss whether wife, sisters, and grown-up daughters should support themselves rather than have a man support them.

Rose Scott: In reply, Scott left aside the contradictory assertion that men's wages were higher because men had dependents to support, yet women and men were paid equally in professions based on 'excellence'. Nor did she tackle the proposition that if women were paid a living wage, as grown-up daughters and sisters they would relinquish dependence upon fathers and brothers. Rather, she highlighted women's lack of industrial conditions and challenged the very notion that women and men were paid equally at all, whatever women's training, talents, or abilities. The law of demand and supply clouded the issue, but even if professional men and women were paid equally, which she doubted:

> … what a small number of women [this] embraces. Certainly, as teachers, as mistresses of post offices, with [identical] training, [identical] or even greater responsibility, women are paid less than men, and are [precluded from rising] to rise to the highest position of the service …'

Furthermore, far greater importance lay in being 'one of a represented class' than Badham recognised, for if working women had the vote 'they would', Scott supposed, 'very soon gain that eight hours a day and other reforms' already secured by working men for themselves and vital 'for 89,000 women earning their living in New South Wales alone', 6000 of whom she reckoned supported husbands and children.

Why these ***Economist*** and ***Sydney Morning Herald*** wrangles? A strange mixture of class, ideology, party politics, life experience, kowtowing to projected notions of what *men* want, versus setting women centre stage as independent beings with economic standing, public status, and private rights?

Political ideology played a part, some women believing women's rights were intimately connected to notions of community ownership of resources and an end to capitalist order. Although the political divide was not invariably one of socialism and women's rights versus capitalism and men's rights over women, socialist ideals did create differences between women at nineteenth-century's end, as they did in the late 1940s and into the 1950s. Disputes following Street's adherence to the communist cause and support for Russia, and later the role played by women's organisations such as the Union of Australian Women (UAW) (many members belonging to the CPA), led them to splits. The 1960s and 1970s saw such differences, too, with liberal feminists versus socialist feminists versus radical feminists divided principally on strategy and class perspectives.

Socialism was at the heart of Badham's assault. In 1895, for Badham and friends, socialism was the menacing scourge. The ***Economist*** recounted her assertion of its being 'a grotesque impertinence' if she were to 'discuss the merits or demerits of Socialism or any other political scheme' in a paper addressing women's need to repudiate 'meddling in politics'. Women were even more at risk than men in this radical madness:

> There is something in Socialism which appeals to one of the highest instincts of a woman's nature: I mean the desire to help the weak and suffering, … an offshoot of the maternal instinct … It is therefore easy to see how socialism may attract women, for socialism, in whatever way we may regard it, is, after all, nothing but a gigantic scheme of state interference with people's private

> affairs. … [T]here is in the world a great deal of poverty and distress on the one hand, and grasping covetousness on the other; the good things of Fortune seem to be very unequally distributed, and socialism undertakes to cure these evils once and for all.

Women ought not, however, to be so easily led astray. Pleading for the vote and for equal pay were *not* the way.

Transcending Politics for Equal Pay

Sixty-five years later, aware of the dangers inherent in claims for equal pay appearing to be driven by one side of politics—particularly the side labelled radical by those opposed not only to equal pay, but to women's rights entire—some women deliberately set out to join conservative political parties as an antidote to contentions that women's rights were a Labour preserve. In 1960, Clara Behrend campaigned for equal pay on the WA Liberal-Country Party agenda. She raised 'The Rate for the Job or Equal Pay for the Sexes', persuading the women's section to vote unanimously 'for' equal pay, then waging a lobbying campaign with the president and members, urging the question be part of the year's annual conference.

Behrend did not resile from confronting her female audience with their own prejudices. A 'bogey' advanced against equal pay was that it would lower the basic wage at the family's expense. Yet 'child endowment and other social services, plus taxation allowances, are blithely ignored'. Contentions equal pay 'will prevent women from marrying; they will be too well off to want to', and 'women will lose their jobs' are 'easily exploded … yet many people, particularly married women … housewives … accept this reasoning without question':

> … one wonders whether such an attitude is merely a rationalisation of a fear that somebody else may end up a bit better off than they are; common justice does not seem to weigh with them. If only they knew it, the [general attitude to women as] inferior beings would undergo a vast change once women were paid according to the jobs they were doing and not by the lesser value put upon their work because of their sex.

Delivering other home truths, Behrend noted that women with 'business and professional training and experience' have realised the value of women's paidwork as equal to men's 'for many years' but are kept busy running two jobs—work during the day and 'keeping the home fires burning' at night and weekends 'as their wages don't permit of paying for the outside help a bachelor can'. But Behrend was even-handed. Women in paidwork did not escape her critique:

> ... business and professional women have fallen down on ... advertising their worth to the community at large [being] too busy with their own affairs and lack of time has caused them to ignore the importance of having the world know what they are doing and the injustice of the system by which they are paid.

The women's section ought not be frightened away from equal pay, thinking conservative ideology ruled it out, she added, saying that 'it has nothing to do with the Labour movement as such, comprising government, employer and employee representatives'. Far from equal pay being a 'socialist plot', women in higher positions were likely to be Liberals and members of more conservative women's organisations, including St Joan's Social and Political Alliance, University Women, League of Women Voters, the Australian Federation of Business and Professional Women (AFBPW)—'solidly in favour of Equal Pay for the sexes'.

So, Behrend gets equal pay onto the 1961 annual conference agenda. A debate staged by Perth Junior Chamber of Commerce follows. In a revealing letter to Arnot in Sydney, Behrend speaks of her apprehensions not only about *perceptions* of equal pay as a left-wing plot, but exploitation of the campaign as a way of promoting socialist causes:

> I am rather concerned at the influx of Labour followers to [the Combined Equal Pay] committee ... some of them definitely 'left-wing'. Have warned Miss Ross of the danger. She and Leila [Roberts] know little about Politics and are an easy prey to such people. Should you be going to the Melb. Conference and see Miss Ross there, you may see an opportunity to back me up on this. I am not so narrow-minded as to want to ban all Labour people but draw the line at Reds and 'fellow-travellers'...

Still, the Junior Chamber of Commerce debate is a coup. 'I am pleased about this,' she writes, for 'some of our members are indifferent, lukewarm, or, in some cases, actively against' equal pay. The discussion will give them a chance 'to air their views and perhaps be talked over to our side'.

The members of whom she speaks belong to one of the organisations she earlier referred to in her women's section speech as conservative, and supportive of equal pay: AFBPW. Not only is her hope that the anti-equal pay members may be converted. She aims at more male support for the cause: '… we do not have many men visitors to the Club and I think it will be a good thing and help to interest them in our Club and its aims.'

In Sydney, women's organisations deal with internal dissent and differences, too, some members continuing to decry equal pay arguments advanced by their leadership. Contrary to notions of support and antagonism dictated by personal circumstances, the divide is not along professional or marital lines. Not a case of married women wanting more for their husbands, spinsters more for themselves. Nor do married women favouring equal pay favour it because they have family responsibilities, or to increase a combined family income. Nor is it teachers 'for', shop girls 'against', or women's organisation member opposed to member of trade union. Often, they are one and the same: teachers and shop assistants are trades union members or members of women's organisations, or of both.

Some spinsters line up against married women, some side with married women. Married women oppose one another, others support their married counterparts in the struggle. Those 'against' sometimes envision equal pay as a challenge to men's rightful pre-eminence. Those 'for' scoff at protestations of male superiority. Trade unionists ally themselves for and against, alongside members of UA, Australian Federation of University Women (AFUW), and League of Women Voters. Sometimes resistance lies in contentions that women don't need equal pay or equal rights. Sometimes it is a case of 'we've won 75 per cent; fair enough, why ask for more?' Sometimes it's that the women's struggle is over. With 'everything' won—or at least as much as we can expect—the struggle, it is said, is obsolete.

When 1960s women burst onto the scene, such arguments are meaningless or swept aside. Invigorated by an energy brooking no resistance, fronting every challenge, women are confident that equal pay will come. How justified was this confidence, how certain the possibilities of achievement? Chapter 11, 'The 1960s—Decade of Radical Change or Back to 1912?' explores women's advances through the arbitration system, the unions, the media, and their own organisations during a decade popularly seen as explosive with excitement, socio-cultural advances, and tossing off restrictive traces of the previous decade. Yet is it a case of two steps forward—and two back? Or whatever the ultimate outcome, are the 1960s an integral part of women's advance towards pay equity?

References

Cases—see Case List

Jean Arnot, ***Interview***, Double Bay, NSW, 1992 (6 April 1992).

Copy survey and responses ***Jean F. Arnot Papers 1916–1969 ML MSS 3147, ADD On 2070/4***, Mitchell Library, Sydney, NSW.

Clara Behrend, 'The Rate for the Job …', Perth, WA, 1960; copy ***Jean F. Arnot Papers 1916–1969 ML MSS 3147, ADD On 2070/4***, Mitchell Library, Sydney, NSW.

Clara Behrend, Letter to Jean Arnot, 1961; copy ***Jean F. Arnot Papers 1916–1969 ML MSS 3147, ADD On 2070/4***, Mitchell Library, Sydney, NSW.

Verna Coleman, ***Adela Pankhurst—The Wayward Suffragette 1885–1961***, UMP, Melbourne, Victoria, 1996.

Irene Greenwood Collection, MU, Perth, WA

Sydney Morning Herald, Sydney, NSW, 1933 (April/May 1933); copy ***Jean F. Arnot Papers 1916–1969 ML MSS 3147, ADD On 2070/4***, Mitchell Library, Sydney, NSW (date unclear, with papers, including UA letter, date known, supporting 1933 circa April/May publication). Copies all letters ***Jean F. Arnot Papers 1916–1969 ML MSS 3147, ADD On 2070/4***, Mitchell Library, Sydney, NSW.

Heather Radi (ed.), ***Jessie Street***, Redress Press, Sydney, NSW, 1990.

Betty Reilly, 'A stitch in time .... ', ***Australian Left Review***, 1983, vol 1, no 8. https://ro.uow.edu.au/alr/vol1/iss81/3/ (accessed 2 June 2006)

CHAPTER 11

The 1960s—Decade of Radical Change, or Back to 1912?

> Men don't seem to mind a woman working, they just resent having to pay her for it.
>
> Eva Pownall, Equal Pay Week Speech
> Federation Hall, Sydney
> ***Daily Mirror***, 30 March 1960

1960. On 15 May, the ***Sydney Morning Herald*** reports Queensland Labour leader Jack (JE) Duggan committing to equal pay, 3 weeks annual leave, and a 35-hour week. On 28 May, for the first time since 1912, the Country-Liberal Coalition wins a second term in office. Equal pay falls off the agenda.

1964. Destination High Court, Garfield Barwick resigns from Parliament. Off Jervis Bay, 82 lives are lost when ***HMAS Voyager***, sheared by ***HMAS Melbourne***, sinks. Double-decker railway carriages run on Sydney's suburban railways, there to stay.

On Thursday 9 April, federal ***Hansard*** records an urgency motion in both houses, the Labour opposition demanding introduction of equal pay and lamenting non-ratification of International Labour Organization (ILO) 'equal pay' Convention 100. The government asserts it's 'honoured its I.L.O. obligations' and, while 'not opposed to equal pay for work of equal value', the Commonwealth Conciliation and Arbitration Commission is 'the appropriate tribunal'.

J. A. Scutt, *Wage Rage for Equal Pay*,
https://doi.org/10.1007/978-3-031-42178-5_11

Mr CH (Charles Harry) Webb (Lab., WA), 'condemns' government inaction, noting that of 113 ILO member countries, 44 have ratified the Convention, 56 introducing equal pay into government departments. Minister for labour, Mr W. (William) McMahon (Lib., NSW), says Australia cannot afford it: £200m annually. Besides, four states have already signalled unwillingness to ratify ILO 100. Australia cannot act, anyway, he adds: major wages and salaries changes, particularly the basic wage, are not for government or federal Parliament, so that's it.

Senate opposition leader NE (Nicholas Edward) McKenna (Lab., NSW) contradicts McMahon. The Commission has already said equal pay, 'social experiments', or 'wide-ranging social change' are not its responsibility. Lacking constitutional barriers, the federal government must accept responsibility, introducing equal pay.

He's rebuffed. Senator JG (John Grey) Gorton (Lib., Vic.), minister for works, denies government obligation. Commonwealth public servants already have equal margins. Basic wage principles should govern wages and salaries, with no special treatment for public servants. Besides, the ILO accepts that the Arbitration Commission sets the basic pay rate. Even then, the Commission should move warily. Equal pay is an Australia-wide question.

Labour presses on. Some from government ranks defect. Senator Ivy Evelyn Wedgwood (Lib., Vic.) renounces her earlier vote against equal pay. If women do the same service for the community as men, she says—they deserve equal pay. Gorton's reaction goes unrecorded. But Hansard captures the mocking and trivialising of women's claims.

'Equal pay for women would mean women have to pay for their share on a date' making women 'one of the mob', says Gerald Collin McKellar, NSW Country Party member. Why abolish 'respect for the female sex'? Besides, 'I'm one of those old fuddy-duddies who believes man is still the family breadwinner', benefitting 'some of the misguided women plugging now for equal pay for equal work'.

'Do we want women drinking in bars with us?' McKellar shoots back at an interjector.

'Yes,' retorts Senator Nancy Eileen Buttfield (Lib., SA) like Wedgwood, reversing her position from 4 years before. Undaunted, McKellar asks: 'Do we want women doing pick and shovel work?' Further, 'girls' dressing 'in tight slacks and matador pants, … hair uncombed, looking unwashed, unwanted, unloved and unhappy' should accept there's 'nothing nicer than … a girl nicely dressed and with her hair combed'. The others 'destroy any respect ... from their boyfriends'. What 'if a man takes a girl out for an outing, what happens then?' ***Hansard*** recorded laughter is no deterrent. McKellar repeats himself: 'She should have to pay for her share ....'

The following day, the 10 April ***Daily Telegraph*** reports 'Senator's warning to women'. The ***Sydney Morning Herald*** leads with 'Critic had the last word'. The matter-of-fact coverage characterising the 1950s equal pay debate is lost.

Opposition Demands, Federal Inaction—So Where Are the Women?

Contradictions abound. The tussle over equal pay resonates in Australian parliaments, federally Liberal-Country Party government against Labour opposition. Existing women's organisations, including the Union of Australian Women (UAW), Australian Federation of Business and Professional Women (AFBPW), National Council of Women (NCW), Women's Service Guilds (WSG), United Associations (UA), and Australian Federation of University Women (AFUW) press on. Trade unions, including teacher, public service, and other white-collar unions come forward or continue lobbying from the 1950s and before. New women's groups, including the Women's Electoral Lobby (WEL), come later.

The 1950s and 1960s Melbourne Drift and Sydney Push were awash with libertarian philosophy and outspoken women, amongst them Glen Tomasetti (of 'Don't Be Too Polite, Girls' fame—the classic feminist trade union song), Betty Burstall (Melbourne's La Mama theatre prime mover), Germaine Greer (***The Female Eunuch***—yet to be written), Margaret Fink (film producer and 'My Brilliant Career'—the film, coming later), Lillian Roxon (subsequently ***Women's Weekly*** 1970s foreign correspondent, living and dying asthmatically in New York), and Liz Fell (the 1970s Australian Broadcasting Commission (ABC) Women's Broadcasting Collective and 'The Coming Out—Ready or Not—Show'). In December 1969, Australia's first ongoing Women's Liberation (WL) group, Glebe WL or the Glebe Group met at 67 Glebe Point Road, inner-city Sydney. Sandra Walker, Julie Gibson, Deidre Ferguson, Lyndall Ryan, Martha Kay (Ansara), and Barbara Levy were soon joined by Gale Kelly, Sue Bellamy, Di Graham, and more.

Yet for women, established institutions changed little. Australia's first female QC, Roma Mitchell, appointed in 1963, became Australia's first female Supreme Court judge in 1965, the year Joan Rosanove became

Australia's second female QC, retiring in 1969 after 50 years in law and no bench appointment. Only in 1996 was Rosemary Balmford made Victorian Supreme Court judge, whilst 1960s parliaments were equally lacking women members, or tolerated miniscule numbers. Women headed no corporation, state, federal, or local government department and, although sometimes on local councils, rarely made it to mayor, much less lord mayor. Initially, still only a handful of women graduated in law, few engineering or architecture, fewer still geology. More studied medicine and science, but specialist and physicist ranks rarely featured women.

Media reporting regressed. Jocularity tinged with sexual overtones, or slighting women's struggle, replaced serious 1950s coverage of equal pay and women's demands for equal job opportunities. State parliaments equivocated. However, gradually, one by one, they met the NSW Labour government challenge, passing equal pay for equal work Acts, replicating Queensland's far earlier 1918 Wages Act, updated in turn by its Industrial Conciliation and Arbitration Act 1961 (Qld) equal pay provision. Nevertheless, terms were restricted to women doing men's work. Just as women in women's jobs missed out in NSW, women in traditional female industries were denied equal pay. Legislation rested on notions that what men did was worthy of commensurate pay rates, what women did was not—unless women sought, and gained, jobs in male domains. The 1912 ***Fruitpickers*** principle was back.

But for all that, some state governments eventually took responsibility for equal pay, unlike the federal Liberal-Country Party government. The 1964 debate typified their approach. Through the decade, the Labour opposition pressed equal pay. The federal government claimed its hands were tied, saying unions must initiate Commission applications. Mimicking the 1950s, this refrain appeared in press releases, media statements, doorstop interviews, and in Parliament, repeated to delegations meeting or seeking to meet with the prime minister or minister for labour.

On 13 September 1960 in Melbourne, federal minister McMahon told an Australian Council of Trade Unions (ACTU) and white-collar union deputation that equal pay for federal government employees was a matter for arbitration. Led by ACTU senior vice-president, JD Kenny, MLC in the NSW Parliament, the delegation comprised representatives of state Trades and Labour Councils (TLCs), the High Council of Commonwealth Public Service Organisations (HCCPSO), Australian Council of Salaried and Professional Associations (ACSPA), and unions with women members. The impetus was the Industrial Arbitration (Female

Rates) Act 1958 (NSW), and Victorian Wages Boards decisions extending equal pay to women. Representing clerks, postal workers, textile workers teachers, and the metals group, and estimating that of 3,000,000 workers more than 800,000 women would be affected by granting or denying equal pay, the deputation urged the government adopt equal pay for equal work 'for the sexes in its employ'.

McMahon reversed the argument, saying nothing prevented trade unions from lodging equal pay claims, yet unions hadn't done so for 10 years. 'Precisely what attitude' government would take, he couldn't confirm, advising that if unions applied, the Commonwealth would 'intervene and present all relevant information to the Commission'.

Neither unions nor women's organisations were satisfied. Even if the federal government couldn't legislate, as falsely maintained, with public servants demanding equal pay, why not take it to the Court as a dispute? Why not basic wage equal pay submission or at least 'present all relevant information'? Why not raise it where already a party, or intervening? Why blame the unions?

When the (Female Rates) Amendment Act 1958 became law on 1 January 1959 and its failure to cover all employed women was criticised, NSW Labour Council had highlighted federal government responsibility in advance. In December, secretary Kenny issued ***Answers to Questions on Equal Pay***, noting that when abroad, Holt as minister for labour and national service 'spoke freely' of Australia's 'wish to participate fully in [International Labour Organization] I.L.O. activities'. Back home, he 'consistently denied' federal government responsibility for equal pay.

Answers to Questions … rebutted a Department of Labour booklet, ***Equal Pay—Some Aspects of Australian and Overseas Practice***, published August 1958. TLCs, trade unions, and women's organisations all disparaged it as marking time or fobbing off. Kenny said it 'contains facts and figures about … Australia but absolutely no promise of action …', perpetuating denial and confirming the government would 'refuse as long as possible' trade union leaders and women's organisation pleas. If the Commonwealth wanted to 'fulfil its International obligations', promoting 'economic equality for women', why no intervention 'in the Commonwealth Court, or at least forecasting … action …?' Arguing against quarterly adjustments in the ***Basic Wage Case 1957***, so keeping wages down—how could it say it was 'powerless to grant equal remuneration for work of equal value to its own employees', initiating action for equal pay in all federal awards? An ACTU petition easily garnering 62,000 signatures was presented to Holt, who promised but failed to put petitions to cabinet. Instead, he 'openly decried' NSW's legislative efforts for equal pay under state awards.

This was standard 1960s fare. Two years before the 1964 federal parliamentary emergency motion, on 1 May 1962 the opposition moved a House of Representatives equal pay urgency motion. Mr EJ Harrison (Lab., NSW) called it 'scandalous' that government obligations under ILO Convention 100 remained outstanding. Minister for labour McMahon called the motion 'capricious and ill-timed', the government *had* 'honoured all its obligations'—so far as possible, 'always' maintaining no opposition to 'equal pay for work of equal value'. But the 'practice … not to ratify any convention' unless all jurisdictions conformed was an obstacle. The states were the problem, for 'many' were 'not prepared to apply … equal pay'.

The prime minister treated the issue non-politically, McMahon added. Women's organisation leaders, ACTU, and Commonwealth Public Service Officers (CPSO) had been given assurances, but the opposition 'capriciously introduced the motion as a political stunt'. The NSW government hadn't assisted women or equal pay, creating an 'unhappy precedent', by passing equal pay legislation—not waiting for Australia-wide agreement.

Yet waiting for agreement might mean waiting forever—women had already waited decades. Harrison, like the NSW Labour government, was undeterred. A federal Labour government would, he said, like state Labour, implement equal pay 'without delay', whatever remaining state governments said or did. Under the ILO Convention, 38 countries had equal pay, 43 for public servants, 77 for teachers. Condemning government inaction, he observed that every government department has '… men and women working side by side doing the same work'; condoning women's lower salaries meant 'the Government wants cheap labour'.

Opposition deputy leader Mr EG (Gough) Whitlam stressed that on 'both sides of the Atlantic', the most highly industrialised countries 'had equal pay rights'. More than half the US and two-thirds of Canada enjoyed equal pay. Constant reminders that Australia has trouble 'selling overseas because of our standard of living [implies] our competitors have lower standards and are undercutting us', meaning 'it's in the national interest to promote equal standards throughout the world', not renounce equal pay for Australian women.

On 4 August 1962, federal government avowals of holding 'cabinet discussions', proved mendacious. The ***Age*** reported the Victorian Equal

Pay Committee (an ACSPA section) writing to Prime Minister Mr RG Menzies, asking if the federal budget would extend equal pay to federal public service women, reminding him of his promise to the ACTU, ACSPA, and Public Service Association (PSA) deputation to investigate and take their representations to cabinet. No personal investigation was undertaken, no cabinet discussion, and no federal budget provision for equal pay.

Two months later, on 24 October 1962, at Department of Labour and National Service estimates, Whitlam contradicted federal government assertions, reiterated by McMahon, of 'no opposition in principle' but 'must wait on the ... Commission ...'. Public service women's equal pay would add £1,300,000 only to the annual wages bill; including overseas civilian employees, excluding local staff, would add £65,000. With no difference in theory between Labor and Liberals, the government's position, if genuine, was obscure: McMahon, Whitlam added, 'is always in favour of virtue tomorrow'.

Mr JS Cockle (Lib., NSW) attacked, saying trade union leaders used 'bullying and intimidatory tactics' towards the Commission. 'People must be shocked by [their] arrogance and un-Australian attitude ...,' when NSW TLC secretary and ACTU Senior Vice-President Kenny 'told 3,000 shop stewards ... that unless the Commission granted the unions' claim for increased annual leave [it] would "cease to exist"'. 'Time' the Labor Party 'recognised its responsibility' by 'inducing the trade-union movement to abide by constitutional processes'.

Women and women's organisations weighed in. On 25 October 1962, headed 'Government lags on Equal Pay', the ***Sydney Morning Herald*** printed another letter by Miss Doris Osborne of Double Bay, NSW Teachers Federation, and AFBPW member. 'Sir, At intervals since 1953, successive Ministers for Labour and National Service have said the Government is "not opposed to the principle of equal pay."' Yet a government 'opposed to the principle could not do less to assist its implementation'. The Australian government supported ILO Recommendations 90 and 100 of 1951 for 'appropriate action' to apply equal pay to all central government employees and encourage application to state and local government department employees. On the 12 April, an ACTU deputation, supported by public service unions, had sought joint federal-state action, without result. Yet the federal government cooperated with the states on other economic and policy matters, including uniform divorce laws, company legislation, uniform restrictive trade practices, and adoption laws.

Why not equal pay? Nonsense, she said, to suggest NSW set an 'unhappy precedent' in the 1958 Female Rates Act, 'merely a first step towards bringing [NSW] into line with the rest of the world'.

Osborne referred to Canada, Ceylon, Chile, Finland, Iran, Israel, Japan, the Netherlands, Portugal, Turkey, US, UK, Uruguay, and Viet Nam extending civil servants equal pay despite not ratifying ILO 100. Protestations of needing the Commission's 'definitive determination' were fallacious, she said, adding that by 1963 the New Zealand Government Services Equal Pay Act 1960 would have phased in civil service equal pay completely. Why not Australia?

Yet by 1964, federal government equal pay estimates soared from £1,300,000 (1962) to 'about £2m'. Responding to Webb's protest that men and women working alongside one another without equal pay meant Australia was disavowing its ILO membership, McMahon denied it. The ACTU could approach the Commission on equal pay, and Commonwealth action extending female employees a male basic wage would compromise any review. Further, four Australian states vowed they 'would not ratify the Convention'. The ACTU had a log of claims for an increase in the ***Basic Wage Case*** right now, he added, so why was no equal pay claim included? The answer was clear: equal pay was not in trade union or workers' interest for (confirming 'worker' meant 'men only') if equal pay were granted, lacking productivity advances, the male basic wage and margins would be unlikely to be increased 'for many, many years to come'. Unions didn't raise equal pay in the Commission, preferring to agitate with deputations and petitions, casting responsibility on federal government, and running a 'dead' campaign to avoid equal pay. As for the Labor Party, they deliberately didn't press the unions to go to the Commission, instead railing in Parliament at the government, blatantly attempting to win female voters' sympathy. The Australian Labor Party (ALP), McMahon implied, hoped to turn women workers' ire onto government, away from unions.

Attorney-general Mr Billy Snedden was blunt. The opposition 'practised a deception to the House and the people of Australia'. Claiming they alone favoured equal pay, Labor was dependent for political support 'basically on the craft unions', but 'couldn't form a government while … relying principally on their support'. White-collar workers were essential for both ALP and ACTU, underlying their support for equal pay, said Snedden, which would not serve craft unions' interests, it diminishing their members' 'wage capacity. Why did the ACTU never raise equal pay? Because 'it fears it would not serve' craft union interests.

But Snedden wanted to have it both ways. Salaried officers' associations would 'make a great mistake' in affiliating with the ACTU and ALP. White-collar workers' interests frequently conflicted with craft union interests. Affiliation 'would submerge salaried officers' interests' in the traditional pattern of party support for the unions.

Unions, the Women's Movement, and 1960s Claims

Throughout the century, claims for equal opportunity with equal pay were reprised, with the 1960s no different. Without access to men's jobs, women lacked not only job rights, but also pay rates. Male industry jobs should be open to women, and men's jobs in industries with significant numbers of women, or women predominating but men holding the senior positions, likewise. Traditional women's work should gain equal status with men's traditional work—say nursing, librarianship, and teaching.

By letter dated 17 September 1960, received by Arnot on 20 September, AFBPW Wollongong highlighted the first claim. Would she 'consider B.& P.W. would be interested in obtaining permission for women to work industry (i.e. steelworks) on shift work … as crane drivers, forklift truck drivers, etc.?' A 'large volume of women' wanted employment in Wollongong, but could not find it:

> The Steelworks currently employs over 13,000 men … insufficient [numbers], and expansion programmes and new units progressively coming into production means we'll be short of labour to glory for many years ahead. We lay hands on every new Australian the Government will give us and have recruiting officers in all countries [trying] to meet our labour needs …

ALP and women teachers' activism encompass the second. In Melbourne in late November 1960, the Federal Conference of Labor Women passed resolutions for a free national health scheme and contributory social service tax, and an Australian constitutional amendment giving 'every woman worker a constitutional right to … wages at the same rate as a male worker doing the same kind of work', plus demanding equal appointment, training, and promotion opportunities. The 27 November 1960 ***West Australian*** reported one delegate saying, 'Australia once led the world' on women's rights; now, 'about 60 other countries … give women teachers equal pay'.

Women marched on May Day and Eight Hour Day proclaiming equal pay and equal job opportunity rights. The 2 May 1960 ***Sydney Morning Herald*** headlined Sydney's May Day march and women's participation in 'Equal pay their baby'. A year later, on 24 August 1960, the WA Teachers Union appointed a two-man, one woman deputation to WA's minister for education demanding women teachers' equal pay, with further deputations scheduled to lobby state MPs. Some 150 annual conference delegates (predominantly male) voted 'for' women teachers as 'the vanguard … ultimately lead[ing] to equal pay for equal work for all women'. On 29 August 1961, all women teachers and 'many male teachers present' at Union's annual conference (totalling almost 200) carried a motion for women teachers to 'receive promotional opportunities equal to [men's]'.

With ACTU backing, Equal Pay Week was held annually through the early 1960s. On late March to early April 1960, NSW celebrated with a Business and Professional Women (BPW) Sydney symposium, a discussion at Labour Council's weekly meeting, and activities at Teachers Federation headquarters, Federation House. In SA, the Trades & Labour Council (T&LC) established an Equal Pay Committee, unlike other states the only organisation outside the trade union movement with Committee representation being UAW. Working with UAW members, the Federated Clerks' Union (FCU)'s Joyce Henriott, Equal Pay Committee secretary, organised Equal Pay Week press releases and public meetings. No white-collar unions affiliated meant the Equal Pay Committee excluded many women workers. Consequently, member Beryl Miller reports, the Equal Pay Committee met with blue- and white-collar unions, creating the SA Equal Pay Council which then featured significantly in Equal Pay Week.

In Perth, a Town Hall meeting began 1960 Equal Pay Week, with Teachers' Union president N. Sampson emphasising that despite identical qualifications and women teachers' work being demonstrably equal to men's, women received less pay. Marriage meant demotion to the Department of Education's temporary list. Women paid heavily for their 2 years' training. If marrying during training, they repaid the bond covering teachers' training expenses. Married women who continued teaching sacrificed superannuation and holiday pay and, like permanent (unmarried) women teachers, were denied male rates.

Sampson shared the platform with Civil Service Association (CSA) past-president Mr AJ Fraser, who addressed contentions that cost rendered equal pay untenable. Agitation for a 40-hour week and other reforms met opponents forever talking of 'dreadful economic consequences' which didn't transpire, he said. Now, opponents prophesied 'rising costs, unemployment and a lowered marriage rate' following equal pay, simply another excuse, as these 'were present already'. Fraser quoted professor Heinz Arndt, Australian National University (ANU) economist, estimating equal pay as a 2 ½ per cent annual national salaries bill rise, £350,000 for WA which if '… spread over five years, the economy could meet without much difficulty'.

In 1961, Melbourne women marched to Parliament House bearing banners and chanting slogans. At a major Perth Town Hall rally on 10 April, speakers included Arnot, flown from Sydney, WT Dowsett, University of Western Australia (UWA) economics lecturer, and lawyer DC Heenan. On Wednesday 12 April, a WSG event featured newly elected UWA Convocation warden, Jean Ethel Rogerson (second woman elected after Dr Roberta Jull, who retired in 1930), as guest speaker. Next day, Arnot spoke on 'Equal Pay, Arbitration or Legislation' at an Adult Education Board symposium.

Anticipating the week, on 4 April, headlined 'Crusaders seek equal pay for women', the ***West Australian*** reported some 25,000 pamphlets would advertise 'equal pay for equal work', with stickers on letters and rear car windows. The Combined Equal Pay Committee, chaired by Miss JM Randell (an International Federation of Business and Professional Women (IFBPW) vice-president), organised the WA campaign. The Adult Education Board symposium was promoted despite—or because of—premier Brand's reiterating yet again 'equal pay was for the Arbitration Court'.

In 1961, officially woman's wage was 75 per cent of the male basic wage under the Arbitration Court's ***Basic Wage Inquiry 1949–1950***. As with other states (except NSW), Department of Consumer and Employment Protection records showed experienced WA women teachers receiving the 75 per cent basic rate plus male margins, making their salaries 80 to 90 per cent of the male rate. Many federal public servants earned similarly. In NSW, the Industrial Arbitration (Female Rates) Amendment Act 1958 (NSW), applying annual 5 per cent increases over a 5-year term, meant female civil servants, teachers, and workers in private industry where unions proved to the Industrial Commission their work was of equal value to men's were receiving 90 per cent of the male rate, expecting 100 per cent in 1963. Still, many women missed out. Consistent the ***Fruitpickers case 1912***, women workers did not qualify for male rates in an industry 'essentially or usually' a 'female industry'.

Like other states, in Equal Pay Week WA's Council for Equal Pay and Opportunity (CEPO) publicised (un)equal pay anomalies. In its 4 April 1961 'Crusaders …' story, the ***West Australian*** said equal pay for WA public servants would cost upwards of 3 per cent in salaries and wages, which 'could be absorbed', just as Australia absorbed the 40-hour week:

> Women [are] beating the drum still more since the Government Equal Pay Act [passed] the New Zealand Parliament last October [supported by] both major parties … N.Z. public servants will advance to parity by April 1963, [over] three years.

Women paid 'the same prices as men' for food, clothing, transport, and housing despite lesser wages, whilst it 'costs as much to support a woman as a man'. Men generally avoided care of dependent relatives—invalids or aged parents—women couldn't. Aged men, unlike single women, had their children 'for support in old age'. Women's 'prevailing feeling …behind the agitation is not optimistic', but belief that the campaign 'would grow', 'crusaders' saying lower pay 'is a relic of Victorian days when women led a sheltered existence beneath their father's roof until marriage' and 'an obvious badge of inferiority'.

Equal Pay Week meant lobbying governments. In 1966, a TLC and WA CEPO joint deputation met Mr O'Neil, minister for labour, then opposition leader Mr ARG (Bert) Hawke. Greenwood, the TLC's Mr JW Coleman, Teachers' Union Mr RG Moore, and CSA's Mr D. Alston wanted an Equal Pay Act, asking why WA was lagging. A state labour ministers conference set for July in Hobart, he undertook to 'seek a meeting on … equal pay legislation in other States'. On Channel 7, Greenwood argued for equal pay, broadcasting talks and radio interviews. A large public meeting twinned with an equally large equal pay dinner at the Nurses Memorial Centre, Kings Park Road. Having heard the Draft Declaration for the Elimination of Discrimination Against Women debated at Geneva the previous year, Greenwood applied it to equal pay, speaking alongside Miss N. Harken, CEPO chairman, Miss Jean Randell, and Miss E. Westhoven of St Joan's Political and Social Alliance. Surveying the hall of 90+ women and men representing government, opposition, public service, trade unions, employer, employees, and women's organisations, Harken confidently declared: 'The writing's on the wall in gold letters.'

A month later, on May 1966, Melbourne hosted a major 'Women at Work' conference. The Victorian Employers' Federation (VEF) with the

Department of Labour and National Service, Australian Industry Development Association (AIDA), and Committee for Economic Development of Australia (CEDA), invited speakers from Japan, the US, and UK, discussing:

- Australia's economy in changed conditions
- women's place in Australia's economic development
- full education and training opportunity for women in industry
- educating public opinion on women's 'new' status

If by omitting equal pay organisers thought it would be ignored, they were wrong. Quizzed, conference director Mr K. von Wolff dismissed equal pay and the questioner with: 'At this stage it is one of the technicalities.' As women primed themselves, making every opportunity to take the microphone, for 40 minutes during the opening unionists—all men—carried banners advocating equal pay, marching in the hotel's entrance. Madge Dawson, from NSW, decreed Mr von Wolff's assessment ill-judged. Equal pay, she said, 'reared its ugly head throughout'.

Yet from the late 1960s onwards, and into the 1970s, the 1930s, 1940s, 1950s and early 1960s, working relationship between women's organisations and trade unions fell away, or at least faltered. Overlap of union and women's organisation membership was less pronounced among newly developing groups and Women's Movement voices. Some women maintained dual membership, advocating joining unions, encouraging membership. However, women outside the labour movement were more likely to be, or be perceived as, trade union sceptics—seeing unions as unsupportive or antagonistic to women's claims.

No longer was it the 1950s argument, exemplified by Street and Rischbieth, of Communists and fellow-travellers. Many women believed failure to achieve equal pay lay with unions not setting women's issues on the industrial agenda. Women's ire was genuine: whatever unions had done, equal pay remained wanting. But those taking up the battle often failed to see that women had fought as unionists and within the unions for women's industrial rights, including equal pay, since unions began, women creating their own unions or joining men's. Yet others, like their foremothers, realised that however male dominated, unions must be brought into equal pay *on women's side.*

Equal Pay for Equal Work? Implementing the Legislation

By 1960s end, earlier agitation and the decade's activism coalesced. States had equal pay legislation implemented or ready. In June 1966, SA minister for labour and industry, Mr AF Kneebone, announced a Bill authorising the Industrial Commission to determine equal pay. Fashioned on the 1958 NSW Act, introduction over 5 years for all government employees, including teachers, began on 11 July 1967. The Industrial Conciliation and Arbitration Act 1961 (Qld) section 12(1)(ii), superseded the Wages Act 1918 (Qld) equal pay provision, meaning the Industrial Commission could 'in relation to a calling or callings' make an award providing 'the same wage … paid to persons of either sex performing the same work or producing the same return of profit' to employers.

In December, Tasmania's Public Service (Equal Pay) Act 1966 (Tas) section 3(4) applied equal pay to government employees 'for performance of work of … same or a like nature and of equal value'. Work 'of the same or a like nature as, and of equal value' meant taking into consideration 'whether female employees performed work … of the same range and volume as … male employees' and performed it 'under the same, or substantially the same, conditions'.

Women entered a new phase of struggle. Interpretation and implementation of the 1958 NSW Act warned women that lack of good faith or judicial will can subvert laws, and union activism is crucial for making industrial legislation work. As ever, financial cost and 'equal work' or 'equal value' were crucial.

The NSW Act was fully implemented by 1 January 1963. The Hon. JJ Maloney, labour and industry minister, reported that for 1963, equal pay would cost the state government about £4,250,000. Meeting the Act's conditions—equal pay for the same work, or kind of work, as men—all women teachers, many public servants, some shop assistants, some in industry automatically received the final equal pay instalment. But to qualify, women must do 'the same range and volume of work under the same conditions' as men. 'Automatically' brought no easy gain. Equal pay remained elusive, for absent equal opportunity, men continued earning more through promotions, training, overtime, bonuses, and benefits women were denied. Besides, for the vast majority, an Equal Pay Act didn't mean women gained it.

Governmental declarations, announcements, and re-announcements, parliamentary shilly-shallying, concerted lobbying by unions and women's organisations. The NSW Labour government introduces an Equal Pay Bill. Endless-seeming debate ensues. More lobbying by women's organisations. Finally, the Bill is carried. On 28 March 1960, the Act in force for some 14 months, a ***Sydney Morning Herald*** 'Staff Correspondent' concluded the effect limited. Progress, measured by 'numbers of women ... affected', was 'slow'. Excluding women working in 'women's industries' (even with men employed) meant:

> Women teachers whose work is of the same nature as and of equal value to ... men teachers, qualify for equal pay; but nurses, [their] vocation essentially feminine despite ... male nurses, do not.

Except for a narrow range of women, Equal Pay Acts did not mean equal pay. Unions asserting members came under the Act must apply to the Industrial Commission. Women not qualifying remained on 75 per cent of the male basic wage. The 'Female Rates' Act made no difference to them, though not all cases were as clear-cut as the nurses. In November 1959, the state clerks' award came up for review. The Commission interpreted section 88D, setting basic principles for its application to new awards.

Re Clerks (State) Award and Other Awards 1959 (***Clerks case***) confirmed the provisions applied to adult females only, not juniors, with the onus on unions to prove the work met the required equivalence of men's. This was the reverse of the war years under the Women's Employment Board (WEB). There, employers had to show work done by women did not equate to that of male workers they replaced, and juniors were covered. Under the NSW scheme, another obstacle obtruded: applications for marginal or secondary rates for females were required to include a case for fixing those rates for males.

Additionally, section 88D required Commission and conciliation committees, in specified circumstances, to insert equal pay provisions as between the sexes in awards and industrial agreements. Where these specific circumstances existed, the same marginal or secondary rates of wages must be awarded for males and females, the total rate of wages payable to female employees calculated by adding to the marginal or secondary rates prescribed percentages of the basic wage for adult males. Where the specified circumstances were not proven, assessment of female employee wage rates continued under rules governing the (differential) basic wage for adult females—not equal pay.

In section 88D applications, investigations were limited to work for which rates were, or were to be, fixed by a particular award or a particular industrial agreement. A conciliation committee or tribunal was not required to look beyond the calling or industry in an application. There was no requirement to look *across* awards. This limited women's equal pay access, by cutting out equal pay for female employees for whom rates were fixed by one award, and were not doing work of the same or like nature and equal value to males' work under that award, but performed work of the same or like nature as, and equal value to, work performed by males under another award. Looking across awards meant significantly more women would qualify for equal pay. This required waiting for the ***Equal Pay Case 1972***.

As for 'work', the Industrial Commission required precise, not generic, interpretation. Work done by a shop assistant-in-charge of a shop fell automatically into a different category from an ordinary shop assistant. Thus, the female shop assistant could not utilise wage rates of the male assistant-in-charge to boost her pay. Contrarily, if male shop assistants earned more than their female counterpart in charge, she could not lay claim to a higher rate of pay based on their both being shop assistants. Nor could she claim she was underpaid because a man doing 'the same' job with fewer responsibilities was paid more. Similarly, work done by a stenographer was different from a telephonist or a clerk, and so on.

The Industrial Commission said it would be equally incorrect to decide that work of individual employees in a particular establishment only should be considered. Specific classes of work under one award should be identified and defined, then work of males and females in each specified class compared. Where the award applied to several establishments, to succeed, applicants must adduce evidence sufficient to prove the work in question was 'the same or a like nature as and of equal value' to work of all males under the award, doing work of that nature: this took the enquiry beyond the one establishment.

New principles for grouping of employees covered by the award in an application made it more difficult for large numbers of female employees to qualify. The Commission decided the common practice up to then—grouping together female employees covered by one award and fixing a common rate, notwithstanding that work performed might differ in range, volume, value, and conditions under which performed, was inappropriate in equal pay applications. This restrictive approach highlighted the connection between equal pay and equal opportunity: while women were denied equal opportunity, under section 88D they would not gain equal pay.

Valuing 'work', the Commission said 'of equal value' did not mean of equal value to employers but the value the Commission or a conciliation committee placed on work. Otherwise, 'the whole nature' of wage fixing would be changed, solely for equal pay cases. As well, 'of equal value' meant 'at least' of equal value, meaning that female employees performing work of the same or like nature as male employees but of greater value would be entitled to equal pay (not more). Range, volume, and conditions of performance should be included when considering the nature of the work and its value. Nonetheless, a tribunal was free to find females' work as of equal value to males', notwithstanding that the work women and men performed differed in range or volume or conditions under which performed.

For comparative work value, the Commission ruled irrelevant females' shorter working life on average as compared to males, and at least discounted notions that females may be less capable than males of assuming higher responsibilities. However, section 88D(9)(b) explicitly ruled out extension of equal pay to 'any awards and industrial agreement provisions' covering employees doing work 'essentially or usually performed by females' but on which males might also work, ruling out 'women's work' as the ***Sydney Morning Herald*** had noted, and reminiscent of the 1912 ***Fruitpickers case***. The onus again rested on unions: here, to qualify by showing the work was not 'women's work'. Making it even more difficult for women to escape this restriction, the Commission said 'usually' and 'essentially' must be read disjunctively, not as a composite. Success required proof of each component.

The Public Service Board (PSB) accepted NSW women teachers (9,600) were covered, plus most professionals—scientists, doctors, dentists, architects, laboratory assistants, and approximately 200 women in the clerical field qualifying through 'male' examinations for promotion to above base pay scale positions. The PSA estimated some 4,000 women members automatically in line for equal pay. But the PSB said librarians and all stenographers, secretaries, and clerical staff machinists—say comptometrists—engaged, like nurses, in feminine work, so fell outside the Act.

Between January and March 1960, applications were made for three categories: five tobacco workers, more than 400 garage attendants, and thousands of shop assistants in the ***Clerks & Shop Assistants case***. Determining the women and men were in paidwork of equal value, the Commission granted women the male basic wage under a formula. Justice Beattie fixed three new awards for shop assistants, for equal pay by stages, receiving male pay rates from 1 January 1963, commencing with 85 per cent of the male basic wage plus the male margin in 1960, 90 per cent plus male margin next, then 100 per cent plus male margin. Newcastle and country shop assistants and country office assistants came under the new awards. Existing awards had (for some years) contained equal pay for women in male departments: groceries and cooked provisions, men's clothing, youths' clothing, hardware, furniture (excluding baby furniture), carpets and linoleum, Manchester, mercury flooring, sports goods, saddlery, wireless sales, motor vehicle accessories, and bicycles. Now, women in soft furnishings, dress materials, furnishing drapery, boys' clothing, household hardware, crockery and glassware, household electrical goods, nursery furniture, napery, and towels (manchester), jewellery, watches and clocks, beers, wines and spirits, travel goods, pipes and cigarette lighters, office machinery and equipment, plastic sheeting, cameras and photography equipment other than film and photofinishing services, and fish (cooked and uncooked) gained equal pay. Office assistants in retail shops missed out, Beattie noting the FCU could raise this later, but not suggesting it for baby furniture sales, baby clothes, or women and girls' apparel. Retail Traders' Association (RTA) NSW secretary, Mr JB Griffin, underscored the anomaly excluding 'about half female shop assistants': female assistants selling goods usually sold by females alone did not qualify for equal pay, women selling goods sold by men did.

April 1966, reporting on the ***Clerks & Shop Assistants case***, the ***Sydney Morning Herald*** noted several unions put equal pay applications on hold pending its outcome. Next listed was the hospital employees' metropolitan award, viz. all hospital employees other than nurses. Meanwhile, librarians sought PSB discussions, exploring whether—women's work or not—they could seek a Commission ruling. University libraries (excluding the University of New South Wales (UNSW)) and others outside the public service, say municipal libraries, paid all senior librarians the male rate. State Library staff were shocked that their rights were questioned. Not only did interpretation of the Act exclude many women workers. If employers refused to acknowledge workers came within it, women workers and women's organisations lacked standing to apply, unions alone being entitled to argue women members' eligibility.

Trade union secretary Griffin was not the Act's sole critic. Rather than quelling women's claims, the Industrial Commission's approach stirred them on. Reporting on equal pay for qualifying shop assistants, the 4 April 1960 ***Sydney Morning Herald*** promoted Sydney BPW's symposium 'Women-Power in Australia'. Two days earlier NSW TLC secretary Kenny was in the news, too, the ***Sydney Morning Herald*** of 2 April reporting his saying women were 'somewhat weary of being a source of cheap labour …'. Men decried 'unfair competition from women': 'If a woman is doing a job equal to a man's, she should receive the man's wage.'

Male chauvinism and whimsy reared. Commissioner Sheehy, ostensibly applying the 1958 Act, in the ***Checkers and Assemblers case 1962*** held 60 women drug warehouse checkers and assemblers entitled to a basic wage at 95 per cent of the male rate. The rationale is obscure—none appears in the reported decision. If the women did men's work, they were entitled to the full male basic wage, if women's work, 75 per cent. Reminiscent of Second World War WEB decisions, apparently for Sheehy, a woman, not being a man, could never qualify fully for men's work—even when that was what she did.

Commissioner Herron in the ***Federated Tobacco Workers' case 1964***, a dispute between Rothman's of Pall Mall (Australia) Ltd and the Federated Tobacco and Cigarette Workers' Union (FTCWU), questioned five females and five males employed on Rothman's South Granville plant's sticking line. The job required picking up tobacco from tobacco leaf bales, shaking to separate leaves, then placing them across a moving conveyor line. Neither Rothman's nor the union raised equal pay, the union claiming the work unsuitable for women. Four of the five women said the work was continuous but not arduous. Herron called it simple repetitive work involving no extraordinary effort, with 'no reason adult females should not be employed' there. His 'firm view' was that equal pay 'must be closely looked at …'. If Rothman's employed women on the sticking line—as employers they were entitled to do—the 1958 Act existed, he must consider it, and the male rate of pay should apply. Equal pay awarded, the women gained 85 per cent of the male basic wage plus the male margin payable immediately, 100 per cent by January 1963, wages rising from £14 0s 6d to £18 18s 0d weekly, £3 7s 6d being the male margin.

Beyond women profiting directly, despite its limitations equal pay legislation had benefits. Taking the argument, prevalent throughout the equal pay struggle, that paying women men's rates would lose women jobs, Herron's finding should have gained what the FTCWU wanted: no women on the sticking line. The ***Courier Mail*** of 20 March 1963 reported Arnot as NSW NCW president speaking during Brisbane's Equal Pay Week, highlighting the fallacy. Contrary to assertions of treasurer Mr Harold Holt, equal pay under the NSW Act 'had not meant undesirable economic and industrial repercussions' for the state. 'It was thought,' she said, that women '… would be out of their jobs and business would go to other States. I have not heard of one woman losing her job …' Arnot said 'industry could absorb [the change] over five years as a wage adjustment'. Women wanting equal pay legislation should 'urge some large group to act as the primary fighting force'.

Arnot believed women should join or join with unions and industrial associations to achieve the goal. She spoke from experience for, once claims met with success, women and sympathetic unions acted. On 30 October 1961, at its biennial federal conference, the Public Services Federation (PSF) supported extending equal pay to 'all working women in Australia'. A motion that the federal government follow NSW 'eliminating different salary scales, based on sex, for government employees' asked state public service associations to seek similar legislation. Another supported women's bureaux in the Commonwealth Department of Labour and National Service and state labour and industry departments, to promote appreciation of women workers' 'special problems', 'socially, economically, and industrially'.

The 1969 Equal Pay Case

By early 1963, the 1958 NSW (Female Rates) Amendment Act had benefited over 20,000 women. Without going to the Industrial Commission, women and unions' demands brought equal pay to teachers (the largest group, 12,000 women receiving identical basic salaries as men), about 600 public service women, including librarians, medical officers, pharmacists, laboratory assistants, cooks, dental officers, and medical technologists classed as doing the same work under the same conditions as men. Union applications brought women equal pay where employers refused. Many more women continued working for unequal pay, nurses one of the largest groups. Buoyed by the impact at state level, and scenting federal possibilities, unions went to the Commonwealth Conciliation and Arbitration Commission.

The Liberal-Country Party government's charge that the Labor opposition was diverting attention from unions' failure to raise equal pay with the federal Commission seems disingenuous when considering the Commission's approach. Not only had the ***Basic Wage Inquiry 1949–1950*** ruled women's work as worth only 75 per cent of men's, the economy able to bear no more, but 1960s Commission decisions illustrated its wariness, even scepticism, toward equal pay justice.

The ***Basic Wage Case 1965*** set a new formula for margins (payments atop the basic wage), denying women automatic rights to margins equal to men's in the same industry. On 6 July, the ***Australian Financial Review*** reported industrial concerns that the decision could depress wage relativities for large numbers of women, a certainty if, when adjusting wages in awards, conciliation commissioners and wage tribunals applied the judgment literally. Thousands of women had margins parity with men. One example was 36,000 women, including juniors, employed by the Commonwealth PSB and receiving male margins: applying the Commission's decision would stop this.

Traditionally, a male employee earning £2,000 a year—£800 basic wage, £1,200 margin—received an additional £30 0s 0d annually in margins, a female employee doing the same work received with margin parity £1,800 a year—£600 basic wage, £1,200 margin. The Commission's new formula calculated annually gave female employees £27 0s 0d extra only. The ***Financial Review*** observed the difference 'may be small', but 'the principle [will] likely loom large' for women. It did. NCW said its members would 'certainly get busy …'.

The ***Basic Wage Case 1965*** proved an aberration. The ***Clothing Trades case 1967*** reinstated equal margins, and even before, the ***Basic Wages, Margins and Total Wage Case 1966*** brought equal pay closer. The Commission held basic wage increases for adult males should accrue proportionately to adult female employees, junior employees, and apprentices. Then, the PSA journal ***Red Tape*** (November 1968) reported on pending federal equal pay claims, saying that if 'breakthroughs' gained equal pay for work of equal value, it would assist the NSW equal pay campaign.

The Commonwealth Conciliation and Arbitration Commission had one claim, the PSA the other. With the ***National Wage Case 1967*** finalised, the ACTU wanted an early hearing. Earlier Mr Leslie Bury, minister for labour and national service, initiated an appeal against an equal pay award made by commissioner Clarkson. Writing to BPW Sydney, Bury justified this saying 'such a far-reaching issue' should be decided by

Commission presidential members, not one commissioner. This provided an opportunity.

The ***National Wage Case 1967*** replaced the basic wage with the 'total wage', now expressed in $Aus (1966 currency change). On 5 June, president Richard Kirby (with justices Gallagher and Moore, and commissioner Winter) decided 'for the present' on 'a different total wage for males and females and ... total wages for many classifications', because of 'existing basic wage differentials and ... quite complex history of basic wages, particularly ... for females ... starting ... from the concept of differing needs and responsibilities of men and women'. Noting male-female basic wages adjustment over time created 'apparent anomalies', with the community 'facing economic industrial and social challenges', Kirby said the Commission 'deliberately' awarded identical increases to adult females and males. His invitation to unions, employers, and the Commonwealth to 'study carefully' the issues raised, with the Commission 'available to assist ... resolution of the problems'—generated the ***Equal Pay Case 1969.***

The Female Scientific Officers' Group (FSOG) asked the Commission to resolve one anomaly, namely 'equal pay for work of equal value'. The ACTU wanted the 25 per cent differential, ranging up to $8.20, between the old male and female basic wage rates, removed. The ***Equal Pay Case 1969***, begun on 25 February 1969, was delayed by a High Court challenge heard in March, and illness of two judges.

First, the High Court. Employers argued Kirby and Moore should recuse themselves as in the ***National Wage Case 1967*** they had raised equal pay. Albeit the Commission's invitation to consider the issues was to unions, employers, and government, the employers said the judges were biased. With the challenge dismissed, Kirby stepped down on medical advice. On 28 April 1969, the hearing resumed, the National Employers' Policy Committee (NEPC)'s James Robinson foreshadowed a dismissal application immediately the ACTU's case concluded: the application was 'clearly outside national wage case consideration'. On 1 May 1969, he sought dismissal because the unions claimed an increase of $8.20 'for all women workers, no matter what industry they work in or what award they work under ... turning the case for equal pay ... into a full-scale national wage claim' and, even then, asking for more!

Forewarned, outside Carlton Trades Hall, hordes of women from the meatworks, with male colleagues, gathered. Marching down Swanston Street they waved banners, chanting slogans:

UNEQUAL PAY IS SEX DISCRIMINATION
MAKE 1969 EQUAL PAY YEAR
EQUAL PAY IS A HUMAN RIGHT
LET'S NOT BUILD ON CHEAP LABOUR
THE TIME IS NOW FOR EQUAL PAY
DELIBERATE DELAY ON EQUAL PAY
MEAT INDUSTRY WOMEN SUPPORT EQUAL PAY

A 50-minute adjournment, then Moore (presiding) said the claim, for the difference between 'the now extinct male and female basic wages', would continue.

Despite repeating obsessively that its policy was for equal pay, and for the Commission to decide it, on 2 May 1969, the Commonwealth's Mr AE Woodward, QC, opposed the claim, telling the Full Bench he was 'not opposed to the principle' but, atop increasing the annual wages bill, 'repercussions' in female-dominated industries—clothing, textiles, electrical engineering and some food industries—would follow. Furthermore, claims 'would cause a major shift in real earnings from male to female wage and salary earners'. Female award fixing history was 'so complex' that the unions' 'simple formula' for equal pay wouldn't work. An award-by-award examination, with 'proper work-value principles ... applied ...' was required. Conditions to be met included 'carrying out the same work as males in range, volume and conditions'. Adopting these principles meant 'females should no longer be automatically excluded from any areas of work ...'.

Thus, by sleight of hand the Commonwealth effectively damned equal pay by arguing it should be accompanied by equal employment opportunities for women, meaning it would take years. Equal opportunity was claimed consistently by women wanting equal pay, but was used now to delay it. The Commonwealth's argument meant, practically, the only way to gain equal pay was accessing men's jobs. Menzies, Holt, Bury, McMahon, Gorton, and others' protestations of equal pay support through the 1950s and 1960s rang hollow.

The employers were even more intransigent. Mr JH Wootten, QC, for Angliss Meat Group (AMG) and Australian Council of Retailers (ACR), took umbrage at the Commonwealth's concession that if the Commission agreed to equal pay, phasing-in of no fewer than 5 years was essential. His two-pronged argument indicated that under no conditions did employers want equal pay. First, Wootten claimed 5-years phasing-in would enable employers to 'evade the issue', creating 'industrial discontent', and segregation of women workers into separate areas to defeat claims. Further, male workers, 'supporting wives and children', would be provoked 'into grave resistance': a curious contention since working men, representing male-dominated unions, presented the union case. Yet it enabled Wootten to conclude, finally, that existing male and female wage differences remained 'appropriate', so the ACTU claims should be rejected 'in their entirety'.

Australian Meat Industries Association (AMIA) counsel, Mr JT Ludeke, wanted the application dismissed, with the ACTU making its arguments in a ***National Wage Case***, 'because the economy is involved'. For the National Employers' Policy Committee, Robinson said the claim would cost $400m to $500m annually.

Meanwhile, Mr CE (Charles Edward) Barnes, minister for external territories, announced that equal pay would apply to Indigenous female public servants in Papua-New Guinea. The wage differential varied from nothing, at the lowest grade of $480 per year, to a maximum of $100 per year, so from 1 July 1969:

> Local female officers doing the same work as, or very similar work to, males, and the same range and volume of work ... under the same conditions, should be paid equally.

Two months before, on 28 April, ACTU advocate Mr RJ Hawke had opened the ***Equal Pay Case 1969*** saying Australian women were treated 'as second-class citizens', 'discriminated against by having their wages artificially lowered'. Old concepts were applied to working women 'irrespective of major changes occurring in recent years'. Discrimination implicit and explicit in earlier cases continued to affect today's working women, he said, adding that women were 'no longer inferior beings, whose lot is marriage and everything that goes with it'. Statistics showed this 'feudal picture' was obsolete. In 60 years, despite 'increasing numbers of women entering industry', 'the archaic method of wage payment' based on the 'old family wage concept' had not changed. It must.

Other union groups began their case on 1 May 1969, then came Ada Norris representing NCW, Powell for the Australian Federation of Women Voters (AFWV), AM (Peg) Magoffin for AFBPW, and Joan Child representing UAW. They argued 'the rate for the job', demolishing the 'equal pay would cost too much' proposition. When figures of $400m and

$500m are put forward, said Magoffin, they are 'meaningless if taken in isolation from other major statistical aggregates in the national economy'. She related the cost 'to the value of the gross national product at factor cost and the wages, salaries and supplements component of the gross national product'. Calculations showed the $400m sum put forward as the cost of granting equal pay was 3.2% of the value of wages and salaries during the 1968 year, 'just a shade over the equivalent of six months rise in the level of wages and salaries right throughout the Commonwealth'. With UAW and AFWV, her stand was that the cost argument was no argument, equal pay 'a matter of simple justice' and Australia is at 'a stage of economic and social evolution ... possible for women to be awarded remuneration based on their education, training, experience and work contribution without discrimination or disparity on grounds of sex alone'. Equal pay would 'motivate girls and women to become educated and trained to the limit of their capabilities, the consequential improvement in quality and quantity of the Australian work force having incalculable economic advantages to Australia'.

On 22 May, case completed, decision reserved, women awaited the judgment. One month later, Thursday 19 June 1969, judgment was delivered.

Gloom replaced initial elation. 'Few women to benefit from wage decision' ran the ***Sydney Morning Herald*** 20 June editorial: 'Leading union and employer spokesmen estimated the number as low as 50,000 women out of a total women's work force of 1,230,700 (excluding domestic and rural workers).' Equal pay was approved, but unions must make separate applications for each classification seeking equal pay, and the usual restrictions applied—men and women working under the same determination nor award covering work performed by both; and work of (a) the same or a like nature and of equal value, mere similarity in names of classifications not necessarily enough; and (b) the same range and volume and under the same conditions.

Unlike most pay claims, there was no retrospective operation or backdating pay rises for applications made on or after 1 October 1969. Three-year phasing-in meant 85 per cent of the male wage for the first pay period on or after 1 October 1969; 90 per cent on 1 January 1970; 95 per cent 1 January 1971; 100 per cent 1 January 1972.

So, 10 years after NSW's equal pay legislation (with its limitations), more than 50 years after Higgins' equal pay for women fruit pickers—equal pay for equal work was affirmed (again). But again, not equal pay for women's work—once more reliant on what men did, and whether any women did, or could be said to do it, too. As in the ***Fruitpickers case 1912***, as with the NSW Act, no equal pay for work 'essentially or usually performed by females'.

On 22 June 1969, the ***Sun-Herald*** believed women should be pleased:

> Editorial: Equality—Of A Sort
> The women ought not to be too disappointed. They have had a win, of sorts.

'Equal pay for equal work' was 'hobbled', no 'big bonanza ahead for the ordinary run of women workers', so 'typists and nurses and those doing similar "women's work"' would have to put up with it, 'consider that work inferior, at least for now.' And whatever the ***Sun-Herald*** said, women could retort that no bonanza came to those 'winning'. No bounty, just simplest wage justice.

If granted in full, the ACTU's claim would have gained women in all industries and occupations, as an essential 'total wage' component, a sum equal to the old male basic wage, making the national wages bill ten times that then paid in wages, or $20m in the first year and $50m in full operation after 4 years, the ***Sydney Morning Herald*** said, whereas the Commonwealth wages bill would rise little, paid to some 7,000 women, clerical to professional, in the public service third division. Employers and federal government could rest easy. What of women?

End of the Decade

In July, ***Red Tape*** lamented 'Disappointing Decision in Equal Pay Case'. Unions and women's organisations said the ***Equal Pay Case 1969*** ignored or sold out their interests. ACTU secretary Souter expressed 'dismay'. Hawke called the decision 'disappointing'. FCU federal secretary Mr J. (Joe) Riordan characterised it 'an outstanding Commonwealth Government victory and severe trade-union movement defeat'. Mr FT Hall, Meat Industry Employees' Union (MIEU) federal secretary, said his union would apply for the meat industry's 3,500-odd female employees, anyway. The clothing industry's 50,000 workers had no such chance, said Mr F Peterson, Clothing and Allied Trades Union of Australia (CATUA) general secretary. Australian Clerical Officers' Association (ACOA) assistant federal secretary Mr S. Imer announced plans to approach the

Commonwealth Public Service Arbitrator (PSA) for 3,000 clerical and administrative staff. The PSA decried 'no advance at all' for their female members. AFWV advocate Powell said she'd 'be surprised if 5 per cent of women under Federal awards received equal pay from the judgment'.

Politicians and ex-politicians weighed in. Mr JJ Maloney, former labour and industry minister responsible for the NSW's 'Female Rates' Act, called the equal pay principle 'outdated'. The decision entrenched discrimination. Restricting women to 'work of equal value to men, or of a like nature' was wrong, he said, wanting 'total abolition of discrimination between male and female rates no matter what the work …' The NSW legislation aimed 'to open the way', but neither federal nor present state government 'made any advance'. Predictably, treasurer and acting minister for labour and national service McMahon was laudatory.

The 20 June ***Sydney Morning Herald*** editorial deemed McMahon's 'memorable landmark' assertion wrong, saying states 'achieved' equal pay already, but the decision was just what the Commonwealth wanted: 'costing very little', 'no significant economic problems', consistent with 'lip service to the concept of equality, [and] never ratifying I.L.O. wage discrimination conventions'.

For employers, Mr FS Buckley, NSW Chamber of Manufacturers president, lamented the 'extra cost burden' on employers, estimated at 'about $50m', with 'about $20m' for state employers. Australian Council of Employers' Federation (ACEF) president, Mr Arthur, agreed, but, '… if … determined to introduce equal pay … it [was] the most logical and sensible method …' Manufacturing, Transport and Engineering Australia (MTEA) president Mr JB Clarkson referenced the limited application, whilst protesting at the 'unions gain'. Associated Chamber of Manufacturers Australia (ACMA) federal president Mr JC Campbell stressed it 'didn't [allow] for a flood of increases in female wages', saying employers readiness to 'engage women' would be unaffected. Mr Gibson, NEPC chairman, wanted 'closest scrutiny of work performed by women' before any equal pay award, advocating stringency in interpreting 'equal work' and proposing employers 'strenuous opposition' to anything further.

The 22 June ***Sun Herald*** editorial did ask 'what next?' referencing anthropological evidence of women's exclusion being 'old as primitive society … animals [having] thought of it first'. Citing 'male bonding' and 'men always sticking together … around the party keg or boardroom table' as 'confirming their superiority in their own minds, making sure they get the gravy …', more than one judgment was required to 'break that down'. The ***Herald***'s 20 June 'Column Eight' was more direct:

> Equal pay … Didn't George Orwell once write, in 'Animal Farm,' …: 'All animals are equal but some animals are more equal than others'?

Media coverage reveals journalists unaware and women not knowing of Higgins' 1912 determination. That the Arbitration Court treated women as fruit-pickers and women as fruit-packers differently, just as 55 years later the Arbitration Commission treats women in women's jobs is no news item, nor part of 1960s women's knowledge of their history. Yet the ***Fruitpickers case*** history is not necessary to generate women's outrage.

Melbourne's D'Aprano adopts direct action. On 21 October 1969, proclaiming distress and disgust, she affixes herself to Spring Street Commonwealth offices building, 'the green latrine'. Chains being expensive, she borrows a length from Painters and Dockers Union secretary, Jim Donogan, buys locks and, shackled to the doors, hands the keys to a woman holding a placard. Police arrive. Journalists ask: 'Do you feel like Mrs Pankhurst?' Told to unchain herself, she refuses. It's lunchtime. The colleague with the keys is off buying sandwiches. The building warden reads a prepared script. 'I have no keys,' D'Aprano replies. 'I refuse.'

A week passes. On 31 October, demonstrating again, schoolteachers Alva Geikie and Thelma Solomon join her. She buys more locks. The chain comes from the Builders Labourers Federation (BLF). D'Aprano drapes the links around the three of them, just long enough to keep one door slightly open. Bending down, people crawl in sideways to enter. The building warden's voice trembles reading his 'text for the day'. Police officers come with bolt cutters. Television cameras whirr. A Commissioner later says he's lucky D'Aprano didn't know who he was, crawling through the doorway, or she 'may have wrapped the chain around his neck'.

Pictured in all their courageous obstinacy, stirring women around Australia, some new, some equal pay proponents of past decades attracted to a more visible stance, some never on the streets before. Incensed at denial of women's personhood, independence, and autonomy downgrading women's worth, D'Aprano's action proclaims a new phase. In progressing earlier women's work, 1960s and 1970s women new to the struggle often overlook the 1950s, or see those women as fuddy-duddys. Yet they discover, and learn all over again, the value of women's earlier efforts.

Individual women's lives illuminate the campaign. Brave 1950s women's truth combines with 1960s women's courage onwards into 1970s mettle. Chapter 12, 'Intermission—Pay and Personalities II', champions women demanding women's history and herstory's truth, discovery and recovery, activists' cooperation in women's struggle-story.

References

Cases—see Case List

AFBPW, *Submission to the 1969 Equal Pay Case*, AFBPW, Sydney, NSW, 1969; reproduced Buswell and Rapp, ***Milestones—***, 1988, pp. 12–14; also in Thoms (comp./ed.), ***The First 25 Years***, AFBPW, Sydney, NSW, 1972.

Jean F. Arnot, 'Embedded in the Soul', in JA Scutt (ed), ***Taking a Stand*** -, Artemis Publishing, Melbourne, Victoria, 1994, pp. 116–28.

Jean Arnot, ***Interview***, Double Bay, NSW (6 April 1992).

Jean F. Arnot Papers 1916–1969 ML MSS 3147, ADD On 2070/4, Mitchell Library, Sydney, NSW.

BPW Wollongong, *Letter to Jean Arnot*, 1960 (17 September 1960); copy ***Jean F. Arnot Papers 1916–1969 ML MSS 3147, ADD On 2070/4***, Mitchell Library, Sydney, NSW.

CE Barnes, ***Statement on Equal Pay for New Guinea Public Service***, Canberra, ACT, 1969 (30 June 1969), ***Irene Greenwood Collection***, MU, Perth, WA.

Irene Bonella, 'A century of pay inequity: …', ***Australian Library Journal***, http://www.alia.org.au/publishing/alj/52.4/full.text.bonella.html, 2003, pp. 1–11 (accessed 11 July 2006).

AJ Fraser, Unpublished Paper (no title), Perth, WA, 1960; copy ***Irene Greenwood Collection***, MU, Perth, WA.

Zelda D'Aprano, ***Interview***, Laureton, NSW, 1994 (April 1994).

D'Aprano, ***Zelda***, 1975 orig pub., Spinifex Press, Melbourne, Victoria, 1995.

Irene Greenwood, *Report to the State Annual Conference of the WA Council for Equal Pay and Opportunity*, July 1966, copy ***Irene Greenwood Collection***, MU, Perth, WA.

House of Representatives, ***Hansard***, Australian Parliament, Canberra, ACT, 1962 (18 October 1962a).

House of Representatives, ***Hansard***, Australian Parliament, Canberra, ACT, 1962 (24 October 1962b).

House of Representatives, ***Hansard***, Australian Parliament, Canberra, ACT, 1964 (April 1964).

Judith Parker, ***Personal Communication***, Perth, WA, 1994 (8 June 1994).

Public Service Federation, *Triennial Conference Papers*, Sydney, NSW, 1961 (30 October 1961); copy ***Jean F. Arnot Papers 1916–1969 ML MSS 3147, ADD On 2070/4***, Sydney, NSW.

Barbara (Callaway) Salinger, ***Personal Communication***, Perth, WA, 1995 (9 October 1995).

Kay Setches, 'No Circuses, No Unreal Promises' in JA Scutt (ed.), ***As a Woman -***, Artemis Publishing, Melbourne, Victoria, 1992, pp. 60–73.

UAW, ***Our Women***, UAW, Melbourne, Victoria, 1969 (June-July 1969); see also G. Robertson, Women's Web, ***Interview—Yvonne Smith***, http://home.vicnet.net.au/~weomnweb/sources/First%20Narratives/YvonneSmith.htm (accessed 26 June 2006).

WA Teachers' Union, *Annual Conference Resolutions*, Perth, WA, 1961 (29 August 1961); copy ***Irene Greenwood Collection***, MU, Perth, WA; 1960 annual conference papers ***Irene Greenwood Collection***, Perth, WA.

CHAPTER 12

Intermission: Pay and Personalities II

'What do you want here?' hooted an interjector … at the lunch-hour meeting for I.X.L. factory girls … 'You never wash a cup!' 'You couldn't do a day's washing,' screamed others. Hastily Mrs. Metcalfe held up her flag of battle—a large double-bed quilt of squares knitted by the Mosman Group of the Guild of Empire. Silence … Mrs. Metcalfe explained co-operation and loving friendship made it … Only [they] could bring success. First in the home, then in industry, co-operation between capital, management, and labour …

It was a most unpleasant afternoon. The Communist women, led by Mrs. Jean Duvanney, interrupted continuously … We [were] proud to belong to the Guild, listening to Mrs. Walsh quietly answering the avalanche of questions … hurled at her while honestly trying to help these people.

Secretary's Monthly Report, 6 April 1934
Empire Gazette, no. 71, April 1936, p. 5

Except in extremely backward societies and among feudal-minded men in modern communities, there is no longer need to prove … women are capable of doing any job men can do and remain womanly.

Dymphna Cusack speaks. It's June 1960. At United Associations (UA) monthly meeting at rooms in Market Street, Sydney, Cusack's paper, *Women in Socialist Lands*, addresses 'Equal pay for equal work and equality … in all laws, rules and regulations', second of UA's aims and objects.

J. A. Scutt, *Wage Rage for Equal Pay*,
https://doi.org/10.1007/978-3-031-42178-5_12

Cusack completed the speech on 18 April in Warsaw, having travelled through the Soviet Union, German Democratic Republic (GDR), Albania, Hungary, Czechoslovakia, and China. Living in France, England, and Italy, 'with brief excursions into Spain, Switzerland and West Germany, and trips to Ceylon and India, to Panama, the Philippines and Hong Kong', she's seen 'the struggle women have everywhere in the Capitalist countries to live decently, to be educated, to be justly paid for their labour, to have equal access to the professions, equal opportunity to develop their talents—in brief, to live full lives …'.

Furthermore, 'Wide travelling has taught me to judge crowds.'

For the UA crowd she addresses, Cusack's invitation is not without controversy. Afterwards, Vivienne Newson writes to WA's Irene Greenwood. 'One of the old girls,' she says, 'was carrying on and on about how there is no more work to do. We women have everything we need, that's her constant cry. Feminism is old hat.' Reading on, Greenwood learns that UA stalwarts fear 'the old girl' will frighten away members. Feminism with no point, what point UA?

'It's been a real trial,' Newson continues. 'When … Dymphna as speaker arose the whole wretched kit and kaboodle blew up. The others didn't want to provide any opening for her to spoil Dymphna's visit and our coup in getting Dymphna to speak.' But what does the organisation want with a SOCIALIST, asks the old girl, enunciating in capital letters? As socialist and women's rights advocate, Cusack doesn't disappoint, observing capitalist countries assert 'woman's place is in the home!' yet 'gets them out of the home paying them low wages because they *are* women'.

The Soviet Union and China accept women engineers, industrial enterprise chiefs, agricultural co-op and commune chairman 'as fact, although the West never ceases being astonished'. Nevertheless, 'in all the Socialist countries [she] has visited … too often … lip service is given to … equality', Cusack observes. Socialist scientists 'can send a rocket around the moon' so 'can surely devise methods [relieving] women in the Socialist countries … of household drudgery …' This, 'as Lenin pointed out', is where 'the real emancipation of women rests'. Yet for all that, 'the Industrial Revolution might never have taken place'.

Pre-dating the meeting, Newson's agility is remarkable. Solving the 'old girl' problem? 'I asked her to introduce Dymphna, then give the vote of thanks,' Newson writes to Greenwood. 'The others thought it was a wrong move. What dreadful things would she say, what jibes would she set in Dymphna's path? They were terrified she'd spoil the evening right from the beginning.'

No More Rights to Be Won?

Yet the old girl, lone June 1960 UA standout, expressed a view heard from others. It's all over, women's rights a given, equal pay achieved, emancipation won. Contradictory contentions arise, too, amongst those newly come to Women's Movement activism: that no activists ever existed before, or women newly arrived will change, almost single-handedly, centuries-old oppression.

In 1972, the Women's Electoral Lobby (WEL) formed amidst notions of women doing nothing or gone moribund since winning women's vote. Ruby Rich, Heagney, Eileen Powell, Arnot, Florence (Flo) Cluff relegated to the past. For many, even these names were unknown. As Joyce Stevens, Australian Labor League of Youth (ALLY) and later Eureka Youth League (EYL) and Communist Party of Australia (CPA) member says, 'many strong and encouraging women ... Ethel Lewis, Ida Sheridan, Audrey Blake, Margaret Walker, Rivka Brilliant and Cath Olive—naming but some' led these organisations, 'with Street and Woodcock in UA and [Union of Australian Women] UAW ...' Yet as Stevens says, although 'admiring them', with 'youthful arrogance [she] regarded their concerns as being of interest only to older women ...' This influenced recording history—and herstory.

For Daisy Marchisotti, at decade's end, 20 years was 'a long time ago', her memory 'a bit hazy', but she believed her 1951 appearance in Queensland's Industrial Court made her 'one of the first women advocates ... to present a case for the Federated Clerks' Union (FCU), Queensland Branch, for equal pay for women'. Yet 1970s women set out to win equal pay as if the 1950s or 1960s rendered no gains at all, overlooking or discounting the ***Equal Pay Case 1969*** and interventions as necessary steps along the way.

Not limited to eras, individuals, or generations, youthful arrogance permeates political movements, particularly where earlier proponents struggled under disadvantages colouring their methods, what they recorded—if they did—and how they and their work are recognised later—if they are. The forgotten and overlooked litter women's equal pay struggle, the few remembered often in isolation as if, single-handed, they won advances. Thousands of women campaigning, lobbying governments, acting through their unions; everyday women standing up at home and at work, fighting through women's organisations, instituting action groups within organisations, beginning organisations afresh, bringing rapprochement between new and existing organisations, are too many to record. All prepared to be reviled, accused as delusional or greedy, marked unmindful of economic stability or men's breadwinner rights, making their mark for equal pay, but relegated to background neglect whilst named women sail into posterity. The many who, names now forgotten in the records or never recorded, had courage, too. They, too, with fortitude and persistence campaigning for an ideal founded in practical realities of women's financial duty toward themselves and their families, and in the justice of a true accounting for the worth of women's work. Without them, those remembered would have lacked—and today would lack—support without which no goal is won.

Remembered Women—And Remembering Women

Some names are known because women's families or supporters are prominent, some remembered because women write their exploits into theses, books, and articles. Sometimes relatives promote them or follow them into politics—unions, parliament, law, women's organisations, women's activism. Yet far more than a backdrop, so many galvanised by injustice and the power of an idea swept into the industrial and political arena to claim wage parity. Their absence from lists of women remembered pays tribute to sheer numbers joining the struggle.

Ellen Violet Jordan* (1913–1982)** elected 1966 to the (then) safe seat of Ipswich West, Queensland Parliament, first Australian Labor Party (ALP) woman and sole female member throughout her parliamentary career despite Irene Longman earlier (1929–1932). 'Treating me as if I were a porcupine … they didn't even have a lavatory for me …,' she said. Musician and teacher, Jordan joined the ALP in 1946. Ten years later, delegate to the Labour-in-Politics Convention, nominated Women's Central Committee inaugural president (1956–1967), then ALP Women's Executive president (1974–1976), she was her local Country Women's Association (CWA) branch president and Queensland Business and Professional Women (BPW) member. Equal pay advocate and agitator, in 1966 she presented her report, ***Equal Pay for Women, to Queensland's Parliament, criticising lack of pay justice progress, particularly when compared internationally. Cut by Parliament's failure to debate her motion: 'That to remove a grave *injustice* … perpetrated on women for many years, this House resolves (a) action … during the current session to introduce legislation for equal pay for equal work, irrespective of sex; and (b) … abolition of discrimination against women in the Public Service', she declared Australia 'one of the most backward of the world's more civilised countries', with Queensland 'lagging behind'. We have failed, she said 'to treat women as "people"'.

Elizabeth Evatt* (1933–)** 15 December 1972, a week after becoming prime minister, Gough Whitlam announced Evatt's appointment as the first woman presidential member of the Commonwealth Conciliation and Arbitration Commission. Heading the Royal Commission into Human Relationships (1974–1977), inaugural chief justice of the Family Court of Australia (1976–1988), as Australian Law Reform Commission (ALRC) president (1988–1994) she chaired the inquiry into women in law and society, publishing ***Equality Before the Law—Justice for Women and ***Equality Before the Law—Women's Equality***. (De)valuing women's paid and unpaidwork at home and out of it formed part of ***Equality Before the Law*** and Royal Commission into Human Relationship deliberations; equal pay was on the UN Convention on the Elimination of All Forms of Discrimination Against Women (CEDAW) Committee's agenda when Evatt was member (1984–1992) and chair (1989–1991). Evatt Foundation Committee vice-president (1992–2005) advancing equality, participation, social justice and human rights, UN Human Rights Committee member (1992–2000), delivering the ***Review of the Aboriginal and Torres Strait Islander Heritage Protection Act 1984*** (1996), Evatt is an Evatt Foundation life member and member of the Council of the Australian Human Rights Centre. On 19 July 1991, she delivered the NSW Women's Advisory Council (WAC) ***Anne Conlon Memorial Lecture***, honouring Conlon's work for women, and equal pay.

For ***Diana (Di) Graham* (1912–2001),** women's economic independence in marriage and at home was crucial to women's industrial and economic rights outside the home. In 1969, joining Women's Liberation (WL) from the Australian Aboriginal Fellowship and the Federal Council for the Advancement of Aborigines and Torres Strait Islanders (FCATSI), she recognised in young women's angry voices '… the same vehemence, distress and four-letter words as those earlier Aboriginal marches and protest meetings'. Joining WEL in 1973, as Probate Action Group convenor she wrote submission after submission to federal and state MPs, successfully gaining abolition of probate duty so that recently widowed women would no longer be in limbo, through household assets being deemed the dead husband's alone. From 1978, Graham co-convened the WEL Family Law Action Group, advocating equal rights to marital assets, acknowledging linkages between women's private and public lives as central to women's struggle for autonomy, equal pay and equal property rights in marriage, separation, and divorce. Celebrating her indomitable advocacy, attended by local and interstate women, ***Diana Graham Commemorative Luncheons*** were held in 1986 at Sydney Town Hall, and in memoriam in 2001, hosted by Quentin Bryce (then) principal, University of Sydney (USyd) Women's College. In 2003, named jointly with Clare Burton for the EDNA 'Grand Stirrer' award, earlier Macquarie University (MacquarieU) awarded Graham an honorary LLD (2000).

Equal Pay Case 1972 Women's Liberation (WL) advocate, from 1975 ***Sylvie Shaw* (1948–)** co-convened (with Mary Owen) Working Women's Centre (WWC) Melbourne, the first trade union women's research and advisory centre in Australia, operating independently under white-collar peak-body Association of Engineers, Surveyors and Draftsmen (AESDA - later Australian Council of Salaried and Professional Associations (ACSPA)) auspices, financed by International Women's Year (IWY) funding, reporting to ACSPA's Council. Atop trade union training, non-English speaking and migrant women workers' rights, occupational health and safety, workers compensation, sex discrimination and equal pay, Shaw established a school-visits program for women in non-traditional jobs, promoted equality in education and trades (working with teachers' unions), developed a Technical and Further Education (TAFE) transition program for women, and spoke in women's workplaces, schools, and to community groups. An Australian Broadcasting Commission (ABC) radio producer from 1979, she taught radio production/media studies at Royal Melbourne Institute of Technology (RMIT) and scripted and produced prize-winning film ***100K A Day***, following two marathon sportswomen's training and participation in women's sport and competition rights (1990–1991). Mid-1990s as a University of Melbourne (UM) Asialink consultant, she coordinated projects promoting Asia and Asians in Australian film and television, then taught media and radio at South African community radio stations and in a Black African township. Later graduating MA, PhD (MonashU), at Australian Maritime College (AMC) she taught communication, environmental and research design and methods to undergraduates and in the MBA program. In 1998, with Catherine E. Rigby she published ***Living with the Edge at the Centre***.

Second youngest of eight, ***Faith Mussing Bandler*** **(1918–2015)** was born on a Tumbulgum banana share-farm, northern NSW, her Australian-born mother of Indian/Scots descent, father from Vanuatu via the 'Sugar Trade' or 'Blackbirding'—kidnapping for indentured labour. At 15, she became a millinery dressmaker's apprentice. In 1941, she and her sister joined the Women's Land Army (WLM), working NSW farms. The denial of women's labour-value in men's work, then ousting women on men's return, propelled her into political action: a Berlin World Youth Festival delegate, in 1951 she toured Eastern Europe. In 1952, Bandler married and, beginning a family, withdrew from activism. Aboriginal activist and women's rights campaigner Pearl Gibbs visited, demanding: 'Get off your behind and give us a hand.' In 1956, they founded the Australian Aboriginal Fellowship. In 1967's constitutional campaign for Indigenous Australian recognition, Bandler worked alongside Street and Graham, promoting activism for Indigenous and women's rights. A WEL founding member in 1972, simultaneously, she recorded her father's life in ***Wacvie***, highlighting his commitment to wage justice. United Nations (UN) Children's Rights Year 1979, she ensured young female Pacific Islander Australians' interests infused WEL's platform.

Queensland Equal Pay Committee's first meeting was held in 1956, ***Kath Thomas*** **(1911–?)** a founding member. Like other union Equal Pay Committees, 1953 Australian Council of Trade Unions (ACTU) Congress resolutions were the impetus. Committed unionist, CPA member and staffing the CPA ***Queensland Guardian***, from the 1940s Thomas was committed to the labour movement. Working for the Queensland Museum, she transferred to the Works Department to do 'more political work'. Campaigning through the union movement, Women's Movement, and Equal Pay Committee, from the early 1960s her Equal Pay Week work engaged unions and women's organisations. An active UAW and Trades Hall Women's Committee member, dedicated to women's economic and political rights, in 1983 she recorded and analysed her and fellow women workers' public service experience for the third Women and Labour Conference, in Adelaide, SA, that year. Graduating from the University of Queensland (QU) in 1932 she had, in her own words, 'been unemployed, and worked in the Queensland Public Service, for unions and in the Trades and Labour Council Research Department'. As a child and young woman from Wynnum and Lindum, Queensland country towns, and throughout her life, Thomas wrote poetry as Kath Watson, her name before marriage.

Community worker ***Diane Alley*** **(1927–)**, born in Ballarat, Victoria, working through the United Nations Association of Australia (UNAA)—convened the Status of Women Committee nationally from 1980, honorary secretary National Council of Women (NCW) Victoria (1968–1974), president (1977–1980), and NCW Australia president. She participated in late 1960s NCW monthly meetings culminating in the NCW ***Equal Pay Case 1969*** submission, then made NCW's ***Equal Pay Case 1972*** intervention application, attending the hearing. Some 20 years later, she prepared and presented the UN Status of Women Committee ***Parental Leave Case 1990*** submission. In 1981, 1982, and 1983, she led three UNAA Status of Women Committee national conferences on women's policy, ***Women and Taxation***, ***Women and Technological Change***, and ***Women and the Year 2000***, then in 1984 co-hosted, with Sharon Firebrace and Merrill Findlay, the ***Women and Aboriginal Conciliation*** conference. In 1998, she joined Meredith Doig, Mary Owen, Lynette Dumble, and others in the Women's Coalition Against the GST, highlighting the proposed Goods and Services Tax (GST) and impact of tax cuts 'benefitting higher income earners more than those on low incomes', mainly women. In 1983 as NCW delegate to the Hawke Labour government's National Economic Summit, she and Bettina Cass, advisor, published a daily women's bulletin. Women's human rights activist Alley appears on the Australian Women's Honour Roll.

Upon WA's Burke Labor government February 1982 election, the premier appointed ***Yvonne Henderson*** **(1948–)** to establish WA Women's Advisory Council (WAC), launched September 1983, after her election to the state seat of Gosnells on 19 February (then Thornlie 1989–1996). Born in Yorkshire, England, arriving in Australia at 8 months with her family, Henderson taught science, was a deputy principal, and held posts in the Southern State Teachers Union (SSTU). A WEL WA founding member and state convenor (1975), she intervened for WEL in the ***State Wage Case 1975*** and in the ***State Maternity Leave Case 1979*** mirrored the ACTU's ***Maternity Leave Case 1979*** submission. The WA Commission (reflecting the federal decision) approved 1 year's unpaid leave for mothers only. As MP, Henderson was minister for productivity and labour relations (1991–1993), and shadow minister for productivity, labour relations, and public sector management (1993–1994). Complementing her WA Arbitration Commission advocacy, in 1988 she was first cabinet member to give birth to and breastfeed her child. In 1996, Henderson qualified LLB, LLM (University of Western Australia (UWA)), subsequently becoming WA's Equal Opportunity Commissioner (2003–2013). When the 7 January 2006 ***West Australian*** speculated upon a woman becoming WA's Supreme Court chief justice, 'Stung by sexism row' quoted her saying that the Weld Club, 'second home to … judges, lawyers and captains of industry', should end its 134-year 'men only' policy, 'opening its doors to women'.

Deferring her Adelaide University LLB studies begun in 1939, ***Elizabeth Johnston*** **(1920–2002)** became SA FCU branch secretary (1942), the secretary joining the Australian Infantry Forces (AIF) when Japan entered the war. Johnston built the union and as SA United Trades and Labour Council (UTLC) delegate was first woman elected to the executive. At war's end, the secretary returned, she continued at the UTLC pursuing women's right to work, demand and obtain higher wages, and secure non-traditional industry employment. Recommencing law studies, in 1958 Johnston went to the Bar, working in her father's firm, Cleland Teesdale Smith, then with her husband forming Johnston & Johnston, serving working-class clients' law and justice. Joining the CPA in 1941, she took on launching the left-wing publisher, Cooperative Printing Press, in the 1980s working at the CPA's 'Red Shed' (The Peoples' Bookshop), as manager. In the 1960s, she marched against the Viet Nam war, assisted in the formation of the Aboriginal Legal Rights Movement (ALRM), and under the Dunstan Labor government worked with the Aboriginal Lawns Trust and Pitjantjatjara Land Rights Committee, influential in drafting the Pitjantjatjara Land Rights Act. Under the ***Sex Discrimination Act*** 1976 (SA), Johnston was appointed Sex Discrimination Board chair with members Deborah McCulloch and Peter Travers. She treasured always George Bernard Shaw's ***The Intelligent Women's Guide to Socialism and Capitalism***, given her by her father.

Helen Prendergast **(1942–)** prioritised improving women's working conditions, emphasising women's entry into non-traditional employment, including federal and state public service, particularly Tasmania; and ensuring women's full, open, equal, and informed opportunities for joining unions. In the 1970s, she worked with Gail Radford (Wilenski), Commonwealth Public Service Commission (PSC), Equal Opportunity Unit head. Active in the Australian Clerical Officers' Association (ACOA), in 1975 Prendergast was delegate to the groundbreaking Women's Trade Union Conference (WTUC) conference in Sydney and in June 1998 participated with Clare Burton in a landmark 'women in unions' seminar, addressing equal opportunity, valuing women's work, and fair industrial conditions. Her union, equal opportunity, and women's wage justice work resonated in the Women's Movement and government, and she worked closely with Edna Ryan, particularly as neighbours during Ryan's last years in Canberra, promoting equal pay and women's political and economic issues. Prendergast's name appears on the Coalition of Australian Participating Organisations of Women! (CAPOW!) Honour Roll recognising her contribution to women in the trade union movement, paid-work, and industrial justice for women.

Former UM Department of Social Work academic associate and senior fellow, ***Shirley Horne* (1922–2007)**, BComm, Dip. Public Policy, was appointed by the Hamer Liberal government to the Equal Opportunity Board (EOB) (now Anti-Discrimination List, Victorian Civil and Administrative Tribunal (VCAT) in 1977, sitting with Faye Marles and Rosemary Balmford on the 1978 ***Deborah Wardley (Lawrie) case***. The EOB found for Wardley against Ansett Transport Industries (Operations) PL which, despite her qualifications, refused Wardley a commercial pilot traineeship. The Australian High Court confirmed the Board's order that Ansett employ Wardley. As NCW Victoria Women and Employment Committee chair, Horne was NCW advocate in the ***Equal Pay Case 1972*** and ***National Wage Case 1983***, and promoted women's rights through research, including the 1996 Council on Ageing (Victoria)'s submission to the Victorian Law Reform Committee on jury representation. At the 1995 NCW Australia Day Women's Ceremony in Melbourne, Horne joined an illustrious speakers list including Marjorie Tipping, Ada Norris, Edith Hall, Beryl Beaurepaire, Deborah Towns, and Gracia Baylor. She appears on the Victorian Honour Roll of 'significant Australian women … past and present', for her Young Women's Christian Association (YWCA) work (May 2001).

Its second day in office after the December 1972 election, the Whitlam Labor government briefed ***Mary Gaudron* (1943–)** as first Commonwealth female advocate in the re-opened ***Basic Wage Case 1972*** (***Equal Pay Case 1972***). Half-a-dozen years later, she sat on the ***Maternity Leave Case 1978*** as Australian Conciliation and Arbitration Commission member. From a Moree, country NSW railway worker's family, studying law at USyd, her first child was born shortly after final examinations, Gaudron was youngest person, second woman appointed Commission deputy president, first NSW woman QC. First woman and youngest person appointed NSW solicitor-general, Gaudron appeared in the 1983 ***Tasmanian Dams Case.*** In 1987, appointed first woman Australian High Court judge since the

Court's 1904 establishment, she told a High Court colleague: 'The trouble with the women of my generation is that we thought if we knocked down the doors, success would be inevitable; the trouble with men of your generation is that so many think that if they hold the doors open, we will be forever grateful.' In January 2003 retiring at 60 years, despite the High Court mandatory age being 70, she became visiting professor, University of New South Wales (UNSW) Faculty of Law, accepted an International Labour Organization (ILO) post and, asked 'why did you retire?' explained: 'Truth is, the best chance of getting a second woman on the High Court was for me to go.' Replaced by a man, 'We muffed it,' she said.

Her widowed father sent ***Yvonne Smith* (1928–2022)** to a private girls' college 'mistakenly believing he would make [her] a lady'. Street's 'Sheepskins to Russia' campaign propelled Smith into EYL, then the CPA (1954–1991). Secretary to the Australian Railways Union (ARU)'s assistant secretary, and UAW Sunshine secretary (elected at its inaugural meeting), Smith supported anti-apartheid, organised meetings on health and with Indigenous Australian women land rights speakers, joined local cost of living council deputations, wrote letters, sold UAW's ***Our Women*** magazine at local post offices, ran fundraising cake stalls and peace-through-art competitions for local schools, spoke at factory gate meetings, trained and organised equal pay speakers at local factories. When she spoke at Pelaco Shirt factory, Williams, Trades Hall Council (THC) Equal Pay Committee secretary, spoke at Kraft Foods. Smorgans meat factory conditions shocked her: employees casuals, first language rarely English, no 'instant dismissal' explanation or redress. Dismissed after a month, Smith became Australasian Meat Industries Employees' Union (AMIEU) secretary (1966–1977), introducing women's inclusion in apprenticeships and gender-neutral terms into the AMIEU award. In 1969, consulted by NCW's Norris, meat trade women's employment conditions and wages were incorporated into NCW's ***Equal Pay Case 1969*** submissions, then Smith and Joan Curlewis integrated AMIEU statistics into UAW's ***Equal Pay Case 1972*** submission. When the Confectionary Union ignored equal pay, she and others leafleted Allen's South Melbourne confectionary factory. As Council of Victorian Employed Women's Organisation chair, she worked with George Seelaf, AMIEU and Bill Richardson, ACSPA, galvanising unions with mostly women members, and reported to federal AMIEU from Mexico City's 1975 International Women's Year (IWY) conference. Smith's ***Taking Time—A Woman's Historical Data Kit*** (1988), lists women's rights milestones, Eve Fesl contributing Indigenous

Australian women's key dates. In 2020 she received WEL's Vida Goldstein award.

In 1979, ***Jeanette Isabel (Jan) Marsh*** **(1948–)** became the ACTU's first woman research officer and industrial advocate, following RJ Hawke, Ralph Willis, and Robert Jolly. She appeared as ACTU advocate and was on the ***National Wage Case 1983*** ACTU team, where UAW, WEL, and NCW put equal pay on the agenda, WEL including childcare. Her advocacy was crucial in the ***Maternity Leave Case 1979***, one of the first 'specific issues' documents circulated by the ACTU in the 1970s being ***Maternity Leave—The Award Explained***, substantially her work, and she conceived the ***Adoption Leave Case 1985*** claim, advocated it through the ACTU, and ran it in the Australian Industrial Relations Commission (AIRC). In the 1970s, Marsh was an NCW Employment Committee and National Women's Advisory Council (NWAC) member advising the prime minister on government policy affecting women (1978–1981). An ABC director (1983–1985), in 1988 she was appointed an AIRC deputy president, then senior deputy president (1989), sitting in ***National Wage*** and ***Living Wage Cases***, and ***Safety Net Review 2004***. As senior deputy president she conducted 15 conciliation conferences (August 2003–June 2004) in the ***Family Provisions Case 2004*** (Australian Federation of Business and Professional Women (AFBPW) intervening), obtaining parties' agreement on some disputed parents' workplace rights issues.

Educated at St Brigid's Marrickville, ***Betty Spears*** **(1926–2012)** went from the NSW Department of Labour and Industry (1942–1947) to unions (1954–1988) until retirement: FCU (1947–1952) to Vehicle Builders Union (VBU) (later the Vehicle Builders Employees' Federation (VBEF)) clerk then office manager (1954–1967, 1967–1988), NSW Trades and Labour (TLC) Equal Pay Committee as FCU representative (with Doris Osborne, Mavis Woodford, Powell, Elizabeth Mattick, Pat Thompson, Dot Chalker, Flo Davis, Carmel (Carmal) Nyhan and others, 1956). Joined ALP's Dulwich Hill Branch 1954, expelled 1956 (on a Unity Ticket at FCU elections), re-joined 1974, serving on the Labour Women's Committee and FCU delegate to NSW ALP annual conference. FCU executive member (1958), vice-president (1959–1971), deputy president (1971–1988), and ACTU Congress delegate (1968–1988), active during National Pay Weeks, following the ***Equal Pay Case 1972*** Spears lobbied for the ***State Equal Pay Case 1973***. NSW Women's Advisory Council (WAC) member (1976–1978), BPW president (1979), at the ***Equal Pay Case 1969*** 30th anniversary she recalled men heading for the hotel from Labour Council meetings whenever equal pay arose, leaving women members and male officials to it and, at the ACTU 1959 Congress, women strategizing in the ladies' room to subvert male delegates' efforts to remove equal pay from the agenda. Men failed, women succeeded, resolution passed. On NSW Labour Council's Scroll of Honour, FCU life member, the annual ***Betty Spears Award*** for a woman trade unionist workplace equality activist, and Tempe ***Betty Spears Child Care Centre*** for bus employees' children commemorate her work.

Anne Conlon* (1939–1979)** was ALP candidate in the 1972 NSW by-election for safe Liberal (state) seat Mosman, WEL holding its first 'Meet the Candidate', 200-strong. June Surtees (Williams) chaired, with WEL member Conlon questioned equally rigorously on equal pay, contraceptives sales tax, abortion law reform, and childcare. Upon the Wran Labor government's election in 1976, Conlon became a member of NSW WAC, then Carmel Niland's Women's Coordination Unit (WCU) senior project officer, her major areas being women in prison, and women and work. She rejected standing aside from politics or declaring politics a dirty game precluding women's participation (due to 'pure' disposition). In 1978 at USyd's Merewether Building, Conlon's incisive speech replaced at short notice a female federal MP who failed to arrive at a major WEL 'Women and Politics' seminar. Joining the political party closest to one's principles, actively working for another world was vital, she said. Otherwise, women delude themselves about capacity to effect real change by standing on the sidelines. ***Gentle Invaders—Australian women at work 1788–1974, co-authored with Edna Ryan, is designated one of four 'fundamental texts for understanding women's history in Australia'. In 1980, proposed by Scutt, seconded Margaret Doyle, NSW WAC established the ***Anne Conlon Memorial Lecture*** commemorating Conlon's contribution to society and women's advancement.

April 1973, ***Elizabeth Reid* (1942–)** became women's advisor on prime minister Whitlam's personal staff. Australian National University (ANU) philosophy senior tutor, she created a post-without-forerunner, monitoring cabinet documents in her role. When an Education Department advertisement for an NT teacher offering additional allowances and accommodation assistance for 'wife and children' came across her desk, Reid negotiated re-advertising, all future advertisements including 'spouse' and children. Thence forth, the Public Service Board (PSB) and most departments sought her overall advice. Women's Liberation Movement (WLM) 1970s member, Reid was committed to redistribution of access to wages and services; legal and moral recognition of women's right to control her own body; dismantling the public-private dichotomy in policies, programs and domestic life; and ending violence against women. She directed significant effort into converting ALP pre-school policy for all children below 5 years, into a comprehensive diversified and integrated children's services program, particularly childcare, and establishing basic preconditions enabling women to lead decent lives: childcare, adequate health services, equitable workforce conditions and educational opportunities, an assured minimum income, and protection from violence. All essential, she said, for women's accession to the financial and emotional independence threshold. Resigning in 1975, Reid worked in the UN on health, particularly HIV/AIDS, later returning to Canberra, ACT, affiliated with ANU. Her work at the Australian government centre impacted long after her departure.

Betty Horsley Olle* (1918–2010)** appeared for UAW in the ***Minimum Wage Case 1974 and ***National Wage Case 1983***. England-born, Crown Derby pottery china painter mother, qualified electrical fitter father, when the Victorian government advertised, her father applied, all arriving in Ormond, suburban Melbourne, in 1920. In 1933, the only girl passing the Intermediate Certificate science examination, longing to study veterinary surgery, USyd impossible: Great Depression, no relatives interstate, family without the money, meant business college, factory office work and observing women machinists' treatment. At Semco Art Needlework, men were managers, did dyeing or dispatch; factory-floor women assembled orders for travelling salespeople: all men. Sacked at 21, called 'bossy and bumptious'—Olle had insisted on the adult wage. Joining the Women's Auxiliary Australian Air Force (WAAAF) in 1941, (un)equal pay swamped St Kilda Road barracks Royal Australian Air Force (RAAF) records section, WAAAFs acquitting men's jobs—without the pay. An under-officer, sending aircrew for training, she and female colleagues didn't receive (equivalent) warrant officer's pay. Later, Peace Movement activist, she was secretary to the 'Red Dean' (of Canterbury) on his Australian visit, travelling the eastern states with him, kept busy by Street (an organiser) writing letters—even on the plane! Following the 1951 Festival for Youth and Students in Berlin amongst 1000 trade union, peace group and political party delegates, she joined UAW, organising International Women's Day (IWD) luncheons, becoming UAW secretary (1968). Launched 1975 by prime minister Whitlam at Customs House, Melbourne, IWD saw UAW gain IWY funding via Reid to celebrate 'the first woman' entering trades or professions. During the ***National Wage Case 1983***, Olle publicised the AIRC's failure to follow-up ***Equal Pay Cases 1969*** and ***1972***, with a UAW press release/photo-opportunity featuring Yvonne Smith, Council of Action for Equal Pay (CAEP)'s Kate MacNeill, and WEL advocate Scutt around a brightly iced cake contrasting men's versus women's wages, garnering wide media coverage with the Full Bench decision.

Mary Owen* (1921–2017)** was, with Sylvie Shaw, co-founder of the WWC Melbourne (1975–1986), working 1984–1986 from the ACTU until it absorbed the WWC. Active in women and girls' education and employment, occupational health and safety, equal opportunity, and affirmative action, through her union work, WEL membership, the WWC, and the ACTU. In 1974, she appeared with Edna Ryan for WEL in the ***Minimum Wage Case 1974. An Association of Architects, Engineers, Surveyors and Draughtsmen of Australia (AAESDA) staff member (1965–1975), in 1979 she published in the journal ***Blueprint*** a comprehensive plan for WWC's around Australia. Later Owen, describing herself as a Women's Liberationist (WL) and trade unionist, lobbied for older people's rights, highlighting sex discrimination in education, employment, promotion, higher-paid jobs, and unequal pay impacting on older women's superannuation. She worked with the Older Women's Network (OWN), meeting at Victoria Trades Hall until her death. Joining WEL in 1972, in 1997 she became a life member and in 2001 was added to the Victorian Honour Roll. The annual ***Mary Owen Dinner*** (1986–2004) celebrated Owen's life and work, hundreds of local, interstate, and overseas women joining this always-overflowing event, purple, white and green recognising suffragettes and feminists.

Sydney, NSW born (25 February), in 1947 ***Deborah McCulloch* (1939–2021)** and family moved to SA. Inaugural women's advisor to Labor premier Don Dunstan (1976–1979), in 1978 she established the first Women's Information Switchboard (WIS), in Adelaide, coordinator seconded from her office, five positions funded from the State Unemployment Relief Scheme. Before becoming a 'professional feminist' (her description), she taught at Adelaide Girls' High School (1960–1969), Darmalan Catholic Boys' High School (1967–1968), Elizabeth High School (1969), then Salisbury College of Advanced Education (CAE) (later SA University) (1970–1976). Poet, writer, feminist political commentator, McCulloch co-founded WEL SA, and was a member, SA Sex Discrimination Board. She worked on the ***Maternity Leave Case 1979*** with the ACTU's Marsh and Kim Boyer, Tasmanian premier's women's advisor. The divide between women in the public service's higher echelons ('femocrats') and women in secretarial roles led her to foster breaking down barriers through flatter structures, anticipating 1980s structural change policies, relating this in 1983 at the third ***Women and Labour Conference***. BA (hons), DipEd University of Adelaide (UAdel), honorary PhD Flinders University (FU), member of the Multicultural Communities Council and executive of Australians for Native Title and Reconciliation (ANTaR) SA (1997–2002), she provided her support message for the Stolen Generation Rally at Parliament House, Canberra, Wednesday 6 April 2000. Her 1996 Senate campaign promoted 'the politics of women, especially in relation to money, power relationships and art, and the politics of the earth in Western culture'.

In 1979, Ivy (Billie) Shore's ***Kondelia ('Della') Nicholas/ Elliott (Xenodohos)*** **(1917–2011)** portrait won the Portia Geach Art Award. In 1953, ACTU Congress delegate Elliott moved the motion establishing Equal Pay Committees in Australia's TLCs, having worked on the FCU Equal Pay Committee, composing the resolution, getting it through the FCU and Congress. Another (male) delegate, protesting at failing to pass his—'of international importance'—called Elliott a 'queue jumper'. One of the first women elected to the NSW Labour Council executive, Elliott was undeterred, though the union circular reporting the motion said Committees would be established under Labour Council 'suspicions' (not 'auspices'—a typographical error …). Working on FCU campaigns for women workers' improved pay and industrial conditions was grim, one involving Lotteries Office clerks working in dingy, damp space akin to a basement—upgraded following a long struggle. Farmer's female department store staff were denied rights to free Saturday mornings, long negotiations culminating in delivery men going on strike, getting Elliott and the FCU delegation a meeting with the premier. 'Farmer's caved in,' she said, free Saturday mornings won. As a 20-year-old, Elliott was a CAEP member, meeting at 7 Elizabeth Street, Sydney, Heagney's home. 'I thought she was an old fuddy duddy,' said Elliott. 'She thought I was a young hot head. Now, I realise how much she did and how long she struggled, how much she achieved and how much effort it took to achieve it.'

A 1997 Sydney Parliament House ***Memorial Luncheon*** acclaimed ***Edna Ryan*** **(1904–1997)** and in 1998 WEL inaugurated the annual EDNA Awards recognising women's contributions to women's advancement. Born into the Nelson family in Sydney's working-class suburb

Pyrmont, Ryan left school at 13. Nearly 40 years later, in 1953, standing as ALP candidate for Mosman, a safely conservative state seat, led her into local politics as a Fairfield Municipal Council alderman (1956–1965), deputy mayor (1958), then Prospect County councillor (1970s). An early WEL member, Ryan convened the WEL Industrial Action Group (IAG), appearing in the ***Minimum Wage Case 1974***. She presented WEL's ***Maternity Leave Case*** **1979**, contributing to WEL's ***National Wage Case 1983*** and ***1991*** submissions. ALP member from 1935, she was an early campaign manager for Gough Whitlam, who later won Werriwa in Sydney's western suburbs. Committed to women's abortion rights, equal pay, education, and job opportunities, after joining WEL Ryan maintained a strong presence in Women's Movement meetings and conferences, providing her papers to the Mitchell and Dixson Libraries Manuscripts Collection, NSW State Library, and the Australian National Library. In 1975 she published, jointly with Conlon, ***Gentle Invaders***, and in 1984 ***Two-Thirds of a Man—Women and Arbitration in New South Wales***. USyd (1985) and Macquarie University (UMacq) (1995) awarded her honorary DLitts.

First woman ACTU president (1995–2000), ***Jennie George*** **(1947–)** presided during the Maritime Union of Australia (MUA) dispute, wharves of major Australian ports picketed claiming union and organising rights, the federal government employing hooded security guards with dogs. Arriving with her family as a 3-year old from Italy in the post-war immigration wave, she became Bankstown Girls High union representative, then Teachers Federation welfare officer campaigning for teachers' right to post-maternity leave return (won early 1970s) and extending incremental pay scales for classroom teachers (predominantly women), next first female NSW Teachers Federation secretary, later president. First woman elected on the ACTU executive (1983), as assistant secretary she became first female ACTU full-time officer (1991), advocating re-evaluation of women's skills through award restructuring. Her ACTU president-elect speech extolled workers' entitlements as teachers, stressing 'never forget the important issues of concern to women'. Federal MP for Throsby (NSW, 2001–2010), George was active on industry policy, job creation, traineeships, and GST impact on pensioners/retirees and low-income earners, mostly women. With (amongst others) Margaret Reynolds (ALP) and Cheryl Kernot (then Democrats leader) an Aboriginal Reconciliation Council member (1990s), in 1998 as an Australian Republican Movement (ARM) delegate she supported 'yes' in the 1999 republic referendum.

Established in 2000, the ACTU ***Jennie George Award*** promotes women's union campaigning, in 2006 jointly awarded to the Liquor Hospitality and Miscellaneous Workers' Union (LHMWU) (now United Voice) (childcare) and NSW Nurses Association (aged-care pay equity).

1972 inaugural WEL WA convenor. ***Patricia Jessie (Pat) Giles* (1928–2017)** was elected WEL's global affiliate International Alliance of Women (IAW) president at IAW's December 1996 Calcutta, India, meeting. IAW board member with WEL's Pat Richardson, she joined Australian feminists Rischbieth (Women Service Guilds (WSG) WA), and Rich (NSW Women's Club) holding the presidency decades earlier. Born in Minlaton, SA, her activism spanned nursing, education, health, then equal opportunity through nursing and as WA Council of State School Organisations vice-president (1971–1974), WA Health Education Council executive member (1971–1980), and WA Discrimination in Employment and Occupation Committee member and chair (1973, 1974), Australia-wide committees established by the Whitlam Labour government to implement ILO C111 on employment discrimination. Completing a BA (UWA), Giles became a WA Hospital Employees Union (HEU) organiser (1974–1980), first woman on WA Trades and Labour Council (TALC) executive (1970s), member of the first ACTU Women's Committee, and HEU advocate in the ***State Maternity Leave Case 1979***, WA's Industrial Commission granting private employment maternity leave. As senator (1981–1993), Giles chaired the Privileges Committee (1988–1993) and promoted equal pay, childcare, maternity leave, health, and working conditions. Following retirement, she was Board of Management community representative, Centre for Research for Women (Curtin, Edith Cowan and MU and UWA). A speaker at the 19th ***Mary Owen Dinner***, on 27 February 1992 she opened the Parliament House, Canberra, Trust the Women exhibition, celebrating 90 years of women winning the federal franchise.

Born Queenstown, Tasmania, ***Eleanor (Betty) Grey* (1923–2011),** BA (University of Tasmania (UTas), 1944), completed teacher training at Hobart's Phillip Smith Training College. In professional and voluntary work, Grey advocated for equity and access to education, equal opportunity, equal pay and status of women, working through Tasmanian Women's Consultative Committee, Launceston Women's Health Network, Zonta International, NCW, ALP, Amnesty International (AI), and other women's and human rights organisations. After teaching at Tasmanian high schools, she became senior mistress at Launceston Matriculation College, then vice-principal of Alanvale College. She lobbied the Tasmanian

Teacher's Federation for a state and federal Status of Women Committee to promote women teachers in union participation and professional careers. With Status of Women Committees established in the Teacher's Federation, Grey became state convenor and national Status of Women Committee representative. Her contribution to women teachers and women's rights continued through Retired Teachers Association executive membership and ALP and Australian Federation of University Women (AFUW) Tasmanian Branch life membership. An exemplary women's mentor, her name was entered on Tasmania's Honour Roll of Women for service to the community and human rights (2005).

Trade union activist, non-English speaking parents, staunchly working-class, leaving school at 14, married at 16, ***Zelda D'Aprano*** **(1928–2018)** saw education and women's independence as intertwined. She worked for the union movement to take women workers' rights equally seriously as male workers and their industrial rights. Completing her Leaving Certificate in 1963, a diverse paidwork and educational background ensured direct insights into sex/gender-, race/ethnicity-based discrimination, particularly in industry. Qualifying as a dental nurse, then chiropodist, she worked as a clothing trade machinist, was a Post Master General (PMG) mail sorter, then an AMIEU clerk. CPA member (1950–1971), joining WL in the 1970s, an active Australian Women's Party (AWP) member, her life experience illuminated patriarchy's influence on employers and trade unions, and 'invisibility' for some Women's Movement women. Determined working-class women would not be forgotten, she straddled the Women's Movement and trade unions. On 19 April 2000, UMacq celebrated 30 years, graduating 3,400 students, and awarding an honorary LLD for D'Aprano. Addressing graduate students, she emphasised speaking with 'own' voice, validating 'own' experience, and ensuring no girl or woman grows up or exists believing herself alone in the women's rights struggle. In 2022, Trades Hall established a fund for a D'Aprano statue on their doorstep, and in May 2023 Jennifer Mann's bronze sculpture of D'Aprano was unveiled by Julia Gillard, Australia's first woman Prime Minister.

Such Clever and Persuasive Women

What of June 1960, Cusack, UA and 'the old girl'?

Newson's gamble pays off. Concluding her letter to Greenwood, Newson triumphs:

> She ran her usual line, but no one had to step in to defend Dymphna or anyone else. Dymphna did it all herself. She included an introduction to her talk, saying she hadn't lived in a single country ... where women and men were equal or the battle over, talked about the struggles she'd been involved in, how she admired the women keeping the struggle going. The old girl was so enthused that at the end she was more complimentary than anyone else! And all sincere. She's been reconverted, and now the others are congratulating me for my perspicacity!

So for UA, at 1960s beginning, anything was possible. Staunchest opponent to be persuaded. Arguments ready. Obstacles confronted. Wise women like Newson standing up. Like Cusack, stars and intellects shining. Critics with the wit to change their minds—like the old girl ... and staunch supporters waging together the struggle to win.

A new decade looms. Equal pay just around the corner. The Commonwealth Conciliation and Arbitration Commission adopting equal pay for equal work, 1960s women—proud radicals—believe it'll embrace equal pay for work of equal value, too. Chapter 13, 'Ingenuity and Intellectual Rigour—Brazen Hussies Arguing Back', has 1950s and 1960s women meeting the women of the 1970s.

References

Cases—see Case List

Diane Alley, ***Interview*** (6 February 2006); ***Personal Communication*** (28 January 2006).

Faith Bandler, 'A Good Innings' in JA Scutt (ed.), ***As a Woman—***, Artemis Publishing, Melbourne, Victoria, 1992, pp. 166–176.

David Black and Geoffrey Bolton (eds), ***Register of Members—***, vol. 2, WA Parliament, Perth, WA, 2004.

CAPOW, ***Australian Women's Honour Roll—'P'***, http://www.capow.org.au/Honourroll/honourroll-p.htm, pp. 1–3 (accessed 12 April 2006).

'Contributors—Kath Thomas' in WLPC (eds), ***all her labours—***, WLPC, Sydney, NSW, 1984, p. 172.

Zelda D'Aprano, ***Zelda—***, 1977, Spinifex Press, Nth Melbourne, 1995.

Kondelia ('Della') Elliot, ***Interview***, Sydney, NSW (June 1994).

Jennie George, ***Interview***, Sydney/Canberra, NSW (6 February 2006).

Jennie George, ***Speech as ACTU President-Elect to the ACTU Congress 1995***, Melbourne, Victoria, 1995 (27 September 1995).

Di (Diana) Graham, 'Through Life …', in JA Scutt (ed.), ***Different Lives—***, Penguin Books Australia, Melbourne, 1987, pp. 178–187.
Kerry Heubel, ***Interview***, Sydney, NSW, 2005 (September 2005); ***Interview***, Sydney, NSW (26 January 2006).
Deborah McCulloch, ***Interview***, Adelaide, SA (31 January 2006).
Colleen McEwen and Emma Jolley, ***ACTU Records***, ABLative No. 7, 1998 (Autumn 1988), http://www.archives.anu.edu.au/nbac/html/%20ABLativeNo7_Autumn1988ACTU.html, pp. 1–4 (accessed 14 January 2021).
Daisy Marchisotti, 'Equal Pay Case, 1951', in E. Windshuttle (ed), ***Women, Class and History—***, Fontana, Sydney, NSW, 1980, pp. 423–429.
NLA, ***MS 9262—Guide to the Papers of Elizabeth Reid***, http://nla.gov.au/nla.ms-ms9262, pp. 1–44 (accessed 8 September 2006a).
NLA, ***MS 7628 Papers of Mary Gaudron***, http://nla.gov.au/nla.ms-ms7628 (accessed 14 January 2006b).
NLA, ***MS 9140 Papers of Edna Ryan (1904–1997)***, http://nla.gov.au/nla.ms-ms9140, pp. 1–16 (accessed 14 January 2006c).
Vivienne Newson, Letter to Irene Greenwood, 1960 (June 1960); copy ***Irene Greenwood Collection***, MU, Perth, WA.
Obituaries, ***Celebrating Elizabeth Johnston, 1920–2002***, http://www.search.org.au/obits/ejohnston.html, pp. 1–2 (accessed 14 April 2006).
Betty Olle, ''Bossy—and Bumptious', in JA Scutt (ed.), ***As a Woman***, 1992, pp. 122–30.
Mary Owen, 'The Women in My Life', in JA Scutt (ed.), ***Living Generously—***, 1995, pp. 243–256.
Helen Prendergast, 'Contribution—Clare Burton', ***Tributes to Clare Burton***, http://www.users.bigpond.com/rj_gj/clare/tributes.htm, pp. 1–11, at p. 8 (accessed 12 April 2006a).
Helen Prendergast, ***Interview***, Lyneham, ACT, 2006b.
Gail Radford, 'Chapter 5—Policy Impact', in ***The History of the Women's Electoral Lobby (WEL)***, Canberra, ACT, 2005, p. 15.
Elizabeth Reid, 'The Child of Our Movement …', in Scutt (ed.), ***Different Lives***, 1987, pp. 8–20.
Geraldine Robertson, Women's Web, ***Women's Stories, Women's Actions: Interview with Yvonne Smith***, http://home.vicnet.net.au/~womenweb/sources/First%Narratives/YvonneSmith.htm, pp. 1–9 (accessed 14 January 2006).
Sylvie Shaw, ***Interview***, Melbourne, Victoria (27 January 2006); ***Personal Communication***, Melbourne, Victoria (28 January 2006).
Fergus Shiel, 'A different kind of justice', ***Age***, Melbourne, Victoria, 2002 (9 December 2002), http://www.theage.com.au/articles/2002/12/08/1038950270361.html, pp. 1–3 (accessed 14 January 2006).
Yvonne Smith, ***Interview***, Melbourne, Victoria (31 March 2006).

Joyce Stevens, 'A Reasonable Exchange' in JA Scutt (ed.), ***Glorious Age—***, Artemis Publishing, Melbourne, Victoria, 1993, 113–121.

Kath Thomas, 'Queensland public service women' in WLPC (eds), ***all her labours—***, WLPC, Sydney, NSW, 1984, pp. 85–92.

Working Lives—Biographical Register: Spears, Betty Monica (1926–), http://www.econ.usyd.edu.au/wos/workinglives/spears.html, pp. 1–2 (accessed 1 September 2006).

John Shields and Andrew Moore, 'The Biographical Register of the Australian Labour Movement …', ***working lives***, http://www.econ.usyd.edu.au/wos/workinglives/register.html, pp. 1–6, at p. 1 (accessed 1 September 2006).

WEL Australia (Marian Sawer), ***Announcements—Vale Edna Ryan 15/12/1904—10/2/1997***, http://www.wel.org.au/announce/edna/, pp. 1–2 (accessed 14 January 2006).

CHAPTER 13

1970s Ingenuity and Intellectual Rigour—Brazen Hussies Arguing Back

> Women have been taught to be silent. Despite accepted wisdom, women do not talk more than men … When women have spoken, our words have been trivialised in a culture dominated by men, listening mostly to themselves. Yet since the late 1960s and early 1970s, women have ceased to pretend to be silent with each other, refusing to relegate our conversation with each other to an inconsequential realm … We have grasped the importance of what we have to say, the value of what we have to say to one another and have recognised the importance of women's voices of the past. More often, now, our voices have broken through the barriers set up by a world subscribing to machismo. We have begun to recapture the voices of our foremothers …
>
> Jocelynne A. Scutt, 'Noisy Women' in Scutt, ***Different Lives—…***, Penguin, Australia, 1987, p. 1

'In a country living on its wits, with half the wits in female heads the underutilization of the potential earning power of women is a frivolous extravagance,' writes a London School of Economics (LSE) academic in the London ***Times*** of 27 April 1970. White Australia celebrates the bicentenary of Captain Cook's arrival, Indigenous Australians mourn it, and Australian Council of Trade Unions (ACTU) president Albert Monk hands over to RJ Hawke. Moratorium rallies pledge an end to the Viet Nam war, in May, led by federal MP Jim Cairns, more than 70,000

J. A. Scutt, *Wage Rage for Equal Pay*,
https://doi.org/10.1007/978-3-031-42178-5_13

marching in Melbourne. In September, 200 marchers are arrested in Sydney, 100 in Adelaide. In October, Melbourne's West Gate Bridge collapses, killing 35 bridge workers. Unionists impose Black Bans on redevelopment of inner-city Carlton. Germaine Greer's ***The Female Eunuch*** is published alongside Shirley Hazzard's ***The Bay of Noon***. In Sydney that July, at 81, Jessie Street dies.

Agitation and Confrontation

Recognising ***Equal Pay Case 1969*** inadequacies, 1970s women and women's organisations lacked a consistent approach. Some took the Conciliation and Arbitration Commission route, with the unions. Some relinquished the struggle, at least for a time, the Australian Federation of Business and Professional Women (AFBPW) no longer seeking leave in industrial commissions or tribunals (1969–1985), concentrating on its core focus of funding young women's scholarships, and encouraging women's professional development. Some—United Associations (UA), Women's Service Guilds (WSG), and Australian Federation of Women Voters (AFWV)—wound up or lost impetus (Street's death—UA and Rischbieth's—WSG), with Women's Electoral Lobby (WEL) adopting their techniques (quizzing MPs and candidates, government submissions—AFWV, WSG WA, Women's Progressive Association (WPA)'s approach) or attracting women who might once have joined longer existing organisations. The Housewives Association (FAAH) continued lobbying against rising household goods and grocery prices, joining the Union of Australian Women (UAW)'s Campaign Against Rising Prices (CARP) which propelled the 1973 Prices Justification Tribunal launch. UAW campaigned against the Viet Nam war, conscription, high prices, powers penalising trade unions and trade unionists, for better living standards, equal pay, maternity leave provisions and allowances, pre-school education, and, internationally (South Africa, Viet Nam, Greece), in solidarity. Like the National Council of Women (NCW), UAW intervened in the ***Equal Pay Case 1972*** and ***Minimum Wage Case 1974***, but the Communist Party of Australia (CPA) Soviet/Mao split catapulted some UAW leaders into the newly established Women's Liberation Movement (WLM). Like Greenwood, some women retained membership of established women's groups, simultaneously joining WEL, Women's Liberation (WL), or WLM.

The 1960s relationship between women and unions fluctuated. Up to the late 1960s, women's efforts to build on (potential) support within unions, and work across class and political party lines, characterised the equal pay struggle. Late 1960s tension between various strands increased, yet despite increasingly articulated scepticism women made continuing and renewed attempts at having unions adopt principles and standards women devised within and outside unions, reflected by the Working Women's Charter and, later, launch of the Women's Trade Union Conference (WTUC). Others were ambivalent or rejected unions completely, generally not for pretentious reasons but considering unions irredeemably male-dominated, a male hierarchy and oligarchy impervious to women's voices, incapable of recognising or appreciating women's qualities, unable to acknowledge fighting for women's industrial rights required the verve and vigour applied to men's rights—or fight for women's rights at all.

WA's Council for Equal Pay and Opportunity (CEPO) was caught between seeking union support and gratitude for it, frustration at the failure to achieve equal pay—and a lack of support from unions in the struggle. Women grappled with the possibility that subversion of equal pay lay at the feet of male-dominated unions combining with the state Industrial Commission. A Supplementary Payment scheme restricted to male wages gave men at least a 10 per cent advantage, whatever the jobs, effectively undercutting Part X, Industrial Arbitration Act Amendment Act 1968 (WA) aimed at equal pay. The psychiatric nurses industry provided a 'classic example', a female psychiatric nurse being entitled to 91 per cent only of the total male rate, not 100 per cent 'as was envisaged when the Union was successful in achieving equal pay for its female workers'. This meant the male worker's receiving (gross) \$53.85, his female counterpart \$39.95, a *reduction* to 74.1 per cent rather than the existing differential of 76.46 per cent applicable before 'equal pay' plus the male supplement. Psychiatric nurses had been first to gain equal pay, predating the Act.

In August 1971, CEPO chairman Rosalind Denny's address published in ***Equal Pay News*** noted CEPO's 13-year campaign for equal pay had 'failures ... and successes'. Though (optimistically) even failures 'in their time may be turned to success', despair at a system ('in every State of Australia') where women lack control permeates. She recounts 'hoping to break the deadlock' the 'previous Minister for Labour, Mr. D. O'Neil assuring us ... he would raise the matter at a Conference of State Ministers to have the anomaly adjusted ...', yet he didn't. Change of government, Australian Labor Party (ALP) in power, February 1971 the situation still looked bleak: '... at Ministerial level we have failed to [meet] Mr. Taylor the new Minister for Labour despite two letters and a follow up letter to the Premier …' 'Unrest' amongst nurses initiated a deputation 'to the Minister for Health, Mr. R. Davies' generating no cause for hope. The Teachers' Tribunal agreed to grant full equal pay to WA women teachers from 1 January 1971, bringing equal pay forward by 1 year, with CEPO urging the government to follow for all government employees. Yet 'the 10% decision hangs around women's necks like the Albatross around the neck of the Ancient Mariner. At one fell swoop it negated all the gains won by award or agreement by women over the years …'

Barmaids 'by agreement with their employers won their claim to equal pay at the cost of an all over rise in the price of beer'. Other women not so fortunate, if the political field was impenetrable, equally so tribunals and unions, the 'complicated machinery' of arbitration providing 'little hope for women' and 'equal pay at the present time [appears] not worthy of Trade Union attention'. Meanwhile, the ***West Australian*** was reporting that real equality of opportunity between women and men 'remains a myth—despite the social changes in … industrial society over the past 30 years …'.

Similar frustrations bloomed around Australia. Some 6 months earlier, D'Aprano (then a Socialist Workers' Union (SWU) clerk), Alva Giekie, and Thelma Solomon created the Women's Action Committee (WAC) with a strong working-class base. Long-time Communist Party of Australia (CPA) and union membership and involvement meant WAC understood trade unions and their lack of prioritising women's issues. Sceptical already of trade union support for equal pay, when no union backing accompanied her chaining herself to government buildings in protest against the ***Equal Pay Case 1969*** and lack of equal pay in public employment, D'Aprano 'felt strongly about' women's need 'to begin fighting their own battles'.

Consciousness raising arrived. Activist groups erupted. On 2 March 1970, WAC's first meeting attracted 14 women, the second, at member Bon Hull's home, 11. On 17 March, the day following, in 'Emancipation is for Ladies Only', ***Age*** journalist Ben Hills reported being 'shown the exit for wearing trousers'. It was 'the order of the boot to end them all', reciting past refusals to admit him to functions was restricted to 'press off-limits' or failure to wear a tie at formal events. Were he a female journalist, he acknowledged, he'd have had no problem: WAC would have let him in.

Women's meetings and conferences followed this pattern, a more upfront and combative stance developing, focused on women's freedom to articulate concerns in the men's absence—their presence infringing on women's rights and inhibiting speaking up and speaking out. Groups adopted a non-hierarchical, non-structured approach, like WAC 'reject[ing] the idea of a structure with a president, secretary or an executive' and abjuring a constitution. D'Aprano and several others were unyielding, D'Aprano attributing her 'vocal opposition' to seeing structures generating power positions, 'people fighting each other to gain the power, glory and status created by the positions'. Not a question of 'woman or man' but 'the position which corrupts' for 'once people get power, they want to stay there ... inevitably go[ing] bad'. She 'shuddered at the thought of women becoming like men in scrambling for power', having 'learnt this lesson the hard way'.

WAC's platform puts women's economic equality (hence equal pay) ahead of every other pressing demand and, although, like other 1970s activist groups rejecting existing organisations' executive structures, on one aspect all united: rate for the job fundamental, equal pay for work of equal value a clarion call alongside equal opportunity. Women's emancipation was, for 'old' and 'new' women's organisations, dependent upon a decent wage for women's work and work women did commensurate with wages for men's work and work done by men, and women's access to all jobs and public offices equally with men.

WAC called for:

Economic Equality

(a) One rate of pay for job performed: Basic salary for all adult workers, plus increments for qualifications and experience etc. necessary
(b) Equal opportunity in employment
(c) Credit to women under the same conditions as men, no male guarantor mandatory
(d) Maternity leave of 1 year with no loss of seniority or superannuation. Maternity allowance at full salary for 6 weeks (ILO recommendation)
(e) Child care, kindergarten, and child minding facilities increased
(f) Part-time work for women requiring it
(g) Retraining centres for women returning to the workforce after childrearing

Social equality demanded 'woman as "sex symbol"' ousted, all business and political organisations, state functions, and public places opened to women; equal education—primary, secondary, and apprenticeships; abortion law reform, family planning facilities 'substantially increased', and 'liberal sex education' for children. The policy clarified WAC's status as a pressure group working for women's equality, members entitled 'to belong to any political organisation of their choosing'.

March 1972, Melbourne Women's Centre was founded, the telephone directory featuring WLM as 'Women's Liberation Movement'. With all members active in consciousness raising groups and part of WLM, WAC disbanded. Demands for women's control over their own bodies, abortion law repeal and abortion on request, freely available contraception, free 24-hour community-controlled childcare, equal educational opportunities, one rate for the job, and equal pay for work of equal value remained central women's liberation planks. Headed 'Equal Job Opportunities and an End to Low Pay', the fifth demand of the Women's Liberation Manifesto stated: 'Employers have no right to pay women less than men, or to keep women in menial jobs' and 'The government must …make it illegal for employers to discriminate against women'.

Despite women's organisations and activism fragmenting, cross-organisational support meant mid-1972 engagement between the WLM Equal Pay Group and UAW, issuing pamphlets in Italian, Greek, and English for distribution at factories, with a Women's Movement '***March*** with the Unions on the opening day' of the Commonwealth Conciliation and Arbitration Commission wage case. Throughout July, UAW and WLM made posters, stood outside railway stations and factories talking with women to and from work, distributed leaflets in local shopping centres and central Melbourne, calling for women to 'help fold equal pay leaflets between 10.00 a.m. and 3.00 p.m. Tuesday to Friday at the UAW …', join the march, and 'sit in the court throughout the case …'.

When the ***National Wage Case 1972*** commenced, WLM sought leave to intervene.

Equal Pay for Work of Equal Value

On 27 January 1972, the day after Australia Day, Aboriginal Australians demanding Land Rights pitched the Tent Embassy outside Canberra's Parliament House. February found Beatrice Faust and ten others meeting in her home at the first WEL meeting, soon organised in every state and territory, a leading force in the equal pay struggle.

WEL's election focus meant quizzing existing and prospective MPs, WEL members attending at MPs offices in pairs; running meet-the-candidate evenings tossing questions in rapid fire at political party representatives; circulating candidates with questionnaires, evaluating answers and scoring respondents out of 10. Non-responses scored zero. WEL's six demands included equal pay for work of equal value, yet WEL's attention centred on the upcoming federal election, not the ***Equal Pay Case 1972***. NCW and UAW took the running with WLM. Irony intruded, for WEL was characterised as reformist, operating within the system, WLM comprising radicals dedicated to working outside and even against the system. Yet in a tightly argued submission, WLM dispatched employers' economic arguments advanced against equal pay claims.

The ***National Wage Case 1972*** began in July, running into months. Women dejectedly anticipated no gain. Despite acknowledged ***Equal Pay Case 1969*** limitations providing little hope of equal pay for most women in paidwork, the federal government joined employers in arguing against widening its scope. Then, on 2 December, the ALP slogan 'It's Time' saw Labor win government after 23 years of opposition. One of Whitlam's first steps as prime minister was to re-open the ***National Wage Case 1972***. The case reconstituted as the ***Equal Pay Case 1972***, Mary Gaudron appointed federal government counsel, the Commission was asked to adopt 'equal pay for work of equal value' in federal awards.

The basic wage was not all. The male minimum wage not extending to women, a major union argument was that—a simple matter of equity—women should receive the same minimum wage as men. No, said the Commission, as the unions' view of the minimum wage as too low 'does not affect the concept'. The 'essential characteristic of the male minimum wage' (incorporating family considerations) mean 'we decline to apply it to females and dismiss that part of the unions' claims'. This meant delay until the ***Minimum Wage Case 1974*** reignited the issue.

With equal pay, the Commission defined its task as 'whether in the present social and industrial climate it is fair and reasonable that the 1969 principle should remain unaltered'. This involved the Commission in 'making assessment of what, if anything, has happened [with] equal pay since 1969 [making] it just and proper ... to alter those principles'. When in July 1972 the ACTU made its original submissions, the federal Liberal government's prevarication on international industrial rights treaties continued. The Commission acknowledged International Labour Organization (ILO) Convention 100 as a foundation for domestic pay equity advances, yet it was not until the Labor government ratified ILO Convention 100 on Equal Pay, ILO Convention 111 on Discrimination in Employment and Occupation, and the UN Covenant on Civil and Political Rights, that they impacted.

Concentrating upon state developments, the Commission nonetheless considered the Equal Pay Act 1970 (UK) and 1972 Aotearoa/New Zealand Equal Pay Bill, saying it should 'reconsider the 1969 principles ... in light of present circumstances'. The conclusion? 'Mere amendment' to the ***Equal Pay Case 1969*** principles was insufficient, 'equal pay for equal work' being '*too narrow* in today's world'. Time 'to enlarge the concept to "equal pay for work of equal value"', award rates for all work done 'considered without regard to [employee's] sex ...'.

Two employer arguments were rejected, first, males would seek to restore pre-existing wage relativities with females; secondly, economic costs. No evidence showed the first occurring after the 1969 decision and, anyway, said the Commission, granting equal pay would not be 'a valid argument' for men to have 'their pre-existing wage relativities restored'. As for the second, endorsing equal pay for work of equal value could result in substantial wage increases when implemented and it was valid to consider implementing the principle to temper its immediate impact, but in the Commission's view 'the community is prepared to accept the concept of equal pay for females and should therefore be prepared to accept the economic consequences ...'.

Equal pay for work of equal value should apply to all awards, adults, and juniors, meaning female rates being determined by work value comparisons without regard to employees' sex: differentiations between Commission award rates 'have traditionally been founded on work value investigations of various occupational groups or classifications', but the male-female award rates gap 'generally is greater than the gap, if any, in comparative value of work performed by the two sexes, rates for female classifications in the same award generally being fixed without a comparative evaluation of work performed by males and females'.

Echoing women's decades-long call for 'the rate for the job', in all cases the eventual outcome should be a single rate for an occupational group or classification, the rate payable to the employee performing the work, whether male or female. Yet the decision highlighted the fundamental problem. All very well to say wage rates must be fixed 'irrespective of the worker's sex', but how to achieve it? In a world valuing men's work more highly, it is not so easy to eliminate sex/gender, even more difficult when those determining work value are bound by conventional ways of viewing the world and work, male-female performance, male and female vocations. Unaware of how wage fixing is permeated with value-laden assumptions, and no sensibilities alerting wage-fixers to their disposition or biases, much less mechanisms to (re)educate them, determining rates regardless of employees' sex is a pious hope, particularly when 70 years of history affirming male-female wage differentials lies between the bench and its newly determined wage-fixing standard.

The Commission faced an additional obstacle to sex/gender blind assessment, so obvious yet so accepted as right as to be unremarkable (to those in positions of power). The bench hearing the claim, the Commission in its entirety, was comprised solely of men. Only on 15 December 1972 was the first woman ever appointed—deputy president Elizabeth Evatt, the second in 1974—deputy president Gaudron.

Commission members were ill-placed to re-evaluate, or evaluate fairly, women's work and capacities of women doing men's work. Inevitably, women's absence from decision-making affects male decision-makers' perception of their own superior abilities—and neutrality. This, in turn, impedes their capacity for work value assessment of women's work, and women working. Lacking acceptance or even perception of the favoured circumstances leading to their being Commission members making wage determinations, while discrimination means few women practicing law or heading unions or employer associations to 'qualify' for appointment, deciding a non-sexed rate for the job runs a serious risk of 'just words'.

Under the ruling, where arbitration implemented the principle, the Commission must exercise 'the broad judgment which has characterized work value inquiries', different criteria continuing to apply from case to case and potentially varying from one class of work to another, as with work value enquiries generally. The Commission did recognise, however, that work value enquiries comparing work and fixing award rates irrespective of sex may encounter 'unfamiliar issues'. However, work value assessment would not always be required. Agreement between parties could apply equal pay for work of equal value. This carries its own dangers, lacking assurance that 'negotiated by agreement' wage rates can or will be set fairly for women. Potentially employers and unions are equally likely to undervalue women's work or capacity for doing men's work, or to see work women do as different from, not as complicated or challenging as, work done by men and, hence, worth less—whatever equal pay principle is ostensibly applied. Not only industrial tribunals and commissions require (re)education in work evaluation and assessment, capacities and skills, for equal pay. Unions, employers, and their advocates require it, too.

Matters not adverted to by the ***Equal Pay Case 1972*** parties would be dealt with as arising. However, the Commission said that some matters parties raised required immediate Full Bench consideration. The six items harboured equal pay negatives and positives. The first barred automatic application of any formula seeking to 'bypass a consideration of the work performed', aiming to quash methods of getting around the equal pay for work of equal value principle. Yet it went on say that 'pre-existing relativities may be a relevant factor in appropriate cases'. The danger is that rather than bringing the women's rate up to that of men's jobs, ensuring equality of rates, relativities between men's and women's rates may be preserved. Despite the Commission's earlier rejection of this as a prospect put in argument, ultimately men may simply be paid at a higher rate, through an increase, whilst women are increased to the original male rate only. Another way relativities might be preserved is by taking women's base rate up to the male base rate, then awarding male workers additional work-related benefits. The Commission could (and should) have spelled out how relativities might be relevant: what would 'appropriate cases' be? Failing this set the stage undercutting equal pay.

The fourth and fifth items cover four aspects:

- Jobs may have similar names, denoting similar or same work; however, job title need not necessarily indicate the same or similar work is being done—generic classifications or classifications covering junior workers may be deceptive, and arbitrators must determine similarity or otherwise of actual work done.
- Differences in work performed may or may not be sufficiently significant to warrant differences in rates, arbitrators determining this by reference to particular work done.
- Under some awards, restrictions exist on performance of work by women, so whether this warrants differentiation in the rate based on relative value of work done is for arbitrators to decide in the particular case.
- Claims based in contentions of greater (or lesser) labour turnover or absenteeism must be rejected.

The reference to job titles failed to recognise that ***different*** job titles rate high in concealing worth of women's jobs and work value: they can ***hide*** similarity of work done or responsibilities and knowledge required for work. The Commission's approach on job titles is biased against women's equal pay, and failed, too, where unnecessary and discriminatory restrictions on women workers consign women to lesser pay rates without justification. Women had to fight this out though anti-discrimination and equal opportunity law. Nonetheless, as exemplified by WEB's limiting women's claims almost as a matter of routine during wartime, that the Commission excluded job turnover and absenteeism was welcome. Here, the Commission arguably showed a perception of bias in assessment.

Effectively recognising gross underpayment of women's work, the Commission said social and economic consequences of its decision would be considerable, requiring implementation over time, delaying women's wage justice. Rates in all Commission awards and all Public Service Arbitration Act determinations were to be fixed fully under the 'equal pay for work of equal value' principle by 30 June 1975—3 years leeway for implementing the decision as affecting public service salaries. Three equal instalments—one-third payable by 31 December 1973, half the remainder by 30 September 1974, the rest by 30 June 1975—'the norm' though 'special circumstances may exist requiring special treatment'.

Finally, ***Equal Pay Case 1969*** principles would apply 'in appropriate cases', the ***Equal Pay Case 1972*** equal pay for work of equal value principle being adopted because 'an injustice might be created in cases based on equal pay for equal work where females could become entitled immediately to male rates under those principles'. Hence, somewhat ironically, the Commission was concerned that there be no injustice ***between women*** entitled to equal pay through the equal pay for equal work principle, and women not qualifying thereby, but doing work of equal value. Yet at base, the issue is not differentials qua women, but the gross disparities between men's and women's wages.

The longstanding injustice of women's work overall being worth less than men's work and that gaining women's wage justice meant showing their work as equal to men's—whether as 'equal work' or 'work of equal value'—was overlooked. The Commission subscribed to men's work as intrinsically superior to women's, more valuable or skilled because done by a male workforce; more meritorious because done by men; the natural, basic measure of work value, or benchmarking work value, Margaret

Thornton's 'benchmark man' (as she termed this phenomenon some 30 years later) infusing 'equal pay for work of equal value'.

Yet women's minds were exercised. Neither placards nor posters were allowed inside Commission precincts. But with Sylvie Shaw presenting WLM's submission for equal pay and an equal minimum wage, Diane Alley for NCW and UAW's Joan Curlewis maintaining the 1969 decision 'deprived women of a basic human right—the right to equal pay for work of equal value', women wearing white T-shirts—emblazoned with 'Women's Liberation' or Texta-Coloured liberation symbols—sat in rows behind. The advocates contended payment of higher wages to men-qua-men was intrinsically wrong, whatever the job. All women had a right to equal payment with men, the distinction between women's and men's work being founded solely in the sex of the person doing it. Unlike the Commission, for women the primary error lay not in the ***Equal Pay Case 1969*** creating a distinction between two different groups of women—those doing men's work and those in traditional women's trades and professions, some achieving equal pay, some not—but in three failures. First, failure to comprehend that workplace segregation limited the decision's scope. Secondly, consistent with it employers could (and did) further segregate the workplace, reconstituting work women engaged in alongside men as 'women's work' by segregating women workers. Thirdly, history, tradition, and culture dictate lesser value of women's work.

When the decision came down, it was—whatever its flaws—an advance. In contrast to 1969, the 1972 equal pay for work of equal value principle eliminated the requirement that for equal pay to apply, the work performed by female employees should be 'the same or of a like nature' as male workers. For 1972, it was sufficient to find equal value between work performed by women and performed by men. Further, a positive latitude applied in assessment of work value. When undertaking work value assessments, comparisons were to apply where possible *within an award* under consideration. But where such comparisons were unavailable or inconclusive—say work performed exclusively by women—work value comparisons could be undertaken *between female and male classifications within the award* and *between female classifications and male classifications in different awards*. This prompted the possibility of 'comparable worth' of male and female jobs being assessed, so that women's work might be upgraded in value by comparing its components and those of men's work in other fields.

The Commission also affirmed that the value of work assessed must be '"worth" in terms of the award wage', not '"worth" to the employer'. This pruned scope for employer-bias in undervaluing women's work or downgrading its contribution to the industry or enterprise.

Following the federal decision, state industrial commissions and wages boards tackled the principle. Yet with equal pay for equal work enshrined in legislation (not so federally), state bodies faced a hurdle not encountered by the Commonwealth Commission. Could state bodies exceed existing legislative terms or interpret them sufficiently broadly, incorporating a work of equal value component, effectively expanding the various Acts' words? Or was legislative amendment required incorporating equal pay for work of equal value? Must women recommence lobbying MPs, governments, and political parties to remove what was, even at its passage or shortly thereafter, acknowledged as inadequate to achieve equal pay for women in all-female (or traditionally female) fields?

This highlighted another irony for women, confronted in the past. An advance for women at one stage—here equal pay for equal work laws—stymies women at a later stage. Would women better concentrated on industrial commissions and tribunals, seeking the broadest scope possible there, rather than lobbying and winning legislative concessions now possibly limiting their industrial demands? Should women refuse to accept half measures (equal pay for equal work) through legislation, hoping industrial bodies will advance the full measure—albeit, perhaps, later?

Justice Cahill, in May 1972 in the NSW Industrial Commission, procured nurses a measure of wage justice by applying the 'what is "just and reasonable"' principle, effectively ignoring section 88D Industrial Arbitration (Female Rates) Amendment Act 1958. Under an agreement ratified by the Full Bench, in 1971, state public hospital nurses gained wages set at 95 per cent of male nurses' rates. In ***Re Private Hospital Nurses (State) Award 1971***, the NSW Nurses' Association applied to bring private hospital nurses within those relativities. Cahill emphasised that 'just and reasonable' means 'no more than "just and reasonable" rates to be prescribe' but equally importantly to ensure 'rates fixed are no less than "just and reasonable"'.

Still, winning 95 per cent didn't mean it was just and reasonable to pay female nurses identically with male nurses. It meant 'just and reasonable' applied by paying women identically with women: private hospital nurses (female) gaining payment identical with public hospital nurses (female). None of the nurses gained equal pay at 100 per cent of the male wage, despite women in nursing having at least equal responsibilities, equal knowledge and experience, and exercised at least equal skills as men in nursing. Not even equal pay for equal work, much less equal pay for work of equal value.

In 1973, the Federated Clerks' Union (FCU) confronted the issue head on, launching a test case in the Industrial Commission under the Clerks (State) Award, claiming women's rates should be fixed on 'the work performed irrespective or the sex of the worker'. The union wanted the ***Equal Pay Case 1972*** applied at state level. It won its claim.

The NSW Commission was more direct than the federal body, Beattie and McKeon (president and justice) saying the time was 'opportune' for introducing 'equal remuneration for men and women workers for work of equal value, meaning … rates of remuneration … without discrimination based on sex'. In acknowledging international standards, effectively endorsing arguments women and the ALP had pursued for years, they cited 'influential factors' as the federal decision and Australian government's 'support [for] implementation'; the NSW government's lack of submissions; the Public Service Board (PSB)'s appearing and raising no objection; and 'the employers generally seeing implementation … as a matter of social and industrial justice', albeit 'pressing strongly for the … [federal] principle to be adopted without modification'.

Additional to the statutory equal pay provision, the Industrial Arbitration Act's basic and marginal or secondary wages distinguished NSW from the federal system's 'total wage'. The Commission cited the ***Marcel Wave case 1929***, distinguishing male and female hairdressers engaged in cutting and permanent waving, never overruled, distinguished or disapproved, remaining in force however wrong, unjust or irrelevant to contemporary needs. Nevertheless, 'equal margins' were implemented variously following the ***Paint and Varnish Makers case***, enabling the Commission to set a margins formula under equal pay for work of equal value. Here, however, the decision exposed naivety or stereotypical bias. All equal pay claims should, said the Commission, commence from an assumption that male and female work is of equal value, the onus on employers or employees challenging it to show error, namely that margins for females were either too low or too high, generating a work value enquiry. Yet faced with different male-female margins, the assumption would be they represent 'true value of the secondary considerations' (factors determining margins) relating to the particular work, 'fixed without regard to sex'. That is, they 'correctly assessed relative value of the work of males and females'. On 'women only' work, where an award 'provides rates of wages only for females ... it will be proper for the tribunal to assume the margins correctly assess the value of work on the basis of the male margins and female margins being assessed in the same way, but again [this] should be a rebuttable presumption'. Had the Commission focused on the reality of award and wage-fixing bias, it would have set precisely the opposite assumption—that the tribunal 'assume the margins *do not* correctly assess the value of work ....'

Ultimately a standard clause provided for equal pay in three instalments, 'equal pay loadings', on 31 December 1973, 30 September 1974, and 30 June 1975. Reflecting on the federal decision—equally applicable to NSW and other states—WL's 1973 Manifesto noted it 'seems favourable at first glance', but 'the full effect ... [awaits] 1975. In other words, we have been "bought off" until then'.

Women Gain the Minimum Wage

Men had the minimum wage. Women didn't. In December 1973, then January-February 1974, unions applied to the Australian Conciliation and Arbitration Commission for award variations. President Moore, justices Robinson and Ludeke, deputy president Isaac, public service arbitrator Taylor, and commissioner Portus comprised the ***National Wage Case 1974*** (***Minimum Wage Case 1974***) bench. Amongst other claims the ACTU sought minimum wage extension to women. But this was not the whole story. Women called for it in the ***Equal Pay Case 1972***, and, apart from D'Aprano's and the ***National Wage Case 1973*** record, that NCW, UAW, and WLM did so then goes unacknowledged. Yet without them, and D'Aprano's 1973 intervention, the ***Minimum Wage Case 1974*** success might have come years later.

Men classified as unskilled or, rather, in unskilled jobs, had the minimum wage. Women filled the lowest categories of paid employment; biases in calculating worth of what women did meant women more often than men were classed unskilled (an impetus behind the 'rate for the job'). But women were denied the minimum wage. As skills measured wages in the arbitration system, by its very nature (payment for *unskilled* work) the minimum wage required something else. The ***National Wage Case 1967*** recognised the minimum wage as, bluntly, a male wage, no prevarication or acknowledgement that 'unskilled' included women, too. A new standard of the minimum wage was set, with an increase being awarded by the

Commission for the first time. In the ***Equal Pay Case 1969***, the ACTU argued for an increase in the minimum wage. Acceding to the ACTU's submission of 'family considerations' being the basis for the rise, the Commission again limited the wage (and rise) to male workers. 'Family considerations' calculated by what a *man* required to keep *his* family at base level.

Thus, one basis of the minimum wage automatically included women—'unskilled work'; the other—'family responsibilities'—artificially applied to men alone, excluded women. '(Male) family responsibilities' won out over '(generic) unskilled work' or '(generic) unskilled workers' as the minimum wage qualifier. '(Generic) family responsibilities' were not considered.

Women's capacity to survive economically through their own paidwork was central to claims for equal pay. Obviously equal pay in work classed 'skilled' was only part of the answer. The industrial reality of survival in the 'unskilled' workforce made extending the minimum wage to women essential. In the ***Equal Pay Case 1972***, women argued the point alongside the ACTU. It was explicitly ruled out.

In the ***National Wage Case 1973***, the ACTU applied for increases in the minimum wage and total wage, not re-running the minimum wage for women argument. Recognising that increasing the minimum wage and total wage would, if successful, create further anomalies for women, potentially undermining the ***Equal Pay Case 1972*** and increasing pay differentials for women classed unskilled, in 1973 the WLM Equal Pay Group intervened, D'Aprano their advocate.

D'Aprano seized the opportunity to highlight women not within the ***Equal Pay Case 1972*** provisions and without a minimum wage. That this was not before the Commission, none of the parties raising it, was no deterrence. For WLM, every opportunity to promote equal pay must be taken. Without unions or governments pursing it, and its being unlikely employers would, lacking women's intervention women's right to equal remuneration would go unrecognised. Nor, in women's organisations' absence, would anyone present scrutinise employer, government and ACTU submissions, and the Commission's response.

Chastising Commission and parties for ignoring women's pay, D'Aprano made an impact. She began with WLM's support of the ACTU claim for an $11.50 a week total wage rise and regular salary adjustments to offset price increases. She noted the parties' Henderson Poverty Commission statistics were slightly outdated, with no-one appearing before the Commission or on the bench being forced to exist on or below the minimum wage. Re-familiarising herself with lived realities, she had returned to work at four industries—electrical trade, textile industry, meat industry, and hospital wards maid, 'an enlightening experience' where women's wages fell below the poverty line. D'Aprano advised her take-home pay in those four positions as $31.00, $34.00, $39.00, and $32.00, respectively. Even with the slight rises secured by those jobs in the 3 years elapsing, none could be assessed fairly as providing occupants above poverty line income. The $71.50 she assessed as necessary for her own needs, above what she received in her current position, indicated that contrary to income-level arguments, people do not adjust their standards of living to their salary. '... it would be unreasonable and unjust for me to assume women could live on any less, [without] enduring some type of poverty'. In WLM's submission, salaries paid to women in all those jobs required uplifting.

Women as workers, and women's (lack of) industrial rights was further confirmed in her appearance that day, obliged to lose a day's pay to do so: a female advocate, representing a women's organisation, she received no appearance payment, nor was paid as part of her job. Submitting women should be granted the male minimum wage of $65.00. D'Aprano declared that without it, women might get a rise when working under awards covering women and men, but would not gain pay parity with their male colleagues. At least, if no minimum wage extension was to be made, the Commission should confirm '... an open mind to a further claim for an equal minimum rate', setting all rates, award and minimum wage, 'without regard to sex'.

Frequently in the law, an argument not initially accepted takes repetition for courts to discover this is what the law should have been all along, deciding the argument is their own, the rationale their construction. Yet theirs reflects submissions once rejected. In the ***National Wage Case 1973***, WLM put the argument for the minimum wage the second time, Shaw (WLM) having made it in the ***Equal Pay Case 1972***. Support came in 1973 from NCW (G Brown) and UAW (Joan Curlewis). It took another year for the Commission to adopt the argument, having exhibited an open mind the year before by giving D'Aprano, Brown, and Curlewis leave to appear. In the ***National Wage Case 1974*** (***Minimum Wage Case 1974***), the Commission invited submissions on that very question.

Betty Olle representing UAW, Edna Ryan (WEL) and NCW (DD (Diane) Alley) seeking leave, intervened. For the Electrical Trades Union of Australia (ETUA) and Federated Photo Engravers, Photo Lithographers and Photogravure Employees' Association of Australia (FPEPLPEAA), ACTU industrial officer Jan Marsh appeared with RA (Rob) Jolly, whilst Gaudron and JF (Jim) Staples, QC, represented the federal government. Revisiting the ***Equal Pay Case 1972*** veto, the Commission said circumstances then prevailing did so no longer. With the unions generally supporting the ACTU case, federal government substantially in agreement, notwithstanding private employers' and Victorian government opposition, the Commission upheld the claim.

'Ever since coming into being in 1966,' said the Full Bench, the minimum wage 'has received special consideration from the Commission'. Claiming (despite D'Aprano's 1973 submissions) lack of 'adequate information about the economic plight of those at the lower end of the pay scale', the Commission had 'been moved to award proportionately larger [minimum wage] increases' than the total wage because the minimum wage was 'entirely within the Commission's control'. Lacking information of 'incidence and effect' of the minimum wage, the Commission 'must continue to use our best judgment in light of movement in prices and the general wage level'. Here, the too-ing and fro-ing of predecessors and the ACTU on whether family responsibilities were part of federal wage fixing was highlighted. Despite generic references to 'worker' and 'low wage earner', men's 'family responsibilities' alone had exercised Australian wage-fixing bodies' care and attention, never recognising that women comprise by far the largest low wage earner category. The Commission observed that limits existed 'to which [it could] go' in aiding low wage earners 'whose needs are magnified by family obligations'. It acknowledged the minimum wage was introduced in 1966 'not as a family wage but simply a wage for adult males', noting 'family considerations' were first advanced in 1969 by the ACTU, further observing 'that arguments relevant to the male minimum wage [were in 1972] presented by the unions and considered by the Commission as including a family component'.

This highlighted an arguably contradictory approach by the ACTU: in the ***Equal Pay Case 1969*** and ***1972*** arguing for equal pay for women, yet introducing family responsibilities into minimum wage computations. Absent cogent arguments from the parties (ACTU, other unions, employers) based on socio-economic and demographic realities of women's family obligations, inevitably the Commission decided against extending the minimum wage to women. Whatever women's organisations as interveners said, the ACTU's emphasis on family responsibilities, moving away from the original 1966 concept of the minimum wage as a subsistence payment based on categorisation of certain jobs as unskilled, meant stereotypes, traditions, and precedent would likely prevail. As indeed they did, until iteration in 1973 (WLM, NCW, UAW) and 1974 breakthrough.

The Commission said it was 'acutely conscious' of complications in effecting 'adequate justice' to widely varying family obligations of minimum wage workers. No available information enabled differentiation between workers' varying needs, awards did not distinguish between married and single workers, and wages did not vary 'according to number of persons dependent on the worker'.

Equally conscious of the information deficit, Ryan, for WEL, drew upon Australian Bureau of Statistics (ABS) material illustrating the fallacy that men alone bore 'family responsibilities', or *all* men wage earners did, or acknowledged them fully, adequately or at all. Women, like men, supported dependants. Such obligations arose not only through marriage. Single women frequently supported aged parents, sometimes out-of-work siblings, even children—sometimes all three. Deserted, separated, or divorced wives often carried financial responsibilities renounced or never acknowledged by husbands. Women living with husbands bore these obligations: husbands lost jobs, failed to find them, ignored wife and children—using income selfishly; others paid housekeeping allowances insufficient to meet family needs, were alcoholics or gamblers.

Before adverting to the accord between all the unions, federal government, WEL, UAW, and NCW, the Commission said that, as it had 'pointed out in the past', it was not 'a social welfare agency' but 'an industrial arbitration tribunal'. It believed the care of family needs 'is principally a task for governments... [so] the family component should be discarded from the minimum wage concept'. Saying a 'strong case' had been made for 'acceding to the claim for equal treatment of adult male and female workers' in the minimum wage, it observed submissions demonstrated 'not only widespread and deep social support but also the economic viability of this concept'.

Extending the male minimum wage to women was a 'logical extension of the equal pay principle', full application scheduled for mid-1975. Cost was 'variously estimated in round numbers at from \$50m to \$200m per annum', said the Commission, 'a very small figure in the overall wages and salaries bill'. However (confirming, although it did not acknowledge or even see the gross undervaluing of women's work), the Commission noted female workers' concentration 'in certain industries, the large proportion ... entitled to the new minimum wage', meaning 'it would be wise to avoid overloading costs of these industries by an immediate full application of [the minimum] wage to adult females'. A 'phasing in period' would 'give industry time for adjustment ...' Under the 'three step process', adult females received 85 per cent of the new male minimum wage from its operative date; 90 per cent by 30 September 1974; 100 per cent by 30 June 1975. The time frame meant the final date coincided with full implementation of equal pay for work of equal value.

Noting the ***Equal Pay Case 1972*** had resulted in 'substantial bridging of the gap between male and female workers', the Commission observed the average Commonwealth award rate for adult females having 'risen from $50.29 in December 1972 to $62.17 in December 1973', a 23.6 per cent increase, whilst for adult males it was 13.3 per cent. December 1973 saw female Commonwealth award rates averaging 82 per cent of male rates compared with 75 per cent a year earlier. So, 'it would be reasonable to expect the gap ... narrowed further with the further phasing in of the equal pay provision since December 1973'. Extension of the minimum wage to women was not, therefore, particularly daunting economically. Nor did it mean that women's wages were substantially increased, as the lowest rates for adult females in most awards 'are now close to the present minimum wage'. All this made the Commission's proposal to extend the minimum wage to females 'economically feasible'.

This recalls the ***Basic Wage Case 1949–1950*** when the Arbitration Court extended a 75 per cent relativity to women. The Court granted 75 per cent because it was what most women were being paid: little or no effect on the economy, little or no impact on employers who could hardly complain if they were already paying that, anyway.

The decision has another resonance: WEL, UAW, and NCW ***Minimum Wage Case 1974*** submissions reflected the WLM ***National Wage Case 1973*** submissions. D'Aprano's research, based in her own industrial and wage earning experience, found women in some industries, at least, were in fact earning less than the (then) male minimum wage. No doubt this was exacerbated by ways minimum wage earners could increase their real incomes through overtime and other job-related benefits, opportunities not generally open to women. Hence the extension of the minimum wage to women was broader in scope than the Commission's remarks appear to suggest. Yet perhaps the most vital element lay in final removal from the arbitration system the nonsense of the family wage as relevant to men only—men alone as breadwinners. That a wage could be set at a minimum subsistence level—then be refused to one group of workers, solely on the basis of their sex; be introduced to cover wage needs of workers in work classed unskilled—yet one group of unskilled workers denied it, because of their sex, illustrates the solidified bias, even bigotry, operative in the wage gap.

The case impacted, with state tribunals beginning minimum wage hearings. In ***State Wage Case 1974***, the NSW Commission created a minimum wage, operating 'independently of award wage assessments both as to amounts and methods'. This was formulated so as not to be confused with the basic wage, which operated as a 'convenient common starting point from which to fix equitable secondary or marginal rates as between [award] classifications … to achieve … just and reasonable total wages'.

So, some 2 years and 6 months after Street's death, the advent of the generic minimum wage, on the one hand, confirmed her and her colleagues' claims that family payments were a government responsibility, not a wages component. On the other, it could acknowledge family responsibilities as generic, not gendered, with wages incorporating a family responsibilities component for both male and female workers. Yet both state and federal decisions were read as extending the minimum wage to women, simultaneously recognising family responsibilities as diverse and a focus for government payments, not wage fixing. The ***Minimum Wage Case 1974*** confirmed that incorporating family claims into wages (particularly as solely a matter of male responsibility, whatever the reality) was misapplying Commission powers and misstating its role. On one level, though, it was a pyrrhic victory. Remembering women winning 75 per cent of men's wages in the ***Basic Wage Case 1949–1950*** because most were receiving it, anyway, now women won the minimum wage because it was about to be abolished, anyway. Or was it that once women got it, it was deemed irrelevant and men's wages must be shored up some other way. Whatever the case, women left the Commission to its own devices until decade's end.

Part of the Union

In 1973 as prime minister Whitlam's women's affairs advisor, Elizabeth Reid secured $3m federal government money for 1975, International Year of the Woman (IWY), funding celebrations and longer-term projects. A grant to the Australian Council of Salaried and Professional Associations (ACSPA) founded Melbourne's Working Women's Centre (WWC). In

Sydney, with Linda Norton, Australian Workers' Union (AWU) communications officer a driving force, $40,000 established the WTUC, a response to affront caused by the ACTU's creating the Trade Union Training Authority (TUTA), its council lacking women, with no reference in its program, aims or objects to women and—or in—trade unions or paidwork. WTUC membership was open to all women unionists, the organising committee comprising women members of the Australian Clerical Officers' Association (ACOA), Australian Miscellaneous Workers' Union (AMWU), Australian Postal and Telecommunications Union (APTU), Australian Railways Union (ARU), Australian Workers' Union (AWU), Clothing and Allied Trades Union of Australia (CATUA), FCU, Mining and Energy Union (MEU), and Shop Distributive Association (SDA), aiming to improve women's union movement status, encourage unions to recognise women workers' special needs, and promote greater participation of women members in trade union movement decision-making.

Just as women of past decades recognised unions' importance in women's industrial rights and equal pay struggle, 1970s women did, too. Yet the 1970s saw a greater public acknowledgement that focusing directly and publicly on male dominance and entrenched male power in unions was vital. Trade union allegiance had meant unionists such as Williams and Heagney did not break ranks with their male colleagues, despite (at least sometimes) spoken misgivings. In the 1970s, women confronted the union role in limited application of equal pay for equal work and equal pay for work of equal value, and other limitations on women's industrial justice, at least in part, to union inertia, obstruction, or hostility. As D'Aprano wrote, when equal pay was denied, but women were 'expected to pay full price for all goods and services', she approached Clarrie O'Shea, Public Transport Workers Union (PTWU) secretary, famous for going to prison in 1969 over the penal sanctions restricting trade union activism. WAC planned a tram ride, women paying 75 per cent of the fare. Not wanting to 'embarrass or alienate' conductors or (as then known) conductresses, D'Aprano asked 'Marxist Leninist and another "revolutionary" of all "revolutionaries"' O'Shea to 'chat them up' to obviate misunderstanding about WAC's intentions. 'Flabbergasted', O'Shea went 'on and on'. Told the action would go ahead, having been discussed 'in all seriousness', muttering and stammering it was 'a very serious matter' he sped away. Gazing 'at his retreating back', D'Aprano reflected there was 'no doubt whatsoever, women would have to do their own fighting …'

A solution was increasing women's union membership, taking union organiser roles and executive positions, or establishing and reinforcing women's activism outside unions but within the industrial scene, through alternative organisations of women who might or might not be union members. For some, it was not a case of either/or, but working through existing union structures to change them by getting women into them, and working outside putting pressure on unions and in particular the ACTU to change.

Tensions arose within the Women's Movement and women's organisations. The split in UAW, some leaders leaving to join WLM, was replicated in other women's organisations and within unions. For years, D'Aprano worked in the union movement, first as workplace representative, then as a clerk, and doing unpaid work, including writing articles for the union journal children's page. Despite applications and soundings out of those in authority, her wish to be a union organiser never happened. Men, often with far less experience or longevity in the union than she, took the jobs. WAC was an outcome of union hierarchy refusal to regard D'Aprano and her abilities seriously—or even recognise them. The Working Women's Charter Campaign (WWCC), established at the 1976 national Sydney **'Unions are for Women Too!'** conference, grew from similar disaffection experienced by women who had been or were still part of the union movement or who, observing from outside how unions were run and dominated by men, had never formally joined a union or were inactive members.

Some women stuck with the unions. Some took an oppositional stance to women who criticised the male leadership or denounced unions as male power repositories lacking interest in or concern for women's industrial rights. In the mid-1970s, the Australian Charter of Women Workers' Rights—incorporating long-lived claims for equal pay and equal opportunity—was centre-piece to this conflict.

In November 1974, at a jointly organised seminar, UAW and the Trade Union Employee Relations Commission (TUERC) called for a guaranteed minimum wage for women and men, including equal margins and equal over award payments. Reminiscent of the 1940s Australian Women's Charter championed by Street and UA, this became the Australian Charter of Women Workers' Rights. The ACTU then produced its own Charter of Women Workers' Rights.

UAW lobbied trade unionists and ACTU Congress delegates to put the Australian Charter of Women Workers' Rights onto the 1975 agenda, with the Builders Workers Industrial Union (BWIU)'s Pat Clancy advancing a resolution that the Charter was a 'good basis for development of a trade union women workers' charter'. Advocating the proposal's adoption 'to formulate a charter in principle', with an elected drafting committee 'to consult with UAW and other women's organisations', the resolution wanted the ACTU executive to finalise the ACTU Charter for the 1976 Congress. UAW was instrumental, too, in the Amalgamated Metal Workers and Shipwrights Union (AMWSU) advancing another resolution, 'Women in the Workforce', incorporating points from UAW's Charter, including policies on the right to work, equal pay, discrimination, retraining, part-time paidwork, maternity and paternity leave laws, union participation, and education (trade union training).

In ***Lightening the Load***, Joyce Stevens' history of the Women's Employment Action Committee (WEAC), launched in 1982, she relates Sydney's National Women's Trade Union Conference (WTUC), 'the largest and most representative national conference of women unionists ever held'. Conflicting views on what was an industrial issue, a range of political opinions and positions on women in paidwork, inevitable. Five hundred and twenty-six registered delegates, one hundred more on the weekend. Two hundred and seventy-three registered delegates with union sponsorship. Workshop proposals 'challenging traditional union attitudes towards women members' in ACTU policies, some wanting 'a "respectable speakers" conference, including Cornell's professor Alice Cook and significant union representation to 'give women sufficient clout in the unions to make headway', plus 'the usual left pressure groups' …

WA Health Employees' Industrial Union (HEIU)'s Patricia (Pat) Giles (opening address) and Norton, WTUC convenor (welcome address) emphasised working together, building on past work in and with unions, to inspire women as equals in the union movement. For Norton, the aim was not 'to mount an attack on unions', breaking down or belittling their traditional concerns, 'awards and conditions they've fought hard for', traditional concerns that 'are ours too'. Women wanted unions to support women's fight for flexible working hours, parental leave, childcare, health and welfare programs, eradicating job-entry barriers. Women didn't want to dominate unions, but to have 'an equal say' in decision- and policy-making at all levels.

Differences came to a head. Stevens describes some participants 'worry that feminists … would succeed in inserting fertility control and abortion' into the draft ACTU Charter, preferring to leave decision-making 'to the more conservative union channels'. Others considered the conference must 'intervene' in finalizing it, persuading women to 'organise and campaign politically to make such a Charter an effective document'. Otherwise, the conference would be pointless. The original program incorporated 23 workshops, 12 on 'Women and Work', 11 covering 'Women and Trade Unions', and none on the Charter. Eventually organisers conceded demands, scheduling a Charter workshop and one on 'Strategy and Implementation'.

From the workshop, a Charter preamble stipulated a women's campaign 'so they [could] take an active part in trade unions and political life, and exercise influence commensurate with their numbers', and encouraging male trade unionists to 'work with women' on implementing the Charter's 15 aims. 'Equal pay for work of equal value—meaning the total wage plus other benefits', was third, equal opportunity for 'occupations and promotion, regardless of sex, sexuality or marital status or race' four, five, and six—covering equal educational opportunity, and equal vocational and training opportunities.

Plus recommending adoption of the Charter and campaign, the workshop wanted a half-hour of the plenary session 'to formulate the ... Charter demands ... [planning] for Charter groups and a campaign around Charter demands'. Conference organisers refused any Charter debate or resolutions, sex education, birth control, and abortion clause the major stumbling block. Some unions were steadfastly opposed to abortion. The way trade union women wanted to handle this was anathema. Any abortion compromise was labelled selling out women's rights. Some women did not understand union history; others understood it, believing 'union women' were 'ganging up' (on whatever side they stood) to stifle debate. Awash with religion and male politics, linked with the 1950s, involving the Groupers and allegations of a Communist union and ALP take-over, what Stevens describes a 'rowdy confrontation', raged, predictable with women committed to the Charter not relishing being controlled. This followed particularly when women had pledged to work cooperatively as an antidote to male-dominated meetings and trade union conferences. Outbursts of anger and frustration erupted. Organisers remained immoveable. At a later WTUC meeting, a resolution proposing a Charter campaign was narrowly defeated. However, many women took the Charter with them from the conference, launching campaigns under the umbrella title 'Working Women's Charter Campaign'.

The dispute did not impede a 'Wages and unequal pay' workshop critiquing the ***Equal Pay Case 1969***, ***Equal Pay Case 1972***, and ***Minimum Wage Case 1974***, negative outcomes listed as:

(a) Unequal over-award payments
(b) Women restricted to jobs with lower pay than for similar work done by men
(c) Women less likely to be offered opportunities for promotion and better paid jobs
(d) Women unclassified in awards before the equal pay decision given unskilled classifications equivalent to the lowest paid male
(e) Women's work value not fully recognised, through women's concentration in certain occupations
(f) Women more likely pieceworkers and more vulnerable to exploitation
(g) Women reclassified to a male classification of lesser seniority—say, a female with 17 years' service to pay and status of a male with 12 years' service

Workshop discussion covered overcoming pay differences, and whether men were entitled to more money, preference, better jobs, more training, and promotion opportunities than women. Battling 'not only male chauvinism', but female workers' 'unwillingness to fight for their rights' was canvassed, and some women's attitude that women 'shouldn't expect to earn a lot of money'. Traditional thinking condemned, participants repudiated 'male as breadwinner', and 'pay as a family wage' concepts. 'One rate for one job, irrespective of sex' was repeated, calls for 'reassessment of how work is valued', and recommendations for eradicating age barriers (junior rates) to equal pay, and greater opportunities for women.

The conference deplored a consistent and deliberate pattern denying women the same wages as men doing comparable or the same work. This was attributed to lower classifications, re-classification, lack of women's promotional and training opportunities for women, classing of jobs as 'women's jobs' with lower pay, non-payment of equal over-award payments, and the 'qualification barrier' 'often used to keep women in low-paid work'. Unions should 'recognise inequities' in female workers' pay structure, taking steps to eliminate them. Existing male and female wage relativities 'must be destroyed'. Until then, the conference concluded, 'true equality in pay will not be achieved'.

Ultimately, whatever differences between union and non-union women, whatever antagonism or failure to prioritise equal pay as an industrial issue, or contradictions about abortion rights, women were adamant. Union action was essential. This did not, however, prevent women from taking independent action.

Working Women as an Industrial Issue

The 1976 WTUC followed the Whitlam Labor government years. May 1974, following a double dissolution when the Senate opposition moved to defer appropriation bills, a Labor government was re-elected, still lacking a Senate majority, and with a reduced House of Representatives majority. In July, Paul Hasluck's term as governor-general ended. Whitlam put John Kerr in his place.

Next April, the Australian Conciliation and Arbitration Commission introduced wage indexation, with quarterly adjustments following consumer price index (CPI) movements. On 11 November, Kerr dismissed the Whitlam government. Parliament was dissolved. On 13 December, a Liberal National Country Party Coalition won majorities in both houses. Malcolm Fraser was prime minister. Meanwhile, through the 1970s, ***National Wage Cases*** ran annually. In 1979, the Commission addressed maternity leave. Women's organisations intervened.

In the interim, women lobbied for laws prohibiting sex discrimination in education, employment, services, accommodation, and credit, winning the Sex Discrimination Act 1975 (SA), Anti-Discrimination Act 1977 (NSW), and Equal Opportunity Act 1977 (Victoria). In August 1997, a major WWCC meeting in Sydney attracted 250 women from most states and the Australian Capital Territory (ACT). The right to paidwork, to organize, childcare, migrant women's needs, and industrial health were priorities, the 1976 Charter amended to incorporate a section on unions and organising, ending with a call for women and trade union activism. Following the meeting, further modifications and additions meant 'The right to work for everyone who wishes to do so' became: 'The right to *paid* work for everyone who wishes to do so.' Expanded categories of discrimination included not only sex, race, marital status, or sexuality, but country of origin, age, religious or political belief, appearance, and (replacing sexuality) sexual preference. Equal pay for work of equal value expanded to incorporate one rate for the job, 'the same total wage plus other benefits, particularly over-award payments', an adequate 'living wage', and an end to piece rates. Now, women's bodily integrity proponents won out, abortion and contraceptive care provisions including the right to free, safe, legal abortion on demand included, and a proscription against 'forced sterilisation or [forced] abortion'. This recognised abrogation of Aboriginal and Torres Strait Islander women's rights, the well-founded fear of genocide arising from Depo Provera.

Increasing Fraser Coalition government attacks on workers and unions led to inclusion of clauses demanding unemployment benefits for all workers registered as unemployed, active development and defence of workers' organisations, and the right to organise against government, court, media, and employer denials. With increasing unemployment and rocketing inflation, the women 'taking men's jobs' theme resurfaced. Heagney's arguments in ***Are Women Taking Men's Jobs*** had a resurgence. A poster campaign developed, declaring:

> When you've spent all day causing inflation and unemployment … it's hard to think of what to cook for dinner!

Union women and women's activity outside unions—primarily the WWCC—surged. Despite not replicating WWCC energy, the ACTU was not idle. Consultations for a 'final draft Charter' ran 'mainly through the male-dominated structures of the union movement', Stevens reported, culminating in a March 1978 Special ACTU Unions Conference addressing the Charter's implementation. Only 62 of 132 affiliated unions were represented. Only 23 delegates were women. Chaired by a man, the conference opened with a written message from ACTU president Bob Hawke. Refusing to be deterred, the WWCC had earlier leafleted 1977 Congress delegates with a 'welcome to the ACTU Charter', suggesting amendments incorporating rights to paid employment and unemployment benefits for sacked married women; sex education; birth control advice, free and freely available contraception; free, safe, legal abortion on demand but no forced sterilisation or forced abortion; and ending all discriminatory practices against women.

Abortion and contraception were not the only reproductive issues women included. One Charter plank—for 'adequate, paid maternity and paternity leave, without loss of job security, benefits, promotion prospects or superannuation'—was pursued when the ACTU launched a test case. WEL intervening, this became the ***Maternity Leave Case 1979***.

A WTUC resolution 3 years earlier pinpointed the importance of maternity leave to equal pay, declaring women workers are not '"temporary" props to a "family" income'. Women do not enter and exit paidwork as if lacking responsibility for their own economic survival, their families not dependent upon their earning power. Determined to take maternity and paternity leave to their unions, demands included:

(a) Retrenchment and redundancy clauses in all logs of claims
(b) Maternity and paternity leave allowing women time off for 'this socially necessary work' without loss of accrued rights
(c) Union hiring and permanency 'by right of working on a job'

In 1979, for WEL, supporting the ACTU claim, Ryan took it further, urging paid maternity leave. The Commission upheld the ACTU's claim. A woman working for an employer for over 1 year qualified for unpaid maternity leave for up to 12 months, with entitlement to return to her job or an equivalent post. So, by decade's end, women had achieved in principle equal pay for equal work, equal pay for work of equal value, the minimum wage, and maternity leave. Childcare was on the agenda. But was it an 'industrial issue'?

Women knew it was. Nonetheless, without union endorsement, employer cooperation of employers—and industrial commission imprimatur as an industrial issue—whatever childcare realities, women's knowledge, like women's experience, didn't count. However, without it, were maternity leave provisions saying a worker could return to her original job realistic?

Rights in principle denote an advance for all women. Yet at the end of the 1970s, as women working in the unions, Women's Movement, and women's organisations realised, in principle and in practice can be very different. The Australian Working Women's Charter and ACTU Working Women's Charter had some impact. Maternity leave potentially increased women's options. Yet women were held waiting for the final year's ***Equal Pay Case 1972*** implementation. As the WL Manifesto reckoned, we were 'bought off' until then, and increasingly through the 1970s, the limited scope of equal pay for work of equal value grew clear. Entering the 1980s, action for equal pay remained imperative.

Calling upon the spirit of Heagney and campaigning of past decades, in Melbourne the Campaign of Action for Equal Pay (CAEP) reconstituted itself, UAW and NCW returned to the fray, WEL took a leading role. Later, the National Pay Equity Coalition (NPEC) began in Sydney. The 1980s saw concerted action on equal pay.

Women were determined not to be 'bought off' again. On whose shoulders, known or unknown, did they stand? Chapter 14,

'Intermission—Pay and Personalities III' provides insights, through individual women's lives representing so many others. Pen portraits reflect the mix of activists in transition from the rate for the job—or equal pay for equal work at 1960s end, then the 1970s equal pay for work of equal value. Women working towards the first goal were the launching pad for those pursuing the second. Both brought gains, achieved and consolidated, foundation for action into the 1980s future and beyond.

References

Cases—See Case List

CEPO, ***Submissions of Service Groups …***, 1970, Perth, WA, p. 1; copy ***Irene Greenwood Collection***, MU, Perth, WA.

Rosalind Denny, 'Chairman's Address—…, ***Equal Pay News***, at p. 4; copy ***Irene Greenwood Collection***, MU, Perth, WA.

Zelda D'Aprano, ***Interview***, Laureton, NSW, 1994 (April 1994).

Zelda D'Aprano, ***Zelda—***, 1977; Spinifex Press, Nth Melbourne, Victoria, 1995.

Geikie's papers UM Archives, ***List of Papers of Individuals from Community, Political and Other Organisations—Alva Geikie***, http://www.lib.unimelb.edu.au/collections/archives/orgnames.html (accessed 16 July 2006).

Irene Greenwood, ***Interview***, Shenton Park, WA, 1988 (June 1988).

Margaret Thornton, 'Towards Embodied Justice … in the Age of the 'New Corporatism' [1999] MelbULawRw 28; (1999) 23(3) Melbourne University Law Review 749 (austlii.edu.au) (accessed 2 September 2022).

Joyce Stevens, ***Lightening the Load***, WEAC, Sth Sydney, NSW, 1991.

'Women in the I.L.O. Employment Programme', ***Equal Pay News***, 1971 (August 1971), p. 14; copy ***Irene Greenwood Collection***, MU, Perth, WA.

'Women's Liberation Manifesto', ***Women's Liberation Newsletter***, Melbourne, Victoria, 1972 (March 1972), pp. 5–6; copy Appendix 1 & Appendix 2, D'Aprano, ***Zelda—***, 1995, pp. 401–3.

Neville K. Wran, 'Murphy—Barrister' in Scutt (ed.), ***Lionel Murphy—***, McCulloch/Macmillan, Melbourne, Victoria, 1987, pp. 15–21.

'Workshop: Wages and unequal pay' in ***Unions are for Women Too!*** 1976.

CHAPTER 14

Intermission: Pay and Personalities III

> In my pre-marriage business career I was reasonably successful …, quickly rising to managing director's secretary, then assuming responsibility for the running of the company—office, stores, repairs sections—during his frequent absences overseas and interstate. Of course I received lower wages than the men whose work I oversaw.
>
> Diana (Di) Graham, 'A Life in Pursuit of Equality' in ***Different Lives***—
> J. Scutt (ed), 1987, p. 179

'Jessie Street - Salute to "A Class Traitor", Kay Keasey's ***Australian Women's Weekly*** tribute, 5 August 1970, shortly after Street's death, carries the epigraph: 'Even at the early age of three, I had instincts … of cause and effect, and the basic need to remove the cause of the trouble'.

Warrior, agitator, lobbyist, thinker—Street was not alone.

When Di Graham discovered her subordinates earned more, she protested. Despite the company's frequently publicising her capabilities in trade journals, it was 'inevitable' 'they' said: 'the government' made the wages rules. As women before and after, Graham—like Street—joined the Women's Movement.

J. A. Scutt, *Wage Rage for Equal Pay*,
https://doi.org/10.1007/978-3-031-42178-5_14

Unjust Ethos, Unequal Practice

In the 1970s and '80s, women new to the struggle joined long-time campaigners. Behind them lay the 1940s, women entering male occupations, rarely paid men's wages, seeing their work still under-rated. Women in women's occupations, seeing—despite their own long-term experience in work equally important—their sisters in men's jobs paid more, realising forcefully that their own work was deemed less valuable than men's. Next, the 1950s. Women sensing unequal pay's deceit, some lobbying collectively for change, some resentful but stomaching it, others succumbing to the dominant tautological ethos that women should not earn as much as men, because women do not.

The 1960s 'equal pay for equal work' brought some women gains. Early 1970s, 'equal pay for work of equal value' reaped minimal numbers because few unions initiated claims. Campaigns continued, 1970s into '80s, women wanting real value measured.

Knowing they were paid less than a man for the same, equally or more difficult, onerous, responsible, productive work created dissonance for women, sometimes engendering a silent shame—although why, when their employers' shameful actions and wage-fixing bodies' ignorance were to blame—or precipitating many into speculating creatively how to instigate change, harbouring a canker that refused to leave. Confronted with an injustice rationalised by some of their sisters, taken by male colleagues as their due, unquestioned by employers and condoned by authority, facing the insult, women developed a fine sense of the ridiculous—to survive, they must, though it lay underneath, like an open wound. Women paid as much, often more, for goods and services. Lower wages meant less power, fewer rights and less say.

In all trades and professions, women uncovered deception. Like Graham, Joan Woodbury earned less than junior men. '… two masters degrees, years and years of experience, working in universities and overseas. It didn't matter'. Arnot's salary was pegged below men of lesser qualifications. Passed over for the head librarian position although acting head, as consolation prize she was dispatched to a United Nations (UN) library indexers conference in Geneva, regularly put on display whenever the NSW State Library wanted a woman to publicly shine. Never did remuneration match adulation.

Women did not class men working alongside them as enemies, responsible for pay differentials—although sometimes scoffing at lesser abilities of those paid more. At least in earlier decades, some ascribed it to governments impervious to women's strengths, intellect, and expertise, or to politicking between powerful groups of men: political parties, politicians, trade unions, employers. Late 1970s, into the '80s, women glimpsed possibilities through anti-discrimination and equal opportunity legislation. Where laws were lacking, women demanded them. With wry amusement, they gazed on men falsely claiming superiority of talent and capability. Despite it, wage injustice did not undercut women's dedication or performance. But it weighted them down.

Dormant endurance erupted with a sense of injustice when ***Basic Wage*** and ***National Wage Cases*** brought home the fraudulence of men's wages and livelihood standing on a different footing from their own. Frustration and anger channelled into union activism, women's organisations, or both. For some, wage differentials drove a lifetime struggle for all women workers.

The Invisible Woman Gets Seen

In late 1950s Tasmania, Dr Anne Matz taught at Hobart High School. Initially languages head, later deputy head, she received 65 per cent of a male salary. 'Coming from Austria, I couldn't believe this', she reflects. 'Returning to Vienna, visiting colleagues and friends of yesteryear, I asked "what about equal pay", they said: "We're not barbarians!" so what did that make *us*!'

Matz joined the Southern State Teachers Union (SSTU). 'At first, I couldn't even be heard. I was invisible. Occasionally someone would intervene for me: "Dr Matz wants to say something." Then I was allowed to speak. After two years I was president of the Southern Teachers, and from then on - no complaints. The ice was broken. Before becoming president I was voted onto the executive'.

Noreen Millar's father was a primary school headmaster. 'I knew nothing of equal pay … I knew some outstanding women teachers. Riding their bikes fifty miles to and from school, everyone respected them. When I began teaching at Devonport, … the caretaker received more money than I –. In Launceston, women staff, strong-minded and community-orientated, dragged me along. Joined the union, became secretary. Lance Barnard, later Whitlam government minister, was president'. Hobart, a new school, her deputy head, a man, on a higher salary. 'It wasn't so much a question of money, but justice. Would you think that's fair?'

BA, LLB, trained teacher, Teachers' Union vice-president, Joan Audrey Burke wrote the Union's equal pay submission then, elevated to the Tasmanian Public Service Tribunal, was unable to present the teachers' case. Millar took over, 'and a shattering experience it was'. On the bench, Burke asked 'telling questions':

> The Chairman finally said he'd had enough of me, I could go. Then - 'Taking into account the case you've been putting up, I shan't open the door for you'. Pinned to my chair, I couldn't move. Hugh Campbell, another tribunal member, got up: 'Noreen, I'll open the door for you'. He did.

Millar was one of the first women advocates in a Tasmanian industrial tribunal. 'A triumph', says Matz.

Yet it ended with: 'You've a very good case, but this Tribunal can't introduce equal pay. Only Parliament can ...' Parliament deferred: "Not for us. It's for the Tribunal". A deliberate stalemate, I imagine', said Millar, 'until forces became too strong'. The Teachers' Union took their case to Parliament. 'Mrs Benjamin was in the Upper House at the time', Matz remembers:

> Phyllis Benjamin helped a lot, introducing us when we handed over our petition and equal pay submission. The men said: 'Did you do this? Incredible.' Retiring in 1968, at 82 or 83 per cent of a man's wage, still no equal pay, the change went through just after. When I retired, three people had to do my work.

Success—Of Sorts

Tasmanian teacher, Joan Woodbury, entered the 1940s NSW struggle when Woodcock was at the forefront:

> She taught me when I was at school, then I addressed envelopes and other clerical work in my first years as a teacher, early in the war. She was a fine teacher and a fine woman, and when equal pay came for teachers, everyone knew it was her success.

Teaching in Broken Hill, then overseas, Woodbury returned to Launceston Teachers' College. She—fully qualified—worked alongside an unqualified male, later becoming first Hobart Teachers' College warden.

'Equal pay started in Hobart in the early 1960s with talk amongst senior women. I was forty by then, and Tasmania was the state with a woman voted in as Teachers' Federation president, then denied her place because she was a woman'. At the first major meeting, 'as many were against equal pay as for it':

> It often seemed we had more support from men than women. Lots of married women teachers were terrified that 'other women'—single ones, like me, would get better jobs than their husbands and be earning as much money.

When the SSTU negotiated for equal pay, Labor was in power. But the Tasmanian Upper House was 'a last resort for dinosaurs':

> The Labor Party said it was for equal pay, knowing full well it could go through the Lower House but be thrown out of the Upper House. We had good strong women leaders, but there were women forcibly against it. We had not only men to defeat, but women, making it difficult for us, politically.
>
> The Women Graduates Association opposed it. Speaking to them, I was howled down by a medical doctor. I said: "Do you get three fifths of a male doctor's pay?" That shut her up …

Harry Leach, Teachers' Federation president, and Brian Miller, lawyer member of the Upper House, advised the debating scheduled. Woodbury took her students into the gallery, 'over three solid years, until the legislation passed … sitting through the debates until the House closed'. Some students 'put up placards outside. While they didn't chain themselves to the railings, they almost did …':

> The final night, artificial insemination of cattle and oyster leases were debated. Equal pay was postponed and postponed, until being the only item left. One member said he'd have supported the Bill if it included the nurses. We couldn't tell him the nurses had decided not to join in. Then there were the waverers, three of them. In the end, they came down on the right side.

When the Bill finally went through, 'the girls went out and danced in the street … too late for the newspapers, and we got two lines in the ***Mercury***. Equal pay was … phased in over five years—and I didn't last long enough to get it'.

Pay, Qualifications, and (In) Equality

In early 1970s Victoria, Shaw, Jessica (Bon) Hull, Geikie and Libby Brooke wrote ***Women in Employment***, never anticipating its impact. Exposing women's exploitation as cheap labour, media coverage, and public debate spurred Women's Liberation (WL)'s intervention in the ***Equal Pay Case** 1972*. Shaw presented WL's submission covering the basic and minimum wage, addressing the 'men alone have family responsibilities' conundrum and advocating the minimum wage for women. The Commission declined. When, in the ***Basic Wage Case 1973***, the Commission addressed proposals to increase the national wage and male minimum wage, D'Aprano's WL submissions focused on the minimum wage anomaly.

D'Aprano found the entire process 'appalling' for '… in front of you, people are arguing about your worth. Your whole worth as a human being is bandied around in monetary terms …', the employers 'see you as a means of profit'. For the trade unionists she was 'a member and payer of membership fees, providing a career for them', ultimately 'sitting on the bench', and 'that goes for the trade unionist sitting up front, too'. Commission members made decisions 'affecting other people's lives, their livelihood, and in some cases their very survival' yet '… no one was interested in sitting down to work out how much the workers had to bloody pay. How much is the average rent? How much does the average family spend on food?' Weren't people 'entitled to a television set and … refrigerator and … all that goes with modern living. No one needs to be a genius to work it out'.

Waiting to be called on, D'Aprano grew increasingly angry at bench and bar-table self-satisfaction. She longed to rise to speak, asking where were the people directly affected by poverty, the minimum wage, the need for increases? Not there, speaking for themselves. She wanted to give 'the toilet analogy' for, nerves intruding, she took several trips to the lavatory and was 'directly affected by lack of toilet facilities for women in this building': women must 'take a lift to the fourth floor, walk two corridors to the building's rear, to use female staff facilities'. Lavatories for press and advocates (all presumed male) were on the courtroom floor. For D'Aprano '… until one is personally affected, all concepts seem remote'.

On leave without pay from the Post Master General (PMG), she felt alone, as if the only worker at the Commission, just as she was the only woman awaiting the call to present submissions at her own expense. No man sat listening or waiting to be heard, worrying about losing more wages, the longer the sitting time. The Australian Council of Trade Unions (ACTU) advocate 'went on hour after hour about the country's industrial situation, world monetary system, world inflation, on and on, all around the world, from heaven to hell, all because workers wanted more money'. D'Aprano thought she was 'better off dragging mail-bags around at work than listening to them day after day', surmising 'the only reason the men could put up with it was because they were well-paid, having power and status going with it'.

Talk of poverty forced D'Aprano to consider her own wage. Calculating she could live on $71.50—just—(less than her PMG wage), she concluded that women living on any less were in poverty. Anyone could assess the minimum they required to survive. Why should the Commission require anyone to survive on less? Next day, she told the Commission it was 'all very well to set wages according to need', but this seemed to apply to some, not others: neither Commission nor advocates, for they couldn't possibly need so much more than ordinary workers. Nor did it seem to apply to women, for therein lay a contradiction. If the minimum wage was set with both family considerations and 'male' as essential characteristics, how could that square with the reality that not all men have family responsibilities and many women do—as sole provider, or households reliant on both parties' wages. Some 25 years later, D'Aprano speculated still, how could the Commission in the ***Equal Pay Case 1972*** decide award rates must be considered regardless of sex, yet simultaneously 'dismiss outright a minimum wage for women' because family considerations determined eligibility, 'continuing this prattle' in the ***National Wage Case 1973***.

As High Court justice, Lionel Murphy said, it takes 'rational argument, over and over' to persuade courts that the time has come. So the ***Minimum Wage Case 1974*** saw capitulation to rationale argument of two years earlier (Shaw, WL), and the year before (D'Aprano, Women's Liberation Movement (WLM)). This time, Women's Electoral Lobby (WEL)'s Ryan, throwing the latest Henderson 'Poverty Line' statistics back to the Commission, employed UN and International Labour Organization (ILO) treaties, women's civil rights and 'twelve bits of evidence' to overthrow the flawed minimum wage rationale of 1966. The WEL submission was brief, Ryan initially showing it to former commissioner Terry Winter, who 'couldn't fault it', suggesting 'reiterating the points at the end, in a summing up'.

Women needed the 'same chances as men in wages', otherwise being 'treated less fairly than men', with 'no chance of saving money to build capital', Ryan said. Evidence included 'a lovely letter from Co-operative

Housing [saying] they took women's wages into consideration [for] housing loans' and the final item, 'the loveliest one' from the Australian Bureau of Statistics (ABS). 'Becoming a bit friendly with the ... people in Canberra', ringing them, 'chasing up statistics on women and pay, and women in single parent households ...':

> Anyway, Miller was the top dog at the ABS. Someone who didn't identify himself rang me, saying: Ask Mr Miller to let you have the latest figures of the Henderson enquiry.

Her anonymous informant advised the report was not yet published, but 'the figure will be very useful to you':

> Talk about a gift from heaven! I asked for it. Arriving the day before I left for Melbourne ... it was the number of fatherless children whose mothers were in the workforce! [In] the Commission it was as if we'd let off a bomb! Everyone wanted to read the letter I had, signed by Miller. When the ACTU [made] its submission, there I was, sitting on this statistic. ... [T]he ACTU was saying it couldn't provide the figures to the Commission, because the report wasn't yet out, and they didn't have the details. It was very funny.

WL/WLM were proven right. Raising the male minimum wage in 1973 without extending it to women left women behind, whilst women gaining equal pay had their progressive increases effectively reduced. Men on the minimum wage gained $9.00 from the 1973 decision, bringing them to $60.00 a week—the same amount women on the total wage received, from the 1972 decision, in steps over two and a half years. In 1974, the Commission extended the minimum wage to women.

Yet, once women had got it, Ryan said: 'It was dropped. There was no minimum wage anymore, no funeral for it, it merely disappeared'. She was right. It was phased out, undercutting the gain, a victory nonetheless. 'We had to win the point', said Ryan.

Shoulder to Shoulder, Woman to Woman

In 1941, with 27,000 other women, ***Valerie (Val) Buswell*** **(1922–2005)** enlisted, earning two-thirds of a male officer's salary. Back to civilian life, she joined NSW Business and Professional Women (BPW) and BPW Hunters Hill. When Evatt's Royal Commission into Human Relationships published its 1977 ***Final Report*** to a hostile Fraser Liberal National Coalition government, NSW BPW held a major briefing. When equal pay languished, BPW Hunters Hill ran a major Macquarie University (MacquarieU) conference. When in 1993, fellow Women's Auxiliary Australian Air Force (WAAAF) June Stone lodged a representative complaint with the Human Rights and Equal Opportunity Commission (HREOC) challenging denial of servicewomen's defence service home benefits, Buswell joined forces. Eligibility depended on field of war or active duty overseas, denied to servicewomen. Campaigning won WAAAFS, Women's Royal Australian Naval Service (WRANS), Australian Women's Army Service (AWAS), and Australian Army Medical Women's Service (AAMWS) the entitlement, wherever having served. Heading Australian Federation of Business and Professional Women (AFBPW) Pay Equity Committee, Buswell briefed counsel intervening in the ***National Wage Case 1990–1991***, ***National Wage Case 1991***, and ***Family Court Counsellors case 1993***. When Arnot turned 90, Buswell and National Council of Women (NCW)'s Joan Ellison established the Parliament House ***Jean Arnot Luncheon***. When Quentin Bryce retired from Sydney University Women's College (May 2003), returning to Queensland as second woman governor, Buswell and Meredith Burgmann hosted a Parliament House send-off. In 2002, the Australian Broadcasting Corporation (ABC)'s ***100 Years*** interviewed Buswell and Dulcie Gillies, 1920s Sunshine Harvester factory worker, on equal pay. In the Workplace Relations Bill 1999 campaign, National Women's Advisory Council (NWAC), Ministerial Advisory Council on Veterans' Issues (MACOVI) and NSW's Council of Ex-Servicewomen's Associations member Buswell spoke: 'In memory of BPW women working hard and long, [for] equal pay …—Jean Arnot, Doris Osborne, Peg Magoffin and many more like them—BPW Australia Division NSW will fight [for] pay equity for all women—in sweatshops, on the factory floor and business and professional women'.

A founding member of the National Pay Equity Coalition (NPEC), ***Clare Burton* (1942–1998)** gave evidence on competency-based systems, performance appraisal, job evaluation methods, and sex bias in job descriptors in NSW's ***Pay Equity Inquiry 1997***. An intellectual powerhouse behind Australian employment equity programs (1980s–1990s), Burton utilised university, public and private sector experience in NSW, Queensland, WA, and her 1998 equal opportunity review of Aotearoa/New Zealand Armed Forces. Crucial to the integration of clerical and keyboard jobs, her work enabled women in keyboard work to expand job descriptions for career opportunities. Growing up on farms in Tuggeranong and Weetangera, now Canberra, ACT suburbs, Burton brought inclusiveness into her work. BA Anthropology (1967, Hons), and PhD (1979) on women's subordination, she taught at Kuring-gai College of Advanced Education (CAE) (now University of Technology, Sydney (UTS)). Taking leave from her associate professorship, she became NSW Director of Equal Opportunity in Public Employment (DEOPE) (1989–1992), Queensland public sector equity commissioner (1992), then consultant. Her contribution to state and federal wage cases figured particularly in the ***National Wage Case 1988*** and ***Pay Equity Inquiry 1997***. In 2003, with Graham, she was posthumously awarded the EDNA Grand Stirrer award. The ***Clare Burton Memorial Lecture*** and ***Clare Burton Award*** commemorate her life and work. Her 1988 monograph, ***Redefining Merit***, is a classic.

Nominating for Port Adelaide 1988 by-election, first Indigenous Australian standing for federal Parliament in SA, ***Ruby Hammond*** **(1936–1993)** is memorialised by the Murray Bridge state seat of Hammond. In 1941, granted partial exemption from the Aborigines Act 1934 (SA), lifting restrictions requiring Indigenous Australians to live on reserves or in restricted areas, meant she was denied association with Indigenous Australians wholly under the Act. Working with Council of Aboriginal Women of South Australia (CAWSA), comprehending poverty's direct interface with legal obstacles confronting Aboriginal people, in 1974 she became executive secretary of the Aboriginal Legal Rights Movement (ALRM) in SA. On 3 May 1973 appointed to the federal Aboriginal Arts Board (AAB), on 11 September 1974, her commitment to women's rights and advancement, particularly Indigenous Australian women, saw Whitlam appoint her to Australia's National Advisory Committee (NAC) for International Women's Year (IWY). Twelve women under Reid's leadership developed themes and programs for 1975 to benefit all Australian women, whatever cultural background, economic status, occupation, beliefs, or ways of life. Growing up in an independent Aboriginal community at Blackford near Kingston in SA, working against sex and race discrimination, through her public service employment, membership of state and federal boards and committees, and at grassroots level, Hammond earned high esteem in Aboriginal and non-Aboriginal communities. In 1977 recognised as SA Woman of the Year, 1992 awarded the Australian Public Service Medal, in 1993 she merited the Equal Opportunity Achievement Award.

***Sharan Burrow* (1954–)** was first woman elected International Confederation of Free Trade Unions (ICFTU) Asia Pacific Region Organisation president (October 2000), and first woman elected International Trade Union Confederation (ITUC), representing 148m workers in 231 affiliated organisations across 150 countries (December 2004). Born into a union family, valuing her great, great grandfather's history of standing for the state seat of Cobar for the Australian Labor Party (ALP) and participation in the 1891–1892 shearers' strike as an Australian Workers' Union (AWU) organiser, Burrow grew up in Warren, a western NSW country town. Studying teaching at the University of New South Wales (UNSW) (1974–1976), commencing her career in country NSW high schools, wanting to improve industrial conditions led to a NSW Teachers' Federation organiser post then Bathurst Trades and Labour Council (TLC) president (1980s). Following George as second ACTU woman president (2000–2010), she spearheaded campaigns for paid maternity leave, lower-paid workers' wage increases (vast majority women), family friendly workplaces, childcare, workers' rights to association, union membership and representation, and against manufactured redundancies and unfair dismissal. A European Climate Foundation supervisory board member, member of the Global Reporting Initiative (GRI) Stakeholder Council and ILO's governing body, Burrow chaired the Multinational Enterprises sub-committee Workers' Group. In Sydney on 30 November 2002, she was a leader of Walk against War with Iraq, and January 2005, in Davos, Switzerland, joined U2 singer Bono's Global Call to Action Against Poverty.

***Juliet (Julie) Richter* (1938–)** headed WEL's Industrial Action Group (IAG), joining the coalition campaigning to amend the Howard Liberal National Coalition government's industrial relations laws, appearing before the Senate Economics References Committee on the Workplace Relations and Other Legislation Amendment Bill 1996. In the NSW Industrial Commission, she presented submissions on award discrimination and enterprise bargaining impact on women workers, and was WEL's representative when NPEC appeared before the NSW Industrial Commission in the Award Simplification hearings and ***Pay Equity Inquiry** 1997*. As IAG convenor, she worked on WEL's ***Living Wage Case** 1997* submissions presented by WEL advocate Julie-Anne Bennett. Active in WEL from the 1970s, Richter (with Elizabeth Windshuttle), wrote WEL's submission lobbying successfully for NSW Department of Premier and Cabinet's Women's Coordination Unit (WCU) (later Department for

Women then Office for Women), and NSW Office of DEOPE. In 1977, she delivered the ***Anne Conlon Memorial Lecture*** 'Women in the Workforce: Looking backwards, going forwards or going round the bend', and in 1998, won the inaugural EDNA award for representing WEL and women's interests in the Australian Industrial Relations Commission (AIRC), in the NSW ***Pay Equity Inquiry 1997***, and lobbying on behalf of NSW Working Women's Centre (WWC).

Philippa Hall **(1953–)** contributed to the NSW Industrial Commission ***Pay Equity Inquiry 1997*** submissions and HREOC in AIRC cases. BA, MA (University of Sydney (USyd)), and MComm, Dip Info Management (UNSW), by 2006, as director, Pay and Employment Equity Unit, Workplace Group in Aotearoa/New Zealand Department of Labour, Hall combined 23-years' public administration in seven agencies, 21-years government equity-related research and policy advice, 17-years public sector management, 12-years collaborative research and report writing, seven-years university research and teaching. NSW Department for Women deputy director general (1996–1998) and, earlier, HREOC senior advisor, MComm (UNSW) lecturer, NSW Department of Industrial Relations, Employment, Training and Further Education Women and Work Unit manager (1991–1993), she worked with the Affirmative Action Agency (AAA), Departments of Industrial Relations and Employment, Primary Industry and Social Security, UTS, and MacquarieU, publishing widely on pay equity and winning an EDNA (2003). Aiming at evidence-based policy development and research, and building support for equity strategies, her postal clerk Aunt Betty's advice 'go for men's jobs—always, you get paid more' was prescient. The ***Sydney Morning Herald*** 'Women and Girls' section (advertising her first post), demonstrated 'we didn't yet have one rate for the job, let alone equal pay for work of equal value'. Today, women's advantage is 'skills, links and a knowledge-base built through influential public and private sector jobs formerly denied women'. Despite continuing discrimination promoting men in powerful jobs, women are 'better positioned than ever' to combine on-the-job expertise with public world activism to change 'how things are'.

Teacher and local community activist in China, as an outworker in Australia, in 1994, ***Qi Fen Huang*** **(1964–)** developed an injury impeding her sewing. Joining Asian Women at Work (AWW) as community worker and organiser, in 1996, she was a FairWear founder and AWW member, campaigning apart from two periods when health and family reasons dictated temporary frontline 'retirement'. Work with NSW Chinese-Australian outworkers prompted the project-funding Mercy Foundation to pursue addressing structural injustices confronting women in outwork/piece-work, leading to the Sydney FairWear campaign. When the Textiles, Clothing and Footwear Union (TCFU) undertook its multi-lingual phone-in for outworkers in 1994, Huang worked as Chinese bi-lingual community worker, then explored exploitation, sexual harassment, and violence reported through the phone-in. A campaign stalwart for industrial rights including outworkers' pay equity, she spoke at FairWear rallies and parliamentary inquiries, worked with outworkers and factory workers, assisted speech writing and submissions for rallies and inquiries. Through community work, Huang supported women individually and in groups, encouraging women to stand up in the workplace, home, and community. In 2005, resigning from AWW due to ill-health, she remained involved in the FairWear Consultative Group, and as support/reference person for FairWear staff. Huang's highlighting outworker/pieceworker issues, particularly amongst women, is acknowledged by FairWear as central to the struggle.

NCW Australia president and International Council of Women (ICW) executive member (1997–2000), NCW Victoria president (1990–1993), ***Gracia Baylor* (1929-)** was municipal councillor (1966–1978), first Healesville (now Upper Ranges) woman president (1978) and Australian Local Government Women's Association (ALGWA) president (1974–1976). Liberal Party member Boronia Province (1979–1985), shadow community services minister (1982–1985), she and Joan Coxsedge, ALP Melbourne West, were the first women elected to Victoria's Upper House. As Equal Employment Opportunity (EEO) for Women Advisory Board member (1999–2002), she reviewed legislation requiring equal opportunity reporting from companies above 500 employees, assisted research and development of women's workplace promotion policies, initiated an annual Equal Opportunity for Women Agency (EOWA) award event for employer achievements, and assisted workshops on Workplace Relations Act 1996 (Cth) changes. Developing and facilitating a Technical and Further Education (TAFE) course, ***Women and Decision-Making 1998–1999***, she led a Hobart, Tasmania workshop addressing women's workforce issues (2000), edited ***Work-Life Management—How to Get the Balance***, and authored ***Economic Security of Women*** (OWA Victoria, 1999) and ***Equal Employment Opportunities for Women*** (Department of Workplace Relations and Small Business, 2000). As MLC Baylor negotiated Miscellaneous Lands Act 1989

(Victoria) terms preserving a Queen Victoria Hospital (built on Victorian Women's late nineteenth-century Shilling Fund) tower, becoming a trustee (1995–2003) of Queen Victoria Women's Centre, chairing from 1999–2002. Secondary school teacher training at Melbourne's Mercer House, teaching (1957–1970), then law clerking (1972–1978) underpinned her politics and women's rights work.

Fran Hayes **(1953–2024)** was senior industrial relations advisor, NSW Office of DEOPE (1980s–1990s), involved in award restructuring and structural efficiency, merit, pay equity, and employment discrimination. As an Australian Social Workers' Union (ASWU) founding member, first national organiser, and federal president (1978–1980), systemic exploitation in this low-paid, overwhelmingly female employment sector (social and welfare work), previously un-unionised, was evident from her Commonwealth Youth Support Scheme (CYSS) work. Entering the Commonwealth Public Service (CPS), Hayes joined the Australian Clerical Officers Association (ACOA), becoming women's officer (1984–1986) and the Trade Union Training Authority (TUTA) trainer (1990s). An NPEC founding member, she contributed to the NSW ***Pay Equity Inquiry 1997*** and Women's Movement Workplace Relations Bill 1996, and Workplace Relations Bill 1999, campaigns. Outside the Senate Workplace Relations Bill Inquiry hearings (October 1999), she said: 'What women want is pay equity and job security, not worsening of their position through substandard work conditions'. Awarded an Edna (with Suzan Virago, Jean Slarke, Rebecca Reilly, and Aileen Beaver) for improving women's workforce conditions, in 1998, she paid tribute to Clare Burton: 'She was the first boss ... proud of my achievements [not] threatened by them'.

Descended from the Wergala and Wamba Wamba people, western Victoria, ***Eleanor Bourke*** **(1943–)** specialises in construction of women and race, human rights and Indigenous Australian women's rights. Co-chairing Reconciliation Victoria, BallaratU adjunct professor, associate professor at SA University, with professor Colin Bourke she reviewed MonashU's Indigenous program for Aboriginal and Torres Strait Islander people's recruitment, retention, progression and graduation, and expanded enrolments, especially in business and science (1977) and devised an Aboriginal Education, Employment and Training Scheme Advisory Structure proposal for ACE (1988). In 1999, with Mick Dodson and Margaret Thornton, Bourke appeared as an expert witness, giving evidence to the Victorian Civil and Administrative Tribunal (VCAT) in

Atkinson and Atkinson v. State of Victoria and ***Yaruga v. State of Victoria***, the first Indigenous Australian professional employment race discrimination claims: non-Indigenous candidates were appointed above qualified Indigenous Australians to a public service and consultancy positions advertised as requiring Aboriginal cultural heritage experience and expertise, qualifications appearing in the consultancy brief and duty statement. As associate professor of Australian Indigenous Studies and director of MonashU CAIS, Bourke spoke to extrinsic and intrinsic worth of lived experience and Indigenous expertise of Elders, exposing biased assessment of work value, qualifications, and merit.

Lynne Fitzgerald* (1946–)** was manager of Tasmania's Department of Economic Development Labour and Employment Unit (2000–2013), Hunt & Fitzgerald consultant (2013–), then elected to UnionsTasmania (originally Tasmanian Trades and Labour Council (TTLC)) (1995–2000), as first woman in Australia to become a state Labour Council secretary. With Elizabeth (Liz) Little, WomenTasmania director, and Scutt, Tasmania's first anti-discrimination commissioner, in the Tasmanian Industrial Commission ***Pay Equity Case 2000 for the first time in a ***State Wage Case*** three women appeared. Earlier, Fitzgerald worked in government and as TTLC occupational health and safety officer, assistant secretary (1992–1994), then Community and Public Sector Union (CPSU) (State Public Services Federation Tasmania (SPSFT)) senior advisor (1994–1995). Born in Sydney's Dee Why, in Tasmania she taught at St Cuthbert's School, Lindisfarne, with Department of Education and Arts southern Tasmania primary schools (1986–1987), then was private secretary/senior private secretary to Michael Aird, employment, industrial relations and training minister in the Field Labor government (1991–1992). As TTLC secretary, Fitzgerald's strategic response included the change to UnionsTasmania, stabilising 'a rapid decline in union density in Tasmania'. An Australian Republican Movement (ARM) 1998 Constitution Convention delegate, long associated with Hobart's WWC and Community Legal Service (CLS), she led the union movement call for peace in the 2003 Iraq war.

Sue Jackson* (1942-)** represented Council of Action for Equal Pay (CAEP) in the AIRC ***Nurses Comparable Worth case 1986, advocating comparable worth. Council of Intellectual Disability Agencies (CIDA) executive officer, she worked in intellectual disabilities services and represented non-government, not-for-profit organisations in Victoria. As Victorian Council of Social Service (VCOSS) deputy director, her work included responsibility for disability policy and advocacy, implementing the Intellectually Disabled Persons Services Act 1986 (Victoria)(now repealed) and development of a State Plan for Intellectual Disability Services. In the 1990s, Jackson worked with the Brotherhood of St Laurence Future of Work Project, assessing Australian labour market changes and social security impact. Awarded a Churchill Fellowship (2000), she examined overseas intellectual disability services developments, focusing on community inclusions and ageing. With substantial non-government community services sector and social policy work experience, she advocates widely on social policy development, and presented the 2006 Australian Education Union (AEU) Disability Conference keynote address.

NSW acute psychiatric hospital social therapist, youth worker at Griffith's Riverina Council of Social Development, then Marrickville Municipal Council, ***Elizabeth (Liz) Little*** **(1952–)** qualified BSS (Bachelor of Social Sciences) (USyd, 1978). Having formulated a community-based rehabilitation program for juvenile repeat offenders at London's Borough of Barking and Dagenham, she returned to local government in Sydney. Next, senior lecturer, School of Social Work, Tasmanian State Institute of Technology (TSIT) at Launceston (now the University of Tasmania (UTas)), then establishing and heading WomenTasmania (Office of the Status of Women (OSW)), Department of Premier and Cabinet and, as Sex Discrimination Act 1994 (Tasmania) commissioner, oversaw sex discrimination claims, research and education. Women and Paid Work Task Force chair (1999–2000), a coalition of unions, business, government, and community organisations aimed at private and public sector culture change, she intervened in the ***Wage Case 2000*** (***Pay Equity Case***). Part-time trainer with Synergy Plus Training (Canberra), she designed and delivered leadership training programs developing skills in change management, negotiation, and ethical decision-making. Department of Justice principal consultant from 2001, Little developed Tasmania's 'Safe at Home' whole-of-government criminal justice response to criminal assault at home and other forms of domestic violence, establishing family violence as child abuse.

Administrator, consultant, editor, public servant ***Kaye Mundine*** **(1947–)** focused principally on race and sex discrimination confronting Indigenous women, working to infuse Indigenous women's rights into equal opportunity and employment programs, fostering valuing of Indigenous women's work. Of Bundjalung descent, Grafton, NSW, born, she joined the Australian Public Service (APS) in the 1960s, after working with the State Bank of NSW (now Westpac). Founding the first APS Aboriginal clerks recruitment program (1980), heading Victorian APS Board's equal opportunity division (1984–1987), she transferred to Canberra's Public Service Commission (PSC) equal employment opportunity unit. Commissioner on the Toomelah Inquiry into Goondiwindi-Boggabilla, NSW, race riots in 1991, elected an Aboriginal and Torres Strait Islander Commission (ATSIC) regional councillor, an Australian Capital Territory (ACT) Corrective Services official visitor, multicultural affairs advisor to ACT chief minister Rosemary Follett, serving on the ACT Aboriginal Advisory Council, her work during Follett's Labor administration (1989, 1991–1995) received Follett's commendation. Twenty years earlier, in 1975, Mundine edited ***Dawn*** magazine for NSW Aboriginal people, was a commissioner for the Catholic Justice and Peace Commission (1980s), and as National Foundation for Australian Women (NFAW) member celebrated its Canberra launch (1989). In 2003, joining South Sydney Council administration, she led on Indigenous programs, colleague Rhonda Galbally saying her 'knowledge, passion, good sense and practical approaches [ensure] South Sydney as a leader in this area'.

Miscellaneous Workers' Union (MWU) (now Liquor Hospitality and Miscellaneous Workers' Union (LHMWU)) organiser in Perth, WA, ***Helen Creed*** **(1953–)** was elected assistant secretary, secretary and, five years later, first female Australian LHMWU president (1985–1995), running childcare worker pay-parity claims, succeeding in NSW and Queensland the week before the Workplace Choices Act 2005 (Cth) removed workers' state industrial tribunal claim rights. Serving on the ACTU executive, Creed was an ACTU vice president (1995), represented the ACTU on the ICFTU Women's Committee, and was elected UnionsWA (TLC) president (2001). Working at Victoria Park CentreLink, then Victoria Park CLC, and with Victoria Park's Youth Accommodation program, May Day 2005 she led the WA labour movement in Nelson Mandela's 'Make Poverty History' campaign. 'The world can no longer afford to ignore the plight of ... women and men living on less than one dollar per day', she said: 'One billion people are unemployed, underemployed or working part-time—the vast bulk women'. Appointed a Board of Tourism WA commissioner for a second term (2006), in January losing ALP pre-selection for Victoria Park, following WA premier Geoff Gallop's resignation, she remained active in politics.

Senior AIRC deputy president (later the Fair Work Commission (FWC)), ***Jennifer Mary (Jenny) Acton* (1955–)** served first as deputy president (1992–1999). APS research officer (1977–1979), Australian Public Service Association (APSA) (fourth division officers) research officer (1979–1981), appointed ACTU senior industrial officer (1981–1992), then 1987, seconded as chief of staff to Ralph Willis, federal employment and industrial relations minister in the Hawke Labor government. ACTU advocate in the ***Nurses Comparable Worth case 1986***, Acton contributed to debates on assessing skills and valuing work, including women's work. LLB, LLM, BEc, MEc, member of the National Advisory Council on Strategy and Resources (NACSR) advising on overseas qualifications evaluation and assessment (1991–1992), and the University of Melbourne (UM)'s Advisory Centre for Employment and Labour Relations (2000–2017), Acton is a Lady Gowrie Child Centre life member (1999).

Teachers Federation member, ***Marie Jovanovich Muir* (1930–2018)**, taught in country, Sydney city, suburban, and disadvantaged schools for 30 years as infant mistress, then primary principal. Campaigning on Commonwealth Aid for Education generated 'The Great Toilet Paper Controversy', the principal, considering his management challenged, refused staff resources: no toilet paper meant cutting newspaper squares for children. Muir secured grocery tissue paper, the Infants Mistress sought Mothers Club assistance, the principal declared staff must supply their own, then finally relented. Working through pregnancy and after her son's birth, in 1961 pregnant again, Muir resigned, returning as a causal, then temporary staff. Told transferring to Broken Hill would gain her permanency, asking for her husband's transfer, too, came advice: 'it may not suit Department exigencies'. Suggesting the policy 'encouraged family break-up', Teachers Federation general secretary, Ivor Lancaster, ensured Muir's permanency. Next, Infants Promotion lists: two-year, not three-year trained, Infants teachers were barred from the First Class Primary School principal promotion list, increased superannuation, and salary. 1950s and '60s discrimination favouring males on lower qualifications, no childbearing interruptions, and a male-take-higher-positions tradition, meant more male school principals. Amalgamating Infants and Primary Lists unfairly disadvantaged infant mistresses. Justice Barbour (NSW Equal Opportunity Tribunal) found for Muir and Marie Breen, but NSW CA and High Court disagreed. Nonetheless, the original proposal abandoned, Infants List three women entered promotion lists at date of appointment. Although men retained 'top of List' status, eventually, appointed Granville South Primary School principal, Muir, initiated multicultural school programs, TAFE running New Opportunities for Women courses. Retiring in 1985, she joined Jessie Street National Women's Library Management Committee (member, 1995–1999, vice chair, 1997–1999).

NSW Labor Council senior executive officer, ***Naomi Steer*** **(1948–)** BA (Hons.), LLB formed the NSW Alliance of diverse groups, including NSW Council of Social Service (COSS), the Australian Conservation Foundation (ACF), NSW Labor Council and Evatt Foundation, on social justice policies (1999–2000). Earlier, as TLC women's officer/organiser, she ran industrial rights, working conditions and equal pay events, supporting activist and union women on federal and state ***Wage Case*** interventions and Workplace Relations Bill 1996 and Workplace Relations Act 1996 (Cth) (1999 amendments) campaigns. Earlier, as NSW MEAA secretary, Steer oversaw the Journalists Judiciary Committee, and was appointed by the NSW Attorney-General to the Professional Standards Council (1995), 'to … improve standards and protect consumers'. As United Nations High Commissioner for Refugees (UNHCR) national director (2000–2022), she travelled to Timor Leste, Pakistan, Afghanistan, and Chad camps, promoting refugee and asylum seekers' rights and conditions, encouraging targeting of aid efforts. She sponsored Now We the People.

With a clothing industry studies diploma (TAFE Tasmania 1998–1999), ***Anthea Stutter*** **(1979–)** BSW (Hons)(UTas, 2005), participated in the UTas SU Women's Officer campaign, Hobart campus (2002), and as Women for Action member (2003) organised writing letters and student newspaper articles, weekly meetings, guest speakers, developing members' public speaking skills, and organising women-only dance party 'Manx'. Chairing IWD meetings, organising IWD 2001, 2002 rallies, Hobart WIIC board of management member (2000–2004), she undertook work experience, policy research, and development with WomenTasmania (2004–2005), trained as a LifeLine Hobart telephone counsellor (2006), then commenced case management with Tasmanian Child and Family Services. At WomenTasmania she researched for the Women's Pay Equity Task Force, analysing the NSW Industrial Commission 1998 pay equity principle, interviewing Tasmanian and NSW women activists, and writing her honours thesis 'Seeking a Pay Equity Test Case in Tasmania' on the ***Wage Case 2000*** (***Pay Equity Case***), evaluating Industrial Commission obstacles for equal pay.

Celtic Studies Foundation director, ***Suzanne Jamieson*** **(1953–)** is associate professor in the Business School, USyd. Australian labour law expert, major research areas workplace equity, equal pay and occupational health and safety. Formerly trade union official and senior public servant, she undertook a major project on international comparisons of gender issues in occupational health and safety law, researched workplace sex discrimination, workplace, and pay issues. Until 1999, she was a National Tertiary Education Union (NTEU) USyd branch executive member, then Senate elected fellow (1999–2005) and member of the Academic Board Staffing Committee. NSW Nurses Tribunal deputy chair, NSW Anti-Discrimination Board member (1998–2008) and member of the Operations Review Committee of the Independent Commission Against Corruption (ICAC) (1998–2006), as NPEC member she undertook joint research and writing of ***National Wage Case 1998***, NSW ***Pay Equity Inquiry 1997*** submissions, and Senate inquiries into the 1996 and 1999 Workplace Relations Bills. She was NPEC advocate before the NSW Industrial Relations Commission and in the AIRC ***HPM Industries case 1998*** with Richter, for NPEC, WEL, and AFBPW. Jamieson was a board member of the Bessie Smyth Foundation (1982–1992) and Evatt Foundation committee member (1982–2005).

Born in Birchip, country Victoria, ***Jennifer (Jenny) Doran*** **(1954–)** worked in private practice, then as occupational health and safety advisor to Jim Simmons, Cain Labor government labour minister (1982–1985). Consulting with employers and unions, drafting the Occupational Health and Safety Act 1985, piloting it through cabinet and parliament, and ensuring successful implementation despite predicted adverse employer and government outcomes, as Department of Employment and Industrial Affairs senior legislation and policy integration officer (1985), Doran established occupational health and safety structures, regulations, and communication on the new law. Representing Victorian Trades Hall Council (VTHC) on the Victorian WAC, as women's officer (1985–1988), Doran formulated the VTHC women's policy. As ACTU women's officer, industrial officer, then senior industrial officer and AIRC advocate, she argued equal pay on a comparator basis: women's (lower paid) work against men's (higher paid) in the same industry or enterprise (***HPM Industries case 1997***, ***Age case 1998***, both settled). Senior advisor then social policy deputy director, Victorian Premier's Office (2001–2005), Doran became Department for Victorian Communities senior policy officer, advising on disadvantaged youth. She attended the 1998 Canberra Constitutional Convention as George's proxy.

Kate MacNeill (*1957–)** was spokesperson for CAEP when it reconstituted in Melbourne 1985. With members of CAEP including Barbara (Barb) Jennings and Di Jackson, she worked on the CAEP's submission for the ***Nurses Comparable Worth case 1986. Her background in law and economics meant she engaged in policy work in the government and non-government sector, before expanding her direction into art history (identity and contemporary Australian art), gaining a PhD, and developing a specialisation in internationalisation of curriculum and experiential learning, as well as cultural management, culture, and communication. Law remaining important in her work, she has focused on intellectual property and censorship. In recognition of her work with the CAEP and equal pay, in 1985 she was among several women funded by the Victorian Women's Trust (VWT) to attend the Non-Government Organisations (NGO) Women's Forum run alongside the UN Women's Platform Conference in Nairobi, Kenya. She is now UM professor and associate dean of education and students in the Faculty of Arts.

Confronting pay inequity in David Jones, Paramatta—via a 'gormless youth … the same age, arriving the same day, receiving about a third more in wages', ***Meredith Burgmann* (1947–)** decided 'money and women's access would answer most problems for women'. At MacquarieU, a survey revealed male senior tutors six times more likely to be tenured. Threat of the Industrial Commission caused a management 'cave in', Burgman joined Federated Australian University Staff Association (FAUSA) (now NTEU). Affirmative Action Committee (AAC) national chair and state president, delegate to Labor Council (1978) and ACTU (1983), she helped launch the National Left Women in Unions Caucus (early 1980s—propelling women onto the ACTU executive), lobbied for the NSW Anti-Discrimination Board, and declared ACTU president George's election (1983) 'one of my political life's highlights'. The 1988 Socialist Feminist Conference set Burgmann, Burton, Hall, Anita Devos, Di Fruin, Meg Smith, Jamieson, Hayes, Danny Blackman, and later Suzanne Hammond to forming NPEC, intervening in the ***National Wage Case 1988.*** Her inaugural NSW Parliament speech (1991) records a NSW Industrial Relations Act equal pay fight, friendship with industrial relations minister Jeff Shaw led to the Equal Pay Task Force and 1998 NSW Industrial Commission's 'equal remuneration principle', and later, wanting to discuss the spectre of enterprise bargaining lowering women's wages,

Burgmann was 'asked to leave an ACTU seminar'. She was NPEC spokesperson, as many members, being senior public servants, were 'civilly dead'.

Before graduating LLB and commencing private practice as an employment solicitor, ***Felicity Rafferty* (1948–)** worked in trade unions, first the Professional Officers' Association (POA), then CPSU ACT branch (1980s–1990s) as an organiser, then food inspectors group secretary, advancing effective regulation of food safety and public health, food poisoning outbreaks and contaminated food arising from governments 'buying out of any enforcement responsibility', 'relying on market forces'. Rafferty advocated for workers' rights in comparative standards of domestic and export abattoirs and, as CPSU ACT assistant secretary, during proposed CPSU restructuring, fought for rights of workers represented by the ACT branch. In 1992–1993, she alerted AFBPW to comparable worth and Family Court of Australia counsellors' wage (in) justice, prompting AFBPW's intervention in the ***Family Court Counsellors case 1993***. ***JIR*** published Rafferty's influential pay equity articles (1980s–1990s), and she was a member (1992–1994) of ACT chief minister Follett's second Women's Consultative Council.

Small country town Victoria, 1930s Depression, environmentalist father, surrounded by shearers—unionist uncles and grandfather—decided politics for ***Molly Hadfield* (1922–2012)**. Mother dying when Hadfield was ten years, leaving school at 13, told nursing was not for her—'you can't do the exams'—she took the dining-room job. Nurses' lunches were left on tables, cold when shifts ended. Sisters and matrons' meals remained in the oven, heating. The hierarchical unfairness mirrored the kitchen-nursing staff distinction preventing Hadfield from meeting nurse cousins and friends on hospital premises. In 1940, city bound, Hadfield made stockings and men's underwear, with time-and-motion men roaming factory aisles clicking stopwatches. Fighting for workers' and tenants' rights when she and her family faced eviction, lobbying for kindergartens, school bus, public transport, community centres, footpaths, roads when moving from Collingwood to newly developing outer-suburban Chelsea. From 1970, weekends in Chelsea, living in inner-city Fitzroy, working at Melbourne's International Bookshop, Elizabeth Street, reading books and running the stall at Women's Movement conferences supported her politics of fair wages, family friendly policies, pregnancy and maternity coverage, aged care and childcare and carers of relatives with a disability. In the 1970s, having promised her dying friend, she assumed care of the friend's husband, his brother, and two sisters suffering dementia. Agitating for complementary medicine, consumer rights and aged care, she led in establishing Frankston Housing for Aged Action Group, achieving worker support for Frankston Housing. Contrasting 1950s and '60s factory workers' conditions badly against poor working conditions of past decades, 'I've been protesting for over fifty years now, suppose I'd better stop', she said. 'But I not while I've a working head and breath in my body …' Fists raised triumphantly at the 1998 maritime workers protests, Hadfield and Edith Morgan appeared on the cover of ***With These Arms***, Maritime Union of Australia (MUA) songs and poems.

On the Strength of Invisible Hands

In 1950s Melbourne, the Liquor Trades Union (LTU)'s Williams enlightened trade union men wherever she could, impelled by 1953 ACTU Sydney Congress reports calling for federal and state legislation 'for equal pay for the sexes in all occupations', and immediate equal pay for their own employees. This motion spawned Equal Pay Committees to 'campaign for legislation', 'arouse … male and female workers' interest in the equal pay demand', and advance executive coordination of 'Equal Pay Committees on a national basis …'.

Yet, the backstory was unknown to Williams: spurred by women's activism within and without the trade union movement, NSW Federated Clerks' Union (FCU) women drafted the motion, ferried it through the FCU, putting it to Congress. Nor did Williams know that Della Elliott approached Albert Monk, ACTU president, saying she wished to move it. Congress rules required delegates to stand in the aisle for the president's call, signifying a motion by hand-waving. For four long days, Elliott leapt into the aisle, waving at every opportunity. Final day, minutes before Congress closing, it came. In a flash at the microphone, motion seconded by a male right-winger from the FCU. It was through.

Neither did Williams and fellow unionists, women and the men working to have motion implemented, know of the stringent dressing down Elliott then suffered. Having beaten another Congress delegate, Jack McPhillips, to the call, he seeing her as usurping his place, McPhillips roundly chastised her. His internationally important resolution overlooked, second place to hers. Why?

Yet around Australia, like Williams, activist women members pressed TLCs, dominated by men. Sometimes, women's activism was subverted.

But claiming a platform, women demand action and change. Built on earlier women's work, that platform was a base for 1960s and '70s women to make their demands. Now, the named and unnamed enter the 1980s. As Chap. 15, 'A 1980s Skirmish into Comparable Worth' affirms, it's time to claim comparable worth.

References

Cases—See Case List

ACT Legislative Assembly, ***Hansard***, Canberra, ACT, 1995 (20 September 1995), http://www.hansard.act.gov.au/hansard/1995/week06/1591.htm, p. 1951 (accessed 20 June 2006).
Jennifer (Jenny) Acton, ***Personal Communication***, 2006 (9 February 2006).
Jean Arnot, ***Interview***, Double Bay, NSW, 1993 (17 May 1993).
Gracia Baylor, ***Interview*** (24 January 2006).
Joan Bielski, 'WEL New South Wales—History ..., ***WEL NSW Women's Electoral Lobby***, Sydney, NSW, pp. 1–5.
Jan Burnswood, 'Tribute to Mrs Val Buswell, OAM', ***NSW Legislative Council Hansard***, NSW Parliament, Sydney, NSW, 2005 (26 May 2005), p. 67.
Val Buswell, 'Eighty Eight's Fair Enough' in JA Scutt (ed), ***Glorious Age*** -, Artemis Publishing, Melbourne, Victoria, 1992, pp. 11–22.
Debbie Carstens, ***Personal Communication***, 2006 (10 March 2006) (FairWear NSW). Thanks also to Daisy Gardener of FairWear Victoria.
Zelda D'Aprano, ***Interview***, Laureton, NSW, 1996 (23 July 1996).
Zelda D'Aprano, ***Zelda***, 1977, Spinifex Press, Nth Melbourne, Victoria, 1995.
Jenny Doran, 'Equal Pay for Women Unfinished Business', ***ACTU—Australian Council of Trade Unions***, 1998 (7 July 1998), http://www.actu.asn.au/public/news/1062718571_20217.html, pp. 1–4 (accessed 20 January 2006).
Jenny Doran, ***Interview***, Melbourne, Victoria, 2006 (21 February 2006).
Kondelia ('Della') Elliot, ***Personal Communication***, Sydney, NSW (June 1994).
Joan Eveline and Lorraine Hayden (eds), ***Carrying the Banner ...***, UWA Press, Nedlands, WA, 1999.
Lynne Fitzgerald, ***Personal Communication*** (31 January 2006).
Di Graham, 'In Pursuit of Equality' in JA Scutt (ed.), ***Different Lives –***, Penguin, Melbourne, Victoria, 1987, 179–87.
Philippa Hall, ***Personal Communication*** (6 March 2006).
Fran Hayes, 'Tribute to Clare Burton', ***Equal Pay Watch, Australia***, http://www.users.bigpond.com/rj_gj/clare/tributes/htm, pp. 1–13 (accessed 20 June 2006).

IATSIS, ***Aboriginal Studies Press—Dawn and New Dawn 1952–1975***, http://www.aiatsis.gov.au/aboriginal_studies_press.htm, pp. 1–3 (accessed 20 June 2006).

Sue Jackson, 'Why Consider a Basic Income?' in VOSS/Good Shepherd Youth and Family Services, ***Income Support***, 1995, pp. 3–7.

Barbara (Barb) Jennings, ***Interview***, Melbourne, Victoria, 2006 (31 January 2006).

Elizabeth (Liz) Little, ***Interview***, Hobart, Tasmania, 2006 (6 February 2006).

Darren Mathewson, ***A tribute to a unionist—Lynne Fitzgerald, Secretary Unions Tasmania, 1995–2004***, www.unonstas.com.au/pdfs/A%20to%20%20unionist.pdf (accessed 15 January 2006).

Anne Matz, ***Interview***, WomenTasmania, Hobart, Tasmania, 1996 (23 May 1996).

Noreen Millar, ***Interview***, WomenTasmania, Hobart, Tasmania, 1996 (23 May 1996).

National Pioneer Women's Hall of Fame, ***Signature Quilt—Women who have signed the quilt & their "Firsts'***, http://www.pioneerwomen.com.au/qult-sigs.htm, pp. 1–20 (accessed 12 January 2006).

Edith Morgan, 'A Strong Commitment' in JA Scutt (ed.), ***Living Generously*** -, Artemis Publishing, Melbourne, Victoria, 996, pp. 154–66.

Marie Muir, ***Interview***, Sydney, NSW, 2006 (11 April 2006).

NFAW, ***Australian Women Biographical Entry—Bourke, Eleanor (1943–)***, http://www.womenaustralia.info/biogs/AWE0305b.htm, pp. 1–2 (accessed 20 June 2006); http://www.arts.monash.edu.au/cais/about/, pp. 1–2 (accessed 20 June 2006a).

NFAW, ***Australian Women Biographical Entry—Mundine, Kaye (1947–)*** http://www.womenaustralia.info/biogs/WE1176b.htm, pp. 1–2 (accessed 20 June 2006b).

NPEC, ***Joint Media Release—20 August 1999—Women meet with Peter Reith***, http://www.wel.org.au/issues/releases/9908reit.htm, pp. 1–2 (accessed 20 January 2006).

Osiris, ***Latest news: HPM sacks male comparators***, 1998 (12 August 1998), http://www.users.bigpond.com/rj_gi/HPM/HPM2.htm, pp. 1–11 (accessed 20 January 2006.

Our Community Matters, ***Welcome by Rhonda Galbally AO, ...***, 2003, http://www.ourcommunity.com.au/files/OCM503, pp. 1–3 (accessed 20 June 2006).

Geraldine Robertson, ***Women's Web - ...; Interview with Molly Hadfield***, http://www.home.vicnet.net.au/~womenweb/sources/First%20Narratives/MollyHadfield.htm, pp. 1–8 (accessed 20 June 2006a).

Geraldine Robertson, ***Women's Web—Women's Stories, - Women's Actions, Interview with Edith Morgan***, http://home.vicnet.net.au/~womenweb/sources/First%20Narratives/EdithMorgan.htm, pp. 1–7 (accessed 20 June 2006b).

Edna Ryan, ***Interview***, Lyneham, Canberra, ACT (June 1997).

Marian Sawer, Philippa Hall and others, 'Obituaries - Tributes to Clare Burton', ***Equal Pay Watch, Australia***, http://www.users.bigpond.com/rj_gj/clare/tributes/htm, pp. 1–13 (accessed 20 January 2006).

State Library of SA, ***Women and Politics in South Australia—The Aboriginal Voice***, http://www.slsa.sa.gov.au/women_and_politics/aboriginal_voice.htm, pp. 1–2 (accessed 20 January 2006).

Naomi Steer, ***Personal Communication*** (1 September 2006).

Naomi Steer, 'Trades Hall—…', ***Workers OnLine***, no. 1, 1999 (19 February 1999), http://workers.labor.net.au/1/c_tradeshall_steer.html, pp. 1–3 (accessed 1 September 2006).

Anthea Stutter, ***Interview***, Hobart, Tasmania, 2006 (15 March 2006).

Anthea Stutter, *Seeking a Pay Equity Test CSE in Tasmania*, BSW Hons Thesis, UTas, Hobart, Tasmania, 2005.

Vale Marie Muir: unionist, feminist and fighter | Green Left (accessed 5 March 2022).

WEL Australia (Liz O'Brien), ***Clare Burton—Obituary: Clare Burton 30 October 1942–23 August 1998***, http://www.wel.org.au/announce/cburton.htm, pp. 1–3 (accessed 20 January 2006).

Joan Woodbury, ***Interview***, WomenTasmania, Hobart, Tasmania, 1996 (23 May 1996).

Neville K. Wran, 'Murphy - Barrister' in J. Scutt (ed.), ***Lionel Murphy—…***, McCulloch/Macmisslan, Melbourne, Victoria, 1987, pp. 15–21.

Women and Work Taskforce Papers, held by JA Scutt (member of the Taskforce, as Anti-Discrimination Commissioner, Tasmania).

CHAPTER 15

A 1980s Skirmish into Comparable Worth

… 'skills', 'merit' and 'credentials' have significant subjective content. 'Excellence' and 'best practice' are equally susceptible to standards favouring the dominant group. For lawyers, it's 'capacity':

> Judges should be chosen for their capacity alone, not in any 'representative' sense. [D]rawing judges from a wider pool of lawyers—particularly women lawyers—could contribute to development of a judiciary more broadly reflecting [community] composition …—but … capacity must be the fundamental criterion.

… the Law Council of Australia's *Submission to the Senate Standing Committee on Legal and Constitutional Affairs* classically illustrates the problem of determining merit and skill according to what 'is': seeing only the dominant group ethos, lacking even (apparently) the capacity to grasp that *values* 'customarily held' or accepted as 'right' by those in power may [contradict] … what excellence, skill, merit, capacity may be if not confined to a narrowly biased perspective …

Jocelynne A. Scutt, 'Credentials, Skills and Merit—…' in ***The Incredible Woman***, vol 2, pp. 63-64

Characterised by rapacious materialism, corporate mateship, and mendacity, the 1980s begin with Cliff Dolan's ascension to Australian Council of Trade Union (ACTU) presidency, RJ (Bob) Hawke contesting the Victorian seat of Wills at the federal election. Shirley Hazzard's ***The***

J. A. Scutt, *Wage Rage for Equal Pay*,
https://doi.org/10.1007/978-3-031-42178-5_15

Transit of Venus is published, Jessica Anderson's ***The Impersonators*** wins the Miles Franklin, Deborah (Lawrie) Wardley makes history as Australia's first female commercial pilot, in her Victorian Equal Opportunity Board win against Ansett Industries, upheld by the High Court. On 18 October, the Fraser Liberal Coalition government is re-elected with a reduced majority. New federal parliamentarians include Florence (Flo) Bjelke-Petersen, Queensland senator, and Hawke.

On 31 July 1981, in the ***National Wage case 1981***, the Australian Conciliation and Arbitration Commission abandons wage indexation. Blanche d'Alpuget's ***Turtle Beach*** reaches the bookshops and, heading the newly created NSW Department of Aboriginal Affairs, Pat O'Shane is first woman to lead a government department in Australia. On 2 September Enid Lyons dies aged 84. Six weeks later, 19 October, so too Dymphna Cusack at 79.

A decade after the ***Equal Pay Case 1969***, ***Equal Pay Case 1972***, and ***Minimum Wage Case 1974***, women turn again to the Australian Conciliation and Arbitration Commission. In the ***National Wage Case 1983***, women's focus is equal pay purportedly achieved. Through the 1980s, women dissect equal pay in principle and practice, proposing equal pay for equal work and work of equal value advance beyond an industrial mantra.

Anomalies, Inequities, and the National Wage

In 1985, Kaye Hargreaves writes in ***Scarlet Woman***: '… many [women] in all kinds of workplaces around Australia state quite clearly they are skilled, want recognition and have a wealth of ideas about what is wrong with their work process and how it could be improved'. Women workers on the shop-floor, through 'health and safety committees, women's committees, shop committees, union meetings and courses during working hours', confronting sexist harassment and sexual harassers, defying workplace bullies, demanding more toilet paper in lavatories and hand-driers in washrooms, women on strike, are effecting change. Not 'solutions imposed from above', but women 'becoming more powerful' is prioritised. Yet, must it be either/or—shopfloor versus Commission?

Following the ***Minimum Wage Case 1974***, until 1983, no women's organisations intervened in ***National Wage Cases***. The Commission's acknowledged pay inequity, yet the ***Equal Pay Cases 1969, 1972***, and ***Minimum Wage Case 1974*** seemed sufficient. The onus to apply for 1969, 1972, and 1974 principles extended to women workers in job categories or industries unions covered was rarely discharged. Just as with ***Basic Wage Cases***, ***National Wage Cases*** ran with no recognition that equal pay is essential to basic or national wage setting.

Women lobbied within union power structures—for organiser and executive positions, changes in union practices, policies incorporating women's issues as industrial matters, equal opportunity, and anti-discrimination laws. Women's wages reached 83 per cent of men's, higher than anywhere apart from Scandinavia, but plateauxed. Worsening economic conditions and industrial disputation late 1970s to early 1980s affected all workers. Yet, without women advocates raising equal pay and women's industrial conditions in industrial bodies, the issues were invisible or misconstrued, women's economic rights of lesser importance. The situation facing women through the 1980s to 1990s requires outlining wage movements generally, and Commission wage fixing.

In the ***National Wage Case 1978*** (***Wage Fixing Principles Case 1978***) the Australian Conciliation and Arbitration Commission conducted a 'complete' wage fixing principles review—omitting equal pay. Unsurprisingly, the outcome affected women's wages and pay relativities. Changes to wage fixing principles affect all wages; set without attention to historical differentiation in male and female wages, women's concentration in work-fields, and traditional women's work undervaluing, outcomes will increase already existing differences or, unintentionally or unwittingly, undermine efforts designed to adjust male-female wage relativities fairly.

Most significant for equal pay in the ***Wage Fixing Principles Case 1978*** was Principle 7, work value changes, catch-up community movements, and anomalies. Wage indexation (CPI wage adjustment) aimed at safeguarding against wage increases outside wage indexation. Changes to rates other than CPI adjustments were severely curtailed, including limitations on work value adjustments. As work value directly affects equal pay, this was doubly significant for women.

National Wage Case (April) 1975 changes to the work value principle meant wage increases outside CPI adjustments were allowed only for:

- changes in work value including changes in nature of work, skill and responsibility required; or
- changes in conditions under which work was performed—ordinarily, this would apply to some classifications in an award only, although in rate cases might apply to all classifications; or
- catch-up of community movements.

This potentially left women out in the cold. For equal pay, work value (re)assessments are essential. Women's existing wage rates incorporate failure over time to fairly value their work. If a change in the nature of work or conditions under which it is performed occurs, or a catch-up of community movements, a wage rise should be effected. However, if this is the only way to gain an increase, historic systemic differentials remain.

The Commission said the ***National Wage Case 1974*** (***Minimum Wage Case 1974***) achieved appropriate relativities between and within awards, establishing 'a firm base on which indexation could be applied'. Yet, relativities for women were not achieved. Apart from any other work value and women's work arguments, equal pay under the ***Equal Pay Case 1972*** principles came in three steps by 30 June 1975, not before. The Commission ignored that in 1974 women (potentially) qualified for equal pay had not yet achieved it. It ignored women covered by other awards, whose unions had not applied for equal pay.

In the ***Wage Fixing Principles Case 1978***, the Commission re-emphasised that the work value principle must be applied strictly. References in the 1975 (April and September) decisions to 'changes in the nature of the work, skill and responsibility required or conditions under which workers performed' were 'exhaustive' of factors substantiating a work value case producing a pay rates rise. When, in the ***National Wage Case 1976***, the Commission rejected the unions' request for relaxation of work value principle parameters, its narrow scope was confirmed, recurring in 1978. Wary of 'contrived' work value agreements and other circumventions of wage indexation to gain wage increases, the Commission overlooked provision for genuine cases—women missing out through past omissions.

Nonetheless, a potential avenue for women arose when the Commission introduced the new 'anomalies' principle. For decades, women's organisations had claimed women's wage rates were anomalous. The Commission anomalies claims procedure was strict: every claim 'arising out of the anomaly or special and extraordinary circumstances will be processed by the Anomalies Conference and not otherwise', with unions required to initiate claims. But the chance was there.

The anomalies principle continued in the ***Wage Fixing Principles Case 1978***. The Commission reiterated its ***National Wage Case (September) 1975*** position, referring to history (though not to history affecting women's wage setting), again limiting wage fixing, not providing scope for women's wage parity. However, it did provide a possibility for women through the anomalies and inequities process. Under 'inequities', the Commission listed conditions applicants must satisfy: inequities where employees performed similar work but were paid dissimilar rates without good reason again 'must be processed through an Anomalies Conference and not otherwise'. Resolution required:

- work similar to the other class or classes of work by reference to nature of the work, level of skill and responsibility involved, and conditions under which the work is performed;
- classes of work compared as truly like with like in all relevant matters, without good reason for dissimilar pay rates;
- existing, in addition to similarity of work, some other significant factor making the situation inequitable—but a historical or geographical nexus between the similar cases of work may not of itself be such a factor;
- rate of pay fixed for class or classes of work being compared with the work as a reasonable and proper rate of pay for the work, not vitiated by any reason such as an increase obtained for reasons inconsistent with the Commission's guidelines as a whole;
- rates of pay in minimum rates of an award not being compared with those in paid rate awards.

With inequities, overriding considerations applied:

- pay increase justified on the merits;
- no likelihood of flow-on;
- economic cost negligible;
- increase a once only matter.

With increasing Fraser Coalition government cutbacks in public sector employment, declining exports and rising imports, corporate downsizing, Tasmania's Franklin and Gordon Rivers demonstrations, Queensland attacks on civil liberties, and protests against repressive policies, growing poverty, and a widening rich-poor gap, industrial agitation swelled.

On 9 January 1981, the Commission conceded the past decade's wage fixation system was 'broken', calling on parties for an alternative to overcome 'difficulties … bringing down the system'. Opening the ***Inquiry into Wage Fixing Principles 1981***, the Commission identified the choice: a centralised or decentralised system, its character and 'what principles if any should apply to each'. In the upshot, wage indexation was abandoned. All parties endorsed centralised wage fixing with national wage adjustments 'as the main source of wage increases'. Yet, the Commission effectively lost control, with continued rising costs, inflation, and wages—for some. Centralised wage fixing ended.

As the industrial scene altered, political changes occurred. Over 1981–1983, state governments reversed political colours. Beginning with Tasmania in May 1981, the Franklin and Gordon Dams campaign precipitated reversal from Labor to Liberal. Elsewhere, conservative governments fell to Labor. Two years after the Tasmanian election, on 3 February 1983, Hawke replaced Bill Hayden as federal parliamentary Labor party leader, just as Liberal-National prime minister Fraser called an election. Two weeks later, the Australian Labor Party (ALP) won government in WA. On 5 March, Labor won power federally. In April, after twenty-seven years of Liberal government, Labor won in Victoria. In November, SA followed suit. The stage was set for a new industrial policy and wage fixing direction. Women, through the Union of Australian Women (UAW), National Council of Women (NCW), and Women's Electoral Lobby (WEL), looked once more toward the Commission.

'National Wage Guidelines' Versus Equal Pay

In April 1983, following change of government federally, the National Economic Summit convened. Attended by men representing themselves, their corporations, or industrial organisations, few women were invited: Joan McClintock one of two Australian Council of Social Service (ACOSS) representatives: NCW's Diane Alley with advisor Bettina Cass, WEL's Eva Cox, and Scutt. The aim was ideas, plans, and policies for Australia's recovery—economic, export, and industrial problems had attenuated employment and economic growth.

Endorsed by all except Queensland government representatives, the Communiqué included a centralised wage fixing provision as the 'most equitable means of ensuring wage justice', simultaneously ensuring wage increases did not stimulate unemployment or inflation. Parties should prioritise 'the option of a return to a centralised system under … the Australian Conciliation and Arbitration Commission', progressed by a conference convened by the Commission president.

In 1982, two days before the festive season, the Commission imposed a wage pause—suspension of improvements in pay and conditions, running to 28 June 1983. In the ***National Wage Case 1983***, the Commission said 'the seriousness of the economic situation, the worst since the 1930s', coming out of 'the combined effect of a deep and prolonged international recession, serious drought and substantial increase in labour costs' drove that decision. The eight federal, state, and territorial governments agreed on economic grounds. In May/June 1983, several unions applied for changes (referring to the ACTU-ALP Prices and Incomes Accord), but on 28 June, the Commission continued the pause indefinitely.

Meanwhile, April through June, in the ***National Wage Case 1983***, the President's Conference convened, finding general agreement on national productivity in wage fixing, having a strong impact for the major part of the subsequent 13 years of federal Labor government. The President's Conference said the objective of the centralised system 'should be to increase real incomes through time in line with productivity'. Further, national wage cases should consider distribution of gains in national productivity; productivity gains should not be double counted; and possible distribution of national productivity taking forms other than wage increases should be conceded.

No women's groups or representatives were invited to the President's Conference; hence, nothing on equal pay. However, the Conference did approve flat rate increases generally, essential for lower wage brackets. A 'feature of a workable centralized system' was agreed as to 'no extra claims except where special and extraordinary circumstances exist …', there being a role, however, 'for a limited and genuine provision covering changes in "work value"'.

For equal pay proponents, 'special and extraordinary circumstances exist' with women denied equal pay routinely, and women's work routinely undervalued. However, there was no assurance the Commission agreed. As well, reference to work value could be positive for equal pay claims. Yet, referencing 'changes' in work value indicates a failure to address women's claims. An equal pay principle concentrated on *changes* inevitably deprives women workers of redress for past inequalities and underpayment borne because women's work has not been valued equally with men's. Where changes mean women's work is even more valuable, that should be an additional boost to wage rates, rather than the sole factor for increasing women's pay relativities. Limiting women to *changes* in work value means underlying and structural components of unequal pay go unaddressed—to the detriment of women's pay packets.

Two final Presidential Conference points confirmed that in a centralised wage fixing system, 'conditions of employment are relevant factors' for consideration, with provision made 'for special and extraordinary circumstances based on anomalies and inequities'. The anomalies and inequities provision held out equal pay's greatest hope. Women could attempt arguing that denial of full worth and value of work done by women and in women's traditional fields created an anomaly vis-à-vis women's wages, and that unequal pay so created is an historical inequity. Whether the Commission would accept this under the anomalies and inequities provision was another question.

The ***National Wage Case 1983*** was the first under the new federal Labor government. All parties and interveners, including employer organisations, state, federal, and territory governments, women's organisations, and the Local Government Association (LGA) agreed with the proposed return to centralised wage fixing. Differences on quarterly versus half-yearly CPI adjustments, and flat money adjustments versus rates calculated on a minimum or basic wage concept did not undercut this. Hence, the application asked the Commission to:

1. adjust wages paid by 2.2 per cent and 2.1 per cent (4.3 per cent) to maintain real value of wages as of December 1982.
2. increase by 2.2 per cent all allowances expressed in monetary terms.
3. provide a centralised system of wage fixation based on automatic quarterly cost of living adjustment for each subsequent quarter.
4. maintain real wages over time by incorporating a further claim of 9.1 per cent, representing CPI movements for June, September, and December 1982 quarters, not taken into account in general wage level adjustments, and taking into account economic progress.
5. implement other variations applicable in the Prices and Incomes Accord context.

The ACTU said it was necessary to implement the Prices and Incomes Accord vis-à-vis wages and allowances; maintain real value of wages during 1983; ensure a stable and equitable basis for wage fixation; remove current uncertainty as to the future wage fixation method; and take into account any other 'fair and just' reasons in the Commission's view. NCW, UAW, and WEL supported the ACTU's submissions. Noting different emphases, the Commission concluded as central to all three interveners was that the female workforce in major part is 'employed in unskilled and low wage areas, ... less unionised and includes [many] part-time employees', hence 'more vulnerable in a decentralized system' through their 'weaker bargaining position'. Generally correct, this missed the vital point stressed by WEL that 'unskilled' misrepresents women and women's work—'skill' being the essence of women's work value submissions.

The Commission set down 11 national wage-fixing principles, with the caveat that the Commission would 'guard against any Principle other than Principles 1 and 2 (on wages and conditions generally) being applied ... to become a vehicle for general improvement in wages or conditions'.

Principle 1 approved wage and salary adjustments on a six-monthly CPI basis, unless the Commission were 'persuaded to the contrary'. February and August Commission sittings would apply a uniform percentage adjustment, deciding otherwise only in 'exceptional circumstances', if a 'proper case' were established for indexation of over award payments.

Under Principle 2, 'National Productivity', the Commission said it would consider (by application and not before 1985) whether productivity should support an increase 'in wages and salaries or changes in conditions of employment'. Yet, this constant emphasis upon and return to productivity characterising the 1980s was problematic for women and equal pay. In a system imbued with notions of women's lesser productivity and women's traditional work's lesser productive contribution, without constant reiteration and acknowledgement of this systemic failing, women lose out. Lacking vigilance, the differential between women's and men's wages grows. Through the 1980s, women remained dependent upon unions to shape wage claims comprehending women's contemporary productivity and highlighting past ignorance of the real productivity of women's jobs. If the unions made such claims, the outcome depended upon the Commission making assessments and decisions with equal comprehension. Women could hardly count on this.

The remaining principles were concerning, too. Principle 3 said no application for a national wage adjustment to an award would have Commission approval unless all unions in the award gave an undertaking not to pursue any extra award or over award claims, 'except in compliance with the Principles', for their duration. But on any reading, this meant that women not yet having gained equal pay must bring claims within the 1983 national wage guidelines. A union attempting to do otherwise in seeking equal pay for women members left all its members denied the national wage adjustment. Consistent with Gaudron and Bosworth's 1979 proposition that the equal pay struggle is made over and over, this presented unions with the dilemma confronting the NSW Teachers' Federation in 1951, when told by the Public Service Board (PSB) that while their equal pay claim remained on foot, no general pay rise claim would be entertained.

Perhaps unsurprisingly, in the ***National Wage Case 1983*** the Commission viewed women's wages traditionally. Ignoring its own contradictions, in one short paragraph it dismissed women's claims as 'inconsistent' with the system it proposed and 'inappropriate' considering unemployment levels. In the instant of recognising women were denied wages commensurate with their work, were grossly underpaid, their work grossly undervalued, it denied women the right to pursue claims for recognition of the work's real value. Effectively sanctioning this as 'how things should be', it implied (age-old proposition) that women must await propitious times for wage justice. Apprehensions of interveners NCW, UAW, and WEL were confirmed—national wage guidelines were for men and men's wages only.

Simultaneously, in determining no claims could be made unless conforming to 1983 national wage guideline principles, the Commission essentially (and contradictorily) asserted that women had equal pay (that the ***Equal Pay Cases 1969/1972*** and ***Minimum Wage Case 1974*** had fixed women's unequal pay) or, if they did not, the 1983 national wage guidelines would comprehend women's claims. Not only was this not so, evident from the Commission's contention that women's claims (though actually valid) were inconsistent with national wage guidelines and inappropriate. It was far from the view of women's organisations.

Horne (NCW), Olle (UAW), and Scutt (WEL, with Cecelia Clarke) contested 1969, 1972, and 1974 had brought women equal pay. The Commission summed up their submissions in a single sentence, namely, 'that in female occupational areas … implementation of the Commission's equal pay decisions [was] not accompanied by proper work value exercises'. The interveners said far more.

From June 1976 to March 1983, said WEL, award rates of pay for males rose by 84.6 per cent, for women, 83.6 per cent. Even this was deceptive:

> … *actual earnings* … (not just award rates of pay), [provides] a less encouraging picture … Rates of pay may have moved in parallel, but the gap between male and female earnings remains …

> In 1972 females earned 65 cents for every male dollar. By 1975 [when equal pay for equal work, and for work of equal value should have been fully implemented] it was 76 cents, after an initial improvement levelling out to about 78 cents in the dollar.

Part-time paidwork emphasised differences even more. With only 25 per cent of women in fulltime paid employment, including part-timers meant 'female earnings [were] further depressed': from 60 cents for every male $1.00 in 1972, by 1981, it was 67 cents.

'In short', WEL said, 'a gap remains …', through:

- barriers to equal pay implementation;
- some employers' circumventing ***Equal Pay*** and ***Minimum Wage Case*** decisions; and
- systemic labour market imbalance.

Hence, an Amalgamated Metals, Foundry and Shipwrights Union (AMFSU)'s 1980 survey showed unfavourable differences in female and male earnings:

- $5.00 per week or more in 51 per cent of cases;
- $10.00 or more in 43 per cent of cases;
- $20.00 or more in 18 per cent of cases;

WEL said the Commission determined all jobs in this class as worth the same pay rate. Over award payments and/or allowances could account for some differences, and 'maybe female process workers don't do jobs paying allowances'. Allowances and over award payments might explain some earnings differentials, however some arise from female process workers' under award payments.

In 1980, of 15,720 process workers, 7.8 per cent of male process workers versus 17.8 per cent of female process workers received under-award wages. A later AMFSU survey showed no male process workers paid under-award wages, but under-award wages paid to approximately 10 per cent of female process workers. Allowances and margins for skill, sex-discriminatorily applied, also enabled circumvention of ***Equal Pay Case 1969*** principles.

Reclassification of jobs along sex/gender lines provided a perennial escape-hatch from 1969 equal pay for equal work, said WEL: women and men previously working alongside or on the same or almost equivalent tasks regrouped, with 'women only' work areas confined to tasks now classed exclusively female, men on tasks classed exclusively male. Equal pay for equal work was undermined by the very nature of its terms: equal pay for women in men's jobs or doing men's jobs. This led to the ***Equal Pay Case 1972***, reconstituting equal pay claims to equal pay for work of equal value. However, said WEL, the 1972 Commission formulation had not worked.

As determined under the 1972 equal pay for work of equal value formula, categories of women's work were first compared with categories of work within the same award and, only if this failed, could across-award comparisons be made. Women were clustered in a relatively small group of awards, unlike men with far greater scope in work-fields, and within fields of work. Therefore, comparing women's work with women's work was pointless, as tasks done in 'women's work' rarely gained equivalence with men's in 'men's work'.

Yet, if cross-award comparisons were made, women could still miss out: tribunals compared women's work with men's work of a lesser value, rather than with more highly regarded men's work. WEL endorsed Margaret Thornton's 1981 observation that the significant gap between women and men's wages is reinforced by sociological, economic, and judicial factors. The principle of equal pay for work of equal value was undermined, she said, if unions endeavoured to demonstrate women 'are engaged in work identical in nature to a predominantly male classification', referring to the ***Universities (Equal Pay) Case***:

> Such an approach is inappropriate [for] women clerical workers since the number of men involved in keyboard and transcription work is miniscule. This work [is] stigmatised as *per se* inferior, justifying a low rate of pay regardless of other administrative duties performed.

It meant clerical workers would never gain equal pay for, with no equivalent tasks carried out by men, there were none with which women's tasks could be compared—or industrial tribunals could equate to women's work. Even computer technology, with men predominating in fields such as programming, could not cure the problem—so long as male dominated industrial bodies did not, or could not, see men's (computer programming) keyboard work as equivalent to women's (clerical and secretarial) keyboard work.

Despite the Commission's ***Equal Pay Case 1972*** directive that women's work value enquiries be conducted, many work value enquiries were undertaken on male occupations, upgrading pay for men's jobs, but work value enquiries on work done by women were rare. A 1978 test case by a married Rockhampton woman established the right to work irrespective of marital status, and a woman was granted pro rata long service leave after ten years' service with an SA insurance company. From 1977–1979 few women participated in work value cases:

> … nine thousand ancillary workers in [NSW], all women, gained half pay for about ten weeks a year during school vacations, when previously receiving no pay. Amongst [all] cases … the only women apart from ancillary workers were some process metal workers having their over-award pay indexed and an unknown number of workers in the Food Preserving industry receiving an over-award payment.

Ultimately, the Commission not only failed to acknowledge WEL's arguments, it ignored WEL's recommendation that atop returning to centralised wage fixing, to ensure implementation of its equal pay decisions, the Commission should:

- immediately make all female occupations subject to work value enquiries, with each award up for variation undergoing a work value enquiry, government and Commission assistance being provided to unions;
- devise an adequate and effective mechanism for restructuring work assessed by reference to work value criteria, including a standing panel of Commissioners to hear female occupation work value enquiries to develop expertise in women's paidwork and skills, abilities, capabilities and tasks, offering a permanent invitation to women's work value claims;
- provide an adequate and effective work restructuring mechanism to take into account special and extraordinary circumstances based on anomalies and inequities.

Rejecting WEL's proposals, the Commission said such 'large scale work value inquiries' would 'provide an opportunity for … additional tiers of wage increases', inconsistent with the centralised system proposed and 'would be inappropriate in the current state of unemployment especially among women' ('now is not the time'). Furthermore, many issues raised by WEL were 'for management, unions and governments', not awards.

Incongruously, this recognised the degree to which women were cheated of remuneration equivalent to their jobs, simultaneously confirming an attitude of acceptance that women should continue denial of their rightful wage. Not only that, using the anticipated large scale of work value enquiries to say 'no' to them meant that rather than seeing women's wage injustice as reason for embracing WEL's proposal, the level of injustice was used to justify rejecting it.

No Comparable Worth?

The 1958 NSW Industrial Arbitration (Female Rates) Amendment Act (equal pay for equal work) specifically excluded nurses. This pattern was consistent: nurses and nursing omitted—whether legislation or ***Equal Pay Cases***, state and federal. Nursing, like librarianship and secretarial work, was women's work. Without men (traditionally) doing it, lacking men's work and pay rates to be measured against, women choosing nursing could not be 'in' equal pay for equal work. What of equal pay for work of equal value? In the 1980s, nurses under federal and state awards demanded their claims be heard.

Despite general and psychiatric nurses' early 1960s demonstrations over pay and conditions, belief that dedication prevented nurses from industrial action remained strong. Nurses had never gone on strike. In the 1980s, this changed. Nurses realised that dedication to their work should not deny its proper valuation. Devalued work meant inferior industrial conditions. Both risked patients' care.

In mid-1980s Victoria, industrial turmoil accompanied nurses' work (re)valuing claims. First, withdrawal of labour from non-nursing duties—cleaning, scrubbing, delivering food trays, emptying bedpans. Nurses continued services directly patient-care related, a humanitarian measure underpinning the nurses' claim—nurses trained and employed for nursing duties, not nursing aids. Royal Australian Nursing Federation (RANF) Victorian Branch secretary, Barbara Carson, and Jenny Gibbs, president and Peter McCallum Hospital director of nursing, led negotiations. Nurses' determination becoming plain, the Victorian government offered half-measures, removing some banned duties from nursing, insisting others remain. Nurses rallied, filling Dallas Brooks Hall. Protracted discussions preceded strike action affecting theatre admissions (hospitals' moneymaking activity). The RANF believed a proper wage valuation of nursing was impossible, while non-nursing duties remained with nurses. Clear demarcation between professional work of nurses and State Registered Nurses (SRNs) (formerly nursing aids) was essential to any major work value case.

Strike action under incoming RANF secretary, Irene Bolger, played out during the ***Registered Nurses (Salaries and Career Structure) Reference***) (***Registered Nurses (Vic.) case 1986***, running in the Victorian Industrial Commission. A mass Myer Music Bowl meeting followed the government's initial response to RANF salary proposals. Nurses voted an indefinite strike, to end following a weekend break. The first-ever hospital or institution-wide strike, nurses were out for 86 days.

In the Australian Conciliation and Arbitration Commission, shortly before, ACT nurses argued a test case on equal pay for work of equal value. In the ***Nurses Comparable Worth case 1985–1986***, threshold questions asked whether:

- ***Equal Pay Case 1972*** principles remained available to be implemented; and
- ***National Wage Case 1983*** guidelines didn't affect equal pay for work of equal value applications.

The Commission acknowledged the ***Equal Pay Case 1972*** required male-female rates comparisons, first within an award then, where unsatisfactory, comparisons 'with female classifications in other awards' and 'in some cases', male classifications in other awards.

Jennifer (Jenny) Acton, ACTU and unions' advocate, said this allowed for pay rates comparison outside a particular occupation. The Commission saw this as equating the 1972 equal pay principle with 'the doctrine of comparable worth'. The Confederation of Australian Industries (CAI) in turn said that the ACTU was 'seeking to redefine the 1972 decision', whereas the 1972 decision requires work value inquiries limited to 'like work' in the 'normal manner' of work value inquiries, inconsistent with comparable worth.

Arguably semantic, what is 'like work', what 'comparable worth'? Other than its being a 'method of job evaluation used in the USA to implement equal pay legislation', the ACTU provided no definition. Interveners supplied answers.

For the Council of Action for Equal Pay (CAEP), Susan (Sue) Jackson said comparable worth was a points system mechanism evaluating rates for different occupations, sex being irrelevant. The federal government summarised UK, US, and Canadian positions, saying comparable worth is 'subsumed in what Canadians [call] pay equity', limited to 'gender discrimination', comparisons 'limited to an employer establishment'; the US applies it 'to adjust both male and female rates'; the UK adopts 'a different approach ...'

Considering the ***Equal Pay Case 1972*** principle, the Commission might have acknowledged it explicitly concerned inequality of pay rates between women and men, setting a principle to address the problem directly, namely comparison between women's and men's work, and women's and men's rates of pay. In other words, 'like work' must refer to work carried out by men, which is 'like' or similar to work carried out by women. Only by comparing women's and men's work, and women's and men's rates of pay, can men's job-worth or value privileging be addressed. Comparing women's work with women's work, raising women's pay to some other group of women's pay, compounds the problem, differentiating between women's and men's work, isolating evaluation of worth, and hence, pay rates for women's trades and professions. Comparing underpaid women workers' pay rates with other underpaid women workers' pay rates to overcome unequal pay rates based in sex/gender is futile.

The best-known system was developed by US job evaluation consultants Hays Associates. But critical review is essential of job and job components 'worth' and 'valuing as such techniques are subject to sex bias themselves. As Burton, Raven Hag and Gay Thompson illustrate, no method is immune. Put simply, comparable worth measures women's job components, comparing them with value or worth of men's job or their components, to overcome sex/gender wage disparity. First, do wage levels of female-dominated jobs accurately reflect 'an explicit and consistently applied standard of value' across all paidwork, or are wage levels 'depressed artificially' because women hold the jobs. Secondly, what jobs (or job titles) may be undervalued. Job content or attributes (behaviours, tasks, functions) must be described comprehensively and consistently, to be compared with 'job content or attributes across categories of work'. Deciding on worth of job content and attributes requires pinpointing content and attributes. Then worth can be measured:

- this job (done by women) consists of 'x' attributes or content;
- wage is 'y';
- attributes or content are 'like' or 'akin to' attributes or content of that job (done by a man);
- wage for that job is 'z' (or 'y' plus 'm');
- therefore, wage for the (women's) job should be 'z'.

Despite its potential, the Commission concluded ('on the limited material before us') comparable worth and related concepts were at the 'widest' capable of applying to 'any classification' said to be improperly valued, 'without limitation on the kind of classification to which … applied, with no requirement that work performed is related or similar'. Industrial relations backgrounds of countries referenced differ greatly from Australia, with 'different approaches … in each' of them. US comparable worth 'refers to value of work in … worth to the employer', postulating 'sex-based wage discrimination exists if employees in job classifications occupied by women are paid less than employees in job classifications filled primarily by men, if the jobs are of equal value to the employer, though otherwise dissimilar'. This, said the Commission, ran counter to the ***Equal Pay Case 1972***, which explicitly opposed work value being determined by value to the employer.

The analysis was disappointing. Advocates sought assurance that the ***Equal Pay Case 1972*** intended wage parity between women and men, not women and women. Reference to US comparable worth incorporating value to the employer, ruling it out for Australia, was an obfuscation. So was the contention of the term's use in the Australian context 'lead[ing] to confusion' as 'inappropriate and confusing to equate … with the 1972 principle of equal pay for work of equal value'. Referencing confusion in comparable worth could not obscure confusion surrounding equal pay for work of equal value. A clear and unambiguous statement of what equal pay for work of equal value meant, how work value was to apply in assessing women's jobs against men's jobs, like with like—and what constituted like jobs was needed. If the Commission itself required guidance, why reject WEL's ***National Wage Case 1983*** 'standing equal pay bench' proposal?

If concerned comparable worth might apply to alter relativities between men's wages, why? Work value claims traditionally conducted in the Australian system affect male wage relativities. Applying comparative worth to adjust women's wages would not impact on men's, unless the

Commission allowed it. Just as equal pay for work of equal value explicitly addressed women's job undervaluation, comparable worth would apply women's job evaluation, providing a means of applying equal pay for work of equal value.

The ***Equal Pay Case 1972*** hypothesised equal pay's arrival by 1975 (three-step implementation). Now, advocates tell the Commission that whole categories of women remain outside, awaiting application to their profession or trade. The extreme exception taken to comparable worth seems rooted in equal pay implications for work of equal value if comparing women's jobs and wages to men's, rather than other women's. On the one hand, the Commission was prepared to give to women through the ***Equal Pay Case 1972*** yet, on the other, not too much—not uncommon for women's rights.

Employing terminology foreign to the Commission some outside presumed inept. Bound by precedent, courts and tribunals do prefer familiar language, fitting their idea of what the law is and should be. But familiar language is unserviceable if not serving ends sought. Women's rights advance through terms making explicit women's disadvantage or denial of rights—take Mackinnon-Farley's sexual harassment and Swart-Lawton's sexually transmitted debt. Words challenge and change perceptions and understandings. Language shifts boundaries. Ten years later, in the NSW Industrial Commission ***Pay Equity Inquiry 1997*** comparable worth was unremarkable.

In 1986, however, having stressed its comparable worth rejection, the Commission addressed whether the ***National Wage Case 1983*** guidelines precluded further 1972 claims. The unions and ACTU argued the 1972 decision stood. Wage fixing principles not unlike the 1983 directives existed from 1975 to 1981, operating alongside decisions implementing the 1972 equal pay principle. In no case, said Acton, did Commission or state tribunals 'consider themselves constrained' from 'continuing to implement the 1972 decision'. The Tasmanian government said the 1983 guidelines governed applications under the 1972 decision, so the ACTU erred in pursuing the present case and should wait the forthcoming ***National Wage Case***. The Victorian government said the 1972 decision remained functional. The federal government agreed it remained available for awards never adjusted by it and, for flow-on of any 1972 adjustments for nurses and women generally, said 'the … matters should be processed as Anomalies through Principle 6(a) of the 1983 Principles' to 'prevent claims … becoming vehicles for general pay increases'. The PSB supported this, saying assertions that the 1972 decision had not been 'properly applied' should not allow wholesale re-opening of equal pay cases previously determined.

For employers, the CAI opposed the nurses' claims on the merits and under national wage guidelines. The ***Equal Pay Case 1972*** remained 'available to be implemented' in individual awards only, where 'different rates of pay for males and females performing the same work' existed, or female rates differed from those 'pertaining to the same work performed by males in other awards'.

The State Public Service Federation (SPSF), CAEP, and NCW agreed with the ACTU, with variations. For the SPSF, the 1972 decision related not just to discrimination in particular awards, but set an in-principle decision of non-discrimination generally. NCW supported the 1972 decision as affirming community and government commitment to eliminating sex discrimination, saying 'it would be turning back the clock' for current wage-fixing principles to bar its continued application. The CAEP said that nursing being a predominantly female occupation, 'equal pay for work of equal value' was not implemented, because 'rates [were] set with an historical gender bias based on a needs concept'. The only way to 'eradicate this vice' was implementing comparable worth, not Principle 6(a) of the guidelines. Comparable worth meant female rates of pay in predominantly female occupations would be re-assessed on a case-by-case basis ...

Launching a full-scale rebuke of CAEP, the Commission asserted it had not analysed ***Equal Pay Case 1972*** applications, nor 'attempt[ed] to justify its submission by reference to award rates', possibly indicating 'a different position' from actual rates of pay. Later (clearly a Commission sore point), it reiterated criticism of 'no analysis of [its] decision or methods' for fixing awards or determinations to indicate 'inequalities were reflected in award rates of pay'. Further, 'many of the factors mentioned' were 'not readily amenable to award wage prescription' and (another thrust) 'not related to the issues raised in these proceedings'.

Reflective of the ***Basic Wage Inquiry 1949–1950*** attack on the Australian Federation of Business and Professional Women (AFBPW)'s Audrey Turner (contention of lacking in expertise—unfounded), WEL in the ***National Wage Case 1983*** ('irrelevant matters'—childcare, vindicated in the ***National Wage Case 1988***), and CAEP (comparable worth, embraced in the ***Pay Equity Inquiry 1997***), this sidestepped the Commission's own responsibilities. With equal pay claims rarely before the Commission, a deficit in equal pay expertise was inevitable. Adopting

WEL's ***National Wage Case 1983*** equal pay panel approach would have assisted the Commission in ensuring equal pay's implementation. What's more, that panel would have sat on the ***Nurses Comparable Worth case 1985–1986*** itself—possessing three years' knowledge and expertise from equal pay claims preceding the nurses' application.

The Commission did, nonetheless, agree that, as the ACTU, unions and supporting interveners argued, decisions from 1975 to 1981 showed the Commission 'remained fully committed' to 1972's equal pay for work of equal value decision, and claims could be made where the principle was not applied already. However, further arguments did not win the day, as where the unions and ACTU (like the CAEP) deemed Principle 6(a) not a 'suitable mechanism' for processing the nurses claim and ACTU's Acton said neither was Principle 6(b). The submission here was that the nurses' applications were not affected by the national wage guidelines because the ***Equal Pay Case 1972*** required a case-by-case approach—each application 'tested on its own merits', with 'strict tests to establish appropriate rates', and incorporated its own flow-on protections in applying to female rates only.

Contrary to ACTU, unions, and supporting interveners, the Commission said the 1983 national wage guidelines applied, specifically requiring all wage increases other than for prices and productivity movements to accord with guideline principles 4–11. Equal pay claims, tackled between 1975–1981, did implement the 1972 decision in particular awards, with flow-on limited to other classifications in the awards or classifications outside, so claims didn't conflict with basic centralised wage fixing concepts. However, the Private Hospitals' and Doctors' Nurses (ACT) Award 1972, minor because most nurses come under state awards, meant any increases from the ***Nurses Comparable Worth case 1985–1986*** applications had 'serious' flow-on implications. Presented as a test case, an effect wider than ACT nurses in private hospitals and doctors' surgeries was intended. The proceedings were 'part of a wider movement to increase salaries for nurses throughout the country', therefore, said the Commission, the applications 'carry great potential for undermining the current centralised wage fixing system'.

For the Commission, maintaining the wage system as it was, without real potential for women gaining wage justice, was necessary. 'Disruption to the system' meant economic consequences (paying women what their work is worth), repeatedly a reason for withholding equal pay.

The Commission said future award applications that had not applied the 1972 decision should henceforth be processed under Principle 6 of the ***National Wage Case 1983*** guidelines. As all parties recognised 'special factors may be relevant to a review of nurses' salaries', the Commission said progressing the claim 'through the Anomalies Conference should involve the raising of all those issues ...' Yet, reference to the ***National Wage Case 1983*** was an exercise in sleight-of-hand. There, WEL alone raised women's occupational issues, the Commission challenging their relevance, saying they should be pursued through government. Thus, although the Commission had not engaged with WEL's submissions in 1983, indeed ruling out its capacity to do so, it now used the fact that WEL had addressed occupational issues then to shut out their now being put by the CAEP.

An Anomalies Conference proceeded to decide if nurses pay constituted an anomaly within the 1983 guidelines. On 2 April 1986, the Commission president found an arguable case, referring nurses rates in awards and determinations to a Full Bench, together with claims based on changes in the nature of the work (***Nurses Comparable Worth case No. 2 1987***). The following May, the Full Bench delivered its decision. Meanwhile, the Victorian Industrial Commission proceeded to hear the ***Registered Nurses (Salaries and Career Structure) Reference 1986*** (***Registered Nurses (Vic.) case 1986***).

Victorian nurses claimed substantial salary increases and a new career structure, winning work value changes and anomalies claims. Anomalies, because (a) registered nurses above first year grade 1 had never received benefit of the 1972 equal-pay principles; and (b) nurses going into alternative occupations generated substantial short-fall of nurses. Work value changes involved greatly increased patient-nurse dependency, with 'intensified nursing experience' at all sick and elderly care levels.

The RANF anomalies case rested on award history.

Nursing was designated as women's work or work for females, the 1938 award containing classifications titles 'clearly female, eg matrons and sisters', with a single rate for each job, dependent on years of service and bed numbers supervised. Salary for a third year sister was £3 0s 0d weekly or 1s 2½d hourly, lower than any male rate in the 1939 International Labour Organization (ILO) ***Year Book of Labour Statistics***. The award first identified male rates (male nurses only) in 1948, from the outset greater than respective female rates, reasons being unstated. Shortly before 1948, nurses (unlike the Women's Australian Auxiliary Air Force (WAAAFS),

Australian Women's Army Service (AWAS), and Women's Royal Australian Navel Service (WRANS)) had performed in the war zone, but men's nursing prowess was now seen as more valuable; or family responsibilities, real or fictional, carried the day; or simply that being men, the work must be worth more. For nurses, 'male means more' became explicit in 1961, a new clause setting the male rate at the 'appropriate female rate plus 33 ½ percent'.

Two anomalies appeared, one identified, one overlooked. Some ten years earlier, in the ***Basic Wage Case 1949–1950*** the Arbitration Court set women's wages at 75 per cent of men's, determining women should be paid less because they predominated in the field. Ignored—or simply accepted as right—this was incontrovertible evidence of work value being downgraded by sex.

As for the second factor, the male rate valuation was precisely the reverse of what operated in other occupations with male and female rates prior to the ***Equal Pay Case 1969***. In predominantly male awards, the female rate was set as a (lower) percentage of the male rate. Applying equal pay for equal work, women's rates could be based on male standards or work value levels. For nursing, equal pay was applied (anomalously) by moving female rates to a higher proportion of the female rate, not the rate for the job based on male work value. The Victorian government acknowledge the move was 'distorted by the award history', with progression to equal pay following that approach.

The Victorian Commission concluded that the ***Equal Pay Case 1972*** had not been applied to nurses under the Victorian Registered Nurses Award. The award covered 'predominantly female employees, originally expressed in female terms', rates 'depressed back in 1938, … set upon the basis that it was females … doing the work …'. A comparison of current wage rates between registered nurses and Victorian Public Service rates for predominantly male groups—farm produce inspectors, meat inspectors, animal health assistants—confirmed women nurses' wage rates as consistently lower.

The CAI's submission that nurse shortages did not assist the demand for pay rate rises failed. The Victorian Commission adopted justice Maddern's language in the ACT nurses Anomalies Conference, saying a shortage (a) despite a large potential supply of nurses; (b) with fewer than half all qualified nurses actually employed as nurses; and (c) where a large number of nurses work in other occupations or are not in the active labour force, is 'arguably special and extraordinary'. Evidence showed 'hundreds of qualified nurses' working as shop assistants in one Melbourne company; only about 60–70 per cent of registered nurses employed; and a large pool 'working in other occupations or ... not currently in the active labour force'. This could establish an anomaly, symptomatic of under-evaluation of nurses' work, and relevant to any nurse salary review. Lack of career structure for those not wanting to enter administration or teaching was raised, too, the RANF favouring a career path, even over wage increases, as did more junior nursing levels.

'Alleged causes' of nurse discontent—car parking, rosters, and authoritarian attitudes—were, said the Commission, 'apparently being considered' in other forums then, finding the anomalies proven, set increased salary levels, and a career structure. A significant impact on nurses' work value was anticipated.

Turning to work value, evidence supporting work changes formed a major part of the RANF case. The Commission said most evidence did not warrant creation of a new classification, not being 'a significant net addition to work requirements ...'. Acquisition of more knowledge and skills on the job through in-service training is a 'normal feature of professional activity', so could not qualify unless 'extraordinary'. Similarly, new equipment and procedures, if a 'refinement of what already exists', lacked sufficient 'net addition to work requirements' to meet the 'work value change' test.

Two criticisms. First, the anomalies outcome was linked to 'work value'—eliding the two, so undermining the nurses entitlement. Secondly, on work value, the RANF concentrated upon *changes* in nurses' work for increased pay levels, overlooking past undervaluation, including failure to assess fairly nursing components unrelated to technological advances. Technological advances and other changes require calculation into work value assessment as an add-on, not the sole or most substantial basis of an equal pay for work of equal value claim. Nursing was undervalued from the start.

As it was, the Commission accepted one factor only as significant for work value: the 'whole area of increased patient dependency', a *change* due to modern conditions. Since January 1982, patients had shorter hospital stays, moving from intensive care into general wards earlier, then to nursing homes and district nursing services. Combined with new equipment and procedures 'enabling operations on older and sicker patients', the overall nursing experience was intensified at all levels of sick and elderly care. This meant more nursing attention and expertise. But where did that leave wage levels set prior to this change? Despite acknowledging historical under-evaluation of nurses' work, plus acceptance of the feminised nature of the profession dictating this, the RANF did not pursue, vigorously or at all, this central aspect of its equal pay claim.

As for increased nurse professionalism by offloading non-nursing duties onto nursing aids through 1980s industrial action, the Commission determined this irrelevant: otherwise employees could seek wage increases by off-loading 'lower functions'. Yet, bearing in mind male-dominated work areas, where job levels and demarcations on a hierarchical basis traditionally resulted in higher pay, creating a career structure with wage increases as workers travel from lower-classified jobs to higher levels, this is disingenuous. Rules applying to men's traditional areas of work were ignored in women's wage setting, maintaining women's lower wages. This point was not taken.

Finally, the Commission said transferring nurse training from hospitals to tertiary institutions might affect work value, leaving this open for a future wage claim. However, if wages increased because nurses train in tertiary institutions, gaining degrees and diplomas, this could deny the value of traditional on-the-job training. Not valuing in-house training fairly in comparison with on-the-job skills and qualifications in traditional male areas requires redress. Failure to assess this with a fair value and commensurate pay rate means future wage fixing inevitably begins from a lower (or continuingly unequal) point again.

Nor was this point taken up.

Comparable Worth or 'Male to Female' Comparisons

In the ***Registered Nurses (Vic.) 1986 case***, the Victorian Commission calculated work value as 'what's changed', following the federal ***National Wage Case 1983***, with nurses missing out on fair assessment of work done in the past. The inability to recognise this failing infused the 'what's changed' finding, too. That patients were more dependent upon nurse care at an earlier stage meant nurses took over work done by doctors and intensive care professionals. The work did not change, only who did it. Yet, the Commission did not value it at doctors' or intensive care professionals' rates. That *nurses* (a woman's profession) were doing the work automatically downgraded work that had been done by far more highly paid professionals.

Was the Commonwealth Commission's approach any better? Having altered the goal posts from the ***Equal Pay Case 1972***, limiting work value to *changes* on the job, despite wage rises, nurses lost out there, too. The anomalies provision could have applied to historical undervaluing of nurses' work, but the ACTU did not incorporate this perspective. Even the change-focus failed to bring an equivalence between women's and men's work.

In the ***Nurses Comparable Worth case No. 2***, the RANF identified eight work value changes:

- increased patient dependency;
- intravenous therapy, new drugs and new drug administration techniques;
- work orientation changes and devolution of responsibility from medical officers;
- technological changes and new procedures;
- staff shortages;
- differences and changes in nursing techniques and functions;
- changes in isolation and infection control through multi-resistant bacteria and new diseases;
- changes in education necessitated by the other work value changes.

Except for Telecom nurses, these changes were agreed for all nursing staff categories in each classifications' duties and responsibilities. Emphasised were: training; required skill, knowledge and responsibility; work environment changes, required versatility and adaptability; quality of functions performed and nurse care in exercising responsibilities; surgical and medical procedures developed through advanced technology, new drugs, new methods of drug administration and drug therapy. University degree status of nurse education, amplified turnover of patients, with more acute treatment in hospitals and community nurse responsibilities (as in Victoria), warranted an increase. This explicitly recognised that qualified nurses undertook (often without supervision) procedures formerly performed by medical staff. Again, wages not rising commensurately meant that despite tasks not changing, simply the status of the person doing it, work value decreased—a sex-biased outcome.

Similarly with anomalies. Neither the federal nor Victorian case resulted in nurses' pay rising to an equivalence of medical practitioners or male workers with like health and life responsibilities. Nor, in either case, was work devolved upon nurses acknowledged as work of equal value to that work when done by doctors—at least not in salary terms. Yet, at least some components of nurses work not only equalled doctors' work—it *was* doctors' work.

Beyond these tasks, nurses' work is equally relevant as general practitioners' to patients. Doctors alone do not bear health, wellbeing, life and death responsibility. This falls equally—sometimes more—upon nurses. Why not acknowledge nurses' work as equivalent to doctors' for determining salary levels? Doctors' lengthy training singles them out for a higher salary, yet formal (paper) qualifications are not the sole measure. Work value involves training, skills, expertise, responsibility ... Does the differential lie not only with the male/female divide, but professional status? But why are medical practitioners seen as more 'professional' than nurses? Doctors and nurses historically connect with unseemly odours, pestilent flesh, blood, germs, disease, and with cleanliness, white coats or uniforms, purveying knowledge and exercising skills to preserve health and life. Doctors are elevated by the professional label. Nurses remain associated with bedpans. However impeccable their uniforms, the image does not give them professional standing akin to doctors—at least in the west, even when nurses acquire jobs passed on from medical practitioners. Is nursing even a 'profession'—or an 'occupation'?

Traditionally, doctors' contribution to health and patient care occupies a realm superior to nurses. Why? Because they and their profession are, generally, male. Surgery cannot be done without the doctor, yet nor without nurses. Equally fundamental to patients, nurses provide patient-doctor interface. Absent nurses, doctors' rooms and surgeries would not serve patients. Patient nurse-time frequently exceeds, often greatly, doctor-time.

But the 1980s ***Nurses cases*** didn't see this. One problem lay in work value and anomalies: new features required for work to qualify. As the original technologically orientated work of nurses was never recognised, granting pay rises on a new technology-base, deprived nurses of having the old (original) technology valued at its proper level. 'People-base' was never properly valued—as it never is, whatever the occupation (it is 'women's work'). Baby and maternal health nurses work mainly in preventative medicine, not valued equally (or more) as technologically or surgically based health care. Nor is nursing recognised as equally life-and-death as doctors or medical officers' work. The ***Nurses cases*** passed over why surgical techniques in an operating theatre—patients comatose—are valued more highly than preventative medicine and life-giving therapies delivered to those fully conscious. Albeit essential to operations, before, during, and after the patient is anaesthetised, this work is not equally worth doctors and anaesthetists' work. Why is nursing graded less valuable than removing a diseased organ? Why therapeutic nursing skills, essential after operations, worth less than excision of a body part?

In 1988, women tried again. In the ***National Wage Case 1988***, the Commission was asked to critically address its own guidelines. A 'full and comprehensive reassessment of work value of work traditionally performed by women' was necessary, said National Pay Equity Coalition (NPEC), to ensure award restructures do not entrench existing relativities between male and female held jobs by merely 'replicate existing skills hierarchies', 'perpetuating … equal pay cases indefinitely'.

Guidelines set by the ***National Wage Case 1986*** and the ***National Wage Case 1987*** two-tier wage system, continuing until the ***National Wage Case 1988***, militated against equal pay. The general increase distributed to all wage and salary earners constituted the first tier. The second allowed additional payments for wage and salary adjustments, based on 'genuine flexibility, within determined limits', depending on 'facts in particular cases and … particular circumstances' of industries or enterprises. Second tier increases were neither retrospective nor uniformly distributed, and did not come into effect at identical dates. Anomalies claims were processed under the second tier, inequities claims through the Anomalies Conference and 'not otherwise'.

All ***National Wage Case 1987*** parties—unions and employers—were, noted the Commission, substantially in agreement, 'recognising the serious economic situation and need for restraint'. All supported a two-tier system with provisions 'remarkably similar in content', designed to 'improve productivity and efficiency at the enterprise or industry level to improve [Australia's] productive base and … competitive performance'. A 'restructuring and efficiency' principle would 'improve public and private sector efficiency', a measure by which a second-tier claim could be determined. This included changes to work and management practices, reducing demarcation barriers between jobs, multi-skilling, training and re-training, and broad-banding, aiming at encouraging workers to upskill, using these skills in their jobs, eliminating multiple workers (each assigned to a particular task) when one could do all tasks. The incentive was that workers who increased their skills and did (what had been) more than one job would be paid more.

The Commission granted $10.00 as the first tier wage increase, setting a four per cent limit on second tier rises.

Unfortunately, no women's organisations intervened in the ***National Wage Case 1987***. Non-unionised workers (mostly women) and those in unions with lesser industrial clout (ditto) were ignored. Though not acknowledged, it was obvious from the outset that women workers, distributed in far fewer occupations and more highly segregated than any other Organisation for Economic Cooperation and Development (OECD) country, would miss out on second-tier increases or at least get them far later than highly unionised workers with high industrial strength.

The predictable happened. If women gained second-tier rises, they waited longer for them, with no compensation for lapsed time. Percentage based, the lower the pay rate, the lower the raise. Women missed out all around. This, and ***National Wage Case 1987*** anomalies and inequities principles, meant women desperately needed their claims to be represented in the Commission.

Saying the equal pay principle should be incorporated into national wage principles because no national wage could be set properly without it, Scutt as NPEC ***National Wage Case 1988*** counsel noted no wage fixing principle of the past fifteen or so years had facilitated the 1972 principle or elevated equal pay. Following the ***National Wage Case 1987***, with equal pay legitimately raised only through the anomalies and inequities principle, a claim could succeed as an anomaly only by conditions of a special and isolated nature. For inequities, work must be shown as similar to work with which compared—like with like; no good reason must exist for dissimilar pay rates; some other significant factor must create the inequity (history might not qualify); comparator pay rate/s must be reasonable and proper for the work for which paid, and comply with Commission principles; and minimum rates awards could not be compared with paid rates awards. Pay increases required merits justification, with no flow-on potential, negligible economic cost, and as 'once-only'. Finally, anomalies or inequities Anomalies Conferences were restricted to peak union council applications only.

NPEC said access for 1972 equal pay principle claims should continue, with women's paidwork incorporated into national wage guidelines, including 'an equal opportunity assessment' of any award restructuring proposals and training packages, plus measures ensuring women 'equal access to enterprise training schemes and ... external, accredited, formal education'.

At base, for NPEC, Scutt argued past equal pay claims had not compared women's work with appropriate categories. Restating that the ***Equal Pay Case 1972*** said women's work would be compared not only within awards but *across* awards, Scutt said there was little point in comparing women's work within awards. This generally meant comparing women's work with women's work, or undervalued work with undervalued work (often the same). For women, gaining equal pay through comparison required comparison *across* awards, with strict attention to nominating comparators and which (men's) work would be compared.

A revealing exchange followed. President Maddern protested that not all women's work was undervalued and not all women under women's awards received unequal pay. 'Fitters and turners are paid less under their award than secretaries under their award', he said. Yet (came the reply) is the Fitters and Turners Award the appropriate comparator? For secretarial keyboard skills, male jobs utilising keyboard skills is a more apt measure, the relevant award one covering computer programmers employing keyboard skills. Then, for secretarial executive capacities, an award covering men exercising executive capacities as comparator. An expostulation matched the president's expression. That secretaries and computer programmers had anything in common was dire. Secretaries and executives? Never.

Over the 1980s, Commission decisions undercut the earlier decade's victories, in truth ignoring ***Equal Pay 1969*** and ***1972*** decisions and disregarding women's wages as demonstrably unequal. The Commission failed to follow through on its earlier decisions, not even ensuring their implementation. Not advancing claims, unions failed, too.

Earlier, stereotyping of women as lacking financial obligations beyond personal expenses, these supplemented by dependence upon a husband or father, militated against women's pay justice. Belief was that by showing the fallacy of the 'men alone head households' notion, 'men alone breadwinners', wage setting would ensure unequal pay was undone. When this didn't happen, women had to question industrial and wage fixing bodies' cognisance of their own biases.

Male Bias, Women's Worth

Despite the ***Nurses Comparable Worth case 1985–1986*** disappointment, comparable worth excluded as 'irrelevant' to Australian wage fixing, the ACTU projected the 1980s ***Nurses' cases*** as a victory. Of sorts. It established a career structure for Victoria's nurses and nurses under federal awards, conforming to nurses' awards in other states, or prospective changes. So too with pay rises, but in-built bias against valuing nurses' work was not overcome, with a failure to grasp, in real terms, the degree of devaluing nurses' work. Neither historical nor contemporary wage injustice, both requiring attention, was considered effectively.

Ultimately, this was unsurprising. Acknowledging the 1938 and subsequent awards confirmed lower pay for nurses because they were paid as women in a women's profession went only one step of the way. The Commissions acknowledged something was wrong or went wrong in valuing nursing as women's work. But 'why'—necessary to inform a proper outcome—escaped them. Neither critically confronted their predecessors' locking-in of nurses to lesser rates of pay because nurses were women, doing women's work *seen by their predecessors* as of lesser value. The 1980s ***Nurses cases*** carried no antidote.

Unequal pay was viewed as if it came unbidden, from nowhere. Even talk about breadwinners, heads of households, changing social and family structures failed to attend the real issue. Neither Commission confronted their complicity as men making women's work determinations, (de)valuing what women were doing. Neither did they question that they were men doing men's work—decision-making on federal and state bodies, appointed by all-male governments. Justice Judith Cohen on the ***Nurses Comparable Worth case 1985–1986*** and the ***National Wage Case 1983*** was one of a handful of women ever appointed to any Australian industrial tribunal. When Cohen, deputy president Marsh and commissioner Pauline Griffin sat in May 1989 as a Full Bench, this gained Australia-wide media coverage, 'first time ever' headlines. Photographs and footage of three women on the bench were so remarkable as to generate front-page and news-lead items.

Women's absence from decision-making, the sole preserve of men or men predominating, affects what is seen as comparable worth or comparable work, what of equal value. That, time and again, through the decades, national and state wage guidelines were written without reference to equal pay and women workers' lack of it testifies to decision-makers' failure, ignorance of women's work value and inability to see subversion of equal pay decisions as inevitable without annual incorporation into national and state wage guidelines. It confirmed, for the 1980s, failure of employers and worker representatives—unions—to recognise women as legitimate in the paid workforce.

Traditional assertions of justice as blind rest upon notions that law, in not distinguishing between litigants, treats everyone equally, making justice neutral—and fair. As Anatole France said, the law 'in its majestic equality, forbids the rich as well as the poor to sleep under bridges, to beg in the streets, and to steal bread'. Yet, who will sleep rough, who dine rich? Meanwhile, so long as vagrancy laws exist, the poor have no right to sleep under bridges.

Whilst women are denied payment of their work's worth, women will be the poor and remain poor. Meanwhile, the legal system's neutrality maintains a mythical vigil, a sex/gender infused blindfold standing between women's work and its fair assessment. France's insights are more than matched by women writers informed by their own experience of working at less than male pay rates, facing obstacles men create. Chapter 16, 'Alarums and Excursions—Facts, Fictions, Fallacies and Fancies' celebrates women of imagination—conscious of women's retrograde industrial conditions, (un) equal pay, and claims for women's industrial rights, taking themselves off to factories and offices, in wartime and peace. Struggles waged in fiction, women using their own experiences and those of women around them, plays out in the march toward women's wage justice. Australian women write the politics of their lives in story as in history.

References

Cases—See Case List

Australian Government, ***National Economic Summit Communiqué***, AGPS, Canberra, ACT, 1983.

Clare Burton, Raven Hag and Gay Thompson, ***Women's Worth—***, AGPS, Canberra, ACT, 1987.

Lin Farley, ***Sexual Shakedown—***, McGraw Hill, New York, NY, USA, 1978.

Anatole France (Jacques Anatole Francois Thibault, 1844–1924), ***Le Lys Rouge (The Red Lily)***, 1894, http://www.classicreader.com/bookloc.php/sid.1/bookid.2422/ (accessed 30 July 2006).

Ann Game and Rosemary Pringle, ***Gender at Work***, Allen & Unwin, Sydney, NSW, 1983.

Mary Gaudron and Michael Bosworth, 'Equal Pay?' in J. Mackinolty and H. Radi (eds), ***In Pursuit of Justice—***, Allen & Unwin, Sydney, NSW, 1979, pp. 161–69.
Catharine Mackinnon, ***Sexual Harassment***, Yale University Press, New Haven, Conn., USA, 1979.
NPEC, ***Personal Communication***, Sydney, NSW, 2006 (26 June 2006).
Rosemary Pringle, ***Secretaries Work—***, Allen & Unwin, Sydney, NSW, 1988.
Judith Resnick, 'The Relevance of Gender, Race, and Ethnicity to Adjudication', in AF Hill and EC Jordan (eds), ***Race, Gender and Power in America—***, OUP, Oxford, UK, 1995.
Edna Ryan, 'Equal Pay, Comparable Worth and the Central Wage Fixing System', ***Australian Feminist Studies***, no. 6, 1988, pp. 7–16.
Edna Ryan, ***Interview***, Canberra, ACT, 1996 (April 1996).
Jocelynne A. Scutt, 'Librarians, Lawyers and Law Reform ...' in JA Scutt, ***The Incredible Woman***, Artemis Publishing, Melbourne, 1997, vol. 1, pp. 185–211.
Jocelynne A. Scutt, 'Nursing as a "Women's Profession"—' in JA Scutt, ***The Incredible Woman***, vol. 2, 1997, pp. 147–64.
Christine Short, 'Australian Women's Pay 1907 to 2002—', Paper presented to *14th Women, Management ... Conference*, 25–26 July 2002, http://www.lmsf.mq.edu.au/resource/pay_equity/2003_short.pdf, pp. 1–30 (accessed 29 July 2006).
Margaret Thornton, '(Un)equal Pay for Work of Equal Value', ***Journal of Industrial Relations***, no. 4, 1981 (December 1981).
Ronnie J. Steinberg, '"A Want of Harmony" ...', in Helen Remick (ed), ***Comparable Worth—***, Temple University Press, Philadelphia, PA, USA, 1985, pp. 3–27.

CHAPTER 16

Alarums and Excursions: Fictions, Fallacies and Fancies

> Knowing she had no means of support and was desperate for work, the manager offered her less than the single girls, who were receiving only half the male rate anyway. The pittance was enough for food, but not for lodging. Josie set her teeth and accepted it.
>
> Ruth Park, ***Missus***
> Nelson, Melbourne, 1985, p. 137

> There's a name for a man who lives off women.
>
> Dorothy Hewett, ***Bobbin Up***
> Australasian Book Society, Melbourne, 1959, p. 115

Filling the doorway, the faces of a group of Australian Army Medical Women's Service (AAMWS), back from New Guinea, yellowed from Quinine Sulphate liberally pumped into them, warding off malaria. The AAMWS flock in, greeting Mary Parker with the curious glances of those newly returned from abroad, and the war zone, whilst she surveys the comfortable Women's Service Club lounge. As the AAMWS plan their sightseeing days, flicking through a Sydney guide to sights and entertainments, Mary Parker's magazine falls from her lap. Full of unreal stories, the way you'd wish things would happen, not as they really do, not like real life.

Mary Parker watches the clock. She's meeting her sister Alice at a quarter past one for a doctor's appointment. No ordinary doctor.

J. A. Scutt, *Wage Rage for Equal Pay*,
https://doi.org/10.1007/978-3-031-42178-5_16

In wartime Sydney, Mary Parker's is oh, such a commonplace story. *He* is married. To a woman who 'doesn't understand him', *he* says. *He* says, the marriage 'is over'.

Mary Parker, excited in her uniform and more excited out of it, finds to her chagrin those promises of wedding-whites and happy ever after untying like the ribbons looping her in just-a-one of the unreal stories, how she'd wished and things would happen.

So, now—*their* union's centrepiece, that baby-child ending only weeks of embryonic existence splat on an operating table, destined for a bucket.

Aliens on Our Own Soil

Challenge faces equal pay on many fronts, pregnancy and childcare rendering *her* a less valuable contributor, downgrading *her* work's value. Absence through giving birth to children and female employees' potential to leave, despite building their skills, experience, and earning capacity on the job, disadvantages employers, the argument runs. So why give women equal pay?

Come in Spinner's Mary Parker was neither alone in her pregnant anxiety, nor in seeking a backyard abortionist or, coming for women much later, a doctor and legal termination. Through the 1980s, fertility, pregnancy, breastfeeding, childcare, and childrearing were, as throughout the nineteenth and twentieth century and now in the twenty-first, central to women in paid employment, and women's paid employment.

The ***National Wage Case 1988*** was a breakthrough. The Australian Council of Trade Unions (ACTU) and Australian Conciliation and Arbitration Commission acknowledged childcare as an industrial issue. This—children and paidwork linked—was no news to women. If men in the ACTU and on the Commission had no wives or partners to look after their children or take childcare responsibility, they'd have reached the conclusion far earlier. (Just as the Women's Electoral Lobby (WEL) proposed, and the Commission ruled 'irrelevant matters', in the ***National Wage Case 1983.***)

Industrialisation meant women working more often outside the home. Nineteenth-century movement into factories, shops, and offices expanded baby farming as women's home-work, caring for children of women working outside. Simultaneously, fertility rates fell, prompting the 1903 Royal Commission On the Decline in the Birth-rate and On the Mortality of Infants in New South Wales. So dissatisfied with the outcome, member Octavius Beale, piano-maker and father of 13 children, marrying his wife's sister two years after the first Mrs Beale's death, persuaded prime minister

Alfred Deakin to appoint him sole commissioner on a Royal Commission into Secret Drugs, Cures and Foods (December 1906–August 1907). Beale deplored women's limiting their families deliberately, by artificial means. The NSW Royal Commission's 1904 report concluded just this, saying: '... the cause or causes of the Decline of the Birth-rate must be a force or forces over which the people themselves have control'.

Decades later, the ***Maternity Leave case 1979*** declared unpaid maternity leave an industrial right, state Industrial Tribunals (including WA's ***State Maternity Leave case 1979***) following. The ***Adoption Leave case 1985*** replicated maternity leave provisions for adoptive parents, and the ***Parental Leave case 1990*** added to the industrial pantheon, sharing women's 12 months maternity leave with fathers. Next, the ***Family Leave case 1994***, ***Personal/Carers Leave case 1995***, ***Parental Leave for Casual Employees case 2001***, and ***Family Provisions case 2005***, though paid maternity leave was another matter altogether. The Maternity Leave (Commonwealth Employees) Act 1973 extended paid maternity leave to federal public service women (12 weeks paid, 40 weeks unpaid), but for women workers generally (and state public service), it was a fight for the future. More remote was an holistic approach encompassing women's paid workforce reintegration: little value in maternity leave or paid maternity leave if, once having borne a child, obstacles delay women's return to paidwork or, once there, they are treated as careless of their careers, as in ***Hickie v Hunt and Hunt***, or making unreasonable demands upon employers as with women teachers in ***State of New South Wales v Amery***, or a Hansard writer in ***State of Victoria v Shou***, or are simply treated poorly. Believing they have an entitlement to bear children and maintain paid employment, women suppose their work will be equally valued, not that their pay rates will suffer after giving birth. However, expectations and reality too often operate disjunctively.

In the 1970s, Shulamith Firestone's ***The Dialectic of Sex*** asserted women's childbearing would willingly, without struggle, be ceded to artificial wombs. This, she said, would relieve women of an impediment to participating freely (that is, like men) in the workforce. By the end of the 1980s, despite developments in new reproduction technologies (NRTs), including in-vitro fertilisation (IVF) and embryo transfer (ET), women's wombs remain vital to reproduction. Through decades, paidwork and pregnancy were diametrically opposed or, at minimum, created undeniable dilemmas for the vast bulk of women. This was so in the 1920s when women kicked up their heels as flappers, the '60s when women embraced the sexual revolution, and the 1980s when women went full tilt to enter the corporate world. Despite 1940s provision of state childcare centres accompanying women's war effort, pregnancy remained problematic. Spanning 1900 through and into the '80s, the world of work existed as an alien land for babies, children, and pregnant women.

'I will give you babies,' she had whispered in the dark, lying shyly in Frank's embrace, that precious week of final leave, days swaying in the wonder of happiness now, and the magical dream of a future planned enchantment. Yes, Barbara would divorce him, he'd said. No difficulty, he'd said … Barbara was fine, he'd said. Never understood him. Wouldn't block his way. He said.

'I will give you babies,' she had said. 'Not right now, my darling,' he had said. 'It's good care I'm taking of that,' he'd said, a smile, laughing. 'Just imagine our little Corporal Mary coming now! A nice advertisement you'd be for the Australian Women's Army Service'.

Now she's waiting, Mary Taylor, under the clock in the Women's Service Club ladies lounge, £40 0s 0d paper-wrapped, bumping against her heart. Waiting for Alice and the doctor's surgery.

When Cusack and James wrote ***Come in Spinner***, they took time out in the Blue Mountains east of Sydney, spending a few weeks' bush holiday together. Back from London in 1938, James joined Cusack and other Australian writers-at-home 'fired with Miles Franklin's burning conviction' that 'without an indigenous literature people can remain aliens on their own soil':

> An unsung country does not fully exist nor enjoy adequate exchange in the inner life.

So, too, lacking a literature peopled with women's lives and concerns, women remain aliens in their own land. The soil tilled in women's lives, undervalued, unremembered, publicly unrecorded, is denied its existence. Women's footsteps along the pavements, their deepest thoughts amidst the darkness of night-time bedcovers, their drudgery over stoves, the joys of a lifetime—ignore these, and deny half the world's story. Lacking a literature chronicling the existence of women's inner lives, the contradictions lived alongside men, and women in the world of women, and in joyous independence, the Australian story, whole, remains untold.

Just as history has denied women's existence or acknowledged it as merely an add-on to the lives of men-who-make-history, women in fiction and women fiction writers have led problematic lives. As Tilly Olsen's ***Silences*** acutely relates, time to write is ever in issue, but pen and paper are ever less costly than oils and canvass, film and camera, bronze, marble, limestone, porphyry, or granite—and the large space the sculptor requires. Paradoxically, the power of the pen extolled, women had more chance of writing. Franklin wanted the Australian story to have a literary existence and, through ***My Brilliant Career*** and beyond, she wanted *Australian women's story* to feature equally in that narrative. Women's socio-political, economic, and cultural positioning in the world and the nation affected women writers and their fiction. Money, income, and wages were significant: lack of equal pay played out at all levels, in every endeavour, for women writers too.

Fiction—As the Economics of Women's Lives

In ***Exiles at Home***, Drusilla Modjeska makes no bones about 1930s Australian women writers using their own experience, focusing on women's socio-cultural experience to interrogate women's survival 'within the structures of marriage and sexual morality'. In the 1940s and '50s, concern with 'women's situation and domestic morality did not disappear, but was rephrased in the universal language of "human" problems and an exploration of wider social manifestations of power'. Modjeska says the 'primacy of personal and sexual conflict was inverted so that in the later novels social and political conflict [gained] precedence over the personal'.

In this period, Australian women novelists displayed a tangible resonance with the political and industrial struggle for women's economic rights and wage justice for women.

In ***Come in Spinner***, Cusack and James relate women's endurance in making money to live through women's war. Wound into a cavalcade of laughs, tears, and struggle lies the economic burden confronting women responsible for children, aging parents, ne'er-do-well husbands and hangers on, and for themselves.

Swift on the horizon in Cusack and James' wartime Sydney, always a just cause, equal pay surely a just cause then. Women recruited alongside men, in the armed services. Women in essential industries, taking positions vacated by men off to the front. Women in jobs held prior to war, jobs deemed necessary by a government's emergency powers. Volunteering, women at work raising money, manufacturing, making light for the war effort. Equal pay, in all circumstances—just. But how likely?

Sydney, the 1940s. The Yankee Invasion. Aussie servicemen's anger and aggro, their women duchessed, wooed away with nylons and Chanel No 5, wining, dining, and free packets of cigarettes. Women juggling children's care and long factory hours, working under Manpower auspices, making uniforms and boots. Working nights in Kings Cross brothels and dosshouses, sending money up the country to a sister caring for children whose fathers are dead, or away at war, or disappeared by their own design or that of some inventive and calculating mind via a landmine or blazing bomb, or ack-ack guns. Or women working overtime in beauty parlours, shampooing, massaging, colouring; plucking eyebrows, doing make-up, pedicures, manicures—for wives and daughters of the crème de la crème or, more likely, the nouveau riche and jumped up merchants making fortunes out of drinking and gambling dens, raking their cut of money circulating from arms deals and pay-packets of men on rest and recreation leave.

Come in Spinner speaks through women's words and lives braced in an international conflagration over which they have no control, lives changed irrevocably by war, marriage on-the-run, gambling and black-market gluttony. Women in a world of good time girls winning champagne and orchids, or scoring £12 0s 0d for a first night service to GIs. Here they come, the GIs, seeking fun and sex, whatever the price the innocent runaway pays drinking a drink shot through with a Mickey Finn and, bearing the consequences, swallowing a drunken dark alley rape.

1930s Depression years, Cusack worked in NSW country high schools, teaching, writing all the while. James, working in London's Fleet Street journalism, spent time in East End voluntary social work with parents and school children. Wartime, living in Sydney with her own young children, ever on the search for accommodation, dealing with work's complications as Royal Prince Alfred Hospital public appeals officer, weathering erratic hours and social functions. Organising fundraising committees, editing the Royal Prince Alfred ***Gazette*** in an office above Martin Place, shouts and laughter seeping into the room, with the military bands' boom! boom! boom! in the air.

Home from the country, working a Kings Cross block of flats briefly, as caretaker, Cusack went back teaching in rural schools, or lecturing for the Army Educational Service until war's end. At Albion Street Children's Court in Surrey Hills she did school counselling, when James did voluntary public relations work. Foreground and backdrop to ***Come in Spinner***, winner of the 1946 ***Daily Telegraph*** novel writing competition, it provided the characters, colour, light and the darknesses of stories woven into a book taking almost two years to complete—then running through revisions and ***Daily Telegraph*** demands for cutting by 50,000 words and toning down.

Cusack, James, and Franklin's correspondence reveals a ***Daily Telegraph*** dictating that ***Come in Spinner*** be less true to women's lives. The graphic reality of women through the war, the abortions, predatory exploitation and assault, yet the power of women glorying in new job authority, grasping gladly independence (economic, despite lower wages continuing) and swelling choices was more than the ***Telegraph*** anticipated the market to bear. For the editorial world, the community eschewed too knowingly written, the lives women were caused to live—or their freedom—during those years. Women's finances meant many took money for sex, or accepted gifts in exchange. For the ***Telegraph***, readers did not want to know so graphically the economic hardship and sacrifice suffered, when women's wages failed to reflect the real cost of living. What it really cost a woman to live.

Ironic, for community and public knew. Of course, the women did. As the men with whom they kicked up their heels—or took off their shoes, or more. And the men as employers still, or newly, getting work from women at less than the work's worth, less than the women's due. All their lives, all their living, resonated as ***Come in Spinner***.

Anything for Counting—In Fiction or Truth?

From the voice of ***Come in Spinner***, Angus McFarland is impatient. Reaching out to press the bell again, his hand thinks better of it. But by God, if people had to put up with what men suffered in France in 1917 …

Nowadays, women lost their femininity fast, husbands and fathers—not a word. Helen! His niece! Weather-beaten lack of style. Just wicked, Olive, letting a young girl grow into neglect. Deborah could give a few lessons on skin and hair. No excuse, up early and late, mannishly mustering, trucking, working it like a brute. Couldn't that mother of hers put her foot down. Abnormal, this fervour for trousers, sex starvation underneath it all … Well, he'd tell 'em how men coming home wanted their women. Helen? No polish, no charm, no grace, no diction. Never!

So, Helen McFarland the worker, albeit an unpaid one. Droving on the family's station for the war effort, taking no money. None offered. Her work part of the landscape, except when decried as unwomanly. As a worker, unrecorded in any women's employment census, Gross National

Product (GNP) contribution uncounted for, though figuring by its output. Her production consumed by the enterprise, entering the books attributed to the men owning the land and the cattle. Her right to a wage, a fair one at that, goes unmet, unremarked, with women seen simply as doing what they do, unpaid and never mind equal pay.

Paradoxically, it's not the actual work done that is the problem, but that it's a woman doing the work. Women's work in the home, unpaid, is invisible. With changed circumstances as for Helen—conditions of war—her work differs from that of her sisters at home, working for nothing, their work seen as nothing. But the mirror reflects them identically. Helen McFarland does men's work, but the wages for it when done by a man pass her by. Women work elsewhere for nothing, so her work, too, requires no payment.

In circular fashion, this intrudes when work value is assessed for paidwork by wage fixing bodies. If some women work for nothing, diligent in doing so, why should others be paid, or be paid more highly than a pittance? (Or a modest sum.) Why pay women like a man, who's not working for nothing, doesn't dream of it—a family to support (or should or could or will be in the future)?

When Angus McFarland abhors Helen's doing something different from the women remaining at home, different from what she did in the past, he does not comprehend the work as valuable, counting for something. It discounts Helen as a serious contestant in the femininity stakes, no more.

This contradiction—of women seen as working differently so subjected to ridicule or disdain, yet simultaneously their work being unseen, invisible or of no worth—occurs not only for Helen McFarland-as-stationhand. Women written out of the paidwork equation, their work invisible or adding no value, never mind being paid for it—occurs not only in the pages of ***Come in Spinner***. Life in rural Australia includes country towns, too, with women's unpaidwork and absence from the census as workers.

'It's just positively disgusting', highly indignant, Aunt Edith declares, 'how you're always hanging about that man. Doesn't he know better than finagling a young girl like you'.

Aunt Edith won't have it. Shannon Hicks—of Tennant's ***Ride on Stranger***—different class background from Helen McFarland. But no different in working for no pay. Nor for her inclusion as a worker in any census. Shannon—all work and no pay, never mind *equal* pay. After all, equal to what?

As Burton, Hag, and Thompson explain, ignorance in assessing worth of jobs held predominantly by women arises twofold. First, jobs undervalued in initial analysis of job's worth, or factors comprising the job. Secondly, judgements of what a job is worth influenced by what it is paid—current or market wages. And that some women do the job for nothing influence estimates of worth when others seek payment for the job.

Shannon—ever in and out of *that man*'s room.

'Why can't you pick some nice companion of your own age?'

Or if needs must hanging round the boarders, why not one or other of the pleasant, lady-like women who'd like her entertaining them? There's the 'nice people' here, Aunt Edith says.

Aunt Edith, listing all the 'choice pests' inhabiting boarding-houses, the hulking great Bertie Bargos youths pouncing out at grabbing from behind. The roustabout with the everyday blasted 'hello' at every new dish and a 'What's this mush?' The lady and child, freckled face reddened beneath ruthlessly brushed hair sprouting up his scalp.

'No, I'm full,' squirming up, does he want more dinner. 'Say, "No, I'm full, *thank you*,"' sniffing, his mother corrects. 'One of these days that kid's neck will be broken,' rages Beryl, conspiring in many a fantastical scheme for taking it on. 'We could lure him into the traffic,' Cheryl suggests.

'Just why Ma puts up with this mob …,' says Beryl. 'It'd take a million to make it worthwhile to stand their manners'.

Early morning 'til dinner time it's cooking and cleaning and washing-up, between washing and polishing and scrubbing and laundry. Shannon older and grimmer, daily despairing, ever more work-blighted, hair greying in silent strings, slogging at Headtown hostelry, Clayton Residential drudgery hurling her into the grave, mourning to Beryl, 'If only I could run away …'.

'Why not?'

'Because,' head slanting sideways, ruminating. 'A girl's got to have a job.'

'Cheer up, kid. Payday's tomorrow.'

'I get no pay.'

Shannon Hicks, born to Mr and Mrs Hicks, fourth in a four-daughter family, a burthen neither contemplated, although Ada Hicks knows her woman's lot. 'Enough to make you believe in more lives than one,' she pronounces, woebegone. 'Something dreadful I must 'ave done, born a woman. Take a man's good life, never mind married or single, never a worry, but a woman! Life just one long worry. Stricken every month, or half-mad on the horizon because she's not. Having children, not having children. Trapped in a one big worry of life. Why not just label us a crowd of criminals.'

Crying now, Mrs Hicks. 'Just born a woman. All we are, paid back, no money showing for it. Fourth in six years! So how this body's got to stand it I just can't say.'

Economics of Women in Service

Tennant, Cusack, and James were not the first to relate women's economic and social position lived in outback and rural Australia, country towns and cities. From the British invasion, Australian fiction was thick with women's lives, women on women's wages or lack of them. Australia's literary ranks overflowing with these novelists embracing the politics of women's struggle for independence, the pressures on women faced with marriage as an economic choice, yet with no real choice, like Mrs Hicks, childbearing a woman's duty—not always born with equanimity, and not always fulfilled.

These fictions illuminate wage fixing historically and in contemporary guise. Social values and priorities are intrinsic to job evaluation and thence to wage fixing and equal pay. Even if, in the 1980s, a woman has real choices for marriage, childbearing, career, the historical impact of marriage and childbearing on evaluating women's jobs and the work women do in men's jobs remains. As Burton, Hag and Thompson say, eliminating wage discrimination requires 'more than tampering with internal differences in wage rates' within an organisation, industry, or enterprise. It involves 'challenging social evaluations of the work men and women do …' Sex/gender discriminatory wage outcomes arise from evaluating caring for material assets more highly than for people; valorising masculine physicality over mental effort; and setting formal credentials above qualifications gained from experience outside formal educational institutions. As writers, women based stories on the world around them, acutely understanding these inbuilt biases and their consequences, yet with engaging humour, subtle wit, and stubborn strength. For Ada Cambridge's ***Sisters***, the kitchen sink, the sewing machine, the factory, the wedding ring combine in the joyous clamour and tragedy of the Pennycuick sisters' fortunes, just as for Henry Handel Richardson's Mrs Richard Mahoney in ***The***

Fortunes of Richard Mahoney, Franklin's Sybylla Melvyn of ***My Brilliant Career*** and ***My Career Goes Bung***, and Rosa Praed's ***Fugitive Anne***—otherwise Mrs Anne Bedo.

Like their characters, these authors knew well the social constraints governing women's lives and their impact on work and wages, if women earned any. Equally alert to the necessity of moving beyond boundaries carved out by patriarchal society, they knew this lay at the nub of women's need to retain economic independence and a sense of their own worth and dignity. As women and writers, Cambridge, Richardson, Praed, Franklin, their contemporaries, predecessors and successors could not but be aware. They, their friends and colleagues, all the women around them, lived lives constrained, or suffered the consequences. Yet consequences came, too, if these social and cultural limitations were not denied or thrown off.

So, when the fortunes of Richard Mahoney go bad and Richard Mahoney goes mad, Mary tosses and turns in bed a'night, worrying about his survival, hers, and that of Cuffy and Luce, the children. What's to be done as the wife of the once-respectable town doctor, no skills, little money, and a family to feed? With a pitiful £40-odd standing to his credit in a Melbourne Bank, 'her own poor remnant of Tilly's loan, and everything else gone in a last mad slaughter—deeds and mortgages, letters and securities, down to the last atom of scrip, Richard piling and burning them all, till the dispatch-box was empty'. (How, now, to prove his shareholdings? Or what wasn't owing on the mortgage?) The house at Barambogie a burden, and the Shortlands lease—months to run—how to cover payments and what if they didn't?

Take in boarders? She couldn't. So—*what* could she do? Wanting to work, needing the money, but what work? Despairing, unburdening to old Mrs Spence, solid backstop and friend in anxiety. 'What can a woman do, except teach? I married so young, lack the youth and the brains, what schooling have I had …' Their destiny she sees in the Benevolent Asylum.

Mrs Spence wonders, 'Has it never occurred to you—Government service?' Sage white-cap nodding, it's work as a postmistress suggested.

Mid-nineteenth century gold-rush time, out on the flats at Bendigo and Ballarat. Up to town by coach or train, exiting at Spencer Street Station, hardly anticipating its far later Southern Cross renaming. Mrs Richard Mahoney visiting her doctor-husband in the Kew madhouse, fighting to take him home, back into her care. Tossing at night, awake on the hard hessian palliasse beside him, her friend's words ringing in her ears, sounding out any chance of rest. Postmistress. Rent-free house with the job. A wage—payment enough to rear a family, a postmaster's salary? Husband and children kept together, putting aside fears of parting from them … Paying off those rents, a millstone around her neck, weighing her down like an anchor weighs a ship at port. Yet! The humiliation of working for a living. Publicly listed as a … she, a public woman, a postmistress! Her name—*Richard's* name—and what about listing her age? Some man as her manager. Managing alien young men herself. What of their class? What about her silent friends? Acquaintances, strangers, raising eyebrows at Mrs Richard Mahoney humbled. It would show who *were* friends, yes. But would she be up to the post?

Doubting, doubts dispersing. Taking it on, training alongside men, little knowing she's broken the glass ceiling, or at least driven a fissure into it, before anyone coins the term. Postmistresses few, earnings on a standard scale. Not two, but one—a male scale for a man's job. Not knowing she's in advance of Higgins' ***Fruitpickers*** ruling that women picking fruit should earn men's wages for a man's job, what she first anticipates as public humiliation of being a woman working, a working woman, a century and more later we see as a woman's win, equal opportunity gain and rate for the job. Her earnings her own, she's equal to a man. Doing the work.

Half a century on, her husband left behind her, Ruth Park's Josie Capper of ***Missus*** doesn't doubt her accounting prowess. But is the world ready for a woman accountant, set up in business, taking on the books of every factory and bakery in town? The government paying Mary Mahoney's monthly salary didn't quibble, her arithmetical and money-handling skills as good as the next man's. But is the private sector ready for Josie Capper's entrepreneurial aspirations?

Cambridge knew what obstacles stood in women's path when seeking an independent life in a world of powerful men. She understood well women's need to marry, and marry well. In ***Up the Murray***, ***A Marked Man*** and ***The Three Miss Kings***, she wrote of bondage as the meaning of marriage, not romantic dreams' fulfilment. Holding up to scrutiny the tale-of-marriage harboured in the wild imaginings of girls led into the garden by glittering golden youths, standing subdued yet glorious at their side and coveting only the touch of a gloved hand, for her and her readers it was a story left wanting.

In ***Sisters***, Cambridge has the Pennycuick daughters poised to sail forth splendid into Melbourne society—all but the plain Mary Pennycuick—until a bevy of ills besets them all. Mary, falsely claiming betrothal to the manly Guthrie Carey, young, widowed, and supposed lost at sea. Mr

Pennycuick rushing swiftly into decline upon Captain Carey's unexpected return from the dead exposing his daughter's wicked fancies. Mr Pennycuick, banishing his loathsome child for her lying tongue and hurrying his own abrupt departure from good health upon news of her hasty marriage to penniless clergyman, Goldsworthy. Mr Pennycuick's fortune slurrying even more hastily, pitched into bankruptcy's black pit. Mr Pennycuick following his shares and land holdings into a grave marked only by the simple headstone distinguishing it from the pauper's grave.

No access to a job and equal pay for Mary Pennycuick, plain, unprepossessing, no training at all. Mary, miserable and defeated, punished for fairytale lies of betrothal, banished from home. But can't anyone marry, if only in the right place, right time? Goldsworthy's there, and on time. His to rescue: her from drowning, he from his lonely life of modest means. Clergyman, church, manse, modest stipend—for Mr Goldsworthy, Mary Pennycuick's the catch of the day. So catch her he does, yet, he the fish reeled in from the stream.

Once caught, her independence lost in law—her work lacking work-value. Never mind she supports Goldsworthy, he lacking financial survival without her, their children-to-come winning starvation without her household contribution. Mince cooked in 55 different ways is not even half of it. Making something out of nothing, much out of little, influences industry's determination, replicated in industrial decisions, that women's needs being few means women's wages should be fewer.

For the Pennycuick girls, marriage is career, just as for Praed's ***The Bond of Wedlock***, and Anne Bedo's flight from husband, hearth, and home. ***Fugitive Anne: A Romance of the Unexplored Bush*** has her run from a drunken, brutal husband. A different life, no husband, but a job? A wage, not work unpaid? A fair day's pay for a fair day's work, wage justice for women?

In ***Missus***, Josie tries it. Moving in with her Aunt Alf, leaving wastrel, gambling husband Noel Capper behind, set on the path of independent businesswoman. Married, pressed to resign from Universal Providers, the Capper family firm. No one employs a married woman. For Josie, deprived, resentful, smarting at having her paidwork taken, it's learning more in a month of marriage than in five years of courting. Raging shouts and anger, the house-of-the-honeymoon subsides into sullen silence. Then—the shock of discovery. Her husband's a common crook, embezzling money for years. Prosecution and prison facing him in Trafalgar, he runs. So, is it 'stand by your man', weekly visits behind bars once he's captured, waiting dutifully upon his release? When Josie chooses independence, the Trafalgar gossips glee in their dissection. Of her. Not him.

Park's Josie recognises hypocrisy and injustice in Trafalgar's moral attitude. Still, recognising and scoffing doesn't change it, nor enable Josie to earn a living. Out in the world of Aunt Alf and necessity, a sympathetic priest finds her a job doing the butter factory books. She takes the post at the rate the manager offers, less than the unmarried girls who are on half the male wages, anyway. Yet, ever resilient, ever the optimist, setting up in business, 'Josie Capper Accountancy'—she waits. No clients. No customers. No books to keep. The drapery shop owner, a woman, her last hope. Dashed. 'Never would I hire a professional woman' the retort. Stressed, distressed, and desperate, Josie pleads. 'As a professional woman yourself …' Silence. Then, 'Good day, Mrs Capper'.

$$$$$ and the Single Girl

Yet for Steve, out amongst the pea pickers, doing men's work on company finances and men's work in the fields earns no employer or co-worker prejudice. A different life for her, from that of Josie Capper, born Josephine Kilker of Trafalgar, southeast of Brisbane, northeast of Sydney, dusty and dry, NSW country town.

An independent woman, Eve Langley's Steve of ***The White Topee*** is not much taken by conformity. Her wardrobe, pants, shirts and six panamas, one for each day shading the blinding sun, like her creator taking work that follows the seasons. Langley worked with Bluey, her sister June, at pea picking. Now in ***The White Topee*** she's taken up bookkeeping and accounts, with forays into the fields picking tealeaves. '*Bon giorno, tutti*', she says, unlocking the office door. Papers lie, cool on the desk. The typewriter's black glitter stands in its rich Babylonian glory, awaiting her touch with a deft pair of hands. Dry tealeaves drifting in from the ovens lie strewn on the shadow-dappled floorboards. Steve grabs an old broom, sweeping before sitting to type, Mr McLachlan's correspondence a diminishing pile.

Steve will never marry. Nor Franklin's Sybylla Melvyn—or …? Single or married. Children, no children. Family, no family. What difference to wage justice?

Before the family wage was overridden by the ***Equal Pay Cases 1969*** and ***1972*** and the ***Minimum Wage Case 1974***, laws governing women and children were replete with contradictions. The family wage ignored women's responsibility for their children, as if it had no financial component (at least for women-as-mothers). Yet, when women mothered illegitimate children, they were responsible entirely for the children's health, wellbeing, care, and support, financial and otherwise. The family wage made no concession: women with illegitimate children, like women with children born in wedlock and women with no children received the same wage, substantially less than the family wage. For single women, mothers or not, the proposition that they had a husband to support them meant the family wage did not apply to increase their wage, but decreased it. Just as industrial tribunals manufactured future children (and even wives) for men to extend the family wage to them, they conjured imaginary husbands and fathers of unwedlocked women and their children (where they had them), providing imaginary financial support. Men received money, even without wives or children. With children (and no husbands and, sometimes, no fathers or no paternal support, or dependent husbands or fathers through illness, disability, drunkenness, gambling addiction, profligacy), women received no money for the added burden (children and/or improvident husband or father—sometimes both) or the deficit (no husband or father's support).

Yet married or unmarried, where a woman killed her child, the law held her responsible, whatever the circumstances. When in England Mary O'Donoghue killed her child of 35 days, she was tried for murder, convicted, and sentenced to death, although the judge 'accepted evidence of insanity due to childbirth and lactation effects'. Susan Edwards reports O'Donoghue's signed confession saying she killed her child because she 'had nobody to mind him and no money'. On appeal, the argument that puerperal derangement could last from two to six weeks after childbirth won. The 1922 Infanticide Act applied, her death sentence commuted to life imprisonment. Better label a woman mad, than grant women equal economic rights.

Similarly, for Australia, such cases had no impact on equal pay. Nothing for women to guard against financial distress, despair, and desolation. Instead, make women guilty of manslaughter, not murder, if killing their infants of any age up to a year when suffering hormonal changes, construing infanticide under the Criminal Code Compilation Act 1913 (WA), section 595; NSW Crimes Act 1900, section 22A; Criminal Code Act 1922 (Tasmania), section 332; and Crimes Act 1958 (Victoria), section 6. The expediency of mental derangement satisfied legislatures and industrial tribunals holding the line against wage justice. Yet, women novelists pursued these contradictions long before industrial commissions acknowledged their retrograde policies. As late as the ***National Wage Case 1983***, the Commonwealth Commission told WEL that childcare was for government, not them. It took five more years and the ***National Wage Case 1988*** to change their minds.

Though never knowing it, never paid it, never offered it, Franklin saw equal pay as a right. She knew, too, how different life could be without marriage-as-vocation. Three years after ***My Brilliant Career*** appeared in 1901, she moved to Sydney from NSW country Monaro. Freelance writing took her to Sydney's literary and feminist circles, then abroad. Joining Alice Henry in 1907 at Jane Hull House in Chicago, she worked in the women's trade union movement, co-editing, then editing, ***Labour Voice***, the union's feminist magazine. Seven years later, the First World War, and back in Europe, nursing, then cooking in Macedonia, for those bombed out of their homes. Knowing then, as before, that women were paid women's wages, not men's—if paid at all, and women were denied men's education and training, then were refused men's jobs and access to them.

From the 1970s, Equal Opportunity and Anti-Discrimination Acts became law around Australia and federally, complementing Status of Women Acts passed earlier (exemplified by the Status of Women Act 1921 (WA) pressed for by Cowan). This meant women had equal education rights and employment opportunity, and preventing women from entry or precluding them from jobs on sex/gender grounds was unlawful. Theoretically, equal pay could come through discrimination claims. Yet, legal action is expensive and debilitating, and employers are far better resourced. The very crux of the claim being lack of wage justice makes finances to sustain it less likely, with pressure to settle by compromise if pursued.

'Sooner a bear dancin' on its hind legs than any woman who takes to writing'. Big Checks is an old man, reeking toxicity and taken to life as a tramp, one step down from the tea-agents populating the bush, he roams the tracks as a broken-down swell. 'Bears performin' 'd be more natural, too', he sneers ... 'What with women getting' the vote, how much longer d'you want to live?'

'But don't you think it's fair enough. Women have brains'.

'Brains! Monstrous, that is, brains in a woman's head!'

Central character of ***My Career Goes Bung***, Franklin wonders what it is about women with talent that terrifies men. Assuming for themselves mental superiority, casting women as 'weak-minded, feeble conies', yet 'getting in such a mad-bull panic' when a woman attempts to express herself. Petrified with alarm, off they go 'strutting and blowing' no shame nor humility, conditions fashioned 'comparable to a foot race, them with all the training and the proper shoes and little running pants'. For women its 'harness and winkers still on 'em, lucky if they get to start at scratch'. Hollering and yelling, men claiming first place—the second, the third and all places that count. Women not up to it, be 'against NATURE', so it would. Yet where is the courage that stands stricken at the thought of fair play? No self-respecting woman 'could possibly *respect* men, no matter how strong an appetite she might have for them'. But 'to be sorry for them, as some women pretend, is mawkish', and carrying dissimulation too far.

Written as parody, ***My Career Goes Bung …*** garners strength from the histories of Franklin and women like her. Sybylla Melvyn and 'I', like Tennant's ***Ride on Stranger*** Shannon Hicks, are misfits in a world expecting women to marry and be still. Neither Shannon nor Sybylla, nor 'I' content to enter it, succumb to that status, take the suffering and the silence, wordless, still. Tennant married (a teacher), but worked (for no or unequal pay) as chicken farmer, barmaid, book reviewer, journalist, Australian Broadcasting Commission (ABC) assistant publicity officer, Unemployed Workers' Union (UWU) organiser, church sister, publisher's literary advisor and editor. Like Franklin, she wrote of what she knew, making sure she knew it. Of women's role in paidwork and out of it, weaving the struggle for career and industrial justice, for paidwork and wages, her consistency matched reality as continually woman's lot.

'I cannot pay you', says Mr Litchin to Beryl and Shannon. Querulous in his cantankerous moaning, he's 'a poor man'. 'Ruin, betrayed, my feet bare in my shoes full of holes. See!' Dragging up both trouser legs, rolling them up to the knee. 'I am ruin', grouchy in his complaining. Beryl and Shannon exchange smiles, lowering their eyes. Mr Litchin turns up his eyes, pleas heavenwards. 'Look at the li-tt-el gurrl laughing', he groans. Then he too begins to laugh, nodding in his chin-driven chuckles. 'I am a funny man, I am funny, eh? All ladies love me. Efen littel gurrls, rude, laffin' little gurrls'.

Leaving, Tennant's Beryl takes coat and bag with her, patting Mr Litchin on the shoulder. Strong and tall, leaving Shannon to it. Joseph Litchin, talking everyone into a coma with his self-pitying exhortations of misery and rage, extravagant in his efforts to exhaust his audience. 'A pound a week and all you can eat at midday', he says.

Like Langley and writer, poet, playwright Dorothy Hewett, Tennant knew the value of familiarity with her subject. 'I have long borne the reputation of being an observer of human behaviour, a binocular naturalist objectively recording wildlife in human form', she writes in her 'Introduction' to ***The Battlers***. She sought the society of unlettered and poor people from choice, taking pleasure in their company and gaining more by it than from those more learned. Laughing this off as mere perversity of quaintness was, for her, to ignore the importance she placed in knowing her material and, better still, living and communicating with people whose lives meant life for her at a human level. Not the acidic story-writing of the white wine set (as she termed it), those drinking in an hour all the money her people could live on for a week. The people making up her books' identities, not those of the white wine consumption, lived lives bearing character for recording.

The imperative for recording *real* lives and political action led Hewett into inner suburban Sydney, Redfern factory work. Like ***Come in Spinner***, ***Bobbin Up*** was written for competition: for Hewett, the Mary Gilmore Novel Competition. Completed in 1958, eight weeks of the coldest Sydney winter on record, Hewett's 'Introduction' says ***Bobbin Up*** was written on the end of the laminex kitchen table. Working into early hours, children abed, money and coal run out, warming hands over the electric stove. A job with ***Common Cause***, the miners' paper, fallen though. Same old same old: 'they didn't believe in employing married women'.

Dorothy Hewett wasn't even married, yet her wages supported three sons and Les Flood, her partner, their father. For two years, she'd worked as advertising copywriter for a mail order firm, her advertisements for shoddy goods printed in catalogues shooting out through the country's length and breadth. In the 1950s, women were still agitating for recognition that women, like men, had dependants. So long as a living wage related to men only, employers would hardly acknowledge Hewett and her fellow workers' needs and responsibilities. Women's award wages didn't even support themselves adequately, much less children and errant, ill, or simply unemployed husbands, never mind other relatives.

In ***Bobbin Up***, 16-year-olds advance their ages for adult earnings, rather than 'slavin' their guts out for a kid's wage'. Women's wages are pigeonholed for expenses, just as men's are: food, rent, children. But there's additional expense. It's not just in wartime women need help in the backyard, skills ranging from professional to mediocre and to downright butchery. Not for nothing is a backyard visit known as going to the butcher. Truth concealed in the everyday language of the everyday expedition for the housewife.

For Mary Parker, the £50 0s 0d her erstwhile ***Come in Spinner*** boyfriend sends by wire arrives too late. The £40 0s 0d scrabbled together, savings and layby payments put off 'until next week', plus £5 0s 0d from South Pacific's *Mi Lady* beauty parlour fellow workers is all she has, making that appointment she must make, waiting now under the clock for her sister. Enough to pay a medico's shaky-hands.

Twenty-five bob's the going rate for the ***Bobbin Up*** women, and that's not enough, either. Still, for Marge it's not death that's the problem—this time. Sitting sipping scalding hot tea, either side of the little deal table, it's getting 'in the family way' again. She's said this to husband Arth the night before, if it happens, she'll 'bloody well drown meself''. Indicating toddler Cheryl 'large as life' across the room, 'somethin' from the chemist last time, cost me twenty-five bob … I'd not be without her, now she's here' Marge declares, but still …

Like the rest of them, Marge and Lil know there's no sense crying, whether to keep a job or for a Housing Commission flat. Or for a fair day's wage for a fair day's pay—or rate, the same as a man's. Meanwhile Nell, listening to news of cutbacks, layoffs, slashed wages and rosters, tries to think herself into the women workers' skulls. Tomorrow's payday, 'with Old Holler, Spender, the mill manager, and Union officials already got together, deciding whatever the textile industry and Employer's Federation wanted'. Two or three days a week—not enough for anyone to live on. Married women 'd be first for the sack. 'Hard to predict what any women would do, the factory women even more unpredictable.' Fighting mad, then fizzling out? Shutting up, taking what's dished out? Sticking out their jaws, dogged, gritty, fighting?

She'd been in a strike once. Seen women unite and fight, with resourceful courage no one believed possible … All the while cooking tea and putting the kids to bed, 'while the union made deals with the boss behind their backs' and women made up twenty-eight per cent of the Australian workforce,// keeping the country rich. Then, along comes the union organiser, 'stepping daintily over the wool waste', briefcase in hand, 'fat, round-faced right-winger full of words and wind', all 'false cheerfulness', he says, 'Well, girls. What goes? …' Ingratiatingly yet insouciant he suggests 'ironing this thing out between us?' Well, thinks Nell, 'There's a name for a man who lives off women.'

So, in ***Bobbin Up***, Hewett showed women together in strike action, consistent with the world outside fiction—her factory-floor experience. Through ***Bobbin Up*** she countered the historical stereotype, women's inability for strike action because (again false stereotype) incapable of collective action.

As women's voices have gone unheard in history, or heard less, not listened to, not publicly recorded, or drowned out by louder voices spoken deeper into male-held microphones, assumptions made from a masculinist ethos are projected as truth. This truth-about-women-workers jars against the truth-in-fiction written by women living through the experiences addressed in their work. Stereotypes pinning women like moths on a board too often project themselves as the story of the woman-in-history. Stereotypes envision and promote women as limited to roles and ways of working. The conflict between (some) labour histories and (some) fictional representations shows the fiction as rightly representative, the historical inapt.

On mainstream labour history and its negation of or passing over women's or gender issues, Pocock points out that failure to see women in the landscape affects detrimentally our understanding of the work world, how it operates and its dimensions. This has implications not only for history and historical analysis, but illustrates how other parts of the industrial schema fail to embrace, understand, or acknowledge women's interests and contribution. This follows for wage justice and the equal pay struggle. For Pocock, differences in 'power balance, employment situation, occupation, domestic location between women and men' impact on 'participation in industrial activity, management, unions, agreement making, and institutional influence and effect'. Feminism has argued alongside this 'the necessity of seeing and analysing the link between paid and unpaid work, between the private and the public, between the domestic front and the paid workplace', leading some to propose a definition of work based in 'the "total social organisation of labour" incorporating all forms of labour in the broadest sense, including voluntary household, formal workplace labor and so on …'.

From what they saw, experienced, and understood, women novelists explored the working lives of women through eyes depicting a 'total social organisation of labour'. The moral is that experience can bring with it a better understanding and perception of what is happening on the ground, in turn promoting a better accuracy of recording—whether labelled history or fiction. So, too, a *desire* to see, to describe, and to envision, enabling it to be seen by others, provides possibilities for a more informed understanding. This is the value women's fiction, written when women historians in the formal or academic sense were rare, brings to women's work history and the equal pay struggle.

Yet Jack Looks Out for Himself …

Just as Virginia Woolf in the twentieth century and Arundhati Roy then and now have used non-fiction and fiction to promote ideas, making claims for women's justice and, for Roy, the underprivileged, so too Australian writers and thinkers—Langley, Tennant, Park, Jean Devanny, Oriel Gray, Hewett …

As Hewett, Tennant, Marjorie Barnard, and Florence Eldershaw (M. Barnard Eldershaw), James, Cusack confirm, in both fiction and fact employers greedily figure in every age, every decade. There are those who care little or nothing for workers' industrial rights or safety, wage justice and equal pay, seeking profit above all else. Women are ever vulnerable, and whilst this ethos predominates, society is at risk and women's exposure as low-paid workers even more acute.

With the ***Nurses Comparable Worth case 1985–1986*** repudiating comparable worth, toward the end of the 1980s unions running equal pay for work of equal value claims nonetheless endeavoured to have women's wages lifted commensurate with men's. But without confronting historical underpayments based in embedded undervaluing of women's work and wages as Cusack, James, Franklin, and the others related, equal pay for work of equal value claims failed—although necessary steps along the path—limited by traditional ways of regarding women's work. Occasionally, women's work was contrasted to men's for re-valuing. But work value tests were not focused nor applied to refute unequivocally existing notions of women's (lesser) work value.

Sex/gender bias in wage fixing was replicated in claims made to overcome it, confirming the endemic nature of sex/gender blindness in wage fixing. This opacity does not eliminate differential valuing of paidwork. Rather, it encapsulates a refusal to acknowledge lack of objectivity in wage fixing of women's work, and none in comparisons of women's and men's paidwork.

Entering the 1990s, women's organisations diverge—intervening in ***National Wage Cases***, and demanding industrial laws incorporating anti-discrimination provisions. Now, centralised wage fixing itself is threatened.

Enterprise bargaining looms. Cooperation and collaboration are no longer the touchstones for measuring Australian society. Writers so eloquently extolling women's economic struggle for independence, valuing and self-worth, escaped the uncaring individualism characterising the 1990s. To achieve equal pay, Women's Movement women must now learn to confront and challenge a new wage fixing system. Chapter 17, 'Enterprising Women Confront Enterprise Bargaining—"I'm All Right Jack" versus 1990s Woman' takes women into the final twentieth century decade.

References

Cases—See Case List

Novels—Text (Paraphrasing and Words)

Ada Cambridge, ***Sisters***, Hutchinson & Co, London, 1904; Penguin, Ringwood, Victoria, 1989, pp. 87–93.

Dymphna Cusack and Florence James, ***Come in Spinner***, 1951, Classic Edition, Angus & Robertson, Sydney, NSW, 1994.

Miles Franklin, ***My Career Goes Bung***, 1945, Virago, London, UK, 1981.

Dorothy Hewett, ***Bobbin Up***, Australasian Book Society, Melbourne, Victoria, 1959; Virago, London, UK, 1985.

Eve Langley, ***The White Topee***, Angus & Robertson, Sydney, NSW, 1954.

Ruth Park, ***Missus***, Nelson, Melbourne, Victoria, 1985.

Rosa Caroline Praed, ***The Bond of Wedlock***, FV White, London, 1887; reprint Wentworth Press, London, 2012.

Rosa Caroline Praed, ***Fugitive Anne***, John Long, London, 1902/1903; reprint Valancourt Books, Richmond, VA, 2011.

Henry Handel Richardson, ***The Fortunes of Richard Mahoney,*** William Heinemann, London, UK, 1930; Text—Text Classics, Sydney, NSW, 2012.

Kylie Tennant, ***The Battlers***, Angus & Robertson/Pacific Books Edition, Sydney, NSW, 1987.

Kylie Tennant, ***Ride on Stranger***, Angus & Robertson, Sydney, 1943.

Clare Burton, Raven Hag and Gay Thompson, ***Women's Worth***, AGPS, Canberra, ACT, 1987.

Department of Premier and Cabinet, ***Industrial Relations and State Service Management***, http://www.dpac.tas.gov.au/divisions/irssm/BAK/careers.html#parental, pp. 1–3 (accessed 16 October 2006).

Susan SM Edwards, ***Women on Trial***, MUP, Manchester, UK, 1984.

R. Grams and DP Schwab, 'Systematic sex-related error in job evaluation', ***Academy of Management Journal***, vol. 28, no. 2, pp. 279–90.

Irene Greenwood Collection, MU, Perth, WA.
Florence James, 'Introduction' in F. James and D. Cusack, ***Come in Spinner***, 1951; Angus & Robertson, Sydney, NSW, 1994.
Drusilla Modjeska, ***Exiles at Home***, Sirius Book edn, Sydney, NSW, 1981.
Carmel Niland, ***Personal Communication***, Sydney, NSW, 1979.
Marilla North (ed), ***Yarn Spinners***, Brandl & Schlesinger, Sydney, NSW, 2001.
NSW Royal Commission On the Decline in the Birth-rate and On the Mortality of Infants in New South Wales, ***Report***, Government Printer, Sydney, NSW, 1904.
Barbara Pocock, 'Labour Relations and Work', ***Journal of Interdisciplinary Gender Studies***, vol. 5, no. 2, 2000 (December 2000), pp. 10–26.
Powerhouse Museum, ***Births Of A Nation—Women, Childbirth and Federation***, http://www.powerhousemuseum.com/pdf/education/teachersnotes/births_of_a_nation.pdf, pp. 1–16 (accessed 13 October 2006).

CHAPTER 17

Enterprising Women Confront Enterprise Bargaining—'I'm All Right, Jack' Versus 1990s Woman

The Women's Bureau has ... found:

- women earn less than men in all occupations;
- women in women's occupations earn significantly less than men in men's occupations;
- considerable variation exists between pay ratios across occupations regardless of conventional occupants of those occupations.

Women's Bureau, DEET,
Australian Women's Employment Strategy* –*1988–1989 Report
Canberra, ACT, 1989, p. 5

... differences between women and men's allowance earnings exist in:

- blue-collar occupations of tradespersons, plant and machine operators and drivers, and labourers and related workers, where women earn between 9 and 28 per cent of men's allowance earnings;
- areas like sales and personal service, women workers' earnings from allowances were slightly higher than those of male workers';
- management and administrative areas, [the] few women ... earn significantly more from allowances than men, largely because more female managers are covered by awards than their male colleagues.

'Men earn more allowances than women'
Equal Pay Unit Newsletter, no. 3, July 1982, p. 6
ACTU, Melbourne, Victoria

J. A. Scutt, *Wage Rage for Equal Pay*,
https://doi.org/10.1007/978-3-031-42178-5_17

Ever optimistic, despite economic rationalism infecting government policies, the 1990s open to possibility, women persist in hopes for equal pay.

On 4 March 1989, Canberra gains self-government. On 11 May, the Australian Labor Party (ALP)'s Rosemary Follett becomes ACT Assembly chief minister, first female Australian attorney-general, first female Australian head of government. Under three years later, electors vote her and her party into office again. Just three days before, on 12 February 1992, Carmen Lawrence, WA Labor premier, becomes the first woman leading a state government. On 7 August, heading the Victorian government, Joan Kirner adds another first. Five months more, on 6 February 1993, Roma Mitchell, QC, becomes SA governor, first woman to hold vice-regal office in Australia. Later that year, first Queensland female governor, Leneen Forde, follows.

Church women are on the move, too. On 24 January 1992, ordained in Aotearoa/New Zealand, reverend Dawn Kenyon becomes Australia's first-ever female Anglican priest at Southern Cross, WA. That year, opposite the Supreme Court where for years men alone have held office, on International Women's Day (IWD) St George's Cathedral sees the first Australian ordinations of women. Almost a year later, on 5 December, five women are officially ordained in Adelaide as Anglican priests, while the decade sees Mary Gilmore and Mary Reibey grace the face of banknotes, the first Australian women after Carolyn Chisholm to do so.

Then—governments defeated, Kirner and Lawrence lose office. Economically, women fare poorly. From a high of 83c in the (male) $1.00 at 1980s end, women struggle to maintain this differential, bearing the brunt of unemployment and depression as lowest-paid workers. Follett and her chief minister successor, Kate Carnell—leading the Liberal Party to office mid-decade—end the decade as the only Australian female heads of government ever elected to office. That modest statistic gives no hint of improving.

Men's Principles, Women's Wages

The ***National Wage Case 1987*** restructuring and efficiency principle effected a substantial wage fixing change, as did the 1988 structural efficiency principle, each affecting women's wages and equal pay. Because, unmindful of women's work and industries differences, wage-setting focused on *male* workers, their traditional industries and work, women were bound to lose out. They did.

Under the 1987 principle, the Australian Industrial Relations Commission (AIRC) limited wage increases for 'genuine' paidwork restructuring to improve efficiency and enhance productivity according to needs and requirements of the industry or enterprise. The 1988 wage fixing system built on the restructuring and efficiency principle, structural efficiency being key. Wage increases were dependent on changes to structures limiting industry or occupational productivity and efficiency. Removing award provisions discriminating against sections of the paid workforce was a new element.

In the ***National Wage Case 1988***, the AIRC said 'proper application' of the restructuring and efficiency principle required trade unions, their members, and individual employers working together to remove obsolete working methods inhibiting restructuring and limiting productivity. Some were 'inadequate for the task', some had made 'positive efforts', the best had derived benefits 'producing immediate efficiency and productivity improvements' supporting future improvement. Yet the AIRC was not satisfied the principle should continue 'as understood and accepted by many parties'. For some, the principle's usefulness was exhausted. The rest couldn't be expected to utilise it effectively. Still, any new wage system 'should build on steps already [encouraging] greater productivity and efficiency'.

The AIRC said job satisfaction should be enhanced through setting skill-related career paths; eliminating multi-skilling impediments; creating appropriate relativities within awards and at enterprise level between different categories of worker, flexibility and efficiency through working patterns and arrangements, and minimum rates for classifications in awards with appropriate relativities; updating, etc., respondents to awards; and addressing discriminatory award provisions. Were women included? Each aim could promote women and equal pay. However, the results indicate this was neither intended nor what occurred. For example, 'appropriate relativities' was not directed to relativities between women and men's wage rates, or workers in traditional women's fields and men's work, but to wage rates in fields of men's work, or generally. The focus was male wage rates, and fairness of relativities between them.

To monitor progress of the structural efficiency principle's application to individual awards, the AIRC implemented a review process. This could have focused on whether equal pay was proceeding through structural efficiency, but didn't, even as an 'also'.

At the first ***National Wage Case Review (February) 1989***, the Australian Council of Trade Unions (ACTU) proposed reviewing minimum rates awards 'to ensure classification rates and supplementary payments in an award bear a proper relationship to classification rates and supplementary payments in other minimum rates awards'. The ***National Wage Case 1989*** incorporated this into the minimum rates adjustment principle, providing minimum rates adjustments would be available under five criteria, relating mainly to timing.

Pay rate irregularities was a ***Review (February) 1989*** focus. The AIRC expressed concern about widespread examples of different rates of pay for employees performing the same work under federal awards (notably, not about women vs men's work—a sex bias lapse), saying that for too long inequitable relationships existed among various employee classifications, related to:

- different attitudes in adjustment of minimum rates and paid rates awards;
- different attitudes toward inclusion of over award elements in awards, whether minimum rates or paid rates awards;
- inclusion of supplementary payments in some awards, not others;
- different attitudes toward consent arrangements and arbitrated awards.

The AIRC acknowledged not only a problem of different wage relativities between employees under the same award, but for employees covered by other awards in one establishment. Such relativities 'can vary from workplace to workplace and may bear no resemblance to the relativities set in the award or awards concerned' with 'inevitable' 'feelings of injustice', industrial disruption, unwarranted 'flow-on', and leap-frogging, creating economically unsustainable general wage increases. Of course all this resonates with the equal pay struggle. Yet again women's wages and equal pay were ignored. The focus on the general workforce situation and wage rates confirmed 'general' meant 'men's industrial conditions and pay'.

In the ***National Wage Case 1989***, the AIRC followed up problems pinpointed in the ***Review (February) 1989***. It established minimum classification rates for a metal industry and a building industry tradesperson, saying that achieving a 'proper and lasting reform of awards', considering 'structural efficiency' compliance and fixing minimum award rates as a package, with priority to structural efficiency.

The ***National Wage Case 1988*** and ***1989*** and ***Review (February) 1989*** pinpointing wage relativities discrepancies yet ignoring women's wages redounded unfairly against women. If (as the AIRC acknowledged) inappropriate differences existed in pay rate relativities within and across awards generally, women's pay rate differences would be more pronounced. As the ***Nurses Cases*** acknowledged, women in female occupations carry a negative historic and social pay rates burden. Therefore:

- historically, women's work being valued less than men's requires that devaluing being addressed before women's wages can be assessed fairly with men's.
- as contemporarily women's paidwork is valued less than men's, meaning lower pay rates accrue to women as workers in women's industries,

the AIRC's failure to incorporate this into the 1980s principles meant women's pay rates continued to lag behind men's, women running the risk of falling even further behind. Correcting relativities between men's pay rates through structural efficiency and minimum rates adjustment principles made this inevitable.

Linking pay increases with multiskilling affected women's rights to wage justice, too, ignoring existing multiskilled elements of women's jobs. Under the old system, now sidelined by new wage principles, men were rewarded by pay rates for skill and proficiency in 'one task' jobs. Jobs classed 'skilled' were specialised, skills 'valuable' when concentrated upon one task, or a clearly defined job—crane driver, or forklift driver (not driver with forklift and crane-driving skills); tailor, or garment salesman (not garment worker combining tailoring and wholesale or retail skills); and bulldozer driver, or circular-saws man (not forest worker with bulldozer and circular saw skills) paid more. Men gained higher wage rates by 'moving up'—going from saws man to crane driver, crane driver to supervisor, supervisor to manager ... Women were 'generalists' (in the new language multiskilled or multitasked), jobs covering a range of skills never rewarded on their individual merits. A woman as secretary did keyboard, shorthand, executive and management work, supervising, training—yet 'secretary' was her categorisation and pay rate. Now, being already multiskilled, women had fewer opportunities to gain pay rises based on acquiring *new* skills. Women lost out both ways: under the earlier system, the very fact of having more than one skill, the skills they had being downgraded in monetary terms—they were not the specialists men were; under the new system, they had fewer if any chances to achieve multiskilling afresh. The assumption was that women must have been paid for their skills already (if seen as 'skilled')—disentitling them from higher pay for multi-skills. Of course, women were often classed unskilled, whatever skills they exercised.

Nonetheless, the 1990s saw several attempts at gaining wage increases in women's industries under structural efficiency and minimum rates adjustment. Following an anomalies conference and inquiry into the Child Care Industry (ACT) Award, in 1990 the AIRC heard the ***Child Care Industry (ACT) Award 1985 case (Child Care case 1990)***. 'Members of this industry's workforces, from whom the community expects much, have,' said the AIRC, 'been disadvantaged', forming a lowerpaid workers class the ***National Wage Case 1987*** identified, so coming under the ***National Wage Case 1989*** minimum rates adjustment principle. The AIRC said the childcare industry award fell within pay rate irregularities requiring attention.

Relating to the ACT Child Care Industry Award 1985 and NT Award 1986 only, the ACTU and Federated Miscellaneous Workers' Union (FMWU) said the issues were germane to Australia's childcare industry generally. Seen as a test case, thirteen ACT, NT and Victorian inspections, many witnesses, and 'voluminous written material' exposed the AIRC's limitations on assessing women's work.

Rather than identify and assess actual components of work done, the Full Bench (justice Ludeke, deputy president Marsh and commissioner Laing) concentrated on childcare workers' formal (Technical and Further Education (TAFE) certificate course) qualifications. This entirely overlooked the components or skills of the job: everything lay in formal qualification, nothing more. An extraordinary oversight, not only that the bench ignored its own history of job assessment, but that the unions let them get away with it—even colluded in it.

The AIRC compared the formal childcare workers' qualification, components, and industry status, with the formal qualification of engineering tradespersons in the Metal Industry Award. Emphasising that the classifications 'Child Care Worker Level 3' with one year's service, and 'Engineering Tradesperson Level 1, Metal Industry Award' 'could [not] be "compared" in the conventional sense', the AIRC said they could be compared 'by reference to the training requirements for each classification'. The AIRC used 'level of competence [to] be attained' by both classes of worker: each must hold a certificate awarded in a TAFE college course. The *formal qualification of 'TAFE college course certification'*, by reference to wage rates applicable to the Engineering Tradesperson Level 1 provided the measure of work value and, hence, a table of wage and salary levels for each level of childcare worker, from 'Child Care Worker Level 1' through 'Child Care Worker Level 5', 'Director Level 1' and 'Director Level 2'.

Acknowledging meaningful comparisons are possible across job-types is important. It provides workers in traditional women's fields with possibilities of their work gaining recognition at higher levels of pay consistent with workers in traditional men's fields. However, it isn't enough simply to take as a comparator a traditional men's field. The tendency to value more highly components of men's work or elevate qualifications in traditional male fields intrudes—in this case, blatantly.

Two factors feature significantly. First, the formal qualification measure: why was a Child Care Worker Level 3 with one year's service seen as equal to someone with the formal qualification Engineering Tradesperson Level 1, Metal Industry Award, where no requirement for one year's service exists? Even on formal qualifications, childcare workers' expertise was subjugated to 'superiority' of a male dominated trade—engineering. Secondly, despite no fewer than *13 inspections,* no attempt appears to have been made to assess (for wage setting) value of actual work done in the childcare industry by childcare workers, or even tease out job components.

Far from the Child Care Worker Level 3 plus one year's service equalling the Engineering Tradesperson qualification, the childcare worker's is superior. Childcare worker and engineering tradesperson hold a TAFE certificate, with childcare workers holding an extra—one year's service. Atop of simply looking at numbers—TAFE certificate plus one year's service versus TAFE certificate without one year's service, of what does one year's service consist? Twelve months' direct on-the-job experience.

Blinkered vision meant the AIRC failed to recognise the comparison was unfair, contrarily seeing it as validating childcare workers' salary or wage levels by matching to the engineering tradesperson scale. The AIRC virtually says the childcare worker's wage rate is 'equal' (or fair or just) because since the childcare worker qualification is better than the engineering qualification, no challenge can validly be made to fixing the raised wage levels—shades of Higgins' efforts to sustain Arbitration Court decisions decades before. So, in the ***Registered Nurses (Vic.) case 1985*** nurses missed out by not having the formerly doctors' tasks valued as 'doctors' tasks in setting nurses' salaries. In the ***Child Care case 1990*** childcare workers miss out by having their work value downgraded to that of engineer tradespersons.

The AIRC recitation of competency attainment indicates that equivalence of qualifications (the TAFE classification), comes with completion of the actual course. TAFE Register guidelines for award of a certificate in childcare and engineering tradesperson courses are identical. The AIRC then acknowledges that many childcare workers gain the certificate after two years' fulltime study or its equivalent, with Level 3 and higher appointment dependent not only on the TAFE certificate, but performing prescribed duties for levels in the classification structure, including:

- working in charge of a group of children age range 2–12 years;
- developing, planning, implementing, and evaluating in conjunction with the director a developmental program;
- supervising qualified workers caring for the group of children;
- liaising with parents;
- ensuring a safe environment;
- ensuring up to date records maintained for each child;
- developing, implementing, and evaluating daily routines;
- being responsible to the director for assessment of students on placement;
- ensuring adherence to the centre or service's policies.

As for engineering trades persons, Level 1, NSW required them to undertake trade courses in TAFE streams 3211 and 3212, the primary function to ensure students receive a sound education basic to skills and related knowledge of their trade. Workers continue their apprenticeship while attending the course, attendance for 864 tuition hours required, courses for 'a specific trade requiring a high degree of practical skill usually in a wide range of related activities', performed with a minimum of supervision and direction.

Are these respective requirements equivalent? The AIRC acknowledges they're not, but accepts it's appropriate to provide a pay rate equivalence:

- both must have work experience complementing academic studies, both taught a range of skills calling for exercise of responsibility;
- childcare studies students have approximately twice the number of academic training hours as metal and engineering students;
- two-year courses in childcare studies the TAFE Register rates *at levels higher than the levels for which certificate trade courses are accredited.*

The Child Care Worker Level 3 rate of salary after one year's service should be $407, the rate for the Engineering Tradesperson Level 1 ... Why?

The AIRC is ultimately responsible for the outcome, downgrading childcare qualifications in seeing them as equivalent to a lesser (male) standard. Yet the ACTU and FMWU suggested the comparison. This does not absolve the AIRC for when, on its own assessment, it acknowledged lack of equivalence, it should have questioned why the ACTU and FMWU saw the comparison as apt, and what other comparator existed. An alternative was, in observing the childcare worker's qualification as higher than the suggested comparator, to confirm it warranted a higher pay rate. At bottom, the AIRC could (and should) have investigated childcare work value—value of work on the job, setting wage rates accordingly, the formal qualification as part of the work value assessment.

Why so undervalue childcare workers' qualifications in the first place, by advancing an inapt comparator? Why did neither ACTU nor FMWU see the need to put a case based in the *real* value of childcare industry women's work by reference to the work-content or a comparison with a male qualification and men's work in a male dominated field being a true or at least more apt equivalent?

A barrier to assessing childcare work value is the industrial arena's long-standing difficulty with women's work. Childcare, after all, is what women do at home, in the ordinary course of (most of) their lives, unpaid. How to value work all women do (or are believed or understood to do), and all (or most) men's wives do some time, including wives of men on industrial commissions and tribunals. Babies and young children are fed, clothed, talked with, read to, laughed with, played with, have nappies changed, and are potty-trained by women working, unremunerated, as mothers. The vast bulk of childcare is sans payment, no wage or salary. Industrial arena actors assessing work value are accustomed to not putting a value on women's traditional work. After all, the everyday work women do domestically just happens, without training and absent college, TAFE or university qualification. From this perspective, the work does not become different simply because done outside the home, by formally qualified childcare workers. What work value can accrue to nappy-change, spooning baby-food into an eager or resisting mouth, sterilising and filling a baby's bottle, then ensuring its placement in the right mouth at the right angle, at the right time? How to determine work value on setting down a child to sleep, washing a baby's face and hands before setting them to play in a bouncinette or tinker with a jigsaw or doll? For older children, what is the calculable value of setting them to building a castle from blocks or constructing toy railway or car-racing track, reading to them or supervising their own reading? How value care and responsibility by workers emulating care and responsibility of mothers working for no pay at all? What about management skills? As every woman who has ever worked as a mother knows, time and task management are essential to the role.

Ultimately, trade union advocates, like industrial commission members, have seen women get on with this work without fuss, without wages, in their own homes. Some have been those women and, however committed to the principle and goal that women's work is valuable, demanding proper valuing, this commonsense home-ground knowledge, observation or experience stands ready to subvert efforts to adequately envisage and calculate work value for childcare components in the paidwork world.

'Women's Issues' as Industrial Issues?

Just as the 1980s demonstrated industrial arena inadequacy vis-à-vis nurses' work, so the 1990s with childcare. Further, despite International Labour Organization (ILO) agreements, acceptance of women's workplace issues as industrial remained elusive. Unless women intervened, commissions ignored women's workforce participation or failed to grapple with its real value. Unless catapulted by women's agitation into advancing it, unions too often failed to promote female members' rights. The 1980s warning signs anticipated the 1990s, where policies of both major political parties at federal level undermined women's industrial rights. The ALP promoted enterprise bargaining, demoting centralised wage fixing. The Liberal National Coalition took privatisation further, through individual contracts (Australian Workplace Agreements (AWAs)). Women's industrial conditions worsened, equal pay more distant.

In the ***National Wage Case 1983***, Scutt for the Women's Electoral Lobby (WEL) argued childcare for workers as essential to any industrial system, especially one purportedly endorsing women's wage work. Lacking comprehensive childcare as industrial necessity, women upon whom major responsibility for dependent care (children and ill or elderly family members) falls cannot compete equally in paidwork, nor gain equal pay. Nonetheless, the ACTU did not support WEL, failing to address childcare as crucial. As for the Australian Conciliation and Arbitration Commission, its response was that, like 'many of the problems ... WEL raised', childcare was 'for management, unions and governments [not] award provision'. The incongruity was apparent, considering the preceding ***Maternity Leave Case 1979*** and later ***Adoption Leave case 1985*** where the Commission recognised maternity and adoption leave as necessitating award provision. What, after all, does it benefit women if, taking time away from paidwork to bear a child or care for a child adopted, they cannot return because childcare, or affordable childcare, is unavailable? Leading women to believe childbearing is industrially supported by maternity leave as an award issue, then—refusing to accept childcare similarly—leaving women in the lurch when seeking return to work, exhibits gross disregard for women, as women and as workers. It misunderstands industrial reality and is unsound economically and strategically: why lower economic standards and productivity, through loss of productivity and expertise, simply because women workers are now mothers? This was a focus of the Australian Federation of Business and Professional Women (AFBPW) ***National Wage Case 1990–1991*** submissions.

In the ***Nurses Comparable Worth case 1985–1986***, the Council of Action for Equal Pay (CAEP) was similarly told factors it addressed—'differences in hours worked between males and females, differences in over-award payments and differences in promotional structures'—were 'not readily amenable to award wage prescription and ... not related to the issues raised in [the] proceedings'. Yet each is at the heart of women's pay rate differences. In them, the CAEP reprised in part WEL ***National Wage Case 1983*** submissions. The Commission's response mirrored its 1983 response to WEL and just as the ACTU did not support WEL in 1983, three years later the CAEP felt betrayed.

In the ***National Wage Case 1988***, concentrating on valuing women's work vis-à-vis men's, the National Pay Equity Coalition (NPEC) confronted unambiguously the Commission's notion that, additional to childcare, clustering of women in certain trades and professions was 'a matter for management, unions and government' not it (or state industrial bodies) in setting award provisions. By this time, the ACTU accepted childcare as an industrial issue, an entire childcare section in its submissions. However, the ACTU continued to lag in overlooking labour force stratification, despite Australia's prominence as principal Organisation for Economic Cooperation and Development (OECD) offender.

Two years later, from the early 1990s, the ACTU moved further away from women workers' central concerns, advocating enterprise bargaining replace centralised wage fixing, despite its predictably negative impact on lowerpaid workers, principally women.

That the 'industrial issue' concept is not neutral follows not only from unions and industrial commissions' failure to take up maternity leave and childcare until propelled into it by women's submissions or women unionists' prompting. Danger money or loadings, (protective) clothing, rates for dirty-work, away from home allowances are male-focused. Garbage collectors' work legitimately warrants allowances for dirty-work, this feature of nursing overlooked—until men enter the profession; window cleaners and deep-sea divers' conditions support rates for dangerousness, whereas dangers in social work or nursing did not, despite sexual harassment and sometimes violence. Similarly with teaching, no danger money, despite women teaching classes and students classified as 'worst', whilst male teachers were favoured with 'top' (better behaved) classes. This reflected the failure to cover women's occupations with occupational health and safety agreements.

Nor is the question 'what is an industrial issue?' neutral. Although individual AIRC members (and its precursors) might exhibit a sensibility as to nature and conditions of women's work (for example deputy president Joe Isaac, ***Equal Pay Case 1972***, ***National Wage Case 1983***), not of its own initiative are women workers' concerns embraced. Women's organisations as interveners made submission after submission, meeting scorn and derision, then later—sometimes years later—industrial bodies adopt them, forgetting their original dismissal as inadequate, irrelevant, or just plain wrong.

In the 1990s, in a rare confluence, the ***National Wage Case 1990–1991*** saw the AIRC agree with AFBPW that centralised wage fixing be maintained, preserving the possibility of improving relativities between male and female wages. This, despite the ACTU's submission advocating enterprise bargaining, so raising not only ACTU ire but that of the federal Labor government. At the following ***National Wage Case 1991***, women lost out, centralised wage fixing went by the board, and enterprise bargaining began undermining fair(er) Australian wage setting and, with it, hopes women had maintained over more than a century of equal pay becoming a reality.

Undermining Industrial Rights and the Equal Pay Principle

Lowpaid workers in Liquor Trades Union (LTU) jobs, like other lowpaid workers, depended for rises and improved industrial conditions upon concerted union action through centralised wage fixing. Unions representing higher-paid workers with industrial muscle ensured lower-paid workers' interests were promoted. At federal and state level, centralised wage fixing meant lower-paid workers' rights through flow-ons from more powerful union gains.

The strongest unions represent male dominated work. In industries where part-time workers or casuals predominate, workers' power to sustain or improve working conditions is far less than with fulltime workers dominant. Where work is classed essential to productivity and withdrawal of labour impacts negatively upon profit levels and output, strongly unionised male fulltime workers have considerable bargaining power. Through centralised wage fixing, stronger unions gained higher wage rises and improved industrial conditions for their members, lower-paid workers benefitting, through maintained wage levels and updating of their awards consistent with updating of higher-paid workers' awards.

Benefits flowed to women, generally occupying lower-paid industries and trades, or classed as unskilled workers. Under centralised wage fixing, women's complaints of relatively poor conditions, underpayment, undervaluation of work and lack of equal pay were well-founded. However, male-female wage and conditions relativities were fairer than in countries where individual contracts or collective or enterprise bargaining prevailed. At 1980s end, Australian women workers were second only to Scandinavians in equal pay. In Sweden, Denmark, and Norway, male-female wage relativities reached approximately 87 per cent to 90 per cent. In Australia, the figure was 81.7 per cent for fulltime workers. Including part-time workers' wages saw this fall to 67 per cent. However, both figures well exceeded Japan's relativities for male and female fulltime workers in paid employment (55.7 per cent), and the part-time figure was closer to relativities for US fulltime women workers (70.3 per cent). Japan and the US utilise enterprise bargaining and individual contracts for wage fixing.

On 15 July 1989, AFBPW's major conference 'Pay Equity, The Gender Gap—Justice Delayed is Justice Denied', revitalised equal pay as a site of women's struggle. Initiated by Buswell and Arditto of Business and Professional Women (BPW) Hunters Hill, the conference wrapped up with a debate between Burton and Scutt on lobbying federal and state governments for Equal Pay Acts (Burton), or taking arguments once again to the AIRC (Scutt). The pro-AIRC argument was that, having set down equal pay principles, the AIRC must be pressed to make them work. That an onus lay on ACTU and unions to initiate claims should not preclude the AIRC from referencing its own equal pay decisions in national wage setting. Why not require ***National Wage Case*** parties to incorporate equal pay into submissions? Why not implement WEL's ***National Wage Case 1983*** standing equal pay Full Bench proposal? Why not call on parties to the 1969 and 1972 Equal Pay decisions for a progress update? As to equal pay legislation, women had waited too long for industrial bodies, the ACTU and unions to effect equal pay as a practical measure: decisions fine on principle, short on implementation. The efficacy of state and federal equal opportunity and anti-discrimination legislation was questioned, too. Equal pay laws (depending how framed) could broaden categories of those entitled to bring claims (say individuals or women's organisations, Working Women's Centres (WWCs) and the like), provide compensation payouts for women workers denied equal pay, and require application of equal pay principles with all wage rises.

No real conflict: women's organisations' intervention in ***National Wage Cases*** would not prevent them or other women's organisations lobbying for equal pay laws. Those focusing on equal pay laws could equally demand industrial bodies take seriously their own decisions. In the 1990s, the two sides worked cooperatively on tactics. NSW AFBPW Pay Equity Committee invited NPEC members Burton and Hall to join discussions before the ***National Wage Case 1990–1991***, precipitating action in state industrial commissions, too.

AFBPW's ***National Wage Case 1990–1991*** intervention saw for the first time:

- albeit implicit in D'Aprano's Women's Liberation Movement (WLM) ***National Wage Case 1973*** intervention and interventions in the ***National Wage Cases 1983*** and ***1988***, explicit objection to making wage guidelines as if women's wages and equal pay were irrelevant, emphasising the guidelines could not be set without them; and
- at least since the 1930s or 1940s, representation was accepted as remunerative work for counsel and instructing solicitor—adopting pay principles for women's work.

Most critical was retaining centralised wage fixing.

The AIRC said the ACTU claim for enterprise bargaining met 'broad support' though 'a marked divergence of opinion' on implementation, but AFBPW, 'though supporting other aspects of the ACTU claim, opposed the enterprise bargaining proposal' and, later, AFBPW 'expressed outright opposition to the enterprise bargaining proposals', concerned it would 'worsen women's position'.

AFBPW referred to the Department of Employment, Education and Training (DEET) Women's Bureau assessment, that 'no necessary correspondence' exists between negotiated pay rates and equal pay. Collective (or enterprise) bargaining resulting in compromised pay rates 'may contribute to fixing women's rates of pay below those established through work value assessment'. Practical problems include contracting out work to avoid pay equity, and difficulties facing unions wanting access to 'complete and accurate knowledge of job information and wage-setting practices, … crucial to pay inequity identification'. Difficulty increases where 'the male comparison group is in another bargaining unit or an unorganised unit'. How could or would other unions in an establishment share access to information—should 'disclosure clauses' be negotiated into collective agreements? That enterprise (or collective) bargaining requires union representation was another concern, AFPBW noting that the ACTU submission of some 200 pages plus appendices devoted one and half pages to women's wages, as did the federal government's, prompting little confidence that women's wages would be pursued under enterprise bargaining.

The AIRC devoted part of its decision to pay discrimination, noting 'the alleged persistence of discrimination against women and danger it might be exacerbated by enterprise bargaining proposals urged … by major parties' was an issue additional to those 'debated most extensively' in the case—including scope for wage increases, superannuation, and enterprise bargaining generally. Addressing pay discrimination in detail, AFBPW 'did not assert that any awards differentiate explicitly between male and female workers', but that 'the wage fixing system evaluates skills and job attributes' so that work typically performed by women 'tends to be devalued relative to work typically performed by men':

> The AFBPW asked the Commission to convene a [Work Skills Value Enquiry (WSVE)] to require all aspects of skill evaluation, including those [having] a bearing on the relative evaluation of male and female work. It also opposed the proposed movement toward enterprise bargaining, arguing that this would adversely affect women.

Acknowledging negative consequences of enterprise bargaining for women workers and wages for women's work, the AIRC said it 'could not predict the extent of disadvantage female workers [would] experience' if approval were given—but bargaining generally and particularly for over award payments—'places at a relative disadvantage … the labour force where women predominate'. Parties and interveners might give this issue more attention 'in future considerations of enterprise bargaining' the AIRC suggested.

AFBPW's proposed WSVE aimed at setting guidelines for employers, unions, and the AIRC to ensure its equal pay decisions could be implemented effectively. For AFBPW, Scutt said the WSVE would 'clarify, in providing guidelines to employers, unions and the Commission, how skills, responsibility and conditions of work are to be measured and considered for award restructuring, implementation of the structural efficiency principle, and wage determination'.

Contending this would 'prove nebulous', in rejecting it the AIRC nonetheless affirmed continuing need for equal pay review, asserting current principles (including 'special case' provision) 'already provide ample scope for review of specific instances where work typically performed by females is allegedly undervalued'. Confirming 1972 equal pay principles 'continue to apply and would be a relevant consideration in any such case', moving on smartly the AIRC paid minor attention to women's legitimate pay claims. The ACTU, federal government supporting, 'called upon the Commission to ensure that the structural efficiency principle is implemented in a non-discriminatory manner'. Here, the AIRC acknowledged citation, by the ACTU, of cases where 'in its view, implementation of structural efficiency has led to discrimination, for example, lack of training for some part-time employees'.

The Industrial Relations Act 1988 (Cth) incorporated direct reference to discrimination, requiring (by section 93) the AIRC to 'take account of' Racial Discrimination Act 1975 (Cth) and Sex Discrimination Act 1984 (Cth) principles. This did not advance the matter, however, for the AIRC went no further than reiterating that parties appearing before it in individual cases 'should raise any issue relevant to those proceedings they consider inconsistent with' section 93 requirements.

Yet imprecations are not enough. If industrial commissions (and unions) do not know what they are looking for, or cannot comprehend how they undervalue women's work, saying the issues should be raised hardly advances equal pay claims and wage justice. AFBPW's call for a WSVE aimed to provide sorely needed assistance to the AIRC and parties, enabling them to develop a grasp of the institutionalised structural nature of sex/gender based discrimination in industrial conditions and wage setting, to establish a means of systematically overcoming it through guidance for valuing women's work. That this proposal was rejected as unnecessary, viewed as 'nebulous', confirmed not only the AIRC's failure to accept limitations of existing wage discrimination mechanisms, but failure to understand work components can identified to expose underlying assumptions and presumptions causing women's work to be devalued and underrated. The notion that individual cases can achieve equal pay further corroborates the problem. (Un)equal pay is not isolated to single instances, nor able to be combatted by a one-off approach. Systemic discrimination requires a structural antidote.

For WSVEs, AFBPW proposed the Affirmative Acton Agency (AAA) (later Equal Opportunity for Women Agency (EOWA)), federal Industrial Relations Department Pay Equity Branch, DEET Women's Bureau, and state equivalents be called on for expertise and the AIRC 'should explicitly recognise the principle of equal pay as a central component of national wage fixing, adding the AIRC:

(a) must confirm its continuing commitment to its own equal pay determinations;
(b) in approving award restructuring agreements and agreements implementing the structural efficiency principle must ensure equal pay principles are not overlooked or inadequately considered;
(c) should ensure that under all agreements women have equal access to training and retraining programs, appointments, and promotion;
(d) should ensure women's traditional industries, work, trades, and professions under the AIRC's jurisdiction provide, through restructuring:
    1. career paths; and
    2. adequate and proper recognition of value of work done by women, and the skills utilized by women, in those industries, work, trades, and professions.

Ignoring all this and its own dismissal of enterprise bargaining in the ***National Wage Case 1990–1991***, six months later, on 30 October 1991, in the ***National Wage Case 1991*** the AIRC acceded to the ACTU and industry. Enterprise bargaining was set for Australia's wage setting, centralised wage fixing effectively abolished. Thus from 1 December 1991, under the Industrial Relations Act 1988 (Cth) section 112 (consent award if 'in the public interest') or 115 (memorandum of agreement—certified agreement), the AIRC would approve enterprise bargaining agreements made between parties bound by minimum rates or paid rates awards, subject to requirements, none covering equal pay obligations or ensuring women's and lower-paid workers' (mostly women) wage rights would be maintained.

When an agreement expired by effluxion of time, responsibility lay with the parties to seek renewal or replacement. For workers unable to negotiate gains through enterprise agreements, awards remained, leaving them with terms, conditions, and wages set by the AIRC. These workers would inevitably be disadvantaged, because awards would not be updated and improved through flow-ons from stronger unions taking claims through the Commission: stronger unions would be negotiating with employers in enterprises solely for their members in that enterprise or part of it. Wage increases negotiated by strong unions through the enterprise bargaining process would accrue to their members alone, without impacting on lower-paid workers' wages. If the enterprise agreement related to one part of the enterprise only, there might be flow-on to other parts, if workers had union representation and hence ability to gain their own enterprise agreement. Even then, the AIRC raised localised flow-on as a possible negative impact.

For workers outside enterprises where strong unions prevailed, and non-unionised workers in all enterprises, enterprise bargaining spelled a growing divide. Within enterprises, danger remained that weaker unions and workers lacking similar bargaining power would languish in relatively poor industrial conditions, a growing gap between their wages and conditions and those of stronger colleagues.

As women's paid workforce position remained unchanged, women less likely to be unionised, more often members of weaker unions, the scene was set for backtracking on advances in male-female wage relativities, and a growing industrial conditions divide. Women would remain reliant upon the AIRC, rather than negotiating enterprise agreements or being recipients of conditions and wages negotiated through them. So it happened, AIRC endorsed enterprise agreements in the years following the ***National Wage Case 1991*** negotiated predominantly male industries and male jobs: enterprises centred on jobs traditionally held by men.

In 1992, almost ten years after WEL in the ***National Wage Case 1983*** raised over award payments as significant in (un)equal pay, the Labor government amended the Industrial Relations Act 1988, affirming the AIRC's capacity to take over award payments into account. This could be heralded as an equal pay advance, but so long as unions sought over award payments as recognition for work and productivity, so long as work and productivity were rewarded by employers with over award payments, and so long as work value and productivity were assessed along sex/gender lines, sex/gender bias in total remuneration would remain. In 1951, ILO's C100 Equal Remuneration Convention recognised this, defining remuneration as:

> ... the ordinary, basic or minimum wage or salary and any additional emoluments whatsoever payable directly or indirectly, whether in cash or in kind, by the employer to the worker and arising out of the worker's employment.

C100 calls for equal pay for work of equal value, incorporating equal remuneration so that base pay equality cannot be claimed to eliminate sex/gender wage discrimination. True wage equality is grounded in base pay *plus* other in cash or in kind paidwork benefits.

For Australia, legislative confirmation that wage justice necessarily meant remuneration equality for women and men was an important step. Yet this came simultaneously with manufactured obsolescence, led by the ACTU and Labor government, ultimately with AIRC's acquiescence, of centralised wage fixing. The result: any allowances, benefits, and all other additions to basic wage or base pay (in the award system 'over award payments') will generally be gained by workers belonging to strong unions, in highly unionised areas, with negotiating power with employers through enterprise bargaining. In other words, above base payments would not accrue to women equally with men, whatever the Industrial Relations Act might say. Hence, not unlike the ***Minimum Wage Case 1974*** extension to women just as the minimum wage was phased out, this was another pyrrhic equal pay victory.

In amending the Industrial Relations Act 1988 the federal Labor government moved further from centralised wage fixing, consequently dividing workers in strong versus weak unions and non-unionised workplaces, downgrading AIRC involvement in conditions and wage setting. AIRC enterprise agreement endorsement removed wage fixing from community and public interest into a privatised realm, employers setting wage levels ostensibly based on productivity in consultation with unions. Unlike centralised wage fixing, unions other than those directly involved in an enterprise agreement could not join. Unless the federal government was an employer and, hence, party to an enterprise agreement, it had no role. Governments had no intervention power when enterprise agreements were before the AIRC for endorsement. Nor was there provision for intervention by employers or employer groups, nor for interest group intervention. Women's organisations had no role in enterprise agreements.

Awards remained as a 'safety net' in two ways.

First, an enterprise agreement must meet 'no disadvantage' and 'public interest' tests, measured by reference to the award covering workers prior to the agreement. Public interest had a limited scope and 'no disadvantage' simply meant an enterprise agreement should not disadvantage workers by fixing terms and conditions below levels struck in the award immediately predating the initial enterprise agreement. Once employers and employees advanced to their second enterprise agreement, no relevant award existed by which terms could be measured. A global test meant provisions in the original award could be undercut without censure at second enterprise agreement stage, and thenceforth.

Secondly, a safety net provided for lower-paid workers through the AIRC award system applying to workers unable to negotiate enterprise bargains or employer agreements. A growing division between higher and lower-paid workers, haves and have nots, ensued, steadily more pronounced, anticipating an even greater breakdown in wage setting fairness when in 1996 federal Labor lost power.

The ***National Wage Case 1991*** enterprise bargaining scheme did not propose replacing the award system entirely, nor phasing out AIRC wage fixing involvement. However, it paved the way for Howard Liberal National Coalition government individual contracts and non-union negotiations without union involvement, with even more serious implications for equal pay.

Going (Further) Backwards—Towards Survival of the Fittest

When the Liberal-National Coalition government comes to power federally, centralised wage fixing is declining. The ACTU-led push to enterprise bargaining through the ***National Wage Case 1991***, promoted by the federal Labor government through its Industrial Relations Act, now leads to the Liberal Coalition government's AWAs and conservative industrial policies. Nineteenth-century employer right stages a comeback, ordinary workers, particularly lower-paid, the losers. With less industrial clout, perceived as lacking skills, their labour less valuable and, hence, less valued, realistically ordinary workers cannot negotiate individual contracts with increased benefits and improved conditions. Flexibility is the employer's prerogative, their interpretation of what flexibility means preeminent. Contradictions proliferate. Public servants, academics, and human resources managers attend seminars and conferences, endlessly discussing family friendly workplaces. Ordinary workers' conditions deteriorate. Some employers stand by or promote industrially sound workplace conditions. Yet more exploit increased deregulation.

Measures supporting post-maternity return to work and time out for childbearing, childrearing, and childraising then, later, caring for older family members—mothers, fathers, elderly aunts and uncles, adult children, or partners with a disability—are traded off, taken away or not provided by employers.

Despite rhetoric promoting flexibility as a key employee advantage, workers comply with employer-set working hours suiting the workplace, not accommodating employee family and living needs. For ordinary workers, benefits and improved conditions are insubstantial. Those at the top—chief executives, executive directors, large private and public sector businesses managers—gain, awarded higher and higher incomes and better conditions, frequently including bonuses for implementing economic rationalist policies through downsizing—terminating employees at least company cost and demanding more work (called productivity) from fewer workers, whatever their cost, whatever the stress to those remaining.

The Workplace Relations Act 1996 (Cth) replaces the Industrial Relations Act, heralding a free enterprise regime. Although retaining the AIRC to oversee minimum wage fixing, supervise awards not eliminated by enterprise bargaining or contracts, and arbitrate disputes, the Workplace Relations Act establishes the Office of Employment Advocate (OEA) to oversee individual worker-employer contracts—AWAs. This role could be filled by the AIRC. Now, the OEA must build processes and expertise, effectively duplicating the AIRC, yet lacking experience or expertise. The changes provoke concern for the AIRC's future, spurred by the Liberal Coalition government's consistently negative views about its wage fixing role.

In 1996, the legislation before Parliament, women's organisations rallied, lobbying government, opposition, and minority parties, particularly the Australian Democrats, with roundtable conferences and meetings in Sydney, Melbourne, and Adelaide, Melbourne sending a delegation to Canberra—meeting MPs and holding a Parliament House press conference. In Adelaide, on Thursday 20 June 1996 women staged an information and organising forum at Pilgrim Hall, planning a Senate Economics References Committee Inquiry submission. Leaflets called the Workplace Relations Bill a 'threat to Women's progress towards equal pay', placing women 'at a clear workplace bargaining disadvantage', award provisions threatened, AIRC role restricted, paid rates awards covering public sector women—teachers, nurses, social workers, etc.—abolished, 'breaking the government's promise that no one will be worse off … and more'. In Sydney, trade union women and WEL, AFBPW, the Young Women's Christian Association (YWCA), and Women's Economic Think Tank (WETTANK) representatives meet with Peter Reith, industrial relations minister. NPEC confers with Democrats leader, Cheryl Kernot, resulting in retention of Sex Discrimination Act 1984 (Cth) provisions albeit efficacy questions remaining), and an amendment requiring an annual Workplace Relations Department review of the new laws' impact on women, workers of minority ethnic background and youth.

However, the Workplace Relations Act was harsh on women and unhelpful to equal pay claims, incorporating problems created by enterprise bargaining, compounded by AWAs. Power and negotiating capacity became even more pronounced, militating further against equal pay. Admonishments that the AIRC should 'take account' of domestic discrimination legislation and international family responsibilities law set in the Industrial Relations Act continued into the Workplace Relations Act 1996 (Cth) did not help. What does 'take account' mean, particularly when the AIRC took no positive steps to ensure compliance with its own equal pay decisions, and had to be told national wage guidelines cannot be set without reference to the equal pay principle? If its own equal pay decisions had so little practical relevance to its broader decision-making processes and already existing general wage fixing responsibilities, it was difficult to see that a legislative obligation to take account of the Sex Discrimination Act 1984 (Cth) or ILO Family Responsibilities Convention could have much impact. Nothing in the Workplace Relations Act instituted training for members in provisions, scope or import of the Sex Discrimination Act (or any other discrimination laws, conventions or treaties), and no education program was established around the Act's provisions, application, and operation. The notion that the AIRC (or OEA) would automatically know or understand the legislation is remote from reality. So, too, any contention it would through its own resources understand how sex/gender discrimination impacts in the workplace, wage setting, and conditions.

Nonetheless, by every intervention, submissions based in women's work realities, traditional and non-traditional jobs, and working lives, women's organisations devoted years to educating the AIRC and its forerunners. The AIRC (with its state counterparts) could develop equal pay as a rights issue, with women's labour market expertise centre-stage. However critical of the AIRC the Women's Movement might be, women's groups had used the AIRC's open processes. Equal pay advocacy from a women-centred perspective and argument that national wage guidelines must incorporate equal pay principles came from them. The AIRC's ***Equal Pay*** and ***National Wage Case*** decisions could be explored, inadequacies and direction for improvement highlighted for future interventions.

The AIRC set the equal pay pace in the ***Equal Pay Cases 1969*** and *1972*, and the ***Minimum Wage Case 1974***. Women interveners' advocacy was crucial, highlighting, in cases following, the need to keep women's wages and equal pay on the agenda, women as advocates. The educative impact was real. Despite limitations, the AIRC progressed towards equal pay. Now, the Workplace Relations Act provided the OEA with no mechanism for hearing intervener submissions, no process for arguments by equal pay advocates, and no AWAs transparency.

The Workplace Relations Act provided for two types of industrial or workplace agreements:

- collective agreements—under the federal corporations power or made in Victoria (it having referred the state's industrial power by the Commonwealth Powers (Industrial Relations) Act 1996 (Victoria); and
- individual agreements or AWAs.

A Division 2 agreement was a collective agreement between employees and corporations, the federal government, or Victorian employers. A Division 3 agreement was a collective agreement made in prevention or settlement of an industrial dispute.

Employer negotiations realistically require union representation or at least agents coming to the table from a position of strength. Women's organisations acted. The National Council of Women (NCW) published ***Work-Life Management—How to Get the Balance***. AFBPW advocated joining unions. Traditionally like NCW amongst the more conservative of feminist groups, positioned towards private sector rather than public job market, promoting women's business interests and individualism rather than workers' collectivism, AFBPW had already been defiantly activist in AIRC interventions. The Workplace Relations Act precipitated AFBPW into a collective and union orientated approach. Women's union membership rose.

The 'public interest' admonition provided potential for holding down women's wages. Contentions that the economy will not sustain equal pay, employers will be disadvantaged or cease to hire or retain women at wages commensurate with men's can be incorporated into 'public interest' by advocates or commissions disposed against women's wage justice. How (some would ask) can it be in the public interest if the economy is damaged or deflated by increased women's wages? How (they ask) is public interest fulfilled if employers are deterred by high wages from hiring women or keeping them on as employees? In the ***Equal Pay Cases 1969*** and ***1972*** these arguments did not prevent the Commission from deciding equal pay for equal work and equal pay for work of equal value. However, contentions that women's wages should be limited or capped resonates in poor economic times. Industrial myths that women's work is not as valuable as men's, women don't need the money men do, women are not responsible as household head for family upkeep, not breadwinners, put commitment to care of family ahead of personal paidwork ambition, meant women were rightly concerned at public interest being defined against women's interests, unfavourably for equal pay.

As for individual agreements, the Workplace Relations Act provided for corporations and federal government to make AWAs with OEA approval. Aware that union membership may be insufficient, unions representing women tending towards lesser strength and power, women's work being taken for granted or not adequately valued, AFBPW published and widely distributed ***Why Should Women Play Snakes and Ladders*** and ***The Workplace Bargaining Game***, explaining the new industrial relations system and encouraging women to develop negotiating strength and expertise. Women must familiarise themselves with the AWA system which required individual skills, as well as identifying negotiators to overcome power imbalances in workplace.

Some themes carried through to the new regime, including enterprise agreements under the Industrial Relations Act. The Workplace Relations Act set generic requirements covering collective and individual agreements by the no-disadvantage test, identical to that in the Industrial Relations Act. Lacking a relevant award, one or more suitable awards could be construed to assess an agreement. However, because it was a global test, an agreement could be approved under the no-disadvantage requirement, even if not meeting individual components of an award or legislative requirement. If it did not, in AIRC or OEA estimation, on an overall assessment disadvantage employees covered by it, then the no-disadvantage test was met, meaning the agreement must be approved. Even if a collective agreement did not meet the no-disadvantage test, the agreement would be certified so long as the AIRC deemed it not contrary to the public interest. The specific example provided by the Workplace Relations Act was where the agreement was part of a reasonable strategy addressing a short-time crisis and would assist in a business revival. Workers' rights to fair industrial conditions were subjugated to employer demands, contingent on the employer's shaping an argument that its business survival required downgrading workers' conditions and rates of pay.

This had potential to affect detrimentally both male and female workers. However, once again myths made women more susceptible, likely to be 'first cab off the rank' where employer demands demoted terms and conditions. Women's purported 'reserve army of labour' status feeds into such a regime. Furthermore, being disposed to support the employer or place the employer's interests ahead of their own, women could be prompted to trade off conditions and pay.

In addition to the no-disadvantage test, conditions governing certification of collective agreements required that employers take reasonable steps to explain the terms to everyone covered (taking individual circumstances—youth, language, sex/gender—into account); employers should not coerce employees; and employees should have reasonable time to consider terms and their agreement, majority acquiescence required. When aimed at settling an industrial dispute, additional provisions governing AIRC approval included satisfaction that the agreement would indeed settle it, preventing further industrial disputes between the parties, or preventing generation of an employee dispute.

These conditions simply replicated constitutional requirements governing AIRC jurisdiction. The difference between the Workplace Relations Act regime and centralised wage fixing system was, however, that in the past strong or powerful unions (in male dominated industries or workplaces) appeared with employers to settle agreements (awards) or prevent further disputes about wages and conditions in those industries or workplaces, the AIRC's decision covering a wide range of workers. Now, ***Living Wage Cases*** were supposed to govern lower-paid workers.

As for AWAs, OEA approval depended upon OEA satisfaction that the AWA included:

- anti-discrimination and dispute resolution provisions as prescribed by the Workplace Relations Act regulations (otherwise model provisions were applicable);
- no provisions prohibiting or restricting disclosure of details of the AWA by either party to another person;
- a nominal expiry date, not more than three years after AWA date of commencement;

And was:

- upon filing with the OEA:
  - signed and dated by each party, signatures witnessed;
  - accompanied by an employer declaration containing all required provisions, plus before signing, the employee was provided with an OEA information statement and a statement whether or not the employer offered an AWA in identical terms to all comparable employees;
  - confirmed by the employer to have been provided to the employee with any other information indicated by the OEA;
- given to a new employee at least five days and, to an existing employee at least fourteen, before signing;
- explained to the employee the AWA's effect, between time of the employee's first receiving a copy and time the employee signed it;
- genuinely consented to by the employee; and
- offered, by the employer, in identical terms to all comparable employees, unless the employer did not act unfairly or unreasonably in failing to do so.

The Workplace Relations Act itself effectively acknowledged that just as some workers would not be included in collective agreements, AWAs would not be negotiated with, or pressed upon, all individual workers not under collective agreements. This acknowledgement came through the ***Living Wage Case*** safety net, fixing wages for workers, at minimal levels, commensurate with the economic argument—however misplaced—that lower wages increase employment.

Australian Bureau of Statistics (ABS) figures showed over 60 per cent of 1.6m paid workers on minimum wages were women. Approximately 75 per cent of workers earning less than $600 per week were women, mainly in hospitality (accommodation, cafes, restaurants), elementary clerical, sales and retail. Whatever qualifications, experience, talents, capacities, and abilities they brought to their work or learned on the job, these workers were classed unskilled, their work dismissed as basic and hence insufficiently valuable to warrant employer-union negotiation for collective agreements, or individual negotiation for AWAs. For these workers, it was unrealistic to suggest employers negotiating individual contracts would provide high or higher levels of wages than the going rate, if that. If AWAs were offered to unskilled workers, no reason to expect employers would set wages beyond the minimum, or industrial conditions beyond the lowest levels. For hospitality workers (including accommodation, cafes, restaurants), elementary clerical, sales and retail, family responsibility and paid maternity leave hardly figured.

In addition to sex/gender, many lower-paid workers come within additional disadvantage, including non-English speaking or migrant backgrounds, comprising some three quarters of low-paid workers, Indigenous Australians, youth, workers in non-unionised workplaces, and/or small business employees. These added barriers made women workers even less likely to have AWAs containing higher wage levels and improved industrial conditions. Hence, ***Living Wage Cases***—first heard in the AIRC, then by the Fair Pay Commission (FPC) under the Work Choices Act 2005 (Cth)—were crucial.

If ***Living Wage Cases*** did not deliver wage rises abreast of wage increases gained by higher income workers (mainly men) and inflation through collective agreements, the wages gap increased.

At 1990s end, a 'second wave' of industrial relations changes, amendments to the Workplace Relations Act, came before Parliament. Again, women organised, in 1999 WEL and NPEC appeared before the Senate Committee of Inquiry and met with the minister. NPEC organised a

Sydney rally, speakers from NPEC, Asian Women at Work, and the Association of Non English Speaking Background Women of Australia joining WEL, AFBPW, YWCA, Women's Information Referral Exchange (WIRE), and National Council of Single Mothers and their Children. Outside the Senate Committee hearings, Suzanne Jamieson declared the Workplace Relations Bill Mark II 'an Arachnophobiac's nightmare'; women must not be entangled in the 'web of lies' woven by the workplace relations minister.

Chapter 18, 'Alarums and Excursions—The Inside Story' explores women's response to the Liberal Coalition government's changes of the 1990s. Women's organising, planning, and analysing government proposals infuse Women's Movement action.

References

Cases—See Case List

Women's Bureau, DEET, ***Discussion Paper No. 5—Pay Equity—Survey of Seven OECD Countries,*** AGPS, Canberra, ACT, 1987.

Meredith Burgmann, ***Personal Communication***, Sydney, NSW, 2006 (26 June 2006).

Clare Burton, ***The Promise and the Price***, Allen & Unwin, Sydney, NSW, 1991.

Clare Burton, Raven Hag and Gay Thompson, ***Women's Worth***, AGPS, Canberra, ACT, 1987.

Val Buswell, 1993, ***Personal Communication***, Sydney, NSW, 1993 (June 1993).

Brad Norrington, ***Jennie George***, Allen & Unwin, Sydney, 1998.

CFMEU, ***As a Union Movement We Chose Enterprise Bargaining: … (CFMEU)***, http://cfmeuvic.com.au/storage//documents/Horses%20for%20Courses-10%20years%20of%20enterprise%20Bargaining.doc, pp. 1–33 (accessed 2 August 2006).

Naomi Steer, 'News—Spiderman Strikes as Women Sink Second Wave', ***Workers OnLine***, no. 37, 1999 (29 October 1999), pp. 8–9, http://workers.labor.net.au/37/print_index.html, pp. 1–42, at pp. 8–9 (accessed 7 August 2006).

NSW Pay Equity Taskforce, ***A Woman's Worth …***, Sydney, NSW, 1996 (August 1996).

WEL and NPEC, ***Joint Media Release***, Sydney, NSW, 1999.

CHAPTER 18

Alarums and Excursions: The Inside Story—Women Working for Women in the 1990s

Women's Liberation Manifesto

We are economically oppressed: in jobs we do full-time work for half-pay, in the home we do unpaid work fulltime.

We are commercially exploited by advertisements, television, and press: legally we often have the status of children.

We are reared to feel inadequate, educated to narrower horizons than men.

This is our specific oppression as women. It is as women we therefore organise.

We demand:

1. Women Have Control Over their Bodies: We believe this is denied us until we can decide whether to have children or not and when we have them.
2. Repeal of Abortion Laws: Abortion on Request—Abortion is an essential part of birth control. Contraception without the right to abortion means the State controls our bodies if we become pregnant unwillingly. Women should have the right to decide whether to have an abortion.
3. Freely Available Contraception: More education on contraception … at an early age, and contraceptives must be easily available and free on social security. Doctors should have no right to refuse contraception on their own moral grounds.

J. A. Scutt, *Wage Rage for Equal Pay*,
https://doi.org/10.1007/978-3-031-42178-5_18

4. Free 24-hour Community Controlled Childcare: Government must provide full childcare facilities Australia-wide, free, staffed by qualified women and men. Centres must be under the control of those using them, to prevent bureaucratic 'baby dumps'. Women must not have to bear individual responsibility for care of children.
5. Equal Job Opportunities and an End to Low Pay: Employers have no right to pay women less than men, or keep women in menial jobs. Government must ... [make employment discrimination illegal]. Although, initially, the 1972 equal pay decision seems favourable, the full effect will not become apparent until 1975. [W]e have been 'bought off' until then.
6. Equal Educational Opportunities: [For] women to have real equal opportunity, all schools must stop streaming women into 'service' jobs reflecting the wife/mother role—cleaners, teachers, nurses, secretaries, social workers—... Sexual bias in curricula must be eliminated. The education system must play a large part in undoing women's conditioning to accept an inferior role, by encouraging women to assert themselves in all fields.

Women's Liberation Newsletter, March 1973, pp. 5–6

Monday, 5 May 1996.

It is precisely ten weeks since federal Labor losest power and the Liberal-National Coalition government takes over, John Howard sworn in as prime minister on 2 March. It is nine weeks since Peter Reith, holding the federal seat of Flinders, becomes industrial relations minister. It is eight weeks since he announces sweeping changes to employer and workers' rights, changes to industrial conditions and ways of achieving them, and an end to the Australian Industrial Relation Commission (AIRC)'s pre-eminence in wage fixing. The Workplace Relations Act 1996 (Cth) is on its way.

Over morning coffee, in a small office at the Young Women's Christian Association (YWCA) in Elizabeth Street, Melbourne, members of the Victorian Women's Coalition (VWC) (set up in December 1992, two months after the Kennett Liberals defeat Joan Kirner's Labor government) meet. For almost ten years under premier John Cain (May 1983–1990) and Kirner (1990-October 1992), the Labor government held office. Whatever criticism inevitably following any government defeat, women had been heard, lines of government communication accessible, achieving positive gains.

Now, it's different.

Organising to preserve women's rights from an attack coming from the neo-conservative philosophy afoot in the state of Victoria, the word went out. Meeting at Collingwoood Town Hall, hundreds of women flooded into the main hall and broad passages, overflowing into the street. Under the slogan 'Women are Watching', working groups formed with convenors, e-mail, and telephone contact lists (e-mail revolutionary, then) shared, charged with keeping abreast of changes and protesting against everything inimical to the rights of women. Victorian Trades Hall (VTH) women's officer Jenny Draddy, centrally organising, mailed letters, made telephone-tree calls, sent out e-mails to those advanced into this new technology realm.

Three years on, and VWC members are concerned for women's rights not only at state level, but federally too.

Women for Workplace Justice

It's 8.30 am. Lily D'Ambrosio, Australian Labor Party (ALP) member since 1983, later state organiser (1994–1999), then MP for Mill Park (2002-), wields pad and pen for jotting down minutes. Apologies come for Barbara (Barb) Jennings, Joy Samuels, and Frances Gleeson. Draddy speaks of the Liberal-National coalition's Workplace Relations Bill and its dire consequences for working women. Her suggestion for a roundtable of key women's groups to decide what can be done is adopted enthusiastically. Someone says National Pay Equity Coalition (NPEC) members in Sydney are drafting amendments for Australian Democrat MPs, to introduce at committee stage.

Someone suggests inviting Jennie George, Australian Council of Trade Unions (ACTU) president, to address the roundtable, plus a feminist lawyer, and historian Marilyn Lake. Draddy is assigned to draft an invitation letter and investigate funding possibilities for a delegation to Canberra. Group members begin drawing up a list of potential roundtable invitees, agreeing to make calls encouraging attendance. Draddy, Jenny Holmes of Ormond College, Leonie Morgan of Emily's List, and D'Ambrosio agree to call other active VWC members.

The next meeting's set: a fortnight later at Thresherman's Bakehouse in Faraday Street, next-door to the old Carlton Movie House. The day, a Monday. The date, 20 May 1996.

On 7 May, from VTHC, Draddy faxes George:

> I have organised the Victorian Women's Coalition (VWC) and Feminist Lawyers to auspice a Women's Round Table on the proposed Federal Industrial Relations Legislation.

> We intend inviting over 30 women's community groups … to provide information on proposed [Industrial Relations] IR changes and alert women to the potential impact for women [and] nominate a delegation to send to Canberra to lobby the Democrats and Greens. I will also make an offer to provide speakers … on the proposed legislation.
>
> [Y]ou are very busy, but … would you address the round table [for] the union movement. We will issue press releases about the meeting and decisions [from] the forum.
>
> Melanie Young a Victorian Barrister who works for unions and a member of Feminist Lawyers will give an overview of the Legislation … Professor Marilyn Lake has also agreed to speak …
>
> … we can schedule for your availability …
>
> Yours sincerely …

In Melbourne, Women for Workplace Justice are on the move.

Lobbying the Minister

Meanwhile, under the banner 'Women's Industrial Relations Legislation Campaign', women in Sydney are organising. Burgmann, Jamieson, Suzanne Hammond, Buswell, Arditto, Di Fruin, Hall, Burton, Jude Stoddart, Anita Devos, Vicki Marquis, Caroline A., Richter, Ann Reich, Hayes, Karen Coleman, Cathy Bloch, Jill Biddington, Ann Reich, Meg Smith, Bennett, Scutt, Martina Nightingale, Jessica Laurence (writing a thesis), Meg, Wendy Caird, Eva Cox, Ann Sherry, Betty Johnson, Doran, Kaye Loder have had some success through a delegation to Reith about the federal government's industrial relations direction.

In April 1996, Reith's office initiates a consultation with the Australian Federation of Business and Professional Women (AFBPW), Association of Non-English Speaking Background Women of Australia (ANESBWA), Women's Electoral Lobby (WEL), Business Council of Australia (BCA)'s equal opportunity manager, Council of Business Women (CBW), and Women's Economic Think Tank (WETTANK).

Meeting on 10 April in Sydney, subject the government's industrial relations policy. Copies of the twenty-nine-page discussion paper arriving the day before leaves little time for preparing detailed comment. Nonetheless, in one-and-a-half hours, major concerns are canvassed with the minister. At meeting's end, Reith invites written comment and advice as soon as possible, for what he says will be 'active consideration'. Acknowledging a battle pending in the Senate to get the Workplace

Relations Bill through, he says the government wants flexibility where possible to minimise the fight. Reith ends the consultation by extending an invitation to meet again, the women generally optimistic about the government's preparedness to act on their advice to retain anti-discrimination, human rights, and equal pay provisions in the new law.

Later, taking advantage of another trip by Reith to Sydney on 15 May 1996, they fix another appointment, meeting ahead with senator Vicky Bourne (1990–2002) to clarify the Democrats' position, keep them informed of Sydney women's lobbying, and ensure open communication lines for future strategising.

In a follow-up letter to Reith, they confirm their understanding of major issues emerging during the meeting, noting agreement:

- objects to include assisting employees balancing family and work responsibilities, with workplace diversity respected and valued through anti-discrimination provisions on race, sex, ethnicity, age, etc., grounds;
- AIRC requirements to 'take into account' the Sex Discrimination, Racial Discrimination, and Disability Discrimination Acts would be retained;
- awards section to include anti-discrimination objects;
- AIRC continuing to scrutinise CAs—CAs [Certified Agreements] required to be non-discriminatory, all employees to get a copy five days before put for approval;
- WWC [Working Women's Centre] funding budgeted for by the Industrial Relations Department and guaranteed (pending any Audit Commission intervention);
- section 143 –AIRC makes new awards in a simplified manner, no new awards discriminatory ...;
- the OEA [Office of Employment Advocate] will be independent, established in Sydney with $2m in funding;
- the OEA will be empowered to prosecute breaches of minimum conditions, with provisions for penalties/back-pay;
- the Award Review Process combined with award simplification and include anti-discrimination provisions, managed by the AIRC;
- enterprise bargaining reviewed and reported on every three years;
- written directions from the Minister ... to the OEA regarding non-discriminatory service delivery; further input from women's organisations will be sought/welcomed regarding OEA establishment;

- women's organisations will have input on AWA [Australian Workplace Agreements] regulations, specifically on standard enterprise bargaining, a final statement ... indicating understanding and collection of data for disaggregation and analysis based on ethnicity, gender, and age;
- redundancy a minimum condition.

Concerns raised, but without agreement:

- retaining equal remuneration for work of equal value within the AIRC's ambit;
- removal of section 170M relating to consultation requirements for CAs.

Further issues claimed by Reith as government policy and in projected legislation but inadequately or not addressed include contentions that the Human Rights and Equal Opportunity Commission (HREOC) can address equal pay under the Sex Discrimination Act: individual complaints cannot tackle systemic issues, and equal pay cases would be 'cumbersome, lengthy, [with] damages rather than rectifying the problem'. As well, notions of 'valuing diversity' and 'reflecting it in consultative requirements' for CAs were unrealistic.

The Sydney women do not leave it there.

On 20 May, at 2.54 pm, Draddy receives an urgent fax from Bloch, Trade Union Choir member, trainer and speaker at the Trade Union Training Authority (TUTA) NSW Centre in Camperdown. Subject:

'Women's Rights at Work Under Threat: what we can do!'

Two days earlier, following an urgently called meeting in Sydney, Burton, Hall, Buswell, Arditto, and others have drafted a statement for women's groups to send as an open letter to Reith, prime minister John Howard, and all federal MPs:

WOMEN AND THE *WORKPLACE RELATIONS BILL*: STATEMENT OF CONCERN

My organisation expresses concern about the impact on women of the *Workplace Industrial Relations Bill* about to be introduced ... We welcome consideration given by the Minister … to concerns already raised by women's groups about the *Bill*, and amendments [accommodating] some of these concerns. We are encouraged by retention in the proposed Act of the object **'helping to prevent and eliminate discrimination'** in the workplace, and insertion of new objects to **'assist employees to balance work and family responsibilities'** and **'respect and value diversity in the workforce'**.

However, we are particularly concerned about:

- **narrowing the equal pay definition to include only minimum award pay instead of whole pay …**;
- **stripping awards to a bare minimum number of provisions, …**;
- **active promotion of secret non-union individual agreements (Australian Workplace Agreements, or AWAs) as the basis for employment conditions,** …;
- **absence of any scrutiny by the OEA prior to certification of an AWA …**;
- **reduction of the safety net standard the AIRC is to apply in union-negotiated agreements …**;
- **removal of special requirements to consult with and inform disadvantaged groups in a workplace …**;
- **abolition of paid rates awards, and their replacement with minimum rates awards. …**.

These changes go far beyond the Government's claimed mandate for industrial relations reform. Many changes were not even mentioned … during the election campaign. The *Workplace Industrial Relations bill* should not be rushed through this parliamentary sitting.

… the Government should encourage full community discussion by:

- **distributing the draft Bill for public discussion;**
- **calling for community submissions on the Bill;**
- **conducting public hearings** …

We ask all political parties to recognise our concerns, particular in community discussions, and not proceed … until these problems are solved and the people have had their say.

The three-page fax received by Draddy in Melbourne contains this open letter plus a covering statement and campaign form for completion and return by individuals and organisations to the Women's Industrial Relations Legislation Campaign, aiming at a coordinated response.

'Women need to take action!' The fax emphasises:

> We are a coalition of women's organisations coming together to ensure women's workplace rights are not undermined by proposed changes. We need your support to win more time for proper consultation of women's, community, and trade union organisations and a proper assessment of impact on women and other vulnerable workers. We need to ensure all recent gains in women's workplace rights and economic independence are not wiped out in one go!

Women wanting further campaign and Workplace Relations Bill information, to distribute information, provide mailing lists, attend meetings, donate to campaign costs, provide other support—are encouraged to return the campaign form.

Campaigning Around the Round Table

On 29 May, the VWC's 'Round Table on the Proposed Federal Industrial Relations Bill', held at the YWCA from 6.00–8.00 pm, with Cheryl Wragg, VWC (facilitator); Melissa Stead and Sarah Lantz of the National Union of Students (NUS); Melanie (Mel) Wheeler and Helena Spyrou for Network of Women in Further Education; Natalie Savin for the Victorian Women's Trust (VWT); Barbara Lewis and Draddy of VTHC; Jill Kidd, Jenny Holmes, Beth Ripper, Morgan, Jennings, Joy Samuels, and Gleeson of VWC; Joanne Prior of Queen Victoria Women's Centre; Patricia Khor of Australian Council of Professionals/Business and Professional Women (ACOP/BPW); Ayfer Akalin of Women in Industry and Community Health (WICH); Karen Mackay of Australian Neighbourhood Houses and Learning Centres (ANHLC) (Neighbourhood Houses); WEL's Owen and Bennett; Celia Haddock and Lynne Wannan of Community ChildCare; Union of Australian Women (UAW)'s Goedecke; Paula Gerber-Jones of National Association of Women in Construction (NAWC); Anita Minicevic, Ethnic Communities Council of Victoria (ECCV); Judi Fisher for Uniting Church; YWCA's Ann Drummond; Meryl Sexton of BPW and Queen Victoria Women's Centre; Gwen Ince, Victorian College of the Arts (VCA); Feminist Lawyers' Sarah Rey and Young; and Misha Schubert of WEL and the YWCA. Apologies are registered for Scutt and George, ACTU industrial officer Doran representing George.

Speaking for 30 minutes, questions following, Doran outlines the Workplace Relations Bill provisions, their implications for women workers and those seeking entry or reentry to paidwork. Earlier, the 35 women present break into four smaller groups, asking: 'What do we want to find out ... What do we want to achieve this evening?' Questioning is sharp, focused.

The roundtable ends with women returning to the original four groups, tackling: 'What are our major concerns ... How do we Respond?' reporting back their Action Plans to a final plenary session. In principle support for a Canberra delegation is agreed, with three working groups set to develop strategies:

- Information kit and publicity;
- Lobbying for the Canberra delegation;
- Fundraising for the Canberra delegation and other campaign activities.

Another Melbourne roundtable is organised, for June.

The week before it, the Industrial Relations Lobby Group meets, resolving a three-woman delegation to go to Canberra. A letter goes to all participating women's organisations, seeking funding assistance and asking for copies of publicity or publications around the issues. The group resolves that ahead of travel to Canberra, meetings will be arranged with Victorian federal MPs, including Democrats senator Sid Spindler (1990–1996) and Lyn Allison (senator elect), and Liberal senators Judith Troeth (1993–2011) and Kay Patterson (1987–2008).

The group agrees delegation members must be representative of a variety of Victorian women's organisations, with a detailed understanding of the legislation and its impact on women, listing Scutt, VWC; Bennett, WEL; Schubert, WEL and YWCA; Khor, BPW; and Wheeler, Network of Women in Further Education (NWFE). Canberra appointments are for Democrats leader Kernot, Tasmania's independent senator Brian Harradine, WA Greens senator Dee Margetts, Judy Moylan, family services minister, Jocelyn Newman, social security and assisting the prime minister on women's affairs, and Reith. Contacting Bob Brown, Tasmanian Greens senator elect is prioritised.

12 June 1996

The second roundtable endorses Industrial Relations Lobby Group resolution, the Canberra delegation set for 18 July 1996, a timetable framed around the Senate Inquiry into the Workplace Relations Bill, scheduled to reconvene on 22 August to finalise its report. The roundtable decides to review and revise the Publications Group's 'Women's Impact Statement', copies provided to participating organisations and the Canberra delegation as the key Canberra document.

Adding to Sydney women's organisation concerns, Melbourne women identify losses:

THE COALITION'S INDUSTRIAL RELATIONS POLICY WOMEN'S IMPACT STATEMENT

Loss of the Independent Umpire

Currently the AIRC has power to settle industrial disputes, fix wages, conditions, and act as independent umpire [this] role important for closing the female-male conditions and wages gap …

Loss of a Bargaining Position

The legislation strongly encourages making individual contracts (Australian Workplace Agreements—AWAs—with seven minimum conditions only). Many women will have to 'negotiate' with their employer by themselves, accepting whatever they are given … At least the Victorian system maintained awards as an individual contract for existing employees as a bottom line for workers to negotiate new agreements.

Loss of Regulation of Part-Time Work

Women comprise 75% of Australia's part-time workers. Industrial awards will no longer contain such protections as minimum shift length, restrictions on casual worker numbers and rostering …

Loss of Award Protection

Awards will be reduced to 18 entitlements, when most currently contain over 35 entitlements. … Many women such as nurses, teachers and public servants are under paid rates awards, where the actual, not the minimum, rate of pay is stipulated, meaning they will have their pay cut and awards stripped.

Loss of Equity between Women's and Men's Pay

Lip service is paid to equal pay for work of equal value. Processes [from] the early 1900s to detect and remedy under-valuing of women's work are removed. In Australia, when award wages alone are considered, the wage gap is 6.2% for women working full-time, but when all forms of remuneration are included increases to 20.7%. The AIRC [loses] power to remove discrimination in award and over award payments.

Loss of Public Scrutiny

AWAs, individual employment contracts, will be secret, with no body to ensure they comply with basic legal requirements and properly provide for women, particularly NESB women. The OEA will not scrutinise the agreement unless an employee complains. Few will be prepared to make complaints. The EAO will assist both employers and employees.

Loss of International Human Rights

Australia is currently a signatory to human rights conventions such as the Equal Remuneration Convention, CEDAW [Convention on the Elimination of All Forms of Discrimination Against Women], and International Covenant on Economic, Social, Cultural Rights. The AIRC need no longer take these into account.

Loss of Training for Workers

The Federal Government is withdrawing its support of the Trade Union Training Authority [TUTA] which ran ... assertiveness training courses for women, negotiating skills, employment rights, sexual harassment, affirmative action, juggling work and family responsibilities, many empowering women ...

Loss of Confidentiality and Representation by Unions

The right of entry for unions to employer premises to check for underpayments and other breaches of law, existing for decades, will be severely limited ...

Apprenticeships, Traineeships and Workplace Training

Today, ... relevant vocational skills and qualifications [are essential]. Access to vocationally oriented skills training has been a gateway into paidwork for young women seeking work and older women seeking better work. The proposed ... changes will reduce by 20% payrates for women in apprenticeships and traineeships, restricting vocational training access to women lacking other means of financial support. The changes support employers to pay women less than their current wage if a woman worker undertakes vocational training at the workplace when upgrading her vocational skills and qualifications.

Arrangements are made for the Canberra delegation to travel at month's end, meeting MPs on Thursday 27 June. A press conference is planned.

In Sydney, action continues, too. Copies of NPEC's Workplace Relations Act submission are sent to senators Harradine, Newman, Margetts, Kernot, Natasha Stott Despoja, Spindler, John Faulkner, Bob McMullen, Grace Grace, and senator elect Brown, along with federal attorney general Darryl Williams (an after-thought—his name appears in the ***NPEC Minute Book*** in a different pen). Seventeen additional women MPs are targeted, and the ACTU, Council of Business Women (Ann Sherry) and Council for Equal Opportunity. Copies are distributed to WEL's national office, to AFBPW and are faxed to Draddy at VTHC, Jude Elton at United Trades and Labour Council (UTLC) (SA), Di McAtee at WA Trades and Labour Council (TLC), Lynne Fitzgerald at Tasmanian Trades and Labour Council (TTLC), Jacqueline King at the ACTU in Queensland, and Steer at NSW Labor Council. Others listed include George, Evatt, Franca Arena, Burton, Scutt, and Cox.

The women draft three different letters. Opposition are offered a briefing on the Bill and women's concerns, plus questions demanding government answers. Government members receive suggestions for amendments and briefing offers, advised that the women will answer any questions. The third letter provides information, promoting opportunities for placing material in newsletters or with the media, and asks 'tell us what you've done' to alert women, MPs, and others to detrimental implications of the proposals.

In a cooperative distribution of effort, Fruin signs the cover letter. The post office box address is Meg Smith's.

Women Wanting Change—And Lobbying to Get It

Sydney and Melbourne women's activism has not gone unnoticed. Under the heading 'Anger over women's role in IR law', on 28 June 1996 the ***Australian Financial Review***'s Katherine Murphy recounts 'renewed pressure [on government] from a coalition of women's groups, claiming the new Workplace Relations Bill is anti-family and disadvantageous to women workers …' Reminiscent of D'Aprano's 1969 demonstration at Spring Street's Commonwealth Offices, Murphy reports on a rally planned for Melbourne the following Friday, outside the Senate Committee inquiry into the bill.

Murphy names the new coalition as Women for Workplace Justice, 'comprising groups such as [AFBPW] and Network of Women in Further Education', members including women lawyers'. She reports that coalition spokeswoman Scutt said it would 'lead a campaign against the new legislation, passed by the House of Representatives last night …', adding that the legislation must be 'exposed for what it is—a direct attack on women workers' wages and conditions'. Further, writes Murphy, University of Newcastle (UNewcastle)'s director of the Employment Studies Centre, Dr Roy Green, 'said it was unlikely the new bill could achieve co-operative workplace relations and higher productivity', calling for the legislation to be 'substantively amended or rejected'.

In Canberra, Murphy attends the press conference. She is not alone.

Ita Buttrose is alert, too.

On her Radio 2GB program, interviewing Scutt on 28 June as a Victorian Women for Workplace Justice Coalition delegate, business woman, media identity, and publisher Buttrose is direct. What of women's difficulty negotiating work terms and conditions commensurate with their capacities, abilities, value, and worth? What will AWAs mean for women?

It is not rhetorical.

Arguably the most powerful woman in Australia, Buttrose is the woman most likely to possess the clout to determine content of an AWA, most likely to possess the greatest negotiating savvy held by a woman in the business world. ***Australian Women's Weekly*** editor under Kerry Packer's Australian Consolidated Press (ACP), she was first woman editor-in-chief of a major daily newspaper, heading Sydney's ***Daily Telegraph*** and ***Sunday Telegraph***. She was first-ever female board member of Rupert Murdoch's News Ltd. Australia.

The ***Herald Sun***'s Chris Lacy follows up, reporting on 2 July 'Ita calls for united front' and that same day in 'Women in Business' writes more substantially of the Buttrose-Scutt exchanges. Clearly, when this most powerful woman acknowledges negotiating AWAs is unlikely to bring adequate—much less equal—recognition and remuneration to Australian women, any contention that the new industrial regime will advance women's industrial rights and promote equal pay is not only thrown open to question. And so it proves, through 1997 and 1998 …

As with previous decades' efforts, women's 1990s organising has impact. Anti-discrimination measures are retained in Reith's legislation, and the Department of Industrial Relations (later Department of Workplace Relations) must review regularly the new regime's impact and effect on women, workers of minority race background and origin, and youth.

But ultimately none of this can advance equal pay rights, nor insulate women's pay rates against the negative impact of enterprise bargaining or individual contracts. Whilst keeping a watch on what is happening federally, equal pay focus returns to state Labor governments.

By decade's end, the Workplace Relations Act has operated for over three years. The Howard government believes it's not gone far enough. AWAs have not replaced enterprise agreements or awards. Workers continue their union membership, and unions remain central to wage negotiations and agreements. The AIRC continues a wage-setting role.

Planned?

August 1999. Reith announces the new industrial laws' second stage.

Friday, 3 September 1999.

Inner Melbourne, Trades Hall on Carlton's Victoria Parade/Lygon Street corner, the meeting room opposite Reception, women unionists gather. Seated together, Carol Andrades, labour law firm Ryan Carlyle Thomas solicitor, and Ellen Kleinmaker, succeeding Draddy as VTHC women's & equity officer. They've drafted a submission to the Senate Employment, Workplace Relations, Small Business and Education Committee—Inquiry into the Workplace Relations Legislation Amendment (More Jobs, Better Pay) Bill 1999.

They'll finalise the submission to send by closing date—17 September 1999.

'Unfortunately', Kleinmaker tells the women, 'We don't have much time'.

That week in Sydney, the Monday immediately before the Friday of Melbourne women's meeting, women sit around the president of NSW's Parliament's Upper House conference table. It is 30 August. Burgmann, president (1999–2007) runs the agenda, reviewing a 20 August meeting with Reith, now minister for workplace relations and small business. The delegation included AFBPW's Buswell, WEL's Hammond, Hayes of NPEC, with YWCA and WETTANK representatives, two women's organisations representing employers—the Australian CBW and Council for Equal Opportunity in Employment.

Victoria's submission provides foundation for a joint AFBPW, NPEC, and WEL submission to the Senate Inquiry. Industrial relations consultant Hayes and Community and Public Sector Union-State Public Services Federation (CPSU-SPSF) industrial officer Hammond arrange to meet the following week to work on it. Hall joins the working party, with Kathy Hancock.

Hammond is off overseas on 13 September.

The others don't have much time, either.

Nonetheless, the submissions make the date. Sitting in Melbourne and Sydney, the Senate Committee hears from the women. Articulate in writing and presentations, it makes no difference. Changes happen. They're not good for women. Equal pay—now more often 'pay equity'—recedes.

Acting on Other Fronts

A reactionary ethos predominates industrially, its impact affecting equal pay. Women are going backwards. Under the rubric of economic rationalism, collectivism earlier evident in Australian political and industrial life is not just under challenge, but demolition. AIRC centralised wage fixing is relegated to a rump. No longer do the strong unions prompt and promote better wages and conditions not just for themselves but for less powerful unions and workers. Now, it's every man for himself, with women—apart from some who've managed the scramble up the ladder to middling-range positions—left behind.

Through the 1990s, industrial rights have suffered sustained attack. As the growing 1990s emphasis upon corporate business being central to progress and private enterprise as superior to public sector bites, a shift beginning in the 1980s, women's position is more precarious. Equal pay faces a newly pronounced challenge.

Not only are low-paid women workers disadvantaged. The 1990s herald economic differences between women unmistakably manifest, some in relative positions of authority and power, garnering pay packets and benefits previously unavailable to women. Equal opportunity and 1970s and 1980s-Women's Movement agitation, building on historical campaigning, has had an impact, but not as imagined back then. The growing global divide between haves and have nots is replicating in the world of women and work.

Yet the 'I'm All Right Jack' philosophy has not driven out all concern for women's collective wellbeing. Evident as it is that in the prevailing political climate equal pay claims have no leverage at federal level, already women are seeking alternatives. From the mid-1990s, NPEC has lobbied the NSW government. In 1996, directly responding, minister for industrial relations, Jeffrey (Jeff) Shaw, MP (1991–2000), sets up a Pay Equity Task Force reviewing pay equity—not only the theory, but the practice.

The Pay Equity Task Force reports, with eleven recommendations. Women's organisations focus on **Recommendation 2**:

> That an inquiry into work value be undertaken by the NSW Industrial Relations Commission, by Ministerial Reference.

NPEC drafts terms of reference.

So women and women's organisations can and do join forces with trade union women; often, though not always, one and the same. Once again history demonstrates the cross-overs between and amongst women, Women's Movement women sometimes joining more conservative women's organisations to work as members; women belonging to unions and women's organisations; creating alliances and connections across party lines, union lines and women's organisation boundaries. Women's capacity to sustain equal pay momentum would be more limited, more circumscribed, without this collaboration women activists built, developed, and maintained.

Without knowing it, in this, women echoed Indigenous Australian poet and activist Lilla Watson's words:

> If you have come to help
> you are wasting your time.
> But if you have come
> because your liberation
> is bound up with mine then
> let us work together.

With this spirit, the Pay Equity Taskforce Report and its recommendations unlock new possibilities, not only for NSW women, but around Australia. From 1990s' end, into the 2000s, through Chap. 19, 'Forward to the Past, Back to the Future—Beyond the New Millennium', women tackle the states for a more sympathetic hearing on women's right to industrial equity, pay justice, and a fair day's wage for a fair day's work.

References

Cases—See Case List

Meredith Burgmann, ***Interview***, Sydney, NSW, 2006 (26 June 2006).

Ellen Kleinmaker, ***Personal Communication***, 2006 (16 February 2006).

NPEC, 1999 (30 August 1999) Minutes, insert to ***NPEC Minute Book***, 1995, fn 16.

NPEC members, ***Interview***, Sydney, NSW, 2006 (26 June 2006).

Senate Select Committee Submission, *Women for Workplace Justice Project*, VTHC, Melbourne, Victoria, 1996 (June 1996); copy in VTHC File No. 29.55, Part 1, 1996.

Lilla Watson, 'Sister, Black is the Colour of My Soul' in JA Scutt (ed.), ***Different Lives—***, Penguin, Ringwood, Victoria, 1987, pp. 44–53.

CHAPTER 19

Beyond The New Millennium—Forward to the Past, Back to the Future

> In the fashion industry, lots of women come from a non-English speaking background and, because of the language barrier, have … hesitation in talking. Take something simple in the clothing factory at lunchtime. The workers would love to have a microwave oven to warm their lunch. Their employer … asked the workers to put their lunch on the ironing board. Sometimes their lunches turn out only just warm, not hot enough, or sometimes they even get a still cold lunch … they dare not say a word because they are so scared and afraid.
>
> Perhaps some … people sitting here do not understand, would not even believe, how … this could happen … it happened in my factory. If the workers do not even dare to request such a small item, how can they discuss their awards and rights with their employer.
>
> Rainbow Chen, Asian Women at Work
> 'Evidence: Economics References Committee', ***Reference: Workplace Relations … Amendment Bill 1996***
> Australian Parliament—Senate, 1996

Like the 1990s, the first decade of 2000 begins problematically for Australian women. In 2000, few women sit on corporate boards, none heads a major company, although several lead government departments. Yet, increasingly pre-eminent is the view that both women and men suffer gender disadvantage; hence, funding and government programs for

J. A. Scutt, *Wage Rage for Equal Pay*,
https://doi.org/10.1007/978-3-031-42178-5_19

women must be mirrored for men. Systemic sex/gender discrimination realities are disregarded, or not even comprehended. Still, there are pluses.

In politics, on 18 August 2001 against all predictions, former Australian Broadcasting Corporation (ABC) journalist, member for Fannie Bay, Clare Martin leads an Australian Labor Party (ALP) administration (2001–2005) in the Northern Territory (NT) for the first time in history. This sparks regeneration of women's calls for parliamentary representation, leadership, and recognition of women's rights and abilities. The spark is rekindled in 2005 when Martin repeats the feat, historically winning two elections in a row as ALP leader (2005–2007). Around Australia, despite ups and downs, women MP numbers generally have been rising, with women in ministries in all states and territories, and federally. Indigenous Australian women gain representation—first, WA's Carol Martin (2001–2013), then three NT members simultaneously—Alison Anderson (2001–2016), Barbara (Malarndirri) McCarthy (2005–2012), and Marion Scrymgour (2001–2005, 2005–2012), one in Tasmania (Kathryn Hay (2002–2006)), one in NSW (Linda Jean Burney (2003–2016)).

An all-woman team led by Scutt appears in the High Court (in ***Osland v The Queen***—leave to appeal and appeal) for the first time in Australian history. A woman—Patricia (Pat) Leary—holds commissions as Tasmanian Industrial Commission president and Australian Industrial Relations Commission (AIRC) senior deputy president. Three are state governors—Queensland's Bryce (2003–2008), SA's Marjorie Jackson-Nelson (2001–2007), and in NSW, Marie Bashir (2001–2014). Women are judges and magistrates in every state, territory, and federally in numbers unimagined 10 years before. Judge Antoinette Kennedy is elevated from WA District Court judge to chief judge (1985–2004, 2004–2010). Two women head superior courts, one federal, and one state. Diana Bryant is Family Court of Australia chief justice (2004–2017), where Evatt was first chief judge (1976–1988). Yet, Marilyn Warren's 2003 appointment as Victoria's Supreme Court chief justice, third female Supreme Court judge and first female chief justice appointed in its 152-year lifetime, provokes ***Herald Sun***'s 26 November 2003 censure: what of male barristers' career prospects? The ***Sydney Morning Herald*** 21 September 2005 reports a second woman's High Court appointment, solicitor-general commenting she's 'without baggage of any kind', lacking 'any sort of extreme views'. Declaring she's 'not a crazy feminist' is deemed complimentary.

With 'remuneration' replacing 'wages' in comparing male and female incomes, hopes rise. But as incomes fall, job-casualisation grows, women more vulnerable, pay equity recedes. Federally, centralised wage fixing is virtually moribund. At state level, contrary messages continue.

In the 1990s, Victoria and WA initiated centralised wage-fixing departures, emphasising individual employer-employee contracts. In October 1992, the incoming Kennett Liberal government disbanded the Victorian Industrial Court. Downgrading the Industrial Commission, abolishing awards, it stressed individual wage contracting. In 1996, it eliminated the state's industrial role, referring powers to federal Parliament. The 1999 Bracks Labor government made no change. Equal pay remained firmly in federal hands. In WA from 1993, the Court Liberal government altered the industrial system radically, a two-stage legislative plan removing unions from the arena, individual contracts centre-stage. In 2001, Geoff Gallop's Labour government reversed the individual contracts push, but enterprise bargaining remained, centralised wage fixing passé, mirroring federal law.

Statistics increasingly revealed women's wage parity in free fall. Childcare privatisation created burgeoning centres, a major revenue source. Reproduction of children requiring care and need for women's paidwork outside the home sustaining income and shareholder profits, concerns about childcare cost and conditions escalated. With union prompting, low payrates of childcare workers came under industrial commission scrutiny.

Women lobbied the federal government on stages one and two of the industrial regime introduced through the Workplace Relations Act 1996 (Cth) and Workplace Relations and Other Legislation Act 1999 (Cth). Concurrently, women turned to state industrial commissions to argue pay equity.

Tasmania Introduces Pay Equity

The NSW ***Pay Equity Inquiry 1997*** made recommendations for a pay equity or equal remuneration principle, not implemented until the ***Crown employees [librarians, library assistants, library technicians and archivists] award 2002***. Hence, on 6 July 2000, following submissions by Fitzgerald, Tasmanian Trades and Labour Council (TTLC) (UnionsTasmania), Little, WomenTasmania director as Women in Paid Work Task Force (Pay Equity Task Force) chair, and Scutt, Anti-Discrimination Commissioner, the Tasmanian Chamber of Commerce and Industry (TCCI) opposing, in the ***State Wage Case and Review of Wage Fixing Principles 2000*** (***State Wage Case 2000***) Tasmania set the precedent:

9 *PAY EQUITY*

9.1 In this Principle, 'pay equity' means equal remuneration for men and women doing work of equal value.
9.2 Applications … will be dealt with according to this principle.
9.3 [A]pplications require assessment of value of work performed …, irrespective of [worker's] gender … to ascertain value of the work rather than … changes in [work] value … The Commission may consider the nature of the work, skill, responsibility and qualifications required by the work and conditions under which [it] is performed ([having] the same meaning as … for Principle 8—Work Value Changes—[looking for example at changes in work, skill, responsibility or conditions under which work is performed]).
9.4 A prior assessment … of value of the work …, and/or prior setting of rates for such work, does not … presume the rates of pay applying … are unaffected by [employees'] gender … The history of … rates … will be a consideration. The Commission shall broadly assess whether past valuation …has been affected by the [workers'] gender …
9.5 [O]peration of this principle is not restricted by … other wage fixing principles. However, the Commission will have regard to the public interest requirements of Section 36 of the [Industrial Relations] Act [1984] [principally 'public interest', 'economic position of the industry' and 'the economy'].

Lacking explicit reference to discrimination (unlike the Workplace Relations Act 1996 (Cth)), the Industrial Relations Act 1984 (Tas) sections 20 and 36 stipulate 'equity, good conscience and merits of the case', and 'subject to provisions of any Act dealing with the same subject-matter'. The Anti-Discrimination Act 1998 (Tas) 'deals with the same subject matter'—employment, referencing direct (less favourable or unequal treatment) and indirect ('equal' or differential or disparate impact) discrimination based on, amongst other attributes, gender, marital status, parental status, and family responsibilities. No award can be made or maintained at variance with these provisions, and if the Anti-Discrimination Tribunal upholds an award, enterprise, or industrial agreement discrimination claim, Industrial Commission action will ensure all workers under the award or agreement benefit.

The Tasmanian and NSW cases were the first addressing equal pay after the ***Equal Pay 1969*** and ***1972 Cases***, where states followed the federal lead. Albeit some elements called for by Fitzgerald, Little, and Scutt were overlooked, Tasmania's pay equity principle stands as their achievement, historic also in three women appearing for the first time. Nonetheless, five principal failings emerge in addition to disregarding the need for Tribunal instruction in women's work value. First, no remuneration definition—potentially remedied by International Labour Organization (ILO) Convention 100. Extensive preliminary argument in the NSW ***Pay Equity Inquiry 1997*** on this, commissioner Glynn's interim ruling (four and a half pages), pending final determination, highlighted its importance. Does 'remuneration' include over-award payments, a longstanding point of industrial contention, women's wages suffering from a consistent lack of over-award payments, contrasted to men's. Without definitional clarification, this debate would continue in Tasmania.

Second is failure to affirm explicitly that finding gender causation or discrimination based on sex is unnecessary to apply the principle. Fitzgerald cautioned the Commission that equal remuneration applications involve at base an assessment of value of work performed in an industry or occupation, workers' sex being irrelevant. The requirement is to determine *value of work* not *changes in value of work*. Valuation can consider 'skill, responsibility and qualifications required by the work' and conditions under which performed, and may consider 'labour market supply and demand, productivity and profitability' so long as *assessed without sex of the workers affecting them*. Factors identified in Pay Equity principle 9.3 are:

- 'ascertaining value of the work rather than ... changes in value of the work'; and
- taking into account—
  - 'nature of the work, skill, responsibility and qualifications required by the work'; and
  - 'conditions under which the work is performed'.

Danger lies in not explicitly eliminating proof of sex/gender as a required cause or discriminatory factor, leaving the Commission open to falling into the trap of pursuing it or demanding it of applicants. Requiring proof of sex/gender underlying the devaluation contradicts the tenet that where work is traditionally performed by women, or women predominate in a particular industry, workplace, or enterprise, work has not been properly valued by reference to nature of the work, skill, responsibility, qualifications, and conditions of work performance. It places a two-step burden upon applicants. Reference to 'assessment of value of the work performed … *irrespective of gender of the relevant worker*' does not help, focusing on the *present worker*, subject of the application, a different question.

Third: disregarding history in undervaluing women's work and traditional trades or professions. Though the principle says value, not changes, is key, it does not emphasise history as central to socio-cultural perceptions and expectations (or lack of them) in sex/gender pay disparity (leading in turn to the pensions gap). It may avoid the 1980s equal pay struggle, where changes in work or occupational requirements were required, concentrating on technological advances in nursing, for example, but this is not assured. Denying historical undervaluation of women's work and trades, professions and occupations undermines pay equity. Considering contemporary socio-cultural attitudes influencing women's work value, omitting specific reference to history means—more likely than not—historical undervaluing will be overlooked. Where unions argue it, employers will use absence of specific mention to assert its irrelevance.

Fourth: no statement that comparison may be undertaken 'across and within industries and occupations, between different classifications in the award in the application and/or between classifications in different industrial instruments', with 'more than one comparison … used if required'. Nothing precludes this—why not say so? The NSW ***Pay Equity Inquiry 1997*** recommendations proposed its inclusion, consistent with the ***Equal Pay Case 1972*** equal pay for work of equal value principle.

Fifth: no assistance on remedies for pay (in)equity, very different from work value *changes* in Principle 8, which provides considerable detail on remedies. If guidance there, why not here, far less understood, far more based in subjective assessments, traditional assumptions? All three advocates proposed detail, and its lack contradicts Fitzgerald's caveat that pay equity 'shall not be implemented by reducing current pay rates'. An open list of remedies included: reclassification of work; new career paths; incremental scales changes; reassessment of classifications or skills broadbanding; reassessments of definitions and position descriptions; amendments to generic descriptions of work not properly describing the value of work; changes to remuneration rates; changes to work conditions and practices to require equal employment opportunities.

Institutionally, industrial commissions' socio-cultural milieu supports a predisposition to undervalue women's work, inevitable where work done predominantly by women is, by its very nature, not classed valuable or is valued less. Components are neither recognised nor appreciated, much less valued fairly. Explicating remedies provides wage-fixing bodies with some guidance for confronting this. Furthermore, education and training for industrial bodies in evaluating work traditionally carried out by women is essential.

Albeit also omitting compulsory training and education, the NSW equal remuneration principle generally avoids Tasmania's omissions. The NSW ***Pay Equity Inquiry 1997*** was crucial, women in government and outside it, in advisory positions, as independent lobbyists, academics and advocates, urging in-depth consideration of women's wage disparity, a culmination of women's past campaigning. Despite regression of relativities between women and men's rates of pay, equal pay was back on the agenda.

The Backstory—NSW Takes the Initiative

On 10 November 1997, NSW attorney-general Shaw (1995–2000) establishes the ***Pay Equity Inquiry*** under the Industrial Relations Act 1996 (NSW) section 146(1)(d), a Work Skills Value Enquiry (WSVE), rejected by the AIRC as 'too vague' when AFBPW proposed it in the ***National Wage Case 1990–1991***. So, where in the past, state industrial bodies generally followed federal decisions, now NSW commissioner Leonie Glynn has the initiative. The ***Pay Equity Inquiry 1997*** reports on Christmas Eve—24 December 1998. Now, from the late 1990s and into the 2000s, state bodies lead. The AIRC loses ascendency.

Three women's organisations—National Pay Equity Coalition (NPEC), Australian Federation of Business and Professional Women (AFBPW) and Women's Electoral Lobby (WEL)—maintain a roster for each sitting day: Richter (WEL), Ruth Jost (NPEC and AFBPW), with Gail Gregory (NSW Labor Council), Ruth Small (Public Service Association (PSA) NSW) and Karen O'Connell (Human Rights and Equal Opportunity Commission (HREOC)) alongside employer organisations and unions. NSW Teachers' Federation (Brenda Seymour), Shop Distributive and Allied Employees' Association (SDAEA) (J. Duncan), Independent Education Union (IEU), NSW ACT Branch (Pam Smith), National Tertiary Education Union (NTEU) (Carolyn Allport),

Construction Forestry Maritime Mining and Energy Union (CFMEU), Mining and Energy Division (Lisa Doust) and Australian Liquor Hospitality Miscellaneous Workers Union (ALHMWU), Miscellaneous Workers Division (Rondell Millane) appear. Jost delivers the joint AFBPW-NPEC-WEL submissions.

Terms of Reference require the Industrial Commission:

- To inquire and report upon:
  - Whether female-dominated occupations and industries [work] is undervalued in remuneration paid relative to work in comparable male-dominated occupations and industries …
  - The adequacy of tests and mechanisms for ascertaining work value and the extent to which, or at all, they are inequitable [regarding] gender.
- In developing recommendations [for] remedial measures …, to [consider], but not be limited, to:
  - Current work value tests;
  - Minimum rates adjustment process and other industrial mechanisms including productivity;
  - Job evaluation techniques;
  - Discrimination and the Anti-Discrimination Act 1977 (NSW) and Industrial Relations Act 1996 (NSW);
  - Relevant international labour and other conventions, including … ILO Convention 100 and 111 and … CEDAW [Convention on the Elimination of All Forms of Discrimination Against Women].
  - Mechanisms and processes [bringing] pay equity matters before the Industrial Commission.
- In [conducting] the Inquiry, and [making] recommendations …, to [consider] the public interest, [as] to:
  - Objects of the Industrial Relations Act 1996(NSW);
  - Likely effect [on] the New South Wales economy, in particular, [protecting] the [State's] employment base … and any adverse impacts on [women's] employment opportunities …; and
  - Inter-State comparative rates.

With counsel assisting and research staff, the Commission took evidence from experts and workers, canvassing historical, cultural, economic, and legal issues. Some 20 industries and occupations were nominated to provide evidence on 'women's work' classification, or predominance of women workers in given areas or fields, including designated workplaces. The Employers Federation challenged the entire Inquiry, objecting to procedure, challenging assisting counsel's appointment and approach, and opposing all nominations and workplaces (including piecework/outwork locations), and the seven basic areas (with subsets or comparators) accepted by the Inquiry for investigation.

Nine industries and their workplaces were reviewed: childcare workers; clerical employees and metal tradespersons; hairdressers and beauty therapists; motor mechanics, librarians (including public sector librarians); geoscientists; nurses and coal miners (including clinical workers—private sector and public hospital nurses); outworkers/pieceworkers; and seafood processors. Selection criteria included demonstrable female domination, a male comparator or industry, and a prehistory of study in that female occupation. Industries featured payment types, including over awards and penalty rates; notoriety for low female wages; significant female employee numbers; having had pay claims based on pay inequities, or mentioned ahead of the Inquiry; public sector; and number of nominations.

First: defining comparable worth or value: 'comparable'—'able to be compared', criteria for determining 'comparable value', or 'comparable value of work' including:

- incidence of over award payments;
- alignment of qualifications;
- work of employees, male and female, covered by different classifications of one award;
- work in an industry undertaken inside, and outside, factories;
- recognition of qualifications, including post-trade qualifications.

The Employers Federation contested 'comparable worth': women's work was not undervalued, required no higher remuneration and, if pay equity were an issue, companies and industries bearing the burden could not sustain women's pay rate increases, heralding disastrous consequences for the NSW economy.

Predicting a regressive impact on women's employment, Australian National University (ANU) emeritus professor, Helen Hughes, agreed with the Employers Federation, providing an instructive counterpoint to Burton's evidence. Hughes said women in the lower socio-economic strata, lacking qualifications or skills and generally in lower-paid, low skilled or unskilled jobs, would suffer, with some 'professional and para-professional women in the public sector' gaining wage increases to other women's detriment. Pinpointing childcare and hairdressing, 'where demand ... is highly elastic', raising wages would likely 'result in a shift from formal to informal sectors, where wages are low'. Raising grocery check-out workers' wages would likely 'accelerate mechanization' and high-level unemployment. Albeit 'well meant', proposals risked detriment to those they intended to help, widening the gap 'between low income women and their families and high income women and theirs'. Without higher productivity, comparative (or comparable) worth 'would be a "dead weight" on the economy'.

So—mirroring ***Equal Pay Case 1969*** and ***1972*** arguments: the economy cannot sustain equal pay, paying women their work's worth loses women jobs, reprised in early 2000, Sydney and Adelaide paid maternity leave exchanges: 'Paid maternity leave could cut jobs: PM', ***Sydney Morning Herald***, 18 October 2001, 'Paid baby leave an investment', ***Adelaide Advertiser***, and the ***Australian***, 'Goward's pet scheme isn't such a great deal'. When the ***Sydney Morning Herald*** 26 June 1998 published Hughes' 'Why pay equity isn't fair', summarising her Inquiry submission, ***Pay Watch Australia*** concluded her 'right-wing ideologue' 'notoriety' gained attention for her 'erroneous, outrageous, and inflammatory views' including 'some particularly insulting references to the NSW Industrial Commission ...'.

Yet, internal contradictions overwhelm Hughes' argument. That pay equity ignores productivity to the economy's detriment, with increased pay levels leading to inflation, loss of jobs and business demise, is offset by her conclusion that jurisdictions applying comparative (or comparable) worth show no significant remuneration changes, so running cases 'would ... create costs for employees, employers and arbitration institutions (that is, for taxpayers), without any return'.

For Hughes, reassessing women's work value by reference to men's work or fields primarily occupied by men, or in occupations and industries where women predominate, is misguided. Comparing librarians' work, skills, and remuneration to geologists' is muddle-headed. Women's representation is low in 'skilled intermediate production and transport ... [with] negligible proportions of apprentices and trainees ...', whilst women constitute 11 per cent of tradespersons only, descending to one per cent if hairdressing and dressmaking are excluded. Overcoming pay differentials requires women to enter men's fields, taking up men's work, she insists, but women 'opt for hairdressing, sewing and cooking' with 'favourable working conditions [but] relatively low skills and low responsibilities'.

Yet, assuming 'relatively low-skills' and 'low responsibility levels' in hairdressing, sewing and cooking is precisely what lies at the heart of pay (in) equity. Equal pay requires recognising women's work as equally valuable as men's in both traditional and non-traditional fields *and* equal opportunity access, promotion and benefits for women in both. An exchange between Hughes and counsel assisting demonstrates Hughes' problem:

Q. … [with] groups such as hairdressers, sewing and cooking having as you describe relative low skills and responsibilities, … what are the skills and responsibilities compared to what other group?

A. Well …, there are … a million … tradespersons … predominantly male. By and large … training and skills of engineers and professionals, metal workers, plumbers, electricians, all sorts of skilled tradesmen have much higher responsibilities than hairdressing, sewing and cooking and they get higher pay.

… If I was seriously interested in improving [women's] condition …, and reducing the earnings gap (and I am and have been all my life) then …, 'Why don't we have any women motor mechanics? Why don't we have any women plumbers? Why don't we have other skilled tradesmen, for example, electronics tradesmen where women are said to be specially suited with other skills?' … why don't … women move into those high skilled, high earnings professions, trades?

…

… I mean hairdressers, tailors, and cooks. Chefs are tradespersons but … they are not always, by and large, not as skilled. They don't require the training … of a motor mechanic or metal trades worker or electronics worker. Their training is much more limited. Hairdressers have very limited training compared to those trades …

Q. … [A]ssessing the position of one [trade or tradesperson] as opposed to the other …—apart from training are there any other criteria or considerations … to determine the relative position of one as compared to the other?

A. [Objectively] training provides the basic difference in base pay and then … you get different career progressions [with] certainly more career progression being a metal worker right up until high supervision provisions with the possibility of moving into technical skills and additional training, whereas hairdressing [doesn't have] the same range of skills the metal worker has.

…

Q. [Y]ou have used the term 'higher skills' on several occasions … On what basis do you say male trades have higher skills. What do you mean by 'higher'? What is the determination of a particular ascription of those skills?

A. … the demand for a product, supply and demand for labour in purchasing that product as well as training experience and so on determine remuneration and … in an increasingly open … trading world, skills are rewarded by pay. So, I conclude that since those trades have a higher pay, they are higher skilled …

The exchange exposes assumptions founding the pay equity argument: why should certain trades (mainly comprising men) be valued more highly than others (mainly women). Why classify them more highly skilled, with more complex training and greater responsibility? Hughes falls into the trap of concluding 'higher skills, more complex training required, greater responsibility' *simply because those trades are more highly paid*. This circularity highlights the need for the Pay Equity Inquiry and WSVEs, just as AFBPW advocated. To say hairdressers have few skills, cursory training and minimal responsibilities indicates little knowledge, or perfunctory thought.

Burton's evidence differed markedly. Both agreed (in Hughes' words) 'the condition of women in Australia' must be improved, reducing the earnings gap being crucial. On reasons for the differential and overcoming it, they parted company. For Burton, women's work is under-remunerated because women do it, history and societal elements featuring. Supporting comparable worth, she put job evaluation systems, their utility, applicability, and assistance in pay (in)equity centrestage. Inevitably, both their substance and implementation harbour sex/gender bias. Systems must incorporate knowledge, experience, and responsibility as inherent elements of predominantly female jobs, with attention to junctures where sex/gender bias could misshape or hinder assessment. Being systemic, the problem requires clear standards and detailed guidelines, despite their potential for dismissal as bureaucratic and time consuming. Regular use, with concise application, reduces time and resources required.

A multiplicity of sources create hurdles militating against pay equity. Hence, a focused, disciplined approach requires education and attention paid to past lessons. Considering the words of an award is insufficient. What lies behind is vital. Just as job analysis is fundamental to exploring whether job descriptions, duty statements and appointments breach sex/

gender discrimination laws, it is basic to determining jobs-worth in wage terms. As Burton says, that it takes time or is difficult to 'achieve high quality job analysis ... doesn't mean the journey is not worth the effort ... The difficulties shouldn't mean that people give up on what is a right and proper goal'.

Job or skills analysis setting past wage rates has been influenced by who has done it—perspective, understanding, socialisation, cultural and socio-economic awareness; what jobs have undergone analysis or work value assessment; who has been industrially active, ensuring those jobs are analysed and rated; whose work value claims have been entertained; how seriously claims have been considered and assessed. Against this backdrop, Burton deemed the goal of a job evaluation system with a high level of gender neutrality achievable. Existing systems such as Hay, developed without gender bias awareness, inevitably contain bias, particularly in skills identification and weightings. A misconceived knowledge base 'compounds the problem as you multiply and add up to get the problem-solving score'. Fundamental design problems mean implementation requires 'a strong equity eye throughout'.

In noting the failure of existing job evaluation systems, Burton pinpointed the unreliability of points systems where a 'veneer of objectivity' exists because points factor systems use numbers. Yet judgements are required, meaning informed and systematic assessments of skills, responsibilities, and accountabilities—often unrecognised in female-dominated occupations—are imperative. Position descriptions contain biased assumptions about skills required and what are skills, meaning systematic consideration of job requirements is imperative, job analysis 'critical and fundamental'.

Burton proposed remedial action building upon the Industrial Relations Commission work value assessment role, incorporating work value elements previously unrecognised. This meant employing expertise to develop an equal remuneration code of practice including standards for 'different evaluation or assessment systems ... [providing] comprehensive guidance about how gender equity in pay setting could be enhanced'. Monitoring and documenting outcomes by gender should, she said, 'extend to performance-based pay and superannuation'.

As raised by WEL in the ***National Wage Case 1983***, AFBPW, NPEC, and WEL's joint submission confirmed inadequate assessments of women's work value. Like WEL (1983), NPEC (1988), and AFBPW (1990–1991, 1991), the submission noted that despite the 1972 equal pay principle 'explicitly requiring proper work value assessments of women's work ..., this was largely ignored'. When conducted, work value assessments compared female classifications with other (undervalued) female classifications, despite the 1972 principle that labour market sex-segregation may flag work value comparisons between female and male classifications in different awards.

Highlighting work value consent arrangements predominating in the NSW industrial system, the submission observed that agreement between male union officials and male management representatives on classifications and rates for women's work frequently meant setting women's jobs to the lowest award classification, paid at the lowest rate. Intentional bias in (de)valuing women's work and women's jobs is unnecessary. Sex/gender discrimination, entrenched and systemic, almost inevitably affects consent outcomes, to women's detriment. Women are active in unions, are industrial advocates, and participate in making enterprise agreements, yet are not always involved in consent agreements, even where the central issue is women's wages and industrial conditions. Women's involvement should be mandatory, but women may be equally or even more disposed to undervalue women's work and women's occupations.

Underlining Australian Bureau of Statistics (ABS) figures confirming the 'high watermark' for women's earnings immediately before enterprise bargaining and the demise of centralised wage fixing, the submission observed:

- in assuming women and men compete freely in the labour market, human capital theory cannot explain 'gender pay gap reality', ignoring access to education, training and ability to work full-time influencing highest income levels;
- occupational segregation doesn't explain the gap completely, and saying women's self-selecting occupations to balance work and family is responsible ignores practical reality—'choice' is limited by labour market structure and segmentation, custom and practice, and women predominantly bearing primary domestic and family responsibilities through domestic labour division and lack of childcare;
- fewer women join unions, with less bargaining power and less likelihood of accessing formal or informal enterprise agreements with increased earnings: 'While awards remain the dominant determinant of pay and conditions for 59 per cent of workers in female-dominated

workplaces, this [follows] for only 21 per cent of workers in male-dominated workplaces';

- skill is socially constructed, privileging work traditionally performed by men, devaluing work performed mainly by women, women's traditional work historically defined unskilled or explained by women's 'natural attributes', men's defined skilled or semi-skilled, justifying substantial pay and classification structure differences, earnings reflecting traditional notions of 'male' and 'female' work, ignoring 'the real complexity or responsibility of work actually performed by women';
- existing tests and mechanisms measuring work value overlook that classification of essential work skills, and undervaluing women's skills where they are seen, constitutes gender bias at every point: description of women's jobs, division into elements, determining value of elements, measurement and weighting of elements, and money-value quantification;
- bias can be eliminated from work value assessments, but generally lacks the 'deliberate, comprehensive and sustained approach' required;
- women 'get around half the over awards men do', making over award payments crucial to pay disparity, but women's are based on individual performance, not the collective basis awarded to men: men's industries tend to run based on over award payments attracting workers, women's on individual merit—probably arising from awards featuring in unionised areas—women less likely to work in unionised workplaces, women's workplaces less likely to be unionised;
- merely asserting conformity of over award payments with market rates fails to answer whether over award payments are allocated non-discriminatorily. If a sex-related pay difference exists through an over-award payment made to male and not to female-dominated occupations, evidence alone can rule out discrimination, and employers must bear the onus of showing market-based justification for the differential.

Over years, these points were made in AIRC submissions—sometimes identically, sometimes in less sophisticated form, sometimes direct experience, sometimes substantive research. Each should have been applied in wage fixing and work value exercises. However, industrial commissions operate according to the very prejudices and biases identified by women's organisation interventions, illustrated by some matters being ruled out—AIRC response to WEL's 1983 childcare submissions (not industrial matter); Council of Action for Equal Pay (CAEP)'s 1986 comparable worth (not appropriate); AFBPW's 1988 plea for WSVEs (unnecessary); the Women's Liberation Movement (WLM)'s 1973 minimum wage claim (not before the Commission). This happened when WEL raised over award payments in the ***National Wage Case 1988***: earlier, margins were within Commission jurisdiction, until the basic wage and minimum wage were applied equally to women and men; then the AIRC said over award payments were outside its scope. This facilitated unequal margins for women and men (if women gained margins at all).

The basis on which over award payments accrue is fallacious, as AFBPW, NPEC, and WEL submitted. Saying men's industries require over award payments 'to attract workers', women's do not, contradicts market realities. Since the 1980s, nursing was cited constantly as requiring encouragement for nurse-numbers to grow—say, the 1987 Victorian government Inquiry into the Nursing Profession or 2002 federal government Critical Review of Aged Care Nursing. Why, then, no over award payments or over award payments commensurate with men's industries to attract women into nursing or aged care? Or take the construction industry: over award payments do not follow industry trends or highs and lows—disappearing in times of high interest rates and low need for recruitment, returning with low interest rates and construction industry booms.

When, in the ***Pay Equity Inquiry 1997***, citing education, training, and fulltime working capacity as affecting women's competition in the market, AFBPW, NPEC, and WEL raised issues the AIRC had declared (in ***National Wage Case 1983*** and ***1988***) as outside basic wage or national wage setting. When reiterating women's lesser bargaining power and lower membership of unions, AFBPW, NPEC, and WEL repeated AFBPW's ***National Wage Case 1990–1991*** submissions, and AFBPW and WEL's in the ***National Wage Case 1991***. In the ***National Wage Case 1990–1991***, the AIRC heeded those concerns, ruling against enterprise bargaining. In the ***National Wage Case 1991***, sweeping concerns aside, the AIRC ditched centralised wage fixing, approving enterprise bargaining, despite that earlier acceptance of women's disadvantage under it.

In critiquing skill as socially constructed, AFBPW, NPEC, and WEL contrasted industrial valorising of components of work done by men as skills, routine classification of women's work as unskilled or lesser skilled. Pinpointing gender bias in all existing tests and mechanisms for measuring work value, their critique encompassed work value processes in Australian industrial commissions and wage-fixing bodies. In referring to custom and practice, including responsibility for domestic and family care and paucity of childcare (not then incorporated into the wage fixing equation), AFBPW, NPEC, and WEL raised custom and practice—exemplified by the AIRC—of classification as 'not industrial issues', not for wage fixing, but for government or others—including, as appeared, women workers themselves (as women were doing, in any event).

Yet, traversing AFBPW, NPEC, and WEL's ***Pay Equity Inquiry 1997*** submission shows conditions are not immutable, and change can—and does—occur. In the 1990s, government legislated to put over award payments within AIRC purview, although (as with the ***Minimum Wage Case 1974*** example), abandoning centralised wage fixing in favour of enterprise bargaining minimised the impact. As for homeground and dependants' care, women's persistence ensured their ultimate recognition as industrial issues, through the ***Maternity Leave case 1979*** (WEL intervening, Ryan appearing), ***Adoption Leave case 1984***, ***Parental Leave case 1989–1991***, ***Family Leave Case 1994***, ***Personal/Carers' Leave case*** (see also ***Supplementary Award Simplification case 1998***), ***Parental Leave—Casual Employees—case 2001***, ***Working Hours Case 2002***, and ***Work and Family case 2005*** (WEL intervening, Richter appearing).

Reinforcing the need to make an argument over and over, the ***Pay Equity Inquiry 1997*** generated another evolution: recognition that entrenched biases in work and skills evaluation exist, require acknowledgement, and need wage-fixing mechanisms to address them. This sidelined the AIRC's declaration more than 10 years earlier that comparable worth was a foreign notion, giving CAEP ***Nurses Comparable Worth case 1985–1986*** submissions short shrift. The NSW ***Pay Equity Inquiry 1997*** vindicated CAEP, and AFBPW in its WSVE call, the next step being a pay equity principle.

To apply whenever the Industrial Commission exercises powers affecting remuneration in consent and non-consent agreements, including approving enterprise agreements and award making, variation and review, the AFBPW, NPEC, and WEL principle encompassed three elements:

- Broad criteria requiring work value investigation, rates set by objective methods free of sex bias and following ILO conventions, transparent in 'factors of value employed, weightings attached, and translation of assessed value into remuneration';
- Examples listed of factors for work value assessment, including skill, responsibility, qualifications, conditions, experience, and so on, tra-

ditionally considered by the Commission, and specifying factors significant in traditionally female dominated work—say, interpersonal skills, nurturing, dexterity, coordination and so on;
- Recognising that if fixing remuneration 'legitimately involves consideration of factors such as labour market efficiency, capacity to pay, working conditions, effect on employment etc.', a non-exhaustive range of legitimate considerations requires specification, with a mandatory requirement that a factor be identified clearly, weight attached to it documented, and each consideration addressed free of sex discrimination.

Transparency is basic, essential for clarifying whether work value assessment considers competently all essential factors for wage determinations absent infusion of historical and contemporary weightings against women's jobs and occupations. Wage fixers must be clear and precise about factors relied upon and how they are considered. Parties must know how (upon what factors and basis) wage rates are set. Only then, can fairness in wage fixing be seen and agreed, flaws in wage setting identified, mistakes remedied, and guidance provided for future work value and equal pay claims. It is fanciful to expect sex/gender discrimination and socio-cultural values undercutting pay equity will disappear overnight. Addressing entrenched bias is an ongoing exercise.

AFBPW, NPEC, and WEL emphasised that women as interveners and expert witnesses are essential when parties rely on an evaluation method showing women and men's work is of equal or comparable value, or that rates are impacted by being classed 'women's work' as where, for example:

- work value margins were, historically, set by the workers' sex, heralding undervaluation of women's work;
- operative wage-fixing principles impeded examination of cases raising equal pay implementation, historic undervaluation of women's work or changes in relative value of women's and men's work;
- rates set affected by sex stereotyped assumptions about women's income needs leading to under remuneration of women's work for its value;
- form of employment contract and/or lack of bargaining power led to a lack of capacity to demonstrate and secure remuneration for the full scope of factors contributing work value in female dominated work, awards, over awards and agreements, resulting in undervaluing;

- a 'significant informal sector has, through unfair competition against the public interest, undercut rates awarded ..., depressing award rates and contributing to under remuneration of women's work for its value';
- industrial instruments have incorporated market rates affected originally by sex discrimination, an example being through first award setting principles and procedures;
- exercise of market power by an employer or group of employers has caused women's work to be under-remunerated for its value.

Yet, lacking access to income sources of other bodies appearing in the Commission—namely, employer organisations or unions, the financial and resource burden women and women's organisations bear requires attention.

The Commission recommended replacing existing equal remuneration principles with the new pay equity principle, applying to the Commission's full range of functions and all instruments—awards, enterprise agreements, industrial dispute resolutions, as an essential feature of every awards review under the Industrial Relations Act 1996 (NSW), section 19. A statutory provision should ensure equal remuneration and conditions of work for women and men doing work of equal or comparable value affirmed through a provision outlining:

- Remuneration defined as in ILO Convention 100 (Equal Remuneration Convention);
- Work value assessment to be objective, transparent and non-discriminatory, assessing the true value of work, not whether there have been changes in work;
- Gender causation or sex discrimination is unnecessary;
- Comparisons of work value allowed across and within industries and occupations between different awards and with more than one comparison if required;
- The use of comparisons as useful only because it gives a guide to the reliability of rates of remuneration;
- The essential ingredient being equal or comparable value, the proper basis for comparison is not restricted to similarity of work: multiple factors could be considered, including history of the female-dominated industry or occupation; award histories and their varia-

tion; availability of credentialing and institutional arrangements in a particular industry or occupation;

- Over award payments, or their lack, considered in making comparisons. However, components of over awards must be properly identified, and over award payments due to labour market factors should be excluded;
- Assessment of undervaluation in itself ('undervaluation simpliciter'), not requiring a comparison between male and female rates of pay;
- Rates of remuneration no longer presumed as properly assessed in female-dominated industries and occupations, under equal pay principles or work value, including under previous processes, such as the Structural Efficiency principle or Minimum Rates Adjustment.

The new pay equity principle should clarify that award history must be accounted for when considering women's work and occupation pay rates, necessarily taking a broad approach, including whether:

- the work has some female characterisation;
- female employees' skills are undervalued in themselves;
- remuneration is undervalued through occupational segregation, women's concentration in part-time and casual work, and low unionisation;
- women's traditional work, including features such as dexterity, nurturing and interpersonal skills, has been assessed in a gender neutral way and given sufficient weight.

In the absence of previous work value assessments, an assessment should be undertaken as part of award review, with male rates of pay not reduced by the principle's operation.

Remedies addressing undervaluation could incorporate reclassification of work; career paths; incremental scales changes; reassessment of broad banding of classifications or skills; reassessments of definitions to ensure accurate descriptions of work. An evolutionary or incremental approach should be adopted to minimise adverse economic or employment consequences. Further, a claim should be advanced to the Commission for application of the equal remuneration principle—a union making a claim, with an employer supporting its female employees in reassessment of work's worth; or union and employer bringing a claim cooperatively. The government—employing many women in female occupations—librarianship, nursing, social work—and responsible for the Commission Inquiry—had to act. This meant considering which female occupation and women workers it would advance for wage reassessment, which unions would participate mindful of members' pay parity claims.

The ***Pay Equity Inquiry 1997*** did not fully embrace AFBPW, NPEC, and WEL's recommendations. Anti-Discrimination Act 1977 amendments, broadening its scope beyond individual claims or class actions, to cover systemic employment and remuneration sex/gender discrimination, were not endorsed. Still, the Commission proposed Industrial Relations Act changes advancing the pay equity principle and preventing diversion from its focus on pay (in)equity, and onto a search for sex/gender discrimination:

- clarifying the distinction between undervaluation and discrimination;
- distinguishing 'discrimination' from 'equal remuneration'; and
- ensuring a focus on pay equity in all deliberations under the Act.

Yet, its being held at all, like its outcome, was directly attributable to women's organisations and individual women. One crucial advantage was women's position within as well as outside institutions. Burgmann, Legislative Council president, lobbied attorney-general Shaw in parliamentary corridors, pushing for the Pay Equity Task Force, then for the Inquiry. Women's organisations lobbied, then intervened in the Commission. Women in the bureaucracy, notably Hall as Department for Women deputy director and earlier at Department of Industrial Relations managerial level, added duel insider and women's organisation engagement, particularly NPEC, with reciprocal support to AFBPW and WEL. Women in positions of (some) power played a crucial role.

Not only did the NSW lead propel Tasmania. The ***Pay Equity Inquiry 1997*** and recommendations provided a model for women and women's organisations pressing governments, unions, and commissions in their respective states to address women's wage justice.

Pay Equity in the States

First, a wobble. Though post-dating the ***Pay Equity Inquiry 1997***, the ***Childcare Industry (ACT) & (NT) case 1999*** was a textbook example of how not to do it. The focus there on formal or academic qualifications ignored childcare workers' on-the-job activities and skills: changing nappies, selecting and preparing nutritious food, setting daily and weekly programs commensurate with infants and children's age ranges, engaging children in age-specific activities, undertaking surrogate parent and health and safety responsibilities. The Commission even downgraded the value of the qualifications it 'assessed'. Other jurisdictions (say, negligence as in ***Commonwealth v. Introvigne***) assess responsibility for children's care, making monetary assessments and findings. Why not in fixing pay rates?

Next off the mark was the Queensland Industrial Relations Commission, taking the NSW approach with its ***Pay Equity Inquiry 2001***, commissioner GK (Glenys) Fisher presiding. WA followed, John Kobelke, minister for consumer and employment protection, commissioning a report by Drs (Trish) Todd and (Joan) Eveline. Then Victoria, minister for industrial relations Rob Hulls establishing a Pay Equity Working Party under Dominica Whelan, AIRC commissioner.

Despite different modes, findings were consistent: the mid-1980s two-tier wage system and award restructuring approach had at least a plateauing effect on women's wages, ensuring a continuing Australia-wide female-male wage gap, failing to improve since the advent of enterprise bargaining.

The Victorian Working Party determined that whatever the measure, a gender pay gap 'as great as 18.4% [exists] based on total weekly earnings for all full-time adult workers', with the gap 'somewhat lower at 11.2%' when including full-time non-managerial employees only, whilst 'no substantial improvement in women's pay as a percentage of men's' eventuated since 1986. The Working Party noted the gap is 6.1 per cent for total hourly earnings of part-time employees, 'considerably lower than for full-time employees', and 'attributable to … the overwhelming proportion of part-time workers [being] women—almost 72%'. Women in part-time work experienced a far greater decline in wage parity, relative to men in part-time work, 'in the order of … 8.4 percentage points for female employees' as against 2.1 percentage points for male employees. On part-time versus full-time, the Working Party concluded '… while women in full-time employment may have increased their earnings this [is] not replicated to the same degree for women in part-time employment', 'a major concern' due to significant numbers of women in part-time employment. Even then, a wage gap remains between women and men in full-time paid employment.

As AFBPW argued in the ***National Wage Case 1990–1991*** and ***National Wage Case 1991***, despite female-male wage differentials, under the centralised wage-fixing award system, women gained greater fairness relative to men's wages. The ***Equal Pay Case 1969*** and ***Equal Pay Case 1972***, for all their deficiencies and lack of their principles' practical application to the fullest, meant Australia led in pay equity for women, second only to Scandinavia. With women less likely to be included in enterprise bargaining agreements negotiated by strong unions in male-dominated occupations and industries, women workers remained dependent upon the award system applying only to the lower-paid. The outcome of ***Living Wage Cases***—employers seeking the lowest possible increases, the Australian Council of Trade Unions (ACTU) minimal rises—left workers (mainly women) obliged to accept them.

In the ***Pay Equity Inquiry 1997***, Hughes had predicted obsolescence of the pay gap, through young women (she asserted) moving into male-dominated occupations, gaining male-level wages and salaries. Working Party research showed women's segregation into women's industries and occupations remained unchanged. The Working Party was mindful, too, of the US 'tipping point': women moving into male-dominated areas, feminising occupations, whereby employers devalue the work. Rates of pay drop.

For Queensland, undervaluation of women's work was attributed to no career path, female characterisation of work, absence of effective work value examinations, low unionisation, lack of or inadequate recognition of qualifications, and a large casual employees contingent. Research into childcare as an occupation confirmed childcare workers' labour as 'arguably undervalued'. Similarly for dental assistants, the Commission's case study providing parties an opportunity to:

- 'analyse, assess and value work in a gender neutral way by "unpacking" skills of a female dominated occupation'; and
- comment on 'the elements of the draft pay equity principle'.

Private and public sector employment of dental assistants, dentists, and dental assistant trainers meant evidence from both sectors was available. That women fought for entry into the field, yet gender wage disparity resulted, counters the proposition that women have only to enter male-dominated fields to achieve equal pay.

In WA, calling for submissions, the Inquiry received 18 responses from large and small employers, unions, professional associations, a government department, individuals, and women's groups. A Reference Group held a joint and smaller meetings, the latter covering specific interests. Stakeholder and expert interviews found women in the WA labour market were, 'on average, paid less than men in WA': of all Australian states, WA had 'the largest gap between men's and women's wages …':

> In the February 2004 quarter, WA women employed full-time earned, on average, 22.6% less than their male counterparts whereas at a national level the corresponding gender wage gap was 15.2%.

Yet, WA women's activism and political gains relative to other states are impressive. At nineteenth century's end and early twentieth, WA was ahead, women enfranchised in 1899 (second to SA—1894), first woman MP (1921), first female minister (1949), first ALP MP (1925), then first female senator (1943). Greater pay inequities may stem from the centrality of minerals and mining economically, exemplifying the need for reassessments of women's work value: metals and mining jobs are no more responsible, difficult, or dangerous (even less so) than jobs where women predominate—say nursing and childcare. WA's earlier accession to enterprise bargaining and workplace agreements, predating their introduction federally or in Victoria is relevant. Enterprise bargaining and Australian Workplace Agreements (AWAs) federally affected women's pay rates, a likely explanation for WA women's depressed wage relativities.

The WA Inquiry endorsed a pay equity or equal remuneration principle, concluding 'economic, social and political consequences for individuals, business and governments' result from wage inequity, with pay equity:

> … fundamental to gender equality, [increasing] women's labour market attachment, financial independence and life choices, all part of expressed government policy. For business, gender pay equity can result in … a more committed workforce [and] better utilization of women's paid workforce participation—thereby addressing labour market supply concerns.

Similarly, the Queensland Commission recommended an equal remuneration principle: practical, easy to use and understand; relevant to new, emerging and established industries, occupations and callings; and providing a balance between competing interests, applied in making or amending awards, making orders under the Industrial Relations Act 1999 (Qld) (Equal Remuneration part), arbitrating equal remuneration industrial disputes, and in valuing or assessing employees' work in women's industries, occupations or callings. Patterned on NSW, it recommended financial provision in bringing pay equity claims, and Industrial Relations Act amendments to ensure awards, enterprise or certified agreements and QWAs—Queensland Workplace Agreements—incorporate pay equity, otherwise not coming into effect.

The Queensland Commission also proposed a measure from WEL's ***National Wage Case 1983*** submission, mirroring NSW's dedicated pay equity commissioner: a panel (two commissioners) hearing undervaluation claims and Industrial Relations Act (Part 5)(as amended) pay equity applications, commissioners on full bench hearings sitting with commissioners from remaining members, to consolidate case law development.

In WA, the Inquiry pinpointed lack of attention to gender pay equity in existing wage-fixing principles, recommending Industrial Relations Act 1979 (WA) amendment by a Part akin to the Queensland Act, addressing equal remuneration specifically. As in Queensland and NSW, general legislative amendments were recommended to clarify how the Act 'can improve gender pay equity'—focusing on objects, 'award modernization and aspects of enterprise bargaining'. The Minimum Conditions of Employment Act 1993 (WA) required amendment, to promote 'an effective minimum wage system, ... [and] more extensive leave provisions to allow workers to better balance their caring and paid work responsibilities'. Further, '[as] women are represented disproportionately amongst casual employees', recommendations followed to ensure compliance with industrial standards for casual employees, and casual employment research.

The WA Inquiry strategies included 'pay equity audits' (government—mandatory, private sector—voluntary) as 'an effective means [for] groups and industry parties [to understand] ... the gender pay gap ... building their capacity to implement equal remuneration'. Also, training for women to build their capacities, and for employers and employees generally prompting awareness of gender and its impact on remuneration and the workplace. Finally, the Inquiry recommended a 'high level Steering Committee' and 'Pay Equity Unit'.

Lacking a state commission to implement it (Victoria having relinquished its industrial powers to federal Parliament), the Victorian Working Party proposed no pay equity principle, recommending that the Victorian government take up pay equity with the federal government, advocating a

Workplace Relations Act 1996 (Cth) review. Advances in Queensland, NSW and Tasmania should be pursued federally, because women under federal legislation should have equal jurisdictional opportunities as in state industrial relations systems 'now adopting more innovative principles' than the federal Act.

The Working Party favoured the Queensland model, focusing on undervaluation of women's work, industries and occupations, recommending a commitment by government, employer organisations, and unions to a gender pay equity campaign, plus union gender pay equity training, and training modules for employer associations and members. The Equal Opportunity Act 1995 (Victoria) individual claimant model required amendment, to introduce a more systemic approach to employment discrimination through 'gender audits'. Consistent with the WA Inquiry, the Working Party recommended a Pay Equity Unit, collection of data, gender pay equity audits, and an overall Pay Equity Plan of Action implementing Working Party recommendations.

Promising in all this was the apparent states' shift toward progressing equal pay. Pay parity having slowed or halted, this was at least promising.

Librarians, Geologists, and Childcare Workers

Yet, what price recommendations without implementation? In late 2004, the WA ***Report on the Gender Pay Gap*** was released for public comment. Six months later, on 29 April 2005 at a University of Western Australia (UWA) Todd and Eveline conference 'Gender Pay Gap: Assessing Possible Futures in a Post Inquiries Era', the consumer and employment protection minister honoured one of the WA Inquiry's recommendations. He announced a Pay Equity Unit 'for an initial three years' (the recommended period) 'to implement strategies to reduce the [WA] gender pay gap'. Otherwise, little movement was evident in WA, or Victoria.

In NSW and Queensland, public sector and union women promoted implementation of Commission recommendations. Unsurprising, considering the librarians' longstanding equal pay struggle, the first NSW case was the librarians, library technicians and archivists' claim, their skills, capacities, qualifications, job components, responsibilities, and conditions of work compared with geologists', pay rates contrasted as gender-bound. As one of the occupations in the ***Pay Equity Inquiry 1997***, the claim's formulation and progress was assisted by the Inquiry's research, and government was amenable to correcting a decades-long gender gap. Yet, the ***Re Crown Librarians, Library Officer and Archivists Award Proceedings 2002*** award covering librarians, librarian assistants, and archivists, and recognising librarianship as a profession in occupational and sociological terms, did not come without a concerted effort by the PSA, women involved directly in the claim, and AFBPW, NPEC, and WEL—intervening jointly to support the claim.

Both NSW and Queensland Commissions then entertained childcare workers' claims, with cases run in Victoria, NT, SA, and the ACT. ***Re Child Care Industry (ACT) Award 1985; Child Care Industry (NT) Award 1986 case 1990***, and ***Re Child Care Industry (ACT) & (NT) case 1999*** were recognised as inadequately addressing childcare workers' competencies, skills and responsibilities, and their appropriate remuneration level, the underlying historical foundation always ignored. In WA, even without a pay equity or equal remuneration principle, a childcare claim was before the Industrial Commission. Nonetheless, absence of the principle and employers' procedural points generated delays. On 31 March 2005, the LHMWU secured a new award in the Queensland claim. In WA, with no determination before the Workplace Choices Act 2005 (Cth) came into effect (March 2006), the federal system was the only option, if the new Act's narrow parameters could accommodate pay parity. With no federal equal remuneration principle, the new Australian Fair Pay Commission (FPC) lacking wage fixing experience or gender gap expertise yet primed to set minimum wages, confidence plummeted.

Tasmania, ahead in July 2000, by 2007 year's end had come to a halt. The Australian Services Union (ASU) produced a substantial Pay Equity Campaign Kit, on 7 May 2002 lodging a claim with Tasmania's Industrial Commission to vary the Community Services Award. Adjourned for discussions between parties, re-listing would occur only with 'complete exhaustion' of discussions, said deputy president Watling. A predominant view was that claims were 'too costly' and 'too complicated'. Unlike NSW and Queensland, in the ***State Wage Case 2000***, the Tasmanian Commission had required no extensive research into selected women's occupations or trades and professions dominated by women for guidance. In NSW and Queensland, the research burden had fallen at least in part upon the Commissions rather than unions. Running the ASU case meant the union must produce its own research, with resource implications. Not insignificantly, too, the ***Wage Case 2000*** advocates were no longer there, and those now in their roles had other priorities.

As history shows, following through on industrial arena wins is essential and, as the ***Equal Pay Cases 1969*** and ***1972*** showed, industrial commissions cannot be counted on to implement their determinations. Yes, unions must pursue claims. Yet, commissions cannot absolve themselves from responsibility to ensure their determinations have effect. The struggle for equal pay is dependent upon institutional readiness to take decisions and claims seriously, upon unions accepting women's pay justice as valid, and women's organisations and individuals' readiness—and resources—to press them.

In ***State of NSW & Ors v. Commonwealth***) (***Workplace Relations case 2006***), the High Court ruled the Work Choices Act 2005 (Cth) valid. In early 2007, what this meant with the vast bulk of wage claims thereby removed from state industrial bodies into the federal arena remained unsettled. Yet, however badly women do in the pay stakes, history shows women's best chances for fair pay rates come through centralised wage fixing, not individual bargaining power, leaving lower wage earners dependent on a 'living wage'. The 2007 federal election saw 'work choices' swept away. However, enterprise bargaining remained triumphant. As Chap. 20, 'Remembering and Forgetting—Women, Working Together and the Struggle for Equal Pay', asks, what direction now for women's ingenuity, persistence, optimism, and effort?

References

Cases—See Case List

AFBPW, NPEC and WEL, *In the Matter of the NSW Pay Equity Inquiry (No. 6320 of 1997)—Final Submissions*, AFBPW/NPEC/WEL, Sydney, NSW, 1998a (3 July 1998), pp. 1–10, http://www.users.bigpond.com/rj_gj/inquiry/womenorgs1.html (accessed 14 June 2006).

AFBPW, NPEC and WEL, *Final Submissions—Oral Presentation*, NSW IC, Sydney, NSW, 1998b (3 July 1998), pp. 1–10, http://www.users.bigpond.com/rj-gi/inquiry/clossub.html (accessed 14 June 2006).

ALIA, ***Review of the Gender Pay Gap in Western Australia***, Perth, WA, 2004 (May 2004), http://alia.org.au/advocacy/submissions/wa.gender.html, pp. 1–6 (accessed 12 August 2006).

ASU, ***Pay Equity Campaign Kit***, http://www.asu.asn.au/tasmania/payequitykit.doc, pp. 1–19 (accessed 12 June 2006).

ASU, 'Pay Equity Campaign—Community Services Award', ***Tasmanian Branch News***, 2002 (7 May 2002), pp. 1–11, at pp. 7–8 (accessed 12 June 2006).

Meredith Burgmann, ***Interview***, Sydney, NSW, 2006 (26 June 2006).

Business Victoria, ***Pay Equity Inquiry—What is the Pay Equity Inquiry?/The Advancing Pay Equity report***, http://www.business.vic.gov.au/BUSVIC/STANDARD/1001/PC_50526.html, pp. 1–3 (accessed 12 August 2006).

DEST, ***Australian Aged Care Nursing: A Critical Review of Education, Training, Recruitment and Retention in Residential and Community Settings***, DEST, Canberra, ACT, c2001, http://www.dest.gov.au/archive/highered/nursing/pubs/aust_aged_care/3.htm, pp. 1–4 (accessed 11 August 2006).

DOECEP Labour Relations, ***Gender Pay Gap—Review of the gender pay gap in Western Australia***, http://www.docep.wa.gov.au/lr/LabourRelations/Content/Current%20Issues/Pages/Gender (accessed 12 August 2006).

Philippa Hall, ***Interview***, 2006 (26 May 2006).

Helen Hughes, 'Equal Pay for Work of Equal Value ...?' ***Issues Analysis***, No 2, 1998 (26 June 1998), pp. 1–15.

Rosemary Hunter, ***The Beauty Therapist, The Mechanic, The Geoscientist and the Librarian: Addressing Undervaluation of Women's Work***, 1st Clare Burton Memorial Lecture, Women's Executive Development Program, ATN WEXDEV, Sydney, NSW, 1999.

Inquiry into the Nursing Profession, ***Study of Professional Issues in Nursing***, Department of Health, Victoria, 1987.

John Kobelke, Minister for Consumer and Employment Protection, ***Brief Ministerial Statement—Gender Pay Equity Report***, Legislative Assembly, Parliament House, W. Perth, WA, 2004 (Friday 26 November 2004), http://www.ministers.wa.gov.au/kobelke/docs/speeches/genderpayequity.pdf, pp. 1–5 (accessed 11 August 2006).

LHMWU Childcare, 'Real work: Real pay. Queensland campaign for child-care pay underway', 2004 (9 March 2004), http://lhmu.org.au/childcare/news/2004/1078967144_6579.html, pp. 1–5 (accessed 13 August 2006).

Minister for Industrial Relations, ***Media release—Gender Pay Gap Set to Widen Under Howard's IR Reforms***, Melbourne, Victoria, 2005 (8 March 2005), http://www.dpc.vic.gov.au/domino/Web_Notes/newmedia.nsf/3981a41eabfaf43bca256d64007ae1a5/a8e3a68dce74e174ca256fbf0010b2ac!OpenDocument, pp. 1–2 (accessed 12 August 2006).

NWCC, ***Pay Equity for Women in Australia***, AGPS, Canberra, ACT.

Steve O'Neill, ***Current Issues—National Wage and Safety Net Claims and Outcomes 1991–2005***, Economics, Commerce and Industrial Relations Section, Parliament of Australia, Parliamentary Library, http://www.aph.gov.au/library/intguide/ECON/safety.htm (accessed 12 June 2006).

Pay Equity Inquiry 1997, Trns pp. 2534–2538, 'Intra and Inter Occupational Gender Wage Differences', http://202.92.124.6/workandfamly/payequity/report/statistical/intra'+and+inter'+occupation (accessed 12 June 2006).

Pay Equity Inquiry 1997 (1998), Terms of Reference, http://202.92.124.6/workandfamily/payequity/report/into/the+terms+of+reference.html (accessed 12 June 2006).

Royal College of Nursing, Australia, *Submission to the Australian Council for Safety and Quality in Health Care Discussion Paper: Safe Staffing*, Melbourne, Victoria, 2003 (December 2003), http://www.rcna.org.au/content/acsqhc_safe_staffing_submission_05_jan_04.pdf, pp. 1–13 (accessed 11 August 2006).

Trish Todd and Joan Eveline, ***Report on the Review of the Gender Pay Gap in Western Australia—Executive Summary and List of Recommendations***, School of Economics and Commerce, UWA, Perth, WA, 2004 (November 2004), http://www.docep.wa.gov.au/Ir/LabourRelations/Media/Gender_Pay_Executive.pdf, pp. 1–12 (accessed 12 August 2006).

Victorian Pay Equity Working Party, ***Advancing Pay Equity***, Victorian Government, Melbourne, Victoria, 2005.

CHAPTER 20

Conclusion: Remembering and Forgetting—Women, Working Together and the Struggle for Equal Pay

> I was but one of a band of local women who set out purposefully to secure certain reforms, and we all kept on until we got them ... We won, as we expected, for never, never would we admit defeat, even when the battle seemed to be against us.
>
> Margaret Ogg, co-founder Queensland Women's Electoral League
> quoted Patricia T. Fallon
> *So Hard the Conquering—A Life of Irene Longman*
> PhD Thesis, Griffith University, Qld, 2002

Twenty years into the twenty-first century, more than one hundred years after the National Council of Women (NCW) prioritised equal pay in its early 1890s inaugural platform, pay inequity persists, repercussions staining women's careers and lifespan. In October 2006, the Australian Institute of Family Studies (AIFS) reported a 'dramatic rise' in mothers with a child under one year returning to paidwork, from 20 to 38 per cent 1981–2004. Although proportionately low compared with many Organisation for Economic Cooperation and Development (OECD) countries, upon a child's reaching four or five, 60 per cent of Australian mothers again worked for money. Still, only 53 per cent of women over fifty-five had superannuation, versus 69 per cent of men, with far lower balances for high-income women than high-income men: of all women forty-five to sixty years, half held only $8000 in superannuation. Australian

J. A. Scutt, *Wage Rage for Equal Pay*,
https://doi.org/10.1007/978-3-031-42178-5_20

National University (ANU)'s Dr Simon Kelly attributes this to late entry into superannuation schemes, 'different workforce participation patterns', and lower earnings when balancing children and paidwork. By 2022, the estimate was $19,107, but Australian Taxation Office (ATO) figures show the pay gap at 13.8 per cent, the superannuation gap 23.3 per cent. Men aged 55–59 hold an average $51,000 more than women—'the equivalent of over three-and-a-half years of contributions on the median national salary of $70,000 per annum'.

In 2007, the forecast federally for women and equal pay was bleak. Delivering the 8th Clare Burton Memorial Lecture, Barbara Pocock concluded: 'We are an increasingly unequal society', Australia's trajectory 'among those in the developed world leading it backwards on key indicators [including] length of fulltime working week, employment precariousness, hostility of work regimes to parents, and collective bargaining'. A few women were doing relatively well—compared with other women, not with their male counterparts, but little indicated women's incomes or capacity to plan for retirement were improving. However, 2007 brought Kevin Rudd's Labor government to power federally, following swelling protest at the Howard government's vaunted 'Work Choices' laws biting workers and stultifying the equal pay campaign, much less improving pay equity. In 2010, Julia Gillard led Labor to power again, a minority government, succeeded by Rudd in 2013, thence to a Liberal National Coalition government from 2013 to 2022, headed variously by Tony Abbott, Malcolm Turnbull, and Scott Morrison, then May 2022 and Anthony Albanese's Labor. Australia's record on women's economic status in the twenty-first century reflects these political changes.

In 2007, Australian Bureau of Statistics (ABS) tables for average weekly earnings showed the vast bulk of women still far behind. Relativities between women and men's incomes decreased over-all, with no sign of positive change. Average weekly total earnings was $700.60 for all employees, $838.80 for males as against $554.70 for female employees. For fulltime adult non-managerial employees, the ratio of female to male average weekly ordinary time earnings was 89.2 per cent. For fulltime junior non-managerial employees, the ratio of female to male average weekly ordinary time earnings was 94.5 per cent. Though suggesting progress, reality showed otherwise: average weekly overtime earnings for fulltime non-managerial employees $66.00 for males, $12.40 for females, even more starkly revealing actual take-home pay differentials, through male workers scoring substantially more overtime. As always, job segregation remained significant in male/female earnings disparity. Unsurprisingly, average weekly total earnings for fulltime adult non-managerial employees ranged highest in the mining industry—$1410.70 (dominated by men), lowest in cafes, restaurants, and accommodation—$641.70 (a major field for women). By 2022, ABS figures showed women's average weekly ordinary fulltime earnings 'across all industries and occupations' as $1609.00 contrasted against men's average weekly 'ordinary fulltime earnings' of £1872.90—meaning 'on average, women earned $263.90 less than men'. The current 'national gender pay gap' is 14.1 per cent. To earn a man's average annual salary, a woman must work 60 more days after the end of the financial year (30 June), making Australia's 'national equal pay day' 29 August 2022.

Pay Equity in Upward Motion

Initially, it lay with the state industrial system to provide movement through in-principle advances on pay equity. Following the historic NSW Industrial Relations Commission ***Crown Librarians, Library Officers and Archivists Award—Re Applications under the Equal Remuneration Principle 2000*** (***Crown Librarians case***) win, in ***Re Miscellaneous Workers Kindergartens and Childcare Centres &c (State) Award*** (***Childcare Centres case***), childcare workers sought similar advances.

In the ***Childcare Centres case 2006***, the L:iquor Hospitality and Miscellaneous Employees' Union (LHMEU) NSW applied to replace the existing consent award (covering primary contact staff, other than teachers, employed at pre-schools, long daycare and out-of-school-hour centres, plus non-contact staff—cooks and cleaners), seeking a new classification structure with increased wages 'properly reflecting employees' qualifications, skills and responsibilities', and changes in award conditions. With women more than 95 per cent of staff, the childcare industry 'was overwhelmingly dominated by female employees whose wages had historically been undervalued'.

Hearing from parties, interveners, and expert witnesses, the Commission acknowledged the importance of work performed by 'the predominantly female childcare workers employed in this State', their responsibility for care and education of children mostly below school age having 'significant value, as is the skill and complexity of their work'. Underscoring this was the 'increasingly detailed attention' from 'all arms of government … to regulation of the industry'. Agreements approved by the Commission over the years meant pay rates failed to reflect the work's value 'properly and adequately', the ***Childcare Centres case 2006*** resulting in a new industry award with increased wages. Seen as a win culminating decades of equal pay struggle, the case illustrates the elusive nature of equal pay, arguments mired in assumptions and analyses influenced by disputed notions of women's work and women's worth. It showed the impact of pay equity inquiries and cases from the twentieth century's end yet failed insofar as it perpetuated undervaluation and underpayment of women's work and women workers.

An award history lacking comprehensive work value assessment together with consent agreements, meant industry changes and skills required of workers were 'not reflected in award rates', including licensing requirement changes, accreditation, training and regulation, health and safety requirements, and child protection and privacy obligations. Low wages, poor conditions, lack of promotion and career advancement opportunities created 'significant problems for recruitment and retention of qualified childcare workers', advancement dependent on employees being considered 'qualified' or 'advanced'. Evidence further confirmed a recurring feature of women's traditional work—no over award payments. The LHMEU initially fought for workers' pay increases on a comparison between wages in industries traditionally dominated by male employees. However, the claim finally rested upon a comparison with wage levels of pre-school teachers, part of the childcare industry. The employers' counter application argued for 'substantial decreases in wages' for all pre-school employees—a danger with pay equity claims and, considering stereotypes and attitudes, making women's industries more likely to suffer unequal pay in the first place, an increased risk where a female dominated industry is used as a comparator.

1990s studies revealed an hourly pay gap of up to 32 per cent between predominantly male industries and industries almost wholly female dominated, identifying childcare as a 'sex-typed industry subjected to stereotypical views' of women's abilities and 'suitability for working with children', doing 'caring and household-related work'. Evidence showed remuneration levels impacted by suppositions of no learning required, no training necessary, wages based on innate ability. Expert evidence established these assumptions lacked foundation, had no research base, and were, bluntly, biased. Contending women are 'naturally' good at childcare because women are women and childcare is women's work (circularity incarnate) generates claims that because women can do it, it cannot be too difficult and requires no training.

Expert witness Dr Lyons addressed the Queensland Commission's contention in the ***Childcare and Kindergarten Employees' Award—State***

case 1991 that childcare work 'is "simple"', trained and untrained workers 'perform[ing] the same work and exercis[ing] the same responsibilities'. Lyons said that over 90 per cent of students, staff, and parents of children in childcare services concluded training for industry work was essential for both males and females, ability being 'a learned skill, not coming naturally to either sex'. Valuing childcare work appropriately for skill, ability, and work is impeded by inadequate sex/gender-reliant or sex/gender-linked remuneration assessment, based in stereotyping. Crucial interpersonal and communication skills are 'not necessarily given the same value as "mainstream" skills, such as use of machinery and technology, or exercising management or supervisory responsibility', with essential teamwork skills overlooked. Confronted with this, the employers in the ***Childcare Centres case 2006*** denied teamwork was a significant factor or had relevance to childcare, or that it was overlooked in previous assessments, noting its necessity and existence in other industries and classifications. Yet that teamwork exists elsewhere cannot counter its being disregarded in childcare, so not factored into work value and wage calculations. All it means is that employers identify its existence in other industries, showing greater readiness on their part to recognise teamwork in other occupations.

Ironically, the self-same problems Lyons identifies could limit his own view—actual work being done and skills exercised clouded by existing notions, or (e)valuation infused by them. The question is not only why 'use of machinery and technology' is deemed superior and worth more than skills employed in childcare but why is 'exercising management or supervisory responsibility' not seen as relevant or a part of childcare work? Childcare workers exercise substantial management and supervisory responsibilities—over the children for whom they care which, on reflection, surely requires superior training and skill.

Overcoming undervaluing women's work—here, childcare—requires at least a three-fold approach:

- isolating, assessing, and valuing skills or abilities different from those seen as existing and traditionally valued in male dominated jobs, giving them a fair and proper value, translating into money-equivalence;
- isolating skills and abilities in female dominated jobs to determine those the same as, or similar to, aptitudes recognised and valued in male dominated jobs, then determining their equal remuneration;

- reassessing the meaning or scope of traditional skills or abilities, to determine whether they in fact exist in female dominated jobs albeit with a different orientation or focus securing their devaluation, as contrasted with that placed upon them in male dominated jobs.

This was not done in the ***Childcare Centres case 2006***, leaving childcare workers still out of pocket, the full value of women's work still unaddressed. The outcome increased childcare workers' wages and improved conditions, necessary considering how the occupation was previously regarded and remunerated. Yet the task remained unfinished, illustrating a continuing element of the equal pay struggle. Comparing women's wages in one female dominated industry, occupation, or profession with another female dominated industry, occupation, or profession might achieve equal pay between women, but won't achieve equal pay. It ignores completely the nub of the matter—differentiation in valuation of women and men's occupations, trades, and professions.

If the equal pay problem lies in undervaluation of women's work, comparison of women's work in one field with women's work in another hardly helps metamorphose male and female wage equivalence. Further, it implies or asserts that women in the comparator occupation are properly paid—in other words, theirs is equal pay. Yet as theirs, too, is a female dominated occupation this is unlikely. Indeed, using a female dominated occupation as the comparator can (as argued in the ***Childcare Centres case 2006***) promote the idea that workers in the comparator occupation are *overpaid*—even less likely.

In the ***Childcare Centres case 2006***, underpaid childcare workers' incomes were measured against underpaid pre-school teachers. Once accepting women's lesser power in the wage-setting marketplace and stereotyping of women's professions and occupations means women are underpaid relative to men, these defects must (unless categorically discounted) apply across the board (including teachers), not just (for example) childcare. Why compare wages two underpaid industries?

Of course employers argued pre-school teachers were overpaid. Of course they argued that rather than increasing childcare workers' wages relative to pre-school teachers, pre-school teachers' rates of pay should be decreased. The argument of teacher-overpayment cannot be separated from the female dominated nature of teaching as an occupation. Influential in contentions that teachers' pay rates should be reduced is the known composition of that profession.

Had the comparator been a male dominated occupation or profession, say engineers or computer programmers, employer submissions would have focused differently, relying on arguments contending engineers and computer programmers are being paid more because their work is superior in value. They would dispute relativities between engineers and computer programmers' qualifications versus childcare workers, and lack of relativities between components of engineering and computer programming, and childcare work components. They would have to assert superior formal qualifications and components of male dominated occupations involving greater complexities, higher levels of education and training, and skilling requiring more lengthy periods of experience. Absolved from having to find any evidence base for such differentiation, they didn't need to argue any of this.

Still, at least the state bodies addressed equal pay and pay equity directly, accepting the lower pay of childcare workers was associated with the sex/gender of workers, requiring redress. On the federal level, there was no such acceptance. Under 'work choices' there was no advance upon the ***Equal Pay Case 1969*** equal pay for equal work or the ***Equal Pay Case 1972*** equal pay for work of equal value. A limited understanding of women's work value remained, with no federal pay equity principle. Federally, women's wages were moribund.

Pay Equity in Downward Drift

With state industrial systems to the fore, the federal industrial system moved in the opposite direction, the downward drift beginning with the move from centralised wage-fixing. As the Australian Federation of Business and Professional Women (AFBPW) in the ***National Wage Case 1990–1991*** pointed out, then AFBPW again with Women's Electoral Lobby (WEL) endorsement in the ***National Wage Case 1991***, this was predictable. Maintaining a centralised system for lower-paid workers only (through the ***Living Wage Case***) as with the Australian Labor Party (ALP) federal government's approach from the early 1990s until losing government in 1996, disadvantaged all lower-paid workers. Their often non-unionised position, perceived and real lack of industrial power, and designation of their jobs as unskilled, made this inevitable. Their conditions, too, were set at minimum standards, without improvements gained by higher-paid workers filtering down.

Difficulties confronting female dominated industries and women workers in the federal industrial system were confirmed by the NSW Industrial Relations Commission in the ***Childcare Centres case 2006***. After pointing out that the Miscellaneous Workers Kindergartens and Childcare Centres &c (State) Award parties (union and employers) had failed to attend to undervaluation of the work before this claim, the Commission said this was compounded because:

> … these female employees, working with vulnerable children in their care, have … themselves been unable to negotiate appropriate rates of pay directly with their employers, on an over-award basis. The serious personal consequences … has been graphically illustrated by the evidence here led.

The Australian Industrial Relations Commission (AIRC) acknowledged, in the ***National Wage Case 1990–1991***, the deficit for women's wages in replacing centralised wage fixing with enterprise bargaining. Yet it failed to adopt AFBPW's recommendation for a Work Skills Value Enquiry (WSVE), implying (and doubtless inferring) it was sufficiently equipped on skills, abilities, and valuation of women's work, professions, and occupations. The state inquiries confirmed their error, the ***Childcare Centres case 2006*** illustrated the canyon between unions, employers, and industrial bodies' capacity to evaluate skills, abilities, and worth of women's work.

Traditional and historical classification of so much women's work deemed unskilled or poorly skilled, whatever its real attributes, left women under federal awards less highly paid than men in lower-paid categories. Unlike state industrial bodies, through the 1990s and into the 2000s the AIRC, despite its equal pay decisions, eschewed real understanding of those entrenched factors, making no effort to try. It failed to understand or investigate, even superficially, comparable worth, shunning any need to grasp or explore its wage fixing relevance to gender biases dictating pay rates.

Commendable in a climate increasingly hostile to women's issues, the Australian Council of Trade Unions (ACTU) endeavoured to run an equal pay case during that decade, senior industrial officer Doran the advocate. The ***Automotive, Food, Metals, Engineering, Printing and Kindred Industries Union v HPM Industries case 1997*** (***HPM case 1997***) covered two categories:

- Some 300 process workers (women) earning $413.90 (including $27 over award payment), compared to seven general hands (men) earning $426–$443 (including $58–$76 over award payments). Doran said the women undertook general assembly work, 'some quite skilled involving hand tools, a range of machines, extensive testing and inspection, making products vital in the public interest'—smoke detectors, surge protectors in electrical switches and general power points and power boards. Men 'delivered around the factory the components for the products', HPM arguing the men's work was 'more important to the company' and 'heavier' albeit women had 'most workers compensation claims for physical exertion'. Claim: process workers $30 wage increase = highest paid general hand.
- Twenty-seven packers (women) earning $440.50 doing work of equal value to twenty-two storepersons (men) on seven different rates. Claim: packers $77 wage increase.

All men had access to a 'merit evaluation' undertaken by supervisors after one- and two-years' service, generating a three-tier wage structure. Women missed out altogether. Men with longer service had higher rates of pay, denied to be based on service; long serving women didn't.

The application was dismissed based on its not being enough 'to show women are on the same classification, nor that according to competency standards (a skills evaluation process in the Metal Industry Award) the women's jobs require at least the same, and in most instances more, skills than the men'. The ***HPM case 1998 (No 2)*** then went to commissioner Jim Simmons, resulting in a work value inquiry aimed at showing the women's work was of equal value. Ultimately resolved by consent agreement, there was no recognition that women's wages and pay (in)equity should always be addressed in general wage cases. The ***Living Wage Cases*** continued this blind spot, failing to see that equal pay must be confronted every time generic wage rises are pursued, pay (in)equity being endemic and embedded in wages and wage fixing. Failure to see this meant further entrenching male-female wage disparities and gender bias.

Women are dependent upon unions for improving male-female pay relativities. Yet in seven key policy objectives identified by the ACTU Congress of 2000, equal pay came fifth only, even then framed as 'improvements', not achieving equal pay outright:

- [I]ncreases in real wages for union members;
- Living Wage for all workers;
- Strengthen and extend collective bargaining;
- [G]reat income security for union members through the strengthening of the award system and through adjustments to the award system to maintain and improve the standards in the awards;
- Reduce and overcome income inequality, and achieve improvements in equal pay;
- [A]dequate resourcing of wage increases in the directly-funded public sector and the income-supplemented not-for-profit private sector; and
- [F]airer distribution of economic wealth.

The ACTU had some success, achieving the $13 wage increase sought in 2001, award rates up to and including $490 per week, $15 per week for rates above $490 up to and including $590 per week, and $17 per week increase in award rates of above $590 per week.

The ***Living Wage Case 2002*** resulted in an $18 per week increase in all award rates, ultimately fairer than the previous year's graduated increases. The ***Living Wage Case 2003*** resulted in a differentiation between increases for the lowest wage rates and higher levels in the lower-paid sector: $17 per week in award rates up to and including $731.80 per week, $15 per week increase in those above $731.80 per week. Lower-paid workers continued to suffer negative differentials in wage rises and industrial conditions. A significant cause of this difference between, in the main—female and male workers—was enterprise bargaining. Hence, with women the majority on lower wages, rather than improving male-female wage differentials, the system promoted by the ACTU exacerbated it. Nevertheless, this is the system the ACTU advocated and continued to press as the best wage fixing system, despite the ACTU's own publications confirming the negative consequences for lower-paid workers and equal pay:

> … The ratio of female to male average earnings has not moved significantly since the commencement of enterprise bargaining, and the current position remains unsatisfactory.

By the 2003 ACTU Congress, equal pay had risen to four out of the seven goals listed as 'overall objectives' for the next triennium:

(a) [R]eal wage increases for union members;
(b) [S]ubstantial improvements in award minimum wages;
(c) Build and extend collective bargaining;
(d) Improve pay equity for women;
(e) Remove wage discrimination impacting upon young people, causal workers, and others; and
(f) Build union membership and organisation through campaigns over wages and employment conditions.

Yet 'building and extending collective bargaining' preceded equal pay. The 2003 Congress listed item three of its objectives under collective bargaining as 'prioritising ... the achievement of equal remuneration for work of equal value'. But this meant that (if met—and steps for attainment were unclear) women under enterprise agreements might move toward equal pay, but women reliant upon the minimum wage would not. Equal pay for all women workers, in all industries, occupations, and jobs, not just workforce sectors or some women workers, was the goal claimed by Heagney and her cohort last century. They understood that if professional women or women otherwise advantaged gained equal pay, others may be left behind—detrimental to campaigning and pay rates. Splitting the struggle redounds against the potential for women at the bottom to win. Numbers not only provide strength, but their arguments and ballast are essential to success for all. Sections of a movement must not be bought off.

Enterprise agreements and their negotiation by consent excluded all but a few women, meaning little likelihood of equal pay's advance, which requires multifaceted approaches, anyway. Publicly funded childcare or, at minimum, financial support for safe and stimulating childcare; adult-dependent care—its lack disadvantaging women juggling paidwork with home-based responsibilities and payment for services; equal educational outcomes and employment opportunities—and revised work value. Women's low wages compound disadvantage: women having fewer funds to allocate means wages of child or dependent care workers will be low, too. Those workers in turn need funds for their own children and other dependants' care, pressing them into paying as little as possible. The cycle of low pay, underpaying women dominated industries and occupations, continues. Lacking explicit recognition in ***Living Wage Cases*** of the centrality of unequal pay, work value claims required case-by-case action.

Paid maternity leave and comprehensive return to work policies underpin equal pay. Since the late 1980s with childcare an acknowledged industrial issue, the ACTU pursued childcare, paid maternity leave, and work and family life as industrial issues. A draft policy explored at the 2003 Congress proposed childcare assistance to all families earning under $100,000 annually, cost calculated at more than three times (then) current federal childcare spending. Fifteen hours free childcare per week would go to parents, with cost of further hours capped at 15 per cent of income. Nevertheless, profit-driven childcare saw ACTU president Burrow reporting that 174,500 children had 'missed out on childcare places' in 2002, childcare costs 'rising 17 per cent' from 2002 to March 2003. The proposed government funding increase 'would still be about $3 billion less than the average investment in childcare by [other] OECD countries'.

The ACTU ***Work and Family Test case 2003*** aimed at 'creating flexibility and choice for workers with young children, including increased unpaid leave for new mothers, more flexible working hours and the right to return to part-time work. Yet this could not militate against inbuilt bias against women and equal pay in enterprise or collective bargaining. Nor could it reverse the realities of its own analysis, of women left behind through:

- dependence upon the ***Living Wage Case*** for wage increases;
- comparatively rare inclusion in bargaining agreements; or
- where included, subject to:
  - consent arrangements omitting equal pay; or
  - agreements without union, employer or AIRC addressing women's work value.

As Pay Equity Plunges … (No) Fair Pay?

In 2003, the ACTU stipulated unions would, in collective bargaining, 'seek … wage outcomes that, as a minimum, retain real value of wages and secure a fair share for workers of productivity growth and improved profitability or efficiency', committing to five collective bargaining principles:

(a) [L]egislative change [guaranteeing] the right to collectively bargain and facilitate multi-employer and industry-wide agreements.
(b) [C]o-ordinated approach to bargaining, with maximum involvement of delegates and members.
(c) Priority to equal remuneration for work of equal value.
(d) Inclusion of claims, … for improved hours of work, increased job security, improved conditions for casuals and other [precarious-

employment] workers ..., better work-family balance, delegates' rights, protection and portability of employee entitlements, and paid training leave.
(e) Adequate resourcing of wage increases through collective bargaining in the public sector and publicly funded not-for-profit sector.
(f) [C]oncern at effect on bargaining of employer-based individualised performance pay systems.

Yet retaining real value of wages would not improve women's underpayment through (un)equal pay. Nor would the imprecation that equal remuneration for work of equal value have priority necessarily produce that outcome. Saying 'give priority' is one thing; ensuring it—and the desired result—another. As the ***Childcare Centres case 2006*** showed, those dedicated to an equal pay outcome can get it wrong or, at least, not quite right. In a world where, perennially and endemically, women's work is undervalued and re-evaluating worth of women's work and women's work value constitutes a struggle, this is inevitable. Enlightenment is not automatic.

As for awards, the ACTU (with unions generally) affirmed a commitment to 'restoring the relevance of award rates of pay through (a) inclusion of bargained/market rates in awards; (b) national wage case applications; and (c) campaigns to lift minimum rates of pay'. Yet simultaneously it acknowledged workers under the award system as in a 'low pay crisis', dependent upon a rump of a system which only fifteen years earlier had regularly secured wage increases and improved industrial conditions for *all* workers under awards. How the award system could be restored to a pre-eminent position or even one bringing real wage justice to low-paid workers was obscure, when the least powerful workers were isolated within that system. The majority being women compounded the problem.

As a possible antidote, the ACTU committed to 'an independent and comprehensive inquiry into low pay', examining:

(a) Causes of low pay and inequality;
(b) Income levels needed to achieve a decent standard of living;
(c) Role played by job insecurity, causal employment, labour hire, and contracting;
(d) Enterprise bargaining impact; and
(e) Levels of executive salaries and fairness of ... income setting for all workforce levels.

However federal government action confronted the ACTU, unions generally and workers. ACTU resolutions could not compete with changes under the Workplace Relations Act 1996 (Cth), 1999 amendments, and the Workplace Relations Amendment (Work Choices) Act 2005 (Cth). Coming into effect on 27 March 2006, the Work Choices Act 2005 finally neutered the AIRC, establishing the Australian Fair Pay Commission (AFPC) for minimum or living wage setting. This in turn removed any chance for the AIRC to embrace state industrial bodies' pay equity advances. AFPC composition and disposition made it unlikely it would comprehend, much less address, pay equity realities. Incoming AFPC member Judith Sloane's Harvey Nicolls Society speech decrying any role for anti-discrimination legislation and principles in the industrial sphere and indicating a lack of understanding of over award payments' impact on (un)equal pay gave no cause for optimism.

States and territories lost a role in wage fixing, except for state or territory government employees and non-corporate employers (about 15 per cent of the workforce). Privatisation of many previously government activities and growth of joint government and private sector businesses removed many employees from the state system into the federal regime. The Work Choices Act 2005 exacerbated enterprise bargaining problems for equal pay, increasing with Australian Workplace Agreements (AWA)s. For some employees, awards—reduced in scope and effect, and effectively marginalised—remained. Lauded as the future for wage setting, AWAs made each employee responsible for her/his negotiations. Award transparency and workers knowing terms, conditions, and entitlements attached to their job category disappeared. The AFPC set minimum conditions limited to annual leave, personal (including sick and carer's) leave, parental (including maternity) leave, and maximum ordinary hours of work. With minimum and award classification wages, also set by the AFPC, these comprised the 'Fair Pay and Conditions Standard'.

Introducing the Bill, workplace relations minister Kevin Andrews reprised the Workplace Relations Act 1996 theme of greater 'choice and flexibility in our workplaces'. The AIRC lost compulsory conciliation and arbitration power, becoming a 'voluntary dispute resolution service' only. Union rights were truncated.

Equal pay expertise built in state commissions was marginalised, no longer relevant to the vast bulk of women workers and traditional women's work. Looking back to the Arbitration Court's 1904 origins, after a century in the field the AIRC comprised male and female members, the

ACTU and other unions had women leaders, greater numbers in membership and higher positions than ever before, yet the system was now sidelined. With Ryan and Conlon's ***Gentle Invaders*** call for women's essential role in wage fixing advancing, the system changed. Women had to start over, this time educating the AFPC. Yet—hope arrives.

Another Chance for Equal Pay?

Nine days after the Howard government defeat, on 3 December 2007 Kevin Rudd is sworn in as Prime Minister. Addressing the global financial crisis, the Australian economy slowdown, and facing recession, in October 2008 a $10.4b stimulus package materialises, then in February 2009 a further $42b. For industrial relations, an award safety-net system is introduced, unfair dismissal laws are restored, AWAs will be phased out over five years, and the AFPC is replaced by Fair Work Australia (FWA). The Workplace Relations Act 1996 is repealed.

In July, the Fair Work Act 2009 (Cth) comes into effect, FWA later becoming the Fair Work Commission (FWC). Modern awards cover workers not under enterprise agreements, which remain despite their negative consequences for equal pay. Still, national employment standards must be incorporated into all industrial arrangements, whether awards or agreements, section 61(3) stipulating minimum standards as:

- Maximum weekly hours
- Requests for flexible working arrangements
- Offers and requests for casual conversion
- Parental leave and related entitlements
- Annual leave
- Personal/carer's leave, compassionate leave, and unpaid family and domestic violence leave
- Community service leave
- Long service leave
- Public holidays
- Notice of termination and redundancy pay
- Fair Work Information Statement—containing the above provisions.

The stage is set for a new offensive on pay equity and comparable worth.

In 2010, lodging an application with FWA for an Equal Remuneration Order (ERO), with the Health Services Union (HSU), Australian Workers

Union of Employees Queensland (AWUEQ), United Voice (UV) and Australian Education Union (AEU), the Australian Municipal, Administrative, Clerical and Services Union (AMACSU) set the ball rolling. The ***Australian Municipal, Administrative, Clerical and Services Union and Ors v. Australian Business Industrial case 2012*** (***AMACSU case 2012***) posited a causal relationship between undervaluation of work in the private sector, namely in the social, community, and disability services industry and its character as female dominated. Wage rates and classification structure in the Queensland SACS Award were addressed, FWA awarding pay rises of 19 to 41 per cent to some 150,000 Social, Community and Disability Services (SACS) workers (mostly women)—phased in over eight years. The decision set annual wage reviews by FWA and, recognising obstacles to industry bargaining, awarded an additional 4 per cent rise in loadings. This was followed by applications for clerks: Australian Municipal, Administrative, Clerical and Services Union and Ors, preschool and primary schoolteachers: ***Independent Education Union of Australia 2021*** amongst others, meeting with varying degrees of success.

Differences surround comparators, for example. The preschool workers case began with three union applicants, being reduced to the Independent Education Union (IEU) when UV and AEU claims foundered, having pressed for male comparators being employees covered by the C5 and C10 levels in the Manufacturing Award 2010: ***Application by United Voice and the Australia Education Union 2018***. FWA determined this to be an inapt group by which to measure work value equivalence: ***Application by United Voice and the AEU***. The IEU's original comparator group was rejected, too, by the application of the principles set out in ***Re Equal Remuneration Decision 2015***. Two essential stages are applied in ERO matters. First, the FWC 'must reach a state of satisfaction' that for the employees to whom the order will apply, 'there is not equal remuneration for work of equal or comparable value'. This is a jurisdictional prerequisite for making an ERO. 'Satisfaction' is measured by a 'comparative exercise' where an identified comparator group has three elements:

1. the two groups perform work of equal or comparable value;
2. are of the opposite gender; and
3. are unequally remunerated.

Once established, the FWA/FWC has a discretion to make an ERO, circumstances relevant to exercise of discretion including:

- circumstances of the employees to whom the order will apply;
- eliminating gender based discrimination;
- capacity to pay of employers to whom the order will apply;
- effect of any order on delivery of services to the community;
- effect of any order on a range of economic considerations, including any impact on employment, productivity, and growth;
- effect of any order on promotion of social inclusion by its impact on female workforce participation; and
- effect of any order on enterprise bargaining.

The IEU comparator group ruled out by FWC was male primary school teachers employed in the government and catholic systemic schools in NSW, on the basis that:

1. early childhood teachers in long day care centres and preschools perform work of equal or comparable value to male school teachers in the comparator group;
2. early childhood teachers are an overwhelmingly female group, and the comparator group is (by definition) entirely male; and
3. male government and catholic systemic school teachers in NSW earn significantly more than early childhood teachers.

The rationale for rejecting this comparator was that albeit the nominated sector workers were male, they were part of an industry that is almost wholly female. Hence at last the lack of logic in comparing women's work with women's work to establish equal pay is confirmed. Yes, the men of the proposed comparator were paid more than women, but bringing preschool and primary school teachers up to their level would not be to introduce equal pay. Working within a female dominated profession, men generally rise to the top level position and secure the highest pay rates—not because they are better at the work, but because they are men. Just as male nurses under the Victorian Award in the 1940s were paid at 'base wage female level + the-nurse-is-a-man top up', this is what was happening for these more highly paid (male) teachers. They could well have been paid below what the work was really worth, because their pay began from an inadequate and undervalued base—women's pay in a female dominated industry. (Though the example was crushingly obvious evidence of males coming into a female dominated profession or trade and gaining higher pay, simply because they were men. At least Higgins didn't award male fruitpackers more than female fruitpackers in the ***Fruitpickers case 2012***.)

The FWC confirmed the comparison as 'effectively between two female-dominated vocations, which does not assist achieving the remedial purpose of [remedying] gender wage inequality [obsolete] and [promoting] equal pay'. NSW Department of Education figures showed female teachers constituted 82 per cent of public primary school workers in 2016, 81.7 per cent in 2015, and 81.3 per cent in 2014. Thus, work performed by primary school teachers was 'not characteristically male work and therefore ... wage outcomes for primary school teachers could not be explained as either the manifestation of considerations unique to male workers or some form of advantage enjoyed predominantly by male workers'. Once again, women equal pay advocates from decades past and continuing were vindicated, though consistent with volte-face sans acknowledgement.

The alternative comparator was accepted, namely male professional engineers:

1. overwhelmingly male;
2. paid higher remuneration; and
3. performing work of comparable value.

This, FWC said, led to a 'substantive contest between the parties' as to 'whether early childhood teachers performed work of equal or comparable value to professional engineers ...' Six early childhood teacher witnesses gave evidence—and two professional engineers—to establish or rule out the comparison. Yet for those familiar with undercutting women's work value, the question is around the wrong way. Shouldn't one ask: is professional engineers' work of equal or comparable value to early childhood teachers'—that is, valorising the latter's work? That the question is asked as it is—as if care of youngsters at their most crucial development stages is considered lesser than the work of engineers so paid less—illustrates the fundamental problem underlying not just women's work value, but work value altogether. The natural position is accepted as 'women's work the lesser'.

Nonetheless, the ***AMACSU case 2012*** put equal pay back into contention. Building on the Queensland ASU case covering SACS workers, the FWC endeavoured to make equal pay real. In May 2009, Queensland Industrial Relations Commission found SACS work 'historically undervalued relative to public sector comparators and work in other sectors', arising from its female-dominated character. 'Gender was at the heart' of the undervaluation, including 'origins of NGO community services in voluntary work and subsequent government funding of the sector', industrial issues and 'historical industry features', together with 'cultural devaluation of care work'. Under the Fair Work Act 2009, SACS workers gained wage increases of between 18 to 27 per cent based on historical undervaluing. Natasha Cortis and Gabrielle Meagher analyse the Queensland case: ***Queensland Services, Industrial Union of Employees v. Queensland Chamber of Commerce and Industry Ltd*** (***Queensland Services*** case ***2009***). Celia Briar and Anne Junor analyse the ***AMACSU case***. Each analysis emphasises historical elements. One key significance was 'reinforcing relevance of the concept of "skill" beyond its historical origins in male trades'.

The ***AMACSU case 2012*** ran when the universal Modern Awards system was being introduced to provide a basic floor from which future wage claims would be launched. Valorising the deficit of history to ensure historic components would be incorporated into the equation of work's worth was vital at this time. The ***AMACSU*** applicants called workers and expert witnesses to expose the depth of skill, knowledge, expertise, creativity, and competence wrapped into the industry. As Briar and Junor recount, SACS workers 'are more highly qualified than the Australian workforce overall', in 2006 'across Australian community service industries in general':

> 64.6 percent having a post-school qualification … a sharp increase from 53.0 percent 2001: for SACS workers, the proportion with qualifications was slightly higher … Yet SACS workers are low paid compared with other occupations with similar demands and responsibilities … In 2010 … the annual full-time salary rate for community sector SAS workers under the relevant Modern Award, in rounded figures, ranging from $A39,000 in the second lowest grade to $A59,000 at the most senior level … Even at the top of the salary range, the most senor community sector managers earning less than the $A65,000 being the national annual equivalent of average weekly adult ordinary time earnings …

Seventy-nine care workers gave evidence. Twenty-three site visits were undertaken. Reading the case and Briar and Junor's analysis brings home with enormous force the extraordinary scope of SACS work. So much is intensive; so much not factored into the paidwork component; so much high-level responsibility. Taking two paragraphs at random from Briar and Junor is illustrative:

> Working at the level of problem-solving and solution-sharing Disability staff had to be expert coordinators … constantly required to assess urgency and importance of simultaneous calls on their attention, any one of which could become a crisis. As demands arose during the day they frequently prioritised tasks and streamlined movements to remain within deadlines, thinking quickly on their feet in challenging situations …
>
> Finally, the skill of keeping a potentially chaotic situation under control, [restoring calm] after an emergency, a requisite skill if clients could relax, flourish and learn … Staff collaboration was a key to overcoming resource barriers and shared creation of techniques for forestalling emergencies. Developed by staff, and changing with the changing client base, these techniques were structured into day to day work, generating an orderly and enjoyable workplace … [W]ith the Manager of a women's refuge and manager of a small community-based women's health centre, through daily team meetings and development of practices such as half-an-hour a day of meeting time with phones off the hook, these women conferred with staff on a daily basis developing systems of practice reflecting a shared philosophy and allowing any crisis, such as the sudden threat of violent intrusion by a client's partner to be managed to be unobtrusive to clients …

'Donations' of time (of money foregone) included:

- unpaid overtime 5–10 hours weekly, mostly catching up with case notes and administrative work, sometimes to assist clients in crisis; unofficially 'on call' during evenings and weekends—especially staff dealing with clients in crisis or at risk;
- eating lunch at the computer;
- sleepovers, covered by an allowance, not an hourly rate—three or four hours only of an eight hour sleepover being paid;
- attending community development meetings in the evenings.

The case concluded as 'the most significant in the past 20 years', its greatest significance lying in affirmation of historical value: recognition of 'what is' (and has ever been) work value—not work value based on 'changes'. Yet problems remain—applicable to traditional women's work and providing an obstacle to fair and proper remuneration—namely, 'where's the money coming from' because the care sector when government run is dependent upon revenue and priorities, and when private sector run has an inbuilt resistance to prioritising pay and services over profit. Further, although the ***AMACSU case 2012*** had an Australia-wide effect with federal government involvement, support and $2b advanced toward costs, work value cases tend to be run on localised lines—specific to states or territories (generally being state/territory employees). Finally, establishing a solid base for a Modern Award, what of future wage negotiations—remaining dependent upon ***Living Wage*** outcomes, whilst 'strong' industries represented by strong unions negotiate enterprise agreements with commensurate outcomes in pay and industrial conditions, again leaving women's work, jobs, occupations, and professions behind.

A Future for Pay Equity

What, then, is to be done?

In Denmark, twenty-five years after the introduction of the ***Equal Pay Act*** 1974, the gap between women's and men's wages persisted. Government and Parliament said 'further steps required'. In June 2001 the Equal Pay Amendment Act dispensed with secrecy requirements covering remuneration, meaning employees could discuss wages openly. Transparency as an essential wages system feature if unequal pay is to be addressed is acknowledged: absent transparency of pay rates in individual enterprises, government departments, and corporations, pay inequities based in systemic sex/gender discrimination cannot be seen, much less be redressed. The Board of Equal Treatment (EOB) or a trade union with one or more members in an enterprise with over ten employees could require an employer to compile and disclose wage statistics.

Ten years before, in 1991 in the ***Danfoss case***, the Danish Union of Commercial and Clerical Workers (Handels - og Kontorfunktionaeremes Forbund, HK Industri)(HK) won a European Court of Justice determination that:

- if a pay system is not transparent; and
- a claimant proves a pay difference between male and female workers;

the burden of proof that pay differentials are not based in or do not incorporate sex/gender discrimination lies with the employer.

On the one hand, the ***Danfoss case*** was a major advance, but the victory was hollow. Proving a pay difference is difficult if wages are concealed and statistics unavailable. The Equal Pay Amendment Act was vital. Ironically, whereas Australian pay rates were transparent in the past, through the awards system, the Danish problem followed Australia's move to enterprise bargaining, thence to AWAs and secret terms concealing wages and conditions. Any real chance of proving differential pay rates means claimants must first be able to show there is disparity in them. The Fair Work Legislation (Amendment)(Secure Jobs, Better Pay) Act 2022 (Cth) (Secure Jobs, Better Pay Act) has reinstated possible transparency of earnings—a potential enhancement of earlier reporting mechanisms under the Affirmative Action Act 1986 (Cth) and Workplace Gender Equality Act 2012 (Cth) (an equality indicator being 'equal remuneration between women and men'). Ending the wages cover up effected by the Howard government's Work Choices, employees are no longer prohibited from disclosing remuneration information or sharing details of employment terms and conditions 'reasonably necessary to determination remuneration outcomes' including weekly hours of work.

Yet ultimately challenging wage inequity cannot be left to individual workers or (possibly) worker groups or the Sex Discrimination Commissioner. Class actions may work, however the right to initiate them is not always favoured by governments, viz the Howard government (1996–2007) explicitly denying access to Federal Court Act 1977 (Cth) class action provisions for Migration Act 1958 (Cth) claimants. Although governments change—they change again, meaning the risk of regressive action remains ever open. And even if class action rights exist for discrimination claims, as recognised in the pay equity principles established state by state in the early 2000s, gaining equal pay should not rest upon the need to prove sex/gender discrimination. A systemic problem requires redress encompassing the systemic nature of pay inequity, as proposed by AFBPW in promoting the WSVE (work skills value enquiry) approach. Adopted in the NSW ***Crown Librarians case 2002***, this breakthrough faltered due to embedded preconceptions about 'women's work' and 'work value', exemplified by the ***Childcare Centres case 2006***. Traditional job and work value stereotyping must be ended for WSVEs to implement equal pay, and ensuring this across the board is essential, for pay rates set by optimal WSVE action require annual review so that workers do not again fall behind.

The advances under the Rudd-Gillard governments heralded further possibilities. The change of government again—to Abbot-Turnbull-Morrison (2013–2015, 2015–2018, 2018–2022) did not result in a reversion to the extreme Howard industrial program. Women's wage growth was stronger than men's wage growth over the period 2013–2019, up by an average 2.8 per cent annually compared with 2.1 per cent for men, contrasted against 2013–2018 where women's annual wage increase averaged 4.3 per cent, men's 4.5 per cent. This needs to be tempered by the reality that women's underpayment remained—and remains—stark. The 2022 change of government re-opened equal pay prospects. In addition to the 'non-secrecy' pay provisions introduced by the Albanese government, measures in the Secure Jobs, Better Pay Act 2022 were designed to enhance potential for ending the pay gap. The Fair Work Act 2012 objects now require that in interpreting and applying the Act consideration must be given to promoting job security and gender equality. The need to achieve gender equality applies to modern awards and minimum wage setting by the FWC, meaning this principle must apply to annual wage reviews henceforth. Further, a new equal remuneration principle provides that in equal remuneration and work value cases the FWC:

- can consider:
  - comparisons between occupations and industries; or
  - if work has been undervalued based on sex/gender historically;
- is not limited to comparing similar work and needs no male comparator;
- is no longer required to find discrimination based on sex/gender:
  - if considering a comparison; or
  - if work has been historically undervalued based on sex/gender.

This picks up on proposals by AFBPW in their equal pay submissions to the AIRC in the ***National Wage Cases 1990–1991, 1991*** advocating WSVEs and Clare Burton to the NSW ***Pay Equity Inquiry 1997***. Similarly, institution of expert panels on pay equity and the care and community sector to make EROs implements the WEL 1980s proposal to the AIRC. Both measures acknowledge that appointment to industrial commissions or tribunals does not mean members comprehend sex-based biases, stereotyping or undervaluation of women's work (including their own), much less have expertise in the field, a noted failing. Banning advertisements containing pay rates that would breach the Act complements earlier campaigning, too, in the decades ago banning of 'jobs for men and boys' vs 'jobs for women and girls' advertisements. Other measures include flexible work (assuming this favours workers albeit harbouring possibly greater potential for employee exploitation through what once was called 'split-shifts'—lobbied against in the 1970s by unions), and addressing sexual harassment. 'All workers' are included in the sexual harassment prohibition—employees, contractors, subcontractors, outworkers, apprentices, trainees, students, and/or volunteers, plus prospective workers and third parties including clients and customers. 'Stop sexual harassment' orders are designed to prevent future harassment, and claims can be addressed by mediation, conciliation, and compensation (though this can be problematic). A model clause for modern awards and enterprise agreements that the employer agrees to '*no* non-disclosure orders' (NDAs) in mediated sexual harassment claims is essential. NDAs favour sexual harassers and employers wanting to cover-up sexist and sexual harassment and bullying, never advantaging claimants albeit too many are persuaded there is benefit in being gagged about their well-founded claims.

The Secure Jobs, Better Pay measures are an advance. Yet through the last thirty years of legislative fluctuations generated by changes of government, enterprise bargaining, despite its negative impact on women's wage justice, remains. Enterprise bargaining was breaking down from about 2012. Collective agreements declined in coverage of employees, with more and more employees resorting to the awards system: between May 2014 and May 2021 employees covered by collective agreements fell by 2200, with award coverage increasing by 798,700. Yet this was not seen as an opportunity to reconsider the approach fundamentally. Rather, the Secure Jobs, Better Pay Act remains committed to collective agreements and enterprise bargaining. The *Bills Digest No 34, 2022–23* outlines efforts to improve them by introducing better access so that collective agreements 'are negotiated in good faith and genuinely agreed to by a representative cohort of the workers to which they apply', with parties having access to arbitration and no unilateral terminations of collective agreements reducing workers' entitlements. However, one principal variation drawing employer ire is a partial acknowledgement of the inept application of the enterprise bargaining-collective agreement approach if wage fairness is sought, particularly when it comes to equal pay: multi-employer bargaining.

Although some provision for multi-employer bargaining existed under the Rudd-Gillard changes, these limitation to low-paid jobs was seen as an impediment which is now eliminated, with an opening particularly provided for industries including childcare, cleaning, aged care, and disability services where recognition of the real value of work failed women, the dominant workforce in these areas. Three 'streams' provide:

- Single-interest—workers with 'common interests' can bargain together across businesses;
- Supported—businesses in low-paid industries must negotiate with a union;
- Cooperative—businesses can opt-in to a bargained agreement.

In June 2023 on the day of multi-employer bargaining came into effect under the Secure Jobs, Better Pay Act, the AEU (Victorian Branch), United Workers' Union (UWU) and IEU early childhood educators lodged a submission under an application for a 25 per cent pay rise for early childhood educators across the industry. This comes on the heels of aged care workers gaining a 15 per cent wage rise under their award (adding $AUS 141.10 to their weekly pay) with $AUS 11.3b committed to the sector by federal government. With a state government three- and four-years kindergarten expansion program planned over the next ten years (requiring more than 11,000 additional early childhood teachers and educators), AEU Victorian Branch President Meredith Peace said these 'essential community workers ... must be supported and must be offered fairer wages and better conditions'. The aim is to ensure uniform industry-based agreements.

Yet again wages and conditions are dependent upon an industry-based approach which cannot take advantage of the industrial clout exercised by unions representing workers in male dominated sectors where higher wages and better conditions are achievable by reason of that clout, premised on the basis that male jobs warrant pay and conditions that are not replicated in female dominated sectors. Centralised wage fixing recognises that the stronger the union, the better acknowledged as significant the industry, the better the conditions and the wages will be, with benefits flowing to all workers. Hence, whatever the AEU, UnWU and IEU gain, it will not be backed through continuing annual reviews under centralised wage fixing. Two limbs are essential to overcome the wage, pensions and superannuation gap: a properly implemented WSVE (which, hopefully, may come through the AEU, UWU and IEU application—though beware women being locked into lower rates than 'real' equal pay for the period of the agreement) plus an annual review generated by the strongest unions making a case for wage rises and improved conditions that will have a universal application and flow on effect—that is, centralised wage fixing.

A return to centralised wage fixing is essential. Consistently confirmed, centralised wage fixing brought Australian women closer to equal pay. This differs from the present system of enterprise bargaining notwithstanding the 2022 changes. Under enterprise bargaining before this change, a few individual women might be advantaged, but enterprise bargaining did not advantage the vast bulk of women. Even for the few, advantage needs to be seen in context. The comparison which shows women as doing well is one more often looking at women's incomes as against other women's incomes, rather than between women's and men's incomes. Any proper calculation needs to look at women's incomes vis-à-vis men's through enterprise bargaining, and between outcomes from ***Living Wage*** and enterprise bargaining outcomes. Women's wages are fixed through the annual Fair Pay Commission which addresses the pay of those who are not in strong unions that gain through enterprise bargaining. Multi-employer bargaining can help by instituting what is, potentially, a WSVE approach, but what of annual reviews?

A return to centralised wage fixing does not require a return to state/federal systems with potential state/federal system disparity. The ACTU's proposal in the first decade of the 2000s for a national industrial relations system encompassing wage fixing for all workers would enable greater equal pay success. All women would benefit, rather than cases being brought state by state where female dominated industries or occupations are not under the federal system. WSVEs would be undertaken with Australia-wide impact, just as, by federal government involvement, the ***AMACSU case*** did so. The WEL standing bench to undertake Australia-wide WSVEs would—as intended—build expertise to ensure historic undervaluing of women's work is undermined and ended, itself at last being relegated to history. Yet maintaining momentum built through WSVEs, keeping abreast of economic changes, wages growth, and industrial condition advances remains problematic without action recognising that the present system won't do it.

Were centralised wage fixing returned on a national level covering all workers, this would mean a consistent pay equity principle applying Australia-wide, facilitating WSVEs in all women's trades, industries, and occupations across Australia. Annual ***National Wage*** or ***Living Wage Cases*** run with ACTU and unions no longer hived off into their own enterprise bargaining strongholds would set basic standards and minimum wage levels across the board. Applying the nationwide pay equity principle, national, or living wages could never be set in ignorance of women's work value. AFBPW, NPEC, United Associations (UA), Union of Australia Women (UAW), Council of Action for Equal Pay (CAEP), and WEL's admonition that national wage fixing cannot be done without incorporating equal pay could ensure women's occupations do not fall back once having gained historical value through WSVEs.

Neither the ACTU nor the ALP has endorsed centralised wage fixing for the future, committing to enterprise bargaining despite its disadvantages for women and all lower-paid workers. Nevertheless, the Canberra Jobs Summit held 1–2 September 2022 (leading to the Secure Jobs, Better Pay Act) declared government, employer, union, and broader community support for initiatives 'building a bigger, better trained and more productive workforce, boosting real wages and living standards, and creating more opportunities for more Australians'—including women. Goals for women included 'equal opportunities' as a 'central objective of [government] economic and fiscal policy' and amending the Fair Work Act to 'strengthen access to flexible working arrangements, make unpaid parental leave more flexible, and strengthen protection for workers against discrimination and harassment'. Women featured in 'improving access to jobs and training pathways for women, First Nations people, regional Australians and culturally and linguistically diverse people …'. Pay equity was tangentially covered in a revival of requirements for business reporting publicly to the Workplace Gender Equality Agency on their gender pay gap, and the Australian Public Service (APS) on set targets for improving gender equity in the public service.

Workplace relations laws would, said the communiqué, be 'modernised' by 'making bargaining accessible for all workers and businesses'. Yet it isn't lack of accessibility to enterprise bargaining that keeps women's wages and conditions down. It is lack of collective action by ACTU and all unions—strong, less strong, and weaker, working together through centralised wage fixing with the goal of improved wages and industrial conditions of all. Remembering WEL and NCW almost half-a-century ago at the 1983 National Economic Summit, had NPEC, CAEP, WEL, NCW or AFBPW been invited to the Jobs Summit in 2022, equal pay would have taken its rightfully prominent place, a non-negotiable goal for government action, public and private sector, nationally and locally, a goal determined to be won. Still, the White Paper foreshadowed by the Albanese government would cover amongst other matters 'ensuring women have equal opportunities and equal pay'. But how? The Secure Jobs, Better Pay Act incorporates some positive advances, yet the deficit in its failure to recognise that the problem of the wage gap—leading to the pensions and superannuation gap which militates even more egregiously against the economic security, financial independence, health and human rights of women—requires centralised wage fixing to end it.

Reigniting philosophy and policies based in collective values, a cooperative and collegiate approach to industrial outcomes, is what is wanted. For well over 100 years women have joined hands, working through women's organisations and unions for equal pay. It is time for women's persistence through this long, long struggle to be honoured by government and union action, embracing WSVEs to establish the real value of women's work, and reinstating Australia's unique contribution to workers' rights in the industrial arbitration and centralised wage fixing system, which holds out the real hope for the goal to be gained.

Otherwise, differences between rich and poor will continue, women's work remaining undervalued, women populating the realms of the poor and underpaid, in unequal and inordinate numbers, being passed over as if women do not count, and pay equity—so hopeful of fulfilment—remaining simply hope—or hope unfulfilled.

References

Cases—See Case List

ABS, ***Employee Earnings and Hours, Australia, Preliminary, May 2002***, Canberra, ACT, 2006, http://www.abs.gov.au/ausstats/abs@.nsf/e8ae5488b598839cca25682000131612/c52cf2bd22d8a45dca2568a9001393bc!OpenDocument, pp. 1–9, at p. 2 (accessed 31 October 2006).

ACTU, ***1927–2002—Key Achievements***, ACTU, Melbourne, Victoria, nd.

ACTU, ***Wages and Collective Bargaining Background Paper***, ACTU, Melbourne, Victoria, 2003, http://www.actu.asn.au/Archive/Congress2003/Papers/WagesandCollectiveBargainingBackgroundPaper.aspx, pp. 1–2 (accessed 2 December 2006), p. 1.

Michaela Anderson, ***Gender Differences in Retirement***, ASFA, Sydney, NSW, 2005 (May 2005) http://ofw.facs.gov.au/women_and_ageing/downloads/older_womens_financial_decision.ppt, pp. 1–14 (accessed 1 November 2006), p. 2.

Kevin Andrews, Minister for Workplace Relations, 'Second Reading Speech', ***Hansard***, Australian Parliament, Canberra, ACT, 2005 (November 2005), p. 1; also ***Second Reading***, 2005.

Australian Government, *Gender Pay Gap Data*, https://www.wgea.gov.au/pay-and-gender/gender-pay-gap-data (accessed 14 September 2022).

Brianna Boecker, 'Early childhood educators push for 25 per cent pay rise in multi-employer bargaining submission', *Women's Agenda*, 6 June 2023, Educators push for 25% pay rise in multi-employer bargaining (womensagenda.com.au) https://womensagenda.com.au/latest/early-childhood-educators-push-for-25-per-cent-pay-rise-in-multi-employer-bargaining-submission/ (accessed 6 June 2023).

Celia Briar and Anne Junor, 'Inequality and Low Paid Women Workers—Care, Skill and Value in Social and Community Sector Work', Paper presented at Gender, Work and Organisation Conference, Keele University, 26–28 June 2014.

Natasha Cortis and Gabrielle Meagher, 'Recognition at Last—Care Work and the Equal Remuneration Case' ***Journal of Industrial Relations*** (2012), vol 54 (3), pp. 377–385, http://jir.sagepub.com/, http://jir.sagepub.com/content/54/3/377 (accessed 2 August 2022).

Department of Industrial Relations, ***Estimating the Coverage of a New Industrial Relations System***, Brisbane, Queensland, 2005

Jenny Doran, Equal Pay For Women Unfinished Business (actu.org.au) https://redirects.ausunions.io/actu-media/archives/1998/equal-pay-for-women-unfinished-business (accessed 2 August 2009).

Anthony Forsyth, 'There's one big reason wages are stagnating', ***The Conversation***, There's one big reason wages are stagnating: the enterprise bargaining system is broken, and in terminal decline (theconversation.com) https://theconversation.com/theres-one-big-reason-wages-are-stagnating-the-enterprise-bargaining-system-is-broken-and-in-terminal-decline-183818 (accessed 1 June 2023).

Geoff Gilfillan, 'The extent and causes of the wage growth slowdown in Australia', *Parliament of Australia*, 9 April 2019, The extent and causes of the wage growth slowdown in Australia – Parliament of Australia (aph.gov.au) https://www.aph.gov.au/About_Parliament/Parliamentary_Departments/Parliamentary_Library/pubs/rp/rp1819/WageSlowdown (accessed 2 June 2023).

Suzanne Hammond, 'NSW Report—A Great Day for Pay Equity', ***Inkwel—State/Territory Reports***, Canberra, ACT, 2002 (April 2002), http://www.wel.org.au/inkwel/ink0204/states.htm, pp. 1–8, at pp. 2–3 (accessed 16 April 2006).

Jobs and Skills Summit | Treasury.gov.au https://treasury.gov.au/employment-whitepaper/jobs-summit (accessed 20 September 2022).

Simon Kelly, see Matt Wade, 'A super shock for boomers', ***Sydney Morning Herald***, Sydney, NSW, 2006 (24 October 2006), http://www.smh.com.au/articles/2006/10/23/1161455665709.html (accessed 24 October 2006).

Michael Lyons and Meg Smith, ***Gender Pay Equity, Wage Fixation and WorkChoices: Forward to the Past?*** University of Western Sydney, Sydney, NSW, 2006, http://www.qwws.org.au/filestore/OWOL%20Papers/PDF/Lyons%20and%20Smith%20FINAL%20-%20DONE.pdf, pp. 1–38 (accessed 13 August 2006).

Jaan Murphy, Scanlon Williams and Elliott King, 'Fair Work Legislation Amendment (Secure Jobs, Better Pay) Bill 2022', *Bills Digest No 34, 2022–23*, 7 November 2022, Fair Work Legislation Amendment (Secure Jobs, Better Pay) Bill 2022 – Parliament of Australia (aph.gov.au) https://www.aph.gov.au/Parliamentary_Business/Bills_Legislation/bd/bd2223a/23bd034#_Toc118721749 (accessed 29 May 2023).

Sherrill Nixon, 'Free child care for every family: union push', ***Sydney Morning Herald***, Sydney, NSW, 2003 (1 July 2003), http://www.smh.com.au/articles/2003/06/30/1056825336183.html, pp. 1–3 (accessed 3 December 2006).

Osiris, ***Latest news: HPM sacks male comparators***, 1998 (12 August 1998), http://www.users.bigpond.com/rj_gi/HPM/HPM2.htm, pp. 1–11 (accessed 20 January 2006)

Osiris, ***Summary: decision of Justice Munro (19 May 1998), HPM decision (4 March 1998) Commissioner Simmonds, Summary of Arguments***, http://www.users.bigpond.com/rj_gi/HPM/HPM2.htm (accessed 20 January 2006)

Barbara Pocock, ***The Labour Market Ate My Babies: Work, Children and a Sustainable Future***, Federation Press, Sydney, NSW, 2006.

Edna Ryan and Anne Conlon, ***Gentle Invaders***, Nelson, Nth Melbourne, Victoria, 1975.

Jocelynne A. Scutt, 'The Privatisation of Justice—Power Differentials, Inequality, and the Palliative of Counselling and Mediation', ***Women's Studies International Forum***, vol 11, no 5, pp. 503–20; also in Scutt, ***The Incredible Woman—Power and Sexual Politics***, vol 2, Artemis Publishing, Melbourne, 1997.

Phoebe Shields, 'The Super Gender Gap', *Proactive – Finance*, 24 August 2022, https://www.proactiveinvestors.co.uk/companies/news/990854/the-super-gender-gap-how-can-women-safeguard-their-superannuation-990854.html (accessed 14 September 2022).

Judith Sloan, ***Worse Might Be Better?***, http://www.hrnicholls.com.au/nicholls/nichvol6/vol1612o.htm, pp. 1–8 (accessed 3 December 2006).

Andrew Stewart, 'Work Choices in Overview: Big Bang or Slow Burn?, ***Economic and Labour Relations Review***, vol. 16, no. 2, 2006, pp. 25–35; [2006] ELR Rev. 2, http://www.austlii.edu.au/au/journals/ELRRev/2006/3.html#Heading4, pp. 1–25 (accessed 4 December 2006).

Matt Wade, 'A super shock for boomers', ***Sydney Morning Herald***, Sydney, NSW, 2006 (24 October 2006), http://www.smh.com.au/articles/2006/10/23/1161455665709.html (accessed 24 October 2006).

Ed Austin-Woods, 'IR Reform Series: Multi-Employer Bargaining', ***Australian Business Lawyers & Advisors***, 12 September 2022, IR Reform Series: Multi-Employer Bargaining – ABLA (ablawyers.com.au) https://ablawyers.com.au/resources/multi-employer-bargaining (accessed 29 May 2023).

Index

J. Scutt, *Wage Rage for Equal Pay*,
https://doi.org/10.1007/978-3-031-42178-5

B

I

GPSR Compliance
The European Union's (EU) General Product Safety Regulation (GPSR) is a set of rules that requires consumer products to be safe and our obligations to ensure this.

If you have any concerns about our products, you can contact us on

ProductSafety@springernature.com

In case Publisher is established outside the EU, the EU authorized representative is:

Springer Nature Customer Service Center GmbH
Europaplatz 3
69115 Heidelberg, Germany

www.ingramcontent.com/pod-product-compliance
Ingram Content Group UK Ltd.
Pitfield, Milton Keynes, MK11 3LW, UK
UKHW020833290926
15470UKWH00004B/1324
9783031421778